The Encyclopedia of Popular
Antiques

The Encyclopedia of Popular
Antiques

General Editor
Michael Carter

octopus

First published 1980 by
Octopus Books Limited
59 Grosvenor Street,
London W1

© 1980 Octopus Books Limited

ISBN 0 7064 0963 9

Printed in Czechoslovakia

50 399

Endpapers   A collection of 17th and 18th century English silver-gilt. (Christies/Cooper Bridgman)

1   Jewelled locket containing portraits by Nicholas Hilliard *c.* 1590. (Private collection/Cooper-Bridgman)
2/3   French silver gilt chocolate jug with its own burner, cream jug and silver bowl. (Louvre/Cooper-Bridgman)
4/5   The Lion and the Unicorn, Staffordshire figures by John Walton of Burslem, *c.* 1830. (Hanley Museum & Art Gallery/Cooper-Bridgman)
6/7   A fine 18th-century interior – the James Gibb Drawing Room from Henrietta Place, *c.* 1728. (Victoria & Albert Museum/Cooper-Bridgman)
8   Italian *cassoni* made in 1472 for the marriage of Lorenzo di Matteo de Morelli and Vagia di Tania de Francesco de' Nerli. (John Freeman)

Contents

Pre-1500   10

Sixteenth Century   60

Seventeenth Century   84

Eighteenth Century   146

Nineteenth Century   256

Twentieth Century   360

Care and repair   374

Glossary   386

Collections to visit   392

Index   394

PRE
1500

Introduction

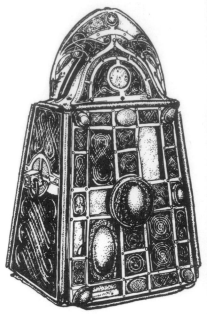

The collapse of the Roman Empire in the 5th century A.D. profoundly affected the known world politically, socially and culturally. From the point of view of craftsmen in the decorative arts, they were now cut off from the skilled centres of craft-making in Byzantium and the Near East as a result of the chaos following the collapse.

The extent to which the European craftsman relied on Byzantium, Syria and Egypt for both knowledge of his skills as well as artistic inspiration became apparent when the crafts of the cabinetmaker, the glassmaker and the gold and silversmith went into decline. It was to take some 500 years for these crafts to be relearned and for a sophisticated and distinctive European style to emerge.

Nevertheless a style did emerge around the 11th century – the Romanesque style – which some authors believe was an imperfect form of the later Gothic form, while others regard it as a complete style in its own right. As the name suggests, Romanesque borrows from Roman as well as Byzantine styles – or at least what craftsmen and architects remembered of classic styles. The style was particularly characterized by its use of carved ornament, notably plant and animal motifs worked somewhat crudely and suggesting a certain barbaric energy, which no doubt reflected the social and cultural life of the times. In England the Romanesque style became known as the Norman style. With the exception of churches and their ornament, little Romanesque art survives.

The shrine of St Patrick's Bell c.1100.

By the 12th century Europe was beginning to re-order itself. Society was dominated by the Church so that it is not surprising that the first truly European style, the Gothic, emerged in the design of churches and was to be triumphant in the cathedrals of Europe. The cradle of Gothic art is the abbey church of St Denis, near Paris, which was rebuilt around an older structure in 1140–44 by the Abbot Suger. Although the Abbot had to retain much of the original structure he created a circular string of chapels around the old church, by virtue of which in his own words, 'the whole church would shine with the wonderful and uninterrupted light of most luminous windows, pervading the interior beauty'. Suger had achieved his dream of raising the Church of France to new heights in the light of the theological and political philosophies of the time.

The inspiration provided by the church of St Denis gradually spread over the whole of western Europe. At the same time other forces were at work which eventually ensured that the artistic forces behind the Gothic movement were applied to more than church design – to furniture, metalworking, gold and silversmithing, embroidery and so on. There were substantial differences between Romanesque and Gothic society. While both were feudal, Gothic feudalism was more ordered and more stable, which encouraged the craftsmen who eventually, with merchants, lawyers, teachers and so on came to constitute a new middle class. In addition, Romanesque society was male dominated while in Gothic society women played a greater role leading to a new sense of romanti-

Introduction

cism. All these elements led to a revival of interest in the decorative arts.

Gothic art is characterized by its emphasis on vertical lines; furniture for instance was severely rectilinear and was usually solid and massive. It was also relatively crudely constructed. In Italy, the Gothic style, introduced in the 13th century, never achieved the popularity it enjoyed in the rest of Europe, possibly because Italians were happy with their own individual styles which were a combination of Romanesque, Lombard and Tuscan styles, and the Gothic, when it arrived, was simply combined with them. Illustrative of this partial acceptance of the Gothic was the emphasis on horizontal lines rather than vertical in the construction and decoration of furniture. The Italians also used a greater variety of decoration of furniture, for whereas in the rest of Europe carving was predominant in the early Gothic period the Italians used gilding, painting and intarsia and other techniques as well. It was partly this wider variety of styles and techniques in Italy that encouraged the birth of the Renaissance in that country in the 15th century.

The primary inspiration for Gothic decoration was of course church architecture – pointed arches, buttresses, floral motifs such as vines, maple leaves and cress as well as animal forms treated after the style of the grotesque gargoyles to be found gazing down from the Gothic church. Gothic gold and silverwork followed these motifs as well and like furniture was both massive and heavily decorated.

Gothic style developed within itself becoming more elaborate and decoratively richer in the 13th century, a phase which is called the High Gothic style. Once again it was church architecture that provided the impetus and inspiration to carry the movement to even greater heights. When, in 1194, the newly rebuilt cathedral at Chartres was destroyed by a fire which engulfed the city, building on a new cathedral was begun immediately. Finished in 1220, the new cathedral is generally considered to be the first of the High Gothic buildings.

The particular accomplishment of the Gothic craftsman-artist was stained glass and in no period before or since has the craft achieved such mystical qualities of light – precisely that quality that Suger was seeking when he designed his church.

The Gothic style reached maturity in the 13th and 14th centuries. The so-called Rayonnant and Flamboyant styles which appeared in France from 1275–1375 and 1375–1515 respectively represent the penultimate development of the Gothic style.

The Rayonnant ('radiant') style was associated with the royal Paris court of Louis IX (St Louis) who fulfilled the medieval idea of the 'saint-king'. The richness of the Rayonnant style reflected the growing wealth of the royal house and Louis made every effort to spread and transform the art and architecture of France.

Even as the French artist was exploring the ultimate possibilities of the Gothic style however, the seeds of the Renaissance were germinating in the provinces of Italy. The Renaissance ('rebirth') is now no longer regarded as being an abrupt transition of the medieval world to the modern world, for its true origins can be traced to the periods before the Middle Ages and the medieval can be found lingering well into the Renaissance.

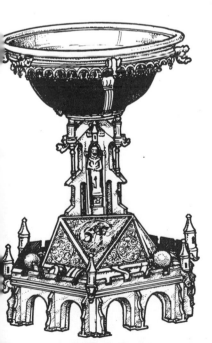

Gothic salt probably made for Louis XI of France, c.1460.

Above all the Renaissance was a time of change in man's attitude towards himself and the world around him. He gradually turned away from the supernatural world, its values and ideas, to a concern with the natural world. For the first time the world was being viewed without the spectacles of religion – it was being humanized in fact. The art of the Renaissance was a celebration of the natural world and of man himself. The traditions on which the Renaissance was to base its new synthesis were those of classical culture which were now being rediscovered 100 years after the fall of the Roman Empire. The particular achievements will be reviewed from the vantage point of the 16th century by which time all of Europe had fallen under its influence.

Furniture

The network of spectacular Gothic cathedrals that sprinkled the 15th century European landscape with towers, pinnacles, statuary and spires manifested the wealth and strength of the main force of internationalism in the Middle Ages, the Christian Church. Commerce also united European societies, but although mercantile exchange, ecclesiastical splendour and courtly extravagance all helped shape interior styles in the late medieval period, they in no way provided the degree of domestic comfort taken for granted today.

Throughout Europe, common houses generally consisted of a single room only, and their stark furnishings revealed a low standard of living. Even in rich aristocratic establishments, interiors were likely to be more showy than comfortable. European nobility constantly moved among their various estates and as they travelled they took with them the sparse furnishings. The dominant features of late medieval furniture were necessarily those of adaptability and easy transport.

This furniture reflected in miniature the Gothic architectural style. This was possibly connected to Arabic sources and was related to the earlier northern Romanesque style of the 9th and 10th centuries. Characterized by pointed ogival arches, cusps, tracery and stylized flame-like carving, the Gothic mode flourished in northern Europe from the 13th to the 15th centuries. The imposing fabric of cathedrals, such as Notre Dame, with sculpture and stained glass executed on a large scale, provided a pictorial medium for presenting the Biblical text to a world that lacked printing and literacy.

Ecclesiastical furniture followed this style, echoing on pews and misericords such features as tracery, arcades and Biblical figures and scenes. Domestic furniture shared the same ornament, and by the 15th century also included the profile 'romayne' heads derived from Italian Renaissance interpretations of Roman coins, and the Flemish-inspired linenfold panelling.

Gothic furniture was sparse. Chairs, chests and tables that date from before the 15th century are rare; hangings were the real furnishings of medieval interiors, and it was the collection of tapestries, velvets, silks

Finely carved early medieval chair from Scandinavia.

and leathers that dominated rooms with their presence and colour. These materials, many produced in Italy and Spain, far outweighed the status and worth of the wooden pieces they dwarfed. Sets of elaborate textiles, called *chambres* in medieval French inventories, together with metal-work were the most ornate of the decorative arts. The rich wall fabrics of the Coronation Room of Queen Jeanne of Burgundy were embroidered with 1,321 parrots and the ducal coat of arms. The poor building insulation that made these hangings necessary also popularized the footstools that kept feet off cold floors. Also heavy tapestries almost totally cloaked medieval beds.

Even in wealthier homes, rooms were not assigned exclusive functions, and the few pieces of furniture that each house contained were moved according to necessity. Life often centred around a large hall which accommodated eating, entertainment and casual socializing. Such halls generally included a long high table for the manor family; this table, and the rows of tables set beneath it at right angles, were taken apart into their component trestles and planks at the end of meals and removed to make way for whatever activity was to follow.

Etiquette required that high tables, four-poster state beds, and princely seats be elevated on a dais. Canopies were hung above the same pieces, and even children's cradles and press cupboards that displayed collections of plate were similarly distinguished.

Tables were made of softwood and oak as well as stone and marble. Trestles were of two kinds: those with separate splayed legs and the column type which rose from a spreading base. Two surviving tables of the latter kind are at Penshurst Place in Kent. Each has three large trestles supporting an unattached board some 8 metres (27 ft) long. The trestles are cruciform, wide at the top and bottom with a waisted centre. Fixed tables were also in use and were known as dormies or dormant. A type of pedestal table is known to have been in use that had a round or hexagonal top supported on cruciform or column pedestals. Library tables, designed for individual use, had screw pedestals.

Few cradles have survived from the Middle Ages, but it is known that among the nobility at least, two cradles were used: a daytime or state cradle and a night cradle.

In addition to being easily dismantled, furniture of the late Middle Ages tended to be plain and serviceable. The woods most often used were oak, walnut and pine. Construction methods progressed from the crude, hollowed-out tree trunk chests of early medieval England to assemblages of wood planks and finally to the more durable panel-and-frame construction introduced possibly in Flanders towards the end of the 14th century.

The chest was the most common piece of furniture in the Middle Ages. It was used to store bridal dowries, to transport belongings, to safeguard valuables such as books and imported spices, as well as to sit on. Italian Gothic chests were often gilt and were generally uncarved, being painted with religious scenes. French chests were carved with Gothic arches, tracery and figures. Those from Spain were often leather-covered, and bound with iron. During the Renaissance, chests developed domed tops, possibly to facilitate their fixture to animals when being transported.

The next most common pieces of furniture after the chest were the various forms of seating. The most usual style of stool had two pairs of curved or straight legs each pair of which crossed in the centre to form an X; opposite legs were joined by horizontal beams or bars which supported a hide or cloth seat. These early stools were designed to be folded but by the 15th century they were no longer portable, having developed a high back. One stool common throughout Europe was the backstool. This was a three-legged stool with a triangular rush or wood seat; one of the legs was extended up above the seat and given a short cross-bar so forming a back – and headrest. They were still being made in the 17th century.

Another 15th-century stool was the slab-ended stool made from a length of plank, supported at either end by two vertical planks which had their edges shaped like buttresses; a piece of wood in the shape of a trefoil or Gothic arch, for example, was cut out of the base of each 'leg'.

In general, Gothic interiors were equipped with few of the accoutrements of easy living that the following centuries would introduce. The sharp contrast between the minimally comfortable furniture that people used, and the ostentatious and expensive embellishments displayed in the rooms around, only began to diminish during the Renaissance.

In the 15th century the Gothic style began to wane. The flamboyant and perpendicular Gothic exhausted itself in its final stages. It gradually gave way throughout Europe to Renaissance influences which had originated about two centuries before in Italy, where the Gothic mode had never been completely established. There, a turn towards humanism in religion in the 13th century transformed the medieval preoccupation with religious salvation into a glorification of man and the world. Simultaneously, the papacy and the rigid feudal system declined favouring aristocratic and mercantile families such as the Medici, Gonzaga and Sforza, who embraced the new age of expansion, exploration and unprecedented wealth.

The patronage fostered a revolution in European thought and art, which originated in Florence. It fast spread to the rest of Italy and gradually permeated northern Europe. Revived studies of classical architecture, arts and literature revitalized antique principles, manifest in the corporeal realism of paintings such as Giotto di Bondone's fresco cycle at the Arena Chapel in Padua, and in the classical proportions of buildings such as Filippo Brunelleschi's Pazzi Chapel at Santa Croce, Florence.

The resurrection of classical architectural forms and concepts brought with it a profusion of acanthus leaves, griffins, urns and other details taken from ancient villas and temples, introducing a repertoire of motifs that would appear on furniture for centuries to follow.

Rivalries of patronage and artistic display among aristocratic families resulted in the building of expensive palaces and villas in Italy and elsewhere. These villas disseminated the Renaissance style, attested to the new social stability and demanded the production of new and finer furnishings.

Early Renaissance interiors continued to be draped with brightly-coloured textiles, but as the period progressed it saw the introduction of

Italian 'Savonarola' chair c.1550.

a variety of new furniture forms, which increased in abundance everywhere. At first, classical ornaments were merely added to traditional Gothic furniture. Gradually, however, although the types of woods used remained largely unchanged, Renaissance architecture, painting and sculpture led to the application of classical architectural motifs and naturalistically carved animals, figures and foliage. Italian and French chests of the 15th and 16th centuries often combined elements such as Gothic arcades and religious figures with classical columns and cornices.

Furnishings and interior decoration developed from the classic restraint of the early Renaissance to an increasing opulence during the 15th and 16th centuries. Walls were hung with cloths of gold, Italian silks and velvets, imported oriental carpets, Spanish leathers, and tapestries woven with mythological and Biblical scenes. Artists such as Sandro Botticelli and Domenico Ghirlandaio frequently executed wall frescoes of allegories, hunting scenes, landscapes with birds and animals and architectural views.

Wooden wainscoting, often with contrasting marble panels or intarsia (inlaying or marquetry) decorations, also covered room walls. Coffered and panelled ceilings, such as Leonardo da Vinci's gold and azure stellar composition in the ballroom of the Castello at Milan, were colourfully painted.

These interior schemes, opulent in themselves, contained collections of paintings, sculpture, silver and gold plate manuscripts, musical instruments and maiolica. Furniture was still scarce, but increasingly refined Italian Renaissance woodworkers ornamented their walnut cabinets, beds, chairs and other pieces with rich carving and marquetry.

The Italian cassone, box-like and painted in earlier periods developed into an architecturally-schemed chest with strong cornice and base, classical pilasters and panels, and ornaments of arches and refined classical mouldings. Cassone were usually the most skilfully and elaborately worked pieces of furniture of the period. Made in pairs by specialist craftsmen, they were designed to hold a bride's trousseau, though they were also used for holding household items.

The cassapanca, a form of chair derived from a chest with back and sides, eventually became the honoured seat of the head of an Italian household. It was fitted with cushions and often raised on a dais as were the carved or inlaid throne seats, with panel-backs and canopies, found in patrician ceremonial apartments. *Sgabello* stools, with narrow triangular backs, were carved and inlaid. The folding, easily-transported X-shaped Savonarola chair was upholstered with leather or fabric. Cabinets acquired the friezes, pediments and columns of Renaissance architecture; their front panels were often inlaid with intarsia *trompe l'oeil* scenes which themselves depicted open-doored cabinets with contents or architectural vistas revealed. Four-poster beds with canopies of rich velvets, silks and tapestries were often gilt and raised on a dais. Large tables, with vase-shaped end supports joined by stretchers, were frequently covered with tapestries or exquisite lace, as were the *credenze* or sideboards, that developed during the 15th century.

The flourishing court of Renaissance Spain eagerly adopted the decorative elements that Italian craftsmen introduced to the already unusual *mudejar* style, a medieval form which had resulted from the amalgamation of Arab, African and Mediterranean influences, and which was characterized by geometrical interlaces, polygons, stars and foliage motifs. In furniture, *mudejar* derived much of its effect from the native materials, so varied and exotic by northern European standards, of cypress, orangewood, chestnut, walnut and poplar and from the increasing imports of rare metals and semi-precious stones from the Spanish American colonies.

The many-drawered Spanish *hembra* evolved into the elaborate *vargueño*, a writing desk on a stand containing tiny, brightly-painted and gilt drawers, columns, doors and carvings.

The *sillone de frailero*, which superseded an earlier X-shaped seat derived from Italy, was square and solid, with horizontal, sometimes curved, arms. Large decorative brass nails attached the leather to the back and seat, and a hinged stretcher pierced with a geometric ornament joined the legs. The characteristic Spanish table, with a thick walnut top projecting above a frieze of small carved drawers, also came into use during the Renaissance.

In Northern Europe, where oak was commonly used, the Netherlands led in the adoption of Renaissance forms, disseminating the style to Germany, Scandinavia and England through circulated prints such as those by Cornelius Floris (active in the 1550s), who introduced Renaissance scrolled ornament and grotesques to the Low Countries and Germany in mid-century. Engravings by Hans Vredeman de Vries (1527–c.1604) and his son Paul (1567–c.1630) accelerated the diffusion of northern Renaissance design.

Italian ideas had begun to influence French styles well before the end of the 15th century. Architecture was the first to feel the effects, followed shortly by furniture. The French Renaissance is divided into two periods: the François I style which covers the reign of Charles VIII (1483–98), Louis XII (1498–1515) and François I (1515–47); and the High Renaissance or Henri II style (1547–98).

During the first period Gothic and Renaissance styles were mixed; for example scrolls and arabesques were combined with pinnacles and pointed arches. It was not until the reign of François I that the Gothic style completely disappeared. A great deal of furniture in France until the 16th century was intended to be portable, years of political upheaval having made this necessary. This is an important reason why the new style took time to reach its full expression.

Ceramics

There are very few ceramic bodies and techniques associated with the art of the potter which were not originally introduced by Chinese craftsmen, and even with advanced knowledge of science and technology the present-day potter only rarely achieves the perfection seen on the wares produced by the Far Eastern potters of earlier times.

From the late Neolithic period, about 2000 B.C., potters in Northern China were producing fine, boldly shaped jars for tomb furnishing which were usually formed by the 'coiling' technique and decorated with vigorous designs in red and black clay slips on a buff-toned burnished earthenware body. The slip is clay reduced to a liquid batter, and used for making, coating or decorating pottery. Primitive feldspathic glazes were occasionally used during the Chou dynasty (10th–3rd century B.C.) but it was from the early years of the Han dynasty (206 B.C.–A.D. 220) that the low-fired earthenwares were made to serve a more practical purpose by the addition of a lead-silicate glaze, sometimes tinted green or brown with metallic oxides. During these early years higher-fired stonewares were produced with a 'tight-fitting' olive-green feldspathic glaze, often inspired by the form and decoration of contemporary bronzes. These stonewares were improved when finer pottery shapes were made during the Six Dynasties period (A.D. 265–589) and are known as 'Yüeh' wares.

During the T'ang dynasty (A.D. 618–906) many fine achievements were made in China in all artistic fields, aided primarily by an increase in trade with Central and Western Asia. Ceramic tomb wares still provide the majority of surviving examples of the potter's art; and these may well be inferior to those made for court use, which have only rarely survived. It was during these years that the popular yellow-and-green toned glazes, referred to today as 'egg and spinach', were so widely used.

It has long been considered that it was during the late years of the T'ang dynasty that the Chinese potter made his greatest discovery – a method of producing a white, translucent body, referred to today as hard-paste porcelain. This was made by fusing China-clay (kaolin) and China-stone (petuntse), at a temperature of about 1,350°C (2,462°F). China-stone was used to produce a tight-fitting clear glaze, which could be fired together with the body.

Porcelain of this type was considered to have been made by the 9th century, but the National Palace Museum in Taiwan now claim that true porcelain was being made in China as early as the Wei and Tsin states (A.D. 220–420) and that recently more of these early wares have been discovered, although the earliest porcelains exhibited in the museum are of the Northern Sung dynasty (A.D. 960–c.1127). They include the fine imperial wares of the *Ting, Ju, Kuan, Ko and Chün* kilns. The most beautiful wares made during the Sung dynasty (A.D. 960–1279) rely primarily upon their shape and fine glazes rather than painted or applied decoration, styles which were to become so popular during the Ming dynasty.

Equally worthy of note are the heavily potted wares with moulded or carved decoration under a greyish-green celadon glaze, made during the Yuan dynasty (A.D. 1279–1368). During this time the country was under the power of the Mongols, following the successful onslaught of Kublai Khan.

It was some time during the early 14th century that the Chinese potter began to use the metallic oxide of cobalt as an underglaze-blue decoration, a technique and colour that was later to be used throughout Europe up to the present day. This new form of decoration continued into the

Ceramic jar from the Han period (206 B.C.–A.D. 220).

succeeding Ming dynasty (A.D. 1368–1644) with very little change, and the porcelain factories in the city of Ching-tê-chên multiplied and flourished, producing wares not only for the court but also for the Near East. Many examples can be seen today in the Topkapi Sarayi Palace in Istanbul.

The reign of Yung Lo (1403–26) saw the firm establishment of new ceramic forms. Tastes had also become more sophisticated and the increasing royal patronage of potters helped them develop and show their true skills. Judging by two vases made for a temple presentation in 1351 and now at the Percival David Foundation, London, the art of blue and white had been mastered by the mid-14th century, but it was during Yung Lo's reign that it gained true recognition both at court and amongst scholars.

Yung Lo 1403–24

Characteristic of this period are large dishes decorated with fruit and floral motifs and with either plain or foliated rims. The bases are unglazed and carry no reign mark. Other popular patterns include a bouquet of lotus and other plants tied with a ribbon. The dishes vary in colour from a kingfisher blue to a fainter shade that is said to give 'the impression of drifting like smoke into the glaze'. While many blue and whites of this period show this effect, not all do so.

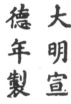

Hsüan-tê 1426–35

The lotus bowl, *lien-tzu*, was also developed in this reign and was made in finely potted plain white porcelain. Decoration was usually in *an hua*, the 'hidden decoration', though underglaze blue was increasingly used as it became more popular. Ewers, based on Middle Eastern designs, with narrow necks and long spouts with a neck support were popular in the early years of the century. The stemcup, which had been in use for centuries, underwent a change in shape, and once again the inspiration seems to have come from Mediterranean and Near Eastern forms that gained acceptance during the Yüan Dynasty.

From the time of the reign of the Ming Emperor Hsüan Tê (A.D. 1426–35) it became a common practice to add a 'reign-mark' in underglaze-blue. This form of mark must not necessarily be accepted as indicating the date of the piece; many marks of earlier periods were often added, some deliberately to confuse, but others merely as a mark of veneration, indicating similarity to wares made in outstanding periods in the history of Chinese porcelain.

The skill and artistry achieved with blue and white during the reign of Hsüan-tê has probably never been surpassed. A Chinese writer of the late 16th century wrote that 'during the Hsüan-tê period potters were inspired by Heaven to produce works of subtle meaning and supreme artistry'. Foreign influences are still apparent in this period, notably in the so-called 'tankards' the shape of which was based on an 8th century Middle Eastern form. Flattened flasks, often decorated with the yin-yang symbol and having two rings attached to the body, were also made in this period.

An exciting new range of enamel colours, fused to the surface of the glaze, were first successfully used during the reign of the Emperor Chêng Hua (A.D. 1465–87). An underglaze-blue outline was sometimes used together with delicate translucent colours, a style referred to as *tou-ts'ai* (contrasted colour).

Vase of the mei p'ing *type, Southern Sung period (early 14th century).*

The porcelain produced during this reign is considered to be the main rival to that of Hsüan-tê, showing a delicacy and refinement not seen before. The shade of blue long used changed and became somewhat paler and a new technique which has been called 'outline and wash' was introduced. The reason, it seems, is that by 1434 the Chinese had received the last consignment of imported cobalt and potters had to rely on the less satisfactory local ore, which was, however, easier to grind and prepare. The more finely ground ore enabled the potter to outline his pattern first and then fill it in with a paler 'wash'.

Early Korean Ceramics

Excavations have revealed that Korean potters were producing grey stoneware vessels and figures for burial purposes during the Silla kingdom (c.57 B.C.–A.D. 935), but it was in the reigns of the Koryō kings (A.D. 918–1392) that many fine porcellanous stonewares were produced, with celadon glazes, which at times rivalled the best examples of the Chinese Sung dynasty. Much originality was introduced, including the then unique technique of inlaying black and white clays into the grey toned clay body, the whole being covered with a watery blue-green celadon glaze.

The coarser wares of the Yi dynasty (1392–1910) still showed a bold originality, which is so much admired by today's studio potters. Iron-brown and copper-reds were often applied to sturdy porcelain forms, and these sometimes acquired a greater charm due to lack of temperature control and the partial burning away of colours.

The Potters of Islam

Collectors of early Islamic pottery are few. Those decorative wares which are today available have in almost every instance been reconstructed from fragments, often recovered from the sites of early rubbish tips. There have been rare finds of pots buried for safety because of fear from invaders, remaining unclaimed until recent years. Fragments of Chinese imported wares, together with local wares which show a close relationship, were excavated on the site of the Mesopotamian city of Samarra, occupied by the Abbasids in the mid-9th century.

The Islamic potter was soon to create more original styles of decoration, and although unable to locate the materials essential for the manufacture of porcelain, their fine earthenware provided ideal grounds for beautifully applied designs in various coloured clay slips and metallic oxides, including lustre.

The technique introduced by the Mesopotamian potter in the late 9th century which was to have such influence in Europe, was the application of a glaze made both white and opaque by the addition of tin-oxide, providing a white porcellanous surface, suitable to receive the limited range of colours offered by the metallic oxides known at that time. Colourful wares in this new style were created in the form of Chinese T'ang period pottery and Islamic metalwork.

The skill of these same Near Eastern potters in achieving a beautiful 'mother-of-pearl' lustre in a wide range of metallic tones can still be seen today on many surviving wall-tiles in mosques and palaces, painted in a wide variety of geometrical, human or animal forms, the latter often showing a Picasso-like quality in the simplicity of line.

Blue-and-white wares are usually thought to have originated in China, where porcelain was being decorated with designs in underglaze-blue from about A.D. 1300, but this same cobalt was being used by the Mesopotamian potter at a much earlier date, during the 9th century. The Chinese are known to have obtained much of the cobalt used during the Ming dynasty from Iran.

Many of the Persian wares made during the 17th century in the style of Ming blue-and-white porcelains were used to fulfil orders placed by Dutch traders, who were having difficulty trading with China during the years of internal strife. Wares of this type were still being made during the 19th century.

Until comparatively recently the term 'Rhodian' was wrongly applied to a class of pottery made in Turkey from the 15th century at Isnik in Western Anatolia. These same wares are often wrongly classed as 'tin-glazed'; they are actually made from a rather low-fired white siliceous body, upon which the high-temperature metallic oxides are painted under a thin transparent glaze. The earliest class, decorated with flowing arabesques and flowers in cobalt blue, date from the last quarter of the 15th century.

Spain and the Moors

The early influence of the Near Eastern potters was first seen in Europe during the occupation of the southern regions of Spain by the Moors. As early as 1154 Arabic writers were telling of the fine 'gold-coloured pottery' which even at that early date was being exported to many neighbouring countries. By the early 14th century lustrewares from Malaga were reaching as far afield as England.

These early Hispano-Moresque wares showed clearly in their decoration the influence of pottery formerly made at such centres as Rayy and Kashan in Persia, and Raqqa in Syria, but in form the Spanish wares were generally more robust in every respect. Many of the pieces were decorated in both blue and 'gold' lustre, the blue being fired at the same time as the rather poor quality white tin-glaze. After firing, the fine thin films of silver or copper oxides to form the lustre were applied, then subjected to a final firing in a low-temperature reduction kiln.

Knowledge of the so-called 'Malaga work' was soon to spread to neighbouring areas, including Granada and Manises, near Valencia. One of the best known and oft-illustrated examples of Manises workmanship is the fine large conical bowl in the Victoria and Albert Museum, London, decorated with a stylized Portuguese sailing ship, seemingly riding upon the backs of four large fish. It is interesting to note that the practice of painting upon the entire ground with what sometimes appears to be quite irrelevant patterns is a device that was continued into the 17th century by the English Staffordshire potters when decorating their 'slip-trailed' dishes.

Hispano-Moresque tablewares were very popular with some of the great Italian families, whose coat-of-arms they often bore, usually upon a tediously painted background of small leaves and flowers, sometimes within a gadrooned pattern.

One of the most common shapes was the cylindrical drug-jar, with a narrow 'waist', usually with an out-turned lip to retain a cord to hold a

Hung-chih 1488–1505

Ch'eng-hua 1465–87

parchment-type cover, the so-called *albarello*. The form originated in the Near East and was later made by almost every European country engaged in the manufacture of tin-glazed wares for the use of the apothecary.

In 1492 the Moors were finally expelled from Spain by Ferdinand and Isabella, but the production of Hispano-Moresque type pottery was to continue in southern Spain to the present day, when the wares are produced for the tourist trade. By 1500 the demand was for lighter and more practical tablewares, and this resulted in the technique of press-moulding being introduced. This made possible the production of shapes previously made only by silversmiths, including ewers, goblets and salvers.

The middle of the 15th century saw Seville as the centre for an interesting ceramic technique which again originated in the Near East. Coloured tin-glazes were kept from intermingling by first incising the design into the prepared clay form, the outline was then filled with a preparation of manganese and grease which acted as a barrier between the colours, a procedure known as *cuerda-seca* (dry-cord).

The Moorish Influence in Italy

The popularity of Hispano-Moresque wares in Italy in the 15th century soon led to them being imitated there. The imported wares were brought to Italy via Majorca and so became known as Majorcan ware or maiolica. The first known use of the word is in a manuscript of 1454. Italy had had its own tin-glazed earthenware as early as the 11th century, but surviving examples from that date are very primitive, painted primarily in brown, yellow and green on a poor quality white ground.

Italian maiolica was at the peak of production from the late years of the 15th century until the middle of the 16th century. Italy had already established a superiority over the Western world in the art of fresco and tempera painting, an art confined primarily to the adornment of churches. The humble potter was soon to treat his pottery as an artist did a canvas, introducing forms which were to offer wide scope to his brush and palette. Indeed, it has been acknowledged that the colourful painted maiolica gave a much truer record of the art of the period than many better known Italian paintings, which over the centuries had suffered damage and been subjected to considerable restoration.

From about 1450 Florence had become a major centre of the pottery industry, producing fine bold forms decorated in a rich palette, sometimes referred to as 'severe', due to their similarity to metal shapes. A much more common class of ware being made in Florence at this time was again being made for the apothecary. The large drug-pots decorated in a thickly applied dark blue with a purple outline are often referred to as 'oak-leaf' jars, due to their having painted backgrounds of highly stylized leaves, somewhat similar to those of the oak. The broad strap-like handles to these larger drug-jars often displayed the badge of the hospital for which they were made.

The last quarter of the 15th century saw Faenza as the major centre for the manufacture of Italian maiolica, having in turn great influence upon the productions of such other areas of distribution as Siena and Deruta. The painting on the early Faenza wares was usually very

Italian maiolica drug jar c.1475.

distinctive, consisting of strong deep blues, purples, drab orange, with bright yellows and greens. The occasional use of heraldic arms or dated signatures of painters sometimes enables a precise date to be given, such as on the service made for Matthias Corvinus, King of Hungary, whose arms are coupled with those of Beatrice of Naples, his bride of 1476.

Some of the most beautiful painted maiolica was made at the Cafaggioli pottery near Florence, a workshop catering exclusively for the needs of the household of Pierfrancesco de' Medici, a member of a younger branch of the family. Similar fine painting in the so-called *istoriato* style is seen on the wares produced at Casteldurante, in the Duchy of Urbino, painted in many instances by Nicolo Pellipario, whose signature on wares made at other centres indicates his nomadic travels.

Glass

Glass is a product of earth and fire, the result of fusing silica (sand) with an alkaline flux (soda), and a small quantity of limestone to harden the mixture. We tend to think of it as only man-made, but glass occurs naturally in the guise of a number of minerals, such as tektites (also termed moldavites), Libyan desert glass and Darwin glass. These are glassy pebbles found in many parts of the world and are thought to be the weathered remains of prehistoric meteorites. Another form of natural glass, utilized by earlier civilizations in toolmaking, is obsidian – a material of volcanic origin and produced by the rapid cooling of viscous lava. Quartz is pure silica and all types of quartz are related to natural glass. However, nearest in appearance to the man-made product is rock crystal, named from the Greek *crystallos* – clear ice. Mined in areas all over the world, it has long been cherished as a precious material suitable for all kinds of artefacts. Stone cutters (lapidaries) delighted in working with this substance, and the technique of rock crystal cutting represents one of the most important aspects of glass decoration.

Glasshouses will obviously be located where raw materials are accessible and of satisfactory quality. In Mediterranean regions, the essential soda would be obtained from certain types of seaweed although, if necessary, some raw materials could be procured from a distant source. The forest glasshouses would replace the soda of southern tradition by potash derived from woodash. The quality of sand – the source of silica – is of great importance to the glassmaker since impurities affect the glass colour and finality. A most important addition to the glass batch is cullet, waste pieces of glass which used to be collected by children and poor families who sold them back to the glasshouse. To form the glass frit (*frittare* – to fry), the cullet and raw materials are ground, ready for melting in the furnace. Glass is a supercooled liquid. It has no crystalline structure and passes into a viscous fluid on heating, without a definite melting point. Three stages are required for heating the frit, beginning with placing it into the melting pot, a preheated refractory crucible which stands in the furnace. The resultant viscous mass is then ready for the refining stage, during which the pot melt is increased to a maximum heat of 1,600°C (2,912°F), when the frit becomes a thin liquid containing air bubbles which give off undesirable gases and water vapour. Impurities rising to the surface are skimmed off with the ladle. Lastly, the frit must be cooled so that by returning to its former viscosity it will be suitable for working at a temperature of about 700 to 800°C (1,290 to 1,470°F).

It may now be shaped by blowing, moulding, pressing or casting and will remain ductile for about 20 minutes. If a longer working time is required, the mass can be kept pliable by brief refining at the furnace mouth. This procedure is also used to polish the finished glass, the so called fire polish. To reduce internal stresses which may result in the glass cracking or breaking, the shaped article must be placed into a special annealing oven or lehr, at a carefully controlled temperature.

By the 18th century, the slightly elliptical glasshouse with its enormous chimney cone had become a familiar landmark. An English Act of Parliament decreed that to enable waste smoke to drift away, glasshouse chimneys were to have a height of at least 15.24 metres (50 ft), and some were built much taller.

Glasshouse pots are made by hand and need special treatment, having to remain in a heating chamber from four to eight months before being tested for additional periods at very high temperatures. Nevertheless, these pots are serviceable only for a period of up to three months at most, because glass attacks the clay. Potsetting is one of the most hazardous tasks even under modern factory conditions. The men receive special pay for this work and there is a tradition of free beer as well.

The glassmaker's tools and techniques are as old as Christianity, although glass was probably made at least 4,000 years ago. The blowpipe made its appearance about the first century A.D. It is a tube made of iron, with a thickened end to gather the molten glass and is protected at handling points by a wooden covering. The lump of glass, termed the paraison, may be taken from the pot with the blowing iron or an iron rod, the pontil. The pontil is used for drawing out the glass and leaves a rough mark where it is broken off, the so-called pontil mark. Both small and large shears are used for cutting off parts such as rims, and pincers and a wooden lipper are needed for shaping.

The rake and ladle are used for skimming off impurities from the frit. These tools are suspended from the arms of the master blower's chair – a short bench with flat and slightly sloping long arms, developed during the 17th century. The term chair also refers to the team of glassmakers working together – the gaffer, or master blower, and his assistants called the servitors and footmen, usually three or four in number. An important glassmaker's requisite is the marver, a polished iron slab for rolling, smoothing or shaping the paraison, and also used for embedding applied decoration in the glass surface.

Advances in technology have enabled greater control in glass manufacture, guaranteeing a larger percentage of perfect output, although the production method remains basically unchanged. Diamond and wheel engraving can now be applied with electrically-powered tools. Mass produced polishing is achieved by placing the glass objects in an acid bath; and acid etching, although applied in earlier times and popularized

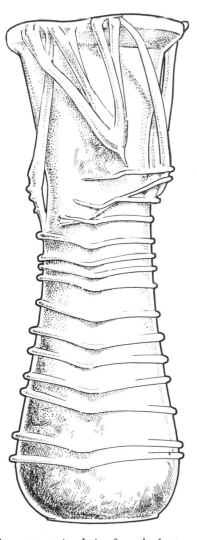

Glass unguent jar dating from the 1st to 3rd centuries found in Syria.

during the 19th century, is now utilized in the fields of decorative domestic and industrial glassmaking. Sandblasting, too, is a modern innovation, although it is a variant of the abrasive technique.

Engraving, either by hand tool or copper wheel, and wheel cutting will always represent the pinnacle of the glass decorator's art. Unlike any other decoration it highlights the refractive property of the material and enhances its brilliancy.

The Ancient World

Glass, as an independent material, made its appearance some time between 3000 to 2000 B.C., although man had prior knowledge of this substance in the form of vitreous glazes. On the basis of some newly excavated material, it is now thought that glassmaking originated in western Asia rather than in the eastern Mediterranean littoral. Hollow glass in very much larger quantities appears for the first time in Egypt from about 1500 B.C.

Early glass centres were favourably situated in the Tigris-Euphrates region, the coastal and river areas of Egypt and along the Phoenician coast in the cities of Sidon, Tyre and Acco. The colourful glass pastes and enamel inlays of Egyptian artefacts bear witness to an abundance of fine raw materials.

The first hollow glass consists of small vessels produced by the core technique, whereby the required form is pre-shaped over the end of a metal rod, the diameter of which corresponds to the required orifice of the vessel. The form is made of clay or straw and sand, probably held together by a cloth bag. The glass mass, ground from larger pieces and reheated frequently to allow satisfactory fusion, is contained in a small crucible into which the glassmaker places his metal dipstick and trails threads of glass around the preformed core until it is covered.

After reheating and marvering smooth, the vessel was frequently decorated by the application of contrasting coloured glass threads, which could be combed with a special tool to create a feather pattern. Since metal contracts when cooling, the rod could be extracted quite easily and the remaining core cleaned out. Handles and feet were applied separately.

Cored vessels represent one of the most delightful facets of the early glassmaker's art. Turquoise and yellow colours dominate; later, almost all colours were applied.

Certain other techniques for shaping glass were available to early craftsmen. Casting glass in open or closed moulds was a logical step, since it was similar to existing techniques of metal and pottery working. Larger vessels and small ornaments could be produced by making a glass paste from powdered fragments and fusing it in the mould. In the mosaic glass technique, the vessel, usually a large open bowl, was built up from slices of coloured glass laid next to each other over a mould forming the shape, and covered by an outer mould. When fused and released from the moulds, the vessel surfaces were ground smooth. Mosaic plaques and *millefiori* glass made from slices of multi-coloured glass rods were produced in a similar manner.

Egyptian artisans were able lapidaries and it is not surprising that they applied their craft to glass. There are reasons to suppose that large glass

Syrian single-handled glass flask.

blocks were transported from their place of manufacture to regions where facilities for glassmaking were not available. This may account for glass objects of similar colour and texture found over widely dispersed areas. Such raw glass blocks were often cut and ground to form a variety of objects.

From about 1200 to 700 B.C., Egyptian glassmaking fell into a decline due to a number of political events and disasters. From the 9th century B.C., the main centres on the Syrian coast and in the Tigris-Euphrates region may have been of Phoenician origin or Phoenician influenced. Phoenicia owned a great fleet of trading ships and Phoenician-made beads and glassware found their way to the most northern parts of the world.

When cored vessels reappeared about 700 to 600 B.C., they had changed drastically in character, and display four distinct design forms: the aryballos, a globular flask with everted rim, short neck and two miniature handles with finials, applied from under the rim to the shoulder; the alabastron, a cylindrical vessel, rounded at the base with short neck and wide, flattened rim and two short handles applied below the shoulder; the oinochoe, a miniature one-handled jug with pinched-in (trefoil) lip and splayed out foot; the amphorisk of baluster shape, with a longish cylindrical neck, handles of the same length and a pointed base ending in a knop or minute disc shaped foot.

Small cored vessels between 6 to 12 cm (2½ to 5 in), rarely larger, were used as containers for perfumes and ointments. Those which were not provided with a foot were either strung up by the handles or rested on specially made stands of metal or glass.

With the coming of Alexander, industry flourished and a great centre was established in the newly founded Egyptian city of Alexandria, where the finest luxury glass was produced by workmen who had emigrated from centres in the Middle East. Asiatic glassmakers brought techniques of colouring, moulding, cutting and engraving. Fine glass seals and glass cameos of many different shades are representative of the excellent workmanship of the new Hellenistic glass industry, and formed part of the luxury ware exported during the first centuries of Roman rule. The so called muzzines, bowls of agate glass made in imitation of semi-precious stones, were still popular during the early 2nd century, and are frequent finds on Roman sites.

The momentous discovery of blowing glass by means of the iron blow-pipe is thought to have occurred during the early years of the first century A.D., and in one sweep transformed the material from luxury to domestic use. Pliny ascribes the invention of glass to Phoenician traders. Irrespective of whether this is true, it does seem that the new technique of blowing must be credited to the glassmaking centre of Sidon, on the Phoenician coast, and this is borne out by the character of the first blown vessels. These are small flasks and ewers in the shape of fruit, especially bunches of grapes and dates, and figurative vessels, particularly single or double head flasks, the latter representing the god Janus. Green or brownish colours are frequently seen in this early group of glasses, which are known as relief glasses.

The new discovery spread very quickly and soon Eastern and

Hellenistic craftsmen had set up workshops for glassblowing throughout the western domains of the Roman Empire.

Much of the early blown glass is a replica of pottery and metal ware of the period, and in the same way as Roman artisans and factories stamped their products with their own mark, so the early glassblowers incorporated a personal stamp or name in the mould.

The Roman Empire

By the end of the first 150 years of Roman expansion, the Empire stretched from Britain to Africa and from Spain to the Black Sea. Stable and prosperous conditions, particularly during the first 150 to 200 years of Roman rule, encouraged trade and industry. Glassmakers from Mediterranean centres followed in the wake of the Legions, and began to establish glasshouses in suitable areas of the western domain.

5th-century glass drinking horn.

Glass made during the period of Roman occupation is frequently termed Roman glass, even though it may have been produced by Syrian gaffers in the Rhineland or a Hellenistic workshop in Gaul. Because of the difficulties in obtaining the vital raw materials, large quantities of glass, especially luxury ware, were imported from Syria, Alexandria and Rome, and it is often impossible to determine the provenance of a piece of Roman glass.

Gold sandwich or *fondi d'oro* glasses present a specialized technique already known to Alexandrian glassworkers who established workshops in Antioch and brought their gold glass to Syria. The method involves placing patterns in gold leaf between two layers of clear glass. In the earlier Syrian pieces the gold pattern usually covers the entire area, up to a defined rim, and there may be additional cut decoration applied to the outer vessel. Gold sandwich glass reaching western territory was probably made in Italian workshops. The majority of gold sandwich glass was discovered in catacombs in the vicinity of Rome.

The earliest examples of free-blown Roman glass are the so called tear-bottles, club formed vials 5 to 12 cm (2 to 5 in) in length. Mainly funerary finds, they supposedly served as receptacles for mourners' tears, but more likely were used as unguentaria, containing perfumes and ointments. Domestic vessels, glass bangles, beads, finger-rings and earrings are common in Roman graves. They may not be elaborate, but provide one of the most spectacular features of ancient glass, the iridescence.

Iridescence or weathering is the result of long exposure to damp earth and air, and the glass surface attacked will become scaly and flake off. Although this disease is not progressive, with prolonged exposure the vessel may deteriorate to the point of disintegration. However, the striking scintillating rainbow effect of the glass surface caused by the chemical reaction of the weathering process is irresistible to the collector of Roman glass, who will not be deterred by a high price.

Roman glassmakers ably exploited the new technique of mould blowing. An attractive and individual group are the Eastern inspired glasses by the maker Ennion and his circle. Mould blown vessels of this group from Sidon and Cyprus are decorated with early Christian symbols, naturalistically patterned friezes, Greek inscriptions, circus scenes and human figures. Inscriptions usually denote the maker's name with added slogans or wishes. Dating from the first century, these pieces must represent almost the earliest glasses signed by their makers. Ennion's branch subsidiaries sprang up quickly in many parts of the Roman west. Most of these related vessels come from Gallic and Rhenish provinces, and British settlements such as Colchester. Few were produced in Italy.

The unmistakeable influence of Syrian gaffers is seen in the group of free-blown glass decorated with applied snakelike threads of opaque colour. These vessels, with or without handles or in the shape of ewers, have their counterparts in the Eastern hemisphere, but were produced in quantity in 3rd century Rhineland. The late W. A. Thorpe aptly refers to this group as Snake Thread (Rhine) Ltd!

On functional lines, several factories produced the practical Roman round or rectangular jar and bottle, an industry which flourished from the late first century. These bottles were largely produced in south eastern Gaul and frequently bear a maker's mark, the name of Frontinus occurring repeatedly. By the late 2nd century attractive vessels emerged, decorated with applied trails and spirals, and during the 3rd century tall jugs with elegant handles become popular. Fragments with painted decoration have been discovered, although never complete, but other finds include dishes and bowls decorated with shallow cutting and engraving. The most consummate *tour de force* must be attributed to the lapidary, and cameo cutting was expertly carried out in Alexandrian workshops.

During the 3rd and 4th centuries, an astonishing cutting technique evolved which has never been equalled. This is applied in the Vasa Diatreta, a mould blown, thick, ovoid or bucket-shaped vessel, which may be monochrome or cased in layers of coloured glass. The coloured casing is so manipulated by the cutter that a contrasting coloured network of delicate pattern surrounds the glass body, held only by some remaining struts. The upper half of these so-called cage cups is usually encircled by an inscription, undercut in the same manner. Figurative cage cups were made by a similar technique.

Glass in Medieval Europe

By the 5th century, a fair number of glasshouses had established themselves in the Seine-Rhine areas, largely with the help of Syrian glassmakers. Important centres were situated in the Lorraine, in Treves, Picardy, Cologne, Mainz, Namur and Liège. This fusion of northern concept and eastern know-how and artistic inspiration resulted in the emergence of a characteristic glass style, which dominates the product of all glassmaking areas in the Roman domain. Free-blown vessels with applied trails or blobs, cone beakers and drinking horns with patterns of applied threads, vases and bowls with trails applied in a diamond pattern – the 'nipped diamond waies' – and finally the intricate claw beaker, were the products of glasshouses affected by the still present but diminishing influence of Rome. The accent at this time was on domestic rather than luxury, glassware, and the 6th and 7th century glasshouses produced a metal of liquid greenish colour prevalent in forest regions where wood- or plant-ash was used as the source of potash alkali, and knowledge of decolorization was non-existent. This forest glass commonly known as *Waldglas*, or in France and the French speaking Lowlands as *verre de fougère*, was of a green or greenish blue colour, as well

Pre 1500

as of a pale amber tone, depending on local raw materials. The medieval slump or, in glassmaking language, the empty ages, had affected Western Europe by the 8th century. The church, which in the eras that followed encouraged and subsidized the arts and architecture, forbade the use of glass vessels for ritual purposes. The foreign elements introduced by Roman colonization in the form of successful competition by Eastern artisans and merchants resulted in persecution and deprivation of oriental and semitic glassworkers and any flourishing of a native glass industry was doomed.

Pre-Islamic and Islamic Glass

Not until the 4th century was the Christian religion adopted in Rome. By this time, the Empire's financial burden had become enormous. Apart from the difficulties of maintaining order and prosperity throughout a vast territory, the army met increasing difficulties in beating back hordes of barbarians which threatened to weaken – and eventually overran – the frontier lines.

In A.D. 324, Constantine I came to the throne to rule his great Empire. Christianity was adopted as the official religion of state and Constantine built himself a new capital, Byzantium, from which to rule. This split of East and West heralded the division of the Empire. In the Western part, isolated forest glasshouses produced simple, poor quality domestic glass, under hazardous conditions. In the East, however, glassmaking continued almost undisturbed under the protection and new affluence of Byzantium and her rulers. Craftsmen were encouraged by special privileges. Under Theodosius II (A.D. 408–450) glassmakers were exempt from all taxes.

Worship of the new religion was expressed by the erection of new temples, and the Byzantine basilica in all its shining splendour required equally sumptuous adornment, which survives to this day in the golden and colourful brilliance of the mosaic pictures decorating walls and ceiling, and made of millions of coloured glass cubes, *tesserae*. This aspect of mosaic art inspired the manufacture of coloured glass windows, representing a large section of glass manufacture. Stone and plasterwork consisted of a tracery of naturalistic patterns with the voids filled by small pieces of coloured glass.

Most of this attractive work was destroyed as a result of Leo III's iconoclastic movement in A.D. 726. This occurrence, as well as the sack of Constantinople in 1204 during the fourth crusade, may be a valid reason for the scanty survival of Byzantine glass, despite a prolific industry. Some pieces of green, wheel-cut glass in the form of cups and dishes are still to be seen as part of the treasure of St Mark's in Venice. This greenish glass colour is responsible for travellers' tales of enormous objects cut from single huge emeralds. The hexagonally shaped Sacro Catino cup at Genoa was originally thought to have been carved from a single emerald, and a solid emerald table on three golden feet, plundered by the Arab commander Musa (710–20) from Toledo, was most likely made of nothing else but Byzantine glass, sumptuous though it must have been.

In A.D. 634 the Byzantine forces succumbed to Moslem invaders and by A.D. 750 a huge Arab empire from Turkestan through Armenia,

12th-century Italian glass beaker.

28

Syria, Persia, Arabia, Egypt, the North African coast and Spain had been created, embracing all important Eastern glassmaking centres. Despite the mixed elements which made up the Islamic population, a distinct Islamic style had evolved by the 10th century. Due to religious ethics, the decoration was initially confined to the ornamental, non-figurative style. Geometrical wheel-cut patterns of ovals and diamonds typify 9th and 10th century glass found in Persia.

A unique group decorated by masterly relief cutting are the so-called Hedwig Glasses, named after St Hedwig, patron saint of Poland and Silesia who died in 1243 and supposedly the owner of one of these vessels, still preserved in Wroclaw.

An innovation, also thought to have originated in Egypt, is lustre surface painting, whereby a metallic colour pigment was applied and fired to form a lustrous film.

Islam's greatest contribution to glass art consists of exquisite and imaginative enamelled decoration. This technique was carried out in three stages. At first, the ornamental pattern was applied in gold leaf and fired. During the second stage the design was traced in red enamel and again fired. Lastly, the design was filled in with coloured enamels and once more returned to the muffle kiln for firing.

Islamic enamel is usually translucent, except for white, which is opaque. The main centres for this technique were Raqqa (1170–1270), Aleppo (1250–65) and Damascus (1250–1400). Glassmaking in Raqqa declined with the city's destruction by the Mongols in 1259.

Aleppo enamelling work is of a more imaginative and refined character than the Raqqa product, partly due to the gradual relaxation of Islamic laws about figurative representation. Musicians, hunters, birds, beasts, flowers and trees in elaborately traced cartouches with trefoil decoration are associated with Aleppo workshops. The celebrated 'Luck of Eden-hall' (Victoria and Albert Museum), a finely enamelled flared beaker, can most certainly be associated with Aleppo workmanship.

Rich, small-scale enamelling is one of the features of damascene glass decoration. The Saracene mosque lamps with overall gilding and enamelling, and elaborate inscriptions in stylized Naksh script created a fashion for glass *à la façon de Damas*, and many specimens have found their way into European collections. During the late 19th century, the French glass artist Joseph Brocard recreated a number of enamelled glass pieces which are almost exact copies of Damascene mosque lamps and vessels.

Characteristic friezes of animals and flowers with the added emblem of the Chinese Lotus indicate the influence of invading Mongols. When Tamerlane invaded Damascus in 1400 and deported all artisans to Samarkand, the glass industry did not survive. A revival took place much later with the aid of Murano workmen, and the best product came from 18th century Shiraz glasshouses, with the typical blue coloured rose-water sprinkler as its most elegant representative.

Venice

After the fall of Damascus and the decline of the Islamic industry, a new element was prepared to fill the void, and for almost 250 years the development and flowering of the European glass industry was determined by the monopolistic aspirations of that great maritime power, the Republic of Venice.

The origins of the Venetian glassmaking industry, even of glassmaking in Italy as a whole, are uncertain. The high Middle Ages in Italy were a time of great social instability. Many of the industrial arts, including glass, seemed to be seeking a new direction. While glass production was sporadic, the industry kept going to satisfy demand. The interest in the art of mosaics in that period led to the development of an industry making *tesserae*, particularly in Ravenna and the Venetian Lagoon area, out of which may have grown a full glassmaking industry. An alternative theory is that the industry may have been established in Venice by glassworkers fleeing from Aquileia and ports on the Adriatic in the face of the Gothic invasions of the time. Aquileia was a glassmaking centre in classical times. Archeological evidence is lacking, however, which would confirm that glass furnaces were in use in those towns in this period.

A third theory suggests that it was monks who fostered the new industry. During the turmoil of the Middle Ages it was a few religious orders and monastic communities that kept alive the spark of civilization. Their particular interests were usually of a technical or alchemical nature – goldsmithing, weaving, book-binding and glassmaking. It is possible that the Benedictines even used small furnaces. One of the most important technical books of the Middle Ages was *Schedula diversarum arta*, written by a Cologne monk around the middle of the 10th century. It gives a detailed account of glassmaking.

The actual answer to the origin of the Venetian industry may not lie in any one of these theories specifically, but rather in a combination of factors and circumstances. The monks, who had several important monasteries in and around Venice, may have introduced glassmaking, but an increasing demand for *tesserae* for mosaics resulted in the establishment of the Venetian workshops.

Certainly well before A.D. 1000 the Venetian glassmakers were at work and were known as *fioleri* because they blew glass phials. Further, by 1268, we know from records that quite a wide variety of objects were being made. It is not until the 15th century, however, that glassware was made that can be confidently dated today. The pieces that have survived from that century are of high quality and include goblets, cups and bowls for special occasions such as weddings or for ecclesiastical purposes. One of the features of this early glass was the wide range of colours in which it was made – dark blue, amethyst, red, emerald green and opaque white. Decoration, which usually consisted of portraits enclosed by medallions or floral crowns, was produced using vitrified colours fired by reheating the object.

Venice eventually became the nucleus for the manufacture of hollow glass, and in 1291 the entire industry was transferred to the nearby island of Murano. This was as much in the interest of safety to prevent conflagration as in the interest of secrecy to prevent any leakage of Venetian glassmaking techniques. Furthermore, it was intended to force buyers to purchase only direct from Venice.

The Murano glassworkers were strictly controlled and heavy punishment awaited the man who was tempted to accept employment else-

Murano glass goblet made c.1480.

where and was caught leaving the island; nor was he always safe from the long arm of Venetian vengeance on foreign soil. Nevertheless, inducement was great, and many glassworkers did escape to foreign lands. In addition, the rival industry at Altare, composed of French and Flemish workmen, imposed no such laws and even encouraged journeys abroad.

The revival of enamelling techniques was one of the earliest consequences of the newly established industry of Murano, and from Venice the art spread to all parts of the Continent where it has been practised ever since, without interruption.

The earliest Venetian enamelling is found on deep-coloured Gothic-style tazza and goblets or standing cups with outsplayed feet, together with applied, crenellated or gadrooned trail around the base of the cup. These mid-15th century vessels were frequently made to commemorate certain events, and a marriage cup would portray the groom and bride. The Berovieri family, distinguished glassmakers and decorators, are credited with this type of work. A special feature of early Venetian enamelling and gilding is a scale-like pattern and the application of bright colour dots. The colours of the enamels were a vivid red, emerald green, blue and white; the motifs were naturalistic – branches, grapes, vine leaves, flowers (especially lily-of-the-valley) and ribbons.

The British Isles

There is evidence that glaziers from Gaul were called to Britain as early as A.D. 680. Glassmaking families from Normandy and the Lorraine found satisfactory sites for their craft in the forest areas of Surrey, Sussex and Kent, and when the fuel supply became exhausted moved to Gloucestershire, Staffordshire and other suitable regions. Laurence Vitrearius (the 'window glassmaker') settled at Dyers Cross in the Chiddingfold district of the Weald at about 1226, and by 1240 was making glass for the Abbey at Westminster. The old glasshouse sites in the Weald yield fragments which correspond with Continental glass made during this period – bottles, beakers and cups of yellow or greenish metal of inferior quality. The industry concentrated on making window glass, though the best was still imported from the Continent. Laurence's son, William 'le verrier', carried on by producing hollow glass and in 1300 Chiddingfold received a Royal Charter.

Between 1350–57, John le Alemayne supplied window glass for St Stephen's Chapel and also produced some 'cuppis to drinke', but elegant table glass came from Venice.

Gold and Silver

Gold and silver, unlike other materials used in the decorative arts, have, until this century, had two distinct and easily reversible functions: they could be made into coin of the realm or into objects of use and beauty. For example, in 1540, François I of France gave the Italian goldsmith Benvenuto Cellini 1,000 gold crowns to be melted down and made into the magnificent salt-cellar which is now in the Kunsthistoriches Museum in Vienna. Conversely, at the end of the 17th century Louis XIV of France, in an attempt to pay for his disastrous wars, enforced sumptuary laws which called in all objects made of precious metal and ordered their melting into coin. This included all the silver furniture that glittered at Versailles when the court was first installed there in 1682. Gold and silversmiths would, of course, also melt down older pieces as a source of metal for their own work. All these factors constitute one of the reasons why little secular medieval gold and silver now remains from which we can judge styles and designs.

The Studley Bowl, a fine piece of 14th century silverwork.

However, from manuscripts and tapestries and from the ecclesiastical pieces which survive in slightly greater numbers, we may infer that throughout the Holy Roman Empire, from the time of the crowning of Charlemagne in A.D. 800, designs deriving from the old Roman Empire began to be augmented with flat, interlacing arabesque patterns of Near Eastern origin. These were brought in by returning Crusaders and by trade through Venice. From this same source, new techniques were assimilated. Vertical architectural features were incorporated in gold and silver vessels, which might also be decorated with human or animal figures or with inscriptions in Lombardic or Gothic script, imitating the use of Kufic script in pattern making.

Mazers are the commonest surviving drinking vessels, made of dense, impervious wood, decorated with a silver lip band and a disc in the middle of the shallow bowl. Later, the low and wide mazer shape became deeper and was gradually raised up on a foot and a stem. There was also a fitted cover. Such cups became objects of great ceremony and the customs associated with passing round such cups at banquets still exist in some societies today. Exotic objects like coconuts (which supposedly had magical properties), ostrich eggs, shells, precious rarities like imported Chinese and Turkish ceramics, minerals like serpentine and rock crystal, were converted into drinking vessels by mounting them in silver gilt. They have often survived because too little silver had been used in their mounting to warrant it being melted later on. Highly prized Venetian glasses were also mounted sometimes, and this goblet shape was copied in silver.

Medieval etiquette placed the greatest importance on the use of a vessel of silver gilt to mark the place at the table of the most honoured person at the gathering, and precedence was regulated by position above and below it. In France, this place was marked by a model of a ship called a 'nef', and existing ones show 15th century goldsmiths' work at its best. In England, a great salt cellar stood in the centre of the high table, the piece itself was often tiered and always impressive, but the salt container was relatively small.

Ewers and basins were much in use, because their decorative shapes made them suitable for display and diners had frequently to rinse their fingers in the course of a meal eaten only with spoons. Attendants took the ewer – filled with warmed and scented water – the basin and a napkin round to each guest and in this way the lavish beauty of the plate was shown off.

In 15th century Florence the verticality of former designs began, in all the decorative arts, to be replaced by a greater horizontal emphasis and

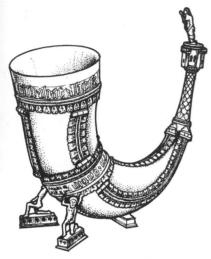

German drinking horn in gold mount c.1450.

by decoration taken from the Greek and Roman precedents. The Renaissance spread outwards from Tuscany, and putti, masks and trophies, acanthus, anthemion and rinceaux gradually superseded the older style.

European Gold and Silversmiths

There are several individual European gold and silversmiths whose work is known from the centuries before 1500. One of the earliest was Vuolvinus (c.850), this name being known from an inscription on the high altar of the church of San Ambrogio in Milan, which reads VUOLVINI MAGIST PHABER meaning Vuolvinus or Wolvinus Master Smith. The altar is the earliest known representation of a real goldsmith and is generally considered to be one of the most beautiful examples of the work of European goldsmiths. The front is composed of bands of enamel framing panels of gold repoussé work and is set with cabochons, pearls and antique cameos. The sides and back are silver, gilt, all framed with enamel bands.

Ugolino di Vieri (c.1329–80), from Siena is remembered for the reliquary of the Sacro Corporale in Orvieto Cathedral, which he completed in 1338. The work, still in the Cathedral but on public view only on Easter Day and the feast of Corpus Domini, stands 139 cm (66.3 in) high and is based on the façade of the Cathedral itself. It is not certain whether the twelve main enamelled panels are the work of di Vieri himself or someone he commissioned for this part of the work. Another surviving reliquary by him is one of gilt brass set with enamel plaques made for the church of San Savino and now in the Museo dell'Opera del Duomo, in Orvieto.

Antonio del Pollajuolo (1431–98) is perhaps best known as one of the greatest Florentine early Renaissance painters, but during his lifetime he was more renowned for his silverwork. It is thought that he was apprenticed to Lorenzo Ghiberti or his son Vittorio at the time they were working on the Baptistery doors in Florence. His first commissioned piece, which he made in collaboration with two other goldsmiths was a large silver crucifix for the Baptistery made in 1457–9. His only other surviving works are reliefs on the Baptistery altar finished in 1483.

Pre-Columbian Gold and Silver

One field of early gold and silverwork that has recently begun to interest collectors is that from the pre-Columbian civilizations of South America, in particular Peru. Certainly the work of these craftsmen is among the most beautiful ever made and an increasing number of pieces are finding their way on to the market in Europe and the United States.

While the Incas are probably the best-known pre-Columbian civilization, little of their gold survives, most of it having been plundered by the Conquistadors and melted down on its arrival in Europe. Pre-Columbian gold was in fact still being melted down in England in the 19th century. The gold and silverwork of earlier civilizations, however, has only been discovered in the last century or so and no doubt much remains to be found.

The first South American goldsmiths were probably from the Chavin culture from the northern Andes of Peru. The techniques they used were confined to hammering and embossing, although they must have known about annealing. Among other objects made by the Chavin, headbands, crowns and ear and pectoral ornaments are the most frequent. Their motifs abound with naturalistic themes, in particular the jaguar and puma which were regarded as gods.

The two cultures which immediately followed the Chavin were the Mochica of northern Peru and the Nasca in the south, both civilizations lasting until about the 8th century A.D. Although the Nasca smiths still relied on hammering and embossing alone, the Mochica were skilled at casting, soldering and smelting. Typical of the Nasca are their funerary and ceremonial masks of which the most curious is the 'mouth' mask which was suspended from a perforation in the nose. The Mochica were both more skilled and artistic than the Nasca. Some of their most beautiful and interesting objects were small figures, about an inch high, of birds and animals which were worn as earrings or as mounts for pins and

From about A.D. 500–900 the Mochica and Nasca were dominated by the Tiahuanaco from the Lake Titicaca area in Bolivia. One of the most remarkable objects of Tiahuanaco origin remaining today is a gold 'whistling vase', composed of two chambers joined by a tube. The front chamber is a human figure with a whistle hidden in the head, while the rear one is a beaker. As the water flowed from the back to the front, air was drawn through the whistle causing it to sound.

The Tiahuanaco were succeeded by the Chimu, who were even more skilled than the Mochica. Among their finest works are beakers of thick sheet embossed with highly stylized geometric and zoomorphic designs and inlaid with turquoise. Their ceremonial knives, with a semi-circular blade supporting human or animal figures intricately worked and inlaid with turquoise must rank as masterpieces.

The Incas overran the Chimu in the 13th century, perhaps attracted by the abundance of Chimu gold, for the metal was sacred to the Incas. From the little Inca gold and silver work that has survived one can judge that their style was sober and restrained but nevertheless possessed of an unsurpassed beauty. Perhaps best known of the remaining Inca gold pieces are the little llamas either cast or built up from plates which were soldered together. An example of the latter technique is the llama now in the British Museum, but this is overshadowed by a cast silver llama with a saddle blanket of inlaid gold and cinnabar now in the American Museum of Natural History in New York.

Gold and silver work of equal interest is still being discovered in other countries of South America, notably Colombia and Venezuela, though the collector should be wary of the flourishing market in fakes.

Clocks

The origin of the first mechanical timepiece is obscure. Although scholars have studied manuscripts dating from the 5th century, it has not been possible to reach any dogmatic conclusions. One difficulty lies in the fact that any references to a 'horologia' can also allude to a sundial or water-clock and not necessarily to a mechanical clock.

One commonly held belief is that the clockwork mechanism originated in the Islamic World where the sciences of astronomy and mathematics were far in advance of those in the Western Hemisphere. Whether this is correct and that descriptions carried back to Europe by the Crusaders engendered experimentation is uncertain, but strong evidence indicates that it was in the late 13th century that mechanical clocks began to appear on the Continent, spreading at a later date to England. The earliest examples were large, iron and weight driven with a verge and foliot escapement. A large bell struck the hours. Apart from small hour markings on the motion wheel and a fixed pointer this was the only method used to indicate the hour. It was not until further technical advancements had been made and the process reversed (the pointer to traverse a fixed dial), that dials were added.

Evidence suggests that the first true striking clocks originated in Italy soon after 1330, for in a manuscript entitled the *Chronicle of Galvano Fiamma* written in 1335, the author, while talking of the church of the Beata Vergine in Milan says 'There is there a wonderful clock, because there is a very large clapper which strikes a bell 24 times according to the 24 hours of the day and night, and thus at the first hour of the night gives one sound, at the second two strokes – and so distinguishes one hour from another, which is of the greatest use to men of every degree.' In an earlier account written by this author in 1306 he makes no mention of such a clock anywhere in Milan.

Although at least one expert suggests that the first striking clock, and certainly the first in England, may have been one at Salisbury Cathedral by 1306, there is more sound evidence showing that Edward III commissioned a striking clock at Westminster in 1365–66 which may have been the first English clock of its kind.

Initially, clocks were made by blacksmiths under the supervision of monks. It must be remembered that prior to the Reformation all learning was the prerogative of the Church and the monasteries the only seats of

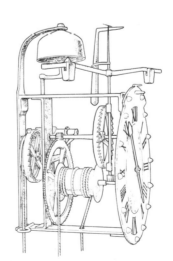

Right: *Early 15th century Italian monastic alarm clock brass and iron;* above: *late 15th century German Gothic domestic clock, iron.*

learning. It was also the monks with their strict hours of devotion both day and night that had the greatest need for a mechanically regulated timekeeper with an alarm bell. However, by the 14th century large public clocks were appearing on churches, palaces and other buildings throughout Europe. References can be found in contemporary literature to clocks on the Church in Milan (1335); the Carrara Palace at Padua (1344), at Rouen (1389) and many other locations. Many of these are no longer extant but one of the oldest clocks in England – that of Salisbury Cathedral (1386) – can still be seen in the North Transept of the Cathedral.

Large dials embodying astronomical data as well as indicating the time of day began to appear as skills grew, while others incorporated automata – a feature especially popular on the Continent of Europe to this day.

Possibly the first astronomical clock was made by the Abbot of St Albans, Richard of Wallingford between 1327 and 1336, which had dials for an astrolabe and showed the motion of the sun (and possibly the planets) and the phases of the moon. A touch of genius was shown however in the clock made by Giovanni De'Dondi, a professor of astronomy at the University of Padua, and completed by 1364. The clock, which was unfortunately destroyed in the 16th century, not only reproduced the motions of the sun and moon but also of the five known planets including Mercury with its unusual orbital patterns. Though it took De'Dondi 16 years to make the clock, its sheer complexity as well as the technical problems he had to surmount suggest he was a man of rare ability.

The earliest domestic clocks were also of iron and were weight driven with a verge and foliot escapement. The movements were held by an open four-posted frame, but although the posts and dials were decorated, the sides were left open. As well as striking on the hour, some had provision for quarter striking or alarm mechanisms. They were intended to be hung on a hook or stood on a wall bracket to enable the free fall of the weights. These early Gothic clocks, as they are generally called, first appeared in Italy and some fine examples have survived to this day. It was, however, only a short time before the craft passed to South Germany with the towns of Nuremberg, Augsburg, Cassel and Ulm becoming recognized centres. Similar clocks were also made in France and Switzerland, but England produced few domestic clocks in this period.

Domestic Metalwork

The development of domestic metalwork is quite similar to that of architectural metalwork, except that in many cases it was the smaller objects of domestic use that preceded the larger architectural applications.

The ancient world was dominated by bronze, and some of the objects made in the first two millenniums B.C. remain unsurpassed for beauty, for example the multitude of hand mirrors made in Egypt, Greece

Domestic Metalwork

Bronze Gothic aquamanile.

and the Roman world. The basic design, wherever the mirror happened to be made, was largely the same as that of a modern mirror: a highly polished disc to provide the reflecting surface, sometimes decorated on its reverse, with a handle which was also usually decorated. The handles of mirrors were sometimes cast in the form of a figure, human or divine, sometimes the periphery of the disc had cast figures of cupids or animals, and sometimes the reverse side of the disc was engraved with an allegorical scene as in some charming Etruscan examples.

But bronze was used for all kinds of things: for votive objects by the Celts, for throne decorations by the Assyrians, for vases, lamps and boxes by the Greeks and Romans, for plaquettes by the Byzantines. The list could be extended almost indefinitely. In China, fine cast bronze was in extensive use by the second millenium B.C. for objects as varied as those made in the West, from hollow vessels to statuettes. The development of Chinese bronzework was unique in many respects.

Iron in antiquity was probably used for domestic objects to a greater extent than is now evident, for rust and other corrosives must have destroyed much, with the result that, apart from a few fragments of various artefacts, one or two andirons (fire-dogs) and similar objects, there is nothing to indicate how widely it was used.

Lead, too, is only represented by a handful of objects, though these are varied in form, among them Egyptian votive slabs, Roman cups and lamps, Greek weights, vases, boxes and plummets.

The same pattern of usage for these metals and alloys continued from the fall of the Roman empire until the dawn of the Middle Ages. Artistically, as may be expected, design was cruder in the early part of this period, yet it often has a barbaric strength and compelling spontaneity. It varies from the relatively simple design and decoration on bronze stewpots made by Huns, to highly decorated cruciform brooches made by Anglo-Saxons. Such a splendid specimen as the wonderful shrine of St Patrick's bell or Bell of the Will appears later (about 1100). This was made to the order of Donal O'Loughlin, King of Ireland (National Museum, Dublin), and consists of bronze worked in a combination of casting, sheet metalwork and forging, decorated with gemstones. Another important work is the font decorated with three-dimensional figures illustrating the life of John the Baptist and supported by bulls, in the church of St Barthelemy, Liège, Belgium (12th century).

The Gloucester candelabrum made about 1112 and dedicated to the Abbey of St Peter at Gloucester, England, is of almost oriental splendour (Victoria and Albert Museum, London). Another handsome 12th century candelabrum, this one having seven branches, and measuring 5 metres (over 16 ft) in height, is in Brunswick Cathedral, Germany; it is said to have been the gift of Henry the Lion, Duke of Saxony. A 12th century bronze door-knocker in the form of a lion and a ring is in Lausanne Cathedral, Switzerland. A bronze thurible of the same century, architectural in form, inscribed with the name Gosbertus, is in the Cathedral of Trier (Rhineland-Palatinate, Germany). Among its architectural details it embodies busts of Moses, Aaron, Isaac and Jeremiah, with Solomon enthroned at its apex. Laton or latten was also used at this time, especially for such utensils as ewers, like the 13th century

German specimen in the form of a lion in the British Museum, London.

Little domestic ironwork survives from before the 12th century. Few large pieces remain, so it is hardly to be expected that smaller works will have survived. However, there are a few fragments which remain: one or two early locks and furniture fittings, and here and there a horse-shoe, but little more.

Lead was widely used, mines being operated in France, England, Saxony, Silesia, Bohemia and Andalusia, yet an insignificant amount survives. Two examples will suffice: a lead sheet in the British Museum inscribed with an edict of Charlemagne, in which he assumes the title of Emperor of the West, and bearing the date 18 September 801; and a 12th century casket in the form of two boxes, one inside the other, which once contained the heart of Richard Coeur-de-Lion, discovered in 1838 in the choir of Rouen cathedral, France and bearing the inscription: HIC JACET COR RICARDI REGIS ANGLORUM (Here rests the heart of Richard King of the English).

With the 13th century came the beginning, especially in France, of a period of brilliant domestic ironwork dominated by the technique of the locksmith and closely influenced by that of the armourer. Such objects made at this early date are very rare, but those that do remain illustrate the virtuosity of which craftsmen were already capable. One such is a pair of wafering irons, a pair of tongs with its terminations in the form of two engraved plates, between which batter is poured, and which are then heated so that wafers for communion hosts are made. Later the irons were adapted for household purposes, such as making waffles. This pair of irons is so elaborately engraved that it is a tour de force in this respect alone, and is to be found in Cluny Museum, Paris.

Despite the rarity of actual specimens of 13th century benchwork, one or two pattern books survive which give some idea of the scope of the work made at this period. One series of designs by the architect Alessandro Romani is in the Public Library at Siena, Italy.

In the next two centuries, and indeed until the 18th century, the objects made by benchwork multiplied enormously. It would be difficult to imagine greater refinement in ironwork than that which was achieved in this work. The vast amount of labour involved, to say nothing of the loving care in making a lock, is almost impossible to assess. There is, on a miniature scale, as much carving in a few square inches as would be present on many a cathedral wall or reredos. The minute jewel-like precision attained in such an uncompromising material, well matches the mathematical construction of Gothic architecture in general. And although the lock is a marvellous specimen, it is by no means unique. Such locks, large and small, are the pride of fine collections at the Cluny Museum, Paris, at the Le Secq des Tournelles Museum, Rouen, and at the Victoria and Albert Museum, London. They were made right up to the latter part of the 18th century, reflecting the taste of the period in which they were made. Sometimes, in the later periods, they were decorated with putti and other allegorical figures. Padlocks also were made throughout these centuries.

As with the locks, so with the keys. The bows (handles) of some 15th and 16th century examples are decorated with arms or monograms, while the bits (the parts that move the wards in the lock) are cut with such complication and precision that they look like gatherings of Gothic lace. Later there was a tendency for the bows to be cast, but the decoration did not diminish.

Apart from locks and keys, the benchworker made many other objects, including furniture fittings (hinges, bolts and key-escutcheons), nails with ornamental heads, judas grilles (which were fitted to doors so the householder could see who was knocking), door knockers, caskets (a very beautiful group), sewing accessories, tableware, bag frames, seals, candlesticks, lecterns, and even statuettes.

The benchworker's tools were made as beautifully as his products. Hammers, vices, chisels, hacksaws, shears, tongs, small lathes and many others were as carefully wrought and as elegantly decorated as the locks, keys and other artefacts that came from their owners' workshops.

The surface decoration of benchwork is finely conceived and applied. Some objects, such as jewelry (even finger rings were made) were gilded all over. But the commonest decoration was by engraving, etching or, especially in the earlier work, by sculpting. Fretwork and castings were also used, the former being sometimes underlaid with leather, velvet or cloth, when it is called *marouflage*. Some doorplates thus decorated are at King's College Chapel, Cambridge, England (early 16th century).

One of the most attractive forms of surface decoration was damascening, also used on fine armour. The name is taken from Damascus, a centre for swordsmiths, where the craft originated; it was perhaps introduced by such craftsmen into Spain during the Arab rule, whence its use must have spread over Europe. It consists of making undercut dovetailed grooves on the object to be decorated, filling them with silver, gold or copper wire and hammering it so that it fills them out, and becomes keyed in position.

Not all of the work was small scale. Large coffers with complicated locks, for containing treasure or documents, were not uncommon. Such a specimen as the 16th century coffer in the Archaeological Museum, Madrid, Spain, must have been almost impossible to penetrate without a key. It is also superbly decorated, especially on the handles, lock escutcheon and even on the actual mechanism of the lock.

Another large object is the wrought iron chandelier in the church of Vreden, Westphalia, Germany (1489). This consists of a big ring of fretwork, around which are Gothic niches containing statuettes of saints, in front of each of which is a little crown surrounding a candleholder. Above all of this, in the centre, is a figure of the Virgin and Child standing on a crescent moon, with rays of glory surrounding them. Above this statuette is a hexagonal structure again decorated with fretwork and with applied lettering; at each corner is a little spire, and the whole is in turn surmounted by two more figures and further spires and at the apex is yet another spire and a little coronet.

Benchwork was used also in Italy, where some of its finest products were lanterns. Four, on the Strozzi Palace in Florence, are in the form of hexagonal temples; they were made by Nicolo Grosso, called Caparra, in 1500. Another, by the same craftsman, derived with variations from the same design, is on the Guadagni Palace in the same city. This classical detailing is completely of the Renaissance, yet the lanterns were made at a time when the Gothic style still prevailed in most other parts of Europe.

Forged ironwork was used for domestic utensils throughout this period, but not much is left. The expensive items made in benchwork would have received special care and therefore have had a greater chance of survival. Nevertheless, some things remain, including items of furniture. Such is the 16th century gilded wrought iron four-poster bed, probably of Sicilian make, now in the Bagatti Valsecchi House, Milan, Italy. It is elaborately wrought with twisted uprights surmounted by bouquets of flowers and with great pyramids of flowers at the foot and the head. An extensive collection of similar beds is in the Sicilian Ethnographical Museum near Palermo.

During the whole of this period bronze and brass continued in use. Bronze cauldrons were cast, usually with legs, but sometimes without if they were intended for hanging from a chimney crane. They usually have two handles and are sometimes decorated with bands, either plain or patterned. The design was probably developed from bronze-age cauldrons made of riveted sheet-metal, such as had been used in the 8th or 9th centuries B.C.

Skillets and posnets or pipkins of various designs were also made. They were a kind of deep pan or saucepan with legs (usually three) and with a long handle decorated with a pattern or with the name of the owner or maker, or with a motto or text. There was a type without legs for use with a wrought iron stand. They were usually made of brass or bell metal, and later were sometimes fitted with cast-iron handles. They were used as early as the 13th century, but were made as late as the 19th century and were known in colonial America; there is one at Mount Vernon, George Washington's home.

Other cast bronze utensils made in the Middle Ages and soon after

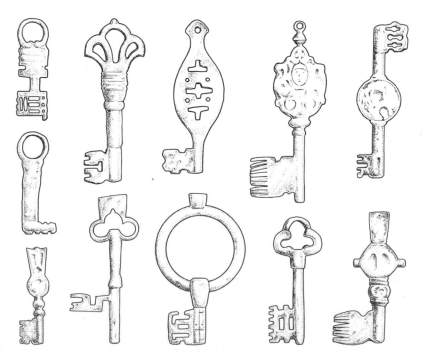

Left: *Some early keys from the Roman, Frankish, Merovingian and Carolingian periods.*
Right: *Elaborately carved Spanish fall-front escritoire dating from the 16th century. Made of walnut, it has inset panels of burr walnut with orangewood crossbanding.*
Following pages: *Casket made in Augsburg, c.1570. The elaborate decoration uses rock crystal and various semi-precious stones.*

Left: *Crystal cross or crucifix watch made by Jean and David Rousseau, c. 1660.*
Right: *A domestic alarm clock of the late Middle Ages, weight-driven, with revolving dial. Height 16 in.*

Left: Tigerware jug with Elizabethan silver gilt mounts. The band at the neck is chased with strapwork. Made in London 1566.

Right top: Aragonese/Castilian ewer and basin in silver parcel gilt, late 16th century.

Right below: A pair of delicately potted openwork bowls made in the reign of Wan-li (1573–1619).

included jugs, ewers, pestles and mortars and candlesticks, some of them elaborately decorated and of beautiful shape. But, as with other things, they continued to be made for long afterwards, and even until the present century. A Renaissance bronze ewer by Desiderio da Firenze is outstanding, with its richly moulded decorations of swags, masks, fruit and other devices.

Laton was much used for memorial brasses, which originated in the Low Countries at about the first quarter of the 13th century. These plates were engraved with an effigy or with emblems and inscriptions. Many brasses have been destroyed, especially on the Continent, but the earliest extant example is at Verden, near Hanover, Germany; it commemorates Bishop Yso Wilpe, who died in 1231. Some of the brasses in England were Continental work, like that of Thomas Pounder and his wife at Ipswich, which is Flemish (1525). But the majority are English; there are about 10,000 examples remaining in England, more in fact than in all of the rest of Europe.

Meanwhile work in cast-iron had been progressing. It was used for early ordnance, which had been made possible by the invention of gunpowder in 1325. The ordnance was as dangerous to those who were firing it as it was to the enemy, but its use persisted, and out of the resulting cast-iron industry which developed in the Weald of England grew the manufacture of domestic cast-iron work.

The cast-iron grave slab was one of the earliest products; it might have been suggested by the memorial brass. One or two early examples still remain. The oldest is in Burwash church, Sussex (mid 16th century) decorated with a cross and has, in Lombardic characters, the inscription in relief: ORATE P. ANNEMA JHONE COLLINS (Pray for the soul of Joan Collins). Another, much closer in design to brasses, is in Crowhurst church, Surrey; it is a memorial to Anne Forster (1591) and bears an inscription, heraldry, figures and a representation of a shrouded corpse. Cast-iron grave slabs were made until the late 19th century, one as late as 1885 is in St Leonard's churchyard, Bilston, Staffordshire.

Pewter

The earliest medieval pewter that has survived comes from the Gothic period and much of it is ecclesiastical pewter. The use of pewter as a substance suitable for chalices can be traced to the Synod of Rouen in 1074 at which the use of wood for chalices was forbidden but pewter allowed where it was not possible to provide chalices of more valuable metals. The Council of Winchester adopted the same ruling in 1076. However a century later the Council of Westminster instructed bishops to consecrate only gold and silver vessels. Nevertheless necessity due to poverty often prevailed and pewter continued to be used.

Sepulchral chalices of pewter were allowed however, indeed every church was supposed to have two chalices – one consecrated for use, the other for burial with the priest. Quite a large number of these have been found over the years in graves at Chichester, Cheam, Gloucester, Lincoln and Westminster to name but a few. The form of most chalices of this period is similar – wide-mouthed, tazza-shaped with an attendant paten.

Other ecclesiastical pewter in use included large vessels for transporting

A fine gold necklace made by the Chimu of South America and probably dated from the 12th century.

wine from the cellar to the sacristy and for the ceremonial washing of the celebrant, and small burettes – pewter bottles for the wine and water – which date from the 14th century. In England these were later called cruets. Two surviving cruets from the 14th century were found in the moats of Weoley and Ludlow castles. Both are hexagonal-shaped with relief-cast panels showing religious scenes and the quality of workmanship is high. Small pewter candlesticks were in use about the same time as burettes, though larger ones as well as hanging candelabra were still made of iron, brass or copper.

Portable pewter bénitiers – vessels for carrying holy water – resembled small buckets and mention of them being used in several 14th and 15th century French churches has been found. Caskets for the Eucharist, incense boats and their spoons, font bowls and small bells were also made in pewter. A pewter font of 13th century design has been found at Cirencester.

The pattern of use of household pewter was quite the reverse of ecclesiastical pewter, for while the use of the latter reached its peak in the 14th century and was declining by the 15th century, household pewter re-emerged at the beginning of the 14th century and was in general use at least by the upper classes by the 15th century.

The earliest mention of domestic pewter is of the export of a few pitchers, dishes and salt-cellars from London in 1307. Until the 14th century makers of pewter were probably general metalworkers rather than specialists but by 1319 four pewterers are known to have been working in London. In 1348 ordnances for the control of pewtering in London were registered, indicating the extent of the growth of the industry.

Jewelry

Good jewelry of any period speaks to us in many ways. It says much of the designer's love of precious materials, it betrays the manufacturer's skills with metals, enamels and stones, it shows, very often, an attempt to express in miniature a notion of perfection and it also says a great deal about the person who purchased it and wore it and about the society in which he or she lived. Jewels were designed not only to be admired from a distance, but also to be handled and the collector or enthusiast is always limited if his knowledge is restricted to viewing pieces behind glass in a museum or shop.

To handle a piece of jewelry is to experience its particular charm, its own special magic, the magic that early craftsmen imbued in all their work. Pick up a fine 17th-century pendant and turn it over. The illusion is not immediately shattered, but sustained through fine modelling and engraving. There is no façade behind which the supports, struts and scaffolding may be plainly seen. Jewels were designed to be viewed in the round, like a piece of sculpture.

Primitive societies recognized this mystical element in jewelry and

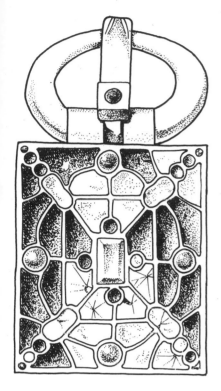

Early medieval enamelled and jewelled buckle from Germany.

buried pieces with their dead as talismans and amulets to serve the owner in the afterlife. With the advent of the Christian epoch, however, this custom was to die out and as a result we know more about the jewelry of classical Greece and Rome than about the medieval period.

Another major contributor to the scarcity of early examples lies within the jewels themselves. The materials used in jewelry have three major elements in common: first, and perhaps principally, beauty; secondly, rarity; and thirdly, durability. It is this last element, the durability of the materials, which allows the continual re-working and remodelling to follow the vagaries of fashion and taste, that has spelt destruction for so many early and fine examples of the art.

The 14th Century

The first decades of the 14th century were an age of Gothic romanticism and love of natural beauty that was reflected in the jewelry of the time. The scope of the jeweller was being broadened by the increasing abundance of gemstones and by the advent of pointed and table-cut diamonds to complement the existing cabochons. Enamelling was also an innovative area, marked by the discovery of translucent enamels around 1300. The early application of the new enamels involved covering a flat relief engraving in silver with a transparent film of enamel so allowing the background to reflect in colour.

One of the great techniques of the Gothic enameller was *émail de pliqué* – the use of translucent cloisonné enamelling on gold. The method was practised only in the 13th and 14th centuries and may have originated in Paris. Notable surviving examples are the falcons sewn on a *pallotto* of brocade given by Archbishop Carandolet (1520–44) to the Cathedral of Palermo.

The increasing use of gemstones in the 14th century led to them being regulated by law and in 1331 a law was passed in Paris forbidding the use of paste gems, while in 1355 jewellers were forbidden to use river and oriental pearls together, or to use coloured foil as a backing for some cabochon-set stones.

Finger rings were popular throughout the 13th and 14th centuries and unlike earlier examples they were not always based on classical designs. Instead, greater attention was paid to simple elegance and refined lines. Two rings of this period, now in the Victoria and Albert Museum, one a sapphire and the other a ruby ring, have such simple, clean lines that could just as easily have been made in recent years. Cabochons were used for rings until the late Middle Ages, while the claw setting continued into the Gothic period, although it began to be overtaken by the use of high collets fashioned to follow the lines of the stone. The lover's ring originated at this time and was often inscribed with simple prose or verse.

As the 14th century progressed more exotic tastes in jewelry became evident at the French Court and throughout Europe jewelry had achieved such social significance that its use was regulated by law to the extent that what a person could or could not wear in the way of jewelry was determined by his social standing.

Head ornaments and belts were becoming fashionable, the former often reaching quite fanciful heights, while belts were studded with gold or enamel plaques on silk or gold tissue. The number of buttons and accessories on all kinds of dress was increasing and any opportunity to wear still more jewelry was welcomed. It was during this period that jewels began to be worn as individual ornamentation, separate from their function as dress adornment and the jeweller towards the end of the 14th century, though still heavily controlled and restricted by the courts of Europe began to show a new freedom of style that eventually blossomed in the 15th century.

The 15th Century

The wind of revolution that blew through all the arts in Europe during the 15th century also had a dramatic effect on jewelry. For the first time the jeweller was able to emerge from the goldsmiths' guilds, where he had been confined throughout the Middle Ages to manufacturing liturgical objects under the patronage of the Church, or jewels commissioned by princes or noblemen, and to develop his art alongside his colleagues in painting and sculpture. Indeed, the new style evident in jewelry of this period may be partly attributable to painters and sculptors such as Verrochio, Pollaiuolo, Brunelleschi and Botticelli, many of whom started their careers in the goldsmith's workshop.

Gothic jewelled brooch shaped like a bird.

Jewelry, thus freed from the constraints of the Church, was allowed to develop freely and become a perfect expression of individual taste, a means of personal expression that was to prove indispensable to the display of prosperity of the emergent mercantile classes. Exploration and trade overseas was already adding to the materials available to the artist craftsman. This, combined with the general increase in wealth evident throughout Europe, accounts for the extraordinary number of jewels which survive even today, testifying to the ostentation and splendour of the time.

Unlike painting and sculpture, Renaissance jewelry was not a rediscovery and celebration of classical Greece and Rome, rather it borrowed from these sister arts, especially sculpture, to develop a pictorial vocabulary of its own. It is likely the general techniques of goldworking had survived since the classical period, but there were very few pieces available for study. Perhaps the only direct link with Greece and Rome was through the revival of the glyptic art (the technique of carving and engraving hardstones) with the result that many classical cameos were copied, imitated, and incorporated into rings, brooches and pendants. Jewellers also borrowed certain decorative motifs from the antique – the arabesque and scrollwork that Raphael had popularized through his decoration of the loggie at the Vatican, and the grotesques inspired by the frescoes discovered in the 'grottos' of the Baths of Petrus.

The emphasis during this period was upon harmony of design and craftsmanship rather than a display of wealth. This is not to say that stones were unpopular, rather they were incorporated into a design for their chromatic value and emphasized through the subtle use of coloured enamel and elaborate settings. The most common type of cutting of this period is the table-cut, where, as the name implies, the stone was roughly faceted so that it displayed a flat top, though many coloured stones remained *en cabochon*, like a pebble. Settings were generally of a square, pyramidal design with the top edges lapped over to retain the stone, very often with the additional ornament of imitation claws. The jewels themselves were nearly always pictorial in design, or at least contained pictorial elements drawn from the wide range of subject matter which the new literature had made available. These included subjects taken from classical mythology, romance and heroic poetry, as well as medieval symbolic images such as the 'pelican in her piety', and, of course, the mythical unicorn.

Perhaps the most original type of jewel to be created during this period was the hat badge or *enseigne*, which derives from the medieval pilgrim sign, and was quickly adopted to display the taste and individuality of the wearer through the choice of subject matter. Many of the contemporary portraits illustrate quite clearly how the jewel was worn. The most notable perhaps, are those by François Clouet, Bartolommeo Veneto and Holbein.

The signet ring served the same purpose as the *enseigne* in exhibiting the personality and individuality of the wearer. These were often set with an intaglio of either contemporary or classical manufacture, or engraved with a device, monogram or cipher to act as a seal. Other rings were more elaborate, often richly enamelled and with caryatid supports to the high collet, or set with portrait cameos or miniatures. Diamonds were used in the natural octahedral form so that the point of the stone protruded from the collet, allowing the owner to use it as a scribe on glass. Rings were also used to celebrate certain events. The most attractive are those connected with betrothals or weddings, most notably the *fede* ring where the bezel is formed by a pair of hands clasping a heart or

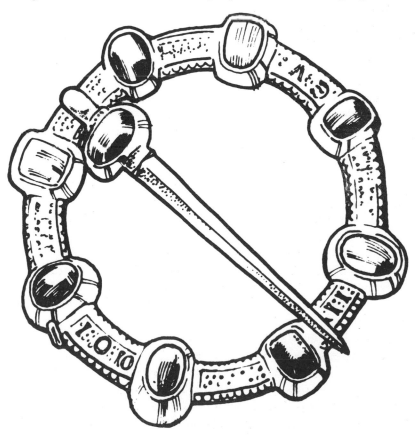

Medieval jewelled brooch.

gemstone. Mourning rings were also popular, the shanks engraved with skeletons, the bezels set with death's heads or coffins. Contemporary portraits indicate how liberally rings were worn, gracing every finger, even the thumb, and very often the first and second joints as well.

Necklaces were worn in profusion and were generally of exceptional length, encircling the throat several times and cascading over the bodice. Many different types were often worn together, contributing to the opulent effect. Chains of plaited wire had survived in popularity since the Middle Ages and were augmented by more elaborate designs incorporating plaques and cartouches enriched with enamelled grotesques and arabesques and set with various gems. Pearls strung into long ropes are also evident in the portraits of the time, and were often hung in festoons at the middle of the bodice from a central brooch.

Embroidery

Embroidery – the embellishing of fabric with stitches – was already a well-established craft in 16th-century Europe. For several centuries professional embroiderers had been among the most respected of craftsmen, their art linked with that of the illuminator. Most of them, at least in England and France, were organized into powerful guilds which, by maintaining high standards of workmanship and by protecting the interests of the embroiderers, helped to ensure the high standing of the craft.

It was customary for the royal courts of Europe to employ professional embroiderers to work heraldic insignia and all kinds of furnishings. The church was also a lavish patron, and although some work was done in monasteries and convents, the best and most valued was made by professional specialists. From early on 'the labours of the distaff and needle' were considered of prime importance for ladies all over Europe, and spinning, weaving and fine needlework formed an important part of every girl's education prior to her marriage.

Border motif from vestments of St Thomas of Canterbury c.1200–50.

In the medieval period the finest of all embroidery was the ecclesiastical work produced in England. Opus Anglicanum, as it was called, was worked with coloured silks and couched gold and silver threads, and the designs – of saints, angels and heraldic motifs – have close parallels in the manuscript illumination of the time. Opus Anglicanum was exported to Europe on a large scale, and although France, Germany and Flanders produced embroidered vestments of a similar style, their quality rarely matched the fine work which came out of the ateliers of London and East Anglia.

The ground for most of these embroiderers was twill-weave, silk-lined with linen. Velvet was used from the early 14th century instead of linen. Other grounds used included samit, taffeta, camoca (a combination of fine camel hair and silk) and, from the 14th century, satin. Some of the most common Opus Anglicanum stitches include *Opus conscutum* – appliqué, *Opus phrygium* – gold work, *Opus anglicanum stitch* – split

Motif from the Ascoli Piceno cope, 1275.

stitch, and *Opus pectineum* – woven or combed work.

Inventories and accounts from the Vatican are a valuable source of information on Opus Anglicanum, for it was favourite with many Popes and the bulk of Vatican embroideries of this time were of this kind. Many of the best examples of this work are ecclesiastical vestments and one of the finest copes now remaining is the Syon Cope in the Victoria and Albert Museum. A study of the copes of the whole medieval period has revealed that there were three distinct periods in the evolution of Opus Anglicanum.

The earliest period is from 1250 to 1275 and the principal features of the designs are saints or Biblical events enclosed by a medallion. Groupings are arranged in concentric circles. Few examples of this period now survive.

The second period is from 1275 to about 1325 and the Syon Cope was made at this time. Rather than being confined by circles, the figures and scenes in the design are ringed by Romanesque quatrefoils sometimes interlaced. Another surviving cope of this period is the Daroca Cope in the Museo Arqueológico, Madrid.

The last period occupies the remainder of the 14th century. Figures now stand under Gothic arches and the scenes are separated by columns. The finest Opus Anglicanum comes from this period.

Chasubles have also survived and a typical example in the Victoria and Albert Museum is in red brocade with scenes from the life of Christ with saints standing under Gothic arches. Mitres were embroidered in Opus Anglicanum though only fragments have survived, such as the remains of one belonging to Bishop William of Wykeham (1367–1404), now in New College, Oxford. The embroidery used both silver thread and gems.

The Victoria and Albert Museum also has an altar frontal from the late 14th century. Worked on a ground of crimson velvet, the figures are appliquéd in gold, silver and coloured thread and surround the crucifixion scene. Palls have survived in greater numbers, many of which are in the possession of London livery companies such as the Vintners', the Saddlers' and the Fishmongers' Companies.

The quality of Opus Anglicanum work began to decline during the 15th century, although a magnificent pall belonging to the Fishmongers' Company which, it seems, could not have been made before 1536, has suggested to some experts that the age of Opus Anglicanum might be extended by a hundred years.

Although the emphasis in 14th and 15th century Europe was on ecclesiastical embroidery, there was at the same time a growing use of domestic embroidery. Woven tapestries, for example, were of importance in furnishing the draughty castles and houses of the rich, and embroidered bed hangings were also invaluable in the cold winters of northern Europe.

There was an increasing use of embroidery for costume and personal adornment. Much of this, whether it took the form of fine linen undergarments or the embroidered and bejewelled purses for which France was famous in the 15th and 16th centuries, was done domestically as well as by professional and religious embroiderers.

Edged Weapons

Flint has been used by men for tools and weapons for hundreds of thousands of years. Man made knives, axes and spears in great quantities. Arrow heads were expendable and were produced in particularly large numbers and, consequently, are still readily available at quite reasonable prices. Generally speaking, the earlier ones are cruder and lack finish, while those of the Neolithic period are polished and well shaped. Many are barbed and most have a short neck which was used to secure the head to the wood or reed shaft. Many primitive cultures continued to manufacture arrow heads of flint long after metal had replaced its use for other weapons. Some Red Indians of North America and the Aborigines of Australia were still making them at the beginning of this century.

Flint is brittle and is unsuitable for constructing long blades, so swords of flint were not practical. When man discovered the secret of melting tin and copper together to make bronze he was able to cast a greater variety of weapons in moulds of clay or stone. Axeheads, daggers, arrows and spear heads and swords were produced all over Europe and

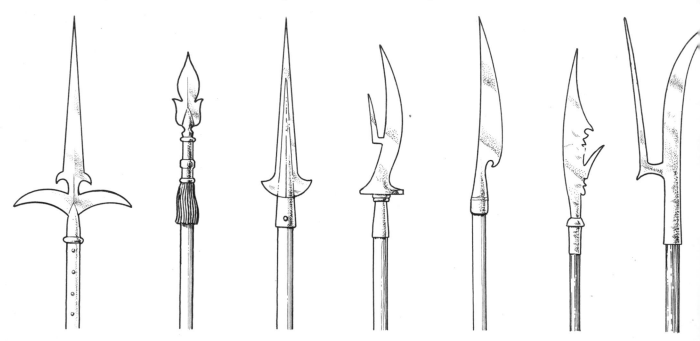

Left to right: *Spetum 1490, partisan 1570, partisan 1580, three glaives, guisarme.*

sufficient have survived to ensure that some still appear on the market: swords are likely to be the rarest and most expensive. Many of the bronzes available today are from Luristan in Asia Minor, and are generally of good quality although unfortunately a number of very good copies have begun to appear so care when buying is essential.

By the 1st century A.D. iron had largely supplanted bronze as the metal for weapons. While iron was better for manufacture it was far less able to survive the centuries. Bronze could resist rust and rot, iron could not and swords dating from the 1st century until the 15th century are extremely rare and very early examples are likely to be little more than masses of blackened rust. The few good quality examples which have survived will certainly be very expensive.

Probably one of the most ancient of all edged weapons was the gisarme or guisarme which receives frequent mention from the 12th to the 17th century in Europe and was a form of long-headed axe that terminated in a sharp, strong point. A little way down the blade a flattened hook projected. In medieval times it was known as a fauchard, while towards the end of the 15th century it is possible that the term 'gisarme' was used to describe the halberd.

The halberd seems to have been of Swiss origin and the first mention of it occurs in 1287, although it was not introduced into France and England until the end of the 14th century. It appeared in various forms

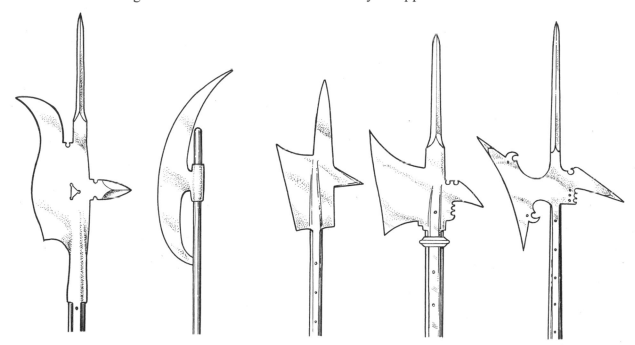

Left to right: *Bill 15th century, berdiche 15th century, Swiss halberd c.1450, German halberd c.1500, Venetian halberd c.1500.*

but was basically an axe-blade surmounted by a spike and balanced by a short fluke at the rear of the blade. By the end of the 15th century the blade had undergone several changes through oblong and horizontally wider to crescent-shaped on some examples.

The great age of the pike began in the late 15th century and lasted until the 17th century. A simple weapon, the pike consists of a long, narrow, lance-like head of steel with lengths of metal running from the head down the pole to protect the latter from sword strikes. At the other end of the pole an iron shoe or point protected the pole base when it was stuck in the ground to resist cavalry attacks. Other edged staff weapons in use in the 15th century included the partisan – usually a long double-edged blade, wide at the base where it was provided with projections of various kinds. The Ranseur and the Spetum were variations on the partisan.

The Voulge was very similar to the gisarme and originated in Switzerlan. The Bill was one of the commonest weapons of the foot-soldier and was derived from the agricultural scythe and so had a crescent-shaped head the inside of which was sharpened while a section of the top of the blade was double-edged. Variants often had the top of the blade dividing into a spike and forward curved hook. The Bill was particularly popular in England. The Glaive had the cutting edge on the opposite side to that on the Bill and had hooks and spurs near the base of the blade.

Until the first half of the 15th century the lance was simply a wooden staff some 3–4.25 metres (13–14 ft) long, fitted with a lozenge- or leaf-shaped blade. During the 14th century jousting lances began to be fitted with a circular hand-guard or vanplate.

Generally the medieval sword had a long, straight blade, usually double-edged, fitted with a simple cruciform cross guard, a leather covered grip and a counter-balance weight (the pommel) at the end of the grip. These swords were essentially slashing weapons designed to hack at armour and mail and some were made big enough to be gripped with two hands. One, known as a hand-and-half, was small enough to be used in one hand but with a grip big enough to hold with both hands to deliver a very powerful blow. A larger version, the two-handed sword, was so large that it could only be used with a two-handed grip.

Very few swords and daggers dating from the 12th–15th centuries appear on the market, but those dating from the 16th century onwards are more readily available.

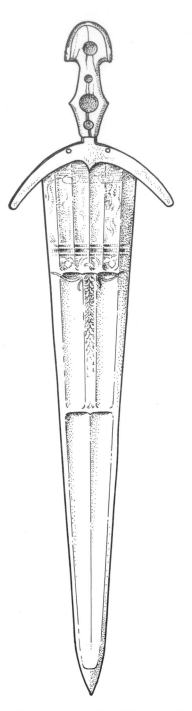

A cinquedea *or Italian civilian sword, 1490.*

16th
CENTURY

Introduction

It is not surprising that the Renaissance, which was in part a revival of classical culture, had its origins in Italy, the heart of the old Roman Empire. Since the new movement represented a change in human attitudes towards the world it made its first appearance in literature and then spread to architecture, sculpture and painting, from where it influenced all the decorative arts. The Italian Renaissance is divided into three periods: Early, 1400–1500; High, 1500–40; and Late, 1540–1600.

Throughout the 15th century a spirit of research which accompanied the new reflections on the world, led to the rediscovery of classical works of literature and the excavations of the archeological remains of the Roman Empire. With every new discovery the artist was provided with further inspiration and stimulus to advance the state of his art to even greater heights. Of particular importance was the rediscovery of *De Architectura*, which were the manuscripts of the Roman architect Vitruvius who worked in the reign of Augustus, and the excavation of the Baths of Titus and the Golden Home of Nero in Rome in 1488.

In 1485 Leon Battista Alberti published his *Ten Books on Architecture* (*De re aedificatoria*) which was a masterly synthesis of Vitruvius' principles and much original material by Alberti himself. He advocated a system of ideal proportions in architectural design, believing that the application of mathematical ratios to building was in itself beauty-producing. Alberti thus made a significant break with all his predecessors and the visible result was a clean, dignified and stately style in which the decoration was primarily columns and pilasters.

The discovery of the Baths of Titus and Nero's home stimulated a leap forward in the decorative arts. The stucco decoration of both buildings with animal, floral, human and grotesque motifs all symmetrically placed was adapted to furniture, metalwork, gold and silversmithing, pottery, textiles and jewelry in the early 16th century.

The Renaissance should not be seen however as a backward-looking search for the glories of a lost empire but as a momentous advance in human culture – a desire not so much to re-create classical culture but to use it as a springboard to the future. The innovations of the craftsmen of the 16th century are a notable illustration of this desire.

The cabinetmaker was, for the first time, primarily concerned with the proportions of his furniture to which he could then apply classically pure decoration. Italian cabinetmakers turned away from oak which was difficult to carve and decorate, to ebony, walnut and so on. Framing was adapted as a method of construction which allowed decorative techniques not used before. Both Italian and Spanish cabinetmakers were influenced by their contacts with Islam. The geometric and naturalistic motifs of Moorish decoration were highly appealing to the Renaissance artist. New furniture forms were also developed, reflecting the needs of a population who were becoming accustomed to more permanent dwellings as the political turmoil of the Dark Ages subsided.

The cassone was a development of the Gothic chest while the cassapanca was a form of sofa which evolved from the cassone as the cabinetmaker sought newer forms. The characteristic 'X' or scissor chair which had been a portable folding chair now became a rigid piece of furniture that was richly decorated. In Spain the chest evolved into the *vargueño*, a type of desk. Tables were no longer designed to be folded away thus opening up a whole variety of forms and decoration to the cabinetmaker.

Italian gold and silversmiths also drew heavily on the surviving buildings of ancient Rome and Greece for their inspiration, tending to use clean, well proportioned lines for the form and to use decorative panels. The smiths of Florence achieved renown throughout Europe for their ingenuity and originality of style and their casting techniques.

Venice, on the other hand, was the centre of the world's glassmaking industry. Although the secrets of making high-quality glass had been lost in the Dark Ages they were rediscovered around the 11th century and by the 13th century a glass industry was established on the island of Murano. Venice began to rise to its pre-eminent position in the 15th century and reached its peak in the 16th century. The glassware of the 15th century though reflecting the splendour of the Renaissance by the use of colour and enamelling, tended to be influenced by silverware of the day and was rather heavy and massive in shape. By the 16th century lighter design had opened the way to more fanciful forms and the invention of *cristallo* was the *pièce de resistance* of the Venetian glassmakers. The fragility of *cristallo* led glassmakers to concentrate upon form rather than applied decoration. Thus glassmaking came of age.

The Renaissance reached France sometime after 1450 at a time when the Gothic style was at its peak. As a result the first effects of the Renaissance were restricted to applied decoration. During the reign of François I (1515–47) the first distinctive Renaissance style came into being and underwent subsequent changes during the reign of François' successor, Henri II, and later (1610) with Louis XIII.

Spain first showed signs of Renaissance influence at the end of the 15th century where it became known as the Plateresque style because decorative work was similar to the fine work of the silversmith. Although the goldsmiths of Spain borrowed much from Renaissance Lombardy in their designs – foliated scrolls, classical heads, mythical beasts and so on – they made a style all of their own and their work is amongst the finest of the Renaissance metalworkers. The skill of the Spanish metalworkers extended to wrought-iron grilles, railings and so on. Spanish tables, as elsewhere, were no longer designed to be portable and were notable for being bound by wrought-iron stretchers.

The Renaissance did not reach England until the reign of Elizabeth I (1558–1603) and even then the transformation remained incomplete, the Gothic style determining form with Renaissance decorative motifs added on.

By the middle of the 16th century in Italy the creative outpourings of the Renaissance were all but spent and until the end of the century the short-lived style called Mannerism was the dominant influence. The Mannerists ceased research into nature and natural appearance as source material and turned back instead to the masters of the High Renaissance

61

such as Michelangelo, and to relief sculpture for inspiration. But around the turn of the century a new style began its march across Europe. The age of the Baroque was beginning.

Furniture

The Renaissance had been evolving in Italy for nearly a century before its influence reached Northern Europe in the early years of the 16th century. The Netherlands were the first to adopt Renaissance forms and it was from there that the style was disseminated to Germany, Scandinavia and England through circulated prints such as those by Cornelis Floris (active in the 1550s), who introduced Renaissance scrolled ornament and grotesques to the Low Countries and Germany in mid-century. Engravings by Hans Vredeman de Vries (1527–c.1604) and his son Paul (1567–c.1630) accelerated the diffusion of northern Renaissance design.

Around 1580 in Antwerp, de Vries published a pattern-book showing strong Italian Renaissance and Mannerist influence in his designs for four-poster beds, tables, chairs, cupboards and other furnishings. The cornices, caryatids, pilasters, arches and other architectural details illustrated in these plates were to be as important for northern European furniture production as his depictions of scrolls, spindles, figures, heavy strapwork and gem-shaped bosses.

Late Renaissance joined cupboards of the Netherlands, particularly those of Antwerp, were characterized by this heavy style. Set on bun feet, they had panelled doors ornamented with rectangular mouldings and separated by pilasters or consoles. Turned supports of spheres, blocks and balusters, the latter often fluted, appeared on Flemish stools, benches, chairs, tables and beds, often joined by similarly turned stretchers.

In Germany, prints executed by Albrecht Dürer (1471–1528), Peter Flötner (c.1485–1576) and the de Vrieses, circulated Renaissance-inspired forms and motifs which furniture-makers had widely adopted by the mid-16th century. Engravings by Lorenz Stöer (active 1555–c.1620) popularized designs for the inlay and marquetry ornament of tables and cabinets, with involved and complicated perspective views that included overgrown architectural ruins, strapwork, rollwork and odd polyhedral forms such as dodecahedra.

In the conservative and more commercially isolated north, stylistic changes occurred more slowly; pieces were heavily formed and enriched with massively carved figures and ornament. Gothic vestiges, such as linenfold ornament on cupboards, lingered well into the mid-16th century.

Application of classical architectural motifs to French furniture forms in the first half of the 16th century created the bold, vigorous François I style. Tables carved with griffins and grotesques, beds with baluster posts and pictorial hangings and panelled chairs, benches, stools and cup-

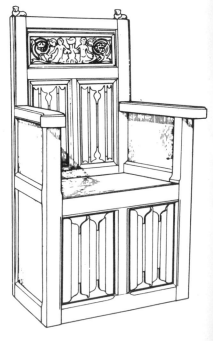

English oak armchair with panelled back.

boards exhibited the initial ripples of Italian influence in their ornament and form. In the second half of the century the integrated, more independently French Henri II style developed, shaped largely by the engravings of architecture and furniture executed by the designers Jacques Androuet du Cerceau (*c.*1520–*c.*1584) and Hugues Sambin (*c.*1520–*c.*1601). Architectural details, fruit and foliage, caryatids and lion, ram and eagle forms ornamented the heavily carved armoires and tables of this period. These also appeared on the characteristic four-doored cupboard in two stages, which was often carved with figures and crowned by a broken pediment.

Du Cerceau's first book of architecture appeared in 1559 and served to establish his reputation firmly. He went on to publish several other books of engraved designs for silver, textiles and furniture as well as architecture, drawing heavily on the silver designs of Hans Brosamer and the engraved ornaments of Polidoro, Agostino Veneziano and Perino del Vaga. He was the first French architect to publish furniture designs in the Renaissance style and despite the fantastic and elaborate style of many of his designs, several pieces of furniture still exist, particularly sideboards and cupboards which are clearly derived directly from his book. Other pieces in which his influence is apparent omit some of his more imaginative details.

It is not known whether Sambin ever actually made a piece of furniture and his reputation seems to rest mainly on interior work for the Palais de Justice in Dijon, notably a wooden screen which separates the chapel from the Salle des Pas Perdu, as well as on his book *Oeuvre de la diversité des Termes, dont on use en Architecture*. Some existing cabinets seem to show the influence of Sambin particularly in the style of their term figures which exhibit the curious fantasy quality typical of Sambin.

The school of Fontainebleau combined the styles of du Cerceau, Sambin and the Italian craftsmen imported by François I and Henri II to decorate the palace of Fontainebleau in the Renaissance manner.

French furniture craftsmanship in the second half of the century showed increasing mastery and refinement of the techniques of carving, dovetailing and joinery.

Tudor furniture

In England the prospering wool trade and the sale of monastic lands after Henry VIII's dissolution of the monasteries in the 1530s led to a national proliferation of manor houses, reaching an extreme form with 'prodigy' houses such as the magnificent Longleat in Warminster, begun in the 1560s. These stately homes were enlarged and multiplied in Elizabeth I's reign, when the expense of entertaining the Queen's entourage, and of improving features that her critical eye might find defective, led to more than one devious scheme to keep her away.

The geometric gardens and curious plans of these buildings, some shaped as their owner's initials (as was the ornament often carved on the furniture they contained), expressed the Tudor delight in intellectual curiosities.

Many English beds, cupboards and refectory tables resembled the massive and bulbous forms illustrated in Flemish and German pattern-books, especially those of Hans Vredeman de Vries. English pieces were generally joined of oak, with turned stretchers and legs that occasionally dominated design, as in the wholly-turned bobbin chairs with triangular seats. Various local woods were combined in the geometric pattern, chequering, and strapwork inlaid into gate-leg tables, beds, chairs and the pilasters that commonly divided the oak wainscoting of room walls.

The use of the word 'cupboard' in Tudor times is something of an anomaly, for although it originally meant 'cup-board' that is a table for cups and plates, it began to acquire partly or fully enclosed sections. Hall and parlour cupboards for instance, were made in two stages, in which either both stages or the upper one only were enclosed by doors; the press cupboard on the other hand was completely enclosed by doors. Food cupboards were often made with doors that had ventilation holes cut into them.

The court cupboard was an Elizabethan innovation and corresponded to the old sense of cup-board for it was an open three-tiered side-table used for holding the family plate. The central and upper stages often had drawers decorated with strapwork. The word 'court' seems to have been derived from the French *court*, meaning short, for these cupboards were rarely made more than four feet high, but on the other hand they were widely used at Court.

Another Elizabethan development was the draw table which, as the name suggests, was an extendable table with two leaves beneath the main surface. The first reference to such a table is in an inventory, taken in 1552, of the Duke of Somerset's furniture. A particular feature of the tables is the large bulbs on the legs called 'cup and cover' from their similarity to silver covered cups.

Chairs of this period with panelled backs and arched crests were carved with strange conglomerations of Tudor roses, Gothic linenfold ornament, dates and grapes, pomegranates and foliage, grotesques, stumpy figures and other motifs ornamented tables, beds, benches and X-shaped chairs.

Ceramics

The 16th century spanned the middle and late periods of the Ming Dynasty in China, a century which finally saw the arrival of mass-produced ceramics and the beginnings of the export trade to Europe. The Portuguese were the first to reach China in 1516, although it was not until 1595, when the Dutch East India Company established itself in Canton, that large-scale exports began.

The craft of the potter was influenced as never before by the Chinese court which for the first time began sending large orders for porcelain designed and decorated in a manner specified by the court. As a result, both the quality and style of porcelains reflected the often widely differing tastes and desires of both the various Emperors and others who had influence at Court, in particular the despotic Moslem eunuchs employed there.

Chêng-tê 1506–21　　*Chai-ching 1522–66*　　*Lung-ch'ing 1567–72*　　*Wan-li 1573–1619*

During the reign of Chêng-tê (1506–21) supplies of 'Mohammedan Blue' became available again after a lapse of some 60 odd years. This was the cobalt ore imported from Persia, that had been responsible for the blue of 'blue and white' since the 14th century. Also at this time deposits of cobalt ore of good quality were discovered near Ching-te Chên. The so-called 'Mohammedan wares' are interesting examples of the blue and white of this period. They were so named because they were heavily influenced by the Moslem eunuchs at the Emperor's court. Most of the articles made were writing table utensils – ink slabs, brush rests, boxes and vases. They are usually inscribed with a motto in Arabic and are often decorated with Mohammedan scrolls or arabesques.

Although the Imperial factories were dominated by the eunuchs, other blue and white pieces of non-Moslem character were also made. These represent a transition between the classical styles of the 15th century and the mass-produced styles of the Chia-ching and Wan-li periods. Bowls, ewers and vases were made in abundance with characteristic 15th century decoration. The blue of this period has a somewhat greyish hue as do some of the wares of the previous reign of Hung-chih (1488–1505). From surviving pieces made in private factories it would seem that some potters at least were making an effort to continue the traditional styles of decoration, regardless of the Moslem influence.

Chêng-tê was succeeded by Chia-ching (1522–66), a devout Taoist, who had little or no interest in governing. Nevertheless, despite the lack of Imperial direction the blue and white of this reign, when produced for the court, was of a high standard. The cobalt deposits discovered in the previous reign were now reaching the potter, who began to use them in preference to Mohammedan Blue.

Because of the Emperor's dedication to Taoism, the commonest motifs were Taoist, in particular a peach tree shaped into the form of *shou*, the Chinese character for longevity. Children at play or *wa-wa* decoration was also popular and indicates a growing trend towards a new naturalism and less use of traditional motifs. Much of the porcelain of this period however, was below Imperial quality as mass production became the order of the day.

The decline of the Ming Dynasty became clearly evident during the reign of Wan-li (1573–1619), a decline which was reflected in the quality of Imperial porcelain. The potter's work was made more difficult by various factors, not least of which was the exhaustion of the fine clay beds at Ma-ts'ang and the oppression of the potters by the court eunuchs who were intent on amassing their own porcelain collections. Nevertheless the period was one of innovation; a pair of delicately potted openwork bowls now in the Percival David collection typify the spirit and skill of the potter when he was allowed the time and resources to be creative.

Italian Maiolica

Italian maiolica, which was well-developed by the end of the 15th century, maintained its distinctiveness well into the 16th century. Two centres of note are Deruta and Gubbio.

The Gubbio workshops of Giorgio Andreoli specialized in the application of a brilliant ruby-coloured lustre. This factory remained in the family until 1576. Deruta, in Umbria, started to produce wares with a brassy-yellow lustre from about 1500, but the fine quality rapidly deteriorated from about 1530. From the late years of the 19th century, the lustres of Deruta have been imitated in a poor manner, by Cantagalli of Florence, who uses a boldly painted cockerel in blue as his mark.

The principal development in maiolica in this century was the style of painting called *istoratio*, pictorial representations of the writings of men such as Ariosto, Ovid, Pliny and other authors of antiquity, as well as the Bible. Painters took their inspiration from both engravings and woodcuts; after 1830 the principal engravings used were those of Marcantonio Raimondi after the works of Raphael. Wares of this latter type were at one time referred to by collectors as 'Raphael wares'. The finest examples of this much copied fashion were produced originally in the workshops of Orazio Fontana in about 1565.

It was during the middle years of the 16th century that Italian potters appear to have become increasingly acquainted with Chinese porcelain, the result being to leave the thick white tin-glaze with little or no decoration, a form of ware (*bianchi*) which soon found favour abroad.

German Salt-Glazed Stoneware

Despite the popularity of tin-glazed earthenware, the use of a clear lead-glaze over the natural coloured clay bodies was to continue throughout Europe and had by the 16th century reached a very high standard. But wares of this type were to take second place in Germany to salt-glazed stoneware, a development which took place towards the end of the 14th century.

Stoneware has all the advantages of a hard-paste porcelain, merely lacking the colour and the quality of translucency. Due to the high content of silicic acid, the material vitrifies at a high temperature and although a glaze is not essential, the appearance and texture were improved by throwing common salt into the kiln at the peak firing-temperature. The resultant close-fitting glaze was often coloured an attractive brown by the previous application of a clay slip rich in iron.

The earliest of these wares were probably made at Siegburg, in the Rhineland, where the tall slender jugs, known as *Jacobakennen* were made as early as 1400. Wares from the 16th century can sometimes be identified by the initials or signatures of such well known Siegburg potters as Knütgen, Symonds, Flack or Oem, all of whom were engaged in producing a wide variety of well designed vessels, including the tall cone-like tankards (*Schnellen*), or the long-spouted ewers (*Schnabelkanne*), wares usually decorated with moulded or carved relief decoration. Examples of these stonewares sometimes have English silvermounts.

German salt-glazed stoneware jug c.*1575.*

Glass

Venice

Towards the end of the 15th century, the Venetian glassworkers began to lose interest in pictorial decoration and sought ways to use it less or not at all, instead giving more attention to the material itself.

The greatest Venetian development was the re-discovery, *c.*1500, of decolorizing agents, resulting in the production of a colourless, transparent glass metal, *cristallo*. To retain its clear property, *cristallo* had to be blown fairly thin, and although brittle it was exceptionally pliable, a joy to the gaffer who exploited this sometimes to the point of absurdity. A distinctive style emerged, resulting in graceful airy shapes and exaggerated winged glasses with applied handles, writhing and snake-like, and sometimes in a clear strong blue colour contrasting well with the colourless body of the vessel. Finials and handles were often additionally manipulated by pinching flat with a patterned tool, and rims were crenellated and wavy. Despite the interest in clear glass, one of the innovations of the late 15th–early 16th century was 'chalcedony' glass, named after the semi-precious stone which it resembles. A variety of objects were made in 'chalcedony' – jugs, plates and ampullae with small spouts.

A significant development was the *latticinio* or lace glass technique. This most decorative glass effect is achieved by embedding opaque white enamel threads in a clear matrix, produced by blowing clear glass into a mould lined with canes of opaque white glass. The canes adhere to the colourless glass mass and the paraison is then manipulated to form a variety of patterns, the *tour de force* being the true criss-cross filigree net (*Netzglas*). The whole is then covered with a layer of clear glass, and the filigree pattern is truly embedded. When the white threads were arranged in spiral or interweaving patterns the method is known as *reticello* ('net-working'). The threads were often so close together that they completely covered the object; colours were not restricted to white, red and blue also being used. *Reticello* was fashionable throughout the 16th century.

Alexandrian colour techniques were successfully revived in the late 16th and 17th century. *Schmelzglas*, a process by which glass of several colours are allowed to fuse and run into each other in a natural stone design in imitation of various agates, is found in graceful forms of Grecian-inspired urn or ewer shapes. It was revived during the 19th century in several countries and particularly by the Italian, Salviati.

Around the middle of the century enamelled decoration fell into disuse and was replaced by *a freddo*, a method of painting on glass without having to reheat the object. Such painters worked particularly on the underside of the bases of plates, glasses and goblets and their motifs were taken from prints and wood engravings of the period.

The Venetian craftsmen also revived a technique of decorating glass after it had been moulded, in which the design – trees, branches and so

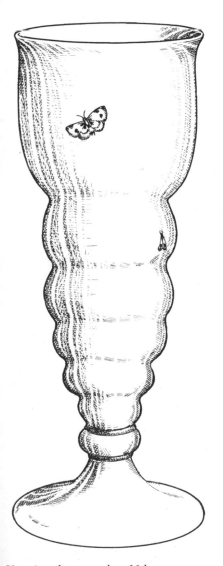

Venetian glass vase, late 16th century.

67

on – were traced around the edge of the object with a diamond or flint. Glass chosen for this type of treatment was usually transparent or deep red or blue. The cuts or incisions were extremely light and feathery, but despite the gracefulness of this work it did not reach the standard of similar Dutch and Flemish work.

One of the most practical inventions of the Italian gaffer is the folded foot. The glassmaker needed a firm base for his vessel and by folding the soft glass under to obtain a foot rim of double thickness, this was achieved. This important innovation was quickly adopted elsewhere.

Ice or crackle glass was another Italian invention but was only short-lived. It was produced either by brief quenching of the hot glass bulb in water, which caused numerous fissures on the surface (which could then be reheated and blown to requirement), or by rolling the glass bulb in powdered glass fragments which adhere to the warm glass, and then further blowing and reheating to obliterate sharp edges. This last method was revived in 19th century France and named *brocs à glaces*. In contrast with the fanciful shapes of plain brown *façon de Venise*, ice glass is of more down-to-earth design – beakers, standing cups – with added decoration applied in the form of gilt lion masks and glass pearls.

All these processes are seen in glass produced in Netherland glass-houses such as Antwerp and Liège, where Altarist and Venetian glass-makers had settled. It is therefore frequently impossible to distinguish between *façon de Venise* made on Italian or Flemish soil.

A branch of glassmaking that began in Venice during the 16th century was the manufacture of mirrors. It is not certain who first used glass in place of metal for a mirror but it is thought that it may have begun in Germany. It was left to the Venetians however to spread the art and to use them in their homes. Early glass mirrors were quadrangular in shape with a frame made of glass held by metal connectors. Both the mirror and the frame were often incised with floral or figurative motifs.

Venice monopolized the Italian glassmaking industry throughout the century. Elsewhere in Italy much of the industry was devoted to producing everyday domestic wares rather than the luxury goods of Murano. In the province of Tuscany, particularly at Empoli, Pisa, Lucca and Florence, the well-known *fiasche* or bulb-shaped glass bottles held in straw were made. There is evidence that the Tuscan glassmakers were attempting to make table glasses in the 14th century, but even by the 16th century they had not achieved the quality of the Venetian product. Some goblets with winged stems, bowls and cups have survived and are described as *alla veneziana*. The glassmakers of Florence became re-nowned for their medicinal and pharmaceutical glass.

With the opening of Eastern trade routes, Venice too commenced production of milk-glass in imitation of the newly imported porcelain. During the 18th century, the Miotti glasshouse in particular responded to the latest fashion with drinking vessels and table-ware in milk-glass (*lattimo*), decorated with exquisite enamelling in bright colours and in black or sepia. By this time, however, Venice had lost her monopoly of the glassmaking industry and this was taken over by Bohemia and England. Each was very different in its concept, but both produced glass of excellent quality and design.

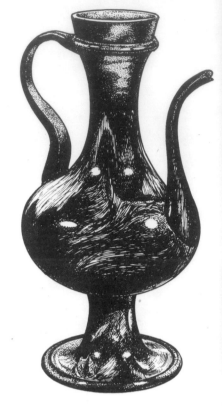

Venetian glass ewer simulating chalcedony c.1500.

Several factors had contributed to this transition. The European glass industry had grown so successful that there was a decrease in glass imports from Venice. Spain and the Netherlands had developed into maritime powers due to the discovery of new trade routes by way of the Cape of Good Hope, and Venice was losing her supremacy on the seas. There was still a demand for mirrors and chandeliers, but a new invention pushed aside the fragile Venetian *cristallo* – the invention of a sturdy glass · metal capable of supporting decorative treatment by deep cutting and engraving, gilding and enamelling by annealing. Bohemia and England shared this success – one with a potash-lime glass composition, the other with the sparkling lead crystal.

England

By 1567 Jean Carré had arrived in London from the Lorraine by way of Antwerp and commenced making window glass by the Lorraine method under licence. Several Continental glassmaking families had already settled in England. The Schurterres in the 14th, the Peytowes in the 15th, and in the mid-16th century the famous Huguenot families of Tyxach (du Thisac), Henvey (de Hennezel), Tittery (de Thietry) and Hoc (de Houx) arrived to lay the foundation of the Stourbridge glass industry.

Carré obtained his licence for making *cristallo à la façon de Venise* at the Crutched Friars Hall, a glasshouse which apparently was already in existence in 1564 or 1565, though seemingly not particularly efficient. Carré therefore sent for Venetian craftsmen, among them the great glassmaker Jacopo Verzelini, who supposedly arrived in London from Antwerp in 1571. There are sources which indicate that he may already have arrived in 1565 and initiated the manufacture of Venetian *cristallo*, and this opens an interesting field of speculation as to the merits of Jean Carré's role in the manufacture of *cristallo* at this early period. Suffice to say that in 1572, after Carré's death, Verzelini was the master of the Crutched Friars glasshouse, and in 1574 he obtained a Royal Patent from Elizabeth I to manufacture Venice glasses for a period of 21 years.

Of the dozen or so glasses associated with Verzelini today, about nine can be attributed to his London glasshouse. The earliest, dated 1577, is in the Corning Museum, New York. Typical features are the stem with hollow mould-brown knop or bulb, bowl of ample size, and of clear, faintly greenish or greyish metal. Diamond engraving in the hatched Italian style is associated with Anthony de Lisle who had come to England from the 'Dominions of the King of France' and applied for citizenship in 1597. A lozenge motif on the bowl and sometimes foot, scrolls, floral sections, friezes of trees, stags and hounds and commemorative inscriptions seem typical of de Lisle's work. Occasionally, Verzelini's glasses are decorated by enamelling or gilding, but this has worn badly. Glasses made at the same period in Hall, in the Tyrol, are in some instances so similar to Verzelini's work that they might have been produced in his glasshouse, and bear testimony to the communication and exchange between glassmakers throughout Europe.

Despite malicious acts by jealous merchants and importers, Verzelini led the industry until his retirement in 1592, and thus initiated the era of monopolies. Sir Jerome Bowes held the monopoly until 1604, when the licence was sold by one profiteer to another.

Bohemian humpen *glass, 1594.*

Bohemia and the German-speaking Lands

Slovakia, Silesia, Moravia and Bohemia are the areas involved in Czech glassmaking. In common with the Rhenish product, the greenish bubbly Waldglas appears in traditional forms. The beaker with applied prunts – *Nuppenbecher* – appears in various modifications: the *Igel* (Hedgehog) with prickles, and the tall *Krautstrunk* (cabbage stalk) covered with pointed prunts in circular arrangement. The antique sprinkler emerges as the *Angster* or *Kuttrolf* with bulbous body and long, slightly twisted glass tubes. The *Maigelein* (a low cup) still appeared in the 15th century. Common vessel forms are the *Humpen*, a tall cylindrical glass of giant proportion, the *Passglas* and the *Stangenglas*, of narrow cylindrical form with applied hollow foot.

With the expansion of the German mining industry, fuel costs rose steeply and in the 16th century a number of small glasshouses and individual glassmakers moved to Bohemia and Silesia where conditions were more favourable. The big landowners and nobility were quick to realize the advantages of possessing large tracts of forest land. They began to set up glasshouses on their estates, attracting glassmakers and their families by granting special privileges – a development paralleled in France.

Baroque and Rococo prosperity, the support by the Church of artisans and artists, and the monastic activities of winemaking and ale brewing all encouraged an expansion in drinking glass manufacture. This in turn proliferated enamelled decoration of a most fascinating kind which flourished particularly during the 17th and early 18th centuries. Scenes from the domestic and political life of the nobility and of influential artisans or tradesmen, Biblical subjects, representation of the 'Seven Ages of Man', the double-headed eagle (Reichsadler) with armorial shields of all embracing lands, and entire families and family trees are enchantingly represented in a refreshing rustic style. Emblems of Trades Guilds and scenic representations, as for instance the Ochsenkopf, a mountain in the Fichtelgebirge, frequently have added inscriptions and permit easy identification. Small beakers, straight or everted at the rim, decorated with brightly enamelled heraldic motifs are usually ascribed to Saxonian manufacture.

Gold and Silver

By the beginning of the 16th century, increasing quantities of silver were being mined in Germany, Austria and Hungary. The mines of India and the Americas further increased the supply. This coincided with a turbulent period in Italy, when in 1526 Rome was sacked, and the consequent dispersal of artists carried ideas to other centres, both in Northern Italy and beyond. Rulers all over Europe now began to vie with each other in the culture and the magnificence of their courts, setting themselves up as patrons and collectors in the manner of 15th-century Italian princes and embracing the new style learnt from Italy, which everywhere gradually

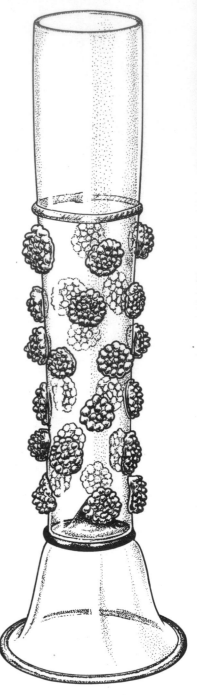

16th-century stangenglas *decorated with prunts, late 16th century.*

German tankard, c.1540.

drove out Gothic motifs in favour of classical decoration.

Court artists were employed to create designs for goldsmiths to follow, an arrangement which can occasionally be detected in the unsuitability of a design for the material in which it is nevertheless superbly executed. Important centres of goldsmiths' work at this time were Paris, Augsburg and Nuremberg. But as the artists who worked in these and other centres came from all over Europe and used designs by Court artists such as Guilio Romano, J. A. Ducereau, Hans Holbein and Cornelis Floris – which were subsequently engraved and passed round lesser workshops – it is difficult to detect any particularly national flavour in work of this period.

The power and prestige of Hapsburg Spain (which also included the Kingdom of Naples) and of the Hapsburg Holy Roman Empire, with a sphere of influence which stretched from Antwerp across Europe to Prague, was enhanced by Spanish control over the rich imports of bullion from the New World into Andalusia. Much of the treasure coming into the Iberian peninsula was used to make objects for ecclesiastical use. Gold brought back from India by Vasco da Gama, who first rounded the Cape of Good Hope in 1497, was used to make a monstrance. Although the goldsmiths of southern Spain were the first to receive the increased supplies of gold, silver and precious stones, it was not until the 1570s that a national Spanish style evolved out of the varied work that had previously been carried on in the many regional centres. From the 1570s, however, the richness and austerity associated with Philip II's building of the Escorial continued to be associated with silver, until the Baroque style emerged in the next century. In the greater part of Europe the clarity of Italian Renaissance forms gradually became obscured because Northern artists, frightened of empty spaces, tended to overload a design with detail. At the same time, a complete mastery of his craft by the goldsmith led to ever greater display of virtuosity. Wenzel Jamnitzer of Nuremberg (1508–85), for example, is renowned in part for his dazzling technique, learnt from Paduan artists.

Jamnitzer's earliest surviving work is the 'Merckelsche' table-centre now in the Rijksmuseum in Amsterdam. The piece is a remarkable example of many of the goldsmith's techniques – embossing, engraving, enamelling and so on, as well as an example of Jamnitzer's penchant for casts of insects, reptiles and grasses. His other surviving pieces include a nautilus shell set in silver gilt, *c*.1570 and the *Kaiserpokal* or Imperial cup, made in 1564, which is less elaborate than many of his table-centres and has a statuette of Emperor Maximilian II on the lid.

Benvenuto Cellini (1500–71) is probably the most famous of all goldsmiths, although our knowledge of his actual skill is entirely reliant on his only surviving piece, the famous salt-cellar made for François I of France and now in the Kunsthistorisches Museum, Vienna.

Sometimes overshadowed by Cellini is the Italian goldsmith Antonio Gentili (1519–1609), who is best known for the magnificent cross and accompanying pair of candlesticks in silver gilt made for Cardinal Alessandro Farnese who gave them to St Peter's in Rome in 1682. The set is still used on the high altar on special occasions. The influence of Michelangelo on the architectural and figurative elements of these pieces is clearly visible. The Metropolitan Museum of Art in New York has in its possession a silver knife, fork and spoon which it is thought may be the only other Gentili work now remaining. The evidence for the authorship of these pieces is a drawing of a spoon, also in the possession of the museum, which is almost identical to the existing spoon and which is signed by Gentili. In addition, the elaborate handles in classical motifs correspond to descriptions of Gentili's work by his biographer Giovanni Baglione.

Between 1515 and 1523, Enrique de Arfe (1470–1545) made a *custodia* – a Spanish portable tabernacle – for Toledo Cathedral which has been described as 'the last word in Gothic ecclesiastical silver'. It stands some 3 metres (10 ft) high, weighs more than 3 hundredweight and is adorned with 260 statuettes scattered amongst Gothic arches and pinnacles. De Arfe was born in the village of Harff in the Rhineland, from which he takes his name. He trained in Cologne and went to Spain before the turn of the century. His earliest known *custodia*, which is also his first known work was made for the Abbey of San Benito at Sahagún. A *custodia* he completed in 1518 for Cordova Cathedral can still be seen, unlike a ten foot high *custodia* he made for Léon Cathedral which was destroyed in 1809 to help pay for the war against Napoleon.

Enrique was succeeded by his son Antonio whose first recorded *custodia* was for the Cathedral of Santiago di Compostella, begun in 1539 and finished in 1545.

In politically restless Northern Italy, a style of decoration evolved from the beginning of the 1520s in which interlacing leather-like straps, ending in curls resembling wood shavings, were used at first to frame, then to decorate and finally to dominate interior decoration. This strap-work was pushed to its extreme in designs for metalwork and all through the 16th century its influence was felt throughout northern Europe. Its nervous uneasiness was allied with grotesques derived from late 15th century Italian revivals of Imperial Roman decoration. Mannerist designers continued to use Renaissance decorative ideas, but gradually the stylish way in which a theme was expressed became more important than the theme itself. To express an idea in *una bella maniera*, to use the then current phrase, could become the only goal of an impoverished mind and brilliant technique might slickly embody a worn out theme.

Tankard, London 1585.

Clocks

It seems likely that the first successful spring was not made before the last quarter of the 15th century, the problem lying in making a spring of sufficient power that would continue to drive a clock without breaking. Brass was probably the material of choice for the first springs. One of the first difficulties that the inventor would have faced is that as the spring unwinds it gradually loses power, driving the clock unevenly. Two solutions to this problem were eventually found – the stackfreed and the fusee. The stackfreed was developed in Germany about 1510 but only survived into the 17th century being superseded by the fusee which was far more efficient. A notebook of Leonardo da Vinci's from about 1500 contains the first known illustration of a fusee and it also seems likely that the first spring clocks came from Italy, although no early examples survive, only references to them in early papers dated 1482 and 1493.

Peter Henlein of Nuremberg was responsible for the first significant technical advances in the spring-clock in the first decade of the 16th century. One of only three suriving clocks of the early 16th century is in the possession of the Society of Antiquaries in London and is signed 'Jacob Zech' (Jacob the Czech). The clock has a year wheel showing the position of the sun in the zodiac and an hour circle that could be adjusted for countries such as Bohemia and Italy that used a 24-hour day. Other than these two clockmakers the only other known one is Caspar Werner.

The first spring driven clocks were horizontal with the cases either drum-shaped, square or later hexagonal. The sides were fully enclosed and frequently highly engraved. Progress was rapid and soon highly ornate and more complicated clocks appeared. Greater accuracy was possible and so minute hands were added. Automata and astronomical dials appeared, together with complicated strike and chime mechanisms. An alternative method of enclosing the mechanism was devised in the early part of the century. The top-plate and dial-plate are fixed to the movement frame while the sides and back are left open. The whole assembly is then slipped into a case which has much of the front open. This method, by providing the large bare surfaces of the case, gave ample scope for decoration.

Centres in South Germany produced the finest clocks at this date. Organized guilds in these areas were particularly strict and by now distinct from those of the blacksmiths, locksmiths and gunsmiths. The Parisian Clockmakers Guild had also been granted a charter by François I, but the Company of Clockmakers was not established in England until 1631.

Left: *Stackfreed mechanism, 16th century.*
Right: *Italian tabernacle clock c.1580. The face and the pendulum movement were later 'improvements'.*

73

The advent of the mainspring opened the door to the possibility of travelling clocks. Although there is some doubt about the authenticity of the story, it is said that Louis XI (1423–83) was the owner of the first travelling clock, which it was said, was small enough to fit into the sleeve of his gown. The clock was supposedly delivered to the king in 1480 by Jean de Paris, so that if the story is true the king owned a clock that was not weight-driven, so preceding the earliest known Italian examples first seen in 1485.

Other than the Zech clock, another clock of German origin from *c*.1550 and now in a private collection, is a further step on the road to travelling clocks. Drum-shaped, with no engraving on the case, it has an iron movement with a tall fusee and large balance, but no balance spring. The clock has a leather travelling case with lock and key.

Drum-shaped table clocks with detachable alarums were in use on the continent from *c*.1540–1600 and many were equipped with leather cases. One late 16th century table clock by Roweau of Paris, which has a circular balance but no balance spring, would appear to be just a table clock except for the fact that the leather case has a window to show the dial, implying that it was not only meant to be carried but was also in operation while travelling.

Watches

Watches undoubtedly developed from portable clocks, the latter becoming possible once the source of motive power was the mainspring rather than weights. It is now thought that the mainspring was possibly in use by the 1450s and it was definitely known by 1477.

There is some uncertainty about who invented the watch but references in *Cosmographia Pomponiae Melas* (1511) by Johannes Cocclaeus point to locksmith Peter Henlein of Nuremberg. However, Italian clockmakers were active in this period and by 1488 small portable clocks and probably watches were being made there. A school of watchmaking in France did not exist until the second decade of the 16th century. Another question that arises in connection with the originator of watches is that while one would expect the shape of the first watch to have been drum-shaped, following the pattern of portable clocks, Peter Henlein's early watches are known to have been spherical. The earliest dated watch (1548) has a tambour case.

Early German movements were made of iron with a verge escapement and foliot with a stackfreed to equalize the power of the spring. Cocclaeus' references to Henlein, however, speak of his watches running for forty hours, whereas watches with a stackfreed run for only twenty-six hours. It is possible that Henlein used 'stopwork' which was a device to prevent over-winding of the watch and to enable the middle turns only of the mainspring to be used, giving a more even torque. Examples of early Nuremberg watches with stopwork are well known. French and English watchmakers preferred the use of a fusee rather than a stackfreed.

Initially these used a gut line, but this was replaced by the chain.

Striking and alarm mechanisms were incorporated in very early watches and, as had happened with some clocks, calendar and astronomical indications also became popular. Dials had only one hand, the hour hand, and were marked in hour and half-hour divisions. Since glass covers had not been invented, either a solid cover was used or one that had been decoratively pierced so that the tip of the hour hand was visible.

Decoration on the dial usually consisted of a star or sun with twelve sunbeams connecting the hour numerals to the centre. Dials became more elaborate as the century progressed, with engraved work replacing the central sun.

Cases of this period fall into two groups – drum and spherical – both characterized by a restraint in decoration which probably emphasized the greater importance of the movement at this time. Many watch cases were pierced so that the movement could be seen. Spherical watch cases were shaped from copper sheet and then chiselled and engraved; drum-type cases were usually cast. After about 1585 the German drum shape was replaced by a circular case with domed front and back covers.

Domestic Metalwork

Patterns of 15th century metalwork continued into the 16th century which saw a few innovations. Firebacks originated around the beginning of the 15th century. They were, it is thought, first made for use in the newly-introduced wall-fireplace, both to protect the wall and to radiate the heat of the fire. The first ones were probably simple slabs of cast-iron, but they soon became decorated. A plain board was used as the basic pattern, and the mould was open topped. After the pattern's removal, decoration was impressed into the sand. The commonest impressions were taken from stiffened lengths of rope, pushed into the sand to form patterns such as pentagrams, triangles, squares and borders. Sometimes the founder would push the impression of his hand or of some of his tools into the sand. Such decorations long persisted and were used alongside more sophisticated decorations on the same backs.

In time, firebacks made from patterns carved in one piece became the norm. The earliest English specimen dates from 1548. Decorations vary enormously and include heraldic devices, flowers and allegorical, Biblical and domestic scenes. Shape also altered somewhat over the years; at first firebacks were simple horizontal rectangles, sometimes with a pointed or curved top. Later they became less elongated and had more elaborate tops; from the end of the 17th century they became roughly square, again with decorative tops, to fit into the newer, smaller type of fireplace. They were made into the 19th century, and reproductions are still cast.

Firedogs or andirons have an even longer history than firebacks. They were used in Roman times, long before the invention of the wall fireplace, when the fire was made in the centre of the house and the smoke escaped through a hole in the roof. Their parts are known as the stauke (the front, usually decorated, upright) and the billet (horizontal) bar. The billet bar supported the logs and the stauke was to prevent them from falling out of the fireplace. The earliest firedogs were made of wrought iron, but from the middle of the 16th century the staukes were cast on to the billet bars. The greatest English centre for the production of the latter was the Weald.

From the 16th century, firedogs became more elaborate, and though the simpler types were still used in ordinary houses and the kitchens of big houses, the more flamboyant types were used in the main rooms of the big houses. Before long they became no more than a decorative adjunct to the fireplace, in elaborately-wrought and highly-polished brass, bronze, steel and even silver.

Cast-iron holloware should also be mentioned (cauldrons, bowls and mortars for instance), which was made in the Low Countries and in England in great quantities from the 16th century onwards. Design followed that of similar bronzework, albeit more simply.

Wrought-iron fire-dog, 1575, height 22 in.

Pewter

Although domestic pewter was well established by the middle of the 15th century, it was not until about 1550 that there was any attempt to move away from traditional designs. The reasons for this are various, notably that pewter was not made in Italy, the birthplace of the Renaissance, and so there was no school of pewterers to lead the way. Possibly as important was the fact that until the 16th century there was no real market for luxury pewterware for the rich were still buying silver. As a result most of the pewter made before 1550 was entirely functional not artistic.

The Renaissance caught up with the pewterer at the same time as did the general increase in wealth which manifested itself in the new middle class. As a result the second half of the 16th century saw the arrival of the age of 'display' pewter, which for the middle class became their answer to the display silver of the nobility. Display pewter was entirely non-functional and is characterized by its relief decoration, for which reason it is sometimes called relief pewter. It originated in France and soon became popular in Nuremberg, but was never enthusiastically received in England. One of the earliest surviving pieces is a tankard by Rolyn Griffet who lived in Lyons from 1528–68. The creator of relief pewter though was François Briot of Lorraine, who is still best known for his masterpiece the 'Temperantia Dish' which was made between 1585–90. The dish is accompanied by a ewer as is another dish he made decorated with the seated figure of Mars. Other surviving pieces of Briot's include a salt cellar and a bowl portraying the figure of Susanna.

The pewterers of Nuremberg were quick to follow Briot's example and relief decoration became even more popular there than in France. The first Nuremberg pewterer to use the technique was Nicholas Horchhaimer who specialized in large bowls with low relief figures. His particular technique of relief decoration was rather different from that of the Lyons pewterers who used engraved moulds. Horchhaimer's technique is known as the 'wood-cut' style since the final product is a flat two-tier relief reminiscent of wood-cuts.

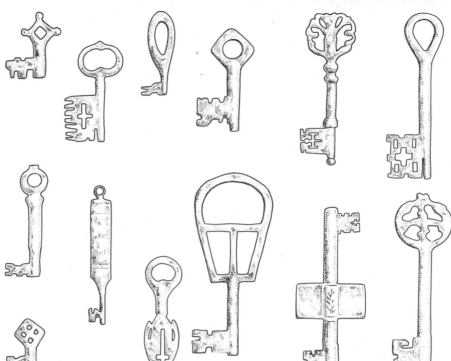

Various types of keys of the 15th and 16th centuries.

Another Nuremberg pewterer working in the same style was Albrecht Preissensin, a colleague of Horchhaimer. The large bowls made by both men are usually decorated with scenes from the Passion or from classical mythology; their small bowls have only arabesque motifs and are much sought after by collectors.

Relief pewter decorated using the Lyons technique was also made in Nuremberg, one of the best-known craftsmen being Kaspar Enderlein who achieved his fame by making exact copies of the Temperantia Dish made by Briot.

Jewelry

The significant difference between Renaissance jewelry and the jewelry of the Middle Ages was that the former concentrated on jewels for the body rather than for dress. The bracelet became popular, false hair was worn and adorned with chaplets of pearls and narrow headbands with a star-shaped gem at the forehead were worn by many women around 1500. Earrings, finger rings and pendants were all worn to set off a woman's body rather than her dress.

The most important jewel during the Renaissance, holding pride of place, is undoubtedly the pendant and it is in this form that the finest examples of the jeweller's art are to be found, many achieving the stature of miniature sculpture. By the beginning of the 16th century, the subject matter of the greater part of these jewels was almost exclusively pictorial or involved in the portrayal of figures in one form or another, often within an elaborate architectural frame. Noted exceptions are the designs by Hans Holbein, the celebrated court painter of Henry VIII. His work mainly emphasizes the use of precious stones for their own sake in an

77

essentially non-figurative composition with the sole addition of coloured enamel and engraving.

The ability to attribute a jewel to a particular country is very rare with pieces made during this period. Holbein was not an artist craftsman, but merely produced designs which were then executed by a goldsmith, probably Hans of Antwerp. This trend was being carried out in the rest of Europe as jewellers issued pattern books of engraved designs which were gradually circulated from country to country.

Pendant design by Hans Holbein.

The infiltration of Renaissance taste and ideals from Northern Italy into the rest of Europe evoked a hunger for the new jewelry in the rising affluent courts of France, Germany, England, the Low Countries and Spain. Benvenuto Cellini, perhaps the archetypal Renaissance artist craftsman, himself worked for a time under the patronage of François I in France, while in Germany, Nuremberg and Augsburg quickly established themselves as great centres of the goldsmith's art, the latter centre claiming Vergil Solis (1514–62) whose widely published designs were extremely influential. Other worthy designers are Androuet Ducerceau, Daniel Mignot, Etienne Delaune and Theodore de Bruy.

The formidable wealth that Spain was to enjoy through the colonization of the Americas and the vast quantities of gold and precious stones thereby made available, rendered the Spanish court an important patron, importing designs and designers from the rest of Europe.

In turn, the jewelry produced in Spain at this time lead European fashions from around 1540 until the Thirty Years War. Typical of the 'Spanish fashion' were very heavy gold chains and pendants hung by short gold chains. In France and England, such chains were usually worn only by men and were particularly popular with Henry VIII. They were also given to ambassadors and other people who had rendered a service to the King. In Flanders and Germany, similar chains were worn by women.

The rise in interest in time-keeping, astronomy and astrology was reflected in the jewelry of the late 16th century. For instance, rings were fitted with watches or miniature astronomical instruments. An example of the former, now in the Schatzkammer der Residenz in Munich, has the watch set in a hexagonal case with a winged lid that opens to show the Crucifixion scene in coloured enamels. An assay mark suggests it was made in Augsburg in 1580. Another surviving ring of this period opens out into a simple astrolabe. Astrology, which had been imported into Europe in the Middle Ages from the Middle East, was in vogue in the 16th century and rings and pendants showing the signs of the zodiac often mixed with Christian symbolism became common. Talismanic jewelry was also popular – a piece of red coral set in enamelled gold for instance, was believed to protect against a blood vessel bursting. A novel type of talismanic jewelry found in Italy was the 'fica'. The 'fica' is a gesture, usually considered obscene, which involves placing the thumb between the middle and index finger of a closed fist or alternatively forming a circle with the index finger and thumb. The gesture however, was also considered protective by the Romans and Greeks centuries earlier and in the 16th century fica-shaped talismans of gold, silver and ivory became popular, the wearers believing either that they would be protected or that they would have an assurance of fertility.

The art of the gem engraver reached its peak in this century with Milan as the undisputed centre. The Milan craftsmen were encouraged by Emperor Rudolph II who personally employed many Milanese cameo-cutters. What has become known as 'Rudolphinian art' was the curious interest of the Emperor in having vessels cut out of semi-precious stones, cameos and gold in pursuance of an ancient belief in the supposed medicinal powers of these materials.

As the 16th century progressed and the High Renaissance gave way to the elaborate ornamentation and excesses of Mannerism, so jewelry quickly adapted to the new taste and fashion. Designs for pendants in particular reflected the peculiarly bizarre nature of all ornament at this time as, gradually, the link with painting and sculpture was abandoned in the search for more and more exotic motifs. Mythology remained a major source of inspiration, but interest also lay in fabulous creatures such as mermaids and mermen, nereids and hippocamps. The large, misshapen baroque pearl, previously thought unsuitable for jewelry, was seized upon to suggest the bodies of such creatures, the figure completed in richly enamelled goldwork.

No element of the composition was left unembellished, or any surface left plain and unenriched with coloured enamels or stones. Dress designs, too, reflect this obsession with decoration in the extraordinary combination of elaborate patterns and rich fabrics, jewelry being used in profusion to add colour and opulence to the general effect.

Throughout the 16th century there had been a gradual move away from minute and elaborate enamelled figures and finely worked gold towards a greater emphasis on gemstones themselves. This trend was to be consolidated during the following century, radically affecting the history of jewelry design. It was a movement which was echoed in all the decorative arts as the elaboration and profusion of Mannerism gave way to the sustained opulence and dignity of the Baroque.

Embroidery

The upheavals of the Reformation as well as outbreaks of bubonic plague took their toll and effectively ended the great days of church embroidery, but by the 16th century needlework was already taking on a new emphasis. It was now based firmly on a secular footing in the courts of royalty and in the homes of the rich, who adorned themselves and their furnishings with an increasingly exotic array of embroidered fabrics.

Blackwork was a form of embroidery widespread in the 16th century but which died out early in the 17th. It consisted of all-over designs of trailing tendrils and leaves interspersed with flowers, fruit and animals worked in black silk on linen. Sometimes gold and silver threads were introduced for richer effect. Blackwork is said to have originated in Spain, where it developed from Moorish work. It soon became popular for collars, caps, cuffs, shirts and other clothing.

Popular English embroidery motif.

Another development was paned or paled work, an example of which in the Victoria and Albert Museum has panels of ivory damask and crimson satin embroidered with gold.

While Italy, France and Flanders excelled in the production of lace and tapestries, England reigned supreme in the realms of domestic embroidery. English ladies covered bed-hangings, cushions, wall panels and, of course, costumes, in a profusion of flowers, birds, butterflies and animals worked in wools on canvas, or silks on linen. They took their designs from woodcut illustrations in newly available books, from herbals and, increasingly as the century wore on, from books of designs especially published for embroiderers. These came from the presses of Italy, Switzerland, France, the Low Countries and England, and continued to be used by many generations of domestic embroideresses.

This habit – which was universal – of using favourite old designs for embroidery, makes dating extremely difficult, and, in the absence of other evidence like a date or supporting document, embroideries are notoriously hard to place within 50 years or so.

A 16th-century development was the working of samplers as a method of recording stitches and designs. The earliest 'exemplars', as they were called, are generally worked in coloured silks on linen and they must have provided invaluable reference material at a time when embroiderers' design books were still rare and expensive. Often they formed long strips of material and were clearly added to over many years.

Although some scholars are of the opinion that the quality of embroidery declined from the end of the 15th century until about 1575, all agree that the Elizabethan period saw a remarkable advance. Probably this had much to do with the ever-increasing popularity of embroidery among lay-people which in turn spurred on the embroiderer's guilds. Elizabeth granted its first charter to the Broders' Company in 1561. The queen herself may have given embroidery new life, being an embroiderer of no small ability. Since most of her clothes were richly embroidered it was inevitable that the middle classes sought to follow the royal fashion.

Swiss Linen Embroidery

Swiss linen embroidery was at its height in this century, declining after 1650. Most of the work comes from the German-speaking cantons, particularly those where linen was also produced such as St Gall, Constance and Schaffhausen. The linen they used was of blue or brown yarn and, because they used only small looms, larger works required the strips to be joined. This in itself provided an opportunity for imaginative work – ornamental overstitching, embroidered braid or lace insertions.

The Catholic Church had always been the prime inspiration for Swiss linen embroiderers and during the 16th century when the Swiss, like the English embroiderers, were studying books and woodcuts for new designs, Bible woodcuts took pride of place. Renaissance motifs were only slowly accepted by the Swiss and certain motifs, such as architectural scrollwork, were never used.

Spain and Italy

Spanish embroidery, though it owed much to the long Moorish tradition, was also influenced by the Incas of South America, for the plunders of their civilization were now reaching Spain. The Incas had achieved

Pair of embroidered gloves given by Henry VIII to his friend Sir Anthony Denny.

high artistic standards in their own textile work and their stylized animalistic motifs were given a new interpretation in Spain.

The standard of embroidery was high and as well as the previously mentioned influences, designs were also taken from the Spanish painters of the day, such as Murillo. Altar cloths, not surprisingly in Catholic Spain, provide some of the more luxurious examples.

Italian embroiderers were also influenced by the painters of the day but took greater pains to imitate as closely as possible even the smallest gradation of shade or colour.

Armour

Metal armour has been used by warriors for thousands of years but, apart from a very occasional excavated piece of Roman or Greek armour, very few pieces pre-dating the late 16th century are likely to be available. By this date the wearing of armour was already in decline, for firearms were changing the face of war and making armour obsolete.

The 16th century had heralded a distinct division of armour into two types depending on its role. On the one hand there was the late Gothic style called 'Maximilian' armour which was used mainly for pageants and display and plain, undecorated armour which was used on the battlefield. The latter is distinguished by the use of chain mail skirts and closed helmets and by the employment of sabbatons instead of sollerets as footguards. Battle helmets consisted of the crown which had a ridge, usually roped down the centre and with two cheek-pieces meeting and fastening at the chin. The visor and bevor were formed of one piece with horizontal apertures to see through and small holes for ventilation. The chain mail skirt had been growing in popularity during the second half of the 15th century and was now in general use. Made of fine mail it usually hung to about the middle of the thighs, though occasionally it reached below the knees. Sometimes it had short slits back and front to facilitate riding.

From about 1500 male fashions in general began to change from close-fitting garments to more ample clothing with slashed doublets. This interest in new fashions was also reflected in armour design which, coincidentally, was under review, particularly in Austria by the Emperor

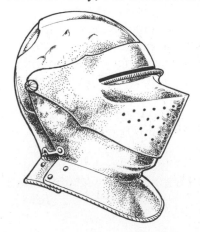
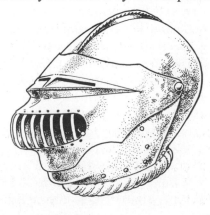

Two designs of the 'Maximilian' helmet, 1500–52.

Maximilian I, with a view to improving its efficiency. The 'Maximilian' style lasted, with a few changes, until about 1600 and was characterized by several supplementary fittings for additional protection and the use of decorative fluting. On the helmet, which was of the closed type, the fluting usually ran from front to back, while the visor was formed of two parts, the upper, or visor proper, which fell down inside the second section or bevor which could be raised independently of the visor.

From about 1545 the fluting on all parts of the armour was discarded because it had been found that a lance meeting the fluting tended to be caught and the point directed to vulnerable parts. The fluting was replaced by rich engravings and *repoussé* work as well as gold and silver damascening. As a result, the armour of the aristocracy tended to become a luxury, lined in velvet or silk, but made of relatively thin metal and so useless as a protection.

The armour worn by the lower ranks however tended to be less uniform. The infantry at this time was made up of pikemen, arquebusiers, canoniers and archers. The pikeman wore a pot-de-fer helmet with a turned down brim from about 1530 until later in the century when it changed to a classic crested helmet and later still to the cabasset helmet. He wore a breast-and backplate but probably only occasionally had arm and thigh armour. In the early part of the century the arquebusier wore little armour but about 1550 he was wearing a type of armour called 'almayne rivets' a name taken from a German system of metal connected by sliding rivets. The cavalry wore mainly half-armour consisting of a closed helmet or casque and a breastplate and tassets which reached to either the middle of the thigh or to below the knee.

During the late 16th century there was an increased use of helmets without face pieces, and these burgonets were worn by both cavalry and infantry. Probably the commonest form is that known as the lobster tailed burgonet which was popular during the period of the Thirty Years War (1618–48) and the English Civil Wars (1642–8). It had a domed skull with a peak through which passed a curved bar, the nasal, which gave some protection to the face. The back of the neck was covered by a flared guard made of several overlapping strips or lames. Two ear flaps protected the cheeks.

Another light helmet was the morion which had a skull with just a narrow brim and perhaps earflaps. Another form had a high central comb and a very pronounced curve in the brim.

Full suits of armour are very rare and many of those which do appear on the market are composed of parts from different armours. A number of Victorian copies also exist and these will seldom deceive the collector for they are usually 'tinny', light and lack the graceful lines of the original.

Although full armours are rare there is a great deal of interest in the collecting of component parts. Helmets are probably the most desirable pieces. Early 16th century examples of the close helm have a fluted surface designed to give greater strength. This style is known by collectors as Maximilian and is very attractive. Some rather crude examples of close helmets may be found and these are usually church helms which were hung above the tombs. They were often put together out of odd pieces and many have a crest fitted.

German breastplate decorated with etching.

17th
CENTURY

Introduction

The word Baroque is thought to have come from the Portuguese word *barroco* meaning an irregularly-shaped pearl. The term did not receive wide usage as a description of the predominant style of the 17th century until the 19th century and, as the translation of the word indicates, it was originally used disparagingly being applied particularly to post-Renaissance architecture. Nevertheless the perjorative use of the word disappeared and the Baroque style came to be seen as an original style with much intrinsic merit and beauty.

Whereas the previous two centuries of the Renaissance were an age of discovery, the 17th century was an age of expansion and the art that it produced, the Baroque, personified this expansive urge. Baroque art has been described as spacious, dynamic, colourful, sensual, opulent and extravagant. It was an age that was to last for over 100 years.

The origins of the Baroque have not been well defined but it is clear that it began in northern Italy around 1600, the full transition taking only a quarter of a century before it spread into most of Europe. It is thought that the Baroque was initially the reaction of papal Rome against the spread of Protestantism and certainly echoes of this idea can be seen in the flight of the Huguenots after the Revocation of the Edict of Nantes in 1685 from France, which by then had become the model of Baroque for the rest of Europe. Ironically it was the Huguenots who were among France's finest craftsmen, and it was they who subsequently carried the Baroque to England and other Protestant countries.

If Rome was the birthplace of the Baroque then Michelangelo seems to have provided the base on which it was built even though he died in 1564. From Popes Paul III (1534–49) to Sixtus V (1580) a successful campaign had been led against the rise of Protestantism after which Sixtus determined to rebuild Rome more magnificently than before as an edifice against paganism. For him, the style of the Renaissance carried elements of the paganism he was opposed to. The building of St Peter's begun by Michelangelo earlier in the 16th century was continued (1606–12) under Carlo Moderna and became Rome's greatest Baroque project. It was in the amendment of Michelangelo's basic plans that the Baroque portentously emerged, but it was left to Gianlorenzo Bernini (1598–1680), the greatest artist of the Baroque if not the originator of true Baroque, to complete the design for St Peter's.

The desire of the papacy to create a pomp and splendour that would shore up the Church and attract more members spread to the nobility of Italy, who had palaces built which reflected the ecclesiastical magnificence. Needless to say the furnishings of these buildings had to match their setting and once again it was Rome that led the way, this time in the decorative arts, particularly furniture.

Exaggeration was the order of the day, in size, scale and proportion. Carving was lavish and the Renaissance sense of proportion was often lost in scrollwork and mouldings. This was the furniture of the sculptor

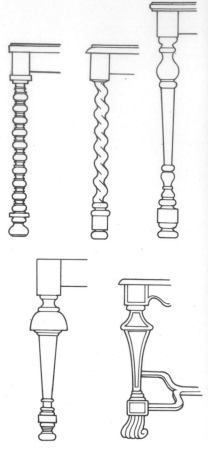

Different styles of turned leg used on 17th century furniture.

with its large leafy scrolls, flower garlands, putti and human figures. Perhaps one of the reasons for the 19th century's derisive attitude to the Baroque was that it was seen out of context. The furniture of this period was designed exclusively for the room it was to occupy; take it away from the painted ceilings and the richly hung walls and its ornateness and massiveness become more obvious. Not all the furniture of the Italian palaces was so designed, for the members of the household lived mainly in smaller rooms above their large Baroque chambers. Here the furniture was of the simpler type common in the 16th century.

As the 16th century progressed the Baroque revolution influenced other Italian craftsmen including goldsmiths, metalworkers and glassworkers. It was in France however that the Baroque was further elaborated into the Louis XIV style, an interpretation of Baroque that spread to the rest of Europe in one degree or another.

The reign of Louis XIV, 'Le Roi soleil', (1643–1717) was a period of French pre-eminence in European history. An age of cultural and political ascendancy for France, Louis' reign saw the origins of an influence on international fashion that still lingers today. Paris replaced Rome as the art centre of the world and French became the language of European courts and diplomacy. The Louis XIV style in the decorative arts was largely due to Louis himself for he believed that art should be in the service of the king rather than the Church as it had been for centuries past. Through his minister Colbert, Louis established academies to standardize style in art, and the style he favoured was a dignified and stately, but still sumptuous form of Baroque. The over-zealousness of the Italians was refined into a new classicism.

In England it was not until after the Restoration in 1660 that Baroque influences appeared. Before that date furniture had remained more or less in the Elizabethan style and other arts and crafts had made little progress for a quarter of a century.

A fuller expression of the Baroque only appeared in England with the reign of William and Mary (1689–1702), after whom the style was named. The Huguenot refugees from France after 1685 played a significant role in the propagation of the Baroque, for many of them were skilled craftsmen bringing with them French techniques and designs at a time when the Louis XIV style was at the height of its fashion. The influences upon English decorative arts were both French and Dutch. Dutch Baroque was characterized by an element of realism which they introduced into their art by their rejection of the old world peopled with angels and saints and their acknowledgement of the new Dutch middle class in which the artist worked not for a sole patron, but for the market.

Furniture

The Baroque era followed the inspired humanism of the Renaissance with inflated statements of pomp, power and splendour. During the 17th century, the institutions of the Church in Italy, the state in France, and the small courts of Germany, spawned materialistic monuments to their own glory in architecture and fine and decorative arts.

In Italy, papal families such as the Barberini, Pamfili, Aldobrandini and Borghese constructed elaborate villas, and filled them with works of art and expensive furnishings. At Versailles, the association of Louis XIV with the sun-god Apollo required the development of an interior setting not quite of this earth.

Initiated by Gian Lorenzo Bernini, the Baroque architectural and sculptural style retained classical elements, but took liberties with principles of symmetry and restraint. Columns became twisted, sculptured figures contorted, carvings expressive and exuberant. Baroque interiors achieved striking effects through a colourful welding together of architecture, sculpture, and painting, which dazzled the eye with splendour and variety. Rising numbers of wealthy merchants, bankers and newly-aristocratic families resulted in a refinement of rules of etiquette and ceremony in order to define rank rigidly. The villas of princes, cardinals and courtiers were replete with devices that filtered and arranged guests and residents to exclude those of lower rank from the more intimate courtly gatherings. Private audiences were held in cabinets and closets, small rooms richly decorated with fine furnishings, hangings, crystal, porcelain and paintings.

Rank determined access to the 'public' *levées* and *couchers* of heads of state, princes and nobility in state bedrooms, where elaborately hung beds were generally enclosed inside alcoves or behind ceremonial balustrades. Rank also determined the allocation of seats: ornate, gilded throne chairs in Italy and elsewhere were reserved for heads of household and state, and progressively less imposing chairs and stools were used according to social position. In Spain, ladies were relegated to floor cushions.

In France, privileged women received in bed, and guests sat on cushions in the *ruelle*, or alley, beside them. Fixed positions of most furniture pieces emphasized the formality of Baroque interiors. Chairs generally lined room walls, and were put back in place there by servants after use.

Intended to impress, these palatial interiors were lined with Turkish tapestries, Genoese cut velvets, Lucchese silks and Spanish embossed and gilt leathers that were exported throughout Europe. Ceilings and walls were painted with brilliant frescoes and self-glorifying messages were not uncommon. Gilding of ceiling panels and wall ornaments became increasingly fashionable.

Although still relatively scarce, Baroque furniture took on the proclamatory aura of the pompous fittings around it. Carved sconces, guéridons and chandeliers provided glittering supports for candles, and their gilded surfaces were reflected in cascades of light by decorative mirrors in elaborate carved frames.

In Italy, large villas such as the Ca'Rezzonico in Venice housed suites of state apartments, including galleries, libraries, dining rooms and salons, all decorated with hangings, gold galloons and fringes, lacquerwork and ivory and marble wainscoting. The furnishings of these rooms were objects of sculpture and art, rather than comfort. Produced by leading contemporary artists, scale, exaggerated style and cost precluded

Top: *Mid-17th century oak country chair with panelled back;* bottom: *Carved hall cupboard.*

casual use. The private family apartments located above the show rooms of the *piano nobile* were furnished very simply.

Baroque furniture was bold, vigorous and sculptural. Naturalistic carving in high relief supported tables, beds, chairs, stools and cupboards, Carved dolphins, eagles, shells, putti and grotesques were combined with volutes, dense scrolling and foliage, and placed beneath seats or slabs of marble to form chairs or tables.

Gilded chairs with outstretching arms and velvet upholstery were carved with broad, ribbon-like forms which twisted and furled to incorporate putti and foliage. Decorative console tables were carved by sculptors such as the Venetian Andrea Brustolon (1662–1732) in vigorous compositions of animals, blackamoors, shells and figures.

Brustolon's training began in his native city of Belluno and was continued, from his fifteenth birthday, under the Genoese sculptor Filipo Parodi whose late Baroque style no doubt influenced him. His earliest known work is a pair of angels for the sacristy altar in the Frari, Venice, probably about 1683 and it seems that much of his life was spent creating religious works for church use. The only furniture that can definitely be attributed to him is a suite, sometimes called the 'negro suite' which he made for a prominent Venetian, Pietro Venier, sometime before 1699 and now in the Ca' Rezzonico, Venice. The chairs of this suite are carved in boxwood, and the arms are fashioned as creeper-entwined branches supported by negros with lacquered heads and arms. The largest piece is a side-table in which Hercules, flanked by Cerberus and the Hydra, supports a platform on which two river gods lie holding porcelain vases with three nude negros supporting yet another vase in the centre of the table. Only two other suites can be tentatively assigned to Brustolon, one made for the Correr family and now in Ca' Rezzonico and the other for the Pisani which can be seen in the Quirinal, Rome. The collection of Lord Burnham in Beaconsfield holds four armchairs similar to the Venier pieces.

Features of the Italian Baroque reached France during the reign of Henri IV, who established craft workshops in the *Grand Galerie du Louvre* on the example of the Florentine ducal manufactories. Aided by cardinals Jules Mazarin and Armand Jean de Richelieu, who wished to establish a national style, Louis XIII continued to promote the emulation of Italian and Flemish achievement in the decorative arts.

In 1661 Louis XIV acceded to the throne, and in 1667 Jean Baptiste Colbert, his minister of arts, founded the *Manufacture Royale des Meubles de la Couronne*, known as the Gobelins after the workshops previously established in 1622. Under the directorship of the artist Charles le Brun, and stimulated by the personal interest extended by Louis XIV, the Gobelins workshop developed into flourishing collaborative manufactories, in which designs of le Brun, Jean Bérain (1638–1711), and Jean le Pautre (1618–82) were completed by craftsmen contributing diverse skills and talents. Among the most prominent were Jacques Caffieri (1678–1755) and André Charles Boulle (1672–1732).

Boulle is undoubtedly France's most celebrated cabinetmaker and his name has been internationally adopted to describe the style of furniture produced in his workshops. In 1672, he was given rooms and a workshop in the Louvre by Louis XIV, where for the next thirty years he made furniture for the Court and the nobility, receiving the title *premier ébéniste du roi*. While he made a great deal of furniture for Versailles, only two fully documented pieces are known – a pair of commodes made for the king's bedroom at the Trianon. It is not certain whether Boulle actually invented the commode but he certainly spent some time experimenting with the concept and played an important role in its development. The original versions of the commode were not unlike the bureau but with fewer drawers which extended the whole width and sometimes provided with doors and the top in either marquetry or marble. While marquetry was fashionable at this time, it was Boulle who brought the technique to perfection. The technique involved glueing together thin sheets of brass and tortoiseshell and then pasting on to the surface a piece of paper on which the required pattern had been drawn. The pattern was cut out with a saw and the layers separated to give two kinds of marquetry, the first called *première-partie* in which the pattern of brass was on a tortoiseshell ground and the other, *contre-partie* which was the reverse. His most magnificent achievement was the *grand cabinet* of the Dauphin, completed between 1680–83, which was later destroyed.

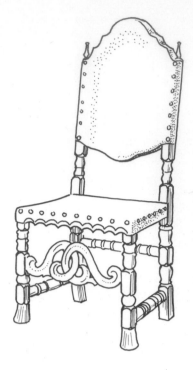

The French Baroque incorporated the exuberance and lavishness of Italian designs, forms and ornamented carving into a more restrained and classical style. Rectilinear gilt upholstered sofas, day-beds and chairs were made at the Gobelins along with other furnishings for the palace at Versailles. Tall, imposing cabinets, bureaux, and commodes were covered with floral marquetry, or the delicate interlacing compositions of contrasting tortoiseshell and brass popularized by Boulle's superb craftsmanship. Heavy ormolu mounts of mythological scenes, masks, lions and acanthus leaves appeared on tables and case pieces.

The Revocation of the Edict of Nantes in 1685, and the great reductions in Gobelins' output which the government imposed for economic reasons, forced many craftsmen to leave France. The designs of Huguenot emigré Daniel Marot (1663–1752) proved especially important in the dissemination of the Louis XIV style.

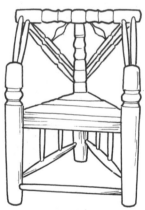

In the United Netherlands the expanded enterprises of the Dutch East India Company brought wealth to the rising class of maritime merchants, who patronized painters, silversmiths and furniture craftsmen. Dutch 17th century interiors were lively and colourful, decorated with checkerboard marble floors, tapestries, portrait paintings, chandeliers and upholstered furniture. Furniture was gilded, crisply carved, painted, lacquered in the oriental manner, and faced with figured veneers. Portuguese and Spanish Baroque influence inspired boldly turned legs and uprights, scrolled feet and caned backs and seats. The tall, straight backs of settles, chairs and daybeds, painted black or gilt, or plain walnut, were richly carved with Flemish strapwork, putti and grotesques.

The naturalism of the Dutch 17th century still-life school, and of sculptor Artus Quellin, was reflected in floral marquetry and inlay compositions executed by craftsmen such as Jan van Mekeren and Dirk van Rijswijk of Amsterdam.

An influx of craftsmen from Germany and Belgium popularized

Top: *Leather studded side chair*.
Centre: *Early oak armchair with sturdy turned posts and plank seat*.
Bottom: *Charles II walnut stool with upholstered seat*.

expensive furniture of ebony; *witwerkers* worked in soft white deal and pine, producing painted pieces for less wealthy purchasers. The tall, double-doored *kas* often had a flat, bold cornice and arched panels separated by pilasters or twisted columns. Tables stood on tapering or spiral-turned legs often with the curves of the apron echoed in the stretchers.

The designs of Daniel Marot, who became Minister of Works to William of Orange after leaving France, popularized ornamented volutés, strapwork and grotesques, and features such as curved chair backs, diagonal stretchers and tapering legs.

Of enormous influence to the Dutch and English furniture crafts at this time were the rare and highly fashionable foreign specimens brought from the Orient in East India Company cargoes. In both countries, oriental cabinets raised on silvered or gilt stands displayed porcelain treasures, and lacquered furniture was especially sought after.

Known in the Orient since the last centuries B.C., lacquer was used to cover boxes, leather armour, bows, chests, household utensils, baskets, earthenware, incense-burners and furniture. The grey resinous sap of the *Rhus vernicifera* tree, *urushi* in Japanese or *ch'i-ichou* in Chinese, was utilized because it hardens, develops a gloss and turns black upon exposure to air. Dyes were added to produce coloured lacquer, and the purified *urushi* was applied in about 30 separate coats.

Various lacquer treatments were used including 'Coromandel' lacquer, with incised and coloured designs; raised designs with mountainous landscapes; mother of pearl inlay; and Japanese *makl'e*, in which the design was formed of sprinkled gold particles on a black ground.

Imported screens were cut up and inserted into European cabinets, secretaires, mirrors and tables, often with total disregard for the cohesion of the oriental scheme. In Amsterdam, before 1610, a guild of Dutch lacquerworkers existed, and pieces were made at about the same time in London and Copenhagen. Although the craft suffered a decline in the mid-17th century, it became increasingly popular in England after the publication in 1688 of Stalker and Parker's *Treatise of Japanning, Varnishing, and Guilding* which provided essential information for professionals. Publications in the following century raised the craft to a level of a fashionable pastime in England, inspiring accomplished ladies to entertain themselves at lacquer-making parties.

Foreign influences permeated England after the Restoration. Early in the century heavy oak pieces still persisted. Jacobean gate-leg and draw tables, presses, benches and chests were ornamented with carved Renaissance foliage and mouldings, grotesques, strapwork and spindles and bosses. Chests-of-drawers, faced with geometric panels which were ornamented with ebony mouldings as well as mother-of-pearl inlay, appeared about the middle of the 18th century.

The widescale rebuilding programme that followed the Great Fire of London of 1668 made great use of walnut, and also popularized the classical interior architectural style introduced to England by Inigo Jones (1573–1652) after the example of the Italian Renaissance architect Andrea Palladio. The Flemish style carvings of Grinling Gibbons (1648–1720), appointed Grand Carver to Charles II, initiated a school of highly delicate and realistic carvings, decorated tables and picture frames such as those in the Carved Room at Petworth House, Sussex, with putti, fruits, flowers, vegetables and birds.

The accession of William and Mary in 1689 brought Dutch craftsmen to England. Carved black, gilt and occasionally silvered chairs and day-beds reflected the Flemish Baroque style, as did the rectangular forms, marquetry and figured veneers, spiral-turned legs and curved stretchers of cabinets, stands and tables. An intricate, lacy form of marquetry known as 'seaweed' developed in England, possibly from the examples in tortoiseshell and metal of André Charles Boulle.

Richly hung state beds, such as the one at Knole in Sevenoaks, Kent, with fabric woven with silver threads, were the prized features of the best 17th century manor houses. They were draped with silks, damasks, brocades, crewel embroidery, mohair and gold cords and fringes.

Top: William and Mary table with drawers, continuous curving stretcher and turned legs; bottom: Queen Anne walnut bureau cabinet.

The production of long-case clocks also became an increasingly important industry in England. As in Dutch examples, they were often enlivened with colourful floral marquetry and small classical or twisted columns on the hoods, and were frequently used to display pieces of oriental porcelain.

The accessories that made life comfortable in European courts, cities and provinces filtered very slowly across the Atlantic, where architectural and decorative styles emerged in much simplified forms often decades after they had dictated European fashion.

Small houses, generally with a maximum of two rooms and a large fireplace, were standard in the colonial settlements of the American east coast until after the mid-17th century. Sparsely furnished, these homes reflected the austere conservatism of religious emigrés, such as the Puritans, and the simple lifestyle of a settlement economy. The essential furniture they contained was serviceable, sturdy and simple, although frequently colourfully painted.

The northern Baroque idiom surfaced in North America in about 1675. Until then colonial furniture continued to be made in the Renaissance style, based on Dutch, German, English or French prototypes, according to the ethnic character of the region in which it was produced. Joining and turning were used for construction: as in Europe, oak predominated, but pine, maple and cherry were sometimes used. Chests formed of six planks and painted with stripes existed side by side with more solidly joined panel-and-frame examples, the latter carved with anglicized classical ornament, such as pilasters and arches, or lunettes enclosing broad acanthus leaves. This ornament showed regional variations.

Bulbous, fluted baluster uprights, showing the influence of Hans Vriedman de Vries, appeared on presses and court cupboards in the English Jacobean manner with knob pulls, 'ebonized' spindles and bosses, chequered inlay, colourful paint and carved figures. Toward the end of the century walnut gained favour, and veneers and dove-tails, together with new pieces such as chests-of-drawers, were introduced.

Immigrants and imports took the primarily Flemish William and Mary Baroque style to America through English intermediaries. American highboys, lowboys and tables were veneered simply with rich walnut burls. European forms including cabinets with convex top drawers and arched panels, and tables and flat-topped highboys with curved stretchers and aprons were adopted, as were carvings of Flemish-style strapwork on day-beds and chairs.

Germany also received the Baroque late in the century, but there the style became rigid rather than relaxed. The small courts of Germany's many principalities translated the already exaggerated ceremonial Baroque in dazzling statements of pomp and grandeur. Yielding to Italian influence and then to the example of Versailles during the first half of the 18th century, court rivalries inspired palaces such as Pommersfelden, Charlottenburg and Belvedere, on which state rooms and suites were lavishly decorated with mirrors, marquetry panels and collections of porcelain.

Engravings of court interiors and furniture designs by Paul Decker, J. J. Schübler, Joseph Furttenbach and Friederich Unteutsch, circulated widely along with pattern-books of designs showing the French influence of Daniel Marot, Bérain and le Pautre. Unteutsch's *Knorpelwerk*, designs of masks and other ornaments disseminated a taste for soft, earlike forms. Especially successful in silver, this 'auricular' ornament was also carved on walnut chairs and cupboards. Engraved and embossed silver furniture was made in Augsburg and Nuremberg, where collectors' cabinets, with miniature drawers and architectural details, were executed in silver, gold, painted glass, boxwood, ivory and precious stones. In Eger, now part of Czechoslovakia, similarly rich cabinets were faced with mythological or Biblical scenes, executed in wood and intarsia in low relief.

For the Brandenburg court, Gerard Dagly produced a refined imitation of ornamental lacquer on various grounds, those on white suggesting oriental porcelain.

Elaborate as these palatial interiors may have been with their halls and state rooms sparkling with gilt mirrors and silver, the Baroque style that the Germans embraced well into the 18th century had begun to decline in other European centres. There, loosened political, social and artistic attitudes had sparked off the more animated Rococo.

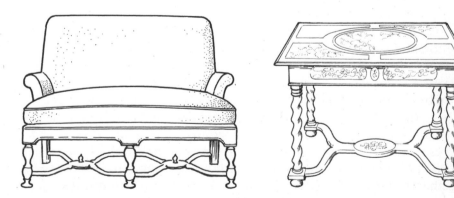

Right: *William and Mary upholstered settee;* far right: *William and Mary centre table.*

Ceramics

Although many original pottery forms were produced in Japan as early as the 2nd millenium B.C., it is the later red-clay *haniwa* burial figures of about A.D. 300–600 which present-day collectors of Far Eastern ceramics find entrancing. Their figures of humans, animals or buildings were placed upon the large burial mound, showing at times a distinct resemblance to those made by primitive tribes of Africa.

The growing popularity of the 'Tea Ceremony' (*chanoyu*) gradually changed from an aid to meditation to a cultured social habit, and by the 16th century notable 'tea-masters' were in need of the various utensils involved. No ordinary tablewares would suffice, they demanded only those considered aesthetically suitable for such a dignified ceremony. Certain areas and potters are today recognized as being outstanding for the creation of these essential wares, where perfection was not necessarily a requirement. The province of Bizen produced wares of heavy, coarse brownish-red stoneware during the 17th century. The similar coarse and partially glazed stonewares of Iga and Shigaraki were also in demand.

Wares of this type are not always readily accepted by today's European ceramic collectors as having any aesthetic appeal, whereas the finer brown-glazed stonewares made in the Satsuma province during the 17th and 18th centuries can more readily be appreciated as fine examples of the Japanese potter's art. Perhaps the best known of all Japanese tea-wares are those of low-fired earthenware, known as 'Raku', a form of ware made by a generation of potters dating back to the early 16th century. Especially beautiful are the hand-moulded forms with soft lacquer-like glazes in black, red or yellow.

It was only during the latter part of the 19th century that Western scholars began seriously to seek knowledge of the comparatively short history of Japanese porcelain. There appears to be little doubt that porcelain similar to that produced in neighbouring China for so many centuries was not made in quantity until about 1620. It was made in a town now known as Arita, which is where the necessary deposits of clay were first located; it is still a source of ceramic materials today.

During the last decade documents have come to light confirming the name of Ri Sampei as the Korean potter responsible for the beginnings of porcelain manufacture in Japan. He worked at Tangudani (The Valley of the Long-nosed Goblins), near Arita, in the province of Hizen.

The earliest Japanese porcelain had much in common with contemporary Korean wares, decorated in underglaze-blue or covered with a celadon glaze, occasionally left in the white. The time was ripe in Japan for the creation of fine porcelains, not only to meet the demands of the local lords, but also to provide wares for the Dutch East India Company. During the troubled times in China in the mid-17th century, this company relied for trade primarily on the porcelains of Japan, though these were very costly in comparison with the wares of China.

It was during the second half of the 17th century that the potter

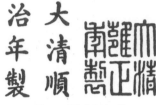

T'ien-ch'i 1621–27.

Shun-chih 1644–61

Kakiemon jar c.1670.

Sakaida 'Kakiemon' introduced a distinctive style of polychrome enamel decoration, which was later imitated by many major European factories. He was born Sakaida Kizaiemon in 1596 and it is said that he acquired the name 'Kakiemon' from the persimmon red colour of the overglaze he used, the Japanese word for persimmon being *kaki*. Kakiemon is thought to be the first Japanese potter to apply successfully overglaze enamels to porcelain. In marked contrast to the Chinese style of decoration which covered whole surfaces, Kakiemon made use of the Japanese style of simplicity and open spaces called *yamato-e*. He was the first potter to use this style. Kakiemon's patterns, in light and delicate lines often with no obvious outline, usually covered one third to a half of the surface area providing a beautiful contrast with the white porcelain. The wares can be recognized by a line of iron red glazing around the rim and called *kuchi-beni*.

Kakiemon's principal colours were of course the soft red persimmon as well as an azure blue, while pale yellow, purple, lavender blue, green and black were supplementary colours used only sparingly. Black or red is used to outline red and yellow areas. Unlike Imari wares which were for everyday use, Kakiemon's porcelains were of the highest quality and even the clay he used was superior to that used for Imari.

It was only in the second half of the 17th century that Kakiemon wares were exported to Europe via the Dutch settlement at Nagasaki. Collections of Kakiemon wares are still to be found throughout Europe. His wares were also popular with the Japanese themselves, as a result of which copies were being produced by about 1672. Most of these were made at Artia and Kutani and are often difficult to distinguish from the originals except that they lack the milk white bodies of the originals.

The most exclusive Japanese porcelain was produced for the *daimyo* Nabeshima, the feudal Lord of the Arita region. Since these wares were made for the *daimyo* or his friends and never made for the commercial market, they were unknown to the West until some pieces appeared at the Paris International Exposition in 1867. It seems probable that the first kiln was started in 1628, though it produced wares of little importance. In 1675 the kilns were moved to a site at Okawachi north of Arita.

Older Nabeshima ware is considered to be the best porcelain ever to appear in Japan, the pure white body having a bluish tinge. Standards of production were high and only some ten per cent of the wares was considered perfect enough to be saved. The early Nabeshima work was blue and white, while later, celadons were also produced. Unique to Nabeshima ware amongst the ceramics of Japan is that the decoration of each piece in a set is reproduced exactly and would appear to have been printed on. In fact the potters first sketched the design on a piece of paper with charcoal, then placed the paper on the plate and rubbed until the pattern had been transferred. After repeating the process on each piece the outlines were drawn in cobalt and the piece fired.

The Netherlands

There appears to be good evidence that Italian-type maiolica was being produced in Bruges during the 15th century, but no examples of this work appear to have survived or can be clearly identified. By the beginning of the 16th century there is ample proof that Italian potters were well established in Antwerp, a centre which was to become the 'nursery' for potters who were to take the craft to other European areas.

It is very difficult for anyone other than the specialist to identify the rare Netherlandish wares made in Italian styles. The colours often appear harsher and the painting cruder – this is certainly so with the Antwerp copies of the Urbino 'grotesques' painted on a white ground. By the end of the 16th century Antwerp had ceased to be a pottery centre of any importance, but knowledge of the technique survived, resulting in the city of Delft becoming one of the most prolific centres for the manufacture of the so-called 'Delftware' for at least one hundred years.

Delftware

It was not until 1609 that Holland, together with six other provinces of Northern Netherlands, first became independent of Flanders and the Duchy of Burgundy. This date roughly coincides with the period when the country first became acquainted with vast quantities of Chinese hard-paste porcelain, which was being imported by vessels of the Dutch East India Company. These were the wares which were going to inspire the Dutch potters in their endeavours to create similar wares in their tin-glazed earthenware. Their pottery became finer. They endeavoured to cover completely all surfaces with a fine white glaze, and their cobalt blue painting was finely applied in the Wan Li porcelain style. Usually, a second clear glaze was applied, at a separate firing, over the tin and decoration, to impart a porcellanous brilliance.

Delftware candlestick c.1660.

Delft was ideally situated as a trading centre for this new industry. Waterways were readily available, giving access to the sea-routes for the importing of raw materials and exporting of the finished wares. The industry was given a further boost during the third quarter of the 17th century, when there was a decline in the Dutch brewing industry, due to competition from England. Many breweries were vacated, only to be speedily taken over as premises by 'Delftware' potters, who in many instances adopted the name of the former occupier. This resulted in such potteries as 'The Golden Flowerpot', 'The Rose', 'The Hatchet' and 'The Peacock'.

Unlike the English potters engaged in the making of tin-glazed earthenware, the Dutch usually marked their wares with registered factory-marks. However, the marks of the finest potters can often be seen on very inferior 19th century wares, the most common being the 'AK' monogram of Adrianus Kocks, who was working at 'The Greek A' factory from about 1686.

The earliest occupant of 'The Greek A' factory was Samuel van Eenhorn, whose 'SVE' monogram can sometimes be seen on beautiful reproductions of Chinese porcelain made between 1674–86. The decoration of the finest Delft can often be recognized by their use of a finely painted manganese-purple or dark blue outline to the design, into which the paler colour-washes are added – a technique called *trek*, which is rarely used elsewhere.

Eenhorn's successor at 'The Greek A' factory, Adrianus Kocks, is probably the name most commonly associated with the finest Delftware. His best known works are the large sets, as designed by the Dutch court architect, Daniel Marot. These include the pagoda-like tulip-vases, and were intended for the apartments of Queen Mary II in the Water-Gallery at Hampton Court. Similar sets can be seen at Chatsworth, the stately home of the Duke of Devonshire in Derbyshire, and at Dyrham Park, Gloucester, maintained by the English National Trust.

Porcelain, such as the Dutch were importing from Japan, also inspired other fine potters, including Rochus Hoppesteyn, who was working at 'The Young Moor's Head' in about 1690. Wares bearing the initials 'RHS' were often further decorated with gold, a rich red pigment and a bright green enamel. Probably one of the most common, yet genuine, marks seen on Dutch Delftware is that of a stylized bird's claw, used originally from 1662 by Cornelius van der Hoeve, who produced some good wares in the Chinese manner. The wares made from the late 18th century until the factory closed in 1850 are very poor quality in every respect.

'The Rose' factory was in operation from 1662–1775, and their blue-and-white plates painted with scenes from the New Testament made a welcome change from the masses of Delft inspired by Far Eastern porcelain.

It was the Delft potters who first introduced the five-piece garnitures, intended for the decoration of high chimney-pieces or the tops of cupboards. The set comprised three covered jars, of Chinese form, and two beakers, with flaring mouths. This form was quickly taken up by the Chinese potters when producing wares for the European market and later produced by several 18th century European factories.

It is impossible to discuss Dutch tin-glazed wares without referring to the prolific manufacture of wall-tiles. Those made during the 17th century were usually quite thick and decorated in colour with fruit and flowers with distinctive corner motifs. Tiles of the late 17th century and early 18th century were only about 6 mm ($\frac{1}{4}$ in) thick and 12.5 cm (5 in) square, and favoured Biblical illustrations, ships, sea-monsters, mounted warriors or men-at-arms, sometimes inspired by well-known engravings, painted in either blue, manganese-purple or a combination of both. There is quite a lucrative business in Holland today in the manufacture of 'tiles for the tourist', often deliberately 'crazed' to suggest age.

The Dutch imported great quantities of English salt-glazed stonewares and cream-coloured earthenwares, which were usually left in an undecorated state, ready for enamel decoration to be added on arrival in Holland. There was also a small production of poor quality creamware made in Holland for the home market, but few factories could compete with the quality and low cost of the English exports.

English Delftware

The term English Delftware is rather an inappropriate one, since Flemish potters were producing tin-glazed earthenware first in Norwich, East Anglia, and later in London by about 1570 – nearly half a century before Delft achieved fame. The production of Jacob Jansen (or Johnson), and other Flemish potters, centred first around Aldgate, in London, neighbouring Southwark becoming a further popular area in the early 17th century. Lambeth, Brislington, Bristol, Wincanton, Liverpool, Lancaster, Glasgow and Dublin were all to become well-known centres of production. All were noticeably within easy reach of the coast, enabling the necessary Cornish tin to be transported by sea. Recent excavations of some early sites have made attributions to specific areas more accurate than has formerly been possible.

Plates or dishes decorated with paintings of reigning English monarchs are very popular with collectors but are also very expensive to acquire. Such datable wares are ideal indicators to the forms of border decoration profiles, and so forth, in vogue at a certain period, but the facial likeness to the characters could hardly have met with the approval of the individuals. The majority of the dishes made before the end of the 17th century had a clear glaze applied to the reverse, to economize on tin, and they usually had a small undercut foot-rim, which would retain a cord for hanging purposes. The popular term 'blue-dash chargers' refers to the blue painted strokes around the rim. 'Dish' would in most cases be a more accurate description than 'charger'.

Earthenware dish by Thomas Toft.

The early English and Flemish potters were actively engaged in making a variety of wares for the use of the apothecary, including wet and dry drug-pots and pill-slabs. The simply decorated ointment-pots could well have been made in either the Low Countries or England.

The popularity of the tulip, and its association with Holland, is seen on many dishes made in the last quarter of the 17th century, the style of painting often having much in common with the early Isnik dishes of Turkey. Unlike most of the Continental faience potters, the British counterpart used only high-temperature colours – blue, green, manganese-purple, yellow and sometimes a poor quality red.

Among the most desirable British tin-glazed wares are teawares, which are extremely rare; flower-bricks, a brick-shaped vessel with perforated top; puzzle-jugs, with fretted designs around the neck. The late wares illustrating Lunardi's balloon ascent of 1784, which took place at Moorfields, near the Lambeth factory, are among the class of pieces sought by today's collectors, even when in poor condition.

'The Potteries'

Due to the fragile nature of the material and the consequent difficulties of transportation by road, the early potter catered primarily for his immediate neighbourhood. But by the middle of the 17th century, the area we now know as Stoke-on-Trent, in Staffordshire, had become recognized as an important pottery centre, with Burslem known as the 'Mother of the Potteries' or sometimes the 'Butter-pot Town', due to the large production of red earthenware jars made for the local farmers for conveying their butter to market. These same potters could, when the occasion arose, produce what might well be termed 'English Peasant-Pottery', dishes or drinking vessels which were decorated by trailing clay-slips of contrasting colour on to the body of the unfired ware, their designs appearing at times to have been suggested by contemporary needlework.

Wares of a similar type were also made at Wrotham, in Kent, and in the London area, where the decoration often included such pious inscriptions as 'Watch and Pray'. All these low-fired earthenwares were covered with a thick lead-glaze, which often had disastrous effects upon the health of the potter.

It was in 1672 that John Dwight set up a factory in Fulham, London,

Highly decorated 17th-century Coromandel lacquer cabinet mounted on a carved and silvered gesso stand.

Right: *Chest of drawers probably by Thomas Dennis of Ipswich, Massachusetts, 1678. Oak and pine.*

Opposite: *Armchair in oak, English, early 17th-century. The straight back, panelled arms and carved ornament are characteristic of the period.*

Below: *Two 17th-century Italian chairs made of walnut and upholstered in tapestry.*

Right: *Wineglass in
the style known as*
façon de Venise, *glass
closely imitating the
Venetian style but
made elsewhere.*
Left: *Elaborate
London-delft posset
pot, probably made at
Fulham c.1670–1710.*

Far left: *The William Grainger candlestick. Pewter relief cast, 1616, and signed with Grainger's full name.*
Below: *Baluster measure (left), c.1700; Tappit hen measure (right), Scottish, late 17th century.*

Salt-glazed stoneware jug by John Dwight.

for the production of salt-glazed stoneware or 'Stoneware vulgarly called Cologne Ware'. Dwight's main production was of German style wine bottles made to the order of specific inns. There is little doubt that he was also occupied in carrying out experiments concerned with the manufacture of Chinese-type porcelain, which at that time was still only being produced in the Far East. Some of his fine mugs of about 1680 are so finely potted, that despite being made of stoneware, they do show a slight amount of translucency by transmitted light.

Two further important potters working in England during the late 17th century were John and David Elers, born in Utrecht and Amsterdam. They claimed they acquired their knowledge concerning stoneware while on the Continent of Europe. The name of Elers is best associated with high quality red stoneware, which they may have been making while working for Dwight at Fulham, but which they were definitely producing at Bradwell Wood, Staffordshire, from about 1693.

German Stoneware and Faience

The most colourful of all German stonewares are the early 17th century tankards made at Kreussen. They are of a dark-brown salt-glaze, decorated with brightly painted enamel figures of the Apostles, the planets, the Electors of the Empire, or hunting-scenes, the decoration has a great deal in common with that seen on the contemporary glass made in both Germany and Bohemia. A further form peculiar to the Kreussen potters is a square or octagonal flask with a metal screw-stopper (*Schraubflashen*). In the latter part of the 17th century Freiberg, in Saxony, was producing a class of stoneware decorated with hand-carved patterns, sometimes picked out with black, white, red or blue enamel colours, often so geometrically precise that the designs were rather dull.

The manufacture of salt-glazed stoneware has continued in Germany to the present time, but usually confined to these made from a grey-bodied clay, decorated with a very bright high-temperature blue. Early German stoneware did not normally bear a recognized factory-mark and collectors should note that the mark of an impressed jug within a triangle denotes the work of S. M. Gerz I, who only started making such pieces in 1857.

Apart from the tiles made from the beginning of the 16th century by the German stove-maker Hafner, very little use appears to have been made of tin-glaze and it was early in the 17th century before Hamburg became well-known as a faience centre, specializing in blue-painted jugs decorated with the heraldic arms of well-known local families. Their dishes were invariably painted in imitation of Chinese blue-and-white porcelain of the Wan Li period (1573–1619).

By the third quarter of the 17th century faience was being made in both Hanau and Frankfurt of a quality to rival the Delftware of Holland, both often using an additional clear lead-glaze to achieve a brilliance akin to that of porcelain. Hanau and Frankfurt faience was sometimes used by well-known outside decorators (Hausmaler) as a ground for fine enamel painting. From the mid-17th century until at least the second quarter of the 18th century, the work of fine painters such as Schaper, Faber, Rössler, Helmhack, Heel and Schmidt, may often be recognized.

Painted Tyrolean bridal bed, inscribed with the bride's name and the date of the wedding 1771.

Glass

In the 16th century the secrets of Venetian glassmaking were reaching the countries of northern Europe as some of the craftsmen of Murano managed to escape the restrictions of the Venetian authorities. By the middle of the 17th century other countries were beginning to develop their own national styles and this was most apparent in Germany and Bohemia where a combination of fine artistic style and technical innovations led to their wares being the most sought after in Europe.

Cutting and engraving is Bohemia's great contribution to glass art. The revival of this craft is attributed to Caspar Lehman (1570–1622), lapidary to the art-loving Rudolf II at the court of Prague. Visiting Italian artisans recalled the work of Cellini with their artefacts in rock crystal and precious stones, and Lehman was inspired to transfer rock crystal cutting techniques to the medium of glass. The brittle Venetian soda glass was quite unsuitable for lapidary work, and it is a remarkable achievement that Lehman did succeed in his objective although a robust potash-lime glass was not developed in Bohemia until about 1670. A splendid armorial beaker of 1605 showing allegorical figures engraved in a broad stylized fashion at the Industrial Art Museum of Prague is the only piece signed by Lehman's hand. The Victoria and Albert Museum is in possession of an engraved panel attributed to this artist. In 1609 Lehman was granted a monopoly for glass engraving which passed to his pupil George Schwanhardt (1601–67), who left Prague for Nuremberg during the Thirty Years' War.

A talented school of glass engravers sprang up in Nuremberg with Schwanhardt's sons George and Henry, H. W. Schmidt and Hermann Schwinger (1640–83) as some of the most gifted. The finest engraving is usually applied to the typical *Nürnberg Deckelpokal*, a tall covered goblet of thinnish metal with a knopped or hollow baluster stem, or both, interspersed by several pairs of flat collars or mereses, an unmistakable feature. Signatures of engravers are frequently present.

Johann Schaper (1621–70), a Nuremberg decorator of both glass and china, produced work in a different genre but of equally high standard. His distinctive technique consisted of delicate enamelling in *Schwarzlot* of landscapes and figures in black or sepia, often seen on glasses so much his own that they are called Schaper glasses – cylindrical beakers on three flattened ball feet. The same medium is employed by Ignaz Preissler (*c.*1675–1733) who, together with his son, worked for a rich Bohemian landowner, Count Kolovrat. Preissler, however, already expressed the Rococo taste of his period with chinoiserie motifs set within garlands and foliage, hunting scenes and vivacious small figures.

The Netherlands

Roman, Merovingian and the common *Waldglas* produced into the 15th century in the Netherlands differed little from glass found or produced elsewhere in Europe. The uses of these glass objects were in the first instance domestic – flasks, bottles, drinking cups and a limited quantity

'Daumenglas' from Germany or the Netherlands.

of window glass were 15th century products. By the 17th century the applied blobs found on Rhenish beakers had developed into the fashionable raspberry prunt, a clever idea which allows a firm grip on a slippery glass. The *Krautstrunk* (cabbage stalk), a large beaker covered with pointed prunts, and the *Passglas*, a tall beaker ringed with applied trails of glass at measured distances and passed around the company with each man emptying the glass to the next ring, enjoyed great popularity.

Flemish 17th century still-life painters have provided an exemplary record of glass forms which were in popular use. Venetian and Altarist glassmakers brought with them all the important developments of their native industry. The elegant flute glass with a short baluster stem is certainly Venetian in origin, but this does not quite apply to that most famous of Rhenish drinking glasses, the *roemer*, although a related form may be seen in the sketches (1667/72) accompanying John Greene's orders for Murano glass.

The *roemer* developed from a prunted beaker into a goblet with a large ovoid-shaped bowl, hollow crylindrical stem set with raspberry prunts, and a spreading foot of spirally wound glass. The early accidental pale green tint was deliberately retained, and an outsize version often appeared as an imposing table centrepiece.

The most notable glass centres were Antwerp, Liège, Brussels, Beauwelz, s'Hertogenbosch and Middleburgh. We know that glassmakers joined these centres not only from Italy, but also from France and Germany. Netherland factories became so prolific that at one stage glass was exported to Venice. In 1585, Antwerp was taken by Spain, but the centres at Liège and Brussels carried on.

Towards the late 17th century glass decoration assumes a new perspective with the emergence of outstanding engraving and cutting techniques exploited with brilliant ingenuity by Dutch craftsmen. Italian inspired engraving techniques seem at first somewhat stiff and unyielding, especially on portrait glasses made to order, but a cursive, calligraphic engraved decoration does appear to have been a purely Netherland technique. The innovation of accomplishing a design in the technique of diamond stippling in the manner of mezzotint engraving produced an effect of exquisite beauty hitherto unknown in glass decoration.

These supreme Dutch glass artists were mainly well-to-do amateurs who frequently signed their work with initials or full name and this, perhaps coupled with some engraved verses, brings a personal charm to this group of Dutch glass. A number of these engravers were women. Anna Roemers Visscher (1583–1651) of Amsterdam introduced fruit, plant and insect forms into the calligraphic design, in the best manner of still-life painting. She is also one of the earliest stipple engravers we know of: one of her glasses incorporating cherries is dated 1664. Anna's sister, Maria Tesselschade Roemers Visscher (1595–1649), and Anna Maria Schurman (1607–78) worked in a similar style. The giant *roemer* was admirably suited for this type of decoration, which was frequently of a commemorative nature. The best known of these calligraphic engravers is probably Willem Jacob van Heemskerk (1613–92), a wealthy cloth merchant.

Fruiting vines, flowers and figures of dancing peasants in the Italian engraving technique were a speciality of Willem Moleyser. The globular long-necked Dutch bottle was greatly favoured by engravers, and was made in green and blue, as well as in a colourless metal. The best known stipple engravers are Frans Greenwood (1680–1761) of Dordrecht, and David Wolff (1732–98).

England

In 1632, a patent was granted to Sir Robert Mansell (1573–1656), a dynamic personality who, in spite of fierce competition and countless deliberately engineered setbacks which lost him a fortune, succeeded in the establishment of a commercial glass industry. In 1615, the famous 'Proclamation Touching Glasses' prohibited the use of wood fuel, and the necessity of utilizing coal effectively created a large industry in the Tyneside region, and brought about the evolution of crystal glass. By the mid-17th century a bottle industry had emerged, and at the end of the century the onion shape replaced the shaft and globe model. A 100 or so years later the bottle neck had grown taller, the shoulder less pronounced, and we see the development of the shape we know today. Bottles with applied glass seals bearing names, initials, crests and dates are desirable collectors' items. One of the earliest intact specimens is the Northampton Museum shaft and globe model, dated 1657.

The first Charter granted to the Company of Glaziers (The Glass Sellers' Company) by Charles I in 1635 was revived in 1664, as the Worshipful Company of Glass Sellers.

By 1660, the monopoly had passed from Mansell to Charles Villiers, Duke of Buckingham (1627–88), who made great efforts to improve trade and started a mirror production at his Vauxhall plate glasshouse. The famous Exeter and Scudamore flutes are attributed to Buckingham's workshops, and it seems that his glass was good, if of rather thin metal.

The increasing demand for glass, which caused a ban on Venetian imports to be lifted, encouraged the Glass Sellers' Company in their researches for a more durable and resistant glass metal. The consequence was the flint (lead) glass developed by George Ravenscroft (1618–81), Crizzling, a defect due to excessive alkaline content and resulting in deterioration and eventual disintegration of the glass, was not entirely overcome until about 1685, but Ravenscroft, who had established his glasshouse at the Savoy in 1673, was in May 1674 granted a seven-year patent to manufacture his crystal glass produced by the addition of oxide of lead. An experimental glassworks at Henley-on-Thames was subsequently set up and by June 1676 the Glass Sellers' Company announced that most of the faults had been eliminated. In 1677 Ravenscroft proclaimed his success by applying the Raven's Head Seal to his finest specimens. At its best, his glass was of heavy metal with excellent refractive properties, of clear and watery limpidity, fusing at a lower temperature than the Venetian cristallo and without the brittle surface hardness. Decorative effects were achieved by gadrooning, vertical ribbing, nipped diamond waies' and attractive rope handles applied to ewers, posset pots, flasks, *roemers* and so on.

While bottles were probably among the first objects ever made in glass, it was not until the 17th century that sturdy bottles, comparable to more modern bottles, were made in England. There is some doubt about who

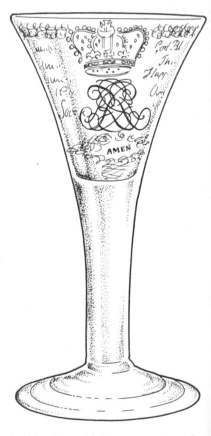

Jacobite glass with drawn trumpet and tear drop in the stem.

108

first made them, for although Henry Holden and John Colnett took out a patent in 1662 claiming that they had 'invented and attained unto the perfection of making glass bottles', a petition was raised against the patent on the grounds that Colnett had made such bottles some 30 years earlier for Sir Kenelm Digby who in turn was the inventor. Whatever the truth, Kenelm has gone down in history as the inventor of the glass wine bottle, although again it is not certain when he did so, for no bottles earlier than 20 years after Kenelm was supposed to have made them (c.1630) have been found yet.

The earliest surviving bottles are two that were found in London and have been tentatively dated around 1657. A third bottle, actually dated 1657 is in the County Museum, Northampton. Bottles of the second half of this century bear a seal showing the owner's initials or name and sometimes a place name and date. The seal takes the form of a raised disc about 3 cm (1 in) in diameter and made by dropping a blob of molten glass on to the body which was then impressed with a metal die.

Seal bottles from this period are rare and most are well-known. In 1949 a list of such bottles then known was compiled. Thirty-eight whole bottles are recorded plus a number of seals by themselves. Today the number is probably over 100 and the recent upsurge in bottle-collecting means that the collector stands a reasonable chance of coming across a seal bottle.

Seal bottles are divided into two groups: those made for innkeepers and those for private use. The two can be distinguished by the innkeeper's use of his inn sign on the seal instead of the crest and coat-of-arms on private bottles. Towards the end of the century, private bottles began to be marked with the name of the drink they contained and were given handles in imitation of their earthenware counterparts.

Early wine-glasses are of several designs, most of them interpretations of Venetian soda-glass which was more delicate. As a result, styles are simple and sturdy. From 1676–95 two basic types of stem are found, the hollow or solid knop stems and the quatrefoil stems. The former are short, with hollow-blown ear-shaped knops, ribbed or plain with collars, though these were soon found to be too delicate and were replaced with solid knops. Quatrefoil knop stems were made by pinching a largish ball knop into four projections with a special pair of tongs. Baluster stems appeared about 1690 and were probably the natural evolution of the urn-shaped knop, which in turn grew out of the simple pear shape. Some examples have a wide angular knop between the stem and the bowl.

It seems likely that the first decanters appeared about 1690 and may have evolved from wide-mouthed bottles blown from soda-glass that had been used for decanting from at least the 1660s. Quart-size bottles of this kind were among the first objects to be made by Ravenscroft from flint-glass.

France

Glassmaking was introduced into Gaul under Roman occupation and post Roman-period glass closely resembles the greenish and yellow-brownish objects found elsewhere. During the 12th century, glazier settlements were in existence in the region of Poitou and immigrant glassmakers gathered, intermarried and created future generations of glaziers. Analogous with Bohemia, the feudal system encouraged the setting up of glasshouses in the forest regions, in Provence and Normandy.

By 1490 the French glassmakers had obtained the right to style themselves *gentilhommes verriers*, a title applying equally to the real and impoverished nobility turned glassmaker. Numerous Huguenot nobles adopted glassmaking and in 1746 forty of these Gascon *gentilhommes verriers* perished on the gallows for their beliefs in the principles of the reformation. Rare surviving 16th-century goblets and chalices show attractive enamelling and a style of design which is clearly Venetian-influenced.

In the 1660s, one of the most able French glassmakers, Bernard Perrot (or Perrotto) inherited the monopoly for supplying glass in the Loire area and the work produced at his Orleans glasshouse is both charming and original. A large number of mould blown beakers, flasks and scent bottles were made in transparent and opaque white, blue and amber glass, showing recurring motifs of hearts, fleurs-de-lys, small figures and sun or moon faces. Perrot also produced an attractive marbled glass and in 1662 developed a process for casting; about that time he began to use anthracite fuel for his furnaces.

A vastly different glass concept is expressed in the so-called *verre filé de Nevers*. This refers to miniature models and grotesques of religious or comic character, made at the lamp by provincial glass enamellers from the late 16th century onward. Nevers figurines are made from hollow blown, very thin glass threads (*verre frisé*), usually wired with copper and placed on a stand of *verre filé* or arranged in groups. Domestic glass was largely imported from the Lowlands, England and Bohemia and not until 1764, when the glasshouse of Sainte-Anne at Baccarat was established by the Bishop of Metz, was a French glass industry founded.

Gold and Silver

In the early years of the 17th century, gold and silversmiths began to turn to less decorative styles than they had used in the preceding century. At first sight it seems logical to assume that this was the result of growing Protestant taste following the Reformation and the polarization of religious attitudes with the counter-Reformations of the 16th century, but this does not seem to have been the reason. Instead, the plainer style was being evolved for people who were chary of spending too much money on the fashioning of plate, over and above the cost of the material, lest it soon would have to be melted again for cash. The Thirty Years' War in Germany of 1618–48, the Civil War in England in the 1640s and the Fronde in France of 1647–53 made people shrink from commissioning expensively decorated plate in large parts of Europe.

Only Holland, at this time triumphant in having liberated herself from Spain – which now began to decline in power – and expanding her empire overseas, enjoyed a confident prosperity. Throwing off the Mannerist grotesques of the 16th century, a new Dutch style of silver-

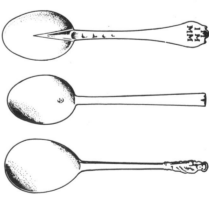

Above: *Apostle spoon, St James the Greater.*
Centre: *Notched end Puritan.*
Top: *Rat-tail trifid.*

ware arose, a style of sinuous fluidity and erotic sensuousness, most characterized by the use of various flowing marine motifs, whose chief exponents were members of the van Vianen family of silversmiths of Utrecht and their pupils. This molten, 'auricular' style, as it became known, spread to Germany and to English court circles before the Civil War. It was followed in Holland by an expression of the prevalent interest in botanical studies in a profusion of embossed flowers, often tulips. This style, too, was taken to England, at the restoration of Charles II in 1660. Dutch interest in pictorial representation showed itself in embossed and engraved plaques and dishes with a religious or classical theme, following engravings of paintings by 17th century artists.

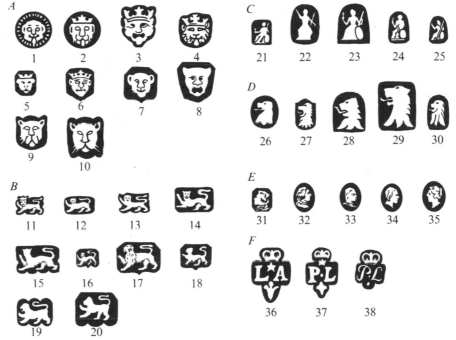

Assay marks used to identify gold and silver

A. Leopard's head
1: *to c. 1470;* 2: *1470–1515;* 3: *1558–92, as before and until 1680;* 4: *1681–9, as before till 1697;* 5: *1719–40;* 6: *1756–1821;* 7: *1822–36;* 8: *1836–96;* 9: *1896–1916;* 10: *since 1916*

B. Lion passant
11: *1544–50;* 12: *1550–58;* 13: *1558–1679;* 14: *1679–97 and 1719–39;* 15: *1739–56;* 16: *1756–1822;* 17/18: *1822–96;* 19: *1896–1916;* 20: *since 1916*

C. Britannia
21: *1697–1716;* 22: *1716–17;* 23: *1731–3;* 24: *1863–4;* 25: *1902*

D. Lion's head erased
26: *1710–11;* 27: *1717–18;* 28: *1725–31;* 29: *1726–7;* 30: *1863–4*

E. Duty marks:
31: *head of King George III (1760–1820), used 1784–6;* 32: *head of the same king, used 1786–1820;* 33: *head of King George IV (1820–30), used 1820–30;* 34: *head of King William IV (1830–37), used 1830–37;* 35: *head of Queen Victoria (1837–89/90), used 1837–89/90*

F. Master's marks:
36–8: *Paul de Lamerie (earliest known work dating from 1711–12, d. 1751); to 1732 in use until 1732;* 38: *used since 1739.*

'A Politer Way of Living'

The middle years of the 17th century saw the introduction to Europe of new tastes in drinking; chocolate, coffee and tea brought from overseas, cooled white wine and hot punches all led to the invention of vessels for their service. Ever since the first years of the century there had been increasing contact with the Far East, following the establishment of trading companies by the maritime nations of Europe. A lightening of Baroque European taste came about, by means of pseudo-Indian, Chinese or Japanese decoration, called chinoiserie, regardless of its exact provenance. Chinoiserie entered all branches of the decorative arts and, with fluctuations in popularity, remained there. Temporarily submerged by the Neo-classical movement of the second half of the 18th century, it was revived again, in an altered form, in the 19th century.

The second half of the 17th century saw the gradual spread of a 'politer way of living'. It now became the custom to use forks at every course in a meal. Previously, two-pronged 'sucket' forks had been used for sweetmeats at banquets, but the rest of the meal had always been eaten with a spoon and fingers. Changed methods of cooking and changed menus encouraged the idea – which came from Italy – of using forks all the time and this made ewers and basins unnecessary, although their decorative function continued.

Strong lead glass was now developed, which displaced both the fragile and highly prized Venetian goblet and the silver wine cup. Glass was preferred because it did not affect the taste of wine, as did silver. Beer was drunk out of tankards in northern countries and the Scandinavian tankard mounted on three feet was popular. Plain beakers were also used for drinking and the Dutch type of beaker was taken to New England and used in some Non-Conformist churches as a communion cup. Flagons were used for serving beer and wine and the pattern, like an extended tankard without a lip, was common for both secular and ecclesiastical purposes.

Greater prosperity led to a proliferation of silver objects being made in Europe and in America, and quantities of teapots, kettles and kettle stands, tea caddies, coffee and chocolate pots, sugar boxes and creamers, waters, salvers and trays were needed for the less formal and more intimate gatherings preferred in the early 18th century. On the dining table would now be placed small, individual salts, casters for spices and sugar, candlesticks, tureens and sauceboats. At the end of the 17th century, sauces were served cold and piquant; double lipped, two-handled sauceboats were put directly on the table. Later, sauces were served hot and so sauceboats were raised off the table on a base or on three feet, so that the polished surface would not be scorched.

Above: *17th-century table candlesticks*, top: *Amsterdam 1642;* bottom left: *Delft 1652;* bottom right: *Montpelier 1695–96.*

Heavy drinking habits called for wine coolers and occasional wine fountains. On the centre of the table would be placed an *epergne*, an arrangement of branches holding assorted sweetmeats in a number of baskets or on small trays.

The dressing tables and writing desks of the wealthy all over Europe and America were graced with toilet sets, ink stands and tapersticks. Silver furniture may still be seen at Rosenborg Castle and at various places in Germany, although all the French examples have perished.

The Huguenot Silversmiths

From the 1660s and all through the 18th century the encouragement given by French royal patronage to the arts led to French taste dominating Europe. Reference has already been made to the disappearance of French silver of the period. In 1685, Louis XIV revoked the Edict of Nantes, which since 1598 had guaranteed freedom of worship in France. This led to a consequent exodus of Huguenot workers, chiefly from the French provinces, into the Protestant countries of Europe, where the extreme elegance and sober and refined monumentality of French classical Baroque taste was assimilated.

In England, the fusion of native and Huguenot taste made this the period of, perhaps, the country's greatest glory in silversmithing. The fusion of styles took nearly a generation, the two styles existing side by side for a while. English goldsmiths carried on with their plain styles which relied for their effect on proportion and surface quality; Huguenots livened their work with their cast and engraved ornament. At the same time however some Huguenots adopted the simple English style, while a small group of English smiths quickly adopted and mastered Huguenot styles. Notable among this last group were George and

Francis Garthorne and Benjamin Pyne. Second generation Huguenots, such as Paul de Lamerie (1688–1751), were capable of producing work of the greatest distinction and simplicity, in which the shape itself constituted decoration enough. They also made pieces in silver-gilt of the utmost elaboration, with cast and applied decoration, skilfully conceived and modelled in the highest sculptural tradition. The beauty of English plate at this time was further enhanced by engraving and flat chasing.

The Huguenot immigrants also widened the range of English silver, for French eating and drinking customs at this time were somewhat different from the English. Among others, the Huguenots introduced the tall helmet-shaped ewer, the pilgrim bottle, the soup tureen and the écuelle, a flat, covered bowl with ear-like handles.

Colonial silver

Early American silver shows all the influence of the immigrants' mother countries, particularly England and Holland. The first indigenous silver industry arose between 1634 and 1650 in Boston and the early styles reflected those current in London in the years 1629 to 1641. Typical decorations of mid-17th century colonial silver include matting, beading and foliate-chased stems. Lacking hallmarks this early silver needs a detailed analysis of style to be dated correctly.

Probably the first silversmith in Boston was John Hull (1624–83), but it was Robert Sanderson (1608–93) who was responsible for establishing the Boston silver industry. Hull and Sanderson had opened a standard Mint in Boston by 1652 where they produced the well-known pine and oaktree shillings and sixpences. The first presentation church silver by these two smiths was produced in 1659 and are important examples of early colonial style displaying real craftsmanship. Collectable silver from this period includes the silver spoons produced by John Hull and John Coney (1655–1722), which have oval bowls and handles that are either trefid-shaped or straight and rectangular with initials engraved on the underside.

The first metalrolling machine appeared in 1692, which meant that silver could now be rolled from ingots. Since this invention reduced the time needed to fashion a piece of silver, prices fell and demand rose. The arrival of the metalrolling machine also gave impetus to a form of decoration known as cut-card work, which had been known in England since at least the middle of the century. The early technique consisted of soldering cut-out patterns, often leaves or strapwork, to plain surfaces. A later development involved the use of several leaves instead of a single one, whilst towards the end of the 17th century the decoration was applied in more than one layer.

17th-century lidded tankards, left: *English 1619;* centre: *London 1675;* right: *English 1699.*

Clocks

Until the turn of the 16th century clockmaking in England had not been widespread. At the beginning of the 17th century there emerged the characteristic English lantern clock. Made of brass, it was weight driven, with a verge and balance foliot rather than a bar foliot. This was to remain virtually unchanged until about 1660 when the latter was slowly replaced by the short pendulum.

A development of the Joseph Zech clock of the 15th century was the square or hexagonal table clocks which were becoming common in the first decades of the 17th century. Like the drum-type clock this clock had the dial uppermost, but it also had a striking mechanism. Made in brass gilt with silver chapter rings, the square clocks usually stood on four feet and the hexagonal ones on three, the feet tend to be claw-shaped and the hammers often appear in the form of grotesque animal heads.

Another clock popular in the early 17th century was the miniature tower or tabernacle clock. These were similar to the lantern clock except that they have a spring-barrel, fusee and gut instead of a pulley, wheel and rope. 17th century examples have brass wheels instead of the earlier steel ones.

The introduction of the use of the pendulum revolutionized clock-making. The first practical application was to a clock made in Holland by Salomon Coster in 1657 to designs by Christian Huygens. It was now possible to achieve a far higher standard of timekeeping. Portable spring-driven clocks made by Coster at this time were enclosed in wooden cases, with the dials covered in velvet upon which a gilded or silvered chapter ring prominently appeared. France adopted a similar style, while clocks using this device were introduced into England during 1658 by the Fromanteel family.

The first English bracket clocks also date from 1658 and were only made in and around London for the first 25 years or so. Architectural-type bracket clocks were popular from 1660–75 and the earliest examples had either plain matted dials, or dials engraved with tulip flowers. The maker's name was engraved on the dial plate below the chapter ring. Bracket clocks often had alarum devices and sometimes a calendar aperture. From 1670 a different kind of case appeared with a handle on top and the pediment gradually gave way to a dome-shaped top.

An unusual form of bracket clock which first appeared not long after the invention of the pendulum was the 'night clock'. It had no hands having instead a revolving dial with the numbers carved through it; a light placed inside the clock enabled the numbers to be read at night.

The introduction of the spring-driven pendulum clock into England heralded the Golden Age for English clockmakers. The main factors contributing to this being the upsurge of awakened interest in the new ideas and concepts carried back to England by Charles II, returning from his exile on the Continent, combined with the many advances made in the field of mathematics which enabled further technological progress

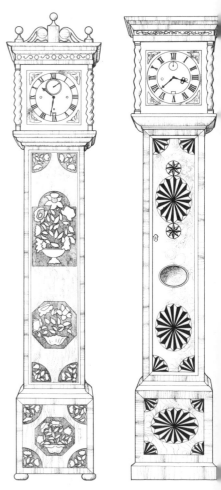

Left: *Longcase clock, John Knibb, Oxford, c.1680;* right: *longcase clock, Thomas Tompion, London, c.1685.*

and the masterly skills of such clockmakers as Edward East, Daniel Quare, Joseph Knibb and George Graham.

Thomas Tompion was one of the greatest clockmakers of all time. Born at Northill in Bedfordshire he was admitted to the Clockmakers' Company in 1671. In 1676 he was commissioned to make the two main clocks for the Octagon Room at the Royal Greenwich Observatory.

In 1671 William Clements produced a clock with a new escapement – the anchor or recoil escapement. It is generally accepted that its invention should be accredited to Dr Robert Hooke (1635–1703). With this escapement the short bob pendulum, as used with the verge escapement, could be abandoned and a longer pendulum with a heavier bob could be introduced. The weights of the weight-driven pendulum clocks were by now encased in a slender wooden trunk, standing upon a wooden plinth so it needed but a slight modification to make the trunk sufficiently wide to accommodate the arc of the swing of the long seconds pendulum. This combination of anchor escapement and seconds pendulum became and remained the standard design for English longcase or coffin clocks as they were initially called.

Bracket clock and movement, Joseph Knibb, London, c.1670–75.
Bracket clock, John Fromanteel, London, c.1685.

Watches

About the turn of the century case styles altered dramatically. The drum shape favoured by the Germans gave way to the oval, round, square and more exotic form cases such as stars, crosses, shells, flowers and birds. Casemaking had now become the task of the lapidist, enameller and a little later the gold and silversmiths. Apart from the cloisonné and champlevé work already seen on dials and cases, there now appeared other forms of enamelwork. Beautiful examples can be seen with scenes painted in enamel. It is generally acknowledged that the fine enamel work of this period was never surpassed.

This type of enamel painting, in which pictures are painted in colours using metallic oxides on a white background enamel, seems to have been originated by Jean Toutin (1578–1644) of Châteaudun in France. It is not known how or when enamel painting began in Geneva. Jean Petitot (1607–91) acquired a wide reputation there (even as discoverer of the method) but this may have been due more to his renown as a miniature enamel painter. While the origins of the industry in Geneva are obscure, it was the Huaud family who raised Geneva to the level of Blois. Pierre Huaud (b.1612) painted his first watches around mid-century and passed the craft on to his three sons. A characteristic of Huaud watches is enamelling on the dial as well as on the bottom of the case.

The relatively fragile enamelled cases necessitated some form of protection. Originally made of stiffened leather, by mid-century these outer cases were of metal covered with leather, shagreen, tortoiseshell and often decorated with piqué work. Perversely the inner case became plainer with the outer case receiving more attention. Although there continued to be made some highly decorative cases, towards the middle of the century there was introduced in England a simple watch with both

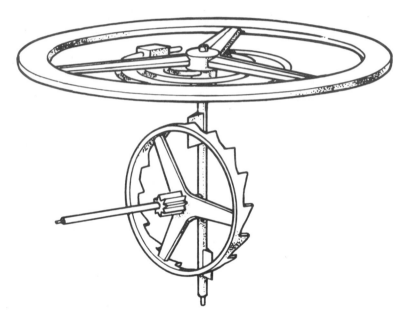

Verge escapement mechanism for a watch. The horizontal wheel is the balance, the lower, toothed one, the escape wheel.

outer and inner silver cases completely devoid of any form of embellishment. This innovation is generally attributed to firstly the Puritan influence and then to the introduction of the pocketed waistcoat.

The lead in the field of watchmaking had initially been held by the German makers, but at a time when watches were regarded not as serious timekeepers but merely beautiful baubles, the French with their natural flair for artistic work rapidly overtook and passed them. The English makers, although somewhat tardy in the 16th century, were to dominate in the 17th with what in modern parlance would be described as a technical breakthrough. This was the successful application of the balance spring to a watch by Thomas Tompion in 1675. There are several claimants to the invention of this device, but in this particular watch by Tompion tribute is paid to Robert Hooke as the inventor. Although the use of a balance spring did not solve all the problems that needed to be overcome before the watch became a precision timekeeper it most certainly did change its role. Cases became much plainer and simpler:

French astronomical clock c.1660. It shows the time, date, phase of moon, quarter day and date of the seasons.

the improved accuracy warranted the addition of a minute hand, and shortly after this a seconds hand.

Geneva was the centre for specialists in rock crystal cases for almost a century. A particularly good example of such a watch, now in the Metropolitan Museum of Art in New York, was made by Jean Rousseau (1606–84), grandfather of Jean-Jacques Rousseau. The bottom as well as the cover over the dial are in rock crystal carved into 12 foils converging on a central hollow. The frame is in gilt metal and the hand in the form of a flower.

A variation on the design of rock crystal watches which also originated in Geneva were the so-called 'abbess watches' made in the form of a cross with the dial decorated with scenes from the life of Christ. Two examples of these watches, one by Jean Rousseau and the other by David Rousseau, are in the British Museum. The former watch employs a fusee with a catgut line, while the other uses a chain instead. Rock crystal watch cases were also made in the shape of flowers, particularly the tulip.

An unusual type of Genevese watch were those made in the shape of a skull or emaciated head, which, it is said, were used by monks who attached them to their rosary beads to remind them constantly of the brevity of life. The skull case was hinged at the rear and opened along the jaw-line. The oldest signed Geneva watch is just such a watch. It is dated 1620 and was made by Martin Duboule (1583–1639). Jean Rousseau also made skull-case watches.

Domestic Metalwork

During the 17th century brass and bronzework continued along the lines established in the 16th century. Some beautiful brass alms-dishes in sheet metalwork were being made, especially in the Low Countries, and also items such as bedwarmers. These bedwarmers, first used in the 16th century, were often made of copper; earlier specimens had wrought iron handles, later superseded by wooden handles. The lids were decorated by engraving, by repoussé or by piercing, sometimes with erotic subjects.

There were, too, skimmers (perforated discs) of brass or copper, and sometimes of tinned iron, used in the kitchen or dairy for operations such as separating cream from milk, and brass chestnut roasters, in form like little warming pans, with perforations all round. Similar objects included saucepans, fish kettles, beer warmers, jugs, pails and innumerable other artefacts, made either in copper or brass, and by sheet metalworking. These objects are usually quite functional and it is therefore often impossible to judge from which country a specimen has originated or what date should be assigned to it. They were used in most, if not all, European countries and also in the USA. Most specimens that one is likely to come across will probably be later rather than earlier in date.

Both copper and brass were used for curfews (from the French *couvre-feu* – cover fire), which were used from early in the Middle Ages to cover the embers of a fire overnight, to keep it smouldering. The curfew was a half dome open at the back, so that it could be pushed against the wall of the fireplace, and was fitted with a handle and usually decorated with repoussé.

Holland was noted for its brass chandeliers, of a type also made in England. The usual pattern consisted of a large central brass ball from which scrolled arms radiated, carrying candle sockets at their extremities. A finial, often in the form of a bird, was provided at the apex of the structure, which was sometimes suspended by an elaborate wrought iron hanger. These chandeliers were made by a combination of casting and benchwork. In England they were most often used in churches and public buildings, whereas in Holland they were commonly found in

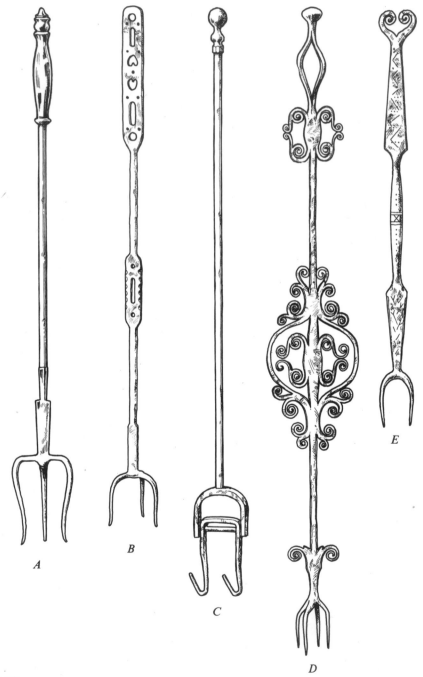

A–C) 17th and 18th-century toasting forks; D) 17th-century toasting fork, length 28 in; E) meat fork, 17th century.

private houses. Excellent chandeliers were also made in Germany.

Bronzework more refined than the foregoing was also made during the 17th century. In France, in the reign of Louis XIV it was used, together with mosaics and coloured stones, for the enrichment of furniture: numerous examples are displayed in the Musée des Arts Décoratifs, Paris. In Italy the many bronze artefacts of the time included candelabra and a profusion of other small objects, with Rococo embellishments replacing earlier decorative elements. In Spain the activity of bronze founders was not great, but some objects, especially for ecclesiastical use, were made.

Domestic ironwork in the 17th century was often attractive, as evident from the many French examples at the Cluny Museum, Paris, outstanding among which is a magnificent chandelier with heraldic embellishments. In the Le Secq des Tournelles Museum, Rouen, is a fine wrought iron lectern consisting of a triangular shaft with scrolled feet, and ornamented with scrolls and leaves. In Italy a splendid instance of how simple forged shapes may be used to make a fine design (the very essence of good blacksmithery) is a cresset of riveted construction on the Saminiati Palace at Lucca. Comparable in conception, but considerably more ornamented, are many cemetery crosses made in Germany and Austria during the same century.

Apart from grand work, simple domestic ironwork at this time was made all over Europe: things such as gridirons, trivets, toasting irons and toasting forks, and so on. Sometimes they are completely functional, but often they are decorated with pleasing and quite rich scrollwork. As already remarked in the case of some copper and brasswork, it is often impossible to judge precisely the country of origin or the date of any given piece.

Continental centres for casting firebacks included Germany and Holland and backs from these areas, imported into England from the time of the accession of William and Mary in 1689, for a time almost

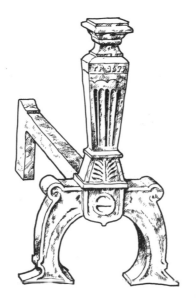
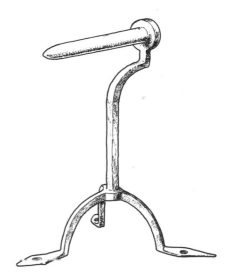

Left: Cast iron fire-dog, 1575, height 22 in; right: wrought iron goffering iron, 17th century, height 8 in.

completely eclipsed the English production. Dutch and German backs are usually more finely cast than the English ones. They are not so thick and are much more elaborate in design, some completely mannerist, others Baroque. Moreover, their subject matter is more varied, embracing, in particular, subjects from classical mythology, allegories of virtues and ideas, and elaborate flower-pieces. French firebacks (and firecheeks for protecting the side walls of the fireplace) from Versailles are exhibited in the Musée des Arts Décoratifs, Paris: they depict the crowned sun, a fleur-de-lys or a royal cipher, supported by sphinxes or griffons (late 17th century) French backs were made into 18th century and carried religious or secular scenes.

During the 17th century there was a considerable increase in the use of lead cisterns in the courtyards and paved areas of houses. Cisterns had been used since the previous century, but such early examples are of the greatest rarity. The 17th century and later specimens are usually pleasingly decorated, a favourite scheme being an adaptation of framed strapwork, with armorial bearings, flowers, cupids, dolphins, stags or classical motifs; they nearly always bear a date. The usual type is box-shaped, but cylindrical and semi-cylindrical types exist, though they are scarcer. The sides and bottoms were cast and welded together, the cylindrical ones being, of course, first curved. Lead pipes were also made but are now rare.

Relief-decorated pewter which originated in France in the second half of the 16th century was continued by the pewterers of Nuremberg until about 1670. Popular designs at the beginning of the 17th century included small disc-shaped plates decorated with scenes from the Old Testament

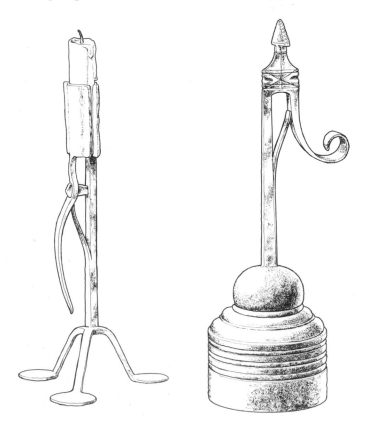

Left: *Rush and candle holder, late 17th century, height 8 in;* right: *rush holder, 18th century, height 10 in.*

such as the Resurrection and the Creation of Eve. These motifs were replaced around 1635 by portraits of the Emperor seated on his horse with portraits of the Electors around the edge of the plate.

By the early 17th century everyday pewterware was becoming more widespread and plates, dishes and small mugs were being produced in even greater quantities than were the large drinking mugs of the 16th century. The earliest datable coherent group of English pewter was made in the first two decades of this century and included wine cups, plates, candlesticks and wine-tasters all relief-cast in vine and rose motifs. Examples of notable English pewter from the second half of the century are the broad-rimmed chargers, often with coats-of-arms engraved on the rims. Another type of plate produced at the same time was the reeded-edge plate made at first with a broad rim and from c.1670 with normal or very narrow rims.

On the whole domestic pewter was never extensively decorated except for a period from c.1660–c.1720 when what has been called 'wriggle-work' was popular on tankards and plates. The softness of pewter does not allow it to be finely engraved successfully, so instead the engraver selected a tool with a narrow, chisel-like blade which was held at an angle and pushed across the metal while rocking the blade from side to side giving a zig-zag pattern.

Pewter is perhaps particularly identified today with tankards and wine measures, not surprisingly, since it has been the metal of choice for these utensils since the 16th century. The earliest datable tankards are of the flat-lidded Stuart type made after 1685. Handles on flat-lidded tankards varied but none of these became standard on the dome variety which instead had a new type of handle with a ball appendage.

Examples of baluster wine measures date from before 1600. Most of the earlier measures had thumbpieces of the ball-and-wedge type, while those from c.1600–c.1670 had thumbpieces of the 'hammerhead' kind. This in turn was superseded by the bud-and-wedge kind.

Jewelry

Throughout the 16th century there had been a gradual move away from finely-worked gold and minute and elaborate enamelled figures, towards a greater emphasis on gemstones themselves. The 17th century was to see a consolidation of this trend which radically affected the history of jewelry design. It was a movement echoed in all the decorative arts as the elaboration and profusion of Mannerism gave way to the sustained opulence and dignity of the Baroque.

Germany, torn by the Thirty Years' War, ceased to be an arbiter of taste. Rather it was France that was to set the standards in jewelry design and dictate style and fashion.

Perhaps the most important influence on the period was the development of lapidary skills, particularly with reference to diamonds, which were being brought back in relatively large quantities through trade with the East. The famous Golconda mines near Hyderabad in India, which were opened at the beginning of the 17th century, were particularly important. Between the late 15th and early 17th centuries, lapidaries had confined themselves to one of two styles: the 'point' or writing diamond, already described, and the 'table', where the top or point of the octahedron is cut to form a square or rectangular plane, the other point being cut to a similar but smaller shape, and the sides roughly faceted. By 1640 experiments in Holland had led to the development of the 'rose' diamond, a vast improvement on previous styles, which at last released much of the true brilliance of the stone. In this cut, the flat-bottomed crystal has a concave surface covered with 16 or 24 triangular facets. The work was sponsored by Cardinal Mazarin, a minister at the Court of Louis XIV; he had seen diamonds from India which had been randomly faceted to remove flaws and how they scintillated. Realizing the potential, he sponsored a number of lapidaries to experiment with the idea.

The appearance of these new stones on the market created an immediate and enormous demand for them, and gold and pearls, until then the most precious materials known, were relegated to second place. Coloured stones, too, benefited from the improvement in cutting techniques, with the result that gems are rarely found *en cabochon* after the middle of the 17th century.

Diamond history of a different kind was also made in this century. In 1650 the Great Mogul diamond was discovered at the Gani mines in India. It has been estimated that it weighed some 800 carats. Towards the end of the century the Mogul sent the diamond to a Venetian cutter, Ortensio Borgis, who unfortunately reduced the stone to 280 carats, a mistake for which he was punished by having all his property confiscated. It is not known what became of this remainder of the diamond.

The first imitation diamonds were also made in this century although there is some uncertainty as to who first made them. George Ravenscroft, owner of the Savoy Glass House in London is commonly credited with the discovery, but Villiers in his *Journal d'un Voyageur à Paris* mentions a Monsieur d'Arre who was making counterfeit diamonds, emeralds, rubies, and topazes before 1675 which was the date of Ravenscroft's discovery. His imitation was a 'paste' glass based on lead oxide, which had a high refractive index and when cut looked like the genuine stone. The imitation was widely used following its discovery.

The new emphasis on stones rather than goldwork and enamel has, however, had an unfortunate outcome: succeeding generations must have coveted the gems more than the settings, for relatively few pieces of good 17th century jewelry have survived the melting pot, compared with the products of the previous century.

Enamelling also flourished during this period, though in a different style. Indeed some of the finest examples of this type of decoration are to be found in the 17th century. The general trend was towards the use of enamelling to enrich and enhance the settings of the stones themselves, rather than to be an essential feature of the design. Watch and miniature cases are an obvious exception and it is in this form that the enameller excelled. Early designs incorporate the moresque decoration so popular during the previous century, combined with elaborately interlaced

Gold miniature case, enamelled in black and white c.1620.

tendril scrolls and strapwork motifs, executed in light-coloured enamel *en silhouette* against a dark background. Occasionally the effect was reversed, a dark decoration against a light background, through the use of niello. Perhaps the most important of all the designers of silhouette enamels is JeanToutin, who was working in Chateaudun during the first decades of the 17th century.

Designs for predominantly gem-set jewelry showed a departure, in spirit and motifs, from the Mannerist style. The Baroque love of naturalistic ornament evident in all the arts, especially ceramics and furniture, was quickly adopted in jewelry as well. Brooches and pendants were soon designed as elaborate foliate scrolls, buds and flowerheads, often supporting several pear-shaped drops, the whole richly set with various gems, often in pea pod-like settings. The reverse of the mount was delicately engraved.

Enamelwork, too, found inspiration in leaves and flowers as a source of decorative motifs. By the second half of the 18th century, designers such as Petitot, Vauquer and Légaré had perfected the technique of painted enamel, where the medium is applied in the manner of paint on to an enamelled ground of uniform colour, usually white though occasionally pale blue, yellow or black. Through this technique, which allows a far greater degree of delicacy than the more common *champlevé* process, flower designs achieved a naturalism and beauty hitherto unknown and seldom rivalled. A further innovation was to model the leaves and flowers in relief by building up contoured layers in the enamel ground. In some instances, the ground was cut away leaving the enamelled blooms alone, and thereby adding even greater realism.

This type of naturalistic flower decoration found its way on to most items of jewelry, not only the pendants and watch cases already mentioned, but also rings, necklace links, earrings and the immensely popular *aigrette*. This last jewel, a hair ornament which usually took the form of a spray of flowers or feathers richly set with a cluster of stones, seems to have been *de rigeur* at all ceremonial occasions. Sadly, few have survived other than in engravings.

Yet another new enamelling technique called *émail en résille sur verre* was practised by some skilled French enamellers. After engraving a design on glass, the cavities were lined with gold foil and filled with a low melting point enamel. Because of difficulties in ensuring sufficient heat to melt the enamel without cracking or melting the glass, the technique gradually lost favour. Miniature cases were sometimes decorated in this way and some belts enamelled with hunting scenes are in the Victoria and Albert Museum and the Wallace Collection.

In dress design, the profusion and mixture of patterns and motifs that characterized the late 16th century were gradually abandoned for a more luxurious and dignified style in rich silks and brocades exemplified in the portraits by Van Dyck. The jewels themselves, rather than tending to be lost among the plethora of decoration and ornament, as was the case in the previous century, focused the attention glimmering with rich colour. Many jewels were worn *en parure*, with matching brooch, pendant and earrings.

An unusual and gloomy fashion was *memento mori*, which complemented the mourning jewelry popular since the 16th century. Fashionable mainly in England, they often consisted of coffin-shaped pendants with a death's head in enamel. One such pendant found at Torre Abbey, Devon, has the cover of the coffin decorated with *champlevé* enamel in black while the coffin contains a white enamelled skeleton. Round the sides is the inscription 'Through the Resurrection of Christe we be all sanctified'. Such *memento mori* became memorials to the death of specific people. A large number of such jewels, for instance, were made to commemorate the execution of Charles I.

Embroidery

England

After the accession of James I in 1603, embroidery in England continued for a while in Elizabethan styles. Spanish work was still popular, appliqué was in fashion and developed into stumpwork, while chinoiserie was in vogue for a few years. Bird and flower motifs in petit point and appliquéd to the cloth were common decorations and designs were based mostly on scroll patterns sometimes with gold and silver thread couching accompanying them. 'Yellow silk' embroidery evolved at this time and consisted of padded panels with heraldic devices embroidered in yellow silk on ivory-coloured satin, which gave a quilted look when they were joined.

Old herbals were still widely used for design ideas as were such books as *Insectorum* by Thomas Moufet, published in 1607 and Simpson's *Flowers, Fruits, Birds and Beasts*.

By the later years of the 17th century, the making of samplers had become part of the needlework education of young girls, who would often make several – perhaps a coloured sampler of stitches, motifs and alphabets, a whitework sampler showing cut and drawn work and embroidery suitable for household linen, and finally an embroidered picture or casket in which she was able to display her most flamboyant skills. Until well into the 18th century samplers were a rich source of stitches and designs and in many cases they provide an impressive record of individual performance.

In time, however, design books became more widely available and fewer adult embroideresses made samplers for their own use. Although they continued as part of the educational curriculum for girls they soon became debased into exercises 'in neatness and perseverance'. They showed fewer and fewer different stitches until by the 19th century they were nearly always worked entirely in cross-stitch. As well as an alphabet and sometimes a child's name, age and the date, they included motifs such as flowers, animals, houses and birds and, nearly always, a pious verse. The whole picture – for this is what the sampler had become – was generally surrounded by a decorative border and was clearly designed to be framed and hung up for all to see.

The later 17th century in England was remarkable for its vibrant

Mid-17th century motif popular on embroidered curtains and hangings.

124

pictorial embroidery. The period after Charles II's restortation in 1660 was one of unashamed luxury, colourful splendour and sensuous excesses of all kinds, and the extravagance of the time is reflected in the array of late Stuart needlework pictures, mirror frames, caskets and keepsakes which have survived to the present day. Some were embroidered in coloured silks in the flat, while others were done in three-dimensional stumpwork, with figures, flowers, fruits and other motifs raised and padded: details of costume-like collars and cuffs were frequently semi-detached and made of needlepoint lace. Although many of the designs were Biblical – the Finding of Moses, Esther and Ahasuerus and the Judgement of Solomon were among the favourites – the figures all wear elaborate Stuart costume. In the background fanciful castles, huge caterpillars, birds, butterflies, cows, lions and flowers, mostly taken from the popular design books of the time, jostle for space with total disregard for the rules of proportion. Their colourful naïvety is charming, and the stitchery, often punctuated with sequins and seed pearls, is breathtaking.

Pictorial panels, however embroidered, were put to a variety of uses. Most frequently they were used to cover the wooden boxes which held the owner's jewelry and trinkets. The scenes around the sides of the box were often from the life of a particular Biblical figure. In some cases the edges of the panels are finished with braid or held with lacquer. The inside of the door is usually decorated with highly formalized flower motifs in laid work. Only the larger boxes were embroidered inside. A particularly beautiful example, now in the Victoria and Albert Museum, was made by Martha Edlin in 1671, when she was only 11, and shows the Seven Virtues, Music and the Four Elements. The rest of her work made as a child accompanies the box and it seems that box embroidery was the first task set a child once she had mastered the basic techniques.

Embroidered mirror-frames are not uncommon, the motifs usually comprising a figure, often cameoed, on each side of the mirror and the rest of the frame filled with flowers, birds, insects and so on. Mirror-frames in beadwork were also made.

Although leather and cloth bookbinding were becoming more common, embroidered binding remained popular until the end of Charles II's reign. Heraldic, floral and pictorial motifs were worked in petit point on canvas, or chain and split stitches on silk, satin and velvet. A large number of such books have survived, the most renowned being those by the nuns of Little Gidding after 1650 and now in the British Museum.

France

Meanwhile across the Channel, the French were enjoying an even more glittering period under Louis XIV. As in England and Holland, the exotic imports of the East India companies stimulated both household and sartorial fashions and gave the French, in particular, a taste for richly embroidered silks. Louis XIV himself had a huge band of embroiderers working for his entourage at Versailles, and anybody who was anybody spent vast sums of money on lace and embroidery for their clothes. Some even sent materials to China to be embroidered with oriental motifs.

17th Century

The chain-stitch embroidery known as tambour work, another Chinese import, was a favourite occupation with French needlewomen from the end of the 17th century, and the habit spread to other countries, especially England, in the mid-18th century. On the whole, the best French embroidery was done by professionals. Many of these were Huguenots and after the Revocation of the Edict of Nantes in 1695 a great number of them fled to England, Germany, Switzerland and Holland where they soon set up successful workshops. Ironically, a proportion of their embroideries found their way back to France.

Louis XIV's minister, Colbert, himself a mercer's son, worked hard to establish France's pre-eminence on all fronts, and especially in the textile industry. As well as encouraging French lace and tapestry he helped to promote linen manufacture at Cambrai, Valenciennes, St Quentin and Lille. Most important of all – for it was probably the most successful – the silk industry of Lyons became supreme in the late 17th century. The colourful garlands of flowers woven on rich cream grounds were as luxurious as any embroidered materials, and they soon became fashionable for the best-dressed people all over Europe.

Chintz made its first appearance in Europe around the turn of the century and was immediately popular because of the brilliance and fastness of its colours. From 1640 the supply of chintz became an important branch of the East India Company's trade and by 1680 demand was enormous. Prohibition of chintz imports by France in 1686 and England in 1700 caused trade to fall but chintz still reached both countries in substantial quantities. Before 1650 chintz was used only as a furnishing fabric but by the 1670s it is frequently mentioned as a costume fabric.

One of the major influences exerted by East India Company imports of printed cottons and chintzes was, surprisingly enough, on the wool embroidered bed hangings so essential to keep out winter draughts in northern Europe and America. Again, these were mainly the province of the domestic embroideress, who worked the bed-curtains and valences – the pelmet-like hangings round the roof of a four-poster bed – in coloured crewel wools on a linen or cotton ground. Her designs for these crewel or Jacobean embroideries, worked in long and short, chain and stem stitches with French knots and a variety of fillings, were frequently taken from oriental originals.

The Tree of Life pattern was much favoured. In this, a swirling tree laden with improbable fruit and flowers springs from a rocky base. Among and beneath its branches hover birds of paradise and all kinds of animals – lions, squirrels, stags, rabbits and insects – which were usually taken not from oriental sources but from the needlework pattern books which had been in current use for most of the century.

America

In the late 17th century, life in the American colonies was beginning to grow less spartan than it had been in the days of the early settlers, and with increasing comfort came an emphasis on domestic embroidery. American wool hangings were at first confined to repeating motifs worked in a single colour, but by the end of the 17th century these had progressed to colourful crewel embroideries similar to those made in northern Europe.

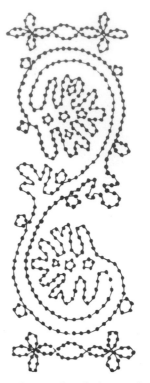

Border motif worked in coral stitch.

126

Americans, as well as Europeans, used knotted pile Turkey work for covering cushions, chairs and other furniture in the late 17th century. Carpets and rugs of Turkey work had originally been imported to Europe from the Near East by the East India companies, and they soon became popular for their hardwearing properties and colourfulness. They were made by pulling wool through canvas or coarse linen stretched on a loom and then cutting it to form a pile. The technique lent itself to formal geometric designs and heraldic motifs in bright colours and was soon made on a commercial scale in Europe. Like many professional crafts, it was also done by persevering ladies at home, and in America Turkey work was more often done domestically than by professionals.

Japanese Swords

Japanese swords made from about 1600 are known as 'shinto' (new swords), and most of the blades still in existence are shinto. This class of swords includes the *Katana*, with a blade length of 53–76 cm (21–30 in), and the *wakizashi* with a blade length between 30–60 cm (12–24 in). Various knives and daggers such as *yoroi-toshi*, a short fighting knife used to pierce armour, were smaller versions of the swords.

The two swords of a samurai were called *daisho*; the *katana*, allowed only to samurai, could be replaced with the shorter *wakizashi* and a dagger, *tanto* or *yoroi-toshi*. On rare occasions members of other classes could carry the short sword and dagger. Also, free peasants (*goshi*) might carry swords at their own risk. The sword and dirk were carried in the waist sash. Although the long hilt on Japanese swords allows two-handed use they were usually used single-handed with a slashing action rather than a thrust, though the point was used with daggers and knives.

Samurai women were not allowed to handle a sword, but they were trained in the use of other weapons such as the halberd. Samurai dominance over other classes was often despotic: sword blades were tested on criminals and even passers-by as well as on iron bars and hay bales.

All the famous swordsmiths were of samurai rank. Smiths were regarded as artists rather than artisans, and founded dynasties and rival schools of swordmakers, some of which lasted for centuries. The Japanese also invested the sword with a religious quality – it was the 'soul of the samurai'. Japanese ideas about swords reflect the mixture of Shinto, the indigenous beliefs, and imported Buddhist ideas: swords were thought to have magical qualities, and to be made of the Five Elements, earth, fire, water, wood and metal. Smiths tended to lead moderate, even ascetic lives; forging was complex and took weeks of skilful work.

The iron and steel from which the blades were made was obtained from local supplies of ferrous ores and a ferruginous sand, although from the 17th century some imported steel was used. There were two basic methods for making blades, one for blades made only of steel, the other for blades made of a combination of iron and steel.

In the first method two pieces of steel of different grades were placed on top of each other and welded to form a billet. An iron bar was then welded to this to act as a handle. The billet was then folded on itself, welded again and hammered out to its original length. The whole process was then repeated at least fifteen times. A special fire was used made from a type of pine charcoal and before each firing a mixture of clay and straw-ash was used to coat the blade, care being taken not to touch the metal with the hands. Occasionally three or four of these billets would be welded together and the above process repeated five times, producing more than four million layers. This method was called *muku-gitai* or *muku-tsukuri* ('pure forging' or 'unalloyed make').

There were several methods of making blades from iron and steel but they all consisted of a soft iron core enclosed by a piece or pieces of hard steel. The core metal (*shintetsu*) was subjected to the folding and welding process followed by hammering out some dozen times. The outer metal (*uwagane*) was made from pieces of steel, from which the slag had been removed, which were forged into a bar, notched, and then folded, welded and reforged some 15 times. A common method of combining the two was to form the *uwagane* into a V-shaped bar into which the *shintetsu* was inserted and welded and the whole then put through the blade-making process again.

Many of the blades of this period exhibited a wood-grain effect called *mokume* made by one of two methods, *hada-gitai* and *masume-tsukuri*. Both methods began with the finished billet and in the former method the bar was randomly dented and gouged and then flattened by hammering or grinding so that the various layers of the bar were revealed. The second method involved hammering the bar on its edge until it became the face so revealing the layers of metal which look like wood-graining. Since the *makume* effect disappeared on tempering it is not visible on the tempered edge.

When forging the hard edge on a sword blade, an almost religious ritual was followed. The smith and his assistant wore special robes indicating their social rank; the smithy was locked and Shinto rites were performed to make it into a shrine with plaited straw hangings and paper flags to prevent the entry of evil spirits.

To produce a hard edge on a sword blade it was covered with wet clay in which a line was drawn about 12 mm ($\frac{1}{2}$ in) from the edge. The clay was removed between the line and edge and the remainder allowed to harden, the blade was then placed in the furnace and watched for the right colour change. The blade was then removed, the clay taken off and the blade quenched. This process produced a hardened, decorative cutting edge (*yahiba*) with a milky white colour where the exposed steel had crystallized.

Characteristic designs were used when drawing the line of the *yahiba*. These included a jagged line signifying a horse's tooth, and a stepped line indicating a road up the mountains. These patterns (*hamon*) may be used to date and value a sword and place it in its tradition or school.

The blade was sharpened and polished over several weeks to produce a mirror finish. The effect of the repeated folding and welding of the original ingot shows in the pattern of the softer surface steel layer (*jihada*) away from the edge. Shinto swords were also often decorated with engraved figures (*harimono*). The tang might then be inscribed with the maker's name, province and the date before the sword furniture and scabbard were mounted. If the blade were to be stored it was mounted with a plain wooden grip in a plain wooden scabbard. Whether stored or worn, a collar (*habachi*) fitted into the top of the scabbard to provide a seal to prevent the damp climate attacking the blade.

Swords are identified by their period, the area where they were produced, and the smith's signature. However, swords were not always signed, and some famous signatures were copied by later smiths. The identification of blades was a touchy subject, even among the samurai. Some 19th century smiths referred to their ancestry when signing blades, others used variations on their name and title. Earlier styles of blades were also copied.

There were several schools of swordsmiths of note working in this century. Probably the most influential was the Horikawa School at Kyoto. Its founder (in 1580) was Umetada Myōju and with his pupil Kunihiro they trained many of the swordsmiths of Kyoto, Osaka, Hizen and Aki who in turn were responsible for the 17th century being one of the great periods of swordsmithing history in Japan. The school made mainly long swords and dirks with the blades engraved with a dragon and sword and showing the *mokume* grain.

The Tsuta School at Osaka which worked from *c*.1650–1700 was affiliated with the Horikawa School and the founder Sukehiro and his son-in-law Sukenao were among the most highly skilled craftsmen of the day, making both long and short swords with *mokume* grain. The founder of the Nagasone School at Yedo, Kotetsu Okisato, became the foremost swordsmith of his time. Working from *c*.1650–1700 he made long and short swords occasionally engraved with the dragon and sword and with *mokume* grain.

In the early years of the Tokugawa, before peace was finally established, swords remained entirely functional and their guards and mounts had little artistic decoration. When interest in more decorative mounts and guards was revived artisans had a long tradition on which to draw for inspiration. Not least was the style set by the Goto School which had been established in 1435 and which was the only style used for court ceremonial wear until 1868. The Goto School is particularly remembered as the creator of relief sculpture in the alloy called *shakudo* made from copper with a small percentage of gold.

In the second half of the 17th century a new school arose, the Nara School, founded by Nara Toshiteru. This school broke away from the rigid traditions of the Goto, using a greater variety of coloured alloys, and a wider range of designs mainly inspired by the painters of Kano. Nara Toshinaga (1667–1737) was the first member of this school to make a distinct break with tradition.

As well as *shakudo*, two other coloured alloys used were *shibuichi*, an alloy of copper with up to 25 per cent silver and *sentoku* a variety of brass which was originally invented in China. These alloys only attained their unique colouration after they had been subjected to a pickling process

129

which oxidized the surface of the metals. *Shakudo* developed a violet-black hue on pickling, *sentoku* a chrome yellow colour and *shibuichi* a range of shades from olive-brown to a colour similar to oxidized silver.

The *hibachi*, already mentioned, was usually made of copper, silvered or gilt, or overlaid with gold, silver or *shakudo* foil. It is either simply polished or engraved with a form of decoration known as *neko-gaki* ('cat scratches'). The *hibachi* can often be a guide to the quality of the blade.

The *tsuba*, or guard, is usually in the form of a flat disc with an opening through which the tang can pass and is the most important of all fittings. More often than not they are made of metal – iron, steel, copper or one of the coloured alloys – on to which the decoration is applied. Some later examples have the front and back in different metals, while during the reign of the Tokugawa Shogun, Iyemitsu (1623–51), guards in solid gold were the fashion. They are decorated on both sides with the edge usually left plain.

The hilt, *tsuka*, was made of wood, preferably a variety of magnolia, which was covered with a piece of the noduled skin of the ray-fish. This in turn was covered by the wrapping, (*tsuka-ito*, 'hilt-thread') made from a single length of silk braid in either black, browns, dark blues or greens. Some court swords lacked this wrapping, while daggers often had the hilt enclosed in wood, lacquer, rattan or metal.

Scientific Instruments

Of all the sciences it is astronomy which has the longest history of an appreciation of the vital role played by precision instruments. Not surprisingly the archetypal and most desirable of all scientific instruments, the astrolabe, was used in astronomy. In the 17th century the astrolabe became obsolete while at the same time astronomy found its prime instrument in the telescope. This century then is a good one in which to review both the history of the astrolabe and the origins of the telescope.

Primarily the astrolabe is a mechanical analogue used to predict star and planetary positions. It could also be used to measure solar elevation, compute the latitude, tell the time and undertake basic surveying. The theory of the stereographic projection, on which the instrument was based, was known in classical antiquity, but the earliest surviving astrolabes were made during the 11th century by Islamic craftsmen living in southern Spain. Even after they became obsolete however, these classic instruments continued to be made in the Islamic world, and are still made in Isfahan by craftsmen who follow the traditional techniques of construction. Such is their attraction that scholars have been studying European and Islamic astrolabes for more than a century.

The astrolabe comprises several parts: The Mater (or *Umm*, in Arabic), is a thick, round plate with a ridge in square section called the limb, and a projecting shoulder (*Kursi*) with suspension ring. This shoulder can be highly ornamented, as in the Islamic examples, or undecorated in

Astrolabe made in Nuremberg in 1632.

European instruments. A hole in the centre of the mater takes a round-headed pin which is slit along its side to take the horse (*faras*) which holds the remaining discs or plates inside the mater. These discs, called tympans (*safiha*), were made of brass and vary in number, each one allowing a different calculation or range of related calculations to be made, depending on the latitude. The rete, which is a skeletal brass disc, is a star map which is placed over the plates. It has an inner offset circle representing the band of the ecliptic. On the back of the mater there is a sighting arm with two aligned pinnules (*alidade*).

In order to use the astrolabe in sunlight, it is held at waist level and turned to the plane of the sun. The *alidade* is adjusted until the sunlight passes through the pinnules and a measurement of the sun's height above the horizon taken. At night, a star would be sighted through the pinnules, the rete set using the appropriate tympan and the instrument was then an exact reproduction of the night sky at that moment.

A principle disadvantage of the astrolabe was that its use was limited to the number of available plates, each one for a separate latitude. As a result, in the 16th and 17th centuries the 'universal' astrolabe was developed. The most widely used one was by instrument designer Gemma Frisius of Louvain which took the vernal equinox as its point of reference rather than the celestial pole. Another type of universal astrolabe was developed by Philippe de la Hire at the end of the 17th century.

The fine metalwork, delicate engraving and graceful lines of an astrolabe have an immediate and lasting appeal. An eye catching feature is the intricately pierced rete whose pointers represent important stars. Products of the Flemish work-shops of the Arsenius family are particularly prized for a very high standard of craftsmanship. Indeed an astrolabe made in 1556 by Gemma Frisius, the uncle and teacher of Walther and Regner Arsenius, holds the world record price for an antique instrument sold at auction, fetching 310,000 Swiss Francs in 1975. This was an exceptionally beautiful astrolabe, a presentation piece engraved with the arms of Phillip II of Spain and Mary Tudor of England.

The telescope was invented in the early years of the 17th century by an unknown spectacle maker, and was given immense publicity by the startling discoveries of the great Galileo. Scientist and layman alike were eager to own and use the new instrument. Initially they were both rare and expensive, and only a handful of telescopes made before 1650 have survived. The second half of the century is better represented. The typical late-17th-century hand-held telescope has a number of cardboard draw-tubes. For portability they all slide into an outer tube or barrel which is normally highly decorated. English instruments of the period are characterized by patches of green and orange on the white vellum cover of the barrel, with a pattern of gold stampings providing further embellishment.

Sundials

The area which is best represented in number and diversity of surviving instruments is gnomics, the science of dialling, or the designing and making of sundials. The various instruments used to set out and calibrate sundials, such as the declinatory, dialling scale, and movable-horizontal-dial, are rare and frequently pass unrecognized. The sundial itself is, however, immediately appreciated as an instrument for telling the time by the sun. That there is a profusion of dials of all sizes, periods, materials and designs, surprises those who have forgotten that watches and clocks need to be regulated to a standard time. Until well into the 19th century, and the spread of the electric telegraph, the sundial was the only way of finding the time once your mechanical timepiece stopped.

Archeologists have recorded Greek and Roman dials carved in stone, but if we exclude these and other mural dials, the earliest sundials produced by European instrument-makers are the horary quadrants made in the late medieval period.

The most frequently seen horary quadrant is that named after Edmund Gunter, whose design was published in 1623. London makers like Allen, Bedford and Hayes in the 17th century, produced fine examples of the Gunter quadrant. Some have a celestial planisphere on the reverse face which permitted the time to be found at night from the circumpolar rotation of the stars. Rather than using silver, brass or boxwood, cheap horary quadrants were printed on paper from a copper plate, and pasted on to wooden boards. There are some nice early 19th century examples of this type, printed in Italy with letterpress instructions on the reverse: *Spiegazione per l'uso dell Orologio a Quadrante Solare.*

In the 16th and 17th centuries Nuremberg craftsmen supplied Europe with a distinctive form of sundial, the diptych dial. Formed from two hinged plates of ivory, the diptych may contain just vertical and horizontal dials on the two inner leaves. More usually it supplements those dials with polar, equinoctial and scaphe dials. In addition there may be tables of epachts (to calculate the date of Easter) lunar and solar volvelles, and dials that indicate the length of the day and the season of the year. Most Nuremberg dials are fully signed – though some bear only the master-sign of the maker. Many are also dated. One craftsman with a distinguished style was Paulus Reinman, active from 1575 to 1609. Reinman's work is often decorated with attractive vignettes, a pair of musicians, lovers talking, hunting hounds. As was the fashion his calibration and decoration is picked out in red, blue and black. Reinman's master-sign was used by Michael Lesel from 1609 to 1629, making it difficult to give firm attributions to some pieces.

In terms of quantity, the Nuremberg dial makers were succeeded from the mid-17th century by the Kompassmacher of Augsburg, whose typical product was the universal equinoctial dial. Working in brass, which in the early period was often gilded, the Augsburg craftsmen had a flourishing trade, printing instruction sheets in German, French and Spanish. Men like Johann Martin and his half-brother Johann Willibrand set very high standards.

Possibly the highest point of Augsburg craftsmanship was attained in the 16th century and is best represented by instruments produced by family dynasties of craftsmen like the Kliebers (1487–1619 in three generations) and the Schisslers (1531–1625 in two generations). Both these families produced wonderful pocket compendia in gilded brass. These dials open out to reveal various universal sundials, nocturnals, astrolabes and perpetual calendars. The compendium allows the instrument-maker to show all his constructional skills in one masterpiece.

Italian, Flemish and less often French and English makers produced fine compendia, but none reached the standards of the 16th century Augsburg masters.

Two distinctly French sundials are those named after Michael Butterfield and Charles Bloud. The 'Butterfield' dial is a pseudo universal horizontal dial adjustable for use over the latitude range 40° to 60° north. The archetypal form has an octagonal dialplate and a characteristic bird decoration on the adjustable gnomon – the beak of the bird indicates the latitude. Made in brass or silver the Butterfield dial was a typical product of the Parisian instrument-makers from about 1675 to 1750. The quality of the craftsmanship is variable, though that of Butterfield himself is consistently good, and is comparable to his contemporaries Bion and Chapotot, and, in the later period, Langlois.

The 'Bloud' dial is one of the few examples of a French instrument of the 17th century made outside Paris. From the 14th century the Ivoirier of Dieppe held an international reputation. In the 17th century a distinct school of diptych dial makers appeared. About 1650 Charles Bloud designed a form of magnetic azimuth dial incorporating a perpetual calendar. He proudly signed his dials *Fait et Inventé par Charles Bloud A Dieppe*. Other Dieppe makers like Senecal, Guérard and Gabriel, Jacques and Jean Bloud produced similar dials. In the Dieppe style they decorated their work with a characteristic border of pecked crenelations.

Three other dials made in the 17th century are also worth mentioning. The cruciform dial was probably first made in the 16th century though surviving examples are likely to be not earlier than the second half of the 17th century. As the name suggests the dial was made in the shape of a cross with vertical dials drawn on the sides of the body and the arms forming the gnomons. A compass was set in the base and when the cross was inclined in the plane of the equator the time could be read on each dial.

The crescent dial was a variation on the equinoctial ring dial and the best-known examples were made by Johann Martin of Augsburg towards the end of the century. In this the hour ring is in two halves fixed back to back and the gnomon is a crescent-shaped bar with its tips lying in the axes of the hour scale. The various pieces of the dial could be folded so that it could be kept in a leather or fish-skin case. Those made by Martin, as well as Johann Willebrand, were beautifully made in silver and gilt brass.

In 1698, Thomas Tuttel designed a self-orienting dial which has two dials, one of which is the usual horizontal dial while the other is an azimuth dial, called an analemmatic dial. When the dial lies horizontally, and is then rotated, the correct time is given when both dials agree.

In its time the universal equinoctial ring dial was very popular, primarily because it is self-orienting and requires no compass to align it. The design was inspired by the astronomical ring of Gemma Frisius and it is most frequently found in the form published by Oughtred in 1652, with two rings set at right angles. There is a pin-hole gnomon on a diametrical bridge, casting a spot of sunlight on to the hour ring. This was the design used by the leading London instrument-makers for over 150 years. French and German makers produced similar instruments, together with the three ring variety which is, however, not at all common.

Most long-lasting of all pocket sundials is the cylinder, pillar or shepherd's dial; this latter name refers to its use in the present century by the Basque people of the Pyrenees. The design is known from 13th century manuscripts, and from that period Continental workshops made them in silver, ivory and wood. One 19th century Parisian clockmaker even marketed cylinder dials made of porcelain; it is a most cumbersome timepiece and cannot compare with the elegant silverware of Schissler of Augsburg, whose cylinder dials contained a set of writing implements, and incorporated an ink well and a sand caster.

Mathematical Instruments

An ability to use mathematical instruments was at one time one of the essential skills of an educated gentleman. For wealthy clients, craftsmen like Giacomo Lusuergh of Modena, who worked in Rome from the late 1660s, produced comprehensive sets of mathematical instruments. Such compendia included all the tools necessary for architectural drawing, surveying, gunnery and computation.

Domenico Lusuergh produced similar work for at least 50 years after succeeding his uncle in 1697. Like other Italian craftsmen of the period, the Lusuerghs produced lavish compendia of mathematical instruments in which technical expertise was complemented by fine engraved decoration.

French, Dutch and English makers of this time tended to produce only pocket cases of drawing instruments, including a sector for computational purposes. Decoration is not found as a matter of course, though there are some notable exceptions. For example, during the first four decades of the 18th century, London makers often engraved an oak leaf border pattern on sectors, protractors and plain scales. This can be very effective on silver instruments, especially when the engraving is filled with niello.

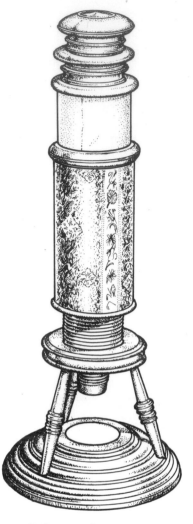

Italian tripod microscope.

One of the most intriguing of all early mathematical instruments is an aid to calculation called Napier's Rods, or 'Bones', since the earliest examples were made from ivory. Boxes of 10 or 20 rods no bigger than a cigarette packet, were used by those who found multiplication difficult – the face of each rod has the multiplication table of a digit from one to nine. The design was published by John Napier in Edinburgh in 1616, and it rapidly became widely known. Few sets are signed and it may be as difficult to ascertain their origin as their date.

The Microscope

Just as the telescope opened new worlds in the heavens so too did the microscope uncover for the 17th century an unimagined kingdom of the minuscule. For 250 years the microscope was the most loved of all the instruments available to the amateur. To be sure, professional scientists used the instrument and made many important discoveries, but from the publication of Robert Hooke's *Micrographia* in 1664 until the end of the Victorian era, ladies, gentlemen and children discovered microscopy as a recreation. Significant developments, both technical and artistic, did not take place in the microscope until the 18th century, however, and it is in that chapter that this instrument will be reviewed.

Turkish Carpets

Among antique rugs, probably the most interesting and colourful group are those made in Turkey – mostly in Asia Minor – in the 17th and early 18th centuries. At that time, the finest of the Turkish products rivalled all but the very best of Persian weavings, and the rugs of Ghiordes, Mudjar, Kadik and Konieh, for example, are still eagerly sought by connoisseurs and collectors, to say nothing of the lovely little Melas rugs.

Most of the Turkish production was in standard rug sizes, with the exception of the Oushak area, which mostly produced standard carpet sizes, and an occasional Ghiordes. So-called Sparta carpets (a corruption of Isbarta), and the similar but more finely-knotted Sivas, were of a much later period and were more of a commercial product. All Turkish rugs are knotted with the Turkish knot.

Ghiordes

The best known of all Turkish weavings, the Ghiordes at its finest is a magnificent rug, rivalling the best in Persia. Examples exist covering several centuries and, even today, pieces from the 17th and 18th centuries still come on to the market. In the *namazliks* or prayer rugs the arch is very typical in form, rather suggesting a Pathan turban, with flat shoulders rising steeply to a point, from which a lamp is suspended. In later forms, this could also be a vase or basket of flowers. Often, in later pieces, there is a form of pilaster inside the edges of the field, acting as support for the shoulders of the arch. The remainder of the field is plain, but the spandrels above the *mihrab* or arch are closely covered with tracery or angular foliate forms. There is a great variety of main border stripes, but they are invariably squared off in quadrangular forms, except when, possibly through intermarriage, the main border stripe from nearby Kulah is adopted.

Knotting varies from coarse 8.75 to the sq cm (56 sq in) to fine 29.75 to the sq cm (192 sq in). The coarser pieces are of a looser texture, with wool or silk warps, though cotton was sometimes used in later pieces. The main colours include a rich red, dark green, ivory and deep blue.

Kulah

The village of Kulah produces a much looser fabric than Ghiordes, and the *mihrab* is the flattest of all the Turkish prayer rugs. The field is almost invariably decorated, usually with vertical rows of flower heads, and the spandrels are covered with small repetitive designs.

Red, blue, a mid-green, ivory and yellow are the main colours used, and there is never any clashing of colours. Texture is loose, with two weft threads between every two rows of knots, the knotting varying between 5.5 and 18.5 to the sq cm (35 to 120 sq in). The border stripe consists of several narrow stripes about 3 cm (1 in) in width in alternate contrasting colours, each bearing minute floral forms at regular intervals.

There are quite a few rugs other than prayer rugs in this category, mostly like a double-ended namazlik, having an identical arch at either end of the field.

Konieh

There is a wide variety of design in this group in almost every part. Borders may vary from several narrow stripes to an exceptionally wide main stripe that is rather too wide for the rest of the design. Positioning of the prayer arch or *mihrab* also varies a great deal, and the fields are rarely plain, mostly bearing small stylized floral forms.

The *mihrab* is stepped and often small latchhooks project from these steps into the spandrel, and so to those of the field. Two threads of red wool wefts across between each two rows of knots, and the backs of these rugs are less ribbed in appearance than most Turkish rugs. Knotting is coarse, varying between 4.5 and 12.5 to the sq cm (30 and 80 sq in) and texture is reasonably firm.

Melas

Although these rugs are characterized by a soft strawberry red, and the designs have an artless simplicity, they offer the widest scope of design in all the rugs in the Turkish group. The variety of design is almost endless, yet there is rarely any hesitation in ascribing a rug to the right category. Generally, the *mihrab* is characteristic in that it is sharply waisted with an angular indentation on either side before the arch ascends at about 45 degrees to meet in the centre. The indentations are often filled, with the exception of a small dividing line, with a triangular piece of the same colour as the field.

Despite this, the rule is broken as often as it is observed. In some *namazliks* the field may be only a long narrow panel running the centre of the rug with a tiny arch at the top, while the rest of the field may be covered with assorted designs or even more, shorter vertical panels.

Rugs other than *namazliks* are quite common, but the variety of invention in design is bewildering. Knotting is coarse, varying from 4.5 to 14 to the sq cm (30 to 90 sq in) and there are usually four weft threads of fine red wool between every two rows of knots.

Ladik

These lovely and colourful rugs may still be found in the auction rooms, though the older pieces are often in bad shape. The *mihrab* generally has a triple arch of which the centre one is higher than the others, while the field is usually a rich red or pale blue. Below the field is a deep panel with a row of reciprocal vandykes from which depend a downward pointing row of stems with leaves ending in what look like pomegranates. These are very characteristic, as is the main border stripe which usually consists of alternate conventionalized rosettes and Rhodian lilies. Colours are mainly red and a lightish blue enlivened by a typical canary yellow, with a certain amount of green and brown. Texture is on the firm side, with from 14 to 24 knots to the sq cm (90 to 156 sq in). The back is ribbed.

Oushak

The carpets of Oushak were some of the first oriental carpets to be seen in the West. There are a good number of examples of these weavings from the 16th and 17th centuries, either in designs with large rounded medallions or with star-shaped medallions. There are also 'bird' Oushaks and examples with the Tamerlane motif of three dots superimposed over two tiny wavy bands, both used as repetitive patterns on a white or ivory field. The principal colours are red, blue and green, and the texture is very loose, while knotting is coarse, varying from as little as 2.5 to a top limit of around 11 to each sq cm (16 to 72 sq in). Warp and weft are of wool, the weft being dyed red.

Makri

Sometimes referred to as Rhodian, these stoutly woven rugs are knotted from thick, lustrous wool of excellent quality, and 18th and 19th century pieces can be found in superb condition, but they are very rare. Like the rugs of Bergama they are rather squarer in format, but they are distinctive in that the field may be divided into one, two or three vertical panels in strongly contrasting colours, each panel carrying a number of disjunct motifs in bright colours.

Ground colours of the panels are usually red, blue and green in rich depth, with a lot of golden yellow and white. The back is not ribbed, and the knotting is coarse, varying between 5.5 to 12.5 to the sq cm (35 to 80 sq in) giving a fairly loose texture. There is a web at both ends, and usually a flat two, three or four cord selvage in bright mid-blue at the sides.

Mudjar

The Mudjar is a rare type that is a joy to find, with borders like tessellated tiles, each tile a different colour from that of its neighbours. Colours include mauve, blue, green, red pink, yellow and ivory. The arch is steeply stepped with three or four lines in differing colours outlining the arch which ends with a vandyke, with disjunct ornaments – often including water jugs – in the spandrels. Above the *mihrab* is a shallow panel carrying a row of vandykes terminating in arrow heads.

Texture is loose and the weave fairly coarse, with from 6.5 to 16.75 knots to the sq cm (42 to 108 sq in). There are two shoots of wool weft between each two rows of knots, the weft being dyed red or brown. The warp is also wool.

Kir-Shehir

Like the Mudjar prayer rugs, the *mihrab* is steeply stepped, ending in a vandyke, with the arch delineated by several parallel rows of coloured lines, but there the similarity ends. In the Kir-Shehir, stylized carnations extend into the centre panel from all round the sides, and there are usually carnations projecting into the sides of the field and spandrels, while the panel above the *mihrab* usually carries a cloudband and rosette design. There are two main border stripes characteristic of this type, one of which consists of sprays of flowers arranged in quadrangular form in different colours, while the other consists of quadrangular arrangements of stylized lilies alternating with cypress trees.

Guns

Of all antique weapons, firearms are probably the most popular with collectors. They have romantic, aesthetic and mechanical qualities which appeal to so many people. Until the mid-19th century each was hand made and unique.

Details of the early history of gunpowder are vague, but it seems fairly certain that it was in use on a limited scale in China during the 11th or 12th century. The story of European firearms begins with a reference to them in 1326 and, by coincidence, the earliest illustrations of a crude gun can be dated to the same year.

The earliest firearms were essentially artillery, primarily designed to replace the older forms of missile weapon used to demolish fortifications. In a very short time the idea of hand firearms had developed and the first handguns were very simple. They were nothing more than a tube with one end closed, and near the closed end a small hole (the touchhole), was drilled through the wall of the tube. A charge of black powder, a mixture of saltpetre, sulphur and charcoal, was poured down the barrel; a ball of lead, iron or stone was then pushed down on top of the powder inside the barrel. A pinch of powder was placed over the touchhole and this priming was ignited by some means or other, perhaps a glowing ember. The priming flared and the flame passed through the touchhole to the charge inside the barrel. As the gunpowder exploded the expanding gas drove out the bullet.

The first handguns had a barrel mounted at the end of a wooden stick, although some were all-metal types with barrel and stock made in one. Examples of these early handguns are extremely rare although similar weapons made at a much later date in the Orient may occasionally be found. Soon the barrel was lengthened and fitted to a wooden stock with the end shaped to fit against the shoulder.

From around the end of the 15th century the matchlock ignition system was developed and this used a piece of cord which had been soaked in a very strong solution of saltpetre and then allowed to dry. If the end of this cord was ignited it smouldered with a glowing tip, burning down very slowly. The match was attached to a simple, mechanical arm which was fitted to a plate set into the stock. When the trigger, set under the stock, was pressed, the arm (the serpentine) which held the match, swung forward and pressed the glowing end into the priming powder and ignited the main charge.

This weapon, known as a musket, was long and heavy, and during the 17th century became the main arm of the infantry of most armies. Seventeenth century muskets rarely appear on the market, and then they are extremely expensive. Army-issue weapons were very plain but some, owned by groups known as the Trained Bands or town guard, were sometimes decorated with inlay of horn or ivory.

One great disadvantage of the match was its vulnerability to wind and weather. Rain could easily extinguish the glowing end and the wind could blow sparks about, a great danger with gunpowder near. Gunsmiths sought other means of ignition which would be less liable to the vagaries of the weather. One solution was known as the wheellock. The idea was basically simple, but the mechanism was rather complex. A steel wheel was fitted with a square-ended axle and the edge of the wheel was roughened by various cuts. This wheel was coupled by a very short linked chain to a powerful V-spring. The edge of the wheel was so placed that it formed part of the floor of a pan set next to the touchhole. A metal arm, attached to the lockplate, had two jaws which held a piece

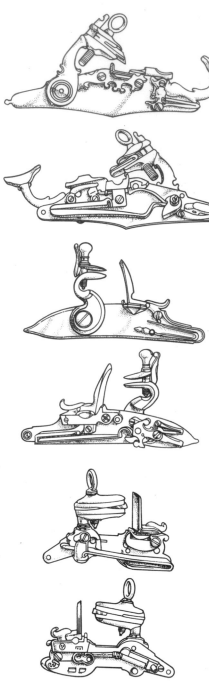

Variations on the flintlock mechanism used on guns during the 17th century

of pyrites – a common mineral. To prepare the mechanism for firing a special key was fitted over the squared end of the spindle attached to the wheel. As this key was turned the wheel also rotated and this movement compressed the spring. When fully compressed a small arm (the sear) engaged with a hole in the side of the wheel, locking it in place. The cock holding the pyrites was swung forward until the pyrites was pressed against the wheel's edge which had been cut and roughened. A pinch of priming powder was placed in the pan and the weapon was ready to fire. When the trigger was pressed the sear was drawn clear of the wheel which, driven by the spring, rotated rapidly. The friction between wheel and pyrites produced a shower of sparks which then ignited the priming powder and so discharged the weapon. This mechanical system of ignition was a big advance on the old matchlock and offered several advantages, being far less subject to the weather. The wheellock was, however, fairly complex and expensive to produce and was, therefore, never issued on a large scale. It was fitted to longarms and pistols, some of which were extremely ornate with the wooden stocks inlaid with mother-of-pearl, ivory, steel, gold and silver. Many of these weapons were works of art in their own right.

The wheellock was fitted to long arms often used primarily for hunting, and since this was essentially a pastime of the rich these wheellocks were often very ornate and elaborate. To ensure greater accuracy, many of these hunting wheellocks were fitted with rifled barrels. They are extremely attractive pieces but their very quality ensures that they fetch very high prices indeed.

Wheellocks were in general use from about 1550 to 1650 but their cost meant that they never ousted the matchlock musket as the standard military firearm.

The matchlock was gradually displaced from the middle of the 17th century, not by the wheellock but by a much simpler system, the flintlock. In place of the pyrites a shaped piece of flint, an even more common mineral, was used. The flint was gripped between the jaws of the cock, which was connected by means of a shank to a shaped metal block, known as the tumbler, fitted on the inside of a lockplate. Bearing down on the tip of the tumbler was a strong V-spring; also pressing against the outer edge of the tumbler was a small arm known as the sear. As the cock was pulled back the tumbler turned and the sear rode over the outside edge and slipped into a small slot cut into the face of the tumbler. In this position the trigger could not disengage the sear from the slot. Known as the half-cock this position enabled the shooter to carry the loaded weapon in safety.

If the cock was pulled further back the tumbler turned and the sear automatically disengaged from the first slot and moved along the edge of the tumbler and then engaged with a second slot. This was the full cock position and in this setting pressure on the trigger disengaged the sear. As the spring was under tension, once the sear was released, it pressed on the tip of the tumbler and caused it to turn rapidly and so swing the cock forward. The flint held in the cock scrapped down an L-shaped arm of metal known as the frizzen, to produce sparks. The short arm of the L served as a pan cover and as the flint pressed on the top section it caused the frizzen to pivot forward allowing the sparks to fall directly into the pan to ignite the priming and so fire the main charge.

There were several varieties of flintlock but the most common form was the French lock which appears to have been first constructed in France about 1610. The miguelet lock is a variant form in which the cock was locked not by a sear pressing against the tumbler, but by an arm which passed through the lock plate to engage directly with the arm of the cock. The common Spanish miguelet is characterized by a short, square frizzen and a squat, square cock.

The flintlock was simpler than the wheellock and by the end of the 17th century the only wheellock weapons still being produced were very expensive hunting arms for the leisured nobility. The matchlock was no longer the standard military issue and generally the only matchlocks still in use after the 17th century were to be found in the East. When the Portuguese explorers first reached Africa, India and, eventually, China and Japan they took with them their matchlock muskets.

The Indian matchlocks are generally quite simple with very long barrels and plain, chunky stocks but the obvious difference between matchlocks from India and those from Europe is that the serpentine arm is set partly inside the stock, unlike the European pattern which has the lock plate mounted on the side of the stock.

Japanese matchlocks are far more ornate and, as befits the skill of their craftsmen, the Japanese produced some very fine quality pieces. Barrels on the Japanese matchlocks tend to be very thick and heavy while the wooden stock does not, like the Indian version, copy the European style. Japanese matchlocks are usually quite short and chunky and they are frequently inlaid or lacquered. The springs on these weapons are almost invariably of brass and the lock favoured by the Japanese was that known as the snap lock. When the arm was at rest the serpentine was pressed down into the pan, a dangerous system for accidental discharges were common. The European style had the serpentine at rest with the arm raised away from the pan.

One great advantage of the flintlock was that it could be produced in any size, large enough to fire a cannon or small enough to fit on a pistol to slip into a pocket or purse. The wheellock may have been responsible for the spread of the pistol but it was the flintlock that made the pistol commonplace. From the 17th century onwards the French style of lock was the dominant version and will be found fitted to pistols and longarms made all over Europe and America.

The shape of the lockplate can be a useful guide in dating flintlocks. The late 17th-, early 18th-century lockplate tends to be rather drooping, almost banana shaped, and is frequently convex in section. As the 18th century progressed the lockplate became straighter, losing that characteristic droop at the rear; it also became flatter in section.

The shape of the cock can also help in dating, for early ones have a very graceful S shape, later versions are less graceful. By the turn of the century many of the cocks are of the ring necked style with the lower S-section being replaced by a strengthened neck. Various improvements were made to the mechanical action of the lock – all designed to reduce friction and make the action more positive. Small metal rollers were

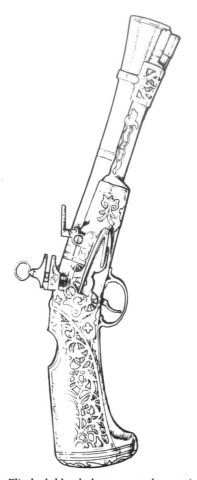

Flintlock blunderbuss, a popular gun in the latter part of the 17th century.

fitted on the lock at points of maximum friction such as the tip of the frizzen where the spring pressed against it – a feature of the late 18th and early 19th century weapons.

Another useful guide, but by no means infallible, is the butt cap on the pistol. As a generalization, and it must be appreciated that there are exceptions to all these general guidelines, the earlier the pistol the larger the pommel or ball at the end of the butt is likely to be. The pommel was usually fitted with a metal cap, and running up the side of the butt were two arms, one on either side. As the 18th century progressed these arms tended to be shorter until, by the turn of the century the butt cap was often dispensed with altogether. If, as on many military pistols, a butt cap was still fitted, the only trace of the side arms was a slight upward curve on the edge of the cap.

Edged Weapons

During the 16th century there was a gradual change from cutting to thrusting as the main method of attack and as armour became more and more effective the sword had to be adapted to offer the warrior any chance of penetrating this protective shell. The solution lay not in cutting through the armour but in attacking the weaker, less well protected spots by thrusting at them. As the Middle Ages progressed, so the swords became longer and more pointed. Another significant change was also taking place, and to obtain a firmer grip the first finger of the right hand was hooked over the cross-guard or quillon. In consequence the top 2.5 cm (1 in) or so of the blade just below the quillon was left blunt and was known as the ricasson.

The next step was to add some form of protection for the finger which was, at first, a simple half loop extending from the quillon. The idea was gradually developed and soon metal rings and bars designed to protect the hand were commonplace.

There evolved in time one of the more common and very desirable types of sword, the rapier. At first they had long, double-edged blades; some were of inordinate length and, consequently, extremely difficult to handle. The hand was protected by an arrangement of bars which virtually enclosed it in a basket of metal. The art of sword play, fencing, developed and the blades were shortened and the edge was blunted and the essence of the rapier was the use of the point. An opponent's blade was diverted by means of a short, parrying dagger held in the left hand. The early ones were ordinary daggers but later specialist forms were introduced.

These left-hand daggers had fairly substantial blades with a simple cross-guard with the quillons having a slight droop towards the point, and a single side ring. A few specialized forms, known as sword breakers, had deep notches cut into the blade. These were designed to catch and possibly snap an opponent's blade.

The Spaniards and Italians developed a form of left-hand dagger which had a narrow, flat blade and long, thin quillons from which sprang a triangular-shaped guard which curved up to meet the pommel. Both rapier and left-hand dagger were often decorated *en suite*. Left-hand daggers were gradually abandoned and by the late 17th century were no longer used except in Spain and areas under her influence, where their use continued until the mid-18th century.

During the last quarter of the 16th century the idea of defending the hand by means of bars was extended and pierced metal plates replaced some of the bars or filled in the spaces between them. Their use was extended and by the early 17th century a single, pierced plate was popular and the size was increased until it was a full bowl with two long quillons. The cup-hilted rapier enjoyed only quite a limited spell of popularity except among the fencing schools of Spain and Italy who retained its use together with the left-hand dagger long after the rest of Europe had dropped it.

The rapier continued in use until around the mid-17th century, but its design changed, becoming shorter and lighter. The quillons were reduced in size and curved down, the knuckle bow was dispensed with and in place of the cup or bars two small shells were fitted one on either side of the quillons. This was the early form of the small sword. During the late 17th century the knuckle bow came back into fashion and the more usual form of small sword was developed. These were delicate weapons weighing very little and fencing with them was a fast moving skill.

The swords themselves were effective weapons but were also regarded by most gentlemen as being part of their costume, in consequence they were often quite elaborately decorated. During the 18th century the hilt was sometimes of silver and it could even be of gold. Even if of steel then the shells might be pierced, the grip enamelled and even set with precious stones. On plainer versions the grip was more often bound with wire. The style of blade varied and there were three main forms. Possibly the commonest was fairly flat, slightly oval in section. The colichemarde blade was very wide just below the hilt (the forte) and narrowed abruptly about one-third of its length, to a very thin section which was the thrusting part of the blade. The third type, known as hollow ground, was triangular in section and gave rigidity with lightness.

The most common style of hilt had a knuckle bow, a small, down-curving rear quillon and two side shells. There were two loops springing from the lower end of the trip and curving over to meet the shells. The size of these is a good guide to the age, for the earlier ones are large enough to insert the fingers but later examples are very small and purely decorative. The small sword was carried in a leather sheath suspended from the belt by means of a very simple hanger, usually little more than a hook to go over the belt and two chains to attach to the scabbard. The small sword continued as a popular item of dress and costume until the 1760–70s, when it was generally discarded. It was a form of sword which continued to be worn by diplomats and other officials.

From the 17th century until at least the middle of the 19th century, few military or naval officers would have considered themselves to be properly equipped without a sword. Most infantrymen, even if the firearm was their main weapon, carried some form of edged weapon. During

Hilt of a rapier owned by Louis XIII of France.

the 17th century the infantry often carried a form of rapier while the cavalry used a much stiffer, broad-sectioned blade. The hilts of these cavalry swords were usually simple with a single knuckle guard, two side rings sweeping out enclosing a pierced plate and uniting behind the grip, and with a small, down-curving, rear quillon. The blade was wide, double edged and fairly stiff.

The British cavalry of the Civil War 1642–49, used a more solid and substantial metal basket with a number of bars which were often chiselled with simple decoration. Some of these swords have a head chiselled on to the basket and tradition has it that this represented Charles I who was executed in 1649 – for this reason they are known by collectors as Mortuary swords.

One specialized form of basket hilted sword is that known as the Scottish claymore. Strictly the term should be used to describe only the large, two-handed sword, the *claidheamh mor*, but usage has meant that it is now applied to the straight-bladed sword with an elaborate metal basket of bars, carried by Scottish troops long after the ordinary regiments had abandoned theirs and still carried today by officers in some Scottish regiments.

Later most of the infantry were armed with a short, light sword known as a hanger. These usually had a fairly narrow, slightly curved blade usually only single edged and often with a brass hilt since this was less liable to rusting. Although Britain withdrew the sword from most of her troops many other countries retained some form of side arm for certain units. Many were designed to serve both as a weapon and tool, being fitted with saw-like teeth on the back edge.

Troops of the latter part of the 17th century onwards were increasingly armed with muskets which, once fired, had to be reloaded before another shot could be fired. The loading process took time and for this period the soldier was useless as far as fighting was concerned. He was open to any attack at this moment and some method of giving him a means of defence was necessary. One of the most universal ideas was the bayonet. Originally it was simply a large knife and its name was derived from the French town of Bayonne famous for its cutlery. The earliest form of bayonet consisted of a short, fairly broad, tapered blade with simple cross quillons, usually quite short, and a plain wooden handle which tapered towards the tip. After the musket had been fired, should an emergency arise such as a sudden attack by cavalry, the hilt of the bayonet could be pushed down the muzzle and the musket was thus converted into a 2.13 metre (7 ft) long pike, clumsy and inefficient perhaps but sufficient to hold off a cavalry attack.

The problem was that with these plug bayonets in position the musket could neither be loaded nor fired. Attempts to overcome this great problem were soon devised and the form developed in the late 17th century was the socket bayonet. This had a straight, triangular section blade attached by a curved neck to a short cylinder just wide enough to slip over the barrel of a matchlock musket and engage with a stud to prevent it slipping off. Even with the bayonet in position the musket could still be loaded or fired without trouble. This socket bayonet remained in use with virtually every European and American army until the mid-19th century and there is little to choose between the various patterns. Some had spring clips so that they could easily be clipped on or removed. During the 19th century a firmer more positive means of attachment was developed which used a lug and spring catch. In the back of the bayonet hilt was cut a shaped slot with a spring catch fitted. This could be pushed over a correspondingly shaped lug on the barrel and the quillon was cut with a hole just large enough to slip over the muzzle. The spring catch engaged with the lug on the barrel of the musket and the bayonet was held safely in position. To release it, the catch was pressed and the bayonet could be removed.

An enormous variety of bayonets was produced and from the 17th century until the present day the output has continued unabated. Until recently these were a cheap collector's item but growing interest and the fact that they were so cheap, led to an increased demand which has pushed their prices up; some examples now realize quite considerable sums at auctions. However, they do offer a most fruitful and entertaining field for the average collector.

Similar in size to the bayonet although less military in nature, are the various daggers produced over the ages. The daggers of the Middle Ages are extremely rare and most collectors cannot hope to acquire any pieces earlier than the 17th century. Most of the daggers had a simple, cruciform hilt and were, in effect, a miniature sword. Blades were sometimes cruciform in section but more usually only slightly oval in section. One special form was the stiletto which usually had a square or triangular section blade with very simple, turned steel quillons and a plain grip, the whole thing light and delicate. Some, known as gunners' stilettoes, have their stiff blades marked off with various scales. These were used by artillerymen as ready-reckoners for sundry ballistics calculations.

One dagger which was very popular with civilians, especially during the late 16th or early 17th century was the so-called ballock dagger which had a plain wooden grip and, in place of conventional quillons, had a guard of two rounded lobes. The distinct phallic shape of the grip did not escape the eye of the people – hence its name. They seem to have gone out of fashion during the first quarter of the 17th century but at the same time in northern Britain, there developed the Scottish dirk which may have owed its origins to the ballock dagger.

The traditional grip of the dirk was of wood, was short and had a swelling at the centre, with two globose guards just like the ballock dagger. The pommel was circular and set at right angles to the blade. Often the grip was carved with intricate, typically Celtic, interwoven strapwork patterns. Dirks were often made using a broken piece of sword blade and this style became traditional and later examples have the blade made to resemble the point section of a sword blade with a false edge and a blunt back edge.

18th
CENTURY

Introduction

From our vantage point in the 20th century it is easy to suggest that the inhabitants of Europe at the beginning of the 18th century had no inkling of the revolutions that were to change the face of Europe and history towards the end of the century. But perhaps this was not so. France at the beginning of the century was the cultural centre of Europe which was almost entirely due to the aspirations of the Sun King, Louis XIV, whose style added new meaning to the word opulence. Yet it was as if Louis' drive to harness the creative spirit of art to the needs of royalty and the aristocracy had exhausted the craftsmen, the aristocracy and the Baroque style itself. Upon the death of Louis in 1715 it was as if, in the words of art historian Helen Gardner, 'all Europe breathed a sigh of relief'. Within a few years the stately formality of the Baroque had given way to the sparkling gaiety of the Rococo.

The word Rococo comes from the French *rocaille*, which literally means 'pebble'; *rocaille* was also used to describe the shell-decorated grottoes which had been fashionable in French gardens since the time of Catherine de Medici. The Rococo style, which was, like the grottoes, primarily an interior style, took the shell as its characteristic motif. In this whole period it was as if the aristocracy, still the patron of the arts, had become aware of their increasing vulnerability in the face of growing popular movements, and were determined to introduced a lighter note in their declining years.

In the period between the death of Louis and 1723, France was ruled by the Regent for Louis XV, Philippe, Duke of Orleans. The style which emerged during this brief period was the *Régence*, traces of which were becoming apparent after the turn of the century. It is generally regarded as being a transitional style between the Baroque of Louis XIV and the Rococo of Louis XV. One of the characteristics of the *Régence* style was the introduction of many new decorative motifs inspired by oriental art notably that from China. Thus dragons, Chinese mythical animals and parasols make their appearance among the classic motifs of the Louis XIV style. It was during this period that the upright shell motif with acanthus leaves sprouting from the base made its first appearance. In many ways it is difficult to draw a dividing line between the *Régence* and Rococo styles, one gradually evolving into the other.

The Rococo style had fully emerged by the early 1730s. It was based on a light and free-flowing naturalism that unlike the Louis XIV style was asymmetrical; curves and irregular forms are typical, though the forms are often completely obscured by gilding, carving and ormolu ornamentation. In keeping with the taste for asymmetry and gold decoration Chinese and Japanese lacquer panels were imported in large quantities and became so popular that the French produced a substitute called *Vernis Martin*. The French cabinetmakers or *ébénistes* were renowned throughout Europe. The essential feature *ébénisterie* was a synthesis of marquetry and bronze built around a shell of inexpensive wood, usually oak. André-Charles Boulle and Charles Cressent were masters of this technique.

In keeping with the new style table and chair legs evolved early in the century into an S-curve known as the cabriole and they were often fashioned to resemble animal legs. Card and dice tables appeared reflecting the leisure time available to the aristocracy, and ladies' dressing tables were made for women who spent an increasing amount of time indulging themselves before Rococo mirrors.

The Rococo salon became the centre of Parisian life just as Paris was the cultural and social centre of Europe. The somewhat feminine look of the Rococo was intimately bound to an age that was dominated by the social tastes of women. At some level women's influence was felt in all the courts of Europe from Madame de Pompadour to Maria Theresa of Austria and Elizabeth and Catherine of Russia. If this age was the last fling of the aristocracy then it was clearly done in style – the artificial reigned supreme and it was even considered bad taste to be 'sincere'.

The Rococo in France became known during its heyday as the Louis XV style and from 1740 to 1760 it became more balanced and spontaneous. Asymmetry was balanced with symmetry; while the form was often symmetrical the surface ornament was an expression of asymmetry. In its final stages the Louis XV style became more moderate and less lavish.

Both England and Holland accepted the Rococo style with mixed enthusiasm particularly as regards to furniture design. In England Rococo was only really fashionable from about 1745 to 1765. This was primarily due to the fact that the English had found their own modes in furniture design and were no longer easily influenced by the Continent. Almost the only feature of the Rococo to reach English furniture was the cabriole leg, first used in the reign of Queen Anne (1702–14). In the same period ornamentation was modest compared to the extravagance of France. Even the animal form of the French cabriole leg became the simple claw-and-ball form derived from the Chinese dragon which is always in Chinese art depicted as chasing the Pearl of Immortality. The most outstanding furniture of the period was that of Thomas Chippendale who created a style which was a mixture of Baroque and Rococo interspersed with Chinese and Gothic detail. English metalwork and goldsmithing also accepted the Rococo.

It was perhaps inevitable that the Rococo itself would come to be seen as excessive and that its de-emphasis on form would lead to a yearning among both designers and consumers for a return to simplicity in form and proportion as well as ornamentation. As if the history of the decorative arts were cyclical the inspiration for a new style after the middle of the century was to come once again from the Roman, Greek and Egyptian empires. The discovery of antique art from the recently discovered cities of Pompeii and Herculaneum buried by the eruption of Vesuvius in A.D. 79 fired the imagination of both designers and public as the century progressed. By the 1770s a classic revival was spreading across Europe which was to influence styles for the next 60 years or so. Since the Neo-classic style spawned several national styles that persisted well into the 19th century it is best reviewed from that century.

Furniture

The accession of Philip of Orleans as French Regent upon the death of Louis XIV in 1715 marked the beginning of a transition from the un-accommodating formalities of the Baroque towards the more animated Rococo. The migration of the French court from Versailles to Paris, where aristocrats and the bourgeoisie began to refurbish their town-houses elaborately and with great concern for style, ushered in an age which focused unprecedented attention on comfort in private life.

In France especially, rooms became smaller: throughout Europe social hierarchies were more relaxed and entertainment more intimate. Rising standards of living and the expansion of the middle classes made the ceremonies of the Baroque passé, and removed the complicated network of symbols of rank that had been incorporated into everyday social interaction.

The release from Baroque court circles, which had been primarily preoccupied by the immediacies of their own pomposity, sparked off in the 18th century a series of quests for the exotic, the whimsical and the refreshing. These yearnings were satisfied in the fine and decorative arts by such light-hearted schemes as Jean Honoré Fragonard's painting of *The Swing*, and the tapestry scenes of the *Loves of the Gods*, woven after François Boucher's example at the Gobelins manufactories.

Continuing trade heightened European taste for things oriental, from tea and porcelain tea-services to the lacquered trays and tables that went with them. In France, comfortable *salons*, where ladies of the *ancien régime* conducted conversations between dandies and *philosophes*, were increasingly fitted through the century with small and serviceable pieces of elegant furniture. Walls were hung with tapestries, silks, or velvets, or wainscoted with fluidly-moulded panels painted in combinations of colours, such as mint green, pale pinks and yellows.

The softening of the rectilinear Louis XIV style was initiated by the designer Jean Bérain and the craftsman André Charles Boulle, with the influence of the Regent's own architect A. J. Oppenord (c.1639–1715), the architects Robert de Cotte (1656–1735) and Pierre le Pautre, and the designers Nicolas Pineau (1687–1757) and Jacques Caffieri (1678–1755).

After the turn of the century, Bérain replaced his earlier scrolling designs with lighter, linear arabesques and fanciful *singeries*. Chairs, tables, bureaux and commodes assumed serpentine lines, stretchers be-came fluid and were gradually discarded; and chairs became lower. Rich ormolu mounts highlighted the curves of cabriole legs, the edges of drawers and the tops of tables, commodes and bureaux. On the elegant, increasingly curvaceous commodes of Charles Cressent (1685–1768), the edging around drawers gradually disappeared, giving way to large compositions spreading over the lacquer or marquetry design of the façade. Cressent became *ébéniste* to the Regent in 1719 and was one of the finest *ébénistes* of all time. It was not until 1751 though that *ébénistes* were required to sign their work with an *estampille* and as a result no

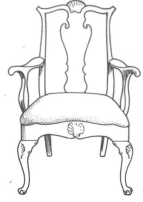

Queen Anne chair with carved back splat and cabriole legs.

Early Georgian chair.

Chippendale's Gothick chair.

Adam-style elbow chair.

Left: *Provincial Louis XV chaise longue;*
right: *Régence chaise longue.*

pieces actually signed by Cressent are known. Many works have been subsequently attributed to him, often on little evidence, but commodes in many collections, including the Wallace Collection and the Gulbenkian Collection, are undoubtedly by him. He designed his own gilt-bronze mounts many of which were inspired by the designs of Bérain, Gillot and Robert de Cotte, and stand as masterpieces of sculpture.

The Rococo and Queen Anne Styles

The engravings of Juste Aurèle Meissonnier (1695–1750) led the early designs of the *Régence* into the exuberant asymmetries and curvaceous naturalism of the Rococo, or Louis XV style. Derived from the lively, cave-like, and sometimes aquatic decorations inside Italian landscape grottoes, Rococo compositions were characterized by illogical combinations of the peculiar *rocaille* scroll, C- and S-curves, shells, foliage, branches and animals, water and flame motifs, and even Chinese figures. Commodes, tables, cabinets and beds assumed fluid shapes. Ormolu mounts became more swirling and elegant, and delicately carved flames and sprays of foliage emphasized the curves of knees, elbows, edges and crests.

These French forms, and the French Rococo ornamental vocabulary, were extremely influential throughout Europe, where chairs and other pieces in the relaxed Louis XV manner were made well into the century in Spain, Portugal, Italy, North America and elsewhere.

The supple, undulating forms created by Daniel Marot, Jean Bérain and the French *Régence* permeated England during the reign of Queen Anne (1702–14). Characterized by curvaceous lines and ornamental restraint, Queen Anne style furniture asserted the first truly English style. As a thriving national economy encouraged more building on the part of landed gentry and middle-class merchants, increased demand for interior furnishings was met by unprecedented standards of skill among London cabinetmakers.

Balanced curves and straight lines gave chairs cabriole legs, vase-shaped splats, horse-shoe shaped seats and undulating backs which followed the sitter's profile. Walnut, and later mahogany, was applied in highly figured veneers to cabinets and tables, or sparingly carved with shells, masks or foliage on the crests, knees and rails of chairs. 'Seaweed' marquetry, japanning on red ground, and judicious touches of gilt coated the flat surfaces of tables, chests-of-drawers, day-beds and settees. Feet were carved as hoofs, hairy paws, trifids and claw-and-ball.

Secretaires and architectural cabinets with arched or mirrored panels were crowned by swan-neck or double-arched pediments, often with ornamental finials. Of Netherlandish origin, these curving pediments were to find extreme expression later in the century on Dutch Rococo case pieces, when curves alternated with horizontal plinths on which porcelain rarities were displayed.

The architecture and furniture of William Kent (1689–1748) promulgated a heavy, Baroque style based on Italian architectural sources, and especially on the Renaissance work of Vicenze architect Andrea Palladio. However, the softer forms of the Queen Anne style persisted, and various elements characteristic of it appeared on furniture well into the century.

In the Netherlands, Portugal and Spain Queen Anne characteristics such as cabriole legs, shell motifs, claw-and-ball feet, and vase-shaped chair splats were transplanted into local styles.

Chippendale's version of a French chair.

The Queen Anne style was adopted in colonial America in the early 1730s, when flourishing trade in the major mercantile centres of Boston, Philadelphia, New York, Newport and Charleston encouraged a desire for large, comfortable and fashionable mansions. Classical architectural details appeared on buildings from the Carolinas to New Hampshire. Houses, such as Westover in Virginia, reflected elements of the English Palladian style, which reached the colonies through such publications as W. Salmon's *Palladio Londinensis* published in 1734, and James Gibbs's *Book of Architecture* of 1728.

Columns and pilasters, swan-neck pediments, and finials filtered on to highboys, long-case clocks, and even the fragile frames of pier-glasses. The favoured woods of walnut, maple, cherry and pine, and increasingly mahogany, were sparsely highlighted with carved shells or foliage, and occasionally offset with inlay in such forms as stars, or with gilded shells on tables, highboys and lowboys. Slender cabriole legs, horseshoe-shaped seats, and feet carved as pads, trifids and claw-and-ball, imitated English fashions long after they had fallen from favour in England. Highboys and secretaires, fronted with doors with arched panels, contained tiers of drawers and pigeonholes. Easy chairs, corner chairs, candlestands, piecrust tea tables on tripod legs and fire-screens, all became more popular.

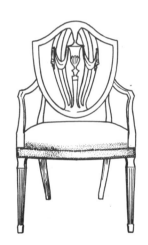

Hepplewhite shield back chair.

Regional differences in furniture-making were sharpened as craftsmanship developed in each area, and immigrant tastes and traditions expressed themselves. Chair splats were shaped with distinguishing silhouettes, those from Dutch-settled New York broader than those from English-settled Massachusetts. The spaces between splat and stiles on Philadelphia chairs resembled birds with bold, inward-curving elongated beaks; the curves of Philadelphia Queen Anne style seats tended to inflect more than seats found on chairs made elsewhere. New York claw-and-ball feet were square in form, while those from Massachusetts characteristically featured raking claws. The cabriole legs of many southern pieces were almost straight. Stretchers generally disappeared during this period, although they tended to persist on Massachusetts pieces, typical of furniture forms produced there.

English Rococo

In mid-century, the French Rococo caught on in England, inspired largely by the engravings of H. F. Gravelot and by improved peace-time relations with France. In England the cave-like *rocaille*, and the cult of

Early wing chair with claw and ball feet.

Right: *Louis XV bureau plat.*
Above: *Bonheur de jour with slightly cabriole legs and metal mounts.*

the picturesque that accompanied it, became popular along with ornaments suggestive of the romantic Gothic and the tantalizing Orient, and the three styles occasionally merged together. As in France, private rooms were made increasingly comfortable by pieces such as small desks, candlestands, fire-screens and work-tables. The most fashionable Rococo interiors featured curvaceous gilt panels, or wall hangings of oriental paper or silk. William Chambers travelled to China in 1749, and in 1757 published his *Designs of Chinese Buildings, Furniture, and Dresses.* Publications by designers and craftsmen such as Thomas Chippendale, Thomas Johnson, Matthew Darly, Matthias Lock, Robert Manwaring and William Ince and John Mayhew, popularized fanciful furniture along with ordinary forms. Their most exuberant Rococo designs were characterized by asymmetrical ornament and whimsicalities. Unpublished cabinetmakers, such as John Linnell, William Vile and John Cob, were equally forceful exponents of the mid-century style.

Cabinets, book-cases, long-case clocks and commodes for the most part retained the basic forms of the preceding Queen Anne period, but many pieces assumed the serpentine shapes and swelling anthropomorphic *bombé* of the French Louis XV style. Gilding and japanning remained in vogue. Twisted girandoles resembling branches, and pier-glasses assembled from C-curves, waterfalls and *rocailles,* captured the effect of rustic naturalism. Increasingly available mahogany, but also pine and gesso, lent itself especially well to crisp depictions of Chinese dragons and pagodas, cusps and pointed Gothic arches, and stylized scenes of peasants, windmills and donkeys.

Many of the chair designs published in Chippendale's *Director* of 1754 had broad square seats, projecting scrolled ears, and animalistic cabriole legs. Settees formed of repeated chair backs were occasionally carved with bamboo-like supports and oriental frets; beds in the Chinese manner, with fantastic dragons perched atop the corner posts, were fashionable but unusual extravagances. Light, gilded seats with serpentine silhouettes in the Louis XV style were common; most of the seats were upholstered with rich floral needlework, velvets, or silk damasks.

The influence of the English Rococo was far-reaching. Contemporary printed designs travelled across the Atlantic, were thrown back to France and reached as far north as Denmark, where chairs showed *Director*-type pierced splats, set between straight wide stiles. The Rococo style characterized by Chippendale's less exotic engravings permeated American design in about 1755.

Rococo in America

In America, the Rococo emerged as a distinctly restrained version of the European style: interiors were hardly as fanciful as their European counterparts, and drawing room walls were ornamented with architectural pediments and rectangular panels rather than gilt cartouches, in a persistence of the Palladian style. Japanning was popular, especially in Boston, but in America the fantastic cult of chinoiserie never crystallized into carved mahogany dragons. The Gothic revival struck no chord in American tradition, and the stylized rustic scenes favoured by mid-century English and French aristocrats could hardly have been adopted as refreshing in a nation still developing vast expanses of wilderness.

Because examples reached the colonies largely through pattern-books, some American Rococo carving is flat rather than sculptural, especially on Boston pieces. Queen Anne forms such as arched pediments, classical details and claw-and-ball feet were retained, and Rococo ornaments and variations added to them.

The superior craftsmanship of Philadelphia cabinetmakers, such as Benjamin Randolph and the English immigrant Thomas Affleck, produced well-proportioned highboys with swan-neck pediments, flame finials, sculptural carvings of foliage and figures, and sculptured busts and cartouches held above the broken pediments. Scroll pediments carved with Philadelphia-style open lattice-work may be found in the cherry highboys from Connecticut executed by Eliphalet Chapin, who worked for some time in Philadelphia.

Some case pieces of Boston, where John Cogswell worked, exhibit the only *bombé* forms found in the colonies; mirrored panels with ogee-curve borders are also found on cabinets made there. The cabinets and chest-of-drawers from the Townsend-Goddard cabinet-making family of Newport, Rhode Island, were exceptional pieces of workmanship, with undercut claw-and-ball feet, undulating concave and convex shells and smoothly executed block fronts.

Tables were of many forms including Pembroke and fold-top card-tables. Serpentine card-tables from New York had rectangular candle supports at the corners and gadrooning on the aprons. Small Philadelphia bird-cage tables, with tilting tops, stood on fluidly curved tripods. Upholstered seats included sofas with sinuous rails and straight 'Marlborough' legs, easy chairs with cartouches carved on the cabriole legs, and local variants of chairs copied from the publications of Chippendale, Manwaring, and Ince and Mayhew. More primitive forms, such as the brightly painted chests and cupboards of German and Dutch settlements in Pennsylvania and New York, continued to be made in provincial areas.

The Rococo in Europe

In Italy, where the landscaped grotto was a long-established source of ornament, the Rococo at times took on an extreme lightness, with chairs and tables resting on shapely cabriole legs comprised of reversing C-scrolls. Delicate effects of underground rock-like growth were achieved in the crisp, crustaceous carvings on the edges of legs, backs and skirts of tables and chairs. Carved shells, lion masks and naturalistic foliage appeared alongside elements of chinoiserie such as peasant figures. Curvaceous gilt structures ornamented with flames, foliage and waves

The traditional and widely-made Windsor chair.

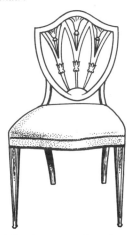

A fine interpretation of one of Chippendale's designs.

Opposite: *Breakfront bookcase with broken pediment made in Charleston, South Carolina c.1790.*
Following pages. Left: *The dining room at Osterley Park, Middlesex, designed by Robert Adam in 1767.*
Right above: *Louis XVI bureau cylindre with ormolu mounts by J. H. Riesner (1734–1806), one of the many outstanding pieces by him.*
Right below: *Writing table attributed to David Roentgen, the greatest German cabinetmaker of the 18th century.*

Left: *American cherrywood drop-leaf table made in the Queen Anne style in the 18th century.*
Left below: *Armchair designed by Giles Greadey in 1730, made of japanned beech with gilt decoration.*

Right: *A dower chest in painted pine and made in Jonestown, Pennsylvania, by Christian Seltzer, dated 1784.*
Below right: *The Maple Room, Port Royal, Pennsylvania.*

supported console tables with serpentine marble tops, and framed Muranese pier-glasses.

In Italy, foreign influence was strong, although Italian Rococo furniture was not as varied, comfortable, or well-constructed as that produced in England or France. Marquetry work was especially skilled in Milan, where German techniques combined with established traditions; the compositions of Piedmont craftsman Pietro Piffetti were especially ornate.

The inclinations towards pompous display among the multitude of small German states produced the palace of Frederick the Great, at Sanssouci, that of Max Emanuel at Munich, and courts elsewhere such as at Würzburg and Frankfurt. The furnishings of these interiors reflected the refinement of traditional German cabinet-making techniques, such as marquetry, and the introduction of foreign influences by Parisian-trained designers such as François Cuvilliés.

German wall painting also echoed the graceful ormolu or gilt ornaments and the characteristically exaggerated *bombé* forms of the commodes, console tables and velvet-upholstered seats beneath them.

The swelling form, a peculiarly German expression of the Rococo, had great influence on furniture produced in the Scandinavian countries. There, *bombé* commodes and serpentine cabinets were covered with marquetry and cross-banding much as they were in Germany, as seen in pieces produced by Mathias Ortman of Copenhagen and Lars Bolin of Sweden. Organic, bulbous forms also appeared in the extremely broad commodes, secretaires and cabinets of the Dutch Rococo. These flatter translations often had wide, chamfered corners, with central ornamental cartouches at the apron and pediment; although the drawers of German *bombé* commodes extended to the serpentine edges, on Dutch pieces the drawers remained rectangular, with veneered strips filling the gap to the undulating side.

The Rise of the Neo-classical Style

The Rococo style reached its peak in Europe in the late 1750s. Meanwhile, the discoveries of Herculaneum and Pompeii just before mid-century had intensified the already popular vogue for continental grand tours among English and French scholars, young gentlemen and dilettanti, who mixed with native scholars and artists at academies and societies in Italy, and inaugurated the classical revival. The aesthetic rivalry between the Italian Giovanni Battista Piranesi and the German Johann Joachim Winckelmann, who defended the supremacy of Roman and Greek civilization respectively, sparked off an increased interest in classical architecture and art as exemplified by these societies.

In England, the Scottish-born architect Robert Adam (1728–92) returned from Italy and Europe in 1758. His publication in 1763 of the *Ruins of the Palace of Diocletian at Spalatro* added to the growing number of volumes of engravings of classical ruins which circulated among aristocratic subscribers who were continually redecorating their homes during the 18th century according to passing fashion. Other publications included Robert Wood's *Ruins of Palmyra* of 1753, and the *Antiquities of Athens* of 1762, by James 'Athenian' Stuart and Nicholas Revett.

By the early 1860s Robert Adam had established himself as the pacesetter and leading exponent of the new 'Neo-classical' architectural and decorative style, derived from free combinations of the grotesques, arabesques and classical ornaments of antique and Renaissance Italian interiors, and from lively French designs such as those of Bérain. While the earlier English Palladians had applied the exterior accoutrements of classical architecture to their rooms, Adam's lighter schemes were based on the interiors of domestic Rome and Pompeii.

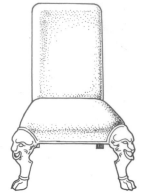

George I chair with lion-shaped legs.

Creating effects of gaiety and movement, Adam covered his walls with colours and a repertoire of delicately interpreted classical ornaments arranged on ceilings, walls, friezes and decorative door and window frames. Adam designed and refurbished entire buildings, harmonizing and coordinating to the minutest detail the schemes of ceilings, carpets, walls, furniture and even in one celebrated case the ornament of a lady's gold watch band to be worn in a certain room. The refined motifs he introduced, including anthemions, palmettes, rinceaux, griffins, bay leaves and peltoid shields, appeared repeatedly with minor modifications within any given room, creating a unified decorative effect. Adam's total schemes also dictated the placement of furniture, as in the chairs which echo the wall ornament in the Etruscan Room at Osterley Park in Middlesex. This is one of several rooms Adam designed in an 'Etruscan' style with terracotta and black ornament derived from Greek vase painting.

Chippendale Rococo chair.

The furniture Adam fitted to these rooms was often executed by John Linnell or Thomas Chippendale. Although it followed no classical examples, it suggested the antique through architectonic forms, straight lines, and classical symbols. Semi-circular commodes, mosaic-topped rectangular side-tables and chairs with lyre, anthemion and oval backs stood on tapering straight legs. Adam's smooth, flat surfaces were enlivened by contrasting marquetry compositions, and inset roundels and plaques painted in the style of Angelica Kauffmann, parallelled by the Sèvres plaques, painted panels and marquetry work found in French Louis XVI furniture and later popular on pieces from Italy, Spain, Germany and the Netherlands throughout the Neo-classical era.

Although many contemporaries found his mature style finicky, the influence of Adam's example at all stages of his career was pronounced possibly because of the charm it captured. Contemporary English and European architects and craftsmen, such as James Wyatt, continued to adopt elegant rectilinear forms, classical motifs and a lightened approach to interior design. The taste for delicacy and attenuation persisted even in the scrolling rinceaux and half-figures of the early 19th century Neoclassical works of the Turin carver Giuseppe Maria Bonzanigo.

Adam-style chair with Neo-classical motif.

162

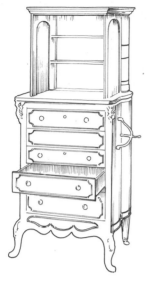

Right: *Demi-lune commode with drawers and two cabinets.*
Above: *Commode-secrétaire with a handle to work the rising mechanism.*

European Neo-classicism – the Louis XVI Style

In mid-century, Neo-classicism was on the ascendancy in France as well, where C. N. Cochin, the Comte de Caylus, and others were busily attacking the Rococo as frivolous. Decorative styles derived from French studies of the classics in Italy were gradually popularized by such designers as the Marquis de Marigny and patrons such as Mesdames du Pompadour and du Barry, in their collections at Versailles and Louveciennes. Craftsmen such as Gilles Joubert (1689–1775), Antoine Foulet (*d.*1775), Jean François Leleu (1729–1807), Jacques Dubois (1693–1763), and the Germans Jean François Oeben (1720–63), Jean Henri Riesener (1734–1806), Adam Weisweiler and Guillaume Bereman, largely shaped the Louis XVI style.

Chairs, sofas and canapés such as those designed by Georges Jacob (1739–1814) had square or oval backs, straight fluted uprights and rails, and tapering legs. Case pieces such as secrétaires, *encoignures*, and chests-of-drawers assumed neat, compact forms made more serviceable by caster feet. The straight lines of the tops and sides were emphasized by ormolu friezes and consoles, and the rectangular panels of flat façades and sides were articulated by ormolu borders. A widespread delight with mechanical devices spawned a variety of complicated combination forms equipped for such varied uses as writing, eating and sewing. Those of Oeben and Riesener were particularly cleverly mechanized, typifying Louis XVI restraint by enclosing a potentially ungainly variety of components, such as springing drawers and dishwarmers, inside smooth surface façades.

Although it remained unusual, the fashion for mechanical devices in furniture spread through Europe to the Netherlands and elsewhere, expressing itself in such pieces as the combination desk-table-chair of the Italian Giovanni Socchi, of about 1810.

Oeben, who managed one of the most flourishing Parisian workshops, produced pieces in a transitional style with studiously naturalistic floral marquetry and cube patterns, but died before the Louis XVI style reached its peak. Floral and picturesque marquetry with classical motifs characterized the early, more truly Neo-classical work of Riesener, but soon after he became *ébéniste ordinaire du Roi* in 1773 he began to produce simpler geometric patterns, and frets enclosing flowers.

Pierre Gouthière (1732–*c.*1813) created delicate, jewel-like bronze mounts comprised of goats, vines and cornflowers and roses, Marie Antoinette's favourite flowers. Sèvres porcelain trays and panels were incorporated in commodes and tables increasingly after about 1760 by

Weisweiler, Martin Carlin and others. Towards the end of the century, English-inspired carved furniture also showed contemporary English influence. Furniture sheathed in the tortoiseshell and brass marquetry popularized by Boulle was considered collectable even during the 18th century, when craftsmen such as Etienne Lavasseur continued to produce it.

The elements of the Louis XVI style were dispersed throughout Europe, where cabinetmakers such as Andries Bongen of Amsterdam produced Neo-classical marquetry compositions, and Giuseppe Maggiolini of Milan sheathed his Louis XVI-style forms with marquetry ornament.

The dissemination of the Adam style led in England to a second phase of Neo-classicism, more accessible to the middle classes because of its use of less costly materials. Pattern-books such as George Hepplewhite's *Cabinetmaker and Upholsterer's Guide* and Thomas Shearer's *Cabinetmaker's London Book of Prices*, both of 1788, and Thomas Sheraton's *Cabinetmaker and Upholsterer's Drawing Book* (1791–94), popularized straight legs and tall light forms derived from Adam's designs. This reductionist form of classicism abandoned Adam's vocabulary of Neo-classical motifs for simplified ornamental schemes comprised of large areas of figured veneers similar to those made fashionable on the mahogany fall-fronts of Louis XVI secretaires.

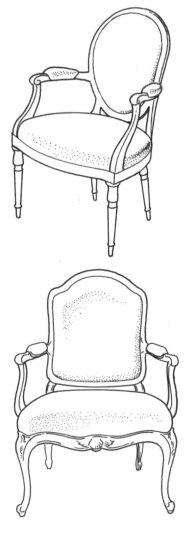

Top: *Louis XVI chair with classical lines.*
Bottom: *Louis XV chair.*

Sheraton, Hepplewhite and Shearer popularized a variety of light forms such as ladies' work tables with silk bags, serpentine-front commodes, tambour desks and cabinets with doors of bronze latticework backed by pleated silk. The backs of settees and chairs were carved with Prince of Wales feathers and classical motifs such as swags and urns.

The purified Neo-classicism of England and France returned to invigorate Italian design, and filtered from there to craftsmen in Portugal and Spain. Light, rectilinear chairs with tapering slender legs, were produced as local interpretations of Hepplewhite and Sheraton designs in Italy and Iberia late in the century.

Louis XVI influence surfaced in Italy in the lyre and oval-shaped backs of chairs, which were caned or upholstered in velvets and striped damasks as in England and France, and in the fluted or spirally-turned straight legs of frequently parcel gilt chairs and side-tables. Marble-topped semi-circular tables and commodes, with gilded friezes ornamented with fluting, guiloches and plaques, exhibited the architectonic preferences that Adam had refined. Other Italian chairs and tables preceded by decades the French Empire style, with elements such as sweeping S-curved arms, curved rear legs, Egyptian hieroglyphics and monopodia, and the horizontal placement at the centre of chair rails of symmetrical, classical foliate motifs in ormolu.

Neo-classical Spanish chairs had straight rails and stiles and oval or arched rectangular backs in the Louis XVI style; their legs often combined vestiges of Baroque capping with French flutes and tapering forms. Chairs with lyre backs and round seats, and caned examples with concave-sided interlaced trapezoidal backs, showed Italian influence. Rectangular console or side-tables, carved or inlaid with attenuated classical ornament, occasionally stood on legs of sweeping S-curved form. Vitruvian scrolls, acanthus leaves, masks and rinceaux appeared on drop-front

Above: *Carved fall-front cabinet with small compartments.*
Right: *Louis XVI commode with concealed drawers.*

desks, commodes, tables and beds.

Portuguese furniture revealed similar ripples of influence. Delicate English-inspired chairs and settees with tapered legs and fluted front rails were ornamented with classical plaques and roundels; marble-topped commodes, semi-circular side-tables and *bureaux à cylindre* reflected the Louis XVI manner.

America

The federation of the American colonies upon the adoption of the Constitution in 1789 established, in American eyes, a republic sufficiently blessed with democratic principles to bear an association with ancient Rome. At the same time the geometric rationalism of Robert Adam's Neo-classical style reached the United States in published pattern-books of engravings by Hepplewhite, Shearer and Sheraton.

Just as Thomas Jefferson would have found appeal in the classical example of Palladio's geometrical Villa Rotunda for his residence at Monticello, American craftsmen were attracted to the purities of geometry and classicism that these later English designs evoked.

After about 1790, geometric forms and surface ornament began to appear on the most fashionable American furniture. Tables and commodes with semicircular plans were made by John and Thomas Seymour of Boston and the Townsends of Newport. Veneered ovals and circles, bordered with narrow strips of cross-banding that emphasized their geometricity, were set in rectangular fields of contrasting colours on the façades of secretaires produced in Salem, Baltimore and elsewhere.

Chests-of-drawers had restrained serpentine façades and simple bracket feet, and the legs of sofas, chairs, sideboards and tables were tapered, slender and straight. The moulded glazing bars on the upper portions of secretaires from Baltimore, Massachusetts, Charleston and elsewhere were arranged in compositions of ovals, circles, and diamonds and squares.

American cabinetmakers also adopted a collection of classical ornaments in more specific allusions to the civilizations of Rome and Greece. Allegorical figures were painted in black and white *verre églomisé* panels on Baltimore furniture; the Boston Seymours inlaid desks with completely flattened *trompe-l'oeil* pilasters; sparingly applied paterae, bell-flowers, eagles, shields and busts all alluded to the classics.

The carved vine leaves and cornucopias that Salem architect-craftsmen Samuel McIntyre applied to his mahogany sofas and chairs similarly reflected the national optimism that pervaded federal America.

Clocks and mirrors were adorned with brass spheres or urn finials, quarter-columns and gilded eagles. Case pieces such as bookcases became increasingly light, and women's secretaires and work-tables, of delicate proportion and ornament, were introduced. Tea-tables, card-tables with folding tops, Windsor chairs, four-poster beds and chests-of-drawers on bracket turned or brass paw feet, all took on the restrained dignity of the Federal period.

Northern Europe

The shapes and ornaments of French and English Neo-classical interior and furniture design, including arabesque wall panelling, rectilinear forms, tapering legs, ormolu mounts and mouldings, and geometrical and pictorial marquetry compositions, were also adopted in Scandinavia, the Netherlands and Germany. However, local traditions distinguished these renditions.

As in the Rococo era, the Scandinavian royal court favoured European styles, and recruited talent from abroad; the Swedish craftsman George Haupt worked in England with William Chambers before returning home. Erik Ohrmark in Sweden, Nicolas Henri Jardin and Joseph Christian Lillie in Denmark, and Lillie in Norway produced furnishings showing Louis XVI and Adamesque characteristics.

The work of Abraham and David Roentgen was highly favoured internationally and their designs were particularly influential in Paris on the development of the Louis XVI style. Abraham Roentgen (1711–93) established his first business at Neuwied-am-Rhein in 1750 after joining a Moravian colony which had established itself there. The furniture which he produced showed the influence of Chippendale perhaps due to the period from 1731 when Roentgen had worked for various firms of cabinetmakers in London. The general style of his furniture was subdued Rococo and while it was attractive his company was often short of money.

Hepplewhite pole screen.

Abraham's son David (1743–1807) seems to have begun managing the firm some time after 1766 and formally took over the management when his father retired in 1772. From the time David began handling company affairs the firm rapidly prospered, almost certainly due to the fact that he was not only a craftsman but also had an acute business sense. He recognized that the Rococo style was no longer in such demand, but even more important from a purely business concern he was aware that he could not rely on local patronage alone for his prosperity. In this he was an innovator for no-one had previously successfully exploited the European market for furniture of quality.

Elaborately carved Louis XVI armchair.

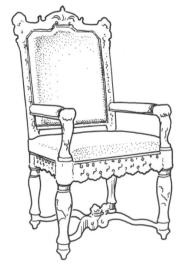

His first major success was a sale of furniture by lottery which he organized in Hamburg in 1769. In 1779 he widened his horizons even further by setting up a warehouse in Paris, the major market for furniture at this time. The venture was an outstanding success for the Court became his prime customer and it has been estimated that over the next years the Crown spent more than one million livres with him. A further indicator of his reputation and success was his appointment as *ébéniste-méchanicien du Roi et de la Reine*. The French Court was not his only Imperial customer. After a visit to St Petersburg in 1783, Catherine the Great became one of his most ardent admirers and purchased a considerable quantity of his furniture.

Left: *Louis XV carved beechwood sofa with Aubusson tapestry upholstering.*
Right: *Louis XVI alcove bed with damask upholstery.*

His business was brought to an abrupt halt by the French Revolution, for his warehouse in Paris was confiscated and in 1795 invading French troops wrecked his workshop at Neuwied. Only a small amount of stock at other depots was saved.

David Roentgen's work was the best expression of German Neoclassicism. In addition he perfected a marquetry technique in which he depicted ribbons, flower baskets and other motifs with extraordinary realism by using a variety of woods of different colours, rather than burning, to simulate shadows and depths. For a time Peter Kinzing was Roentgen's partner and together they specialized in furniture with built-in, elaborate, hidden mechanisms such as secret drawers, compartments or musical boxes.

The Empire Style

The publication in 1802 of the *Voyage dans la Basse et Haute Egypte*, a collection of drawings by Baron Vivant-Denon, who had accompanied Napoleon on his excursion to Syria and Egypt in 1798–1801, heightened the interest in Egypt that Napoleon's campaign had itself generated.

Interiors designed by Napoleon's architects, Charles Percier (1764–1838) and Pierre Fontaine (1762–1853), including those at the Tuileries and the Château de Malmaison, and pieces produced by makers such as F. H. G. Jacob-Desmalter and L. F. and P. A. Bellange, developed the Empire style. This drew on Greek, Roman and Egyptian sources, and became popular from England and North America to Germany, Italy and Spain.

This grand, imperial style achieved much of its effect through massive forms and rich ornament. Although an ornate, propagandistic style, it derived great dignity from its clear forms and classical restraint. Motifs such as eagles, lions, caryatids, griffins and sphinxes, taken from Roman, Greek and Egyptian antique examples, appeared on furniture as ornaments and supports. Tables with monopodia legs, gilt eagle supports, or lion's paw feet, elegant sofas and 'sleigh' beds with sweeping S-curved arms and endboards, and klismos and curule chairs, presented classical motifs on a much larger scale than in earlier classical styles. Rich woods such as mahogany, gilt carving and ormolu mounts of anthemions, stars and medallions, characterized Empire furniture.

The English version of this style, known as the Regency, lasted from about 1790 to 1830, when the vogue for relics of antiquity popularized furniture ornamented with sphinxes, griffins, classical mouldings and other Empire style elements.

Although it reached its peak early in the 19th century, the Empire style represented merely one phase in the evolution of the classical style that would take place in the course of the century when a variety of past idioms would be continually reinterpreted and renewed.

Ceramics

Hard-paste porcelain teapot c.1742–45.

Italy and Spain

Prior to about 1710 the only true porcelain being produced in the world was that of the Far East, but experiments were started in Italy, concerned with the manufacture of an artificial, or soft-paste porcelain, during the second half of the 16th century. This was the Medici porcelain.

The early Florentine wares were made between 1575–87, for what would appear to have been the personal requirements of the Grand Duke Francesco I de Medici. The artificial porcelain body was produced from a white-firing clay, together with a high percentage of frit (glass). The existing pieces, which now number about 60, are almost all decorated solely in underglaze-blue, with the occasional manganese outline, often showing firing faults.

There appears to have been no further serious attempts to produce porcelain of any type in Italy until 1720, when Francesco Vezzi, of Venice, was aided by the renegade Meissen arcanist, C. K. Hunger, to produce a good quality hard-paste porcelain with clays obtained from Saxony.

The wares produced during the seven years of activity were extremely good, primarily tablewares of designs obviously inspired by contemporary silver, usually decorated in strong enamel colours with a variety of subjects including Italian Comedy figures, heraldry, or chinoiseries. Cups and saucers were made with relief prunus decoration in the style of the 17th and 18th century Chinese Fukien province wares.

A further Venetian factory was started in 1764 by Geminiano Cozzi, whose early forms and decoration showed very little originality, the paste material being very grey, but the production of both tablewares and figures was seemingly large and pieces marked with a distinctive form of anchor in red enamel are by no means uncommon in Europe.

The factory started at Doccia, near Florence, by the Marchese Carlo Ginori in 1735, is still active as the Richard-Ginori concern. The early porcelain is often referred to as *masso bastardo*, a grey-toned hybrid porcelain, which at times was hidden under a tin-glaze to make the ware appear more suitable for Far Eastern type decoration. Their early tea-wares were Baroque in style, with snake-like spouts and high-domed lids, but Doccia might well claim to be the earliest factory using transfer-printed underglaze-blue decoration. The coarse prints suggest the use of an engraved wood-block, rather than the English-type copperplate.

Some of the finest quality soft-paste porcelain was produced between 1743–59 at the factory of Charles of Bourbon, situated in the grounds of the Palace of Capodimonte, near Naples. When Charles succeeded to the throne of Spain in 1759, his porcelain factory was moved to Buen Retiro, near Madrid. The only mark ever used at both Capodimonte and Buen Retiro was a fleur-de-lys, in blue, gilt or incised, never a crowned 'N' as commonly supposed. The later mark was used at The Royal Naples Factory established in 1771, and was used during the 19th century at Doccia and also on the late 19th century porcelains of Ernst Bohne of

Rudolstadt in Thuringia. A further Italian factory whose wares are worthy of comment is that of Le Nove, near Bassano. Pasquale Antonibon began experiments as early as 1752, but little success was achieved before 1781, when the concern was leased to Francesco Parolin, and later to Giovanni Baroni, closing in 1825. The early wares had much in common with those of Cozzi, but from about 1780 decorated wares were produced from a fine white porcelain, with gilt decoration comparable to that used at Sèvres.

Germany and Austria

Until at least 1770 the porcelain fashions in Europe were dictated by those of China and Japan. These wares were imported into Europe in increasing quantities and dominated popular taste until the rise of first Meissen, then Sèvres.

For many years a great deal of wealth was spent in the purchase of Far Eastern porcelain for use at the court of Augustus II, Elector of Saxony, King of Poland. In order to try to remedy this vast expenditure, Count von Tschirnhaus was given the task of researching into the mineral wealth of Saxony, in an effort to produce the necessary materials for the manufacture of a true porcelain and fine glass, which at that time was only being made in Bohemia. From 1704, Tschirnhaus was assisted in his experiments by a young alchemist, Johann Friedrich Bottger, who claimed to possess the secret of producing gold from a base metal. Their first combined success was to produce a hard fine-grained stoneware, which could be ground and polished in the manner of a semi-precious stone. This red stoneware had the appearance of the Chinese Yi-hsing ware, usually used to produce the teapots for the European market. Some of Bottger's lower-fired red wares remained porous and so were given a dark-brown glaze, with added gold or lacquer decoration.

Tschirnhaus died in 1708, leaving Bottger to take all the credit for the production of a form of white porcelain, resulting in the establishment in 1710 of the Royal Saxon Porcelain Manufactory, in the Albrechtsburg fortress at Meissen, 12 miles from the city of Dresden. The early Meissen porcelain was made from the white-burning China-clay (kaolin) from Colditz, near Zwickau, and a calcareous flux in the form of alabaster. It was in about 1718 that the correct material of China-stone (petuntse) was put to use, resulting in the Saxon hard-paste porcelain being an even whiter ware than that made in the Far East.

The early white porcelains produced prior to the death of Bottger, in 1719, were mostly inspired by contemporary metalwork, sometimes from the designs of the court silversmith, Irminger. The figures were often modelled after the 17th century prints of Jacques Callot's grotesque dwarfs, who were a favourite subject in the early 18th century, when there was a morbid curiosity in those suffering from various afflictions.

The year 1720 marked a further milestone in their success, being the time Johann Gregor Horoldt was introduced to the factory by the disloyal kiln-master, Samuel Stolzel. He persuaded Horoldt to leave the services of De Paquier at the early rival porcelain factory of Vienna. Within two years, the influence of Horoldt was clearly seen in their improved decoration. A new range of vivid enamel colours was used in a wide variety of patterns, including copies from engravings telling of Far

Augustus Rex Meissen porcelain vase.

Eastern travel, and far more original *chinoiseries* – fairy-land fantasies based on the Court and social life of China (Horoldt's original sketches still exist).

The new enamel colours were also used to depict stylized oriental flowers. These were wrongly termed 'India flowers', as they were developed from paintings on late 17th century Chinese porcelain brought to Europe by the vessels of the East India Companies. These oriental flowers were replaced in about 1740 with naturalistic flower paintings, often inspired by the engravings of recorded botanists. Between 1725 and 1730, harbour-scenes and landscapes were also extremely popular and many are attributed to the painters J. G. Heintze and C. F. Herold.

In 1727 Gottlieb Kirchner was appointed as the first Chief Modeller, his earliest creations being the life-size figures of animals, as requested by Augustus for the furnishing of his Japanese Palace. Kirchner was soon to be overshadowed by the more famous modeller J. J. Kaendler, who was appointed in 1731. Kaendler excelled not only in decorative figures for table decoration, but in designing other large heavily modelled tablewares, including the famous Swan Service for Count Bruhl, who was appointed Director of the factory following the death of Augustus II in 1733. This was a post he retained until he died in 1763.

By 1738 Kaendler had produced a wide variety of small porcelain figures based upon characters featured in the traditional theatre of Italian Comedy, made to 'wander among groves of curled paper ...' (Horace Walpole, 1753). These figures were far more animated when placed upon the simple mound bases of the Baroque period, but by 1750 the more ornate bases, in the now popular Rococo styles, seemed to arrest their movement.

The Meissen factory was occupied by the troops of Frederick the Great of Prussia at the start of the Seven Years' War of 1756–63 and by the end of hostilities the porcelain factories of Europe were looking towards the French factory of Sèvres for fresh inspiration. Meissen was never to recover fully from this disaster, but during the so-called 'Marcolini' period of 1774–1814, novel shapes were produced in the Neo-classical taste. But porcelain was not an ideal body for such fashions, which were inspired by the early Grecian wares excavated at Herculaneum and Pompeii.

The success of the Vienna factory was due entirely to the disloyalty of the Meissen gilder, Hunger, and the kiln-master, Stolzel, who in 1719 deserted Meissen in order to help Du Paquier produce a good quality hard-paste porcelain in Austria. The factory was taken over by the State under Empress Maria Theresa in 1744. It remained under State direction until 1784, when the concern came under the management of Konrad von Sorgenthal, eventually closing in 1866. The unmarked wares of the Du Paquier period were mostly decorated in original chinoiseries and Baroque versions of the popular leaf and strapwork designs (*Laub-und-Bandelwerk*).

The tablewares of the State period showed very little originality and owed much to Meissen. However, the figures tended to have a slightly prettier and more doll-like quality, a charm often lacking in the bold and sometimes harsh work of Kaendler.

K'ang-hsi 1662–1772

Yung-chêng 1723–35

By the middle of the 18th century the materials and techniques concerning the manufacture of hard-paste porcelain was no longer a secret, and those possessing the knowledge were well paid by heads of other German States to part with their knowledge. Johann Josef Ringler, who obtained the secret at Vienna by 'courting' the Director's daughter, is known to have helped in the establishment of at least six other factories.

The collectors of German porcelain are fortunate in that nearly all the major 18th century factories adopted a recognized factory-mark, which was usually applied to the base of the wares in underglaze-blue. Without this aid, attribution to a particular concern would in most instances be very difficult.

Höchst, making porcelain from 1750, adopted as their mark a six-spoked wheel, often reproduced on 19th century wares made elsewhere. Their early figures, attributed to the hand of Simon Feilner, are of a rather coarse porcelain, with a milky-white glaze, but their tablewares were beautifully painted with flowers, landscapes or chinoiseries, with fine quality gilding.

By 1752 Duke Carl I of Brunswick was sponsoring a factory at Fürstenberg, where some good figures are attributed to the hand of Simon Feilner, but the tablewares tended to be extremely fussy. The Fürstenberg factory continues to the present time, still using a version of the original letter 'F' as the factory-mark.

A further factory still in production today is that of Berlin, started in 1761 by J. C. Gotzkowsky and purchased by Frederick the Great in 1763. Many skilled workers were recruited from Meissen, and their early wares, which relied primarily on fine painting, are most attractive and original. The mark remains a sceptre in blue.

Paul Hannong established the porcelain factory at Frankenthal in 1753, having had to abandon his production at Strasbourg due to the monopolies enjoyed by Vincennes. Hannong's early wares tended to be fashioned in the contemporary French styles of Vincennes and Sèvres, but lacked the quality of the fine French soft-paste. The factory passed into the hands of the Elector Carl Theodor in 1762 and continued until 1800. The original moulds are being used today at the Nymphenburg factory, Bavaria. While one must accept Kaendler as the outstanding modeller during the Baroque period, there is little doubt that Franz Anton Bustelli, who worked at Nymphenburg from 1754, was the master of Rococo porcelain sculpture. His models clearly indicate by their carving and postures that he had been trained initially as a woodcarver. Some of his best work is seen in the form of centrepieces for the table, where the entire group appears to be stirring in a placid wave-like motion. The Nymphenburg shield is still used as a factory-mark on modern wares produced from early moulds.

The factory, patronized originally by Duke Carl Eugen, was established in 1758. It cannot be said that it flourished, as the workers were at times compelled to accept their wages in 'seconds' (faulty wares) which they in turn had to sell. The wares of this Ludwigsburg factory can at times be easily recognized by a rather off-white clay, but mention must be made of a charming series of miniature groups, modelled by J. J. Louis. There are several characters in a scene, such as men playing dice,

Angry Harlequin figure by Kaendler .1738.

tailors at work and inn scenes, all of which show great depth of detail despite the diminutive scale.

France

From the mid-17th century various East India Companies had been bringing Far Eastern porcelain into Europe in increasing quantities. In consequence, there was little incentive for potters of other countries to spend time and money trying to produce a similar type of porcelain. It was eventually left to a few French potters, already engaged in the production of faience, to make an artificial or 'soft-paste' porcelain. The wares supposedly made by Louis Poterat of Rouen after he had been granted a patent in 1673 are very difficult to attribute with any certainty. However, some collectors consider a limited number of examples of a thin glassy paste, decorated in an inky underglaze-blue and with the mark A.P., to be the work of Poterat.

Soft-paste porcelain Mennecy teapot.

Records concerning early porcelain made at Saint-Cloud are more readily accepted. Pierre Chicaneau, another faience maker, appears to have passed on his knowledge of the manufacture of soft-paste porcelain to his son and widow before he died in 1678. The widow later married Henri Trou and the factory was continued by their descendants until 1766.

The beautiful creamy-toned soft-paste porcelain of Saint-Cloud was necessarily rather thickly potted and left either in the glazed 'white' state or decorated in underglaze-blue with the so-called *lambrequin* designs, as seen on Rouen faience. Moulded scale patterns, probably suggested by the artichoke, were very popular, and handles of vessels were usually of square or rectangular section. Many saucers had a raised ring to locate the foot of the cup. This so-called *trembleuse* feature was probably first introduced at Saint-Cloud.

Saint-Cloud also produced a wide range of tablewares, snuff-boxes, cane-handles and so on, decorated in the bright enamel colours and gilding in the Japanese 'Kakiemon' style.

The early French soft-paste porcelain factories rarely showed a profit, and it was only by the interest and generosity of wealthy patrons that they were able to survive. This was certainly so with Chantilly, the factory established by Louis Henri de Bourbon, Prince de Condé, in 1725. The production was directed by Ciquaire Cirou, who almost certainly acquired his knowledge at Saint-Cloud.

The Prince de Condé possessed a very large collection of Japanese porcelain, which was to inspire early Chantilly decorators to use so many 'Kakiemon' designs, but such polychrome decoration did not show to advantage on creamy-toned porcelain. Therefore, the majority of pieces decorated in the Japanese taste were given a white opaque glaze.

Following the death of the Prince in 1740, more original styles in French taste were introduced, including a wide range of flower decoration. These designs were later to be taken to the Vincennes factory by the Chantilly workmen, Gilles and Robert Dubois, who helped to establish the factory in 1738.

Chantilly is best known to the collector for the wares made from about 1770, when the decoration consisted almost entirely of sparse floral sprays in underglaze-blue, the much copied 'Chantilly sprig'. The original mark of a French hunting-horn was used during the 19th century by other Chantilly potters making wares in a hard-paste body in the earlier 18th century styles. Samson of Paris also made hard-paste reproductions of the early wares, decorated in the 'Kakiemon' manner.

Some of the most beautiful soft-paste porcelain ever to have been produced was that made at Mennecy. The factory of François Barbin was started in Paris in 1734, under the patronage of the Duc de Villeroy, whose initials 'D.V.' were used as a mark. From 1748 until 1773 production continued at Mennecy, from which time a further move was made to Bourg-la-Reine, where the factory finally closed in 1806.

The beauty of Mennecy wares was undoubtedly due to the simplicity of form. The glaze is well described as having a 'wet' appearance, and probably illustrates better than any other soft-paste porcelain how the enamels tend to fuse into the glaze, rather than lie upon it, as seen with hard-paste. The figures of Mennecy are especially charming and were obviously intended as table decorations, which can be enjoyed from any viewpoint. The popular groups of child musicians were almost certainly inspired by the paintings of François Boucher. Many of the later Mennecy figures were left 'in the biscuit' and had a lot in common with the contemporary English Derby figures.

It is fortunate for today's collectors that the French porcelain factories did not have access to the necessary clays for the production of a hard-paste porcelain until 1769. Instead, they relied upon fine quality soft-paste, such as first seen at Mennecy and then at Vincennes, and we have some very beautiful wares as a result.

The first experiments concerned with the production took place in 1738 in a royal chateau at Vincennes, on the eastern border of Paris, under the direction of a financier, Orry de Fulvy. He was aided by Gilles and Robert Dubois, who claimed to have acquired the necessary knowledge while employed at Chantilly.

It was not until about 1745, when a further Chantilly worker, François Gravant, was engaged, that any real success was achieved. He was aided by other outstanding artists and craftsmen. Precise dating of early Vincennes is difficult, the royal double 'L' cipher was adopted as a mark from the beginning of production, but by no means consistently, and it was not until 1753 that a letter 'A' was enclosed within the cipher. That was the start of an alphabetical dating system (A = 1753, B = 1754, C = 1755, and so on), which continued until 1793.

It was from the Vincennes period that most of the well applied ground colours, including *bleu lapis*, *jonquille* and apple-green, were so beautifully applied. There was also superb engraved gilding used as borders to reserves painted with polychrome enamel floral sprays, scenes after Watteau or Boucher, birds, or chubby cupids. Among the most prolific articles produced at Vincennes were porcelain flowers, which can at times be seen as part of a bocage, used as a background to Meissen figures on *ormolu* mounts. In 1754 plans were put in hand to rehouse the porcelain manufactory in a new building at Sèvres, between Versailles and Paris, eventually occupied in 1756.

The move to the new factory coincided with the occupation of Meissen by the Prussians and marked the start of a period during which the French soft-paste was to surpass that of the Saxony concern in every respect. However, Sèvres was far from successful financially and in 1759 the factory was purchased by Louis XV, from which time it was heavily subsidized as part of the royal estate.

Highly decorated Sevres vase.

Much of the beauty of Vincennes and early Sèvres porcelain was due primarily to the simplicity of decoration, allowing large areas of the fine white surface to be seen to advantage. From the late 1760s there was a tendency to apply enamels and gilding to the entire surface, which resulted in a loss of the sense of fragility. From about 1750 it was realized that some of the ground colours were too intense and various methods were introduced to break up the large areas with various gilt patterns, including *cailloute* (pebbling), *vermicule* (wormlike) or *oeil-de-perdrix* (partridge-eye), which were all very successful. Recent research into the archives of the factory has proved that several terms used over a long period are inaccurate, for example, the rose-pink introduced in 1757 was recorded as simply *rose*, never *rose Pompadour*.

The first porcelain figures made at Vincennes were glazed, but from about 1752 it became fashionable to leave the porcelain 'in the biscuit'. Some of the finest miniature statuary of this type was modelled by Etienne-Maurice Falconet, who was trained as a sculptor. He worked as a modeller at Sèvres from 1757 until 1766, when he went to Russia, where French porcelain was in great demand. In about 1788 the Empress Catherine II ordered a 740 piece service, decorated with her monogram 'E II' (Ekaterina II). Tea drinking played a large part in the social lives of the French court and nobility, and services for the enjoyment of the drink were made in quantity, including cabaret services, which had the pieces necessary for 'tea-for-two'. They were often made to be carried in fitted travelling cases.

Experiments concerned with the manufacture of hard-paste porcelain following the discovery of kaolin (china-clay) at Saint Yrieix near Limoges were successful by 1769 and in 1772 true porcelain was in regular production, although soft-paste was also made in limited quantities until the end of the century.

Following the death of King Louis XV in 1774, both the quality and quantity of the wares rapidly declined, caused to a large degree by competition from the newly established Paris factories. Due to the patronage of members of the royal family, these were permitted to make certain classes of wares previously reserved for the Sèvres factory alone.

The royal porcelain factory was taken over by the new revolutionary regime in 1793 and the mark of the royal cipher was replaced with the 'R.F.' monogram (*Republique Française*), which was used until about 1800. During these seven years very few pieces of any great importance were made, other than those with decoration including revolutionary emblems, sometimes applied together with newly introduced ground colours. These new colours were intended to imitate tortoiseshell and semi-precious hardstones.

Belgium

François Joseph Peterinck was granted a privilege in 1751 by the Empress Maria Theresia to establish a porcelain factory at Tournai, where some very good quality soft-paste porcelain was made until the time of the founder's death in 1799, when the factory passed into the Bettignes family. The Bettignes are better known for their 19th century reproductions of Sèvres, Saint-Cloud, Chantilly, Sceaux, Chelsea and Worcester.

The best known Tournai pattern is said to have been introduced in 1787 to decorate a service for the Duke of Orleans. The naturalistic bird-painting is based on drawings made by Buffon for his 1786 publication *Natural History*.

Because Peterinck engaged some English workmen, there is frequently a distinct similarity to the porcelains of Derby and Worcester. This is especially so with the 'biscuit' figures, and positive attribution can be extremely difficult as there are no factory-marks. The Tournai models would be slightly earlier than those of Derby and probably modelled by either N. J. Gauron, who previously worked at Mennecy, or Joseph Willems, who was working at Chelsea for many years before modelling for Tournai from about 1766.

Holland

The Dutch, who excelled in the manufacture of tin-glazed earthenware, were less successful with porcelain and produced few wares which were entirely original.

The earliest production of hard-paste porcelain in Holland was that started by an Irishman, Daniel McCarthy, at Weeps near Amsterdam, in 1757. The raw materials were obtained from Germany, and resulted in a fine white body, but the decoration of flowers, landscapes and 'exotic' birds was very stilted and lacked the naturalistic colours seen on the contemporary German porcelains.

In 1771 the Weeps concern was purchased by Johannes de Mol, who moved the operation to Oude Loosdrecht, near Hilversum, where further good, but dull, wares were produced with the aid of the arcanist L. V. Gerverot. Following the death of Mol in 1782, the factory was moved yet again by the new owners to Oude Amstel, where production continued under the direction of the German, F. Dauber. The next move, made in 1809, was to Nieuwer Amstel, where the manufacture of good tablewares in the French Empire style continued until the factory closed in 1820.

The factory established at The Hague in 1776, by Anton Lyncker, remained in his family until 1790. The wares again showed very little originality, other than some excellent painting by Leonhardus Temminck in the style of Boucher, often featured on teawares. The mark of The Hague was a stylized stork with an eel in its beak, but because porcelain made elsewhere was often decorated by the Lynckers, the original underglaze-blue mark of such factories as Höchst, Ansbach, Meissen or Tournai are often seen to be overpainted in enamel with the stork-mark.

Denmark

Despite attempts being made to establish a porcelain factory in Copenhagen from as early as 1730, there is little evidence of any real success being made until 1759, when Louis Fournier, who had previously worked at Vincennes and Chantilly, produced a good quality soft-paste porcelain, usually fashioned after French or German tablewares of the period. It was unfortunate that the material proved to be uneconomic and production was halted in 1765.

It was in 1775 that a successful production of a hard-paste porcelain was achieved under the ownership of F. H. Müller, who engaged skilled painters and modellers from major German factories. This concern was taken over in 1779 by the King of Denmark, when the Royal Danish Porcelain Factory was established. The earliest wares were of a greyish-toned body and often decorated with underglaze-blue versions of Meissen designs. It was at Copenhagen that yet another famous service was again associated with the Russian Empress Catherine II, but upon completion the *Flora Danica* service of nearly 2,000 pieces was acquired by the King. The decoration, on the Neo-classical styled service, consisted of botanical specimens from G. C. Oeder's *Flora of the Danish Kingdom*. The painter was J. C. Bayer from Nuremberg.

From about 1780 an increasing number of 'biscuit' porcelain figures were produced, again often inspired by those of France or Germany. After 1835 the Royal Danish Porcelain Factory started their now famous production of figures based on the work of the sculptor Thorvaldsen.

Although Denmark's claim to fame in the ceramic field is associated with the porcelain of Copenhagen, during the second quarter of the 18th century the Store Kongensgade factory, under the direction of Christian Gierlof, produced a wide range of useful wares, including a punch-bowl in the form of a bishop's mitre. Their decoration was generally restricted to the limited range of high-temperature colours.

The rival factory of Peter Hoffnagel at Osterbro, Copenhagen, was producing many typical Scandinavian forms, decorated in blue and manganese-purple, from about 1763.

The decoration of the faience made at Schleswig from about 1758 was somewhat limited due to the monopolies previously granted to other undertakings. Their most common palette consisted of a brownish-manganese together with a grey-green, and their Rococo forms were usually more appropriate to the finer materials of porcelain.

Different cup shapes: (from the top) *London* c.1750; *Bow* c.1752; *Bow* c.1761; *Pinxton* 1796–99.

Other factories at Criseby and Eckernforde were started during the 1760s, but the factory producing some of the finest Scandinavian faience was that at Kiel, under J. S. F. Tannich, whose wares made up until about 1768 are considered to have equalled those of Strasbourg. But later, under Johann Buchwald, there was a marked decline in both quality of material and choice of decoration and palette.

During the 1760s a successful production of faience was conducted by Peter Hoffnagel at Herreboe, where the painting was primarily of high-temperature blue and manganese, applied to extreme Rococo forms.

Sweden

In 1759, as in Denmark, a successful production of soft-paste porcelain was started on the estate of Marieberg, on Kungsholmen in Stockholm, by the German dentist J. L. E. Ehrenreich, but almost immediately the newly erected factory was burnt down and no further porcelain was made at Marieberg until 1766. Then the Frenchman Pierre Berthevin produced wares which, if unmarked, are difficult to separate from those made in France, at Mennecy; this is certainly true in the case of the delightful little covered ice-cream cups.

Following the departure of Berthevin in 1769, the charming soft-paste

From the top *Longton Hall c.1756; Longton Hall c.1755; Worcester, Flight period, 1783–93.*

porcelain was abandoned in favour of a poor quality hybrid hard-paste, which was improved upon in about 1777, when Jacob Dortu, from Berlin, made some excellent hard-paste tablewares in the manner of Sèvres and Berlin, which had now become a far more fashionable factory than Meissen. Production ceased in about 1782.

Great Britain

The British potters were comparatively late starters in the field of porcelain manufacture, but in this respect it must be remembered that unlike the majority of their Continental rivals, they were only rarely subsidized by royal or noble patronage and so were entirely dependent upon the commercial success of their undertakings.

The early factory of Chelsea, managed by the Flemish silversmith, Nicholas Sprimont, was an exception, recent research having proved that Sir Everard Fawkener, Secretary to the Duke of Cumberland, was involved with the factory on a financial basis. In common with many other European factories of the mid-18th century, Chelsea looked first to Meissen for their inspiration, and then from about 1756 to Sèvres.

The years from 1745–70, during which time the Chelsea factory remained independent under Sprimont's direction, is usually discussed under four periods, named after the marks usual at certain dates. From 1745 to about 1749 wares were often marked with a small triangle, and during this 'triangle' period the majority of the wares echoed the form of Sprimont's earlier silver. In about 1749 the quality of the paste was improved, permitting a larger range of tablewares to be made, often marked with a small moulded anchor on an oval tablet, hence 'the raised-anchor' period, which continued until about 1752. It is generally agreed among today's collectors that the Chelsea wares and figures made between 1752–8 were the finest they produced. During this period, when the mark was a small red enamel anchor (red-anchor period), some very fine figures were modelled by Joseph Willems, again mostly inspired by Meissen. Naturalism at the table also extended to the wares and various vessels were modelled to resemble animals, birds, fruit or vegetables.

During the 'gold-anchor' period, from about 1758–70, the small scale figures of about 16 cm (6½ in), previously used for table decoration, were replaced by large ungainly figures, often with a background of bocage and suitable only for side-table or cabinet decoration. During this same period the tablewares were fashioned in an exaggerated Rococo style as popularized originally at Sèvres.

The slightly later production at Bow catered for the less wealthy customer, and by about 1747 a soft-paste porcelain, including calcined animal bone, was being used to produce large quantities of cheap and durable wares, primarily decorated in the Chinese fashion of underglaze-blue. By about 1750 many Bow wares were being decorated in enamel colours, often inspired by the Japanese 'Kakiemon', the Chinese *famille rose* or the German naturalistic flower-painting.

Bow figures were also of a type which would have particular appeal to the mid-18th century Londoner. Popular actors and actresses, such as Henry Woodward and Kitty Clive, were depicted in recognized roles, and national heroes, including General Wolfe and the Marquis of Granby,

177

were made in quantity, together with such characters as Bacchus or figures symbolizing the Four Seasons or the Elements. The early wares of Bow were comparatively simply made, but nevertheless possessed a distinct charm which is lacking in later wares, when both tablewares and figures became very clumsy, with loud and poorly applied enamelling.

The new collector may well be forgiven for confusing some examples of Bow with those made at the small Suffolk factory at Lowestoft, established in 1757 and continuing until about 1799. It is said that one of the proprietors, Robert Browne, actually obtained employment at the Bow works in order to learn the secrets of the production. Until about 1768 almost all the Lowestoft wares were decorated in underglaze-blue, and these examples are in great demand today. Many of the later wares were decorated in enamel colours in chinoiseries, a style of decoration that was probably responsible for that completely erroneous term 'Chinese Lowestoft'.

The Lund and Miller factory, started in Bristol in 1748, was probably the first English factory to produce a porcelain body containing the material soaprock, or steatite. There is difficulty in identifying their early unmarked wares as the factory was taken over in 1752 by the newly established Worcester concern, under the famous Dr Wall.

The new ingredient produced a ware which had almost all the advantages of a true porcelain and the proprietors claimed their products could withstand the temperature of boiling water and so be less liable to crack.

Both Bristol and early Worcester concentrated on blue-and-white, although by about 1756 Worcester were also making some beautifully decorated wares in delicately applied enamelled colours. Worcester was one of the first English porcelain factories to decorate their wares with enamel and underglaze-blue transfer-prints, many from the copperplates engraved by the master Robert Hancock, who had previously worked at the Battersea enamel factory.

Towards 1770, Worcester began to attract several fine painters who had previously worked for Sprimont at Chelsea. From about 1768 their wares were rather heavily decorated, often with the famous underglaze-blue applied as scales, leaving reserves for enamel decoration, of flowers, birds or chinoiseries in rich gilt scrollwork frames. Worcester is the only English porcelain factory to have survived to the present day with an unbroken history.

Other English porcelain factories were soon to acquire knowledge of soapstone and gain access to the material, which was quarried in Cornwall, in the West of England. Caughley, the factory Thomas Turner established in Shropshire in 1772, produced a very good quality soapstone porcelain, decorated in a wide range of patterns, both in underglaze-blue and enamel colours. At least four major Liverpool factories made a similar class of ware, but the decoration was restricted mainly to underglaze-blue.

During the mid-18th century the only porcelain factory in Staffordshire to survive for several years was at Longton Hall, where a glassy soft-paste porcelain was made from 1749–60. Due to the high content of frit (glass), their early wares were subject to high kiln-losses and were

Worcester vase and cover c.1760.

often misshapen, but these difficulties were seemingly overcome by about 1755. Then some simple but highly original figures were produced, together with many tablewares, often of naturalistic form. Some Longton Hall mugs, and other wares, were decorated at Liverpool by the firm of Sadler & Green with enamel transfer-prints.

William Duesbury, who was formerly an independent pottery and porcelain enameller in London, established a porcelain factory at Derby in 1756, an undertaking he likened to 'a second Dresden'. The finest wares produced at Derby were made from the time Duesbury took over the Chelsea factory. During this so-called 'Chelsea-Derby' period (1770–84) many well designed and tastefully painted table-wares were produced in the Neo-classical styles. It was on Derby wares that the fine naturalistic flower-painting of William Billingsley first appeared, alongside the painting of Zachariah Boreman, who excelled in the painting of landscapes of the Derbyshire countryside. The factory was taken over by Robert Bloor in about 1812 and closed in 1848.

William Cookworthy, a chemist, eventually produced a hard-paste porcelain at Plymouth, Devon, in 1768. Although it was near the source of the raw materials of china-clay and china-stone, the undertaking was moved in 1770 to Bristol, probably because of the difficulty of re-cruiting competent potters. It remained in production until 1781. The early Plymouth wares were often badly fired, probably due to difficulty in controlling the high temperatures, but from 1774 when Richard Champion, one of the original partners, assumed control, his claim to produce wares with the hardness of Dresden and the elegance of Sèvres, was well justified. Some extremely fine tea services were made in Neo-classical styles.

In 1781 a group of Staffordshire potters purchased the unexpired years of Champion's patent for the manufacture of hard-paste, and so gave birth to the now popular New Hall factory, where a hard-paste body, with a rather soft glaze, was used to produce a wide range of useful wares until about 1812. Then in common with most other factories making porcelain, they started to produce bone-china, as introduced by Josiah Spode in about 1796, when china-clay and china-stone became legally available to any British potter for the manufacture of translucent ware.

Caughley porcelain was produced at the 'Royal Salopian Porcelain Manufactory' near Broseley in Shropshire from 1775–99. The factory was founded by Thomas Turner, an engraver, who had previously worked at the Worcester porcelain factory. A pottery existed at Caughley before Turner's arrival, but was rebuilt in 1772 as a large porcelain factory with three kilns.

The Caughley works produced a wide and varied range of porcelains, from buttons to dinner-services, and while for a long time it was generally believed that Caughley wares were inferior to Worcester, many collectors now agree that a not insignificant number of Caughley porcelains in the post-1775 period are superior to Worcester wares. If nothing else the early feelings about Caughley ware have meant it is now highly collectable.

Much of the factory's output was devoted to wares with printed patterns in underglaze-blue, and after 1785 when the Worcester works ceased to produce blue and white, Turner's only competitor was imported Chinese products. Contrary to a previous view, it is now thought all Turner's underglaze-blue decoration was done at the Caughley factory and not at the main Worcester factory. The Caughley marks are the word 'Salopian' found on flat-based articles and the initial 'S' in underglaze-blue on a variety of objects; the initial 'C' was also used on hand-painted and other pieces. Turner never used his own initials.

Many of Turner's designs proved very popular, in particular designs such as the Fisherman and Pleasure boat. It was in fact one of Turner's fortes that he successfully copied designs that could be produced cheaply. He also made a series of porcelains that show a French influence in particular in their use of the Chantilly-style sprig motifs in underglaze-blue or overglaze enamels.

The Caughley factory was sold by Turner in 1799 to the nearby Coalport works of Edward Blakeway, John Rose and Richard Rose and continued operating under John Rose for some fifteen years.

From the 1780s there were as many as three factories in Worcester producing porcelain, one of the earliest and most notable of which was that owned by Richard Chamberlain. Chamberlain is said to have been the first apprentice at the main Dr Wall factory in the 1750s and certainly by the 1770s, along with his son was in charge of decoration at that factory. He and his son left the Wall factory in 1783 and established their own decorating business in Worcester in 1786. The porcelain blanks for their business they first bought from the main Worcester factory until about 1789 when they were obtained from Turner's Caughley factory. Of the blanks from Caughley, the Chamberlains enamelled and gilded some to the specifications of Turner while the remainder were sold directly. Eventually the Chamberlains went into the manufacturing side themselves and by 1796 the bulk of their products was of their own manufacture and they had built up a substantial trade.

Wedgwood vase showing the 'Apotheosis of Homer' modelled by John Flaxman.

English Stonewares

From about 1720 Staffordshire and Yorkshire potters were producing salt-glazed stoneware which had been considerably improved by the addition of white Devonshire clay and calcined flints. Apart from 'thrown' tablewares, they also made a large variety of novel forms, such as teapots in the form of houses or camels by the slip-casting method (pouring watered-down clay into hollow plaster of Paris moulds). Other forms of decoration included rubbing cobalt into incised decoration (scratch-blue) and enamel painting.

The early Staffordshire lead-glazed slipwares were soon to be similarly refined to provide wares suitable for the popular beverage tea. The name of John Astbury of Shelton is today used to describe the mid-18th century wares and figures involving the use of applied or trailed clays in contrasting colours as a means of decoration. Similar wares are known to have been made by many other English potters. The name of Thomas Whieldon is similarly used to describe the variegated glazes acquired by the application of various high-temperature oxides under a fluid lead-glaze, which was again a technique used by many other potters during the same period.

Before becoming a Master Potter, Josiah Wedgwood (1730–95), was in partnership with Thomas Whieldon from 1754–9. Wedgwood is known throughout the world for his large production of blue-and-white jasperwares, made from about 1775, during the time he was in partnership with Thomas Bentley (1769–80), but in his earlier years Wedgwood produced some beautifully moulded lead-glazed wares, often aided by the modeller William Greatbatch.

If fired at a lower temperature and then covered with a refined pale yellow lead-glaze, the body of salt-glazed stoneware can be used to produce cream-coloured earthenware. A primitive creamware was being made as early as 1720, but credit is given to Josiah Wedgwood for improving this body to such perfection that he was patronized by Queen Charlotte. His 'Queen's Ware' was in world-wide demand. He produced the famous 'Frog' service for Catherine II of Russia, now in the Hermitage, Leningrad. It was Wedgwood's aim to convert a rural craft into a great industry, and this he achieved. Fortunately, some contemporary potters continued to make wares in the traditional manner. Foremost was the Wood family of Burslem, who are best known to collectors for their figures, many of which were modelled by the nephew of Ralph Wood, Enoch Wood. Ralph Wood died in 1772, but the production continued under his son and grandson. The early wares were decorated with lead-glazes which had been previously coloured with high-temperature oxides, resulting in a much more orderly finish than the figures of Whieldon type.

Recent research has proved that a very large production of creamware and other ceramic bodies associated with the Staffordshire potteries was also taking place during the second half of the 18th century in Yorkshire, including the Leeds Pottery, which started about 1770.

Early American Potters

The first American colonists could ill afford, or have any use for, decorative tablewares. Just as 17th century English potters catered primarily for the farming community, so in 18th century America the potters were producing 'redware' or 'stoneware' vessels for cooking or storage, but when the occasion arose, they too were able to apply their skills to fashion more decorative items. Plates or platters, various sized bowls, some suitable for tea drinking, and a wide range of jugs and pitchers, were made more attractive with brushed, 'splashed' or trailed clay slips of contrasting colours. New England archeologists have found evidence of a wide range of wares, which has enabled the collector readily to distinguish between pottery made in America from that imported from England. Porringers in the form of a large shallow cup with a single 'steadying' handle, were used at the table for multiple foods, together with mugs of tall cylindrical form.

Towards the middle of the 18th century, the American potters, many of whom had migrated from Staffordshire, became aware of the dangers of using glazes with a high lead content. As a result there was an increased manufacture of salt-glazed stoneware, of a type which had much in common with the early German Rhenish vessels, rather than the fine white body of mid-18th century Staffordshire. There was little encouragement for the American potter to try to improve upon the quality of these humble wares, for from the last quarter of the 18th century masses of white earthenware was being exported from England at a price American craftsmen could not possibly match, despite efforts to produce both tin-glazed and cream-coloured earthenware.

Due to the importation of Chinese porcelain, the demand for the more expensive and vulnerable English blue-and-white soft-paste was very low. However, many wares such as Nankin China mugs and salt cellars went to America by way of England, as there was no direct trading taking place between America and China before the American Revolution.

Attempts have been made by many researchers to find proof of the type of porcelain said to have been made by the Savannah potter Andrew Duche, who, according to William Stephens, Secretary to the Colony of Georgia, was making 'translucent' wares as early as 1741. This would pre-date any documented English porcelain. South Carolina also appears to have attracted potters from England. In 1770 John Bartlam was advertising the opening of 'A China Manufactory and Pottery' to be staffed by 'the properhands' from England. A contemporary pottery in the same area was also advertising for fine clays, which were probably required for the manufacture of creamware.

The most important finds concerning 18th century American ceramics were made at Philadelphia, where excavated fragments identify at least 20 examples of the soft-paste porcelain made by Gouse Bonnin and George Morris. These identified pieces include baskets, sauce-boats, cups and saucers, sweetmeat dishes and covered jars. They are decorated in underglaze-blue, having a great deal in common with English porcelains made at Bow, Derby and Worcester. It was a pity that this venture only lasted from 1770–72.

Glass

The Baroque influence seen in English glasses, with their covers decorated by finials of crowns and crosses, elaborate stems and wrythen bowls, declined by the last decade of the 17th century, so heralding the great period of English drinking glasses. Aided by the new variety of available beverages, the 18th century drinking glass emerges in all possible shapes and sizes imaginable. The stem received the greatest attention. The enclosed airtwist spiral (1730–70) was probably derived from the accidental and later deliberate 'tear', an elongated airbubble, cleverly manipulated to form a single or several spirals within the stem. By the mid-18th century the mixed air and enamel twists, the opaque white and colour twist glasses establish the English product as one of the greatest achievements in glassmaking history, and a delight for the collector.

The most elegant vessel is the Newcastle Baluster, tall and graceful with plain or twist stems, knopped, with enclosed tears and generous bowl – an ideal foil for the art of the Dutch engravers. The drawn trumpet, where bowl and stem are drawn from one piece and the foot applied, is one of the earliest drinking glasses already produced in the 17th century. Characteristic of the Lynn and Norwich factories are glasses with bowls manipulated by the gaffer to show horizontal 'corru-

17th- and 18th-century drinking glasses are classified according to major and minor stem groups. Major stem groups: a and b) Inverted and true baluster, c.1685–1735; c) Plain, c. 1730–75; d) Air-twist, c.1745–70; e) Opaque-twist, c.1755–80; f) Faceted, c.1760–1810. Minor stem groups: a) Moulded pedestal or Silesian, c.1715–65; b) baluster, c.1725–60; c) composite, c.1745–70; d) incised, c.1725–70; e) mixed and colour twists, c.1755–75; f) rudimentary.

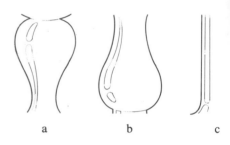

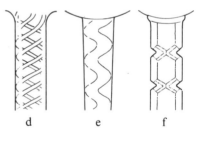

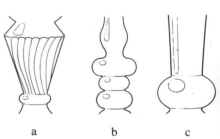

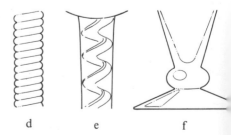

gate' rings. Rarely do we find the famous folded foot in glasses after the middle of the 18th century. Most characteristic is the plain conical foot which should rise toward the centre and have a circumference at least equal to that of the rim of the glass.

Commemorative glasses represent the most fascinating group for the collector. Jacobite glasses referring to the rebellions of 1715 and 1745 are usually well engraved with pertinent symbols, the rose for Stuart, the thistle for Scotland, flowers for initials, Fiat – may it happen, Redi or Redeat – may he return. The rare Amen glasses, engraved with verses of the Jacobite Anthem, portrait glasses picturing the Young Pretender, Irish glass commemorating the ascent of the House of Orange and glasses of William II interest fall into this group. Coinciding with this phase are the Privateering or nautical glasses. Coins enclosed in the stem or foot of the glass are not always a true indication of the age of the vessel, which must be judged on its own merits.

The Glass Act of 1777–8 doubled the duty on lead glass and taxed the enamel necessary for producing white and colour twists.

In 1788, John Robert Lucas, William Chance and Edward Homer founded the Nailsea factory near Bristol. To beat the tax they bought cheap cullet from Bristol's 'white' glasshouses and produced attractive dark green glass objects applied with fused-on enamel chips of various colour, or band and spiral patterns. There is, however, no proof that all the gaily coloured glass objects, rolling pins, walking sticks and friggers (these were made 'at the end of the day' from left over glass remnants) came from the Nailsea factory.

The most gifted representatives of Rococo style in glass decoration were William Beilby Jr (1740–1819) and his sister Mary (1749–97) who worked for the Dagnia-Williams glasshouse at Newcastle. This meant of course that they had available to them the finest glass made at that period. Most Beilby glasses have enamel twist stems, and range from small drinking glasses to large goblets with a generous bucket bowl.

Wine glasses decorated in white enamel with fruiting vines are favourite subjects, but there are also Rococo landscapes with figures and animals. Magnificent heraldic decoration in polychrome enamel is found on impressive goblets and bowls, almost exclusively made to order. Signatures are present on important pieces.

The work of the decorator James Giles (1718–80) was directly influenced by the Adam style. He confines himself largely to gilding, decorating opaque white as well as coloured cut glass with elegant classical designs of garlands, birds, pheasants, grasses and bushes.

The work of Michael Edkins (1733–1811) is associated with colourful enamelling on opaque white glass produced in the Bristol area soon after 1750 in imitation of porcelain, and aptly expressed in delicate *chinoiserie* motifs. Edkins also produced much of the fine gilding on Bristol blue glass made at the Non-Such Flint Glass Manufactory of the Jacobs family. This glassworks was active between 1775 and *c*.1815 making fine blue glass tableware decorated with non-figurative classical motifs.

Gilt decoration of a more rustic charm was produced by William Absolon of Great Yarmouth between 1790 and 1810. Absolon specialized in decorating souvenir ware of blue and white glass.

The English Glassmaker in Ireland

One of the most significant results of the Glass Act was the migration of English glassmakers to Ireland, which was not affected by the English tax regulations and had been granted freedom of trade. The years 1780–1825 are often now referred to as the Anglo-Irish period.

The Waterford Glass House was established in 1783 by George and William Penrose, businessmen with no knowledge of glass manufacturing. However they employed as manager of the factory John Hill from Stourbridge, who, it is believed, brought with him some of the best glass workers he could find from the Worcester area. Hill stayed with the company for only three years and left following an argument with his employers. Before he left Ireland, Hill passed the secrets of his successful glass manufacturing to Jonathan Gatchell, a close friend and a clerk at the Waterford works. Gatchell was duly made manager in Hill's place and went on to become a partner in the firm. It was George Gatchell, his descendant, who eventually became sole proprietor of the company and continued the Waterford factory until the manufacture of flint glass ceased there in 1851.

Although the majority of pieces made at Waterford were a high quality clear glass, some coloured glass was produced. It is also known that the company held a formula for making opaque white glass, but there is no record of any pieces being made in this way. Waterford glassware is particularly known for its use of cutting as a method of ornamentation, although this was not done in any particular style or type of cut.

The Cork Glass Company was also founded in 1783 by Francis Richard Rowe, Thomas Burnett and Atwell Hayes and continued with several changes of ownership until 1818. The Long Bridge Glass House in Belfast was founded by Benjamin Edwards from Bristol. Edwards, a skilled glassmaker, had been brought from England by the owners of the Tyrone Collieries to manufacture glass from local supplies of sand and coal. He stayed with them for some five years before going to Belfast to start his own manufactory. The firm continued until 1826 when it was forced to close after the imposition of the Irish glass tax in 1825.

Not all Irish glass manufacturers marked their wares, but where they did it took the form of raised letters running round beneath the base. This was done by blowing the glass into a mould which had the lettering incised, but the re-heating needed to finish the piece sometimes blurred the mark and occasionally obliterated it altogether. The marks of the three companies previously mentioned are PENROSE WATERFORD, CORK GLASS CO. and B. EDWARDS BELFAST.

Most of the pieces that are marked are decanters, finger-bowls, water-jugs and some dishes. A feature common to most Irish decanters is the short vertical flutes which ornament the lower part of the body. While on many decanters this was the only ornament, others were cut or engraved. Other notable features of these decanters is the use of neck rings and stoppers of either the disc type or mushroom-shaped. The Cork Glass Company seemed to favour three neck rings and the mushroom stopper, while the Long Bridge Glass House more often used two neck rings and upright disc stoppers which sometimes had a central depression enclosed by a border of radiating cuts.

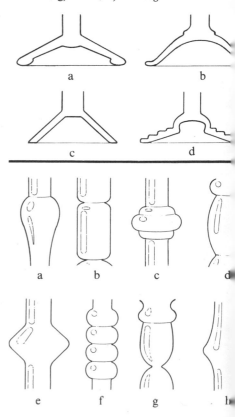

Basic foot shapes of 18th-century English drinking glasses: a) *Folded conical;* b) *domed;* c) *plain conical;* d) *terraced. Some knop shapes:* a) *Drop;* b) *domed;* c) *annulated;* d) *egg;* e) *angular;* f) *bobbin;* g) *acorn;* h) *swelling.*

Advances in Germany and Bohemia

The glass industry in Germany and Bohemia continued to expand in the 18th century and the glassmaker was no less innovative and creative than he had been in the 17th century.

From 1720 to 1745 *Zwischengold* glass techniques were successfully revived in Bohemian workshops and possibly also produced in monasteries. This is a form of decoration whereby gold foil, engraved with a fine needle and sometimes highlighted in brilliant red or green lacquer, is enclosed between two walls of glass, the outer surfaces of which is usually additionally decorated by facet cutting. The majority of existing *Zwischengold* glass takes the form of faceted beakers, but the technique was also applied to bowls and covered goblets.

At Gutenbrunn in Austria, Joseph Mildner (1763–1808) developed a most distinctive variation with medallions or miniature portrait panels of enamel or painted on parchment enclosed within the wall of the vessel. These medallions usually carry the name of the sitter and the date on the obverse. Occasionally a little poem is added – Mildner had a penchant for poetry and created his own.

An individual form of glass decoration in a raised enamel technique was produced by Johann Friedrich Meyer of Dresden (1680–1752). The most delicate and exquisite glass decoration, however, was the technique of transparent enamelling, inspired by stained glass methods. Several of these artists frequently dated and signed their work. One of the most influential was Samuel Mohn (1762–1815) of Dresden, who specialized at first in silhouette portraits on porcelain and on glass, and then turned to transparent enamelling, representing a variety of subjects including panoramic views of landscapes and cities.

The Rise of Glassmaking in America

The first attempts at glassmaking in America were made by English settlers in 1608 at Jamestown, Virginia, an event still commemorated there with the sale of brown glass souvenirs. The earliest successful venture came with Caspar Wistar's glasshouse, established in 1739 in Salem County, Southern New Jersey. Wistar's free-blown glass is characterized by applied decoration of trails, bird finials, prunts and blobs eventually developing into the (South Jersey) lily pad motif. Wistar's glass was clear, in pretty colours of aquamarine, olive green, amber, brown, blue and colourless. The factory ceased manufacture in 1780.

In 1763 Henry William Stiegel, a German-born iron worker appeared on the glassmaking scene. He rebuilt his father-in-law's iron works, named it Elizabeth Furnace, continued to prosper, and consequently invested in glassmaking first at Elizabeth Furnace and then at Manheim, Pennsylvania. Stiegel manufactured mainly table glass and flasks, both in mould-blown patterns. The daisy in a diamond design is associated with this factory – and with enamelled decoration of birds, flowers, hearts and inscriptions in the Continental rustic manner. In 1774 the company went bankrupt and Stiegel, after his release from a debtor's prison, died in 1785.

Since both Wistar and Stiegel employed foreign workmen and imported foreign glass, it is difficult to distinguish with certainty between

American and foreign products, but it seems reasonable for the decoration to have been applied in America.

The third glassmaker to have made his mark on the 18th century American scene was John Frederick Amelung from Germany, who established an ambitious undertaking near Frederick, Maryland. The New Bremen Glassmanufactory, so named after Amelung's home town, employed some 300 workmen at its peak, mostly German and English. Without doubt, Amelung's glass is the finest made at that period. The high standard of Rococo-type engraving and the harmonious lines of free-blown goblets, flasks and tumblers testify to foreign workmanship. A further product was pattern moulded glass in attractive clear colours. After a number of misfortunes, the factory closed in 1795. The workmen were absorbed by other factories, in particular the New Geneva Glassworks founded in 1797 by a Swiss, Albert Gallatin.

Spain, Scandinavia and the Netherlands

Spain was slow to develop a national style in glassware due to the conflict of Eastern and Western influences in that country. It was not until the middle of the 18th century that Spanish glassware improved in quality.

In 1728, the Royal Factory of La Granja de San Ildefonso was established by Catalan glassmakers. Glass production was almost exclusively for the Royal Palace and workmen were engaged from all over Europe. The characteristic late 18th century product is a vessel with engraved and firegilt decoration, as well as enamelled decoration of a rather provincial style with flowers and garlands. Milk glass and coloured glass, sometimes with a mottled effect, was another feature of this factory.

Little figures similar to *verre filé de Nevers* were made in Spain from the 16th century onward.

Although there was early knowledge of glassmaking in Scandinavia, the first factory to operate in the Danish Norwegian kingdom was established in 1741, at Nøstetangen, Norway. German and English glassblowers were engaged and native workmen sent abroad to learn the craft, resulting in glass analogous with the prevailing Anglo-Venetian style.

In 1676, Giacomo Scapitta founded the Swedish Kungsholm Glasbruk factory at Stockholm and supplied the glass for the royal household. Table glass and chandeliers in Venetian-influenced blown glass were produced in these factories. By 1757 two further glasshouses operated in Norway – Hurdals Verk specializing in crown glass manufacture and enamelled glass in small quantity, and Hadeland producing bottle glass. During the later 18th century, some fine German engravers decorated glass at Nøstetangen: Heinrich Gottliev Köhler working in a Rococo style, and Villas Vinter.

By the beginning of the 18th century glass engraving had been developed almost to the peak of perfection in the Netherlands. The Dutch engravers practised both wheel engraving and diamond stippling. The former was already of the highest quality and the 18th century saw diamond stippling carried to the same level due mainly to the work of two men, Frans Greenwood (1680–1761) and David Wolff (1732–98).

Wolff glasses, with their delightful treatment of children in formal dress, putti among clouds, commemorative portraits and allegorical

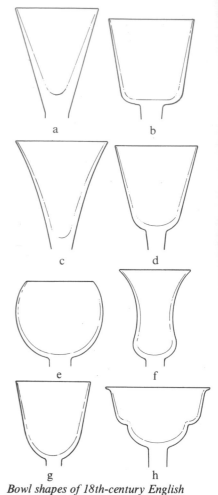

Bowl shapes of 18th-century English drinking glasses: a) *Funnel;* b) *bucket;* c) *trumpet;* d) *round funnel;* e) *cup;* f) *bell;* g) *ogee;* h) *double ogee.*

designs accentuate the charm of Rococo art. Wolff applied his techniques almost exclusively to English glasses. *Façon de Venise* had gone out of fashion and glass *à l'Anglaise* was favoured by most engravers. This was due to the great development of a brilliant English lead glass, seen in its most satisfying form in the Newcastle Baluster as produced by the Newcastle factory of Dagnia – an Altarist family.

The brilliance, whiteness and softness of lead metal combine to make English glass a perfect foil for the Dutch engravers, and as early as 1680 the Bonhomme factory at Liège attempted glass *à la façon d'Angleterre*. By the mid-18th century some good English-style glass was produced, though lighter in weight due to smaller lead content. The new, thicker glass responded well to the growing demand for wheel engraved decoration. One of the greatest exponents of this technique was Jacob Sang of Haarlem, whose work may be seen in the Victoria and Albert Museum, and other important collections.

Gold and Silver

The arrival of the 18th century heralded the beginnings of a new style that was to influence all the decorative arts. The new movement had its origins in France, which, during the first quarter of the 18th century, was undergoing a transition from the majestic style associated with the building of Versailles to a style now called *Régence*.

Gradually, in response to the ideas of French architects, designers and goldsmiths – who once more took their inspiration from Italian sources – the whole of Europe shed the static weight of the Baroque style in favour of a lighter, Rococo mood, which used ideas taken from rockwork and shells in graceful, undulating curves and reversed C-scrolls. The spirit of playfulness was also expressed in the continental use of chinoiserie, to which the asymmetrical nature of this new style was particularly suited.

The Rococo style appeared early in silverware in the use of *bombé* shapes, full of swaying movement because they contained no straight lines. The effect of asymmetry was achieved by applying cast decoration in such a way as to disguise the basic regularity of shape. Some of the

18th-century table candlesticks, from left: *London 1720–21; Paris 1744–45; Paris 1767–68; Amsterdam 1770; German, c.1780.*

finest works ever made appeared in this style, for which 'white' silver was preferred to the majestic quality of silver gilt.

In France, where the Rococo style originated, the designs of J. A. Meissonnier (1695–1750) show a complete mastery. Much silver was melted during the Revolution, but it is still possible to see some of the superb work of Thomas Germain (1673–1748), the greatest French silversmith of the first half of the 18th century. He was the son and the father of highly talented workers, and in addition to his work for Louis XIV and Louis XV, executed pieces for the Portuguese Royal Family, many of which were lost in the catastrophic Lisbon earthquake of 1755.

J. M. Dinglinger (1664–1731) is justly renowned for the works of art he created from 1698 in Dresden for his patron Augustus the Strong, Elector of Saxony and King of Poland. Incredible wealth in precious and semi-precious stones and metals came from Saxon mines and Dinglinger used them to make objects of extraordinary fantasy.

Housed in the Green Vaults in Dresden, Dinglinger's cabinet pieces are perhaps the most famous of his works and they show an early interest in Eastern subjects, of which the Gold Coffee Set and the Great Mogul's Birthday Party, a metre square stage set with over a hundred figures of guests, attendants bearing gifts and exotic animals in gold, silver-gilt and precious stones, are examples. The Apis Altar, his last work, has an Egyptian subject which was not pursued elsewhere in Europe until later in the 18th century.

A portrait of Dinglinger exists, in which he is painted holding his

Silver coffee pots, left to right: *London 1736; Rome 1734–44; London 1730;* above: *London 1711.*

Bath of Diana, an elaborate confection based on a stag's head whose antlers support a chalcedony bowl framed with gold and above which rests an ivory Diana carved by the court sculptor, Permoser. Dinglinger also made jewelry, which was housed in the Jewelry Room of the Green Vaults, on which the great Meissen porcelain modeller J. Kaendler worked as a wood carver. This connection between metalwork and porcelain has an interesting parallel in London, where in 1742 the Liège goldsmith, Nicholas Sprimont, registered his mark and a few years later founded the Chelsea porcelain factory.

The 18th century was a period of great industrial change in Europe with machine processes gradually taking over from the craftsman – and in this England led the way. Until this time, workshops had been small, with a master and some assistants working for commission and for stock. This system was gradually superseded by one in which large general firms collected their stock from a number of specialists who did not need to deal with the public themselves, but could also work on their own account if they wished. Not only did the introduction of machinery make silver production cheaper from the mid-18th century onwards, but the invention of substitutes allowed more people to have what had previously been a luxury. The first of these substitutes for silver was Sheffield plate.

In about 1742 it was discovered that a sheet of copper could be fused by heat to a thin skin of silver and that when put through a rolling mill the two metals would expand in unison and could be used in the same way as sheet silver at a fifth of the cost. Horse powered rolling mills gave

English silver teapots, top row: c.*1710*; *swag-bellied*, c.*1750*; bottom row: c.*1780*; c.*1810*.

way to water power and then to steam. Die-stamping and swaging machines made patterns, copper wire was plated with silver and then drawn out and used to strengthen and to decorate pieces.

At first, one side only of the copper sheet was plated, but later both sides were covered and the edge of the piece where the copper layer was exposed was disguised by soldering on a grooved silver wire, by soldering on stamped out silver mounts or by lapping over the edge.

The various methods of concealing the raw edge allow the collector to distinguish the types of edge and mount and so to date the piece fairly accurately. The simple sheared edge was in use from 1743–58 and involved concealing the visible copper beneath a layer of silver solder or tin. Joseph Hancock introduced the single-lapped copper edge which was used from 1758 until the 1870s. Here, a layer of silver overlaps and conceals the copper edge, but like the simple sheared edge was not satisfactory if the piece was to be subjected to heavy use. The double-lapped copper edge, which was in use from 1768 until the early 19th century, utilized a piece of copper wire which was first silver plated and then flattened and soldered to the edge of the plate. It is often difficult to detect the soldered edge. Another method of concealment, the silver-lapped edge, was in use from 1775–1815. The method consisted of fitting over the edge of the plate a U-shaped length of Sterling silver wire, soldering both sides and burnishing.

Ornamental piercing of Sheffield plate became possible in the 1770s with the introduction of double plating. Piercing of plate had also been dependent upon the development of hard-steel tools, for the use of a fretsaw revealed the inner layer of copper. In the 1770s special hand-operated fly-presses with hardened punches were designed for use with double plate, which left a layer of silver protruding beyond the copper that could be lapped over and burnished until the copper was hidden.

Matthew Boulton (1728–1809) at his Soho factory in Birmingham, England, ensured the highest standards of design and workmanship in

London, early 18th century

Silver tea caddies, left to right:
London 1735–36
Halle 1716
London 1759–60

190

Leeuwarden, 1716

Silver tea caddy, Haarlem 1708.

this new medium, as well as in silver, by commissioning the best designers. Boulton, like his potter friend, Josiah Wedgwood, was one of the first to use industrial processes on a large scale. Subsequently fused plate, as it was called, was made in France and in Russia, though less successfully.

The new industrial methods were particularly suited to the expression of Neo-classical taste, which spread through Europe and America from the 1760s. Once more the artistic impulse came from Italy – architects and artists studying there were influenced by the Roman architect, Piranesi, and by the archeological treasures then being uncovered. For the first time, the artistic initiative which began the new style did not come from court circles, but from intellectual ones. Monarchs, fearful for their thrones, suspiciously regarded it at first as liberal and revolutionary. Again, for the first time, the style was accepted very quickly and within 30 years all over Europe and North America the swaying, Rococo shape was replaced by the chaste, classical vase. Contemporaries refer to this style, which we call Neo-classical, as the 'true' and 'correct' style. Matthew Boulton's description of it cannot be bettered – it evolved, he said 'by adapting the elegant ornaments of the most refined Greek artists and humbly conforming to their style and making new combinations of old ornaments without presuming to invent new ones'.

The publication of numerous engraved designs in this simplified style enabled manufacturers rapidly to produce classical designs in silver and in Sheffield plate for an ever-increasing and prosperous middle-class clientèle.

Sweden had, in the past, been influenced first by German and then by French artistic sources, but at this period in London there was working a Swedish silversmith of great talent, Andrew Fogelberg. His work and that of the English late 18th-century silversmith, John Schofield, expressed in the purest fashion the first phase of Neo-classical taste. However, the finest silver produced in this style was still recognized to come from France and work was commissioned from Jacques Roettiers (1707–84) and R. J. Auguste (c.1730–1805) by many Royal patrons, including Catherine the Great of Russia.

Scottish silverware, notable for its great simplicity, reached its peak in the 1730s and 1740s. Notable silversmiths such as Colin McKenzie and James Sympsone of Edinburgh were making important pieces – tankards, fruit dishes and coffee pots – which for the most part lack any ornament except for finials and magnificent coats-of-arms. Silverware of this period can still be found by the collector. Teapots by James Ker and William Aytoun are sought after, if rare, as are cream-jugs and sugar basins. Spoons of the rat-tail type are more easily found however.

Scottish silverware of the second half of the 18th century is more difficult to distinguish for by this period silversmiths had begun to absorb styles current in England at that time. While the hallmark is the first thing a collector should look for on Scottish silver he will encounter some difficulties. Until 1784, Edinburgh silver had the usual four marks, when in that year the sovereign's head was added. Although Glasgow had begun a date-letter in 1681 it was not used regularly until 1819, while burghs such as Aberdeen did not have a regular date-letter. Town marks can also be an inaccurate guide.

Clocks

While the most significant technical advance in clockmaking in the 17th century – the introduction of the pendulum – had been the achievement of the Dutchman, Huygens, it was the English clockmakers, led by Thomas Tompion, who in the remainder of the century took the greatest strides in the development of accurate timepieces.

The pre-eminence of English clockmakers continued into the 18th century, the early years of which were marked by the invention of the deadbeat escapement in 1715 by George Graham, followed by two important methods of overcoming the problems of the adverse affect of changes of temperature on the pendulum (the gridiron pendulum by John Harrison in 1725 and the mercurial pendulum of George Graham in 1721); these added to the advances being made towards producing precision timepieces. Accuracy of timekeeping was now of imperative importance both to the astronomers and to the seafaring nations. Supremacy at sea both for purposes of exploration and trade depended upon the ability of a clockmaker to produce an extremely accurate portable timekeeper which would enable the sailors to chart their longitudinal position accurately. Both French and English Governments were actively encouraging their craftsmen towards this goal at the beginning of the 18th century. However, although Le Roy and Berthoud of France produced some extremely accurate timepieces, John Harrison (1639–1776) must go down in history as the man responsible for conquering the problem.

The making of the cases now came under the care of the cabinetmakers and naturally reflected the current fashions in their respective countries. The English longcase styles changing from the early ebonized, architectural examples with gilt mounts and twist or barley sugar columns to high domed tops (from 1705), broken arch (from 1760) made of oak veneered in walnut or other decorative woods to the pedimented tops (from 1780) of the lacquered or marquetry cases of the next century. Mahogany only came into use in England in the latter half of the century.

The longcase clock did not achieve the same degree of popularity on the Continent that it enjoyed in England. The Dutch examples were the most similar, but their cases were more elaborate with *bombé* bases, outcurving feet and hoods surmounted with carved figures. Marquetry was extremely popular. Colourful scenes with automata in the dial arch or musical mechanisms were more common. The French examples either emulated bracket clocks standing on matching pedestals or had trunks that curved outwards towards the base with an aperture through which an ornate pendulum was visible. Locally made cases would be simple, but those intended for the more sophisticated town dwellers would be elaborately decorated with exotic woods, veneering and ormulu, but became more classical in design towards the end of the century. Many of the movements, especially those originating from the Franche Comte district, were totally unlike those of the Dutch and English.

Coffee pot made during the 'First' or 'Dr Wall' period of the Worcester factory, 1751–83.

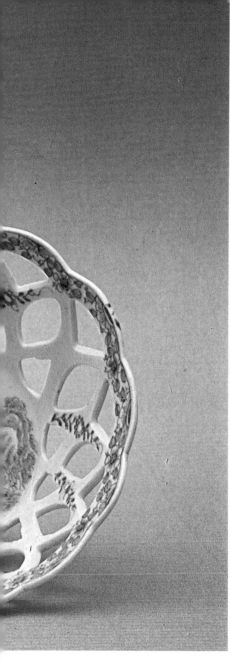

Above: *A collection of Bow porcelain. The cream jug, c.1755 has famille rose decoration. The figure is of 'Winter', c.1760–65 and the basket decoration is in underglaze blue, 1750–55.*

Left: *Two 'First Period' Worcester plates, c.1775, showing French influence in their decoration.*

Right: *Bristol vase and cover c.1775, a fine example of the porcelains produced by this factory.*

Below: 'Botanical' plate produced by the Chelsea porcelain factory during the 'red anchor' period – c.1750–60.
Left: 'Lovers and a Clown' made c.1755, a Derby version of the well-known Meissen group.

Left; *Sevres porcelain ewer and basin in jaune* jonquille, *one of the earliest (1753) Sevres colours. Painted by Catrice, dated, 1763.*

Above: *Lowestoft porcelain*, left to right: *Tea bowl and saucer, unmarked, c.1785; cream jug, unmarked, 1785; coffee pot, c.1770; tea caddy, c.1765.*

Spring-driven bracket clocks were also produced in abundance during this period and followed much the same changes in case and dial styles as the longcase clocks, as well as including many of the same technical innovations. In many instances they achieved an equally high standard of accuracy. English bracket clock cases tended to be relatively plain, although there were more elaborately cased clocks with ingenious mechanisms. These were frequently intended for the Eastern market, as was the extraordinary collection made by James Cox of Shoe Lane, London. Unfortunately, due to local unrest these were never exported and after being placed on display and a few charged to view them, they were disposed of in 1775 by lottery.

The Dutch cases also tended to be more elaborate, but for the most exotic and extravagantly decorated cases it is necessary to turn to the French clocks of the 18th century. During the reign of Louis XV (1723–74) there is little doubt that the clockmaker played a subservient role to that of the casemaker. The movements had to be adapted to fit the cases and not vice versa. Although there are exceptions (the work of makers such as Lulien Le Roy and Ferdinand Berthoud), the consequence was that movements of this period tended to be of a fairly standard pattern. The current Rococo style of furnishings was carried over to the clock cases and masterpieces, often signed by their makers, of boulle work, lacquer or intricate veneering embellished with fine ormulu appeared in abundance. Towards the end of the century many fine porcelain cases appeared. During the reign of Louis XVI cases were still superb but there was a general return to more classical lines and themes and more emphasis on complicated movements.

One of the most attractive clocks to appear in this period was the lyre clock, a type of mantel clock. The dial occupies the lower circular space of the lyre, with the pendulum set above the clock appearing like the strings. The framework of the lyre is usually of marble or bronze the latter decorated with enamel and diamanté.

Another type of mantel clock popular in this period was the so-called 'column' clock, in which the dial was hung from a portico supported by two side supports which take the form of marble columns, caryatids or bronze figures.

Dials were almost invariably of white enamel and were well designed. The dial painters Coteau and Dubuisson became famous at the end of Louis XVI's reign for their beautiful floral work as well as for their zodiacal designs.

Among the styles that reappeared in Louis' reign were the Religieuse, characterized by columns either side of a glass front, a break-arch top and the pendulum swinging below the dial and visible through the front; the Grand Style of Louis XIV also returned, particularly that of Boulle.

Clockmaking in Germany declined during the 18th century. Obviously, clocks continued to be made both of the spring-driven and weight-driven variety, but it was the wooden movements of the Black Forest area that came to the fore at this time. These simple weight-driven clocks with a verge escapement and foliot were made by the farmers during the winter months while outdoor work was impracticable. Tradition has it that the familiar cuckoo clock originated from this area and was first constructed

ineglass decorated with the arms of the
ckmaster of Lincoln, c.1765.

by Franz Anton Ketterer about 1740, and by the end of the century these clocks were being exported throughout Europe. Slowly the anchor escapement replaced the verge and first the escape wheel and the train wheels became of brass, but it was not until the end of the 19th century that wooden plates were finally dispensed with. A few bracket cuckoo clocks were made towards the end of the century, with some examples including a fusee, but generally they retained their simple design and resulting low cost. Their manufacture, although now by factory methods, has continued to this day.

The earliest domestic clocks in the American colonies were those brought by the settlers themselves. Most of these clocks were of the lantern or similar type. There was probably little indigenous clockmaking until about 1700 although the first immigrant who claimed he was a watchmaker was William Davis of Boston who arrived in 1683. In reality, he was probably a watch repairer. By 1698 clock and watchmakers were working in Pennsylvania although no signed examples of their work exist and they too were probably primarily repairers. By 1700 there were sufficient watches and clocks in the colonies to attract artisans from Europe.

The 18th and first half of the 19th century was the age of the hand-crafted clock in America. Since the majority of the early craftsmen were from England, handcrafting was predominantly a variant of the English style. Early domestic clocks were almost entirely tall clocks which came to be called grandfather clocks. A few table or bracket clocks were made in Boston and Philadephia. Wall and shelf clocks were introduced by the Willards of Boston in 1775. The four Willard brothers, Benjamin, Simon, Ephraim and Aaron, were, for some 75 years, the most prominent and influential clockmakers in New England. The most famous of the four brothers was Simon (b.1753). Little is known of his early apprenticeship except that he probably completed it under his brother Benjamin. Some clocks are known however that have case-lead pendulums with the names John Morris and S. Willard, dated 1770 and 1771. Before 1783, when he settled in Roxbury, Simon was manufacturing tall clocks, thirty-hour wall timepieces and a few eight-day shelf clocks all inscribed 'Simon Willard, Grafton'. After 1783, he stopped making the thirty-hour clocks and by 1800 he had developed an eight-day brass clock in a wall-type case which became one of the best-known American clocks.

Watches

The successful application of the balance spring to the watch in 1675, while overcoming one great problem, showed up another – the in-efficiency of the verge escapement. The best accuracy attainable was about one minute a day depending on conditions.

Much experimentation both on the Continent and in England was carried out in attempts to improve upon the verge escapement. George Graham perfected the cylinder escapement about 1725. Although used

Dial and back of repeater watch, made by Daniel Quare and Stephen Horseman, London, c.1720.

in a few English watches, it was not used extensively until the end of the 18th century when the Swiss and French makers dispensed with the fusee and utilized this escapement in their endeavours to meet the demand for thinner more elegant watches. Through persisting with the use of the fusee even in their cylinder watches and declining to adapt the verge watches in order to meet this new fad, the English slowly lost their lead in the overseas markets.

The advantage thus given them was eagerly grasped by the French, who also had the advantage of having at this time an exceptionally artistic as well as technically brilliant horologist – Abraham Louis Breguet (1747–1816). Born in Neuchatel in Switzerland he spent most of his working life in France. Movements of the watches produced during this century included many complicated mechanisms, namely automata, striking, chiming, repeating work, perpetual calendars and so on, as well as incorporating technical improvements needed to achieve precision timekeeping.

Repeating mechanisms for watches had been first used in 1685 by Thomas Tompion. By 1700 half-quarter repeaters had been introduced which sounded a single stroke 7½ minutes after the previous quarter. Five-minute repeaters were in use by 1750.

A notable advance in this century was the introduction of jewelled bearings. In 1704, Nicholas de Duillier, a Swiss mathematician along with two French immigrant workers, Peter and Jacob Debaufre, took out a patent for 'An Art of Working Precious or more Common Stones (whether Natural or Artificial) Christal or Glass and certain other Matters different from Metals, so that they may be employed and made use of in Clockwork or Watchwork. . . .' The patent taken out in England was granted, but when they tried to apply for an extension they were opposed by both lapidaries and watchmakers who then kept the secret to themselves. By 1750 jewelled bearings were appearing in high-quality watches.

Decoration of watches varied over the century. In the first quarter of the century enamelled dials were becoming popular and were in general use by 1750. The so-called 'beetle and poker hands' were standard until around 1800, continental examples often having pierced hands.

Although using many of the previously introduced techniques of enamelling and so forth, the application to cases altered. The paintings were now confined to panels set into a gold case, with the metal being pierced, chased or set with half-pearls or brilliants. The former were characteristic of many Swiss cases, although the French and Swiss designs tended to be similar in most instances. Guilloche or Engine-Turning became widely used towards the end of the century and frequently was further embellished with a coloured translucent enamel.

The pair case is seen more often in the third quarter of the century, the outer case being plain or covered with fish-skin with silver or gold pin patterning. Matt-surface gold and silver dials also appeared at this time.

Repoussé-worked outer cases were common until about 1775, the motifs often being scenes from mythology or the Bible. Repoussé work was at its peak mid-century but continued in varying degrees of quality for a further 25 years. The general aim of the case designer at this period was one of restrained elegance.

Domestic Metalwork

French domestic ironwork of the 18th century was dominated, as it had been in the previous century, by benchwork. This is shown by the collection in the Le Secq des Tournelles Museum, Rouen, in which are fire irons, firedogs, locks, knockers, comfit boxes, cane handles, *necessaires*, chatelaines, needlecases and a host of other objects, all made of chiselled iron and decorated with repoussé, damascening, etching or engraving, and all reflecting the styles of the period.

Italian work of the 18th century is more representative of forging, and includes candelabra, lanterns, beds like those made in the 16th century and well cranes. In Spain and Portugal, sanctuary lamps, candelabra and door lamps and brackets are of particular note; there are some noteworthy large lamps in the cathedral at Lisbon. German work of the time includes chandeliers, lanterns, knockers and small sculpture in steel, many of these things being strongly influenced by French design. Signs for inns and shops of charming Rococo design, made during the 18th century, may still be seen in position in many places in Germany and Austria.

Of everyday artefacts of a kind made all over Europe in the 18th century are sugar nippers and hammers (for breaking up sugar loaves), kitchen knives and pastry jiggers (for cutting out pastry), chimney jacks, and candle snuffers of infinite variety, all made by benchwork. Forged work includes stands for warming plates in front of the fire, and goffering irons with a socket for receiving a heated iron or poker, and over which frills, ruffles and so on were prepared; later, in the 19th century, goffering irons usually had cast-iron bases. There were also various lighting appliances including candlesticks and lanterns of many kinds and

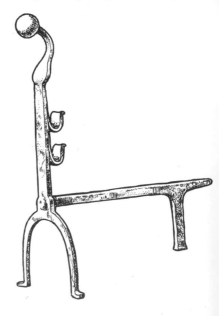

Wrought iron spit-dog, 18th century.

Scottish lamps or cruses for burning oil: these were in the form of two oval, lipped cups, one above the other, the top one to hold the oil and a lighted wick, the lower one to catch the drips. Rushlight holders were another lighting appliance used in poorer British homes. They consisted of small upright tongs set in a base, usually a heavy piece of wood, which held a burning rushlight (a rush dipped in tallow) which was moved along as it burned down. They came into use after a tax was put on candles in 1709 and continued even after the repeal of the candle tax in 1831.

Among other artefacts were sheet-metal spout-lamps for burning oil, which looked somewhat like an odd-shaped kettle on a leg, the spout holding the wick; and sheet-metal candle-moulds and boxes, kettles and candlesticks, some of which, for bedroom use, were fitted with cylindrical glasses. Office candlesticks with two holders and shades, all adjustable, sometimes combined wrought iron and sheet steel, the central stem and scrolled supports of iron, the base (sometimes filled with lead), holders and shades (usually prettily perforated) of steel; these are late 18th or early 19th century.

Firegrates of polished steel and various alloys, including Paktong, were widely used in the 18th century. Made by a combination of black-smithery and benchwork and sometimes casting, they were decorated with perforations that included Rococo and Gothic patterns, classical arcading and Chinese fret. Matching fenders were also made. The fire-basket itself was usually of plain forged wrought iron.

Cast-iron was used for fireplaces, often with great imagination, as on late 18th century hob grates, which consisted of two cast-iron boxes or pillars, often delightfully decorated, connected by wrought iron firebars. Apart from these there were many different designs for framed grates.

Wrought iron fire irons – pokers, shovels, tongs, log forks – varied

Top right: Wrought steel douter, late 18th century; snuffer, wrought steel, late 18th century.
Bottom row: Wrought iron trivets, 18th century.

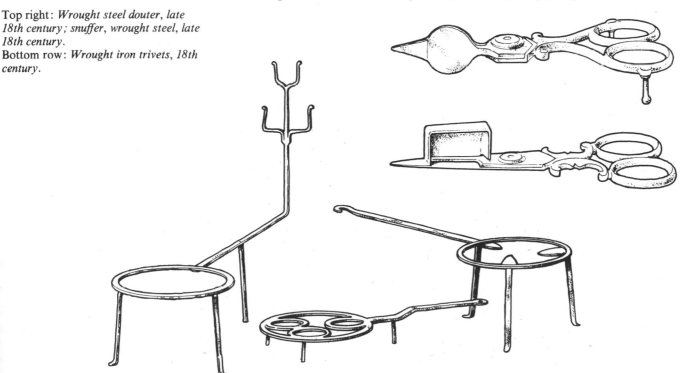

considerably in the elaboration of their design, but basically they have not altered much over the centuries. The more elaborate really differ from simpler ones only in their handles, which are sometimes cast bronze, brass or iron, or of chiselled or forged steel or iron. One basic variation, however, is in the design of tongs, which may be either of the spring or hinged pattern: the former, which have a bow-shaped spring in place of a hinge, were not used until the late 18th century, but the latter were in use as early as the 17th century.

An aspect of sheet metalwork practised widely in the 18th century was the manufacture of japanned ware. It was made in Holland, France and Great Britain, and although each produced good work, that made in France was of the best general quality. The lacquer was applied and re-peatedly stoved at a low temperature, and one stoving could last as long as three weeks. The metal most frequently used was tinned steel, for this helped to give great hardness to the finished surface, but other metals and alloys were also used, including copper and Britannia metal.

Japanned ware covered an enormous range of objects, including trays, urns, vases, tea and coffee pots, candlesticks and snuffers, coffee urns and coal vases. The decoration varied, much of it chinoiserie (for japanned work was at first made to meet a demand for real Japanese lacquer, the export of which was banned in the 17th century), but there were many other forms, still life, flowers, rustic scenes, tortoiseshell and abstract patterning among them. Sometimes japanned work was fitted with bronze, ormolu or gilded steel mountings.

Bronze in the 18th century was frequently of a high standard, especially in France. Two of the greatest French bronze founders of the time were Jacques and Philippe Caffieri (1678–1755). Their output was enormous

Above: *Cast iron fender, late 18th century;* below: *copper fender, perforated and engraved, late 18th century.*

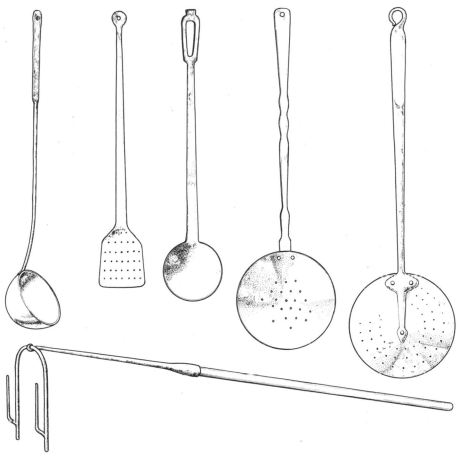

Left to right: *Ladle, 20 in; fish slice, 18 in; ladle, 18½ in; two skimmers, 22½ and 24 in; down-hearth bread toaster.*

and included fine chandeliers, one of which is in the Mazarine library, Paris. A pair of ormolu firedogs by Jacques is in the Wallace Collection, London. The works of the Caffieri are notable for their use of Rococo design. Other French bronzeworkers in the Rococo style included F.-P. Gallien, Fermier Antoine Lechaudel, Georges-Alexandre Moreau fils, who worked with the Caffieri, Feuchère, and Jacques Renard, a fine candelabrum by whom is in Autun cathedral.

Later in the century there was a return to classical style, one of the foremost exponents of which was the bronzeworker Gouthière (1740–1806), whose patrons included Madame Dubarry. At Versailles there are chandeliers by him in the form of a central torch surrounded by four baby fauns playing trumpets. Scrolled arms with rosettes and leaves grow from the bottom of the torch, and each has a candle socket at its extremity.

In Germany, notable work was done in the Potsdam atelier of the Swiss craftsman, Jean-Melchoir Kamble, who made furniture fittings and mountings, mirror frames and clockcases, all of them in French style. In the Low Countries bronzeworkers were also busy, and their work is exemplified by several fine church lecterns, such as in the cathedral at Ypres by W. Pompe (this cathedral also contains a brass baptismal font of about 1600) and in the church of Notre Dame, Courtrai, by Jean Bernaes (1711).

By the middle of the century, brass pattern books were making their first appearance in England as a result of the enormous range of wares

207

now being offered which made it impossible for the travelling salesman to carry a full selection of samples. The collection of pattern books in the Victoria and Albert Museum shows how widespread the use of purely utilitarian brass had become – hooks, hinges, drawer knobs, handles, window catches, coach fittings, locks and traps, to name but a few. Buttons and buckles were widely made in brass and some buttons display high artistic skills. As fashions came and went, pattern books began to fill with snuff-boxes, needlecases, clock faces, scissors, knives, candlesticks, umbrella handles and the like.

Pattern books are usually very difficult to date for the salesmen, or factors as they were then called, showed a high degree of secrecy about the source of their wares, particularly if the craftsman at the source was highly skilled. As a result, pattern books contain no maker's name, no date and the pages are randomly numbered. Only the watermark on the paper, if there is one, can offer any guide to the date of the wares.

Towards the end of the century a larger number of brass articles were being made by stamping rather than casting and many of the early pieces are indistinguishable from the cast items, except for their weight. One exception to this move away from cast brass were candlesticks. From around 1670 English candlesticks had been cast in two halves and had a hollow core. After about 1770, English craftsmen finally mastered the technique of core-casting, although the French had successfully used the method since the 15th century.

Brass, like other metals in this century, was widely lacquered and in the case of brass this treatment not only protected the surface of the metal but also gave it a rich gold appearance. In 1759, Stephen Bedford of Birmingham discovered that the lacquered surface could be worked to imitate engraving; the lacquer, however, wears off in time and few examples still survive.

Lacquers were made in a wide variety of colours and consistencies. Basically they were made from spirits of wine and seed lacquer or from spirits of turpentine and amber. Colouring agents included turmeric, sandalwood, gamboge and dragon's blood.

A group of late 18th- and early 19th-century loving cups.

English brass has always remained unmarked, in part because no guild was ever organized to oversee the brass trade. The Founder Company's members worked in various metals, while the Armourers and Braziers were only responsible for the brass trade in the City of London from 1714. Neither body, however, had an official seal. Another reason for the lack of marks on brass may be that throughout the history of the brass trade restrictions had been placed on the importation of raw brass and it would have been unwise for the enterprising brass maker to mark his work while such restrictions were in force. Where a mark does occur it is usually that of a landowner placed there when an inventory of his household was taken, or of an individual worker determined to be known.

Jewelry

The age of the gem, which began in the 17th century, continued with undiminished fervour in the 18th century, by the middle of which jewelry had become almost exclusively involved with the setting and display of gems, enamel rarely being incorporated into the design except in Spain.

The enthusiasm of the craftsman for this new medium spread to the public, resulting in a fashionable vogue for jewelry the extent of which was unparalleled in the history of jewelry.

The rose diamond, so popular during the 17th century, was soon superseded by the 'brilliant' cut discovered by a Venetian, Vincenzo Peruzzi, around 1700. This new style of cutting was a major contribution in establishing the diamond as the pre-eminent gemstone. Indeed, colour was generally avoided during this period. This is reflected in the fact that diamonds were generally set in silver, gold being reserved for coloured stones. The emphasis on stones at the expense of workmanship meant that jewelry became gradually more and more expensive, placing it even further out of the reach of all but the privileged few.

Early 18th century settings for diamonds reflected the confidence (or lack of it) of the lapidary and the expense of brilliant-cut diamonds. In these early settings the stone was held tightly and open mounts were rare. The rose-cut diamond continued for some 50 years after the introduction of the brilliant cut, backed and firmly held in claw settings before the lapidary found the courage to introduce the brilliant-cut in claw or coronet settings with the stone held above the base. Eventually the back of the setting was opened up. By the time of the Regency, pavé settings, suitable for a group of small stones and with the metal frame almost invisible, were being experimented with for brilliant-cuts.

The expense of jewelry in the early years of the century resulted in a boom in the market for imitations. Since diamonds were so popular, attention was particularly directed towards the production of a cheap substitute. Many materials were used including rock crystal and good quality paste, the most famous of which was invented by a German, Stras, working in Paris. His name has become synonymous with paste jewelry in France. In Switzerland, where the wearing of diamonds was forbidden, marcasites, rose-cut crystals of iron pyrites, enjoyed great popularity, as indeed they did in England and France as well, the popularity spanning the following century, too.

Another diamond imitator which, like marcasite, was to become fashionable in its own right was faceted high-carbon steel. The process is generally supposed to have been discovered in Birmingham, England, but suffered the severe drawback of being prone to rust. Coloured stones and pearls were more successfully imitated in paste, but semi-precious gems were common as well. Among these lowly stones the most popular were turquoise, citrine, agate, cornelian and garnet. Gold itself was the subject of many imitations, the most successful being the famous alloy of copper and zinc invented by Christopher Pinchbeck in the early years of the 18th century.

Stomacher of topazes mounted in silver, Spanish, c.1760.

France remained the arbiter of taste throughout the period, but the Rococo style that held such sway over the decorative arts during the mid-century, especially in France, had little effect on jewelry design other than in the decoration of watch cases and objects of vertu.

Although Thomas Flach published his book *A Book of Jeweler's Work Designed by Thomas Flach in London* in 1736, the designs are formal rather than naturalistic and could be used for anything from furniture to jewelry. It was not until later in the century that designs and patterns specifically for jewelry were created. It took most of the century for the change from formal to naturalistic to take place, but in 1771 Joseph Banks returned with Captain Cook from Australia bringing with him his drawings of botanical specimens which were so acclaimed that there was a wave of enthusiasm for naturalism and particularly highly accurate naturalism. Flowers were given stems and leaves which they had lacked in the earlier formalized designs, stems were textured and even butterflies or dragonflies were attached to floral brooches by tiny spring wires producing the *tremblant* effect. This effect, though not an 18th century invention, nevertheless reached the height of its popularity at this time. Corsage ornaments such as spray brooches achieved a greater and greater degree of naturalism and informality. To these was added a fashion for bows and loops of ribbon and lace, notably the large *sévigné* brooches, (named after the French letter-writer) which had sprung up during the latter half of the 17th century. These brooches were often worn *en parure* with a pair of pendant earrings of *girandole* design, each in the form of a pendant with three drops, the longest at the centre. Designs incorporating feathers and feather scrolls are also frequently found during this period, especially in *aigrettes*. All these ornaments were essentially vehicles for the display of gemstones. The famous chatelaine, however, perhaps the most characteristic jewel of the period, which supported not only watches but also keys, *étuis*, miniature notebooks and seals, was rarely set with fine stones, its decoration relying on the fine working of gold and gilt metal often with the addition of painted enamel plaques.

Although chatelaines made in the early part of the century did make use of gems, such as the watch and chatelaine made by Thuilst for Queen Anne about 1705 of pierced and chased gold, inlaid with mother-of-pearl which itself is set with garnets, information about early chatelaines comes from imitations often in pinchbeck. It was only in the second decade of the century that the chatelaine was used to carry not just a watch but the other items instead.

Echelles were sets of matching brooches exclusive to Georgian times and were made so that they could be sewn on to a garment. They could, for instance, be sewn around the hem of a dress for one occasion and were then removed and sewn elsewhere on the dress for a different occasion. Designs were quite formal, the most popular being bow-shapes.

Male jewelry was largely confined to buttons and shoe buckles. There are still many good examples in existence designed for both ceremonial and day-to-day wear. The former would invariably be set with diamonds, the latter with imitations such as paste and cut-steel. Rings, too, were favoured by both sexes. Apart from signets and clusters, perhaps the most distinctive design of the period is the *giardinetto* where the bezel is in the form of a pannier of flowers.

The second half of the century showed a great revival in enthusiasm for mourning jewelry. Perhaps most typical are the pictorial pendants produced in large numbers during the last two decades. These were usually oval or marquise-shaped (a sort of pointed ellipse), and contained a sepia miniature drawn from the current iconography of urns, weeping willows, broken monuments, angels, doves, and so on. Part of the composition was usually executed in minute strands of hair taken from the deceased and the reverse of the mount was invariably inscribed and dated.

The rise of the Neo-classical movement in the second half of the century brought with it a renewed interest in cameos – an interest which had been waning since the Renaissance. The difficulty and expense of producing cameos in hard-stone led to a serious quest for suitable substitutes. The relatively soft shells of certain large molluscs, when carved, closely resemble sardonyx cameos and the process became increasingly popular during this period, although it was almost certainly also known during the Renaissance. In Britain, large numbers of substitutes were manufactured in paste and ceramic, most notably, perhaps, the well-known plaques produced by the Wedgwood factory as well as the paste copies of antique gems popularized by James Tassie.

Scientific Instruments

The Microscope
From 1650 to 1830 the optical performance of the microscope improved only marginally. During the same period the stand was redesigned and improved by a host of makers. Some specialized in miniaturization, others in elaborate mechanical gimcracks. One of the longest lasting designs is that associated with the London mathematical instrument-maker Edmund Culpeper.

18th Century

The first form of the 'Culpeper' microscope was introduced about 1725 as a modification of the tripod microscope developed by English opticians after an Italian design manufactured by the renowned lens polisher Guiseppe Campani of Rome. As with telescopes of the period, the body tube is pasteboard covered with shagreen, the stained and polished skin of the sting ray. The eyepiece is turned in ebony, the stage, legs and fittings are brass. Culpeper's significant technical innovation was the concave sub-stage mirror that gave improved illumination of the object. For this reason the instrument was known as the 'double reflecting microscope'.

There were almost a dozen design variations in 50 years; the final all brass form of about 1770 was in production for over 70 years as the 'three pillar microscope'. If fully equipped the 'Culpeper' microscope has a range of accessories stored either in the octagonal foot or in the drawer of the tapering case. Culpeper's own work invariably has an oak case, and the attribution to the maker is made from the engraved trade-label pasted in the back of the case. Later models have mahogany cases and less than half of those that survive have the maker's name engraved on the stage or the body-tube. Lately some unsigned instruments have been 'doctored' with the signatures of reputable makers to enhance their value. With a keen eye and a powerful hand lens such fraudulent activity can usually be uncovered.

The recent engraving of signatures should not be confused with contemporary attempts to reap financial benefit from the reputation of a well known maker. The firm of P. & J. Dollond of London were renowned for their achromatic telescopes, indeed for some years they had a monopoly of the manufacture of telescopes with the doublet objective for reduction of colour aberration patented by John Dollond in 1758. Unwary buyers at the end of the 18th century bought telescopes signed 'Dollond' in the fond belief that they were acquiring a product of the house of Dollond. Almost a century earlier the expatriate English instrument-maker Michael Butterfield suffered similar plagiarism from unscrupulous colleagues in Paris, whose sub-standard sundials were engraved BVTERFIELD APARIS.

During the 18th century, Continental microscope makers took up and modified the designs of the market-leading London opticians. The Parisian atelier married brass, silver, wood and shagreen with confidence and to far greater aesthetic effect than their rivals across the channel. There is no English counterpart to the French 'Box' microscope, where the body of the instrument is set on a handsome cabinet inlaid with marquetry, decorated with ormolu mounts, or merely faced with carefully chosen veneers.

On the few occasions when a London optician set out to make an overtly decorative microscope the effect was unconvincing. The great silver microscope made by George Adams for George III in 1761 is certainly a fine and impressive example of mechanical skill, but is also in monumental bad taste. In contrast Alexis Magny, a Parisian maker who worked for clients like Bonnier de la Mosson, owner of one of the most extensive cabinets of instruments in France, produced microscopes that incorporated not only all the latest technical features, but were also of considerable beauty. They were embellished with the Rococo decora-

French octant made c.1786.

212

tions in gilded bronze, and a highly decorated shaped leather casket. These mechanical and aesthetic triumphs of Magny were proudly owned by members of the French aristocracy like Louis XV, the Marquis de Pompadour and the Duc de Chaulnes.

American Instruments

The development of the American instrument-making industry has a history which is quite well represented by surviving instruments. The first colonists had to rely on European instruments, but by the mid-18th century indigenous craftsmen were able to satisfy the desperate local demand for the utilitarian instruments used by surveyors and navigators. The earliest recorded maker of instruments in North America, James Halsey of Boston, is known from a navigator's backstaff dated 1676. Since brass had to be imported from England until the second quarter of the 19th century, the colonial makers turned to the native hardwoods. In New England black-walnut, rock maple, pear, wild cherry and apple were used. These woods were neither sufficiently close grained nor resinous enough to survive the rigours of shipboard use, so that for octants ebony and mahogany imported from the West Indies were preferred.

The classic American instrument is the surveyor's compass, which in the 18th century was made totally of native wood. Like all colonial work, this instrument had no superfluous decoration. The one exception to this general rule is the engraved paper compass card at the centre of the surveyor's compass. It is frequently found with an elaborate design in the central roundel. In the early examples, the style and motifs of the decoration followed English traditions, using, for example, the crown and tudor rose. Not unnaturally, Old World themes were rapidly abandoned after 1776. A common post-independence design has a marine scene as the central vignette. This is an unexpected iconographic feature to find on a surveying instrument, but is explained by the economic desire to use the same copper plate to print compass cards for the surveyor and the navigator.

One area where the colonists had to rely on imported instruments was in the supply of apparatus for college teaching. The apparatus of natural philosophy as it was called in the 18th century embraces a very wide subject area. It includes such items as air pumps, with the associated pneumatic apparatus like Magdeburg hemispheres and guinea and feather apparatus: there are hydrostatic balances, inclined planes and a host of mechanical models to demonstrate the operation and principles of the gear, pulley and lever, also lodestones, magnets and the very wide range of electrical apparatus out of which modern physics evolved.

Not until the third and fourth decades of the 19th century were American instrument-makers, like Benjamin Pike of New York, able to produce all these instruments. Before that time London makers such as Martin, Adams and the brothers William and Samuel Jones, supplied colleges like Harvard and Dartmouth. This is not to imply that London held a monopoly of the manufacture of demonstrative apparatus. In Holland, France, Italy, Germany and even Sweden there were men who manufactured a range of instruments used to explain and illustrate scientific ideas. Much of the Dutch work is of a very high standard with the woodwork echoing contemporary styles of furniture, while the

French makers adorned some pieces with gaily painted patterns of flowers and foliage.

Other Instruments

A contrasting example is the sextant. It has remained an essential tool of the navigator since its introduction in about 1758. It was an improvement on the octant or reflecting quadrant invented in 1730 quite independently by John Hadley in London and Thomas Godfrey in Philadelphia. Unlike the Sikes hydrometer, the marine sextant has run through a series of variations to the basic idea. On design features alone it is possible to date individual instruments to within 30 years or so as a matter of course, and frequently to much closer limits. From an aesthetic point of view the most desirable sextants are those made in the last quarter of the 18th century, solely from brass, their surfaces protected by a clear lacquer.

The orrery was the first scientific instrument to represent the Copernican rather than the Ptolemaic picture of the solar system. The first orrery was made by clockmakers Thomas Tompion and George Graham whose clockwork model simulated the daily motions of the earth and the periods of the moon. Made of silver and ebony this orrery, or 'tellurium' as it was called then, is supposed to have been made for Queen Anne to give to Prince Eugène of Savoy. John Rowley copied this instrument in 1712 for Charles Boyle, fourth Earl of Cork and Orrery, hence the name. The orrery was developed by a friend of Graham, Thomas Wright, who added long moving arms carrying the planets and their moons.

The price of orreries was prohibitive for schools and it was not until 1766 that Benjamin Martin produced a less expensive range. Particularly elegant are the later orreries of George Adams Jnr and Dudley Adams.

The 18th century saw the invention of the first accurate marine chronometer, thus allowing longitude to be determined also for the first time. The first such instrument was made by John Harrison in 1735 as the result of a challenge issued by the British Government in 1713 that it would give £20,000 to the man who made the first accurate chronometer. This first chronometer was very successful on its first voyage, but it was not until Harrison had modified it three times that he was awarded the prize in 1773.

The theodolite, which was invented about 1555 by Leonard Digges, was not improved until about 1722 when a Mr Sisson made a sturdy, compact version of the instrument with a telescope and bubble level. John Bird (1709–76) was a well-known manufacturer of theodolites around the middle of the century.

Pocket globes of the earth, first made in the previous century, were becoming more popular in the 18th century with the rise in interest in astronomy and geography. They were probably invented by Joseph Moxon from Yorkshire in the second half of the 17th century. One of the earliest makers whose globes are still available to collectors today was John Senex (*fl.*1704–*ob.*1740). By trade he was a skilful engraver, making plates for mathematical works, but his speciality was globes. His attention turned to smaller globes after the French astronomer Cassini suggested that he should make compact globes for wide distribution rather than simply to make large, ornate examples for royalty.

Pocket globes of the 18th century were made in two basic designs, one with the globe simply enclosed in a ball-shaped fish-skin case, the inner surfaces of which were also engraved with the global map, and the other with the globe mounted in a cottonreel-shaped base with removable dome-shaped lid, all usually made in boxwood. Another miniature globe which appeared at this time, though not strictly a pocket globe, was the table globe, mounted in a meridian ring slotted into a horizon ring and standing on a four-footed stand with crossed stretchers.

The electrostatic generator, which was developed during the latter half of the 18th century, is an attractive example of an instrument of natural philosophy. The glass cylinder or disc, which is turned against leather rubbing cushions to generate a static charge, is mounted in a mahogany frame. There are large brass condensers set on insulating pillars of glass. It is an impressive artefact, as is its later 19th century equivalent, the influence machine. This was developed by Holz and Töpler and is familiarly known under the name Wimshurst machine, after a common late 19th century design.

Objects of Vertu

Objects of vertu is a term many people find mystifying. Although it is a definition well known among collectors, the meaning is often confused with the word 'virtue'. The expression is derived from the French word *vertu* and means a small object of beauty and rarity. In the 17th century, the word vertu, such as a 'Man of Vertu', meant that he had a particular interest in the fine arts. These objects help to provide an inkling into the elegant way of life in the 18th and 19th centuries.

Articles of a great many kinds were made and were in constant use during this period, such as *boîtes-à-mouche*, these were boxes for holding patches, *boîtes-à-rouge*, boxes for make-up, as well as many different types of receptacles for containing powder and comfits. Fine gold cases were also made for needles and wax, and called *étuis-à-cire*. Other objects included boxes for powder, pills, also vinaigrettes for scent, seals, chatelaines for watches or étuis, cane and parasol handles, scent bottles, buckles and gold boxes.

These gold boxes were often called snuff boxes, although many were never used for snuff, and were distinctive manifestations of the civilized life of the leisured rich in 18th century Europe, just as pomanders for scent had been an indispensable accessory of the Renaissance courtier 200 years before. Gold boxes tend to be studied and discussed in isolation, whereas gold chatelaines and étuis are given their rightful place in the history of jewelry. Yet the designs for étuis and gold boxes were in many cases undoubtedly made by the same craftsmen. The gold box was as much a part of a gentleman's adornment as the buckles on his shoes, the rings on his fingers and the gold cane in his hands. In consequence, the gold box may best be studied as an extension of the goldsmith's craft in the field of jewelry.

Louis XV gold and enamel snuff box, 1766.

18th Century

As with Renaissance jewels and works of art in enamel and gold, the task of establishing the country of origin for many gold boxes and small objects remains baffling. By the second half of the 18th century, most gold boxes were made in France, the main centre of objects of vertu, and bear hallmarks and maker's marks, but neither the English nor the German articles were normally marked, and the problems of attribution are very often insoluble. The development of a purely national style in this field was made difficult by the arrival of foreign craftsmen in centres such as London, Dresden and Amsterdam. Another cause for this was the influx of foreign, particularly French, engraved designs for these objects, which the local goldsmiths copied, often quite slavishly. This section discusses examples of the various styles of European and American gold boxes and objects of vertu produced from the beginning of the 18th century, and will give some idea of the various techniques employed by leading European and other goldsmiths.

Small receptacles for scent, snuff, pills and bonbons were not made in France before 1660. From the literature of the few countries where snuff-taking was well-established before this date, these appear to have been made of shell, horn and tortoiseshell rather than of the costly materials used from the beginning of the 18th century. The first boxes which could vaguely be classed as works of the goldsmith's art were made as early as 1668.

After the death in 1715 of Louis XIV, who disapproved strongly of snuff-taking, the official ban was lifted from the Court of Philippe d'Orléans during the *Régence* period which followed, and lasted until 1723. The production of small boxes began in Paris during this period. Most of the early boxes were of simple design, often in gold with the use of other materials for embellishment. These were very often in the form of scallop shells or oblong shapes chased with reliefs and set with miniatures.

Boxes set with portrait miniatures were often made to be given by the king to visiting diplomats from abroad, the lids of these boxes being set with fine enamel portraits of the king and queen and bearing the Royal Cipher and/or Coat of Arms. These miniatures were thought to have been painted mainly by Jean Petitot, who worked for the French Court from 1607 until his death in 1691. He was by far the most prolific painter of his time. Unfortunately, examples of his work set in contemporary boxes are not known to have survived, as these portraits were remounted by makers such as Adrien Maximilian Vachette at the end of the 18th century, but their general style may be inferred from slightly later examples made by Daniel Govers, who worked exclusively for the Court of Louis XV, and those made by others. Among his most important royal commissions was a box applied on the cover with a monogram of the king and queen in rubies and diamonds on a tortoiseshell ground, the gold sides enriched with enamelled shells, the interior with a double portrait of Louis XV and Queen Maria Leszczyneki. This box was not known to have been presented by the king until 1744, when it was given to a Swiss banker, Isaac De Thellusson.

Many of the recipients of such diplomatic presentation gifts sold the articles back to the French Foreign Ministry when leaving their posts, who re-used them at a later date, or if the style was by then unacceptable melted them down for the materials. By the 1730s, the effect of the Rococo movement was reflected in the design of bijouterie with such objects as boudoir clocks, scent flagons and all manner of small boxes. The first Rococo designs by Juste-Aurèle Meissonier, who lived from 1693 to 1750, displayed asymmetry, for nothing that could be gracefully curved was left straight. Although many larger domestic objects such as candelabra in ormolu survived from this period, it is sad that few truly Rococo boxes remain.

Repoussé is the word used to describe the technique of decorating the metal, where the surface is pressed forward in relief with a matted tooling in the sunken areas to give more emphasis to the raised parts. This type of repoussé decoration was England's main contribution in the field of. valuable objects of vertu. While these Rococo articles were being produced in London, utilitarian wares were being produced in the English Midlands. The Georgian enamellers who fused enamel on to copper to make hand-painted and transfer-printed wares often imitated the more costly bijouterie of the London and continental goldsmiths. The first factory producing this enamel work was at Battersea. This factory was founded by Stephen Theodore Janssen in 1753 with two partners, Brooks and Dalamain, but they were dropped from the firm after its first year of establishment. Although this venture was artistically brilliant, it suffered from commercial instability, and in 1756, three years after it was founded, it was declared bankrupt. The other main factories were Birmingham, Bilston, Liverpool and Wednesbury. These factories produced many fine enamelled wares, usually of a flamboyant nature, as many of these factories were in direct competition with the successful steel toy trade of their neighbours in Wolverhampton, Birmingham and Liverpool were the only factories that imitated the decoration of the earlier factory at Battersea.

Transfer printing, the technique by which the wares were decorated, was an English invention, although it is not certain who first devised the technique, or when, the method involves painting an engraved metal plate or 'blank' with enamel colours, transferring this to a sheet of paper and then to the surface of the porcelain or pottery and firing. The blanks, of course, made possible mass-production and Birmingham was the centre of production of the blanks.

It is often difficult for the first time collector to distinguish between Battersea and Birmingham boxes for both centres used blanks supplied by the other. The Battersea printing was usually better and very little decoration was added to the final print and where it was, only thinly applied translucent enamels were used. In Birmingham however the enamel painter often used the print as a guide to further extensive painting. The decoration on Battersea work usually consisted of classical and mythological scenes, many of them attributed to Ravenet. Birmingham boxes were made in a wider variety of shapes and sizes than in Battersea and on larger boxes and caddies the decoration was inspired by the French artists Watteau and Boucher. Many of these boxes were also decorated with well-printed flowers. The Bilston factory also had a fairly high output of these boxes, in particular snuff, sweet and patch form boxes which imitated the Meissen wares. The decoration of boxes began to change around 1770 as the new Neo-classical mood swept Europe.

Later boxes produced in England for the most part emulated French designs, or alternatively rigidly interpreted Neo-classical designs of Robert Adam, and used, in many cases, similar colourings. In France in the late 1740s, receptacles for snuff and bonbons changed shape, new fashions came in, and enamel appeared as one of the salient elements. At first it was used primarily to embellish floral motifs such as enamel flowers and birds on grounds of mother-of-pearl and lacquer. Among the most attractive examples of this style were those decorated with shells, elaborate flowers and exotic birds, the designs being raised on gold and then enamelled in naturalistic colours. These objects were among the most outstanding and distinctive ever produced.

The Royal Manufactory of porcelain at Sèvres had begun to reproduce imitation flowers in porcelain in 1748. These were apparently first ordered by Madame de Pompadour to surprise her royal lover by presenting him with a mass of summer flowers in mid winter. In ornament, it was a sign of the return to nature that was to become manifest everywhere.

Among the makers most accomplished in this technique was Jean-François Breton in the early 1750s. In the Corbeille of Marie-Joseph of Saxe, who was married in 1747, there was included a box decorated with a hawthorn spray with enamelled leaves and diamond flowers. Others were decorated with fruit as well as flowers in a similar manner. The demand for articles decorated in this manner soon greatly exceeded supply and an alternative was produced in the form of cagework bijouterie. This meant that the object could be more easily produced and a particularly popular model could be almost mass-produced in its various component parts. Occasionally, the retailer, who was not strictly allowed to do so, fitted his own panels into these cagework mounts.

German enamel scent bottle with gold mounts.

These panels were often of oriental lacquers and mother-of-pearl or under glass miniature paintings. Under Guild Law, it was illegal to replace them but it was a rule that must have been frequently contravened. Dutch subjects had been in vogue since 1738 with peasant scenes after Teniers, and subjects were often taken from the painted interiors so characteristic of Dutch painting. However, there is no doubt that this fashion was partly motivated by commercial rather than artistic reasons. During the height of its popularity, the French philosopher and author Diderot exclaimed 'I prefer rusticity to affectation. I would give ten Watteaus for one Teniers'. However, the fashion went out after 1760 as it no longer corresponded with current French taste.

Dutch boxes themselves generally lacked fine craftsmanship and the production of small boxes was restricted to those for tobacco which were very often made in materials such as wood, brass, tortoiseshell or silver. It is rare to find this type of box made purely in gold, and the few that do exist date from the middle of the 18th century and are of oblong or cushion-shape, the lids often chased or repoussé with classical or allegorical scenes and the remainder left undecorated. During the early years of the 19th century, objects were produced in small numbers in gold and decorated with engine-turnings.

French goldsmith craftsmen working during the third quarter of the 18th century developed the technique of box-making with multi-colours of gold. Paris led the rest of Europe in this technique and none of those who emulated it at a later date, not even the Swiss, could reproduce the sculptured effect that the French achieved in such perfectly balanced colours. This technique of decorating in variously coloured gold had been in existence for some time, but it did not fully come into fashion until the middle of the 1790s. The colour of gold could quite easily be changed by mixing it with other metals, the four basic colours being red, green, yellow and white.

Perhaps one of the greatest exponents of this technique, and also one of the greatest French box makers of the 18th century, was Jean Ducrollay. Much of his work dates from this period and although he used many other techniques, his multi-coloured gold articles display a sculptural quality unsurpassed during any later period. By the late 1760s the more fashionable bijouterie makers had restricted the use of four-coloured gold decoration to the more minor areas. From then the borders advertised this technique until the French Revolution. During the last quarter of the 18th century, there were predominantly two fashionable types of decoration used on boxes. In the first group, gouache miniatures under glass took the place of enamel panels. The second group consisted of portrait boxes, which had been made since Louis XIV's portraits had adorned the earliest presentation boxes, but now nearly all these small containers held items for *la toilette* and were made in cheaper materials and produced in fairly large numbers.

The one artist whose work was almost exclusively mounted in gold, as an indication of his standing, was Louis Nicholas Van Blarenberghe (1715–94). His subjects included châteaux, pastoral scenes and townscapes. The late 1760s also brought about a further change in decoration in Europe, which reverted to the Greek influence in styles, not only in objects of vertu but also the interiors of buildings, furniture, fabrics and jewelry. The fashion became so popular that the élite would have been ashamed to appear in public without a receptacle that was not *à la grecque*. The flowers that had previously decorated these articles were now replaced with laurel wreaths and Greek key patterns. Gone, too, were the Rococo shapes, for from then on boxes were either oval, circular or oblong, quite often with the corners cut to allow the ends to be decorated with Grecian pilasters. While the enamelling changed in a more subtle way, with the inevitable scene from antiquity decorating the main areas of these pieces, others were decorated with plain translucent coloured enamel areas showing engine-turned grounds to advantage.

The pinnacle of Neo-classicism before the French Revolution can best be seen in the painted cameo miniatures by Jaques-Joseph de Gault, whose work was exclusively confined to reproducing classical bacchic friezes. The change in style during the 20 years preceding the Revolution in France can best be seen in the works of such makers as Joseph-Etienne Bierzy and Jean-Joseph Barrière.

Boxes and other objects of vertu produced between 1775 and 1791 fall into two distinct groups. The first group made use of bright distinctive coloured enamels with borders of green and red enamel foliage adorned with simulated jewels such as opals, pearls, rubies and sapphires. The other style was more to the Neo-classical English taste with the wide use of single-coloured panels. A goldsmith typifying the pre-Revolution period was Adrian Maximilian Vachette, who worked from 1779 to 1830. He made very successful use of materials of earlier periods, such as oriental lacquers and miniatures by the artist Jean Petitot. His articles were always of a simple shape, often of tortoiseshell with covers or sides containing miniatures by 17th or early 18th century miniaturists. Many of his works were almost certainly made from dismantled objects, but his boxes of the early 19th century period were totally original, with portraits of Napoleon Bonaparte and other members of the Napoleonic Court.

Louis XVI gold and lacquer snuff box, 1775.

Mention must be made of the thriving industry in Germany from the middle of the 18th century. Frederick II, in order to encourage active interest in the goldsmith's craft, forbade the importation of the successful French goldsmiths' work into the country, although many of the styles used in Germany were adapted from the French originals of the day. The articles produced were generally of Baroque inspiration and were usually larger than the products they were copying. With its rich deposits of hard-stones, Bohemia could provide a great number of types of quartz such as cornelian, bloodstone, jasper and rock crystal. Objects were produced in all manner of shapes and designs to attract the collector who was doing the Grand Tour. The styles that predominated during the middle of the 18th century in Germany were those of carved work inlaid in hardstone and also the use of mother-of-pearl and shells.

As well as hardstone and porcelain objects, enamel work on copper was also being produced and the earliest of these factories producing fine enamel work was that of Fromery, in Berlin. This factory must have been the most prolific of all the establishments making enamel wares in Germany in the 18th century. The work produced was easily distinguishable from that of its competitors because of the ornamentation on most of the articles produced by Pierre Fromery and his son, Alexander, who perfected the factory's individual style. They also mounted their work in gold and silver, whereas their contemporaries rarely did so.

The workshops of Augsburg, which had produced the most magnificent silver and gold wares in the 17th century, did not retain very much of the status in the production of objects of vertu, and from the late 1740s the only items produced were those of the Du Paquier factory, many of which were only made to amuse, with painted enamel objects such as playing card boxes and shallow receptacles, painted to simulate letters.

During the Seven Years' War, 1757–63, there emerged enamel boxes with portraits of Frederick the Great and embellished with trophies of war and maps of his successful battles. This was a good way to spread propaganda for the Prussian cause. Although there were many centres in Germany producing bijouterie at this time, Berlin must have been the centre making the most magnificent of all examples of the lapidary craft. These boxes were made for Frederick II, who designed many of them himself and who was also a great patron of the arts. Dresden also became prolific in the mining of quartz and the production of boxes, and it emerged as the prime centre by the 1770s. Again appealing to the Grand

Tourist, Johann Christian Neuber produced many fine examples with the use of classical hardstone cameos in the Italian manner – portrait miniatures and intricate patterns decorating the whole surface of the box in inlaid hardstones. These were very often numbered around the mounts and were usually accompanied by explanatory booklets describing the various hardstones. These charts were concealed in the base of the article and were revealed by means of a secret catch.

Among the centres in Europe embarking at this time on the manufacture of small objects of vertu were the Swiss, who in the 1770s successfully produced multicoloured gold objects such as etuis for various materials and boxes for snuff and powder. The main decoration was classical-inspired and the use of columnar designs adorned with flowers and foliage often taken directly from French styles. This may be accounted for by the fact that many French craftsmen settled in Switzerland after the onset of the Revolution, and at this time enamelling was a prominent feature in all Swiss articles. However, they did not quite achieve the quality obtained by the French goldsmiths. Enamel had been equally prominent in the decoration of Swiss watch cases in the second half of the 17th century, but it had been allowed to become extinct, as the exposed surfaces of the enamel very soon deteriorated in constant use.

The watches made in Geneva in the late 1780s made use of transparent enamel which served as a protective covering for painted surfaces, and this made the whole technique more viable, although enamel articles produced in Switzerland were generally unmarked, except where goldsmiths tried to imitate the earlier marks that the French had used, but this was always unsatisfactory as the date letter and Fermier Generale marks rarely tallied. One of the reasons why the Swiss boxes bear pseudo-Paris hallmarks was because Geneva was under French rule during this period, and wherever the French dominated, they tried to impose their hallmarking system. Signatures do appear on landscape paintings adorning these articles, the main enamellers in this medium having been Jean Louis Richter (1766–1841) and David Etienne Roux (1758–1832).

Geneva, by the 1820s, was devoting much of its time to the manufacture of flamboyantly decorated and jewelled objects for the Turkish market, such as small enamel watches and clocks, singing bird boxes, zarfs (or coffee cup holders), gem-set bonbonnières and scent containers. These items were in many cases over-decorated with emeralds, rubies or diamonds against vivid enamel grounds. It was not until the beginning of the 19th century that boxes produced by the Swiss enamellers developed a truly recognizable style of their own. These boxes were usually of a shallow oblong or oval shape with cut corners or scalloped effects and were painted in various colours with flowers, landscapes or lakeside scenes – these studies were often signed by the artist.

Fruitwood boxes were popular from the beginning of the 18th century on the Continent. In the Low Countries, fruitwood carvers produced some attractive 'form' boxes, most notable of which are those of boats with their hulls finely carved. Ragard of Nancy was the most prolific French producer of fruitwood boxes up to 33 cm (14 in) wide decorated with low relief work. The coat-of-arms of the owner was often present among the decoration. Boxes with pressed decoration appeared around

1770. Most of these were circular, shallow and unhinged. The lids were decorated with classical motifs or portraits which, from the 1790s, became portraits of the monarchs of the time or of commemorative scenes. Napoleon-headed boxes, since they were produced in greater quantities than those of other heads-of-state, are the ones most likely to be found by the collector today.

Tortoiseshell had been used in England since the mid-17th century when it was imported from Jamaica. It was an emigré Huguenot in London, John Obrisset, who became one of the first craftsmen to use both tortoiseshell and horn. His first horn boxes with moulded portrait heads as decoration appeared around 1690. Tortoiseshell was more popular than horn and by the end of the 17th century *piqué* boxes were being made in Holland, France and England. A typically English tortoiseshell box was bun-shaped and was squeezed at its end to remove the lid. *Piqué point* was introduced early in the 18th century as was the technique known as 'hairwork' in which threads of silver and gold were let into the surface of the shell.

American boxes and objects of vertu are little known, but a few fine examples by such makers as Jacob Hurd are in a number of museums in America. The best known example is in the Museum of Fine Arts, Boston; it is engraved with a coat of arms and was presented to William Drummer, Lieutenant-General, Massachusetts (1716–30). Other makers of Freedom boxes (these were boxes presented when high officials were given the Freedom of a city or state) include Charles Le Roux, who was the master goldsmith in New York and was apparently the only maker of Freedom Boxes from the period 1720–43. In the 1780s, Jacob Gerritse Langing was recorded as having made gold Freedom Boxes.

During the last quarter of the 19th century, simple engine-turned boxes for snuff and cachous were produced in fair numbers. Mexico City was also concerned during the latter part of the 18th century and the beginning of the 19th century in the making of small gold objects. In 1786, an Academy was founded there and staffed mainly by European instructor-craftsmen, and the designs bear a very great similarity to European taste. The most interesting and original objects to be produced were boxes to contain cheroots. These boxes were of cylindrical shape with oval cross section and flip-up lid decorated with multi-coloured gold garlands and foliate ornament, and set with square or cushion-shaped diamond thumb-pieces. Objects produced in Mexico were usually hallmarked and consequently dating of these pieces is fairly accurate.

By the 1820s, the fashion was turning from snuff-taking to other forms of indulgence, such as cigarettes and cheroots. In consequence, receptacles for containing these were devised by the goldsmiths of the day. From the onset of the Victorian period, and with the more severe styles of the following decades, there was little demand for elaborate small boxes and associated objects until Peter Carl Fabergé revived and elaborated these objects of vertu. It was not until the Paris Exhibition of 1900 that Fabergé's objects became widely seen and admired outside Russia.

Peter Carl Fabergé was the leading Russian goldsmith during the second half of the 19th century. The Fabergé family originated from

Picardy and with many other Huguenot families fled from France following the Revocation of the Edict of Nantes in 1685, and later settled in St Petersburg, where they became Russian citizens. Fabergé was born on the 30 May, 1846. He was sent to study the goldsmiths' and lapidary craft in all the main centres of Europe and on his return worked under the manager of his father's shop until 1870, when he was given the position as head of the entire concern at the age of 24. The same year, the 'English shop', which was run by two Englishmen called Nichols and Plincke who had run a fashionable jewellers in St Petersburg, was closed and the Court transferred its enthusiasm and patronage to the jewelry and objects produced by Carl Fabergé. It was not until 1884 that Fabergé made his real breakthrough, when he produced a jewelled Easter egg, commissioned by Alexander III for his wife, Maria Feodorovna. This was the first Easter egg of its type to be made, and during the reign of Alexander III and the last Czar, Nicholas II, 55 other eggs were produced.

The Easter celebrations, which are taken more seriously in Russia than in any other country in Europe, are more joyous and holy than Christmas. Easter is also the climax of the Orthodox Church Year, and brought about the lavish giving of presents. A great many more simple eggs than these costly objects given by the Czars were produced for presentation to the whole Court, often in porcelain, and papier-mâché, as well as gold and enamel.

It was the success of these presentation gifts that inspired the Czar to grant a Royal Warrant to the Fabergé firm. Fabergé was undoubtedly the most prolific maker of fine objects during any period and as a craftsman and designer must be placed at the forefront of the 19th-century craftsmen reviving styles of previous periods, but his inspirations were mainly taken from French 18th-century originals and his designs were rarely totally original in all respects. Fabergé produced an enormous range of different objects, including cigarette cases, pill boxes, parasol handles, hardstone animals, snuff boxes, scent bottles, bell pushes, miniature frames, glue pots and stamp dampeners – all of which achieved great distinction in their own right. From 1900 and until the outbreak of war in 1914, the Fabergé workshops were still producing many fine objects to satisfy the demands of European royalty and nobility, but gradually the demand dwindled for such luxurious objects, as twinges of social conscience made themselves felt; and the final blow was dealt by the Revolution. Fabergé escaped to Switzerland under the guise of a diplomat where he died two years later.

Apart from Fabergé, the other silver and goldsmiths, such as Khlebnikov, Ovtchinnikoff Sasikoff and co-operative groups, produced silver and enamel objects mainly in the old Russian style.

An example of the five main marks found on English gold and silver boxes: quality mark, town mark, date letter, maker's mark and duty mark.

Chinese Snuff Bottles

Historians are uncertain as to when the use of tobacco, and particularly snuff, began in China; while it may have been given to the Chinese Court as a gift by foreigners in the 16th century, it is generally acknowledged that the use of snuff did not become popular until the middle of the 19th century. Despite the fact that the earliest dated bottles are from the reign of Shun-chih (1644–61), many authorities believe that the use of snuff dates from later in that century and that these bottles would have been used for a different purpose.

The period during which snuff bottles were made corresponds roughly to the Ch'ing Dynasty and it seems that until the middle of the 18th century the centre of snuff use was Peking in Northern China. Snuff bottles from the Kang Hsi reign (1662–1722) are rare and it was not until the reign of Ch'ien Lung (1736–95), when the arts of China were raised to a high level of perfection and snuff-taking was widely popular, that bottles were made in any quantity. It is these bottles and even more commonly those of the 19th century that the collector is likely to find fairly readily available.

The Ch'ien Lung emperor Hung Li was probably the first emperor to more than occasionally indulge in snuff-taking and it is known that his corrupt chief minister managed to build a collection of 2,390 snuff bottles, details of which were regrettably never recorded. By 1800 snuff-taking was a part of Chinese life and remained so for the next hundred years. The really prolific period of snuff bottle manufacture was in the years 1821–50.

As a rule of thumb, the first porcelain bottles were made in the late 18th century and first half of the 19th, the first enamel bottles between 1750 and 1800, the first glass bottles between 1730 and 1850 and the first interior painted bottles after 1840.

The range of materials used to make snuff bottles is enormous but they have been broken down into eight categories: glass; porcelain and Yi-hsing; gem, stone, rock and fossil; organic material; metal; embellished; interior painted and enamel. The variations on these make a full list impossible here, but glass, for instance, includes cameo, carved celadon, crizzled, enamelled, marbled, opalescent, translucent, transparent and so on. Organic materials include bamboo, betel nut, boxwood, gourd, various horns, ivories and tusks, lacquer, walnut and shell. Embellished bottles will have one or more of the following decorations: damascene, inlaid wood, lacquer or metal, lacquer and nacre and mother-of-pearl. The shape of bottles is even more difficult to classify and no two bottles are exactly alike. Probably the commonest shapes are circular, oval or spade; octagonal, hexagonal, pear or vase-shaped are also quite common.

The decorative motifs on bottles abound with the rich symbolism found in all branches of the decorative arts in China, many of which have been discussed in other sections on Chinese art. Additional motifs found on

224

bottles are worth detailing here. Colour is important to the Chinese, the five primary colours being red, blue (including green), yellow, white and black. Red is the emblem of joy and symbolizes virtue especially truth and sincerity; blue symbolizes heaven, white the moon, black was evil, yellow was the Royal Ch'ien Lung colour and green was the Royal colour of the Ming Dynasty.

Several humans and gods are also portrayed: the Eight Immortals of Taoism, notably Li T'ieh-kuai appears as a beggar with a crutch carrying a gourd from which a manuscript is escaping; Chou Ko-Liang, a famous philosopher of the Three Kingdoms period (220–c.280), is shown riding on a donkey accompanied by servants; Liu Kai, a minister of state in the 10th century is represented with his foot resting on a toad and holding a ribbon strung with five gold coins, for he is the patron of merchants and wealth.

Glass was one of the commonest materials used for snuff bottles and in fact one hears little of glass in China until it was used for snuff bottles. There is some dispute as to whether the earliest glass bottles were carved and later ones blown or vice versa. Regardless of the question of dating however, blown glass bottles can often be recognized by the streaking at the base of the bottle where it was connected to the rod.

The Chinese were masters of imitation and applied their skill to glass bottles by using various metallic oxides to colour the glass. By using opacifying agents as well they were able to imitate porcelain, agate and, notably, jade, which in the best examples is difficult to distinguish from the real thing. Certainly the first-time collector should be on his guard when offered jade bottles.

The glass bottles of the late 18th and early 19th century are unequalled in form and technique. A favourite colour of this period was the 'imperial yellow', which after the Ch'ien Lung emperor's death was used by others outside the court. Overlay glass bottles rank as some of the most attractive of all the snuff bottles, the technique involving the use of one or more layers of different coloured glass over the basic bottle. The technique was used to make cameo-style bottles as well. The highest number of overlays known is four, though some experts believe five may have occasionally been used. The basic colours of overlay glass were clear, white or milk glass, sometimes with the inclusion of bubbles. Variations on overlay bottles include multi-coloured single overlay and seal-type overlay which bear the names or seals of non-imperial workers.

Few porcelain bottles were made before the reign of Yung Cheng (1723–35). The earliest porcelain bottles were said to be jade green followed later by blue, white, purple, yellow and brown. They were not made in quantity until the late 18th century. Porcelain bottles are divided into four categories: moulded and carved, enamelled, underglazed and monochrome or glazed without design. Moulded bottles seem to have appeared in the reign of Chia Ch'ing (1796–1820) and can sometimes be recognized by examining the interior for join marks or signs that the join has been smoothed away. Yi-hsing is a type of earthenware produced near a village of the same name close to Shanghai and while not as aesthetically appealing as other ceramic bottles is of value to the dedicated collector.

Fans

Most of the ancient civilizations of the world have used the fan at some period in their development. The early history of the fan is unknown but it was almost certainly derived from the use of plant leaves to cause a movement of the air. The word 'fan' comes from the Latin *vannus*, which means an instrument for winnowing grain, but whether this usage reflects the first use of fans is uncertain. It is likely that the Chinese and Japanese have the longest continual history of fan use, which in China may date back to at least 2500 B.C. The Japanese were the first to invent the folding fan in the 7th century A.D. The early fans from both countries were made in a wide variety of materials, designs and techniques, reflecting somewhat the social importance that was long attached to the fan. For the Japanese, for instance, the fan is full of symbolism: the rivet-end is seen as the beginning of life and as the fan widens it reflects the widening choices and experiences of life.

In the Middle East the fan may have started life as a fly-whisk, varieties of which are still used throughout Africa today. The sophisticated Egyptians were probably the first to make advances on fly-whisk design and their personal fans became semi-circular structures which fitted into long ivory or wooden handles. Similar fans spread into Rome, Greece and southern Europe, where, as in Egypt they began to gain some symbolic and ritual importance. The *flabellum*, or fly-whisk, was used in the Christian churches until the 15th century, its function being to keep insects out of the chalice during services.

In the 16th century, as the use of the ecclesiastical fan finally died out, the Portuguese reached Japan and China and were able to bring back examples of folding fans. For the next century and a half fans remained very much the plaything of the rich, their surfaces set with gems and precious metals and their handles of ivory, gold and silver. The first folding fans in England probably came from Italy via France in the second half of the 16th century. The most fashionable type of fan in this period was the feather fan made from peacock, ostrich and parakeet feathers. Decoupé fans of paper or vellum appeared in the late 16th century although only two examples from that century are known to exist today. By the 17th century fans were indispensable for the fashion conscious woman and the most widely used type was now the folding fan.

By the reign of Henri IV in France (1589–1610) the fan industry had grown to such an extent that it was necessary to regulate it by law. By 1753 there were over 150 master fan makers in Paris alone.

The first specifically French fan was the so-called brisé type which consisted of many wide continuous sticks and lacked a mount. The continuous surface was ideal for painting. Although they were first made in the 17th century the collector is unlikely to come across examples earlier than the 18th century. Most notable of the brisé fans are *Vernis Martin* which are skilfully painted in thin oil colours and the whole surface then coloured and gilded and coated with a special varnish de-

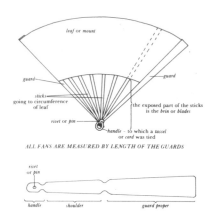

Diagram of how the popular 18th-century brisé *fans were made.*

226

vised by the Martin brothers *c.*1720. The predominant colours of these fans are dark greens and blues.

By the reign of Louis XVI brisé fans had become smaller and their decoration inspired more by Chinese openwork ivory fans. French openwork is characterized by the use of three medallion motifs linked by garlands of flowers often carved in very low relief. The medallions were usually portraits or rural scenes and sometimes bridal scenes.

The French ivory workers of this period were finely skilled, piercing diaper patterns of thread-like thickness. Flat-piercing of horn was employed while less formal fans of perforated cedar and satinwood, either painted or engraved, were made. Cabriolet fans appeared in the mid-18th century. Reversible fans, which could be opened either way thus offering two pictures, were made late in the century from either ivory or sandalwood with the typical three medallion motifs. After the French Revolution French fans underwent considerable changes becoming smaller and less well-painted. It was not until the 1830s that high-quality fans were again produced.

The use of the fan in Europe is most closely identified with the Spanish for it was in their country that fans were most widely used. A high proportion of their carved ivory fans were imported from France and finished by Spanish workers. Spanish fans are characterized by being a little larger and darker than other European ones as well as by having unusual leaf to stick proportions. Painted decoration is often less skilful than on the average French fan. Popular themes included the bull ring, scenes of royalty, great battles and national triumphs.

Boxes

One of the many new and extraordinary wonders Columbus' sailors reported seeing on their travels was the natives of Haiti taking snuff. That was the beginning of a huge tobacco trade which was to have an impact throughout the world. And as a result of that trade we have a rich legacy of snuff boxes to collect and admire.

The tobacco Columbus saw being grown at Haiti was being used both as a narcotic and as a medicament, and news of its properties soon spread. By the 1550s seeds had reached Portugal, probably from Brazil, and from Portugal they reached France in 1560, when the French Ambassador sent home leaves of the plant and instructions on how to cultivate tobacco. The ambassador's name was Jean Nicot and from his name derives the word 'nicotine'. On its arrival in Europe tobacco was generally bought from apothecaries' shops, because it was prized as a medicine.

Until Virginia tobacco began arriving in England in about 1615 Spain and Portugal had a virtual monopoly of tobacco imports from the New World and the habit spread more quickly in Catholic than in Protestant countries. Snuff was made in Tuscany, where tobacco is still grown, and as far away as Russia both smoking and snuff taking were well established by the middle of the 17th century.

By this time the use of tobacco as a medicament had died out and it was frowned on by the churches because its efficacy as a narcotic had been learnt from suspect magic-invoking ceremonies practised by heathen natives. Europeans had become addicted to a pleasant social habit, however, and smoking tobacco and taking snuff stayed on. In America, snuff taking was never very popular, and their tobacco was either smoked or chewed.

In the second half of the 17th century snuff taking became popular in France and from there the habit spread all over Europe during the next hundred years, and it was only in the 1780s when cigarettes were introduced from Turkey and cigars from South America, that snuff taking went out of fashion. During the 150 or so years that the fashion lasted goldsmiths produced superb snuff boxes and French gold boxmakers took their art further than it had ever been taken before, using matchless skills to make boxes of the greatest beauty.

Snuff box carved from agate with gold mounts, German, c.1760.

French goldsmiths belonged to the most rigorously regulated of all guilds, and were members of the only French guild to survive the revolution and continue into the 19th century. Apprenticeship was long and the number of masters limited, penalties for infringement of the guild's regulations were severe, and substandard work could be punished by a sentence in the galleys. By 1740 a special category was created within the guild for those goldsmiths who made only boxes, and each of the techniques used in making a box was practised by a craftsman who specialized only in that particular technique. Each gold box therefore embodied a sum of many expert hands.

A snuff box had to have many attributes. The box had to be airtight and the lid had to fit without a catch: the join between lid and box had to be invisible when the box was closed. When it was open the box had to balance in the hand while it was offered in the complicated ballet-like etiquette of snuff taking. To achieve this balance the hinge, often invisible on the closed box, had to open to a wide angle. In addition, the box itself had to be decorated in the latest fashion to please the intellectual, cultivated, capricious and wealthy society that demanded and got the highest standards in design and execution. Boxes were 'worn' and were made in different styles for men and women, for winter and summer, for different clothes and different occasions, for carrying in a special pocket or for putting on the writing or toilet table. Quite obviously one box would be insufficient for all these demands and a snuff taker would have a range: indeed when Count Brul's effects were sold at his death in 1763, 700 boxes were included in the sale.

Not all boxes were for snuff, they were made also for patches, for rouge, for sweets: Louis XIV disliked snuff exceedingly, so courtiers would take dragees to sweeten their breath. Very occasionally an old box still gives off a scent of aniseed (with which they were flavoured) when it is opened. An acceptable way for a king to give a tip was to present a box with a royal portrait which could easily be removed if the box was exchanged for cash. The amount of decoration was graded to the importance of the recipient: about 1775 the Sardinian ambassador in Paris received the same box three times ever increasingly decorated with diamonds as his position grew in importance, and which each time he sold back to the Royal office from which it came. In general, gem decorated boxes went out of fashion in France in the 1740s because Frederick the Great of Prussia and the Empress Elizabeth of Russia so overloaded boxes with precious stones that they became vulgar.

Early French boxes were often made of tortoiseshell or mother-of-pearl, with delicate designs inlaid in gold: they were also made of semi-precious stone like agate or rock crystal from Germany. Boxes were also made wholly of textured gold chased or engraved with an all over pattern, sometimes to resemble watered silk, sometimes a sunburst. On this surface a design would be applied, a scene perhaps, or a trophy, which was further enhanced by its being executed in *quatre couleur* gold or in enamels. Two enamel techniques were used, either *basse-taille* enamelling, where the translucent enamel was fired and rubbed down level with the rest of the surface of the box, or enamelling *en plein* when an opaque colour was fired to the gold base and further colours painted on to this surface: Pastoral or genre scenes deriving from Watteau, Boucher or Teniers, and floral and chinoiserie subjects were much used.

Gradually the practice grew of making gold box frames and of fitting into this cage-work decorative panels of imported Japanese lacquer or of semi-precious stones, plaques of porcelain decorated in enamel colours or painted miniatures. This encroachment on its regulations was naturally resisted by the goldsmiths' guild, but in 1855 it had to give way and accept a fait accompli. The practice of making boxes *à cage* had been fostered by the *marchands merciers*, middlemen who dealt in all the objects with which these decorative panels were made and who were extremely influential. Much more flexibility in the use of decorative material now became possible, and the cage technique allowed panels to be renewed without destroying the very expensively decorated gold cage. The cage itself changed from the 1760s, in keeping with the general Neo-classical trend, and became more overtly architectural with the division between the lid and the body of the box becoming part of the architectural design.

It followed that in the second half of the century the shapes of boxes changed also, the undulating Baroque and Rococo cartouche shape and the simple round or rectangular box changed, in the main, to the shape of an oval or to that of a rectangle with canted corners. Oval boxes were often decorated with a central medallion of a classical subject either in painted enamel colours or in *grisaille* to imitate a classical cameo. In general, boxes were decorated with subjects taken from paintings and engravings in the current cultural repertoire. An exception is to be found in the superlative work of the van Blarenberghe family who produced gouache miniatures of their own composition for the panels of gold boxes. These miniatures are among the most interesting of 18th century paintings: one box, which originally belonged to Mme de Pompadour shows the unveiling of a statue of Louis XV in what is now Place Vendôme in Paris, another shows the French sculptor Falconet's statue of Peter the Great in St Petersburg. Two boxes, one of which is in the Wrightsman collection in New York, show the town and country houses of the Duc de Choiseul and give valuable documentary evidence about French furniture and furnishings of the early Neo-classical period.

18th Century

Contrary to what might be supposed, Napoleon needed gold boxes to give away as much as his Bourbon predecessors had done and the power the goldsmiths' guild still held over its members meant that early 19th century work continued as fine as before.

The Swiss became clever plagiarizers of French designs and techniques and their boxes with musical or watch movements were popular in the 19th century, partly because the Swiss makers undercut the French by using gold of a lower carat than was permitted in France.

Russian boxes were derived from French originals or made by French goldsmiths working in Russia, though they are characterized by a much greater use of diamond embellishment than would have been tolerated in France. Boxes made by Fabergé at the end of the 19th century were in direct emulation of 18th century French boxes, Fabergé having been challenged by the Czar to do so. Where the current Art Nouveau style was allowed free play, for example in a blue enamel cigarette case asymmetrically encircled by a diamond snake, the combination of contemporary design with high technique was extremely successful.

Probably the earliest surviving English snuff box is one in the Wallace Collection in London which is bottle-shaped and made of fish skin decorated with the Royal cipher in tiny gold nails. A much quoted reference from the 2nd Earl of Ailesbury's memoirs tells us why such boxes were made for the king: the Duke of Lauderdale was continually

Wooden boxes, such as cutlery and tobacco boxes, also reached a high level of craftsmanship.

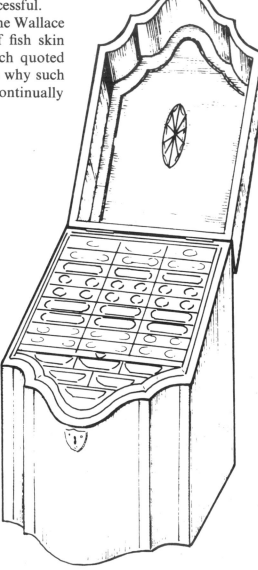

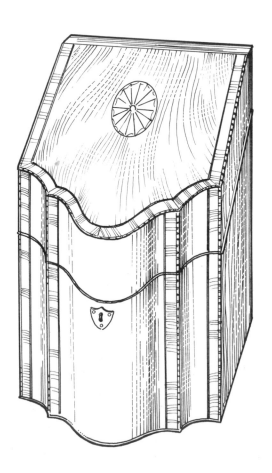

putting his finger into the king's snuff box, which obliged him to order one to be made which he wore on a string on his wrist, and did not open, but the snuff came out by shaking.

Gold boxes of high quality were made in England in the late 17th and early 18th century. In the first quarter of the century gold and silver boxes were either rectangular, oval or bow-fronted and the decoration was usually restricted to a coat-of-arms or an engraved monogram. Lozenge-shaped boxes with inset agate panels were fashionable in Queen Anne's reign and their wide gold borders were engraved or chased.

English stone and gold boxes mounted *en cage* are often difficult to distinguish from similar boxes made in Dresden, where the design for these boxes usually originated. In difficult cases a gold standard test can be used, the English standard at this time being 22 carats while those from Dresden were 18 carats. English boxes with more stone than gold, weight for weight, were not required to be hallmarked.

Just as in Holland, there was a long tradition of repoussé work in high relief in England and boxes of various shapes decorated in this way with classical or mythological motifs became popular around the middle of the century. The influence of the Rococo reached England at this time and many boxes were clearly influenced by Meisonnier and the painter Watteau. Much of the stonework in these boxes was done by Italians resident in England.

In England in the 18th century gold boxes were 'worn' as they were in France and the best, for example by Moser and by Moriset, were equal to the French boxes from which they derived. James Cox specialized in larger boxes incorporating clocks, often made for the export market. George IV had a large collection of superb French boxes which unfortunately were melted down by his hiece, Queen Victoria.

In England and America in the 18th and early 19th centuries, when a man was honoured by being given the freedom of a city, the scroll on which the honour was recorded was presented to him in a gold or silver box. 'Freedom' boxes, as they were called, were the size of large snuff boxes and were obviously designed to be used subsequently as such. These were either oval, with a loose cover, or rectangular and were decorated with the shield of arms of the town or city conferring the honour.

The enthusiasm of the Dresden craftsmen for the semi-precious stones found locally is reflected in the wide variety of shapes and sizes of the boxes they fashioned – baskets, shoes, bases, frogs and skulls to name but a few. A popular Dresden technique was to cement carved stone motifs to stone-panelled boxes. The boxes of Benjamin Gottlob Hoffman are a particularly beautiful example of this technique. One of his boxes, now in the possession of the Queen of Denmark, has panels of translucent cream quartz decorated with sapie, green jasper and carrot-coloured sardonyx moths. Other examples of his work use beetles, dragonflies and ladybirds as decorative motifs.

Dresden goldsmiths were also renowned for their use of a technique called *Zellenmosaik* (cell-mosaic) which is not unlike Italian *pietra dura* work. The boxes, usually oval or round, are made up from small, shaped sections of different coloured stones held by fine gold webbing similar to cloisonné. *Zellenmosaik* was perfected by Heinrich Taddel and the few surviving examples of his work show a preference for rural and pastoral mosaic scenes. Johann Christian Neuber (1736–1808) was also a renowned worker in *Zellenmosaik* and his first known box was made in 1770. An interesting feature of many of his boxes is that he chose the stones for their local interest. Numbers referring to each type of stone were engraved on the gold divisions and inside the box would be a book-let giving the key to the stones. Often the booklet would be hidden in a secret compartment or drawer.

Frederick the Great, whose only hobby in life was collecting boxes, had a collection of some 1,500 and his enthusiasm led him to found an industry making boxes in Berlin. Many of the boxes were designed by Frederick himself. Berlin boxes are characterized by a technique called *reliefmosaik*, which involved materials such as ivory, mother-of-pearl, and coral to the body of stone and gold boxes.

Box of agate with gold and diamond mounts made for Frederick the Great c.1750.

Musical Instruments

Musical instruments are fascinating objects. They range from the simplest instruments, which are designed to be solely utilitarian, to the most sophisticated ones, made and decorated by highly skilled craftsmen. The story of the development of musical instruments is fascinating, and many discussed below were used in folk music as well as in orchestras today.

The early history of instruments in Europe relies largely on musical representations in painting, sculpture and other branches of the visual arts. This is because few instruments have survived from early periods, due to their fragile construction. Also, they were often remodelled into other instruments as soon as they became unfashionable; lutes, for example, were rebuilt into hurdy-gurdies.

In the medieval period, manuscripts form a very valuable source of historical information. When illustrating Biblical scenes, artists often depicted the instruments they knew. Grotesques and other amusing creatures were featured in the margins, playing the instruments. Some-times these representations are not reliable evidence for the musical historian. The length of a trumpet or a bagpipe drone might be exag-gerated to provide a border to the page, or for dramatic effect.

Instruments were also used in still-life paintings; those by Baschenis were composed entirely of musical instruments. Italian wood intarsias of the 15th and 16th centuries included them, and in the 19th century inlaid work to decorate cabinets again used them. Often, this inlaid work was used to decorate the cabinets of musical-boxes. In the designs, lyres, lutes, sheet-music scrolls, aeolian harps, violins, oboes, trumpets and military drums are found. Pottery figurines also make use of musicians and their instruments. In paintings, a pastoral atmosphere is sometimes created by the inclusion of a bagpiper, or in a portrait the sitter might be posed by or with a much-prized instrument.

Right: *English mourning brooch, c.1780, made of enamelled gold set with pearls and tiny diamonds.*
Following pages: Left: *Diamond and silver pendant made in England during the early 18th century.*

Right: *Louis XV ormolu and porcelain mantel clock, the Meissen ground by Scaramouche.*

posite: Decorative boxes from
many (top), Russia (third row left)
France. Dating from the mid-18th
ury they show the superb quality
eved by the goldsmiths and enamellers
he time.

: Two gold watches by London
ers: a repeating lever watch in
-hunter case by Edward Ashley (left)
one with an 'up and down' dial to
w when it needs rewinding (right).

ht: Various Victorian watch-
ements: lever winding mechanism
), minute-repeating mechanism
tre left). Early mass-produced watch
tre right) and a top-quality movement
ked at Kew Observatory, hence the
'W A'.

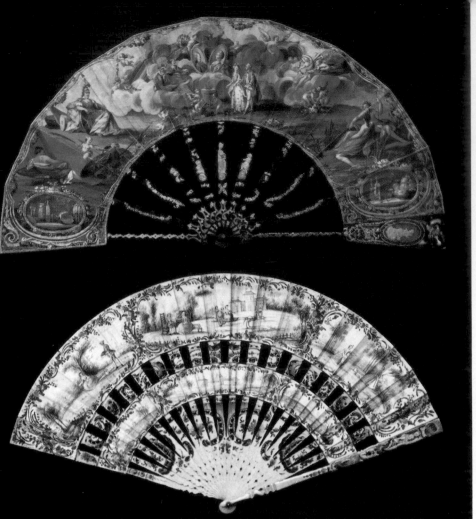

Examples of late 18th-century fans,
showing the variety and quality achieved
in this period. Particularly fine is the
battoir-type fan (top left) showing an
allegory of the wedding between the
Dauphin and Marie Antoinette.
Opposite: *Nest of tables in papier-mâché
c.1960. One has an inlaid mother of pearl
chess board.*

Instruments from the 18th century onwards are to be found in greater numbers; they sometimes are to be found in small music shops, antique markets or auctions. This survey traces the development of the instruments from the 17th century, together with some mention of contemporary folk instruments. The instruments can be grouped together, according to the manner in which the sounds are produced – percussion (bells and gongs), drums, strings and wind.

The first group of instruments are the autophones, these include rattles, bells, gongs, musical-boxes and musical glasses. These are all the instruments which, when struck, produce sound by vibrating. The most familiar members of this group are bells, gongs and musical boxes. Bells can be made out of many materials, the most common being metal. Using casting methods such as *cire perdue* it is possible to design them with very ornate decoration; bells from Tibet and Burma use this technique. In England, large pellet and clapper bells were used on harness for horses. Some of these were made at Robert Wells' foundry at Aldbourne, Wiltshire, England; they were justly famed in the 18th century for their fine tone.

Bells have also been made of pottery. For example, those used in festivities in Naples at the feast of Piedigrotta. Glass bells became very popular in the last century.

Wooden bells and gongs are found in many countries. Some of the bells used on cattle are quite simple in design. The Chinese *Mu-ju* which became popular in dance bands is a very beautiful instrument. The curved fish is to represent wakeful attention and it was originally used as a temple bell. Also from China is the *tamtam*. This is a large flat gong with a shallow rim. Only a few of the best quality came from China to the West; they were expensive to produce and the secrets of their manufacture were known only to a few. The best of these were engraved with a dragon, the rank of the owner shown by the number of the creature's claws.

Musical-boxes have a great fascination for collectors. In the centre of the box is a metal comb which is plucked. Early examples had each tooth fastened individually, but by 1820–30 most combs were formed as a single unit. The 19th century saw the greatest development of new effects; the instruments were also given more elaborate boxes and cabinets. In the early 19th century, the boxes were quite plain, the tone of the movement soft and sweet, but later a harsher tone with great brilliance was achieved. Principal areas of manufacture in the period 1790 to 1820 were Geneva and St Croix. From 1830 to 1860 some of the finest boxes were made by Nicole Frères, Lecoultre and Duconmum Girod.

The international expositions resulted in a large number of inlaid box cases from 1860 to 1870, and the 1870s saw the period of greatest elegance and use of mechanical devices. Makers of that era were Paillard, Bremond, Allard, Baker-Troll and Greiner. The end of the century marked the end of popularity of the large cylinder movements, and the subsequent use of discs. The disc movement was first developed in the 1880s, and these were developed by the firms of Polyphon, Symphonica and Regina.

The second group of instruments is the membranophones – those having a skin which vibrates when struck, drums being the main example.

Top: *Louis XV gold and enamel snuffbox made in Paris by Jean-Marie Tiron, c.1755–56.*
Below: *Four views of an elaborately chased snuffbox in the chinoiserie manner.*

18th Century

The orchestral side-drum developed from the drums used by the Regiments of Foot. The ancestor of this was the medieval double-skinned drum, called a tabor or tabret. Across one of the skins, the lower one in the case of the side-drum, is stretched a snare which causes a rattling sound. Tabors, which are still used in popular music, vary considerably in diameter and depth. The strings used to tighten the skin make criss-cross patterns, often emphasized when the instrument is used decoratively. The orchestral timpani were preceded by the cavalry's kettle drums.

Kettledrum illustrated in Museum Musicum, *1732.*

The large kettle drum was introduced by the Arabs for mounted use and they were played in pairs. They were brought to Europe in the second half of the 15th century and were modified so that they could be placed on an iron stand for concert or church performances, while those intended for orchestral use only were given fixed iron legs. Kettle drums dating from the 16th century had their tensioning screws turned by a separate key, a method which remains in use today on cavalry drums. 17th and 18th century kettle drums were smaller than later ones, the largest having an average diameter of 60 cm (24 in). 'Great kettle drums', made in the 18th century, had diameters over 100 cm (40 in).

The bass drum was first used in the West in the second half of the 18th century, the earliest known specimen dating from 1783. The drum varied considerably between the period of its introduction and the advent of the military version, c.1850. Early models were described as long drums, the wooden shell being 65–75 cm (26–30 in) long with a diameter of 58 cm (27 in). By the end of the first quarter of the 19th century it had become wider and shorter. The modern shallow-shelled bass drum was introduced in mid-century. Unlike the side-drum which was carried against the thigh, the bass drum has a metal ring at the centre of the shell so that it can be carried across the chest.

The tambourine was introduced into Europe from the Middle East in the late 18th century at a time when there was a rise in interest in Turkish music. The European version does not have snares, instead having five pairs or two rows of five jangles. The instrument is a descendant of the hand frame drum of the Eastern Mediterranean.

Instruments in the group of chordophones produce sounds through the vibration of strings. In some, the strings are plucked, such as lutes, guitars, clavichords and harpsichords. In others they are hit – dulcimers and pianos – while with the violin they are bowed.

The lute was introduced to Europe at the end of the 13th century from the Arab civilization. Good lutes are extremely fragile, as the best sound is obtained from thinly wooded instruments. This in-built fragility means that early examples of lutes are very rare. The most famous school of lute makers was at Bologna, where Laux Maler, and his son Sigismund, flourished in the early 16th century. In the second half of the 16th century a large form, the theorbo was invented.

The lute was at its most popular from the 15th to the end of the 17th century, although they were still being made in the mid-18th century. The European version is somewhat different from the Arab one, the latter being played with a plectrum and the former with the fingers, so that it was necessary to alter the tuning. In the mid-16th century the great centres of lute-making were Venice, Padua and Rome. The craftsmen of these centres were mainly of German extraction like Maler, as were the craftsmen of Lyon, the main French centre.

The theorbo, invented in the 16th century, has a longer neck than the normal lute, the main courses being quite long and an upper peg-box providing the long basses. The two heads of the theorbo can be made in either of two ways: with a 'straight' head or a 'junked' head. Small versions of the theorbo, called *tiorbini*, with bodies some 36–40 cm (14–16 in) long. The *chitarone* is a taller version of the theorbo, 175–200 cm (70–80 in) high with the peg boxes having a 'straight' head.

Bass theorbos were over 1.52 metres (5 ft) long, and they continued in use in song accompaniment and continuo until the end of the 18th century.

The mandore is a round-bodied instrument resembling a miniature lute. They were less important musically than the lute, but those made from the late 17th century compensate for this with their use of lavish ornamentation. Manores differ from mandolins in having their gut strings tied to the bridge; mandolins have some metal strings as well, all the strings being fastened to the bottom of the instrument. Early mandores had four or five strings, while in the second half of the 17th century some instruments came to have five or six strings. The 18th century version with six double courses came to be known as the Milanese mandolin and remained popular for most of that century.

The Neapolitan mandolin has several characteristics: the body, with up to 35 ribs deepens in its lower part; the sound hole is fully open and is oval in later examples. The belly has a tortoiseshell plate inlaid to protect the wood and the head is flat and had rear pegs until the invention of machine heads in the 19th century. The fretting is almost always of metal or ivory.

The origins of the guitar are obscure though it has been suggested that it was introduced into Spain by the Arabs. Four wooden instruments excavated in Egypt and subsequently dated at around the 4th–8th centuries, have built-up bodies, an incurve of the ribs and long, narrow necks. Without additional evidence however, it is assumed that the guitar developed from the *guitarra latina* or gittern of 13th century Spain. The first guitar of musical importance was the Spanish *vihuela* which was used in place of the lute in Spain during the later 15th century and into the 16th century. Metal strings have been used on guitars since at least the 17th century, such strings being more effective in hot climates than gut strings. One of the earliest metal-string guitars was the Italian *chitarra battente*, which, like the mandolin, had the strings attached to the base. The back of the instruments is vaulted and there are as many as fifteen pegs.

Towards the end of the 18th century the guitar began to evolve again, heralding the great age of guitars. Several features rapidly changed – vaulted backs were no longer used, sound holes were completely open and the stringing was changed from double course to six strings before 1800, the latter innovation probably occurring in France or Italy rather than Spain. The figure-of-eight head appeared shortly after 1800. The creator of the modern Spanish guitar is said to be Antonio Torres. Working in the mid-19th century, he enlarged the lower part of the body, relocated the bridge developing the tied bridge and keeping pegs rather than using machine heads.

There have been many variations on the shape of the guitar, notably the German *Mappengitarre*, which has the upper swell of the body reduced to points. Round and crescent bodies were also made, in addition to which there were the lyre-guitars of the early 19th century and the American 'harp-guitar', dating from *c*.1834.

The term lyre-guitar is often used to describe a number of instruments built between *c*.1770 and *c*.1840 which were popular among fashionable women as a result of the new Neo-classical mood that swept the decorative arts at this time. The so-called French lyre resembles the classical Grecian lyre more closely than other variants, having a wide body whose shoulders become two curving arms which support the head, from which the fretboard descends towards the body without reaching it.

The lyre-guitar proper is really a six-stringed guitar on which the arms reach upwards as in the French lyre, but are hollow and form part of the soundbox. The arms do not meet the head directly, connecting instead by cross-pieces or bars. A variation is the Apollo lyre first made by Robert Wornum in London, *c*.1810.

The earliest four-stringed surviving violins date from the mid-16th century. Centres of manufacture were round Gasparo da Salo in Brescia and the Amatis in Cremona, both in Italy. The highest point in their development came with the makers Stradivari and Guiseppe Guarneri del Gesu. The beautiful design of the violin is functional, the body designed to amplify the sound, the narrow waist enabling the bow to pass easily across the high and low strings. The t-shaped holes in the belly have an ornamental appearance, but these are necessary for the good production of sound.

By 1800 the violin was being used to display the great virtuosity of solo performers. The age of the public concert demanded a more brilliant tone than could be met by the early design. This was obtained by raising the playing pitch, heightening the bridge, lengthening the playing string and neck, and shaping the finger-board to facilitate maximum dexterity.

In the 19th century another development was the making of cheap 'factory fiddles' from Mirecourt in France, Mittenwald and Markneukirchen in Germany.

The 18th and 19th century dancing master's fiddle, or kit, was an adapted form of the violin that was very portable, sometimes fitting into the master's walking stick. The French pochette, a long and narrow instrument with a rounded back, was even tinier.

The Norwegian Hardanger fiddle is a beautiful example of the folk violin. The oldest is dated 1651, and they are still used to accompany dancing. Like the *viola d'amore* it has sympathetic strings. This instrument is usually beautifully decorated with inlay work.

Miniature violins have been made over the centuries, usually as souvenirs or gifts, but quite playable. Small violins for children became standard in the 19th century and were approximately quarter-size.

The rebec, a bowed chordophone from the Renaissance, evolved from an Arab instrument, the rabāb, which was played in the 11th century. It was a small instrument with a piriform body, short neck and three strings similar in length to those on a violin. The body was either carved from a single piece of wood or was moulded. They were still being made in Italy and France until the 18th century.

The viola, short for *viola da braccio*, is the alto member of the violin family. Until the 18th century it was made in two sizes – the *contralto viola* and the *tenore viola*, the latter being the larger of the two. When the musical distinction between the two became redundant the *tenore viola* was no longer made and many existing ones were converted to the smaller instrument.

The violoncello or cello began life in the 16th century as a bass violin and was known as a *basse de violon* until about 1700. Early examples had four or five strings and were somewhat wider and longer than today's instrument and only became smaller with the advent of the bass violin as a solo instrument. Only at the end of the 17th century did it gain a spike; small cellos were placed on footstools.

Keyboard instruments which have strings also fall into this category. They include the clavichord, harpsichord, spinet and virginal, where the strings are plucked, and the piano whose strings are hit by hammers. The largest of the first group is the harpsichord. It was the principal keyboard instrument in the 16th and 17th centuries, until it reached the highest point of its development in the 18th century. In the second half of the century it was gradually superseded by the piano.

The history of the harpsichord is obscure until the 16th century. Prior

Left: *Italian guitar dating from the mid-18th century.*
Right: *Late 18th-century French guitar with 'C' holes.*

to that time the earliest known reference is by Eberhardt Cersne who refers to a *clavicymbolum* commonly known as a clavicimbalum. The earliest preserved harpsichord, dated 1521, was made by Jerome of Pesaro, of Italy and is in the Victoria and Albert Museum, London. Italian instruments were made of cypress and were elaborately decorated. Flemish harpsichords were made of pinewood. It was not until the 18th century that the harpsichord became an instrument in its own right, having previously been played for practice by organists; even as a solo instrument it was only played by organists until the 18th century.

The piano as we know it was invented by Bartolomeo Christofori in 1709. His work did not become really popular in his lifetime, although Pistoia wrote music for it in 1731. It was the work of Johann Andreas Stein, who invented the different action known as the 'Viennese', that was to direct notice to the instrument. Hearing a Stein piano in 1777 Mozart wrote to his father saying that he liked it far better than the piano by Spathe, and subsequently composed for it. By 1800 the piano had established itself as a solo instrument, although it had to obtain greater power for use in public concert halls. By 1855 the instrument reached the modern form – Broadwood produced his first complete iron-frame for the Great Exhibition of 1851. Square pianos were used until 1860, but by that date the 'upright' had virtually replaced them for use in small rooms.

The last group of instruments are the aerophones – those instruments which produce sound by the vibration of a column of air. In the 16th century this group included recorders, flutes, crumhorns, curtals, shawms, cornetts, sackbuts and trumpets. This group is best described by taking the woodwind first, then the brass. Small wooden instruments in the 16th century were made of boxwood and the large ones of maple. There was little ornamental turnery, this being limited for the most part to bagpipe design. The 17th century marks the period during which the instruments known today developed. Many of the changes began in France, where the wind instruments had continued to be popular. The maker Hotteterre is thought to have been responsible for many of these. Originally a bag-pipe maker, he adapted the jointed construction to the flute, oboe and bassoon, at the same time using ornamental turnery to strengthen the joints.

As well as the change of design from instruments made in one piece to those constructed of several pieces, keys began to be added. The Hotte-terre flute, with three joints and one key, became the standard 18th-century form. The problem of only having one key was that it was very difficult to get notes in tune with the complicated cross fingertips used. The flute was the first instrument to have chromatic keywork, when London flute makers added three closed keys of the type earlier used on the musette. This not only improved the tuning, but also extended the range.

The clarinet was an important 18th-century German development by Denner. It was originally introduced into France to be played in partnership with the horn. After 1750 the bell was elongated, and from 1770 there were five keys.

The 19th century saw the great period of mechanization of the wood-

Clavicytheriun made by Albert Delin, second half 18th century.

wind, firstly through the introduction of the 'simple system', by which each instrument had a set of simple closed keys. These provided accurate notes for each semitone. Instruments were made of boxwood or ebony, with brass and silver keys; from the 1850s German silver was sometimes used. Subsequent methods of construction made keys more reliable and less sluggish. Innovations by Theobald Boehm (1793–1881) made use of ring keys in the clarinet and flute. Although Buffet worked on the design of the oboe using a Boehm system, the eventual arrangement of the modern oboe was the result of improvements on the older models. In Germany, although new techniques were used by Heckel on the bassoon, these were made without spoiling its tone.

Recorders are perhaps one of the earlier instruments that the collector is likely to come across. It dates from the 14th or 15th century and is a development of the *flageol*. Prototypes of the instrument have been traced back to the 11th and 12th centuries. By the 15th century the recorder was being made in several sizes. By 1511 three types, bass, tenor and soprano, were known which in time were each made in two different sizes differing in pitch by a tone. These early recorders were built in one piece and were not tunable. The jointed recorder was the work of Jean Hotteterre in the mid-17th century. It was made with three joints: the head which is cylindrical or slightly tapered in bore, a tapering middle and a foot joint. The little-finger hole was placed on the foot joint, which, since it was moveable, dispensed with the need for a second hole for left-hand players as on earlier models. Many 18th century examples, carved and intricately decorated, still exist. Recorders declined towards the end of that century, but good examples *c.*1800 by Gouldings of London are known.

Horns, trumpets and trombones form today's brass instruments. Horns and trumpets have been used as signalling instruments from time immemorial. Early horns were made from a variety of materials – animal horns often being used. These were sometimes decorated with silver mounts and mouthpieces for foresters and were often held as symbols of office. Long trumpets of metal also have a long history. A pair of trumpets was one of the customary gifts to impress a king. Such trumpets were used on ceremonial occasions and would have been straight with flags suspended from their length. Because of this ceremonial connection, composers have often used their sound to portray battles and pageantry in music.

The great innovation in the history of brass instruments was the valve. Horns in the 17th century were in the form of a hoop, and different horns had to be used for playing in different keys. But by 1715 crooks (different lengths of metal tubing) had been adapted which could be slotted into the instrument when a new length was needed. In 1815, with the invention of the true valve principle by Stokel and Bluhmel, it became possible to play a chromatic scale without even changing crooks.

The valve was also applied to the trumpet, which otherwise had reached its typical form by 1500. The trombone, and its precursor the sackbut, changed less: for the slide meant that it was comparatively easy to change the tube length.

The saxophone was invented around 1842 by Adolphe Sax (1814–94).

He patented his design in 1846 in Paris. There are various forms of the saxophone: the soprano is straight, while from alto down the instrument is bent back to form a curved bell and is fitted with a crook. The sopranino instrument is very rare. Other reed instruments introduced in this century include the *alto fagotto* which is a variation of the *Caledonica* invented by W. Miekle of Lanarkshire *c*.1830. The latter was a bassoon-shaped instrument with a conical bore. The *alto fagotto* was an improved version by George Wood of London. Only one specimen is known and that is in the Museum of Fine Arts in Boston.

Another instrument was the *tarogato* which resembles a soprano sax. It was invented in the 1890s by Schunda of Budapest to replace a shawm (also sometimes called a *tarogato*). The older version had a double reed and pironette and lacked fingerholes. Schunda used a single reed, a clarinet-type beak and keys similar to a soprano sax.

Toy instruments can be looked at as a group. They sometimes reflect developments of the rest of the instrument world but they more often show a continuity which is astonishing. One of the first toys given to a child was the silver coral and bells. This is a rattle made up of a handle of coral (or occasionally mother-of-pearl) to the centre part of which rows of bells are attached, and with a whistle at the top. This was fastened by a link to a ribbon or chain and to the child's belt. Many 17th-century portraits of tiny children show one, an example being the portrait of Elizabeth of Bohemia, daughter of James I of England. Rattles like this continued to be given until the present century.

Many instruments such as May whistles and bull roarers were made by children themselves, or by their parents. Whistles were used both as toys and as signalling devices. In the 19th century they were used in speaking tubes, and also as dog whistles. Many beautiful whistles were made in the shape of dogs' heads, from bone, ivory, metal and even occasionally slate. The potteries produced whistles from clay using the conventional design, but they also produced cheap whistles in the shapes of birds and other novelties that were to be won as prizes at fairs.

Jade

Throughout Chinese history, until quite recently, jade, whose Chinese name *Yu* means 'beauty' or 'purity', was highly venerated. Magical and curative powers were ascribed to the stone and it was even thought capable of bestowing the gift of immortality. Although jade is found in the ground the Chinese did not believe that this was its source; instead it was the essence of water, the congealed semen of the dragon or even the essence of heaven. References to jade occur throughout Chinese mythology; Taoist Immortals lived on jade; Jade Maidens attended the Queen Mother of the West; the Jade Emperor of Heaven rules all other gods and has power over this world and the next; the 'jade gate' is where the spine joins the skull.

Jade is not found in China proper and was first brought to areas such

A jade P'an or sacrificial vessel dating from the Three Dynasties.

as Kansu and Honan in northern central China from the Lake Baikal region of Siberia and later from the Sinkiang mountains and around Khotan in central Asia.

The stone is extremely hard to work without metal tools, yet Stone Age cultures in China used polished jade for tools and for ornamental or religious items such as rings, plaques and the sacred *Pi* disc. During the Shang dynasty (1600–1027 B.C.) jade was largely used for ceremonial weapons, jewelry and musical instruments. Ceremonial knives and the blade of the dagger axe, *Ko*, were made in jade and jade axes were carried by the kings. Jade plaques carved as birds, fish and animals were worn as pendants while jade chimes were used in religious rituals.

In the Chou dynasty (1027–249 B.C.) the use of jade in court ceremonies was recorded in the *Chou-li*: the king or emperor held a jade sceptre, *Chen-kuei*; courtiers held a jade tablet, *Kuei*, against their mouths when speaking to the emperor, and princes and court officials held sceptres or tablets of jade carved in various forms according to their rank. Three jade objects, *Pi*, *T'sung* and *Huang* (a half circle) were included among the Six Instruments of court ritual. In royal burials protective jade objects were placed around the corpse: a *Kuei* sceptre to the east, a tiger to the west, a *Huang* to the north and a short tceptre, *Chang*, to the south. A jade plaque carved in the form of a cicada, a symbol of immortality, was placed in the mouth and the orifices were sealed with jade plugs. Jade tablets were also sent as signs of authority with envoys carrying messages.

Jade carving was refined and developed about 500–200 B.C. with the introduction of iron cutting tools and a rotary lap drill, which allowed the production of hollow ware in jade. Towards the end of the Chou dynasty, Chinese society changed radically, emerging from centuries of feudalism and the arrival of the Han dynasty (202 B.C.–A.D. 220) saw these changes reflected in the arts and crafts, including jade carving. The kind of objects carved in jade increasingly fell into two groups – amuletic and functional. The latter group included such objects as bowls, dishes for food and drinks, toilet boxes and screens as well as personal jade ornaments such as pendants, belt hooks, seals and sword fittings.

The amuletic function of the stone was of course derived from its supposed magical and mystical powers and it was used to protect both the living and dead. As well as the *Pi* disc, the *T'sung* was also used as an amulet. Its shape is usually that of a hollow cylinder or tapering cone enclosed by a rectangle, or alternatively it is cylindrical with four rectangular prisms projecting from the surface. The *T'sung* was the symbol of Earth, which was regarded as a deity. It has been suggested that the *T'sung* might have been used as a sighting instrument as well, by astronomers and surveyors. Particularly beautiful jade amulets are those carved as winged felines ridden by a winged immortal, which are probably derived from large stone figures of winged felines which guarded important Han tombs. Winged felines by themselves, known as *pi-hsieh*, meaning 'averters of evil', were also carved as miniature jades. The *pi-hsieh*, sometimes called the 'fabulous animal', may be a variation of the dragon which appears as a motif throughout Chinese arts and crafts.

The Han dynasty saw the flourishing of various philosophies and religions – the ancient ancestral cult, Confucian ideals and prescriptions and the more mystical but popular Taoist ideas. Beliefs in the magical properties of plants, wood and metal were prevalent. Jade, as the produce of earth and water symbolized the unified principles of Yin and Yang and both form and colour symbolism were important. Jade figures were used in sorcery and rainmaking rituals, and were burned as sacrifices. Witches, *tao niu*, made hollow statuettes in jade, clay, paper or wood and gave them life by placing models of human organs or a small living creature inside. The most striking objects from this period are the jade suits of Prince Liu Sheng and his wife Tou Wan. These suits are made of jade plates sewn together with gold thread. The corpse was dressed in jade in the belief that this would prevent bodily decay.

'Yu' refers to both types of jade known as jadeite and nephrite. They are hard, brittle stones, difficult to differentiate, which resonate when struck. Nephrite is more fibrous and older objects tend to be made in this stone. In pure form both jadeite and nephrite are completely white, though these are rare and more usually some colouring is present. Spinach jade is a green form of nephrite with either black or gold flecks. The oldest jade objects are perhaps made in this colour. Jade also occurs in yellow, cream, grey, brown, cinnabar red, lavender and black. 'Mutton fat' jade has a lardish, greasy appearance, often with red spots, and was appreciated for its rarity. Jadeite was first imported into China in the late 18th century from deposits in Upper Burma. *Fei-ts'ui* is the most valued type of jadeite and is either a brilliant emerald green, or white with emerald patches resembling kingfisher feathers.

The Ming dynasty (1368–1664) and early Ching dynasty (1644–1912) saw the craft of jade carving raised almost to perfection. The early Ming period was not an outstanding one for the jade carver however. In many ways this was a time of transition for the craft and the carver seems to have temporarily lost his way as shown by the colour of jade he chose to work with – usually an unstriking grey or brown and yellow. The decoration was mainly symbolic and the form was archaic though with a curious rugged touch to it.

The mid-Ming period (1465–1521) saw radical changes in the state of the art. It has been suggested that the best jades were usually made within a century of an outstanding ceramic period and the reign of Hsüan Tê (1426–35) was just such a period. Once again the carver was choosing his stone with care and attention and using the natural colourings of the stone as an intimate part of the design. With the exception of the later Chi'ien Lung period some of the finest jades ever made date from these years and are notable for their use of elaborate high relief work.

The excellence of the work continued into the beginning of the late Ming period (1522–1620) but soon began to show signs of decline, a reflection no doubt of the decadence and instability that characterized the last years of the Ming dynasty. There was something of a return to the styles of the early Ming but with better choice of stone. As the period progressed decoration became more ordinary and conventional.

There is little doubt that the jade of the Chi'ien Lung reign (1736–95) reached a level of balance, refinement, skill and decorative imagination

Jade Tui, *or covenant vessel, decorated with earth markings.*

Right: *Sacred jade* Pi *disc, with 'grain' decoration;* Above: *Jade* Tsun, *or sacrificial vessel.*

that has never been surpassed. The emperor took a greater interest in the jade workshops than his predecessors had, which may account to some extent for the quality of the jades. More particularly this reign is the ultimate result of a progression that had been taking place in the previous two reigns. During the reign of K'ang Hsi (1662–1722) pierced work was revived, decoration was mainly floral and the forms were inspired by those of the Ming Dynasty. Few carvings in emerald or apple green jade date from this period. The Yung Chêng reign is notable for its graceful statuettes and the introduction of purely decorative jades. Forms were based on the ceramics of the K'ang Hsi period rather than on archaic models and decoration tends to be symbolic rather than floral and is executed in low relief or engraving.

Embroidery

By the early 18th century furniture in general was becoming more refined and comfortable with an increasing use of decorated fabrics for upholstery. Velvets, silks and damasks were extensively used, but many chairs, stools, settees, screens and even card tables were covered with embroidery.

Sometimes, designs were worked in crewel wools on linen, but more often, especially as the 18th century progressed, wool or silk on canvas was favoured. This either took the form of bold 'Florentine' patterns in flame stitch, or figurative designs in tent and cross stitches. Often, they conformed to the oriental fashion with Chinese figures, pagodas and exotic trees and birds, but by the early 18th century the influence of the Dutch flower painters was bringing a new naturalism to all kinds of decoration. Vases of flowers were inlaid into furniture and worked on canvas for chairs, and flower designs were clearly among the most popular by the 1720s and 1730s. Whole sets of chairs were sometimes covered with fine stitchery and evidence of these mammoth undertakings – which often kept the ladies of a household employed for years – can still be found in old country houses.

Many furniture embroideries were probably worked in silks or in wool with silk highlights, but because of its fragility compared with the robustness of wool, much silk embroidery has perished, leaving the almost certainly false impression that wool was the most favoured embroidery material. In France, where after the Revolution special workmen were employed to unpick embroideries, very little 17th or 18th century needlework in any material has survived.

Comfortable upholstered chairs covered with embroidery or rich velvets continued to be fashionable until the craze for Neo-classiciam began to sweep through Europe in the 1760s and 1770s. After that, the 'best' houses had rows of elegant but much less comfortable chairs ranged round the edges of rooms. Sets of settees and stools were arranged in deliberate groupings in drawing rooms. They would have been too much even for the most indefatigable of needlewomen, and besides, they were much more suitably clad in the delicate striped or flower-sprigged brocades, light-coloured damasks or gaily printed chintzes which became more and more widely available. Women contented themselves with knotting fringes and weaving braids for trimming their furniture.

From the early 18th century styles in screens began to change to cope with the large, draughty rooms of the period, providing great scope for the embroiderer's imagination. At the beginning of the century, the two-fold screen had become complemented by the cheval or horse-style screen and as with furniture upholstery designs were taken from tapestry and were characterized by a central motif worked in tent stitch. Other designs of the period were mainly floral – a bowl of flowers being popular – as well as ribbons, ostrich feathers and pastoral scenes.

During the first half of the century, pole screens were coming into general use and consisted of a rectangular or shaped frame holding the embroidery, fixed to a pole or rod mounted on a tripod base. The frame was designed to move up and down the pole. The best examples of their embroideries are of pastoral scenes – young shepherds and shepherdesses with their flocks, farmhouses, windmills and dovecotes. Sometimes the background to pastoral embroideries is worked with flowers, flower-bowls or baskets rather than landscape detail. Unfortunately as pole screens became more popular the general quality of the work tended to decline, although some fine examples were made well into the 19th century.

Throughout the 18th century both men's and women's costumes were lavishly embroidered. The rich employed professional craftspeople to work flowers, in sprigs, garlands, trailing patterns, bunches and festoons on their clothes, to quilt their petticoats and to beribbon plainer materials. Coloured silks, metal threads and jewels were used for the most sumptuous, while those who chose not to employ embroiderers wore equally beautiful gowns and waistcoats of flower bedecked brocade.

In the furnishing of houses too, the domestic embroideress continued

Satin bed cover designed for Osterley House by Robert Adam, 1776.

252

to work fine household linens and particularly bed coverings, and here the Americans were pre-eminent. In North America, where the winters are particularly cold, crewel embroidered coverlets continued to be made throughout the 18th century, whereas in Europe they had become unfashionable by mid-century. A form of looped embroidery in wool on woollen cloth was also used for coverlets, mainly in New England, from the 1720s until the early 19th century.

It was more usual in America than elsewhere for women to dye and spin their own embroidery yarns and to weave cloth and many of them also printed their own cottons with stencils or wood blocks. Cotton bedcovers with home-printed designs in red, green or yellow, and often quilted, are not an unusual find, and they mostly date from the 18th and early 19th century. Quilting, the technique by which a thick layer of material is sandwiched between two thinner ones and bound by patterns of running stitches all over the surface, was used a great deal to conserve warmth. Candlewicking and embroidery in white on white were also used for American bedspreads of this period. The most celebrated American quilts, however, are undoubtedly those decorated with appliqué or patchwork.

Printed cotton chintzes were imported into America in the 18th century, but they were extremely expensive and were at first luxuries confined to the rich. It was soon realized that if the printed designs were cut out and appliquéd on to a background material, the chintzes could be used much more economically, and it was not long before appliquéd chintz quilts gave way to patchwork in which even smaller pieces of material were stitched together, side by side, to make colourful patterns.

Some American quilts are a combination of patchwork and appliqué and their range is endless, probably because every girl was expected to make several before she married, and it was also customary for quilts, made through the joint efforts of several women (at 'quilting bees'), to be given as presentation pieces.

The different patchwork patterns were given names – Puss-in-the-Corner, Dutchman's Puzzle, King David's Crown and Lincoln's Platform are typical, and these often varied from region to region. Some of them recorded historic figures or events while others are simply quaint. Few give any clue to dating, any more than the materials used in patchworks, since these were often already old when they were put into a quilt.

Another point of interest in American weaving and embroidery is the wide range of discernible national styles. America was colonized by immigrants from almost every country in Europe, and just as they all took with them their own national characteristics, so they took their textile skills, needlework patterns and embroidery techniques. Whereas dating American needlework accurately is almost impossible, it can often be attributed to a specific region, colonized by a particular national group, on the basis of its European stylistic roots.

Among late 18th century gentlewomen, whether in America or Europe, there was a definite tendency towards maximum effect in the minimum of time where decorative needlework was concerned. The developing machine age was already giving people a taste for speed, besides changing the entire face of textile manufacture, and women were no longer happy to persevere for years on a single project like the embroidering of a set of chair covers or the panels of a screen. Instead, they turned to smaller items, such as panels for tea caddies and trays, fire-screens and pictures. These they stitched with gentle and refined designs of shepherds and shepherdesses, rustic views, flowers and wistfully romantic scenes from Goethe's *The Sorrows of Werther* or Sterne's *Sentimental Journey*, in coloured silks on a silk or satin background.

Designs were copied over and over again and most of them were available 'off the peg'. The faces of figures, skies and other details were nearly always painted in watercolours, and contemporary magazine advertisements recommended shops selling embroidery designs complete with the silks for working them.

Interesting variants of the late 18th and early 19th century silk embroideries were the 'print-work' pictures done entirely in black, grey and dark brown silks. They were made in imitation of the fashionable prints of the time and must have been exceedingly monotonous to work. Some pictures of the same period were embroidered as mourning pieces, and these are occasionally worked partly in human hair – presumably that of the deceased. In America, these printwork or 'etching' embroideries were known as 'engraved' work.

Motif used in white-work on a fine lawn fichu.

Scandinavian embroidery

Scandinavian embroidery began to develop along attractive lines in this century. White linen was the most frequently used ground even after cotton began to be imported later in the century. Even silk was used more often than cotton. German and Swiss pattern books began to reach Sweden in the late 17th century but were used mainly by the upper classes. Peasant embroidery remained uninfluenced by the books. The favourite embroidery of the rich was Holbein work – black double running stitches named after Hans Holbein the Younger. Designs were also taken from the Vikings and, more commonly, from the Bible. Personal marks are often present enclosed by a flora wreath. Holbein work was mainly used on bed linen, towels and for window borders.

Away from the cities, Swedish women preferred drawnwork, cross-stitches and counted satin stitches. A particularly difficult type of drawn-work was called *näversøm*, meaning birch-bark embroidery. In this work, threads are drawn out of a piece of linen which was then stretched across a piece of birch bark and the pattern worked through the drawn-thread sections underside up.

In Denmark the famous Hedebo embroidery appeared around 1700. The original Hedebo was done on narrow cloth with horizontally-running designs of small cut-out squares and surface embroidery. This was called *rudesyning*, meaning 'windowpane sewing'. The commonest motifs on Hedebo were animals, birds, flowers and eight-point stars. Long Hedebo were used ornamentally on special occasions but were gradually developed to be used as everyday household objects. Hedebo carries the monogram of the owner as well as the date it was made.

19th
CENTURY

Introduction

Between 1750 and 1850 a number of styles in art, architecture and the decorative arts came and went and the period has been called an age of Romanticism. Essentially the styles of these years paraded the romantic past before a public willing to embrace them enthusiastically.

Romanticism had its roots in England in the late 17th century and began with an interest in Chinese forms and designs. This was supplemented in the 18th century by a taste for the Gothic which had never really died in England, a factor which was in part responsible for the reluctance of England to fall under the spell of the Rococo. In 1718 for instance, John Vanbrugh, architect of the Baroque Blenheim Palace, designed for himself a Gothic house, while the Earl of Burlington built Chiswick House in the Palladian style in 1725; Horace Walpole renovated his Twickenham house in the 'gothick' fashion in 1749–77.

In the mid-18th century, however, the discovery and excavations of Pompeii and Herculaneum turned the taste for the romantic in a new direction, beginning the style called Neo-classical. The art that unfolded as the volcanic ash was removed from the two cities stunned all of Europe. For once, Europe's view of the Roman Empire was not dependent on the ruins that still littered Europe but on the almost perfectly preserved wall-paintings and artifacts that emerged as the excavations proceeded.

The best-known early exponents of the Neo-classic style were Robert and James Adams, the Scottish architects, who visited Herculaneum in the 1750s. On their return to England they began designing architecture, furniture and other decorative arts in the style of the Roman Empire.

English designers were not the only ones to visit the two cities for by the 1770s designers from all over Europe were flocking there and the inspiration they received brought about a rapid dissemination of Neo-classicism throughout the Continent and as far as Russia and America.

In England Neo-classicism became known as the Adam style after Robert Adam. Although an architect, Adam believed that he should design down to the smallest decorative detail, for only this way could design have a sense of completeness. The style he created with his brother James was a remarkable synthesis of classic ornament and his own sense of refinement, elegance and grace. There is probably no greater decorative contrast in this century than Adam's Etruscan Room in Osterley Park House begun in 1761 and the Rococo salon of the Hôtel de Soubise in Paris built in 1737–40. In the former, symmetry and rectilinearity have reappeared and there is none of the massive splendour of the Louis XIV style. The decorative motifs of the Adam style are all taken from Roman art – urns, vine scrolls, medallions, sphinxes and tripods. Following the stucco style they are arrayed sparsely in broad neutral spaces and narrow margins.

It was not until Louis XVI ascended the throne of France in 1774 that the Rococo was finally banished and French craftsmen were given a freedom they had not had under Louis XV, particularly in his later years when craftsmen became eager to explore the new classic style while Louis still preferred the Rococo. From about 1760 to 1770 French styles underwent a transition period in which elements of the Rococo and classic ornament were mixed. Neo-classicism in France became known as the Louis XVI style and in its first phases was a combination of antique art and the Renaissance interpretation of that art, but later it was dominated by Roman architecture and ornament. As the style became more and more popular there was an increasing tendency to imitate more closely antique art which ultimately led to the Directoire style which developed from 1793 to 1804 and anticipated the later Empire style.

Essentially the Directoire style was a more severe version of the Louis XVI style but lost none of the essence of classic ornament. It was very much in keeping with the mood of the Revolution of 1789 in which the lavishness and splendour of the aristocracy in France were all but swept away. Not surprisingly some of the favourite motifs of this style were the symbols of the new Republic – liberty caps, fasces and laurel crowns. The Directoire style took Greek art as its source of inspiration: the most popular Directoire chair, for instance, had a rolled-over back or concave crest rail.

The new style influenced the decorative arts in both England and America after 1795. In England, Sheraton and other contemporary cabinetmakers adopted many of the features of the Directoire, whilst in America, in the first quarter of the 19th century, cabinetmaker Duncan Phyfe created elegant and tasteful furniture reflecting both the Directoire and Sheraton styles.

The Directoire style was to be only a transition style between the Louis XVI style and the later Empire style which was promoted by Napoleon Bonaparte and reflected his dreams of a new French Empire and his desire to be an emperor in the true Roman tradition.

The Empire style was largely the creation of Pierre Fontaine and Charles Mercier, two architects who closely studied Roman and Etruscan style while in Italy. At the turn of the century they were employed by Napoleon to remodel his palace, Malmaison, which subsequently became the basis of the Empire style. In keeping with Napoleon's vision the style copied Roman, Etruscan, Greek and Egyptian styles almost exactly, and possessed a cold formality and elegant severity. Furniture, for example, was mainly rectangular and heavy with large flat surfaces devoid of moulding or other decoration. Even when upholstered the furniture was rather uncomfortable. Carving was not used except on table legs and the arms of chairs; marquetry and lacquering disappeared. Favourite motifs of the Empire period include acanthus, wreaths, winged classical figures, gods and goddesses, sphinxes, lyres, eagles, swans and caryatids.

The Empire style spread throughout Europe during the first quarter of the century; in Italy and Germany the style was imposed by Napoleon's conquering armies. Italian Empire closely followed the French while in Germany the style was interpreted in a lighter fashion. In England the Empire style was called Regency (1800–37) after the period when George, Prince of Wales was Regent. Although the Regency did not copy the continental European style, nevertheless it still tended to copy classical styles exactly.

In France, the Empire style began to decline after 1815; in Germany it evolved into the Biedermeier style. In England by the 1830s the Empire style had been abandoned and was gradually being replaced by an eclectic style, a mixture of late Empire and Gothic that has become known as Victorian. It is probable that the emergence of this style was in part a result of industrialization and mass-production techniques that opened the decorative arts to a much larger population. Renaissance, Baroque and Gothic and so on, were all employed to give the Victorian style its characteristic extravagance which, while often lacking any artistic merit was notable for its quality of workmanship. The Great Exhibitions of the second half of the century were the penultimate displays of the age of Romanticism. While the rest of Europe did not accept the Victorian melting-pot of styles with the enthusiasm of its country of origin the fashion for earlier styles persisted until the end of the century. The ultimate reaction against eclecticism and mass production took various forms. In England the Arts and Crafts movement of William Morris, one such reaction, extended to most areas of the decorative arts, with its emphasis on true craftsmanship. The Art Nouveau movement which originated at the end of the century was an evolved form of the Rococo and which, while emphasizing handcrafting, led to designs that could be mass-produced. These two movements were to have a wide-ranging influence on the styles of the twentieth century.

Furniture

Much of the spirit of the 19th century may be summed up as a growing nostalgia in the face of the machine age. Throughout Europe and North America, change continued, with populations increasing, economies expanding and cities burgeoning. In the course of the century, automobiles, electricity, photography and skyscrapers were to appear.

Internationally, the much-enlarged middle class rose to a point of unprecedented social domination. Change and advance were adopted more quickly in the 19th century, as railroads, widely circulated publications and increased international commerce made communications and international cross-fertilization of ideas more rapid. Technological and scientific developments improved health and hygiene, provided new degrees of comfort and wealth, and introduced mass production.

At the same time, the century's innovations altered established orders and eroded long-standing traditions. Standards of quality, especially in production – a rarity that individual craftsmanship had guaranteed – gave way to the economies, ubiquities and machine-made finishes of mass production. Proliferating factories turned out articles of domestic comfort in great quantities, and put money in the pockets of the masses who manufactured them.

The resulting demographic shift saw, for the first time, a population in which a bourgeois class with an enormous disposable income was the most powerful sector. Its emergence allowed the production on a large

Chest of drawers with writing compartment.

scale of items far below the standards of style and workmanship that a discriminating élite had exacted in the previous century in procuring articles of aesthetic merit. Throughout the century, the defenders of the survival of that discriminating taste rejected innovative products and styles. Past styles were revived and old objects sought out in successive waves of revival fashions, producing an extraordinary eclecticism in interior design and architectural styles.

Of great importance in the development of 19th century design was the series of international exhibitions, launched by the Great Exhibition of the Works of Industry of All Nations, held in London in 1851, largely a result of the efforts of Albert, Prince Consort, and proponents of good design such as Henry Cole (1802–83), publisher of the *Journal of Design*.

Six million people attended the London exhibition, which was housed in the Crystal Palace, a structure designed by Joseph Paxton and made of glass and cast-iron, a strong testimony itself to progress. This and other exhibitions, which followed at intervals into the 20th century, accelerated the dissemination of innovations, and similarly internationally spread current stylistic fancies.

The rise in demand for furniture, and the simultaneous adaptation of technological developments, contributed to changes in the organization of furniture production and in the construction of furniture itself.

In an age that delighted in inventions however quixotic, numerous mechanized processes were perfected to improve the production of articles of interior decoration. Machines wove carpets and printed wall-papers and textiles in increasing quantities. In furniture manufacture, new devices were able to mould, plane, mortise, cut frets, slice veneers, rough out carving, laminate, drill and shape. In America, the New York firm of Henry Belter produced pieces by means of a laminating process in which layers of wood were steamed into curves with the use of moulds.

The first popular piece of furniture to be produced in mass quantities was the simple English Windsor chair, made by firms such as Webb and Bruce of London. The shortcomings of mass production would spur passionate protests among reformers, and ultimately provoke the formation of an arts and crafts movement which championed medieval traditions of hand craftsmanship.

More significant than changes in methods of execution were alterations within the furniture craft. In the mass-assemblage factories that the end of the century would see, craftsmen's contributions were confined to the completion of only one part of the whole piece. Moreover, furniture came to be designed by architects rather than by craftsmen themselves.

The evolution of interior decorating shops, which bought furnishings wholesale from suppliers and proffered hangings, upholstery, furniture and all the other necessities of room decoration, meant that except for the most affluent, the previous close collaboration of client and craftsman in interior decoration came to an end. This severing of the relations, which was traditionally so essential to the furniture craft, accounted for a great deal of the diminution in status of furniture itself. Instead of being commissioned works of decorative art, they became ready-made decorative objects, bought like other necessities.

About 1830 papier-mâché furniture appeared in England, and

although it continued to be fashionable until the 20th century, it never caught on as a major design innovation. Tables, trays, chairs and other pieces incorporated the material, which was often ornamented with mother-of-pearl inlay, gilt, and painted floral designs, but generally coated with imitation oriental lacquer.

Far more consequential was the introduction of cast-iron, which spread from England before the mid-19th century, and because of its durability was widely used in North America in a variety of styles for beds, chairs, garden furniture and small decorative pieces. Brass beds, with light, decorative endboards, were also popular.

Michael Thonet (1796–1871) introduced bentwood chairs that were very popular both in Europe and America. Born at Boppard in Prussia, his style was so innovative and atypical of the 19th century that Le Corbusier chose the chairs for the Pavilion de l'Esprit Nouveau at the Paris exhibition of 1925. Although Thonet had set up his own carpentry workshop to specialize in parquetry in 1819, it was in 1830 that he began to experiment with methods of glueing veneers together and stem-bending beech rods. In 1841 he applied for patents in France, Belgium and England for his bentwood technique and in 1842 went to Vienna and formed a partnership with Carl Leistler who had a furniture factory there. The chairs that Thonet designed in this period were made of glued, then bent veneers, with upholstered backs and seats.

The partnership with Leistler was dissolved in 1849 and Thonet established his own works in Vienna and in the same year he supplied the first chairs, later to be called Thonet Nr 4, to the Cafe Daum.

Thonet was joined in the firm by his five sons in 1853 and renamed the company Gebruder Thonet and from that point on he could lay claim to be the most successful furniture manufacturer of all time. By 1871 he had established salerooms in many of the major cities of Europe as well as in Moscow, St Petersburg, Chicago and New York. The design of his Thonet Nr 14 chair in 1859, which was completely without decoration and was made from only six parts, shows Thonet's concern with cheapness, which no doubt was part of his success. By the end of the century the company, under his sons, was making 4,000 pieces of furniture a day.

A Profusion of Styles

The taste for the exotic, which showed itself in an extreme form early on in John Nash's Hindu–Chinese confection, the Royal Pavilion at Brighton, which he constructed from 1815–21 for the Prince Regent, continued throughout the century. Turkish-style decors, with Persian tiles, hangings and cushions, were not infrequent choices for smoking rooms. Indian furniture, exhibited at the International Exhibition of 1851, was imported to England in great quantities; and oriental ornament enjoyed wide popularity. However, although Japanese examples would greatly influence the wallpaper and textiles of William Morris's arts and crafts movement late in the century, none of these modes played a dominant role in shaping the century's interior design. They did, however, offer refreshing respites from the more standard styles.

Although never surfacing in a pure form, geometric preferences provided much of the basis of furniture designed by Gothicists, including William Butterfield and William Burges. The arts and crafts school would eventually produce furniture formed of simple geometric forms and shapes.

Naturalism, another thread that pervaded the Victorian era, permeated the Gothic style with figures and foliage, the Rococo with scrolling acanthus, the aesthetic movement with oriental flowers, and then achieved its ultimate expression in the organic forms of Art Nouveau.

The dichotomy between expensive and elegantly styled furniture and cheaper versions was to remain throughout the century. Another contrast was the coexistence of several different styles, each of which underwent major modifications. Both middle-class preferences and the persistence of Neo-classicism were crystallized in the German Biedermeier style, expounded by designers such as the Neo-classical architect Karl Friedrich Schinkel of Berlin, and others including Josef Danhauser and Michael Thonet.

Biedermeier furniture was unpretentious and informal. Round tables, secretaires and commodes with flat façades and recessed arches, broad beds and sofas with arms and endboards shaped as swans' necks or cornucopias, were covered with flat veneers that displayed the natural beauty of mahogany, walnut and cherry.

Throughout Europe and North America, Neo-classicism was favoured during the century, managing to survive the vigorous competition of the Gothic revival which superseded the classical mode at times.

In England, buildings such as the British Museum of Sir Robert Smirke (1823–24) and C. R. Cockerell's Ashmolean Museum at Oxford (1839–41) paralleled the Neo-classical work of Schinkel in Germany and Benjamin Latrobe in America. Publications such as George Smith's *Cabinetmaker and Upholsterer's Guide* (1826), Peter and Michael Angelo's *The Practical Cabinetmaker* (1826) and Mesangère's *Album*, championed this late classical mode.

After about 1815, massive mahogany furniture with carved ornament formed with chunky proportions became internationally popular. Known as 'fat classical', furniture in this style was characterized by heavy twist turnings, fattened classical columns, lush, bulging acanthus leaves and thick, tightly wound scrolling ornament. This more stodgy translation of classicism was reflected by French chairs with backs carved as large, thick-leaved palmettes, Biedermeier case pieces with classical ornament and blocky proportions, Italian furniture made by Paolino Moselini, Giuseppe Cairoli and Pelagio Pelagi, and American examples by Duncan Phyfe and Joseph Meeks & Son.

Although elements of a Renaissance revival had surfaced as early as the 1851 Exhibition, this interpretation of classical sources gained great popularity only in the late 1860s and early 1870s in England, Italy, America, Austria and elsewhere. This revival often reflected the Renaissance as it had been translated centuries earlier into various national modes. German pieces recalled the squareness of Hans Vredeman de Vries; French Renaissance style furniture incorporated decorative elements typical of du Cerceau's Henri II cabinets.

Towards the end of the century, rising political nationalism, and the increasing vogue for amassing great collections of antiques, resulted in reproduction styles which revived historical national furniture forms. In

A type of davenport.

England, neo-Georgianism again renewed the Neo-classical idiom. In America, colonial furniture became newly fashionable after about 1870.

Simultaneous with 19th century classicism, various antiquarian styles evolved, generally presumed to be based on national medieval examples of furniture but often drawing more on architectural ornaments and forms. The Gothic mode had long been a popular decorative and archi-

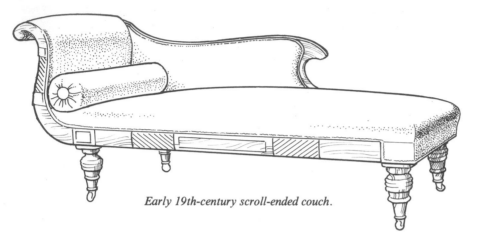

Early 19th-century scroll-ended couch.

tectural style in Europe. Horace Walpole's Strawberry Hill at Twickenham, England (1749–77), was a Gothic folly of monumental scale, and even Robert Adam had worked in the Gothic style.

Unlike the purified geometricity of classical styles from Greece and Rome, European Gothic images and forms smacked of local history, were steeped with the medieval humanism of the familiar and local Gothic cathedrals and provided a picturesque retreat from the galloping advance of modernism.

Publications such as E. J. Willson's *Specimens of Gothic Architecture* (1821–23), Edward Blore's *Monumental Remains* (1826), Henry Shaw's *Specimens of Ancient Furniture* (1836), preached the merits of the Gothic style. Other exponents were Batty Langley, A. W. G. Pugin, the Italians L. F. Basoli and Alessandro Sidole, and the French architect and furniture designer Eugène Viollet-le-Duc.

The Gothic revival was reflected internationally in the furniture of designers and makers such as Franz Xavier Fortner, Johann Wilhelm Vetter, the firms of Kimbel and Leistler of Germany and the Italian Pelagio Pelagi. Others were Aimé Chénavard and P. A. Bellange of France, Joseph Meeks & Son of New York and the talented English carvers W. G. and W. H. Rogers.

In England, and to a lesser extent in North America, an Elizabethan furniture style, which combined Elizabethan, Jacobean and Caroline forms, was favoured in the 1830s and 1840s, when Elizabethan interior schemes were popularized through publications by Robert Bridgens, J. C. Loudon and Joseph Nash.

Country houses with Tudor towers, windows and patterned chimneys were built, and interiors were fitted with oak wainscoting, Glastonbury style chairs, beds and draw tables with Jacobean and Elizabethan strapwork and bosses, and chairs with spiral-turned uprights modelled on

Caroline forms. The latter were imitated in America, along with chairs modelled after Daniel Marcot. In Germany, where the Gothic style had reached a high point in cathedrals such as that at Cologne, country houses with medieval interiors were also built.

Though not necessarily any more archeologically correct, interiors in the Gothic revival style purported to be true to their name. William Burges, Norman Shaw and Augustus Welby Northmore Pugin (1812–52) were among the leading English exponents of this style, and designed furniture with Gothic arches, colonettes, trefoils and other medieval motifs.

Pugin, a devout Roman Catholic who championed the Gothic as the only acceptable Christian style, advanced Gothic design in such publications as *The True Principles of Pointed or Christian Architecture* (1841) and *An Apology for the Revival of Christian Architecture in England* (1843). Pugin designed Gothic style furniture characterized by thick, sturdy oak members, ogival arch-shaped supports, and naturalistic foliate carving.

In the United States, Alexander Davis (1803–92) designed Gothic interiors for Lyndhurst and Ericstan in New York, and supplied them with tables, chairs and other oak furniture with crockets, finials, cusps and quatrefoil. Alexander Roux, John Jelliff and other cabinetmakers produced American Gothic furniture.

In the mid-19th century, a reformist, and more archeologically correct approach to the Gothic style, was adopted in England by architects and designers, including Pugin, William Burges, William Butterfield, G. E. Street and Charles Bevan. The art furniture movement, which preceded the aesthetic movement that eventually evolved into the Art Nouveau style, grew from the work of Bruce Talbert, Sir Henry Cole, Christopher Dresser, T. E. Collcutt, William Godwin and Thomas Jeckyll.

Drawing on Japanese and Gothic sources, these designers produced furniture in the 1860s and 1870s that was simple and decorative, making use of light forms, flat surfaces and dark woods, incorporating richness in carved and applied ornament, stoneware and painted panels.

The Arts and Crafts Movement

Pugin's writings, which preached integrity, propriety and functionalism in design, were of great importance to William Morris (1834–96). Morris took his degree at Oxford, intending to join the Church, but decided he was more interested in architecture and joined the firm of G. E. Street. Finding himself dissatisfied with the new choice, he moved to Red Lion Square in London and, with his friend Edward Burne-Jones, set themselves up as painters under Rossetti. Probably the first furniture designed by Morris was for his house in Red Lion Square. It was made by a local carpenter and painted by Burne-Jones and himself.

It was while working at Street's that Morris first met Philip Webb (1831–1915) and Morris now commissioned him to build a house for him in Bexley Heath which was finished in 1860. Webb, who was more expert than Morris at designing furniture, also designed most of the furniture for the house. This successful collaboration led to the formation of Morris, Marshall, Faulkner and Company, with Webb as a partner and the company's chief designer.

More often than not Webb's furniture was made of plain oak sometimes stained black or green and decorated with lacquered leather or paintings. Ornamentation, however, was kept to a minimum unless he felt the piece justified it, as with some of his pianofortes, and he clearly steered a middle road between opulence and austerity. He left the firm when it was reorganized in 1875, though he continued to supply designs. He was more intent in his later years on his architectural practice.

The company was renamed Morris & Co. in 1875 and throughout its history, as well as giving precedence in design to simplicity, utility and necessity, adopted as its essential principle the tradition of hand craftsmanship in construction, so giving birth to the arts and crafts movement.

Beginning in the 1880s, craft organizations such as the Century Guild founded by A. H. Mackmurdo, the Art Workers' Guild founded by C. F. A. Voysey and the Guild of Handicrafts founded by C. R. Ashbee in England, and societies and guilds of Arts and Crafts in Minnesota, Boston, Chicago and New York, forwarded various interpretations of the arts and crafts movement. The work of Mackmurdo, Voysey, Mackay Hugh Baillie Scott and the Glasgow designer Charles Rennie Mackintosh looked forward to the Art Nouveau style. Mackintosh's tall, straight-backed chairs and slender cabinets, like the uncomfortable, blocky furniture designed by the American Frank Lloyd Wright whom he influenced, was rectilinear and rigid, but its attenuated proportions anticipated the Art Nouveau.

The revival of French 18th and 19th century styles, often termed 'Louis XV' no matter which era was represented, permeated 19th century interior design internationally, providing the decorative schemes for middle-class homes, hotel lounges and palatial suites. Revitalized in about 1835 in England, the Louis XV style was embraced by the French Emperor Louis-Napoleon Bonaparte in mid-century, and gave way later in both countries to the more restrained Louis XVI mode. Publications including George Smith's *Cabinetmaker and Upholsterer's Guide* of 1826 paved the way for a Rococo revival. In Vienna, the Thonet firm and Karl Leistler produced Rococo revival furnishings; in the course of the century, Pössenbacher in Munich, Anton Bembé in Mainz, Giuseppe Cima and Alessandro Sidoli of Milan, J. P. F. Jeanselme and Guillaume Grohé of Paris, William Smee, Collard & Collard, Dowbiggon & Co., of London, J. & W. Hilton of Montreal, Prudent Mallard of New Orleans and Alexander Roux of New York turned out 19th century renditions of Louis XV, Rococo and Louis XVI designs.

It was the modernization of these old styles, more than the seeming confusion about which style was which, that most significantly characterized their 19th century renditions. Antiques were adapted to suit current taste; misinterpretations of Rococo pattern-books occasionally led to exaggerated asymmetries that 18th century designers would never have intended. Rooms were generally more crowded and casual than they would have been in the previous century.

The invention of coil springs and deep-button upholstery led to the production of large, over-stuffed sofas and easy chairs and although these Louis style seats were shaped as three-pronged pinwheels or other sequences of curves, to a certain degree they lost the lightness and

Pedestal work-table.

delicacy of 18th century design.

Balloon-back chairs with cabriole legs and lightweight fly chairs, meant to be moved about easily, were innovations of this style, as was the use of papier-mâché by the Englishman Charles Bielefiled to produce Rococo ornaments and the substitution of putty for wood by G. Jackson and Son of London for their ornamental mouldings. John Belter of New York made great use of his lamination process to produce beds, sideboards, chairs and other rosewood pieces that were highly carved with flowers and foliage in a naturalistic Rococo style.

Art Nouveau

Emerging at the very end of the century, the Art Nouveau style produced furniture which, light, ornamental and organic in conception, was hardly as ponderous as the blocky pieces of the contemporary arts and crafts movement. These were as heavily formed as they were laden with social significance.

Representing the first major break from the traditions that had shaped so much of 19th century design, the Art Nouveau style flourished from about 1893 to 1910. Its dominant feature, curvilinearity, originated from sources as varied as the Japanese prints that enjoyed wide circulation in the West at that time, the French Louis XV and XVI styles, and the flowing, organic decorations on recently popularized Minoan pottery. In the pictorial world, the English artist Arthur Rackham illustrated fairy tales with delicate etchings of attenuated figures and sinuous tangled trees. The architects Victor Horta in Brussels and Antoni Gaudí in Barcelona created buildings and furniture characterized by swirling undulations suggesting underwater or plant growth. Horta's celebration of line and light surfaces seen in his combination of glass and cast iron at the Hotel van Eetvelde of 1895, was shared by Louis Comfort Tiffany of New York, who in the 1880s began to produce lamps, vases and other furnishings of iridescent glass, which hinted at organic movement and growth with their swirling forms and naturalistic motifs such as dragonflies.

Similarly, Art Nouveau furniture was characterized by swirling lines and attenuated shapes, and suggestions of such light, natural forms as curved growing plant stems. Although not a unified international movement, the flowing tendencies of the Art Nouveau style were expressed by European furniture designers including the German Richard Reimerschmird, the Italians Carlo Bugatti and Pietro Fenoglio, the Belgian Henry van de Velde and the Frenchmen Hector Guimard, Emile Gallé, Pierre Chareau and Louis Majorelle. These designers generally achieved decorative effects through a careful integration of form and surface ornament; rich woods, such as cherry, walnut and mahogany, were flatly carved with decorative rounded panels, whiplash curves and swirling ormolu mounts.

The work of Louis Majorelle was exceptionally successful; the cabriole legs he used show the influence of earlier Louis styles, but the attenuated, stretched shapes of his desks and cabinets exhibit a greater freedom and lightness. The rounded, slightly trapezoidal panels and drawers of pieces by Jacques Gruber, and the flowing continuity of line joining crest rail and stiles in the chairs of Pierre Chareau and Sue et

Mare, similarly manifested the natural integration of form that defined the Art Nouveau style.

Although the style declined soon after the turn of the century, its very occurrence freed designers from the series of revivals into which the preceding era had been bound. The qualities of lightness, tensile strength, and integration of ornament and form it embodied foreshadowed the approach to furniture that 20th century designers would take.

Ceramics

During the early decades of the 19th century, the entire ceramic industry of Europe was dominated by the prolific output of British pottery, porcelain and bone-china.

John Rose, who had established a factory mainly devoted to the manufacture of porcelain at Coalport, Shropshire, in about 1797, was to flourish and in turn absorb the concerns of neighbouring Caughley (1799) and later two Welsh factories, Nantgarw and Swansea (c.1820). Coalport is now part of the Wedgwood Group and is still in operation in Staffordshire.

There is still a little confusion concerning the wares made at Caughley by Thomas Turner between 1796–99 and those made by John Rose, who after his purchase continued in production until about 1815, when he transferred the entire manufacture to Coalport. Further difficulties also arise because quite a lot of Turner's Caughley wares were decorated independently by Robert Chamberlain at Worcester. Also, in the early 19th century John Rose was supplying the London decorator Thomas Baxter with 'Coalport White China'. Therefore, attribution is usually best verified by form rather than decoration.

Most early Coalport porcelain is unmarked, but pattern numbers can be a useful guide. Progressive numbers 1–1,000 were used from about 1805–24, after which fractions were used. This resulted in 2/1–2/999 being applied to wares made between 1824–38, reaching as high as 8/1–8/1000. The later numbers are usually accompanied with a recorded and datable factory-mark. During the middle of the 19th century Coalport produced some fine quality reproductions of Sèvres porcelain, sometimes complete with mark!

It had long been the ambition of the painter William Billingsley to produce a fine porcelain. He left Derby in 1796 to establish a factory at nearby Pinxton, financed by John Coke. The limited production consisted primarily of tablewares, very much in the same styles as those of Derby. Sometimes they were decorated with pleasing landscapes by Billingsley himself, in the manner of Zachariah Boreman of Derby. Due to lack of expected profits, Billingsley moved on in 1799 to become an independent decorator, but Pinxton continued in a modest way until 1813. Pinxton used some distinctive handles on their vessels and cups, which are a useful identification aid to the collector.

Having found a new financial backer, Billingsley started to produce a

19th-century 'Etruria' teapot produced by Wedgwood.

beautiful, but costly, soft-paste porcelain at Nantgarw, near Cardiff in South Wales, in 1814. However, within the same year he was compelled to transfer the manufacture to the Swansea pottery of L. W. Dillwyn. There, Billingsley and his son-in-law, Samuel Walker, were forced to make a more stable porcelain, with a so-called 'duck-egg' translucency. In 1817 they returned to Nantgarw to restart their original factory. Stylistically, the early wares of Billingsley had much in common with French porcelain of the Empire Period, but a large amount of Nantgarw porcelain was ruined by the over ornate decoration added in London by the decorators employed by the china dealers Mortlocks of Oxford Street.

Josiah Spode was born in 1733 and at the age of 16 years he was apprenticed to Thomas Whieldon. In 1770 he was sufficiently experienced to take over the pottery of William Banks, for whom he had previously worked. He became a Master Potter, establishing a major ceramic factory, which has flourished to the present day. The son, Josiah Spode II, first produced bone-china in about 1800, taking William Copeland into partnership in 1805. William Spode, the grandson of the founder, died in 1829, and in 1833 William Taylor Copeland and Thomas Garrett became joint proprietors until 1847. From that time the company has been associated with the Copeland family, although now part of the Carborundum group of companies.

The name of Spode is probably best known among collectors for the large production of earthenware decorated with underglaze-blue transfer prints, often illustrating subjects taken from published engravings. Josiah Spode II used fine bone-china to produce a wide range of tea and dessert services and many good quality decorative wares. He managed to survive trading difficulties resulting from the Napoleonic Wars better than many of his rivals. It has been suggested that Spode's stone-china was being made as early as 1805, after he had acquired the patent from W. & J. Turner, but factory records indicate the material was not introduced until about 1813.

A further important name in the field of 19th century English ceramics is that of Thomas Minton, born in Shrewsbury in 1765. Minton was first apprenticed to Thomas Turner at Caughley, to learn the art of engraving copper-plates for the making of transfer-prints. It is said that he was involved in the early version of the so-called 'Willow' pattern, as seen on Caughley. He later worked as an engraver in London and after marrying returned to Stoke where he engraved plates for other potters, including Spode.

Minton's business flourished and in 1793, at the age of 28, he became a partner in a pottery. By 1796 he had built his own factory, where he first appears to have concentrated on the manufacture of blue-printed earthenware, soon to be followed by cream-coloured earthenwares of the Wedgwood type and bone-china. By 1810 Thomas Minton was producing wares in almost the entire range of ceramic bodies being made in Staffordshire at that time, although the production of bone-china was halted between 1810–24.

Recently, identification of many of Minton's unmarked wares made between 1810–24 has been made easier for the collector through the surviving pattern-books. These show not only the form, but a wide variety of original printed, painted and gilt designs, in addition to many patterns which would normally be associated with such contemporary potteries as Spode, Miles Mason, New Hall and Pinxton.

Many bone-china figures and ornamental wares previously considered to be the work of Coalport, Derby or Rockingham, have been confirmed by the pattern-books to have been made by Thomas Minton and his son Herbert, who was in control from 1836. Herbert Minton took John Boyle into partnership from 1836–42, after which he was joined by Daintry Hollins and Colin Minton Campbell in 1842 and 1849 respectively. Herbert Minton died in 1858, by which time the company had 1,500 employees. Today, Minton continues in production as part of the Royal Doulton Tableware Group.

A wide range of commonplace earthenware had been produced at Swinton, Yorkshire, from the mid-18th century, but the Rockingham factory is best known today for the fine porcelain made by the Brameld family from 1826. Many so-called Rockingham porcelains were beautiful. However, they were so expensively decorated that profits were small and despite financial aid from Earl Fitzwilliam closure became necessary in 1842.

For many years a large number of bone-china figures, tablewares and decorative pieces have been attributed to this factory, without the benefit of any evidence. But recent research has enabled present-day attributions to be more accurate. It has, for example, been proved beyond all reasonable doubt that Rockingham made no figures of small 'shaggy' poodles or pastille-burners in the form of little cottages or other buildings. The adopted 'griffin' mark (in red enamel from 1826–30, and in puce from 1830–42), was not used consistently and sometimes is seen only on a single item of a service. The collector should note that any pattern number exceeding about 1570 definitely indicates the work of another factory making similar wares, such as Ridgways.

America

During the first half of the 19th century various types of earthenware were being produced by several potters in the Philadelphia and Trenton areas. These included some admirably printed wares of English type, made by the American Pottery Company of Jersey City. Jugs of 'Parian' type porcelain, with moulded relief decoration and patterns 'pirated' from the English manufacturers, were in great demand. They are known to have been made by the United States Pottery at Bennington, Vermont, and E. & W. Bennett of Baltimore, Maryland.

Also popular during the mid-19th century were vessels with a rich-dark-brown glaze, so called 'Rockingham', a fashion catered for by many American factories. The American 'Rockingham' glaze differs from that associated with the English factory at Swinton, Yorkshire, by having a thicker and mottled appearance. These American Rockingham wares had much in common with *maiolica* ware. This was popular both in America and England. Glazes coloured with high-temperature oxides were applied to wares moulded in relief. The colours usually included 19th century pinks and crimsons derived from chrome.

From about 1826 some very good quality hard-paste porcelain was

H. Chamberlain
& Sons

Chamberlain's
Worcester,
& 63, Piccadilly,
London.

Chamberlain's
Regent China,
Worcester,
& 155,
New Bond Street,
London.

CHAMBERLAIN & CO.
WORCESTER
155 NEW BOND ST.
& No. 1
COVENTRY ST.
LONDON.

CHAMBERLAIN & CO.
WORCESTER

CHAMBERLAINS

Different styles of marking their wares used by Chamberlain's Worcester factory.

made in Philadelphia by William Ellis Tucker and his various partners. Jugs, or pitchers, tea sets and dinner services were well decorated with flower paintings and monochrome landscapes, together with fine gilding. Many such pieces have so much in common with the contemporary French porcelains, that positive attributions can only be made by reference to pattern-books preserved in the Philadelphia Museum.

Art Pottery did not really become popular in the United States until after the 1876 Centennial Celebration, from which time Cincinnati, Ohio, became the centre for this new taste. This attracted many art potteries, including the Rookwood Pottery, which was the only one to survive beyond 1890. Mrs Maria Longworth Nichols, a well-to-do Cincinnati socialite, was primarily interested in the creation of finely designed wares, rather than establishing a commercial success. Aided by friends skilled in the appropriate arts, Mrs Nichols succeeded in producing a wide variety of most interesting effects on wares. These wares were in great demand from 1880, when the first kiln-firing took place, until 1941, when the firm became bankrupt. The early years were very unprofitable, but by 1889 Rookwood Pottery was well established and a wide range of artistic wares was being produced. These included some original underglaze painting, under the direction of William Watts Taylor, who moved the production to large premises in 1892. By 1900 the Rookwood Pottery was the foremost American art pottery.

Zanesville, Ohio, was also a popular centre for the manufacture of art pottery. The foremost concern was the Lonhuda Pottery, originally located at Steubenville and purchased by Samuel Weller of Zanesville as an addition to his existing factory. Their wares had a great similarity to those of Rockwood and included various fruit, flowers and figures

Principal handle-types on pre-Nippon porcelain teapots, sugar bowls, creamers and other pieces. The handle, centre, top row, *was used on chocolate pots.*

painted in coloured slips on a dark ground and covered with a brilliant glaze. Some of their pieces were painted with characters from the works of Charles Dickens, the English author. However, such ill-fitting decoration under a matt glaze cannot be considered too successful.

There is great similarity in some of the matt-glazed forms made by the Grueby Faience Company of Boston, Massachusetts, and those of the Martin brothers, working in London at about the same time. They both seemed to be inspired by the leaf forms, which played such a large part in *Art Nouveau* in many European countries.

Japan

The years 1868–90 saw the growth in Japan of pre-Nippon porcelain wares. These export wares represent a transition period in Japanese ceramics and while the form and decoration show Western influences they still retain their Japanese heritage. Most pieces have no mark or when they do it is usually the potter's name. Characteristically the wares are extremely individual and exhibit a high standard of workmanship.

By the 1870s the kilns of Arita and Seto were producing these wares in large quantities but the blandness that accompanies true mass production is happily absent. The new occidental form is particularly noticeable in the handles and spouts of these pieces. Handles on teapots and chocolate pots were often in underglaze blue and elaborately painted, while the spouts were short and pointed and did not pour well, for the Japanese concept of a teapot was rather different from the Western designs they were trying to imitate. The join of the handle to the body was often quite intricate and pieces of this period can be dated from these handles, later examples showing a clumsiness in design and workmanship.

Many of the pieces were footed and the number of feet – usually three, five or seven – is typical of the Japanese predilection for irregularity in design. Small pieces were made with solid, curved feet and large wares with hollow ones; the feet for large pieces were made in a drain mould and had a small hole on the inside to prevent the build-up of pressure during firing.

Ornamental vases are a perfect example of the blending of East and West, for the true Japanese vase was made to hold flowers and therefore be as unobtrusive as possible. Ornamental vases were made entirely for export. The decoration on these vases was often highly detailed and intricate and often had as many as four kinds of coralene beading on one piece, with the beading on the front differing from that on the back. The beading can be a help when estimating the age of a piece, complex beading rather than the impression of complex beading indicating pre-Nippon wares as opposed to later imitations. Beading on smaller ware is also indicative of this period.

Roses and chrysanthemums are the principally used floral decoration and these are all painstakingly painted, unlike the wares of later periods which use blobs of colour surrounded by the appropriate outline. Floral designs on the front of a piece were usually different from those on the back – often fewer flowers and a different arrangement of colours.

The Artist–Pottery Movement

During the late decades of the 19th century most major industrial potteries were influenced by Japanese taste. Thereafter, designers turned

Chai ch'ing 1796–1820

Tao-kuang 1821–50

Hsien-fêng 1851–61

Vase made at the Rookwood pottery, 1890.

to either the old traditional patterns in vogue during the earlier years of the century, or the simple functional designs made in Berlin, Vienna, Paris, Milan, the various Scandinavian factories and especially England. In Great Britain, the ideas of Keith Murry are seen on Wedgwood wares of the 1930s, clearly indicating that formerly the designer was an architect working with a rule and compass.

It is fortunate that during this same period many skilled potters preferred to use clays as a new means of expressing personal feelings towards their craft. Today, many artist-potters are creating wares destined to be the antiques of the future.

The earliest evidence of the artist-potter obviously under the influence of the Near and Far Eastern potter was seen in the work of the Frenchman Théodore Deck (d.1891), who opened a studio in Paris in 1856 and continued to produce beautiful painted earthenwares in the Islamic manner until he became Director of Sèvres art department in 1887. While Deck is best known for his painting, Ernest Chaplet, who was working at Bourg-la-Reine in the 1870s, later specialized in glaze techniques and produced a wide range of unique effects on both stoneware and porcelain. They often equalled the glazes of the Chinese potter. Similar beautifully glazed stoneware was made in France by Adrien Dalpuyrat during the last decade of the 19th century. His contemporary, Auguste Delaherche, who produced some fine glazed stonewares, sometimes decorated in the *sgraffiato* technique.

The French artist-pottery movement was particularly evident during the 1920s and 1930s, when many original and interesting wares were produced by George Serre, Jean Besnard, Jean Mayoden, René Buthaud and Paul Beyer, the latter reviving the technique of salt-glazed stonewares.

The vogue for artist-pottery was soon to be seen in other European countries, especially Germany, where some interesting shapes and techniques were produced around the turn of the century by such potters as Herman Mutz of Altona. He was strongly influenced by Japanese ceramics and his son Richard also made some interesting stonewares in Berlin, often decorated with attractive 'flowing' glazes. These glazes appear to be suddenly 'frozen' from their liquid state. They were also very successfully applied by Julius Scharvogel, who was working in Munich in about 1900.

Following the First World War, there was a revived interest in Germany and the works of many potters active during the 1920s are to be seen in public and private collections. Foremost of this school was Bontjes van Beeck, a naturalized German of Dutch descent, who was extremely successful with his finely glazed stonewares in the styles of the Chinese Sung period. Since 1946, artist-potters have been working in both East and West Germany. The work of Ingeborg and Bruno Asshoff, working in Bochum in the 1960s, was highly original. They produced many simple shapes as a ground for 'bubbly' glazes.

The artist-pottery movement in Scandinavia was quite strong by the 1880s, when Thorwald Bindesbøll was creating decorative earthenware in Denmark. Most Scandinavian potters of the earlier period seemingly preferred the lower-fired earthenwares to stoneware, and often relied more upon applied decoration than original glaze effects. This was certainly so with Herman A. Kähler of Naestved, Denmark, who had great success with metallic lustres.

The division between the artist-potter and the ceramic industry is not so marked in Scandinavia, due to many factories providing the facilities for the artist-potter to experiment and create individual work. This was in addition to using his talents in designing for a greater production of wares made industrially. This practice has been a great asset to such fine potters as Axel Salto at the Royal Copenhagen Porcelain Factory, Stig Lindberg at Gustavsberg, Harry Stalhane at Rörstrand and Toini Muona at the Arabia factory, Helsinki, Finland.

The first wares which may well be termed artist-pottery in England were similarly sponsored by industry. The factory at Doulton, in Lambeth, London, had been in production since 1815 and their wares consisted of domestic and industrial salt-glazed stonewares. In 1871, students of the Lambeth School of Art were invited to work at the factory to choose jugs and vases to the shape required and to apply their original decoration. This was usually incised, carved or applied in a range of browns, blues and greys. The artists were then required to sign their work. Today, the individual work of such former students as Hannah Barlow, George Tinworth and Frank Butler is in great demand.

Salt-glaze stoneware was also the preference for the now famous Martin brothers, who from 1873 were working at Fulham, London. Later they moved to Southall on the western outskirts of London. Walter and Edwin Martin were trained at the Doulton studios, but much of their work was decorated with floral forms inspired by Japanese taste which enjoyed much popularity following the London International Exhibition of 1862.

It was in 1872 that William de Morgan started a workshop in Chelsea, London, where he specialized in the painting of tiles and pottery in lustres of the greens and blues seen on so much Persian pottery of the 15th–19th centuries. De Morgan's work was quickly appreciated and it became necessary for him to employ more staff, including the painters Charles and Fred Passenger and Frank Iles. Due to the founder's ill health the factory closed in 1907.

In 1905 the Moore brothers' porcelain factory at Longton was sold and Bernard Moore started his own business in Stoke. Moore had experimented with flambé glazes and now made decorative flambé ware using such artists as Hilda Beardmore, Dora Billington and John Adams. Flambé ware was also made by two of Moore's pupils, E. R. Wilkes and J. Howson under their own names. G. L. Ashworth & Bros. of Hanley were also making flambé glazed ceramics at this time.

The now much collected Ruskin pottery was the achievement of William Howson Taylor, the son of the headmaster of the Birmingham Art School. In 1898 he built his own pottery at Smethwick and began experiments with high temperature glazes with the assistance of some craftsmen from Wedgwoods. His experiments were highly successful and he went on to produce a range of high temperature glaze effects, lustres and monochromes, calling the latter 'soufflé' glazes.

Few of these early artist-potters were completely responsible from start to finish for the work they were involved with. Possibly the first true

Dish by William de Morgan c.1890.

artist-potter was the world renowned Bernard Leach, who was initially trained at the Slade School of Art to be a teacher of drawing and etching. Leach then spent about 11 years in Japan where he received training as a potter under a Japanese master. He then returned to England accompanied by a Japanese potter, Shoji Hamada. Together they established a pottery at St Ives in Cornwall. Leach and Hamada worked together, using all locally obtained materials, from which they produced a wide variety of wares, including Japanese style stonewares and traditional English slip-trailed earthenwares.

Many now-famous English potters worked at some period during their training at St Ives, where Leach ran his pottery on a community basis. This enabled them to produce many modestly priced and readily saleable wares, while allowing them to create original and personal work. Michael Cardew, Nora Braden and Katherine Pleydell-Bouverie all owe a great deal of their success to the knowledge gained from the master, Bernard Leach.

Hamada returned to Japan in 1924 and has worked there ever since. His style carries the influence of Japanese folk pottery, English slipware and Yi Dynasty Korean pottery. All of Hamada's work in high-fired stoneware is intended for domestic use including plates, bowls, teapots, bottles, jars and flower vases. This stoneware has a rough texture which contrasts well with the wood-ash and milky feldspar glazes he uses.

Nippon Wares

Nippon wares are those which bear the name 'Nippon' and appeared in the years 1891–1921. The McKinley Tariff Act of 1890 decreed that all articles imported into the United States should bear the name of the country of origin in English. Nippon being the Japanese name for their country this name was used on pottery from 1891 until 1921 when the U.S. treasury ruled that 'Japan' should be used instead since Nippon was a Japanese word.

Early Nippon period wares still showed the blend of East and West characteristic of the pre-Nippon ceramics, while the later pieces become more and more Westernized; handles in particular show Western influence and feet are reduced to small balls of clay. Early Nippon wares still bear the hand of the individual potter but from about 1915 mass production had taken hold and the same moulds tended to be used repeatedly. Also in this period the use of the jigger gradually took hold as a result of which the wares became less attractive. The most characteristic wares of this period were chocolate sets and while the moulds used were almost identical, the quality of the porcelain varies enormously. The finest porcelain is that bearing the Rising Sun symbol.

Glass

The supremacy of Bohemian and German glass, established in the 17th century, continued into the 18th century until it began to be challenged by the English glassmakers. The most serious blow, however, was the

Napoleonic Wars which disrupted trade throughout Europe. When the wars were over and the German and Bohemian glasshouses were in a position to move forward again they found that the English had made even more serious inroads into their markets, with their cheaper lead glass, and that the French Empire style had become fashionable.

The history of Bohemian glass is a history of challenges well met however, and once again the glassmakers were able to rise to the challenge and to usher in a second great age of Bohemian glass. With the exuberance of Rococo swept aside by the Napoleonic Wars and the glittering Empire style lasting for only a short time, the new Biedermeier style was perhaps a logical evolution.

The emerging style, at first necessarily frugal, developed along aesthetic and still Neo-classical lines as expressed in furniture and furnishings of this period. The romantic and intimate character and the preference for pastel shades of blue, pink and alabaster white are echoed in Biedermeier glass. Workmanship is of high standard and this applied to all aspects of the arts and crafts. The finest engraver of this age was probably Dominic Biman (1800–57) of Neuwelt. His specialities were portrait glass and portrait medallions, executed to order for visitors to the famous spas which had become so popular. The engraved work of K. Pfohl (1826–94) is especially memorable for its spirited representation of horses.

Developments in coloured glass in this period were intrinsically bound with the Biedermeier style. One of the most ingenious glassmakers of the Biedermeier period was Friedrich Egerman (1777–1864) of Novy Bor. Apart from his successful pinkish red, and gold topaz, stains, he developed a most interesting simulated stone glass akin to Venetian *Schmelzglas*, the so-called *Lithyalin*. This *Lithyalin* glass resembled marble, and though made in several colour shades was largely produced in a deep red. This marbled glass was applied either as an overlay on transparent coloured glass, or used as an opaque glass mass, decorated by most sophisticated cutting which exploited the marble pattern in an inimitable technique. Egerman signatures are extremely rare.

One of the most prolific artists was Anton Kothgasser (1769–1851) who worked in Vienna. Kothgasser's panoramic views are usually found on that most typical of Biedermeier vessels, the *Ranftbecher* – a plain flared beaker with cogwheel base, further enhanced by an all-over yellow stain. Followers of Kothgasser include Hoffmeister of Vienna and Carl von Scheidt in Berlin, among others. Subjects include floral decoration, romantic figures and verses of dedication, characters from playing cards and animal fables.

A fluorescent green or yellow was achieved in this period by the introduction of small quantities of uranium or vitriol to the glass batch. This technique was developed by Josef Riedel of Dolny Polubny in Northern Bohemia and the colours named *Annagrün* and *Annagelb* after Riedel's wife Anna. Uranium glass was produced between 1830–48.

A solid opaque black glass was patented by Count Buquoy *c.*1820 and in sympathy with the classic revival in the arts was christened *Hyalith* glass. Pleasing classical forms were applied with fine gilding of flowers and insects and *chinoiserie* motifs. Similar decoration is seen on some of

Egerman's products, and it is quite likely that the same artists were employed. *Hyalith* is very brittle with little heat resistance and not much has survived.

The Biedermeier style established a prime place again for Bohemia and Germany, but from about 1850 the industry began to decline. A new upsurge came towards the end of the century with the *Jugendstil* or Art Nouveau, largely due to the efforts of Louis Lobmeyr of Vienna, industrialist and glass designer, who brought together the best Czech and Austrian artists to resume glassmaking on an individually inspired artistic level. Lötz Witwe at Klostermühle, Austria, created Tiffany-inspired lustre glass of great originality as well as exploring a number of other techniques under the direction of Max von Spaun. Bakalowitz Söhne, Adolf Meyers Neffe, the Harrach glassworks, Josef Pallme König and Ludwig Moser & Söhne (the last three still exist), were the most important factories producing art glass. In Germany the glassworks of Count Schaffgotsch' Josephinenhütte, and the Württembergische Metallwarenfabrik, both operating today, made important contributions to glass development into our age. In 1904, the glass factory at Zwiesel set up an influential school for glass techniques.

The Emergence of French Glassware

Despite the fact that glassware had been made in France since Roman times no glass of quality was produced in France until the 18th century. The forced migration of the Huguenots in that century probably ensured that a distinctive style could not appear. It was not until 1764 when the glasshouse of Sainte-Anne at Baccarat was established, by the Bishop of Metz, that a French glass industry was founded.

In 1822, the company emerged as the Compagnie des Cristalleries de Baccarat. The agate and opaline manufactured during the first half of the century was followed by developments of colour glass and the application of excellent cutting and engraving from 1867. Baccarat too produced a fine green and yellow fluorescent glass metal, the *cristal dichroide*. George Bontemps, one of the most imaginative of French glass designers, exploited Venetian techniques at Choisy Le Roi (1823–48) resulting in the manufacture of the paperweight, produced by various French factories.

The first Baccarat millefiori weights appeared in 1846, and if dated will be from 1846–49 inclusive, the last year being the rarest. Dates are preceded by the initial B. In 1848 Baccarat started production of the *sulfures*, enclosing flowers, animals or fruit, and paperweights in the *cristallo-ceramie* technique, the so-called *sulphides*. Baccarat weights are frequently additionally decorated by cutting and a star cut base, and enclosure techniques are also applied to beakers.

The factory of St Louis, founded in 1767, produced paperweights which may be dated between 1847–49 with added initials SL. Snake and reptile weights are a speciality of this factory.

A distinct feature of paperweights made at the Clichy factory are swirl patterns, and some Clichy weights are marked in the pattern with the initial C. Table glass, vases and decanters were made by all these factories, and during the late 19th and early 20th century came up with well designed, pressed glass which was on occasion partly coloured, simulating overlay glass; a signature is present in the mould. Modern Baccarat is always signed in full.

During the third quarter of the century, a new development in glass art emerged, combining historic techniques with naturalistic design. The leader of this Art Nouveau movement was Emile Gallé (1846–1904), designer of ceramics, furniture and glass, and the inspiring force of the Ecole de Nancy. During the various phases of Gallé's creative style, decorative techniques were carried out with incredible virtuosity. Enamelling, gilding, cutting, engraving, acid etching, cameo carving, sandblasting, colour fusion and incrustation were applied in profusion. Gallé's early works, his *verreries parlantes* and *vases de tristesse*, are imbued with poetic spirit and lyricism. His later revival of cameo glass techniques, influenced by the decorative treatment of Chinese snuff bottles in particular, made a tremendous impact and resulted in a real mechanization of cameo carving processes. The consequence was a commercial, factory-produced product which nevertheless did not exclude the development and exploitation of ingenious studio glass techniques on the highest artistic level.

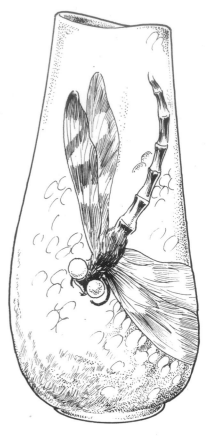

Glass vase made by Emile Gallé in 1903.

Some fine results were achieved by several of Gallé's close followers: Daum Frères of Nancy, Muller Frères of Lunéville, St Louis-Münzthal (signatures Arsale for *Argental* = Münztal), De Vez (real name Camille Tutre de Varreux) of Stumpf, Touvier, Viollet and Cie; Schneider (signed Schneider, also Le Verre Français), Legras of Pantin. Gallé signatures are of incredible versatility and on good pieces in close sympathy with the general style of the decor.

Of the highly gifted individual artists mention must be made of Eugène Rousseau (1827–91) and his pupil E. Leveille, who experimented successfully with crackleglass and inlay techniques; Joseph Brocard (d.1896) who revived Islamic style enamelling, and the group of artists who worked in *pâté de verre*: H. and J. Cros, F. Decorchement, H. Dammouse, G. Argy-Rousseau, Almeric Walter, G. Despret and perhaps also Georges de Feure, a successful illustrator, designer of furniture, furnishing materials, theatre decor and ceramics. In principle, the *pâté de verre* technique consists of pulverizing glass, adding a binder, placing it into moulds and cooking it in the kiln. Signatures are always present.

American Glassware

It is thought that glassmaking was one of the earliest American industries, but it was not until the late 18th century, when more glassmakers emigrated from Europe that an industry of any importance developed.

One of the first styles to emerge was the 'South Jersey' style in free-blown, clear glass in well-balanced forms. By the early 19th century, several New York state glasshouses produced a South Jersey style in pleasant shapes and colours. In addition, by 1815 about 40 glasshouses were in operation in various parts of America, making bottle and window glass.

The war of 1812 and the blockade by the English encouraged home manufacture and by 1840 at least thirty glasshouses produced tableware. English, Irish and French and a little later Bohemian techniques made their mark on the new industry. The Pittsburgh Glass Manufactory, established by Benjamin Bakewell and Edward Ensell from England in

1808, continued trade under various names. In 1817, a group of businessmen purchased the defunct Boston Porcelain and Glass Company and began trading in 1818 as the New England Glass Company. The most dynamic of these partners, Deming Jarves (1790–1869), established his own glasshouse at Sandwich, and in 1826 this was incorporated as the Boston and Sandwich Glass Company.

The perfection of a pressing machine by means of which molten glass was pressed into any desired shape revolutionized the American and European industries. Patents for pressed glass knobs were taken out by Bakewell in 1825, and by the New England Company in 1826. The designer of the metal moulds must be considered the real artist in this glassmaking process. Early American pressed ware is usually of fine quality lead glass, and the utilization of three-part moulds encouraged more elaborate designs. By the 1850s, three-quarters of American glass output consisted of pressed ware. Between 1825–50 the new process was exploited to the full with a very distinctive design, the 'lacy', a pattern with a stippled background which gives the appearance of delicate embroidery or textile. Because of the growing intricacy of these patterns, the moulds had to be exceptionally well made and heated, prior to being filled with a fluid glass metal. 'Lacy' was made in coloured as well as milky opalescent and colourless glass. The pattern variations are almost limitless and even detailed study cannot always ensure definite attribution to one factory or another. The publication *American Glass* by H. and G. S. Mckearin (New York 1941, Crown Publishers), will be very helpful to the collector of 'lacy' ware.

Favourite objects are the charming salt cellars in Rococo and Empire style, and the small cup plates of about 7.5–10 cm (3–4 in) in diameter. Patriotic slogans and emblems were popular elements in pressed glass design. Pictorial and historical pocket flasks were produced from at least 1780 in a variety of colours, and include the charming group of violin bottles and the Jenny Lind bottles. Factory marks occur frequently on moulded glass but not automatically so, and numerous amalgamations and name-changes of smaller American glasshouses need patient research.

By the mid-19th century, renewed Continental influence caused the appearance of some delightful and well made paperweights. Floral bouquets or miniature fruit resting on a *latticinio* bed were the speciality of the Sandwich Glass Company and the work of a Frenchman, Nicholas Lutz, formerly of the St Louis factory. John Gilliland who owned his Brooklyn factory preferred millefiori weights and sulphide enclosures, perhaps French-influenced or an application of Apsley Pellatt's process. Weights of more individual charm were produced by the New England Glass Company and consisted of beautifully coloured single fruit, free blown and near life-size, resting on a clear glass cushion.

The last quarter of the 19th century brings a spontaneous emergence of 'art glass', and with it a vogue for shaded colour glass. This fashion appears to have been introduced with the so-called Amberina glass, shaded amber to ruby red, a creation by the former Stourbridge glass artist Joseph Locke and patented in 1883. Another Englishman, Frederick S. Shirley, followed suit with his Burmese glass a pale yellow to pink patented by the Mount Washington Glass Company and manufactured under licence by Thomas Webb in Stourbridge. Colour shades became more and more exuberant with exotic names: Pomona, Peachblow, Maize, Coral Wild Rose. The Mount Washington Glass Company and Hobbs-Brockunier and Company are perhaps the most prominent from the collector's point of view, with the Durand Glass Company coming a very close second.

In 1864, William Leighton of the Wheeling Glass Factory in West Virginia developed a lime soda glass as a cheaper substitute for lead crystal. This was disastrous for some of the glasshouses producing high quality lead glass and they were forced to cease manufacture. When the New England Glass Company finally closed down in 1888, the factory's agent, Edward D. Libbey moved the Company to Toledo Ohio where cheaper gas was available, and took over the Charter in 1890, with Joseph Locke still as leading glass artist. The Libbey Glass Company is now a division of the Owens-Illinois Glass Company.

The greatest innovator in American Art Nouveau glass was Louis Comfort Tiffany (1848–1933), son of a fashionable jeweller. The company was established in 1878 as Louis Comfort Tiffany and Company, Associated Artists, and in 1880 Tiffany patented his iridescent glass – the 'Favrile'. Tiffany's interest extended to glass exploitation techniques recalling ancient processes of iridescence and corrosion, and re-created these effects by exposing his glass to metallic oxide fumes or by adding certain substances to the glass batch. His iridescent colour creations made an enormous impact on glass art everywhere, and iridescent glass was soon produced by most good and artistic glass factories. Signatures vary from the full name to initials only, or perhaps the trademark 'Favrile'. Tiffany produced a number of artefacts, small boxes and lamps. He had produced stained-glass windows and screens as early as 1872 and applied this experience to the production of most fascinating lampshades. The factory closed in 1932.

English Glassware
The repeal of the Glass Excise Act in 1845 and the 1851 Great Exhibition created a new activity in the glassmaking industry, with interesting results. Richardsons of Wordsley contributed with fine colour enamelling and acid etching. William Fritsche and Frederick Kny, two Bohemians, produced remarkable engraving in the rock crystal style at Stourbridge. John Northwood I (1836–1902) became the first glassmaker to produce cameo glass in the classical style with his replica of the Portland Vase.

It took Northwood three years, from 1873 to 1876, and endless experiments to complete the vase. When the vase was almost finished it first cracked and then broke in two and Northwood was forced to glue the parts together and continue his work. His ultimate method, having formed the dark blue body and coated it with opaque white glass, was to create the general pattern by removing the white layer in a bath of acid, grind as much as possible of the remaining pattern on a wheel and then to complete the detailed work with sharp steel tools using paraffin to give them a 'bite'. This method was eventually used for the manufacture of cameos on a commercial scale.

An entire school of cameo cutters and engravers was formed in the

Marks of the three principal slag glass manufacturers. (See text opposite).

Stourbridge industry with a number of gifted artists: Alphonse Eugène Lecheverell at Richardsons, Joseph Locke (1846–1938), John Northwood II (1870–1960), Joshua Hodgetts (1857–1933) of Stevens and Williams, and the gifted Woodall brothers, George (1850–1925) and Thomas (1849–1926) of Thomas Webb, who financed the best artists with the result that 19th century cameo glass is described as Webb's Cameo glass, even if produced elsewhere. Signatures are frequently present. English cameo work usually shows the relief in opaque white glass on delicate natural shades from brownish yellow to orange and green, and on a distinctive midnight blue base. Stourbridge and Birmingham revived millefiori techniques for the production of paperweights, ink bottles, tumblers and doorknobs from the mid-19th century.

American pressed glass techniques reached England after 1830 and resulted in attractive novelty ware, especially slag glass, so termed because of the deliberate addition of waste material from metal foundries.

The technique of press-moulding is a relatively simple one, but could not be said to be a fully mechanized method of making glassware for it still relied on the skill of the worker. A known quantity of molten glass is first poured into a mould and a plunger then lowered in order to press the glass into all areas of the mould. After removal of the plunger the mould is opened. Due, however, to the rapid cooling of the glass, particularly when used in small quantities, the glass was often not pressed completely to the top of the mould.

The prettiest colour of the English product is light blue. Other shades are purple, cream, white, black and marbled effects, applied in patterned ware in the shape of urns, lattice plates, jugs, dogs, mugs, obelisks, candlesticks, boots and more rarely portraits with inscriptions. The factories mainly associated with slag glass manufacture are: Sowerby's Ellison Glassworks at Gateshead (marks: moulded peacock's head), George Davidson and Co. of the Teams glassworks at Gateshead (marks: lion overlooking rampart, facing right), and Greener and Co. of Wear Glassworks Sunderland (mark: lion facing left, bearing halberd).

Some of the glassware made by these companies, as well as others, is marked with a small raised diamond either on its own or accompanied by the maker's mark. The letters Rd (an abbreviation of 'registered') are to be found in the centre of the diamond and indicate that the design had been registered at the Patent Office. The year, month and day of registration appear in the corner of the diamond. From 1884 only this information with the letters Rd but no diamond was used.

Powells of Whitefriars produced glass in the Venetian style from the 1850s. In the 1890s under the direction of Harry J. Powell, the firm produced some attractive Art Nouveau shapes using a yellow to cream opalescent glass with bluish highlights, as well as slim, tinted glasses with combed and trailed decoration.

A more original development were the sometimes harsh and uncompromising forms of avant garde designers such as Christopher Dresser (1834–1904) and George Walton at the Glasgow factory of James Couper and Sons. Their streaky glass often bubbly and with aventurine inclusions named 'Clutha' (cloudy) was frequently produced for Liberty's, mounted in pewter or silver designed for the Tudric and Cymric range.

Dresser had specialized, while studying at the School of Design in London, in botanical drawing. He went on to become a leading Victorian designer in various fields including carpets, fabrics, wallpaper, metalwork, furniture and silver. He joined Coupers in the late 1880s as principal designer. While many of his designs were original, he also used as models both ancient glass and pottery from Rome, the Middle East and Peru. His designs are often signed on the base with an etched flower with the word Clutha in Celtic capitals curving above the flower and 'Designed by C.D.' below and the word 'Registered' below that. He designed glass for Coupers until the mid-1890s.

George Walton (1867–1933), an architect and designer, was his successor, appointed a couple of years after he left Coupers. His designs were more symmetrical than Dresser's and he also used richer coloured glass, containing aventurine and gold flecks.

Gold and Silver

The Neo-classical style which had swept Europe and America in the last decades of the 18th century had in part been the result of an artistic interpretation of the Roman and Greek styles of antiquity that were being revealed through archeological discoveries. Around 1800 the Neo-classical style moved into a new phase which was fired by the desire to reproduce even more exactly the styles of antiquity, which now also included Etruscan and Egyptian forms. In France the new style became known as Empire which corresponds with the Regency style in England.

Silver gilt was much used in work at this time – it exhibited the highly cultivated taste of the Prince Regent, later George IV. In France, the firm founded by M. G. Biennais (1764–1843) rose to success in the service of Napoleon's Imperial dream and here again the use of silver gilt was preferred. So highly regarded was the British firm of Garrards, that in the 1820s the Paris goldsmith Odiot sent his son to work there and ordered English machines for his Paris workshop.

Garrards had started in 1802 when Robert Garrard senior took control of a company he had partnered with John Wakelin. Garrard died in 1818 leaving the business to his three sons, Robert, James and Sebastian, although from the start it was Robert who dominated and controlled the company until his death in 1881.

Garrards succeeded Rundell and Bridge as Royal goldsmiths in 1830. Much of their financial success was due to the fact that they produced everyday silverware in contemporary styles that were literally good, solid pieces of silver whose weight and value were immediately apparent. Their reputation however was derived from their presentation silver of which they were the leading purveyors, furnishing cups for many well-known races and producing a large number of table-centres.

Edmund Cotterill, a sculptor, joined Garrards in 1833 and by 1842 was being hailed as an outstanding artist. His speciality was racing trophies and among his most notable creations were the Ascot Cup for

Silver coffee pots, top: *Wurzburg, c.1810*; bottom: *Stuttgart, early 19th century.*

1842 which represents an incident at the battle of Crecy and the Queen's Cup for Ascot 1848, depicting a Mexican lassoeing a wild horse.

England continued to dominate the industrial world by producing in 1820 a steam-powered lathe for spinning shapes and by the discovery of the electroplating process. As early as 1814 Paul Storr had made an electrogilt silver goblet, but not until 1840 did the Elkington cousins of Birmingham take out the first patents which led to their revolutionizing and monopolizing the plating industry.

While the fortunes of the Elkingtons were made by mass production of domestic-type wares, particularly for hotels and restaurants, they also tried to rival Garrards and Hunt and Roskell in solid decorative silver. To this end, they employed a number of French sculptors such as Aimé Chesnau, Pierre Emile Jeannest and Albert Wilms. Their most successful sculptor was Léonard Morel-Laudeuil who was with the company from 1859 until his death in 1888. He is best known for the Milton shield which was exhibited at the Paris Exhibition in 1867.

When articles were made in Sheffield plate the copper sheet was silver plated before the object was shaped. In electroplating the object was completed in base metal before being put into the plating vat to be covered with a thin skin of precious metal by means of an electrical current passing through. At first the electroplaters used a copper base which gradually showed through with wear, as it had done with Sheffield plate, then a layer of whitish alloy was interposed between the copper and the silver. This was 'German' or nickel silver, a mixture of copper, zinc and nickel, invented in China and introduced into England in the 18th century. By 1836 the copper base was replaced entirely by one of improved nickel silver, now called 'Argentine' silver.

Another metal, a mixture of copper, antimony and tin which originated in the 18th century and had been used by the Sheffield platers was also electroplated. This was called 'Britannia' metal. The great advantages of using a 'white' base metal and of the electroplating process itself was that when the silver wore away the colour of the exposed base layer was less obvious, and also that the object could be put in the vat for replating as often as was necessary.

Electrogilding was a merciful improvement on the gilding technique which had been used until this time, since although mercury gilding had produced a lasting effect of great beauty it was lethal to the workmen who often used it incautiously.

Electrotyping was a further development of the electroplating process, in which objects could be copied in copper and plated. This was popular with the growing public for revived styles, who were satisfied with electroplate. Usually, a mould was taken from the object to be reproduced, but in the 1840s there was a revival of interest in natural forms and objects which led to the electrotyping of real flowers, leaves and plants and also of small animals and insects – an interesting return to the work of the 16th-century mannerist goldsmiths.

From 1842 G. Christofle (1805–63) in Paris began making electroplated goods under licence from Elkingtons, of Birmingham. All his designs were available both in silver and electroplate, an important selling point, and his use of an 18th-century style was greatly to the taste of

Second Empire France under Napoleon III and the Empress Eugenie.

A turning point in Christofle's career came in 1852 when his nephew Henri Bouilhet joined the company. Bouilhet, who had a diploma in engineering and chemistry, was able to devise a new machine for stamping out spoons and forks as well as developing a method of producing large scale architectural ornaments in single pieces on a commercial scale.

In America the company of Reed and Barton, heirs in the 19th century to the Taunton (Massachusetts) Britannia Manufacturing Company, did not at first make articles in silver at all, but concentrated on the market for electroplated goods. Silver was discovered in the USA in 1859 and the success of the Gorham Manufacturing Company was derived from the consequent lowering in price and the increased supply.

One of the styles of gold and silver work to appear in the first half of this century was a new naturalistic style. With the advances in technology, silversmiths found themselves with the ability to copy exactly all the known historical styles and to simply add naturalistic details to them. Eventually, however, this naturalism began to form the basis of a new advance in design rather than simply an element in design. Amongst the first work of this kind to appear were experimental productions by Rundell's, one of the most notable pieces of which is an 1820s salt cellar designed as a sea-urchin resting on coral.

In the 1840s there was a marked return to classical styles. The copying of Roman articles which had been started by Rundell's, Storr and Flaxman was revived on a large scale as a result of the advances in technology. Copies of the Portland vase were made by Hunt & Roskell in the 1840s. Chinoiserie also reappeared for a short time in the 1840s.

A revival of the Gothic style, in this period, was led by A. W. N. Pugin, who had worked for Rundell's. While much of his work was with furnishings and ecclesiastical buildings he also designed domestic wares. Popular adaptations of Pugin's Gothic style were made by Elkington's such as the tea sets exhibited by them at the Great Exhibition. The popularity of the style persuaded Gough & Co., Elkington's and Henry Wilkinson & Co. to produce silver and electroplate salt cellars, cruets, mugs, tea sets and other domestic wares.

Unhampered by the rigid assay systems of European rivals, the firm of C. F. Tiffany (1812–1902) was able to show at the 1867 exhibition in Paris work which reflected the simpler style stimulated by the resumption, after many years, of trade with Japan. The 'Aesthetic Movement' as the Japan inspired style began to be called, was more palatable to the Western intellectual élite than were the eclectic revivals of previous styles which continued to be popular with the general public.

In 1876, the English designer, Christopher Dresser (1834–1904) visited Japan, buying both for Tiffany and for the South Kensington Museum (now the Victoria and Albert) in London. Dresser's functional designs, drawn with the machine in mind, and made to be executed in either silver or silver plate, were marked by their beauty and simplicity of shape, no decoration blurring the burnished surface. Japanese influence appeared in the shapes he used and the positioning of the handles on his objects.

Artists in many fields were by now concerned to eliminate the grosser evils resulting from the Industrial Revolution. The many popular

Silver teapot designed by Christopher Dresser, 1880.

282

exhibitions from 1851 onwards unwittingly demonstrated supreme technical control allied with appalling design. Throughout the rest of the century designers and artists tried constantly to revert to what was thought to be the golden age of the craftsman when, it was felt, the worker, unsullied by contact with machines, was inspired by joy in the work of his hand and mind.

Christopher Ashbee (1863–1942) was one such thinking artist. He was probably influenced by philanthropic classes organized in Philadelphia by Charles Leland. He founded a Guild and School of Handicraft in 1888 at Toynbee Hall in London, where unskilled workers were taught age-old crafts and where an amateur, hand-made look was cultivated in opposition to the cheaper, characterless, slick finish of the factory.

The firm of Liberty and Co. of London exploited the appeal of Ashbee's Guild style. It was in keeping with the general Art Nouveau taste of the 1880s and also with Liberty's original reputation as importers of oriental goods. From 1899, Liberty's 'Cymric' silver and 'Tudric' pewter fused the influence of Dresser with that of Ashbee. Made by using factory die-stamping and spinning processes, Liberty silver bore hammer marks which made the work look as though it was completely hand-made. In fact, the hammer marks were either included in the die-stamp or added to a spun piece after it was finished. Liberty silver was not cheap, but the use of machine process and hand finish enabled it to undercut firms which would have no involvement with machines.

The designs of the Glasgow architect, Charles Rennie Mackintosh (1868–1928), more influential in continental Art Nouveau than they were in Britain, clearly showed a development from sappy, tendril-like hothouse curves to a tauter, more purposeful and energetic style appropriate to the 20th century.

Russia has not been previously mentioned, because in general silver designs were derived from those prevailing in Western Europe. Since the mid-17th century Russian rulers had encouraged architects and artists from outside to go there to work. Russian museums now held many superb examples of the best European silver which over the years had been presented to successive Czars as ambassadorial gifts. Not all Russian silver, however, was derivative, certain objects developed along their own lines in a particularly national tradition. An example of this was the kovsh, a flat-based boat-shaped vessel with a prow-like handle, which was used as a cup or a ladle. Another was the charka, a small spirit cup of more conventional shape. Both could be decorated in niello or in cloisonné enamel – neither the shape of these cups nor the techniques used to decorate them were to be found elsewhere in contemporary Europe.

Clocks

The 19th century saw many changes in the craft of clockmaking. The demand was growing for a cheaper priced clock for the masses instead of costly possessions for the élite. The French in the preceding century had realized that sub-division of labour and specialization could achieve a greater output without necessarily destroying the quality of the product. It was, however, the Americans who took this concept a stage further. Many of the 18th century settlers had been or became skilled clockmakers. They had one major problem – a lack of metal from which to manufacture their movements. By laborious methods some of them managed to overcome this problem and some fine long case clocks were made in and around Philadelphia. In their attempts to overcome the difficulty, the clockmakers of the New England area slowly developed a characteristic style of their own.

Simon Williard of Grafton, Massachusetts was an outstanding maker of this period. His eight-day brass timepiece, which became known as the 'banjo' clock was patented in 1802 with a further nine improved patents following. The basic shape of the clock almost never changed, unlike the finish. Early examples have simple banded inlay work with an acorn finial and the decorative glasswork was usually done in geometric patterns with 'S. Willard's Patent' in gilt on the lower door glass. It is believed that these glasses were made for Willard by John R. Penniman from 1806–28 and by Charles Bullard.

In 1819, Willard patented an alarm clock, which, so the patent states, 'when let off, it strikes on the top of the case of the clock, and makes a noise like someone rapping at the door, and it will wake you much quicker than to strike on a bell in the usual way'. The cases of these clocks are similar to a lighthouse with the clock face under a glass dome on top of a circular case.

The Connecticut makers with their abundant supply of local wood decided to produce wooden movements. Eli Terry stands out as an important pioneer in this stage in the history of American clockmaking. After accepting an order to make 4,000 movements he had through necessity to devise some labour saving and time saving conveniences. Part of his solution was the standardization of parts and in 1816 he patented details of a weight-driven wooden or brass movement for a shelf clock.

The spring-driven clock was not generally in use in America until the 1840s. The first man to produce them in any quantity was probably Joseph Ives using his lever spring. Although coiled springs had been imported in the 18th century they were too expensive to be used in cheap clocks. Eli Terry's son Silas was the first to devise a method of tempering coiled springs allowing them to be made cheaply. He took out a patent for this idea in 1830.

During the 1840s brass springs were used extensively after Joseph S. Ives patented a method for making them in 1836. At this time brass springs were still cheaper than imported steel ones. By 1850, spring-driven clocks were being made in larger quantities than weight-driven ones and, since steel was now cheaper, few clocks after this date are found with brass springs.

In 1842 Chauncy Jerome shaped history by sending a shipment of his cheap mass-produced spring-driven shelf clocks to England. They had cases of cheap veneered wood, painted zinc dials, glazed doors with either straightforward movements or with the additional feature of an alarm or striking on the hour. These clocks flooded the market and sounded the death knell for the more conservative English clockmakers.

Calendar clocks were popular in America, for over 50 years from 1855. The clocks were of two basic designs, one with only the days of the month around the dial, and the other with two dials, the calendar one being worked by the clock. Some were even more elaborate than this and had the day of the week, the phases of the moon and the tides. Most of them self-corrected for a leap year.

The first calendar clock with a separate mechanism was patented by John H. Hawes of Ithaca, New York in 1853, but it was never put into production. In 1854, William H. Akins and Joseph C. Burritt patented another mechanism a perfected version of which was sold to the Seth Thomas Clock Company, which manufactured the clock until 1876. They continued producing calendar clocks. Other well-known designers of calendar clock mechanisms in this period include Henry B. Horton, whose design was used by the Ithaca Calendar Clock Company until 1917, and Benjamin B. Lewis of Bristol, Connecticut, whose mechanism was used by several companies including Burwell & Carter and the E. Ingraham Company.

One clock mechanism popular with collectors because of its complexity was patented in 1877 by Daniel Jackson Gale and manufactured by Welch, Spring & Company.

In Germany, clockmakers were quick to realize that, if they were to survive, their cottage industry must adopt new methods. One family, the Junghans, were particularly progressive, and in the mid-1860s the business skills of one brother and the knowledge gleaned of 'the American Way' by other members of the family while working in America resulted in the opening of a factory making mass-produced clocks with American machinery. Some of their designs followed those of the Americans so closely that it is in many instances difficult to tell them apart. However, they also continued with their traditional cuckoo clocks, postman alarms, and so on.

The French clockmakers, who had long realized the potential of mass production, continued, notably in factories run by the Japy Frères, to produce movements to a standard pattern for the 'makers' to case as they wished. These roulants appear in every conceivable style of French clock: four glass clocks, the typical Victorian black marble clock, and many elaborate cases and garnitures (the designs of which were copied from earlier styles) and also the carriage clock. The carriage clock was tremendously popular. Possibly its attraction lay in its compactness, wide diversity of quality and style of case decoration, together with the many variations of simple or complicated strike and chime that were available.

Both longcase and bracket clocks underwent some changes in the first two decades of the century, English longcases becoming simpler and more refined in style and the break-arch top of bracket clock cases becoming more curved and the break sometimes disappearing altogether. The 'lancet' bracket clock, so-called because it is shaped like the lancet window, appeared in the first decade of the century. The balloon clock, which was first designed about 1760, reached the height of its fashion just

American clock made by Seth Thomas.

285

after the turn of the century. The inspiration for this clock is variously attributed to the hot-air balloons of the Montgolfier brothers and to typical Louis XV bracket clocks. The latter seems the more likely since the first balloon flights did not take place until 1784. These clocks with their waisted sides are quite plain and usually have a panel of inlay below the dial.

A novel type of clock which was made until 1830 is the tavern or Act of Parliament clock. In 1797, because of a tax placed on all watches and clocks by William Pitt, innkeepers were forced to use cheaper clocks. Although the tax was repealed a year later, innkeepers carried on using this type of clock for some years. They were made of a large wooden, painted dial and a drop case for the pendulum and weight so that they could be hung on the wall. Only a few of the surviving examples are highly decorated.

The English clock industry dwindled, however, as the century progressed. While other countries accepted the new ideas, the English makers insisted on continuing their now out-dated methods which could not meet either the demand or price range of their new customers. A few small factories opened in the mid-1800s, one being the British United Clock Company, but they failed to realize how completely competitive they needed to be. Although struggling at the lower end of the market, the Victorian clockmakers did produce some magnificent pieces of quality workmanship for those who could afford them. In particular, the brass skeleton clock under its glass shade with its varying escapements, frame designs and strike enjoyed a quite remarkable popularity.

In 1851 Lord Grimthorpe and Edward John Dent devised the Great Clock of Westminster, which came to be known after its installation as Big Ben – the most famous public clock in the world. The gravity escapement of Big Ben was a new type perfected by Lord Grimthorpe. The early types of gravity escapement, first invented in 1770 by Thomas Mudge, were unstable, so Lord Grimthorpe devised what is called the 'single three-leg' escapement in 1850 and the 'double three-leg' which he used in Big Ben.

The building of the clock was an event that no doubt was a contributory factor to the numerous orders received by the turret clock manufacturers of that day from many foreign parts. The order books of Potts of Leeds, Smith of Derby and Gillet and Johnston of Croydon make fascinating reading. No doubt this also influenced the making of the huge longcase and bracket clocks made about the turn of the century with their multiple choice of chimes on bells, tubes or gongs.

It would appear that the age of the mechanical clock is nearing its end and will be entirely replaced by those utilizing the quartz oscillator. This has been a natural evolution from the first successful application of electricity to clocks by the Scotsman, Alexander Bain, in 1842. From that date we have seen the progress of many systems of master clocks controlling slave dials (that of Synchronome first patented 1895, and Lowne patented 1901) and the domestic battery clocks (the Eureka first patented 1906 and the Bulle of 1921), followed by the synchronous mains clocks of the 1920s and 1930s. And now, in fact, the digital and quartz clocks are common.

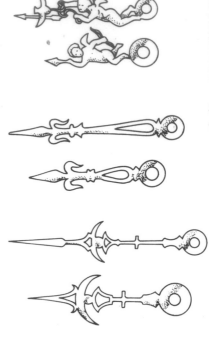

Some of the hands used on French clocks 1850–75.

Watches

The 19th century saw many changes in the watch. By 1830 the cylinder escapement had almost completely replaced the verge escapement and the use of the chronometer escapement gave watches a precision they had not had before. The lever escapement established its supremacy in this century.

Possibly the most noticeable technical achievement was the advent of the keyless watch. The difficulty encountered when attempting to incorporate this feature into a watch with a fusee, heralded the final demise on the Continent of the fusee, although many English makers clung to the key wound verge watch until as late as the 1880s.

The Swiss industry began to emerge from its previous state of quiescence to become one of the major manufacturers. With a widening market the form watch was reintroduced. Now intended primarily for use by the fair sex, these small movements were housed in finger rings, bodies of butterflies, bracelets and so forth. Although Frederic Japy had begun making watches in France by machine tools as early as 1776, it was during this century that true factory methods were generally adopted.

It seems likely that the first watches made in America were the work of Thomas Harland (1735–1807). An advertisement of 1773 declared that he made 'horizontal, repeating and plain gold watches in gold, silver, metal or covered cases', though whether he made these or simply engraved his name on imported examples is now known. His obituary states however that he made the first watch manufactured in America.

After his death, Luther Goddard (1762–1842) bought some watches from his estate, as well as some tools and in 1809 began making watches at Shrewsbury, Massachusetts. Many of the parts he bought from abroad but some he cast in his workshop and had the cases engraved by a local engraver. His first watches were marked 'L. Goddard'.

Two other watchmakers of repute in the first half of the century in America were the Pitkin brothers, Henry (1811–46) and James Flagg (1812–70). By 1835 they had developed a watch which they hoped could be manufactured commercially by standardizing the parts so that they were interchangeable. Even so they had to import dials, hands, hairsprings, mainsprings and jewels. The first 50 watches were marked 'Henry Pitkin' while later pieces were marked H. & J. F. Pitkin. The brothers were never successful at cheap mass production for their watches were still more expensive than imported ones.

It was not until the 1850s that successful production of machine-made watches was achieved, principally due to the efforts of Aaron L. Dennison and Edward Howard. Dennison was trained by James Carey of Brunswick and after working for a repairer for some years he opened his own workshop called A. L. Dennison & Company in 1856. Although the firm was at first making only boxes for the jewelry trade, by 1849 Dennison had turned his attention to the manufacture of watches and persuaded Edward Howard to give him a room in his own factory in

Roxbury, Massachusetts in order to experiment with machinery for watch production. He had little success with his first eight-day watch but by 1854 he had produced over 1,000 thirty-six hour movements with the name 'Samuel Curtis, Roxbury' engraved on the plates. Curtis had been one of Dennison's early backers. Dennison's company at this time was called the Boston Watch Company. Unfortunately the company went bankrupt in 1857 mainly due to a general recession. However they had set the trend that was to be followed by the more successful companies such as The American Waltham Watch Company and E. Howard and Company.

Firms such as Waterbury (1880–1896) and Ingersoll concentrated on the rapidly growing need for cheaper watches. These cheap watches, the products of advancing technology and acceptance of new ideas, were eventually to crush the more conservative English watch trade. The Swiss makers survived, however, by adopting and improving upon the best of the new methods of production. Many of the names appearing on watches of modern manufacture bear names of eminent makers of this century: Jurgensen, Frodsham, Bonniksen, Vacheron, Constantin – their work having been continued by their successors.

As the century progressed, the emphasis changed, with cases becoming plainer. The demand was now for a technically interesting watch that was highly accurate, or for a simple inexpensive model with an adequate degree of accuracy.

Jewelry

The Neo-classical movement which began in the second half of the 18th century was inspired by a new interest in Greek and Roman antiquities which arose out of archeological excavations at Pompeii and Herculaneum from 1738–56. The early style of the movement was a combination of the lightness of Rococo with classical ornamentation, but as Neo-classicism progressed the style became more of a direct imitation of antique art, partly out of an increasing understanding of that art and partly as a reaction against Rococo.

In France, the conscious imitation of Imperial Rome was brought to a head when Napoleon became emperor during the first decade of the new century. His empress, Josephine, quickly re-established a taste for lavish jewelry display. This was made possible by jewels which had been sold or broken up during the early years of the Revolution. The new designs were essentially classical pastiches using laurel wreaths, combined with a reassertion of coloured stones, especially emeralds and sapphires, and the widespread use of cameos: diadems, hair combs and *épingles à cheveux* were especially popular, the hair drawn up on top of the head away from the ears.

This Neo-classical influence was present in most items of jewelry during the first decades of the century and was arguably most effective in the iron jewels produced in Germany during the latter years of the

Chandelier in the Banqueting Room of the Brighton Pavilion, dating from 1817.

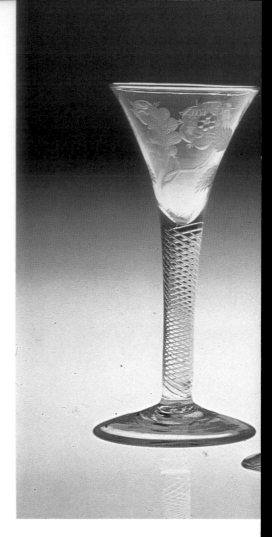

Left: *Ewer by Emile Gallé, c.1870. The body is acid-etched and is mounted in silver gilt. Signed Gallé, Nancy.*

Above: *Engraved wine glasses, left to right: Waisted trumpet bowl with engraved Jacobite emblems, 1750; funnel bowl with Jacobite emblems, 1750; waisted bell bowl with carnation and bee, 1765; Hanoverian funnel bowl engraved with The White Horse of Hanover and a 'Liberty' ribbon; bell bowl, 1765; Jacobite flared bucket bowl, 1760; trumpet bowl with engraved Jacobite motto, 1745.*

Right: *Spode saucer with tea and coffee cups, c.1800. The pattern is based on Japanese Imari ware. Transfer printed earthenware plate, c.1820.*

Following pages: *Deer Park Parlor, Baltimore County, Maryland, c.1800.*

Opposite page: Top: *Two different Staffordshire models of Napoleon Bonaparte* c.*1845.* Below: *Staffordshire figures* c.*1845 of Jules Perrot* (left) *and Carlotta Grisi* (right) *in their costumes for the ballet* La Esmerelda.
Centre: *Early 19th century Hard-Paste porcelain plate decorated with a scene of Saint Cloud, France.*
Below: *The influence of Art Nouveau is very apparent in this silver gilt cup and silver christening set.*

Napoleonic wars. The Prussian government had appealed to the wealthy to donate their jewels to the war effort. In return they were given necklaces, brooches, pendants and earrings in a delicate cast-ironwork, lacquered black, and frequently stamped on the reverse with a motto such as *Gold gab ich für Eisen*, followed by the date of the donation. Iron jewelry continued in popularity well into the second half of the century and Rouen became a great manufacturing centre. The technique adapted itself particularly well to the Gothic tracery motifs of the 1840s.

Jewelry suffered far more from the vagaries of fashion during the 19th century and became, as a result, immensely eclectic. By the late 1820s Neo-classicism had burnt itself out and the poor jeweller was at a loss for new inspiration and motifs. What he could not conjure up afresh he sought in past styles and designs, borrowing from a procession of sources. Among these, the Romantic Gothic, popularized through Walpole's novels and the architecture of Pugin and Burgess, was an important influence during the 1840s and is best illustrated by the knights, angels and gargoyles that decorate the jewelry of the Froment-Meurice and Jules Wiese.

If the Gothic jewelry was largely fantasy, the classical jewels produced during the 1860s were not. Makers such as Castellani, Melillio and Brogden, who had all profited by the immense quantity of previously unknown pieces yielded through excavations at famous sites like Herculaneum and Pompeii, were involved in a re-working of Etruscan and Hellenistic jewelry that was both intelligent and faithful to the originals. Another important source of inspiration was the jewelry of the Renaissance, especially the designs of Holbein. In England, Carlo Guiliano and firms like Phillips of Cockspur St, London, seized on these designs as a vehicle for their superb enamelling skills. Carlo Guiliano, in particular, established an almost unrivalled reputation as an enameller during the 1870s, operating from a shop in Piccadilly; the reputation being continued by his sons working in 'Holbeinesque' and 'archaeological' styles.

The grand exhibitions that took place in Paris and London during the second half of the century had an enormous effect on the spread of new motifs and designs drawn from myriad sources. For example, the Great Exhibition in London in 1851 showed that the fashion for all things Egyptian had had an effect on jewelry design as well. Attention had been directed to the area through the excavations in the Nile valley and the approaching completion of the Suez Canal.

Following the 1851 Exhibition the first major exhibitions were the Dublin International Exhibition of 1853 and the Exposition Universelle in Paris in 1855, which was the first French international exhibition. The Castellani brothers from Rome exhibited their work for the first time at the 2nd English International Exhibition in 1862, though of perhaps even greater interest at the time was the display of Japanese prints and ceramics.

The Paris Universal Exhibition of 1867 showed evidence of the French involvement in Algeria by the appearance of jewels designed around the knots and tassels common to North African dress. Other new designs were less successful. The battery-operated kinetic hair ornaments that

Left: Art Nouveau brooches, pendants and buttons by Child and Child, Ashbee, Henry Wilson and Omar Ramsden arranged on a Mucha poster.

appeared in the same exhibition are a good example.

The four South Kensington International Exhibitions of 1871–74 were conspicuous by the amount of commercial jewelry on show and as an indicator of the popularity of Neo-Renaissance and 'Egyptian' jewelry with the public. The Exposition Universelle of 1878 set the trend of jewelry in Paris for the next 25 years and launched Lucien Falize, Jules Debut and Eugène Fontenay to the forefront of the scene. The catalogues of all these exhibitions will provide the collector with a fair indicator of the trends and fashions throughout the last half of the century.

Other jewelry of the period was less innovative. Spray brooches remained a popular vehicle for the display of diamonds and achieved a high degree of naturalism and informality. This was augmented by the mounting of some of the flowerheads *en tremblant* on a watch spring, so that the bloom literally trembled with the wearer's every move. Many of the brooches show great botanical accuracy. Perhaps most attractive are those produced by Froment-Meurice during the 1840s, the leaves highlighted with translucent green enamel.

Less important items of jewelry tended to suffer from the Victorian flippancy and sentimentality. This latter element was responsible for the great fervour for mourning jewels, a habit especially seen in Britain. Many of them were particularly grisly and macabre. Even items that were not specifically involved with the commemoration of the dead frequently had provision for a hair compartment. Indeed, in some cases jewels were fashioned entirely from the hair of the deceased person.

Birds and insects were fashionable too, ranging from the delicate doves of the traditional Normandy St Esprit pendants, to grotesque lizards and cockroaches. Birds were also a common motif of the mosaic and intarsia brooches widely exported from Rome and Florence respectively and popularized through the medium of tourism.

Male jewelry was restricted to signet rings, watch fobs and chains and tie or stock pins. It is really only in the latter group that designs show imagination illustrated by the enamelled skulls, with articulated jaws operated by a drawstring, characteristic of the Romantic Gothic of the 1840s, and the golfclubs, ships and horseshoes produced during the last quarter of the century with the fashion for sporting jewelry.

In America, comparatively little jewelry was worn before the mid-19th century and in the 1830s and 1840s the home market mainly comprised functional silver jewelry, such as buttons and buckles, made by local smiths. High quality jewelry was imported from Paris and pinchbeck from Birmingham. While there were a few firms in the major cities they were not exclusively devoted to the sale of jewelry. Even Charles Tiffany relied mainly on imported Parisian jewelry until 1850.

In that year the American government began imposing duty on imported jewelry, which rapidly stimulated the growth of home manufacturing. The principal centres for commercial production of jewelry were Newark, New Jersey and Providence, Rhode Island, for both of these cities had a history dating from the turn of the century as jewelry manufacturing centres.

Despite the late American start in the craft, by the 1860s several quite

Lozenge-shaped brooch of diamond and aquamarine by Fabergé.

distinctive styles were evolving which owed much to Tiffany. Examples are gold-mounted tortoiseshell combs and gold jewelry decorated with engraving and Rococo and classical patterns in black and white enamel. American jewellers were also quick to see the possibilities of the recently discovered Japanese decorative arts, or *Japonisme*. It was not until the Centennial Exposition in Philadelphia in 1876, when American jewellers were competing for the first time with their European rivals, that they realized the need to evolve a purely American style.

A great deal of American mourning jewelry can still be found, much of it from the 1860s and 1870s, when it was particularly fashionable, and consists of gold combined with jet or onyx, or gold decorated with black enamelling.

The general appetite for jewelry, which increased dramatically during the 19th century and which spread to most social classes, was greatly served by the production of machine-made pieces, especially in Britain, Germany and Austria. Settings and components stamped out of sheet metal and assembled by hand are common throughout most of Europe from the mid-century onwards. The process was soon adopted in America, too, as a means of producing jewels quickly and cheaply, though at first to predominantly European designs. Originally the process was reserved for gilt metal jewelry but was quickly applied to precious metals as well, largely as a result of the formidable increase in gold resources through the discoveries in California, Australia and South Africa.

Towards the end of the century there was a gradual reaction against the ostentation and ponderousness of the previous 50 years. Diamond jewelry, in particular, shows a gradual lightening and increasing delicacy of design, very often looking to the Louis XVI style of decoration, especially in ormolu furniture-mounts, in swags, garlands and ribbon bows. The technical excellence of the diamond jewelry during the last decades of the century and the early 1900s has seldom been surpassed and benefited greatly from the immense quality of diamonds that were being mined in South Africa after 1868, together with the use of platinum for the settings, a metal which combines good working qualities without tarnishing.

Fine examples of this technical excellence are the products of the Fabergé workshops in Russia. The firm is characterized by an immense attention to detail and a careful choice of materials, specializing in *objets de fantaisie* as well as hardstone sculptures and jewelry. Perhaps the most famous articles that the firm produced are the jewelled Easter eggs which were manufactured every year from 1882 and given by the Czar as presents to his wife.

In Britain, the move away from the excesses of the Victorian era in all the decorative arts is largely attributable to the crusading work of William Morris, whose firm, Morris & Co., had been set up as early as 1861 in an attempt to re-affirm the importance of craftsmanship and integrity to design. In jewelry this meant a reaction against the display of wealth through gold and precious stones to which the art had been confined since the late 16th century. Instead the arts and crafts designers favoured silver and enamel set with agates, moonstones, mother-of-pearl and peridots.

Scientific Instruments

In the 18th century the leading makers of precision astronomical instruments all worked in London. The names of Graham, Bird, Short, Troughton and Ramsden were familiar to astronomers throughout the world. But by the turn of the century German workshops began to compete and then overtake their English rivals. The Mathematical-Mechanical Institute of Reichenbach, Utzschneider and Leibherr, a Munich consortium, led the way, followed by the equally illustrious names of Frauenhofer, Ertel, Merz and Repsold.

In the 18th century brass draw-tubes with wood or leather-covered barrels commonly occur. The intermediate stage when vellum-covered pasteboard was combined with a polished shagreen stained red or green is particularly attractive, especially if the lens mounts and reinforcing ferrules are made of silver rather than horn, ebony or brass. By the latter part of the 19th century nickel, aluminium and chrome plate are used and these hand-held telescopes hold little attraction. At this late date, however, astronomical instruments using the telescope only as a sighting device still retain a strong aesthetic appeal. It is the sheer ingenuity and complexity of the mounting, be it transit, equatorial or altazimuth, that overcomes the drab but hard-wearing finish then applied.

The visual attraction of pieces from German workshops during the early decades of the 18th century was attained by the use of brass with various colour characteristics; a copper-rich alloy highlighting the more usual yellow brass, while the whole instrument was enlivened by the inset circles of silver on which the fine divisions of degrees were marked and calibrated. In the middle years of the 19th century a dark blue-green or black oxide finish was applied to astronomical instruments. This provided a practical and durable finish but the price paid was an immediate reduction in visual impact. Surveying instruments of the period were similarly treated. They are far more common and less intricate than astronomical instruments. In a search to uncover supposed former glories quite a number have been 'restored' by the removal of the original lustreless finish and buffed-up to an unnatural sheen.

In the third decade of the 19th century, with the development of the compound achromatic objective, the microscope came of age as a scientific instrument. From this date development based on sound mechanical and optical principles was undertaken both in Europe and the United States. The workshops of Ploessel of Vienna, Norbert of Bath, Oberhauser of Paris, Nachet of Paris, Powell and Lealand of London, Ross of London, Dancer of Manchester, Spenser of New York, Grunow Brothers of New Haven and Zentmayer of Philadelphia produced excellent instruments. By 1870 the English makers had been overtaken in eminence by American and German firms who continued to adapt and innovate rather than rely on well tried models. Zeiss of Jena led the field, their designs stimulated by the theoretician Ernst Abbe. The 'Jug-Handled' Zeiss remains a classic instrument among microscopists today. A number of French and American firms also produced advanced work. The Bausch and Lomb Optical Company of Rochester are worth particular mention, and it is interesting to note that the leading American microscope makers of the latter part of the 19th century were almost all refugees who had left Germany during the 1850s.

The Sikes's hydrometer was used to test the strength of spirituous liquors for revenue purposes in the British Isles from 1816. The design hardly changed through more than a century of manufacture and the instrument itself was only replaced by more sophisticated methods during the last decade.

The brass hydrometer, covered with a fine film of gold to prevent corrosion, is frequently seen in antique shops sitting in an attractive velvet-lined case with a set of small gilt weights, an ivory backed thermometer and a slide rule in boxwood or ivory. As with any scientific instrument the maker's name is the most reliable guide to date, though where a firm has been in business for two or three generations or more, other pointers are required. A practised eye will know real ivory from the various synthetic ivorines than replaced it, while silver and brass should be readily distinguished from polished nickel and chrome plate. Those with a knowledge of furniture may rely on the way that the case is made and finished. The centre piece, the hydrometer itself, gives few clues to its age. The calligraphic style of the calibration and other engraved lettering can be helpful, but frequently, as with other instruments whose design was long lived, it is the sum of the evidence drawn from the object, its accessories, the case lock and hinge, that provides the experienced observer with evidence of the date of origin.

The barometer, for all its being a meteorological instrument invented by Toricelli about 1640, is the extreme example of the trend to turn the laboratory into a salon. Indeed the vast majority of mercury barometers that survive were made and sold as items of domestic furniture rather than as scientific instruments.

During the late 18th century scientific and domestic barometers ceased to evolve along similar lines. On the one hand the scientific barometer was increasing in accuracy as the demands of science grew more rigorous, while on the other, the domestic barometer stagnated. Nevertheless good examples continued to be made until after 1850. Notable barometer makers were Matthew Berge (*fl.*1802–d.1819), Thomas Jones (1775–1852), Dudley Adams (*c.*1760–d.1819), Nairne and Blunt, W. & S. Jones, Dolland and J. &. E. Troughton. Balthazar Knie (*fl*1743–d.1817), originally a glass-blower of German origin, became one of Edinburgh's most famous makers. Another Scot to gain a reputation in the field was Alexander Adie (1774–1858), an optician who made both domestic and marine barometers. He is also known for his invention of the sympiesometer, a barometer using oil and hydrogen gas instead of mercury thus making for smaller barometers.

During this century the barometer industry in France and Holland is notable for the large number of Italian immigrants – usually glass-blowers – who set themselves up as barometer makers. In Holland, well-known makers included Bianchi, Butti, Pagani and Reballio. Many of the Italian immigrants eventually moved to England for their signatures (often anglicized) are often found on English instruments. One Italian maker who worked in London and Paris was C. Bettally. Others include F. Arione (1802), J. Cetti (1803) and F. Pastorelli (1805).

In the early 19th century, despite the arrival of more and more Italian makers, the English still dominated the industry, but by 1840 the Italians were the leaders. It is likely that many of them did not fashion the entire barometer themselves; instead, as glass-blowers, they made the bulb and tube and other functional parts and hired local workers to make the supportive and decorative parts which were returned to Italians for assembly.

In the first decade of the century the most popular barometer was the straight-tube leather-based cistern type with a simple mahogany frame with rounded top. The tube was either encased or exposed in a groove. Panelled mahogany frames and scroll pediments were also common, sometimes with carved ivory rosettes on the scrolls and ivory or wood inlay work on the cistern cover. Black borders of ebonized veneer were also introduced. Barometers were also given thermometers and occasionally oat-beard hygrometers. Bow-fronted cases were popular and were made until late in the century.

As well as the 'stick' barometer the well-known 'banjo' barometers shared a dominant place. This type of barometer may have originated in France c.1760; the earliest English examples date from 1780–90. C. Bettally was a distinguished maker of this type of barometer and he is particularly remembered for a pair of them supplied to Lord Bute in 1787 that had their cases inlaid and veneered with satinwood.

The invention of the voltaic cell and the development of electromagnetism and current electricity led to many new instruments like the induction coil, the tangent galvanometer and the multi-cellular voltmeter, with the electric telegraph providing both a new means of communication and a large market for receivers and transmitters. The delicate workmanship of the later electrical instruments used for precision measurement is often hidden inside a protective case. Those without some technical insight might not appreciate the subtlety of the design. However, the layman cannot fail to be attracted by the various forms of vacuum tubes with which 19th century physicists studied the effect of high voltage discharge through gases at a high degree of exhaustion. Geissler, Plücker, Hittorf and Crookes all gave their names to vacuum tubes of particular types. If we can no longer be dazzled by the fluorescence of uranium glass in a Geissler tube, we can still be impressed by the skill of the glassblower who was able to insert a small paddle wheel inside a Crookes tube so that it would spin and run along a glass railway when bombarded by rays of 'radiant matter'.

Here was the birth of particle physics, and at a more directly useful level it was with a pear-shaped Crookes tube that W. T. Roentgen discovered X-rays in 1895, and so opened the way to radiotherapy. Most early medical instruments being almost solely concerned with surgical applications have macabre associations that tend to swamp any aesthetic attractions. In contrast the early X-ray tube has a functional form of considerable strength, and would not be out of place in a gallery of 20th-century sculpture. For the collector of scientific instruments, perhaps the most desirable are those made in Germany by firms like Müller of Hamburg, where the etched signature includes the word 'Roentgenrohr' and so commemorates the discovery.

By the beginning of the present century, physics had outgrown descriptive natural philosophy and become a highly mathematical subject. Mathematics itself had advanced considerably and in combination with electrical technology was soon to spawn that master of all our destinies, the electronic computer. In its earlier history, the tools of mathematics were far less awesome artifacts.

Embroidery

By the 1820s a new craze had gripped needlewomen, who were more and more intent on speed and colourful effects. In the early years of the 19th century a German printseller called Phillipson had begun to sell hand-coloured needlework designs on squared paper, and they were eminently suitable for working on canvas with the soft wools of Saxony. The designs – and the wools – spread very rapidly to France, Spain, England and America, where thousands of women spent hours each day working chair and footstool covers, bell-pulls, slippers, braces, card cases and all conceivable trifles with garish flowers, parrots, animals and even whole scenes from old master paintings. Some were highlighted with beads. By mid-century the beads were obtainable in the same variety of brilliant colours as the wools. Other designs included 'plush' stitched features in which a section of the design, for example a bird or a rose, was worked in a looped stitch and then cut to form a pile, giving a three-dimensional effect. In spite of occasional variations of canvas stitchery, tent stitch was by far the most usual for Berlin wool work, or 'zephyrs' as it was called in America (after the yarn used in it).

A large variety of materials were used for working on: the earliest wool work was principally on silk canvas which was made from cotton fibres with fine threads of silk wrapped around them. Silk canvas grounds were particularly used when the object was not going to be subjected to hard wear – pictures and screens were typical examples. Designs on silk canvas, particularly when plush stitch was used, gave the piece a three-dimensional effect. Jute canvas was used when the finished piece was likely to be subjected to any degree of wear and tear, such as cushions and stool tops.

Cotton canvas, which came in a variety of meshes, was made and used in France, Germany and England, the French samples being the better quality. While it can be difficult to distinguish between the French and English cotton canvases once they have been worked, the German canvas was made with every tenth thread coloured yellow and this is still visible on the finished work. From about 1850 the double or Penelope canvas was popular in England. Java canvas was used particularly for making bags.

The use of Berlin wool work on upholstered furniture became more

Broderie anglaise border on a cotton dress, c.1818.

popular as the century progressed. Until 1830, very little of this work was used on furniture for the design of Regency furniture was not suitable for the relatively small patterns that were being imported at that time. By Victorian times, however, embroidery and Berlin wool work had come to mean the same, such was the popularity of the latter. The return of Gothic and Elizabethan styles around 1830 also gave impetus to the use of wool work especially for the *prie dieu* or devotional chair which originated in this century. Floral designs such as roses, passion flowers and carnations are commonly found on these chairs, sometimes along with Gothic tracery and religious symbols. Floral wool work can often be dated by the background colour, pale pastel colours with an airy feel indicating a pre-1850 date, while the use of vivid aniline dyes began in the 1860s. The range of flowers on these later designs also widened to include fuchsias, tiger lilies and suchlike. Religious designs were worked until about 1855.

The sewing chair with its continuous seat and back was also a subject for wool work. One way it was decorated was simply to work a line of needlework about six inches wide down the middle of the seat and back which was covered in satin or velvet. *Bergère* chairs which had closed arms and loose seat cushions were ornamented with floral wool work in the second half of the century.

After the mid-19th century, Berlin wool work began to lose its preeminence, at least in 'artistic' circles. A new movement, aimed at encouraging a more inventive approach to embroidery design and reintroducing many of the stitches which had all but disappeared from the needleworker's repertoire, was already afoot by the 1860s. Known as art needlework, its ideals were fostered in England by William Morris and Edward Burne-Jones, and the movement found its vehicle in the Royal School of Art Needlework, founded in 1872. Its objective was 'restoring . . . ornamental needlework to the high place it once held among the decorative Arts'. Its members were mainly impoverished gentlewomen and its patrons were almost invariably titled. Much of the work was designed by such artists as William Morris, Edward Burne-Jones and Walter Crane.

The Royal School of Art Needlework was most influential in America, where similar schools were set up in major cities in the 1870s and 1880s. The Royal Irish School of Art Needlework, established in Dublin in the 1870s, helped to popularize the new ideas all over Ireland. Other movements took root in Europe and by the end of the 19th century there was a noticeable merging of styles. This common ground, embodied in Art Nouveau, was manifest more in textile design than embroidery which, largely because of the relentless development of industrial technology, was relegated and remains a minor accomplishment. The design of machine-made fabrics, on the other hand, has continued to attract artists of high calibre, and it is probably in this field that one should look for the best examples of modern textile achievement. Although embroidery cannot be subjected to mass production, there has been a growing realization that using some aspects of our industrial age is only sensible. The use of machine embroidery, until recently quite unthinkable, is now included without a second thought.

Netsuke

Ivory netsuke c.*1800.*

Traditional Japanese clothing consisted of robes and a sash. Small belongings such as a tobacco box or a seal case, *inro*, were suspended on a cord with a toggle or pendant, *netsuke*, fastened to the other end. The *netsuke* was pushed down through the sash to secure the object.

Early *netsuke* were probably made of natural materials – pieces of wood, bamboo, roots, horn and stone. *Netsuke* were in use in Japan from about the 14th century until the 19th century. In general Japanese craftsmen took their inspiration from China, and *netsuke* carvers were no exception. Some early *netsuke* were copied from Chinese seals, and were often carved in ivory with Chinese designs and called *karmono*.

Netsuke were used to carry a variety of objects – medicine cases, writing cases, powder flasks, flint and steel, keys, chopsticks, small tea jars and drinking gourds. Some objects such as brush cases and compasses served in themselves as *netsuke*. The introduction and rapid adoption of smoking stimulated the production of *netsuke* and the majority were eventually used to carry pipes and tobacco boxes.

Smoking was introduced into Japan in the mid-15th century but in 1603 the Shogun, Ieyasu Tokugawa, banned the practice. Then in 1605 the first tobacco plantation was established in Japan. However, further bans in 1607 and 1609 made tobacco cultivation a penal offence. In spite of these and other even sterner measures, smoking continued to spread rapidly and was eventually adopted by the aristocracy. By 1639 smoking was part of the hospitality offered along with tea to guests.

Gentlemen, samurai, did not carry smoking equipment, nor did they smoke in public. Men of the lower classes – traders, farmers and labourers – did, and it was they who used *netsuke* to carry their smoking things, including metal *netsuke* to keep their pipe ashes alight.

The impetus to develop the craft of *netsuke* carving came from wealthy merchants in the early 17th century. Under the Tokugawa the merchant class was forbidden to carry swords, while at the same time the samurai were wearing increasingly decorative sword furniture. In order to compete, wealthy merchants commissioned more elaborate *netsuke*. The development of craftsmanship in sword furniture inspired in its turn an increase in the designs, material and quality of *netsuke* carving.

Before 1780 *netsuke* were the utilitarian side products of skilled workers in other crafts. Wood-workers of religious sculptures used their offcuts and musical instrument makers used the ivory remaining from a tusk after a *samisen* plectrum had been cut from it. Imported ivory was expensive and scraps were too valuable to waste. This shows in the typical shapes of ivory *netsuke*: triangular if the *netsuke* is taken from the outer layers of a tusk and pyramidal if carved from a tip.

In the late 18th century the demand for *netsuke* became so great that professional carvers became established, and over the next century produced the finest work in this genre. The best carvers lived in Osaka, Kyoto and Edo and sometimes became retainers on the staff of high ranking samurai, carving largely for their lord and his house. Most *netsuke* are unsigned while those that are often have the carver's 'nom de plume' rather than his real name. A surname is usually lacking since this was only held, along with the privilege of sword wearing, by those of samurai status.

Netsuke craftsmen used a variety of woods, some of which were imported. The most commonly used was boxwood (*tsuge*) which is hard, yellowish and fine-grained. Wood for *netsuke* was either stained brown with the juice of the *kuchinashi* berry, or black with Chinese sandalwood. Alternatively the wood was painted in water colours or lacquered. *Netsuke* of the latter group are usually made from Japanese cypress, magnolia, Paulownia or *keyaki* (Planera japonica). Identification of the woods is aided by the fact that many artists and schools preferred specific woods. Korean pine, for instance, was used by the early Hida school (19th century); yew is particularly associated with the artist Sukenaga in the late 18th and early 19th centuries, while red sandalwood was used by Matsuda Kaneyuki in the mid-19th century. Most of the woods used were suitable for carving (*ki-no-horimono*), although Japanese cypress is fairly soft and was used by the early carvers of Buddhist images and by the famous artist Shuzan (1743–91). In the mid-19th century a technique which used different materials for the various parts of *netsuke* became popular. For instance, a human figure may have his various limbs made from wood, ivory, coral, jade, gold and silver.

Ivory was the second most popular material for *netsuke*, especially in the 18th century when it began to be imported from India. Ivory carving is called *zoge-no-horimono*, and one of the earliest masters of the technique was Ogusawara Issai in the late 18th century. Ivory is a particularly good medium for carving because of its naturally variable graining, which in the hands of a good craftsman can be incorporated in the design. The earliest ivory *netsuke* were triangular and elongated in shape to avoid wasting expensive ivory. Such work was called *sankaku-bori*. In the early 19th century some artists, such as Ryukei began experimenting with tinted ivory, using the juice of the Gardenia berry (*kuchinashi*) to give a brownish-yellow stain, while ferrous sulphate or nitric acid was used to etch the outline in brown-black, and copper sulphate for green staining. Stained ivory of the 20th century, however, tends to be inferior.

Various kinds of ivory were used including narwhal, sperm-whale tooth and wild boar tusk. As with wood, certain artists tended to use particular kinds of ivory. Bunshojo (1764–1838) and Tomiharu (1723–1811) carved in tooth, Ogasawara Issai (late 18th century) in ivory and whale tooth and Kamman (late 18th century) in boar's tusk.

Various kinds of horn were also carved – rhinoceros horn, buffalo, antelope, oxhorn and deerhorn, which was the commonest used. Yellow or gold coloured rhinoceros horn with black veining was also popular. Deerhorn was carved by Shogetsu and Ryukoku in the mid-19th century, although the most famous was Kokusai (mid-19th century).

Nuts that were used for carving *netsuke* included walnut, betel nut and palm nuts. Damson and peach stones were also occasionally used. Only rarely were *netsuke* carved entirely from minerals, but inlay work with malachite, marble, jade, soapstone, mother-of-pearl, coral and ivory is fairly common. The most famous artists using such inlay were Suzuki Tokuku (mid-19th century) and Kagai Dosho (1828–84).

An indication of the age of *netsuke* may be gained from the object and the carving style with older pieces showing a simpler carving style of fewer subjects. Late 18th century subjects include religious and mythical figures from poetry legends and proverbs, signs of the zodiac, masks and dolls. Some of the latter, *negoro-ninyo*, were carved in wood and lacquered by descendants of the priests of Negoro who invented a famous lacquering technique. In the 19th century subjects included real and mythical animals, birds, reptiles, the occupations of daily life, utensils, fruit, vegetables and the seasons. Money, medical figures, trick figures and erotica also served as subjects.

The forms of *netsuke* are also indicative of the age of pieces and the development of the craft. The earliest *netsuke* are *sashi*, thin pieces of wood, bamboo, bone or ivory, about six inches long with a hole at one end. *Katabori*, the largest group of *netsuke*, and the type next developed, include animals, insects, tools, musical instruments and human figures among their subjects. These are all about two and a half inches square. From the 17th century onwards miniature masks, carved as *netsuke* by Kabuke mask makers, were a popular subject.

Manju is the second largest type of *netsuke*. They are a flattish oval or square shape with rounded corners, resembling a Japanese cake and may consist of one or two pieces fitted together. *Manju* were mostly carved in wood during the 18th century, but by the 19th century ivory, bamboo and horn were also used. A sub-type of *manju* is *kagamibuta*, a finely carved bowl of ivory, horn or wood which was valued for its metal lid rather than the bowl. These lids were made in iron or alloys of iron and gold, silver or copper, and some cloisonné, by craftsmen in sword furniture. *Hako*, small boxes, and *ryusa* are other forms of *manju*. *Ryusa*, produced from the 18th century, are hollow forms made on a lathe, and have openwork decoration showing insects, blossoms, birds and arabesques. *Ichiraku netsuke* are relatively few in number, and are woven in thin wire or rattan cane in designs such as baskets, gourds and sandals.

The fashion for wearing *netsuke* disappeared about 1870 when cigarettes and western dress were adopted in Japan. At the same time the demand for *netsuke* by western collectors led to the Japanese regarding them as works of art. A few *netsuke* are still carved but the craft is uneconomical.

Inro and Ojime

Inro are sets of boxes which fit into each other and apart from pipes and tobacco boxes, *inro* were the objects most often carried by means of *netsuke*. The word 'inro' means seal case and the earliest examples, imported into Japan from China, were used for holding seals and an ink pad. The earliest *inro* were thus single or double boxes, and were kept in homes as shelf ornaments. About 1500 the most typical form of *inro*

Inro with five sections decorated with trees and figures.

developed. This was a flattish, rectangular box, about 9 to 10 cm (3½ to 4 in) long by 5 cm (2 in) wide with three to six compartments which was carried with a *netsuke* on the sash. The top and bottom surfaces of the box are called *joge* and can be either flat or convex. The layered series of boxes in the *inro* are called cases, while the topmost section which is not considered a case is known as a *futa*. Each of the cases has a lip which extends upwards (the riser) which fits into the bottom of the case above. Multiple case *inro* came to be used for carrying medicines.

The sections or compartments of an *inro* are joined by a cord and are kept together on the cord by a running bead, *ojime*, which then has a *netsuke* on the end. Open cases and pouches lacked a bead. The *ojime*, up to 1 cm (½ in) in diameter, appear in a variety of materials – carved wood, coral, cloisonné, metal, semi-precious stones, porcelain and rarely, gold. Since it was forbidden to wear gold as jewelry, gold *ojime* were sometimes lacquered to avoid detection. *Ojime* and *inro* may be signed, and on the latter the signature may be on the outside of the base or concealed in the design on the side. It is not usually on the lid. The characters inside an *inro* usually refer to the medicines it contained.

Inro were carried both by samurai and civilians, and were usually made in lacquered wood in black, red and gold though blue and green were also used. Lacquered *netsuke* were commonly used with lacquered *inro* to avoid damaging the latter.

Inro were in use for a relatively short period of time, from the 16th to the middle of the 19th century and since their style and design varied with fashions they are often quite difficult to date. The shape of *inro* varied over the centuries as well as geographically. The round shape – *marugata* – varies from an almost full circle to an ellipse, although the latter are rare. The flat shape – *liragata* – varies from a blunt-ended oval shape to a thin ellipse. Despite the common shapes of *inro* no two were ever made exactly the same. In the early 17th century a tall, narrow cylindrical-shaped *inro* with external rings or channels was popular, while during the reign of Yoshimune (1716–45) a squat horizontal *inro* was introduced.

The decoration of *inro* also varied over the centuries, the earliest influence being Chinese. Examples of 16th century *inro* influenced by China are those carved in red and black lacquer as well as *chinkin-bori* work, where lines engraved on lacquer are made more visible by powdering them with gold. Motifs on early *inro* were kept simple and were usually restricted to mythological beasts or naturalistic designs.

The first craftsman to break with Chinese tradition was Koetsu in the early 17th century. His style has been called 'impressionistic' because of the effect he obtained by using broad simple inlays. More exotic *inro* also made their first appearance in this century, notably those of the Koma and Kajikawa families who worked in gold-lacquer and in the technique called *togidashi*. In this technique the design is first drawn on paper and then traced using heated lacquer on the reverse side. The outline is then rubbed off onto the lacquer surface of the *inro* and lines dusted first with white whetstone and then with coloured, pulverized lacquer. The outlines are then covered with lacquer, allowed to dry and the whole process repeated. Finally the surface of the *inro* is painted with black lacquer and

Lacquer inro with a miniature mask as the netsuke.

ground down until the underlying design appears.

It is generally acknowledged that the finest *inro* were made in the Genroku era (1688–1704) when there was a return to simple designs and the characteristic Japanese use of open spaces as an integral part of the design. By the mid-Edo period (1681–1764) highly decorative *inro* was being made again and by the late Edo (1765–1868) the quality of lacquerwork began to decline.

Inro were made in other materials as well as lacquered wood. Some *netsuke* craftsmen, such as Garaku, Gyokuzan, Issan and Tokaku, carved *inro* in wood, ivory, tortoiseshell or horn. In the mid-18th century Ichimuke Nauka made *inro* engraved with amazingly detailed maps of Japan. Metal *inro* were made in the late 18th and 19th centuries and were crafted either entirely in metal or encrusted with metal motifs in relief. Famous craftsmen in metal include Joi, Yasuchika, Hamano Musayuki and Somin. Ceramic *inro* were also made, though not in any great numbers for they were found to be too fragile and could not be made airtight. Ceramic inlays on wood or lacquer grounds were made by Ritsuo.

Other Miniature Lacquerwork

There were few decorative objects, whatever their size, that the Japanese did not make in lacquerwork or applied lacquer to. A short survey of miniature lacquerwork will give the collector some idea of the more interesting objects he may come across.

A particularly important drinking utensil in the Japanese household was the *sake* cup or *sakazuki*. Often made in sets they are fairly shallow bowls averaging 10 cm (4 in) in diameter and about 2.5 cm (1 in) high, with short, round pedestal bases called *itodo*. Decorative work is usually restricted to the inner surfaces of the bowl, occasionally with secondary designs on the sides or bottom of the bowl. Naturalistic motifs were usually the motif of choice. Cups most likely to be found by the collector date from the 19th and 20th centuries. Some are signed by well-known artists.

Two very important ceremonies are associated with the use of lacquer objects, the tea ceremony and the incense ceremony.

The tea ceremony (*cha-no-yu*) originated around the 9th century as a Zen ritual but did not assume national cult proportions until after the 13th century. Several lacquered articles are used in the ceremony: a cabinet, *cha-dansu*, used for holding the tea utensils; the *satsu-bako*, a tray usually measuring about 12.5 × 17.5 × 10 cm (5 × 7 × 4 in), as well as tea bowls and whisks (*chasen*). Of particular importance is the tea caddy or *natsume*, which is usually cylindrical and some 7.5 cm (3in) high and 6.25 cm (2.5 in) in diameter. It is made from wood called *kiri* from the tree *Paulownia imperialis*.

Incense (*kodo*) has long played a vital role in Japanese social and religious life. It comes in various forms from the cheap joss-sticks to more expensive powder and pill forms. It was burned in a small brazier (*koro*), which stood on a lacquered stand. The pills and powders were kept in beautiful lacquer boxes called *kogo* or *kobako* and the charcoal in a *hitori koro*. This last is usually of bronze or ceramic with a cover of open metalwork. Only occasionally was it made in lacquerwork.

The *kogo* has been known since the reign of the Emperor Konoe

(1142–55) and while the early examples were relatively simple and un-decorated, later ones are among the most beautiful of all Japanese lacquerwork. They are usually fairly shallow boxes, less than 2.5 cm (1 in) high with a cover that is decorated both inside and outside. Decoration is usually in either flat, raised or carved lacquer, or flat or raised encrustations. Some *kogo* have a small, perfectly fitting tray inside. The shape of the *kogo* without a tray varies from round or rectangular to fan-shaped or shell-shaped.

Toys

Strange how a toy evokes childhood, yet all toys were not made for children. Clappers were originally designed to drive away evil spirits, dolls to encourage fertility, corn-husk figures to promote a good harvest, and intricate moving toys were invented to amuse rich men at their banquets. African rattles were mere seedpods. Greek knucklebones were real bones, natural forked twigs were used in Australia while in England wishing-bones and old clothes-pegs were dressed up and became dolls.

Clay was modelled very early on, especially by folk living near rivers where plenty of mud was available. Minute pots and humped-back clay animals came from regions north of India, jointed dolls from Greece; there were also many birds which, when blown into, made a hollow sound.

Sticks and brooms ridden astride were the forerunners of the hobby horse. Hoops came from discarded barrels, and in South America a little wheel on a toy cart came before real wheels were used as a means of locomotion.

About 2,500 years ago kites were flown in the East and eventually it was a kite which led to the first suspension bridge over the river Niagara. Now they take the shape of huge birds, tortoises or flying bats and are beautifully coloured.

During the 5th century B.C., many little figures were made depicting the daily life of the inhabitants of Greece and Rome. Some were made of a mixture of lead, tin and antimony, others from bronze or from clay. Tin was added to harden the bronze and was in great demand, the Phoenicians even going as far as Cornwall in their search for materials. During the Middle Ages, treasures retrieved from sunken ships in-cluded miniature domestic items, and during the 12th century A.D. boys played with toy knights manipulated by strings.

Rattles are probably among the oldest children's toys but it was not until the 17th century that any substantial advances on their design were made. Particularly delightful are the silver rattles of the 18th and 19th centuries with tiny bells attached and often incorporating a whistle. Such rattles usually had coral handles for the baby to cut his teeth on. Hand-bells and drums were also popular in these centuries, the former appear-ing as pairs of handbells played by groups of children and sets of small bells each producing a different note hung together on a tree-like frame and provided with a small striking hammer. Tin drums first appeared in the early 19th century and for a time became even more popular than skin drums.

Copies of pilgrims' badges were made as toys for children and lead soldiers stood upright by means of boards with holes. These figures were made in moulds, many of which have survived. Model trees were often sold flat and later bent into position. The Hilpert family in Germany were famous for their animals and soldiers. Other makers were Gottschalk and Beck, both from Switzerland. Ernst Heinrichsen was busy in Nuremberg, and it was he who introduced the size of 3 cm ($1\frac{1}{4}$ in) for the metal figures and soldiers. Another well-known toy maker, Allgeyer of Furth, also conformed to this scale from about 1848.

Early soldiers are flat and known as flats, though later ones are solid, like the Churchill soldiers in Blenheim Palace which were made by a Frenchman called Lucotte. The first hollow metal soldiers were made in 1893 by William Britain, an Englishman.

Toy vehicles of all kinds, whether road or rail, are useful historic indicators of how means of travel have altered. The first metal trains were coloured by hand, though later the rather brittle colouring was applied by heat. Little tin-plate German cars were assembled by means of tabs and slots, whereas those from France had the joints soldered. The more expensive cars of about 1908 had doors made to open and shut. Children's pedal cars came as early as 1906.

Rubber was an ideal substance for balls and solid rubber balls were played with in Mexico about A.D.700. Hollow animals and dolls were made in two halves and often contained a squeaker, but rubber dolls have never become popular being apt to fade and heavy to hold. Toy aeroplanes were propelled by rubber bands.

Miniature violins have been known almost from the time the full-size instrument was invented. Until the later 19th century they were made with the same precision as the normal violin and were intended to be played. Miniature violins as well as guitars intended only as toys and simply making an appropriate noise were manufactured in considerable quantities towards the end of the 19th century. They were made in wood, papier-mâché and tin, but it is usually only the more accurate instruments that are of interest to the collector.

Probably no other toy is more associated with the Edwardian Victorian nursery than the doll's house. They have been known since the 16th century and were probably first made in Nuremberg. The dolls' houses of the late 18th and early 19th century are more attractive and detailed than the later Victorian houses; to the Victorian child the furnishings were more important than the house itself. The interior of the lavishly-appointed Victorian house was often accurate to the last detail, from the perfect miniature carpets and curtains to the intricate hand-made furniture and upholstery.

Celluloid was used for bath toys and for ping-pong balls. It was made famous by the little Kewpie dolls designed by Rose O'Neill Wilson of the United States in 1913. With their shiny tummies, wide open eyes and tiny blue wings they were instantly appealing. In the heyday of celluloid, pretty goldfish from Japan floated in many baths, but eventually all celluloid toys were banned because they were too inflammable. The material did, however, lead to the present-day plastics.

Buzz toys were introduced into the United States by British soldiers towards the end of the 18th century. German immigrants introduced arks, rocking horses and some of their dolls. Now, over the years, various toys have gradually become associated with specific countries. These include nest toys and pecking toys from Russia, creche figures and marionettes from Italy, silver toys, wooden dolls' houses from the Netherlands, and arks from Bohemia. Early dolls' houses were known as baby houses.

Germany is noted for its toy soldiers and engines, France for fashion dolls and strangely for cheap clockwork toys, Switzerland for intricate automata and England for wax dolls and paper cut-outs. The United States became known for cast-iron toys, intricate fire-engines, cap pistols and Daisy guns. Also from America came the first teddy bears, but gollywogs remain exclusively English.

Not only toys are collected, now their boxes are collected also. Little oval pinewood boxes are especially pretty and contain wooden animals and figures. Cardboard boxes can also be attractive; both oval and rectangular kinds appeared in the early 1880s, many with interesting labels. In times of scarcity even net bags take their place.

Games

Games with balls have a long history. Small glass, marble-like balls have been known for some 3,000 years from the Mediterranean area, though there is evidence that they were used in religious ceremonies rather than as toys. The first European marbles to be used as playthings appeared in Venice in the 14th century. They were made in both transparent and opaque glass of different colours and incorporated some of the innovative glass decorative techniques that the Venetian glassmakers are well-known for, including *latticinio* – coloured strands inside the glass – and the decorative use of air bubbles. They ranged in size from 1 cm ($\frac{1}{2}$ in) to 5 cm (2 in) in diameter.

Glass marbles did not become popular in the rest of Europe until the 18th century and even then many of the marbles were imported from Venice. Later in the century marbles in the Venetian-style were made in France, Germany, England and the Low Countries.

As well as glass marbles many other types were made in the 18th and 19th centuries, including Dutch 'stonies' made from Coburg stone in Germany, Chinamen – large ceramic marbles with black and white bands – and 'bouncers', cricket-ball size marbles made in Sunderland, England, around 1850. The game of marbles was at its most popular around 1870.

Some of the prettiest balls are the porcelain carpet balls which were rolled along the corridors of stately homes in the 17th century. However, a ball often requires something else with it and in medieval games one finds a trap and ball, cup and ball, and bat and ball.

Hoops were mostly for boys in medieval days, but battledore and shuttlecock was played by both boys and girls, the same with diabolo and the much more ancient game of yoyo.

At the end of the 18th century small books appeared extolling obedience to one's parents, and picture cards issued in 1788 also had a moral purpose, for it had been said that many indoor games promoted cunning. In 1815 alphabet cards appeared, and there were sets of ivory letters to help with reading. Some of the books were less than 5 cm (2 in) high and only 35 mm ($1\frac{1}{2}$ in) wide.

Picture cards were cut in halves, the picture being complete when the correct half had been found. Children learnt natural history and geography by these means. The cards were hand-coloured engravings and after 1835 could be hand-coloured lithographs. At first the colours were pale but later the cards were painted in bright colours.

The Victorians and Edwardians enjoyed playing cards and other indoor pastimes. Board games were numerous on both sides of the Atlantic and lucky children shared improving games with their parents. Jig-saw puzzles and picture alphabets taught them much, and many historical facts were learned effortlessly. It was quite usual for a five-year-old child to read.

A card game popular among adults in the 19th century was the 'question and answer' game with the question on one card and the answer on another. When placed in the correct sequence a complete story would reveal itself. A children's card game designed along similar lines was 'Welcome Intruder' which appeared after 1815.

The first attempt at light-hearted rather than educational card games was by Anne W. Abbott of Beverly, Massachusetts, who devised a card game based on a character called Dr Busby. She eventually sold the idea and it first appeared on the market in 1843. Happy Families was played in Britain from 1861 while Animal Grab made its debut in 1890.

Chinese puzzles were unknown to most people in Europe until the second half of the 19th century. Once they became popular however, they were widely imitated and adapted, resulting in such games as the Egyptian Mummy puzzle, the Persian Shah puzzles and The Silver Bullet, a First World War game. At the turn of the 19th century pocket puzzles, which had eight to fifteen pieces arranged in a backed frame leaving one space blank, appeared; each piece carried a letter, number or symbol, the object being to arrange the pieces in a specified sequence. Also popular was the game, still found today, which consisted of a small box containing several tiny balls; the box had to be carefully manipulated until all the balls rested in separate depressions in the base of the box.

Like puzzles, many board games of the 19th century were based on Oriental games. Fox and Geese is probably the best-known of these and it first reached Europe in the late 17th century. Variations on the game include Officers and Sepoys, and Asalto.

Early board games, jig-saws, building bricks and puzzles came in wooden boxes with sliding lids and attractive labels. Inside would be the instructions and the counters. Instead of dice which were considered to promote gambling, a teetotum was introduced which could be of various

313

shape and size. Moral games were still the thing in which virtue was rewarded and vice punished.

The first dissected puzzles were maps. The pieces were large, often being cut around the actual county or country and there was a guide sheet to follow.

The first board game published by Milton Bradley in the United States also had a moral tone. This was The Checkered Game of Life, which came in 1860. Many of the later games were based on banking and earning money such as The Business of Going to Work, and later still Monopoly.

Dolls

The 18th century was the age of the fashion doll, dolls which were dressed in the latest fashions and sent from Court to Court as a method of announcing current trends. The first known account of fashion dolls appears in the 15th century when Robert de Varennes, Court Embroiderer to Charles VI of France, made a doll's wardrobe for the Queen, Isabeau de Barière, who then sent them to Queen Isabella of England.

The rich and extravagent court life of the 18th century brought the fashion doll to its height of popularity. Fashion shows were conducted with dolls rather than live models, though the dolls often reached life-size. Among upper class women it was the custom to keep two dolls dressed according to the fashion of the day and known as 'big Pandora' and 'small Pandora'. The former was dressed in formal attire, the latter in elegant négligé. Probably the best-known maker of fashion dolls in the second half of the century was Rose Bertin who was at first doll-maker to Marie Antoinette and later, after the Revolution, moved her business to London. There was a decline in the use of the fashion doll in the first half of the 19th century as the influence of the Court on public fashion declined and as fashion magazines superseded the doll.

The wooden dolls of the mid-18th century had their heads particularly well made, although with most dolls it is the head that receives the greatest attention, while the rest of the body can be positively crude and may be of rough wood or merely a bundle of stuffed calico with straw to stiffen the limbs. Care is normally only taken on the parts which show after the doll has been dressed. If the doll wears a cap, then only wisps of hair poke out, if a low neck is the fashion then this is finished smooth to match the face; two raggish shoes on wooden sticks may protrude beneath a silken gown, and on jointed dolls it was not until their dresses were short that the joints were put above the knees and not below.

From about 1790 the flat, paper dolls began to make an impact on the market. These dolls, made of paper or cardboard, were sold in cut-out sheets, each doll representing a different class and profession of person. The sheets also carried a cut-out wardrobe. In the 19th century some dolls were made in the image of popular personalities of the day. Since these dolls were also used by adults they may have been the precursor of the fashion doll.

Papier-mâché dolls were first manufactured in the early 19th century in Sonneburg and Meiningen. Initially the use of papier-mâché made from paper pulp, rags, flour, pumice and kaolin was confined to the finishing of wooden heads. A well-known papier-mâché doll was the *Parisienne*, a Sonneburg-made doll but dressed in France and exported from there around the world. A Sonneburg manufacturer, Edmund Lindner, was the first to make papier-mâché dolls that were similar to the life-like Chinese and Japanese examples first exhibited at the Great Exhibition in London in 1851. His first such doll was a baby doll made in 1855, which was given a realistic skin colour by dipping the head first in wax and then in wheat powder. She was given convincing blue eyes and a suggestion of baby hair, as well as moveable limbs.

England was noted for wooden dolls and later excelled in making dolls of wax. Madame Montanari made her name at the Pierotti Charles Marsh, Meech and Lucy Peck all worked in London and Meech claimed to be the maker of dolls for the English Royal family. Unlike their wooden sisters these dolls had well-modelled lower arms and lower legs of poured wax. Their calico bodies fitted tightly into the hollow limbs, the glass eyes were inset and strands of real hair inserted carefully into the warm wax. The Italians also excelled in making wax figures and babies for their cribs.

Wax doll with porcelain arms and moveable eyes.

Rag dolls, often home made, have always been popular and two famous examples are the early Roman doll in the British Museum (who has now lost her remaining blue bead eye), and 'Bangwell Putt' of the United States who now sits comfortably in Deerfield, Massachusetts.

China-headed dolls came from the Continent of Europe. The majority had white glazed heads, tinted pink cheeks, little scarlet mouths, eyes usually blue, and highly glazed black hair. This was sometimes ornamented with pretty wreaths of coloured flowers and leaves. Tiny hands and tiny feet wearing shoes were also made of porcelain, but with soft bodies the dolls could lie down or sit up. As the dolls were sold by length, often they were taller than one would expect from the head size.

To obtain a more natural appearance china-heads would be left in the unglazed state known as biscuit, and in the doll world as bisque. The bisque heads being hollow were soon fitted with weights to enable the eyes to close when the doll was laid down, the lids being painted directly on to the glass eye-ball. When hollow bodies arrived, these also were fitted with gadgets so that the doll could walk, talk or cry and even perform other movements.

Souvenir dolls of the 19th century are popular with collectors as are portrait dolls. The latter were probably derived from the wax figures made by Madame Tussaud. Queen Victoria was a popular subject.

Well known French manufacturers of the past are Jumeau, Bru, the S.F.B.J. and Jules Nicolas Steiner. Famous German names include Heubach, Handwerck, Schilling, Kammer & Reinhardt, Kestner, Simon & Halbig and Edmund Ulrich Steiner. There are many more, but the maker who produced the most dolls seems to be Armand Marseille from Kopplesdorf. His mark AM is incised on the back of the bisque heads, a place where the majority of marks are found. After 1890 the name of the country of origin was marked by law.

Chinese Carpets

It is only in the last few decades that Chinese carpets, previously over-shadowed by the enthusiasm of collectors for Persian carpets, have been given the attention they long deserved. While the quality of Chinese carpets declined at the end of the 19th century, in part due to an increasing use of chemical dyes, one of the most appealing characteristics of earlier carpets was the unsurpassed, subtle use of colour.

A full appreciation of Chinese carpets must begin with an appreciation of the role that they played in the household, for they have never been used solely as decorative floor coverings. In northern China in particular, a feature of the average home was the *k'ang*, a brick or tile platform that was heated from beneath and on which the family would sleep. During the day the family would remove their mattresses and lay the family carpet on top of the *k'ang*. Since the *k'ang* was a central feature of the home so too was the carpet. In their service as house warmers, carpets were also hung on the walls. The symbolic motifs on carpets, which rank closely with the use of colours in determining their appeal today, dictated where a carpet would be situated in the home. Carpets with patterns that converged on the centre were placed on the floor; others were used as wall hangings.

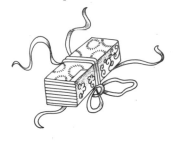

Chinese decorative motifs known as the Four Accomplishments.

The 19th century has been chosen as the point from which to take this brief look at Chinese carpets for with the arrival of chemical dyes the quality of colours in rugs changed completely. Chemical dyes destroyed the sheen and oils in the wool, making it stiff and dry so that the soft modulations of colour attainable with vegetable dyes were impossible to achieve.

The Use of Colour

The earliest carpets known date from about 1600, the time of the Ming Dynasty, and the use of colours was consistent throughout the succeeding two decades or so.

The most widely used colour was blue, derived from the indigo plant which produces shades from pale sky-blue to black. It is possible that the Chinese used blue so much because it did not fade as other colours did, but merely became even bluer. This is useful in determining the age of a carpet, for clear blues suggest a recent carpet, while if all the colours including blue are dim then the carpet has probably been aged artificially.

Blue, though, is rarely used as a ground colour in old carpets, instead brown, white and yellow are used as the grounds for blue patterns, and in particular a soft brown was favoured. Principal shades of brown include fawn, tan, ochre and sand as well as a copper-brown called *ku t'ung sê*. A dark brown was produced using manganese brown, but since this dye is corrosive it gives the effect of incised or punched out patterns. White comes in all shades, while yellow appears in shades from chicken yellow to honey, amber and orange. Most famous of all yellows is Imperial yellow, a pure luxurious colour that was reserved for the use of the court. Mandarin yellow has a touch of orange. Another ground

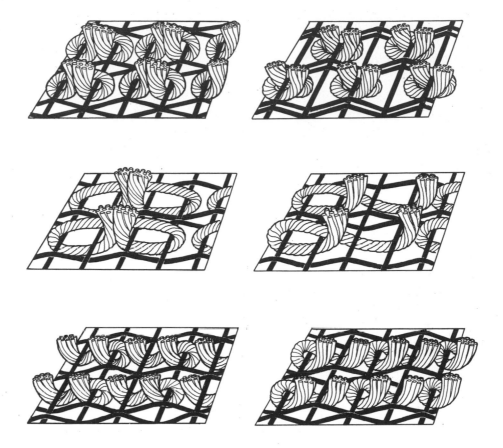

Different types of knot used in Chinese carpets.

colour was a curious red that does not contain any blue and about which there has been much speculation as to its origin. It has been suggested that the carpetmaker was aware of the mellowing influence of time on this colour and may have made it by dyeing the carpet first with a fast yellow and then with a strong red, so that as the red faded the yellow began to show itself.

Black is only used occasionally, while gray is sometimes found in bands running along the outside edge of pre-18th century carpets. Green is very rare until the advent of aniline dyes which produced rather gaudy shades of this colour.

The Chinese were masters in the art of combining colours and, unlike Persian and Caucasian rugmakers, disliked using strong, unrelated colours. Two principles guided them – colour relatedness and colour gradation. Their inclination has been to always use blue motifs on brown grounds or a white and blue, which may have been inspired by Chinese porcelain. This latter combination was popular in the 18th and 19th centuries. Pale yellow and blue were often popular as were carpets simply in varying shades of blue.

Carpet Motifs

The carpet designer was fortunate in having a rich heritage of symbolic motifs on which to draw and he gave free rein to his imagination when it came to adapting and combining those motifs. Chinese carpets contain a greater diversity of motifs than any other oriental carpets and are not simply decorative, but have a language of their own.

317

There is not sufficient space here to list all the motifs used – books have been written on the subject – but an outline will give the potential collector an indication of the way the Chinese used their motifs.

The borders of very early carpets contain either a meander in the form of a T- or key pattern, swastikas, or what is called the hooked cross motif, which consists of C- or S- forms in continuous lines. The swastika is the symbol for happiness or luck and when it is made continuous it means 'ten thousandfold happiness'.

Chinese language characters are used but only three are used symbolically – *shou*, *fu* and *shuang hsi*. *Shou*, which means long life, is the commonest of the three and it is usually found in stylized medallion form in the centre of the carpet. The character *fu*, meaning luck, is more common in embroidery than in carpets, possibly because it is difficult to stylize in the same way as *shou* and is more difficult to knot. *Shuang hsi* is the name given to a double *hsi* character, which means wedded bliss. A single *hsi* is not often used. Carpets with *shuang hsi* motifs were often given as wedding presents.

Naturalistic motifs are widespread and usually highly stylized. The cloud motif is distinctly Chinese despite comparisons with Turkish or Persian clouds and can be found scattered singly throughout the design or in cloud banks. Mountains and water are always found together, since the Chinese name for 'landscape' is *shan shui* – mountain water. The mountains are always shown emerging from the water. Sea and mountains together symbolize long life and luck. Water is depicted in various forms: multi-coloured semi-circles for calm water, square or triangular shapes with dots above to suggest spray, for rough water.

While human beings and gods rarely appear on carpets because of difficulties in knotting them, animals have a distinctive and treasured place in the repertory. The dragon, *lung*, is both the best known and most spectacular animal for it has high significance in Chinese religion and philosophy, representing a powerful god and the master of the forces of nature. Not surprisingly, the dragon became the Imperial emblem. In both form and concept the Chinese dragon is very different from the Western dragon, appearing as a reptile-like creature with snake-like body, four legs and a fantastic head. Almost always associated with the dragon is the pearl, *chin*, which the dragon is constantly striving to reach, for the pearl means perfection. A pair of dragons are often depicted fighting over the pearl. When the dragon was adopted as the Imperial emblem it evolved into two kinds, one with five toes on each foot (the *lung* dragon) being the Emperor's motif as well as that of princes of the first and second rank, while the *mang* dragon with only four toes was used by lesser court officials.

The dragon motif is particularly cleverly used on pillar rugs – long narrow rugs which were used to decorate pillars on festive occasions. When the carpet is viewed flat on the ground, the coils of the beast appear to make little sense, yet when the carpet is wound around the pillar the coils join up and the dragon comes to life. Pillar rugs were usually made in pairs and were favourite gifts.

The phoenix, *feng huang*, is a composite of several creatures and is different from the apocalyptic beast of Ancient Greece, for in China its

Decorative motifs. From top: *Four classic scrolls, cloud collar or lappet, six cloud scrolls.*

appearance heralded a period of good fortune. The creature was a composite of pheasant, swan, crane and mandarin duck and was the symbol of the Empress.

After the dragon, *fo* dogs are one of the best-known motifs associated with Chinese carpets. In mythology, such dogs, which resemble lions more than dogs, were said to be the companion of the Buddha and to guard Buddhist holy places. The male dog is often depicted playing with a ball, the female with a pup between her paws.

The unicorn, *ch'i lin*, also differs from the Western image and some authorities feel the Chinese had two varieties, one with the body of a stag with a long straight horn and the other with the body of an ox and a short, curved horn. The *ch'i lin* was said to live a thousand years and appear at the birth of sages. Genuine stags, *lu*, also appear as motifs, often holding the sacred fungus, *ling chih*, which can bestow immortality, or with a stork, a symbol of long life.

Perhaps the most frequent animal to appear is the bat, *fu*, which since its Chinese name sounds exactly like the symbol *fu*, also means luck. The butterfly appears on carpets from South China instead of the bat. Other animal motifs include fishes, usually the carp, the horse, rabbit, hare and tiger.

The commonest floral motifs are the lotus, peony and chrysanthemum. The lotus is both the symbol of purity and summer and, while they are sometimes difficult to distinguish on carpets from chrysanthemums, can be recognized by their accompanying seed pods. Other floral motifs include plum blossoms, bamboo and peach blossoms, although they are somewhat rarer than the previous three. The only fruits to appear as motifs are the peach, pomegranate and the citron, for each of these three has a meaning unlike other fruits. The peach, food of the gods, symbolizes longevity, the pomegranate signifies abundant male offspring, while the citron is a symbol for happiness since its rind is supposed to develop into petals resembling the classic position of the Buddha's hand.

The two great religions of China, Taoism and Buddhism, are also represented on carpets in the motifs of the Eight Symbols of Taoism and the Eight Symbols of Buddhism. The former are a flower basket, flute, lotus, bamboo clappers, bamboo tube and rod, crutch or staff and gourd, sword and fan. The Buddhist symbols are the canopy, two fish, urn, lotus, conch shell, umbrella, knot of destiny and the wheel of law. Another group of Taoist motifs are the Eight Immortals who were supposed to live in Paradise and represent practitioners of various trades. Other groups of motifs include the Eight Precious Things and the Four Gentlemanly Accomplishments.

Decorative motifs. Left: Ju-i *head;* top right: *diamond diaper border;* bottom right: *key fret or 'thunder' pattern.*

Pipes and Smoking Equipment

The habit of smoking, though now stripped to its bare essentials, was once accompanied by all manner of equipment, while pipes, cigarette holders and the like were considerably more ornate.

The first pipes in Europe were clay pipes which date from the 16th century. The collector has little chance of finding 16th and 17th-century pipes however, owing to their fragility and the fact that they were made to be expendable. By the 18th century the clay pipe was faced with its first rivals in the form of porcelain and meerschaum, materials which could be ornamented to suit the growing demand for more elegant pipes.

Meerschaum is a form of magnesium silicate and was first used for making pipe bowls in Central Europe. It is said that a Hungarian shoe-maker discovered how to 'colour' the material by the use of wax in 1750. Nevertheless it is the process of smoking that largely imparts colour to meerschaum, although the waxing is important. Meerschaum is easily carved and some of the best examples have been compared with *netsuke*. The commonest subjects are human heads and figurines, but the range goes far beyond that. The mouthpieces of the pipes were always made of another material – usually amber, ivory or mother-of-pearl. The hall-mark on the silver band that joins the mouthpiece to the body can be reliable as a method of dating. Where this is not visible, dating is very difficult; there were also a large number of fakes made. Meerschaum did not reach England until the 1760s and elaborately carved specimens did not appear until 1830.

Porcelain pipes were common in Germany and Austria in the 19th century although they were never popular in England. The disadvantage of glazed clay is that it is not porous, which leads to a build-up of liquids in the pipe. The solution to the problem was found around the end of the 18th century. The final form of pipe consisted of a tall, narrow cylindrical bowl with a short stem aligned slightly off the vertical which fits into a Y-shaped porcelain reservoir which collects the condensing vapours; the other arm of the Y takes the long stem and mouthpiece which is usually made of wood, horn, bone and so on. In effect the pipe is an air-cooled hubble-bubble. Decoration on the porcelain bowl was hand-painted until 1850, when transfer printing was introduced.

The meerschaum was gradually replaced by the briar pipe after about 1850. The suitability of briar for pipes was said to have been discovered by a French pipe-maker, who on a trip to Corsica lost his meerschaum, whereupon a local peasant carved him a pipe from the root of a heath tree called *bruyère*. Encouraged by the quality of the smoke the French-man sent samples of the wood to St Claude in the Jura mountains to be carved and there a briar pipe industry subsequently thrived.

Tobacco stoppers, used for pressing down the tobacco in a burning pipe, were in use from the 17th century to the middle of the 19th century. Though simple in function they became a form of miniature art. There were few materials not used for making them: ivory, wood, bone, silver,

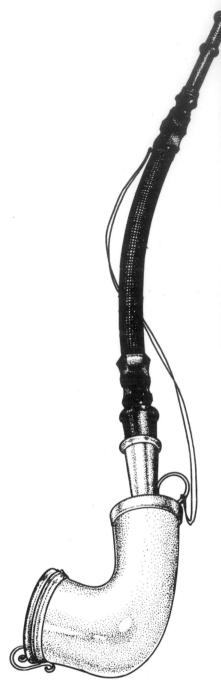

Late 19th-century meerschaum pipe, overall length 38 cms.

pewter and so on, but dating them can be difficult. As a general rule early stoppers had a base designed to be fitted into small bowls and were less than 1 cm ($\frac{1}{2}$ in) wide. Although some 18th century examples have small bases they are more frequently dated or can be judged by the fact that they were often carved to represent figures in period costumes. Another common 18th century theme was single arms and leg-shaped stoppers as well as greyhounds and squirrels. A significant number of stoppers were made by the individual smoker and the collector is more likely to find wooden stoppers than those in other materials. During the late 18th and early 19th centuries more and more stoppers were made wholesale in brass, pewter, bronze and silver in simple designs including the female leg, bent at the knee and wearing a garter. Memento mori stoppers were not uncommon as were stoppers incorporated into a finger ring.

Tobacco jars were intended for storing cut tobacco in the home or shop and usually had detachable lids and were taller than they were wide or long. From the 17th century tobacco jars were usually made from lead. 18th century jars, which the collector is more likely to encounter, were octagonal-shaped with smoking as the theme of the decoration; great events were also portrayed such as the Crimean War and the Peace of 1874. The jars were all painted, often in bright, garish colours. Few of them were dated or marked with the maker's name and the collector has to rely on the style in which they were made. For example, the period from the 1780s until the 1830s was known as the Gothic revival and it was not uncommon to find jars made in ecclesiastical shapes such as fonts and pulpits. Lead boxes were not made after the 1850s.

Wooden jars were never as popular as lead jars (though many were made) because they tended to dry the tobacco; most of them were made with lead or foil liners to counteract this tendency. They were made in a variety of shapes, but most commonly in the form of a turned barrel. Tobacco jars and tea-caddies are sometimes difficult to distinguish, but as a general rule caddies had locks while jars lacked them.

In the 19th century most of the mass-produced tobacco jars were of porcelain and produced at Fulham, Isleworth and at Wedgwoods to name but a few places. Many were imported, particularly from Germany. The most notable examples are the Martin brothers' of 1873–1914.

The tobacco box was a flat, pocket-sized box with a close-fitting lid, most commonly made in brass, but foil lined wooden boxes were also made especially in Germany or Holland. Most boxes made before the 19th century were usually simply decorated.

Printed Ephemera

The development of printing dates from the Middle Ages and since then it has played an ever increasing role in the spread of Western civilization. For several centuries, printing and the publication of knowledge was associated largely with books, but since the 18th century it has come to affect every aspect of our lives. This spread has been assisted by advances in technology and by changes in social patterns. The concept of universal literacy has ensured that our lives are increasingly determined and regulated by printed material, most of which is, by its nature, ephemeral. This, in turn, has encouraged a new pattern of collecting based on an interest in printed material for its own sake. Many now wish to preserve printed material precisely because of its ephemeral nature. Its survival ensures that it acts both as a record and a mirror of the period that produced it.

Although printed ephemera has been collected since the 18th century, it is only in recent years that it has emerged as a major collecting field. Although it is beyond the scope of this book, stamp collecting is probably the earliest large scale interest in ephemera. Following this lead, specialist collectors turned their attention towards other areas of printed ephemera such as early trade cards, book plates and political or theatrical posters. Some specialized in the products of early jobbing printers, which included advertising matter, theatre, travel and sports tickets, invoices, labels, paper bags and other forms of packaging; in short, all material that expressed the business and social life of a period.

These collections were inspired partly by an interest in typography and styles of printing, and partly by an awareness of the changes in social and domestic life provided by the development of advertising. From the efforts of these early enthusiasts there emerged the internationally famous collections of ephemera at the New York Public Library, the American Antiquarian Society, the Bibliothèque Nationale in Paris and the St Bride's Library in London.

Almanacs and calendars represent the earliest fields of interest, partly because the material itself can be of considerable age. In America, Benjamin Franklin's *Poor Richard's Almanack* was first produced in 1732, while the English *Old Moore's Almanac* dates from 1700. A similar French almanac, first produced in 1679, is still published today. Almanacs reflect the religious, social and political life of a community, as do magazines, newspapers and journals, and so the interest they arouse today is understandable. Old magazines and newspapers not only bring the past to life in a very direct way, but also reflect the changing impact of advertising on the public. It is also interesting to study the style and structure of newspapers in an age when there was no means of reproducing illustrations. Children's comics are a recent development in this field, reflecting changing attitudes to education and leisure and interesting applications of contemporary styles of drawing, the range extending from Kate Greenaway to Captain Marvel. Equally, bookmarks, book plates, trade and sale catalogues are keenly collected for similar reasons. Trade catalogues are direct records of a vanished way of life and so can connect the past with the present in a very tangible way, while the old sale catalogues permit the tracing of the history of objects and collections that might still be accessible today. Collectors of book plates can be inspired either by the connection with the famous person who once owned the book, or by a general interest in typography. In fact, a general interest in typography, graphic design and printing technology can produce a collection of broad scope and popular appeal.

The interest in printed ephemera was greatly encouraged by the production of material specifically designed to appeal to the collector, the most obvious example being the apparently endless variety of special issue postage stamps. Other include souvenir programmes and tickets and popular items such as cigarette cards which were designed to increase sales of cigarettes by encouraging the collection of a series of related cards. This cultivation of the collection of the ephemera of the present soon developed into a general interest in the ephemera of the past which was encouraged no doubt by the romantic nostalgia that is a part and parcel of all kinds of collecting.

Some collectors have highly specialized interests and the specialist in matchbox covers, cigarette cards, beer mats or railway tickets is often interested in little else. Such collectors concentrate on the narrow but well-defined limits of their field of study, aided and guided by the societies, conferences and specialist publications that have grown up to serve them. Many of these very obscure publications will in turn become valuable examples of printed ephemera in the future, reflecting an interest that may then be quite incomprehensible. Others specialize in playing cards, Valentine cards, Christmas cards, funerary memorial cards and decorative music covers. The last two are closely related to the colourful pictorial posters of the late 19th century and both express the decorative freedom enjoyed by artists and designers after the development of chromolithography.

A brief review of the history of some of these specialist fields will help the potential collector. The first British pictorial matchbox label appeared in 1830 and showed a comic portrayal of a Highlander and an Englishman smoking with two snakes blowing out a flame. Matchbox labels often commemorated notable events such as the first swimmer to conquer the Channel, Captain Webb, and other famous sportsmen. Japanese labels are often very attractive many being reproductions of the work of famous artists such as Utamaro and Hiroshige. One of the commonest reproductions are those of Hiroshige's drawings of the Tokaido Road, which first appeared on matchboxes around 1900. American labels can also be found although they tend to be expensive. In the period between the Civil War and 1885 match factories proliferated due to a ban on the railroad transport of matches.

It is not known for certain when cigarette cards were first issued but the earliest known date is 1879. The card was American and bore a picture of the Marquis of Lorne who gave his name to the particular cigarettes. A substantial number of sets of cards were issued in the U.S. in the years before 1900, most of them devoted to illustrating the American way of life – girls, baseball heroes and so on. W. D. & H. O. Wills were among the first British companies to issue cards, the earliest examples being with a description, on the back of the card, simply the manufacturer's name and a small design. Cigarette cards were not issued after 1905 in the U.S. The most valuable cards date from the period 1880–1900. The Second World War saw the end of the cigarette card.

Celebratory cards of the 19th century have become popular with collectors in the past few years. Valentine cards were in use by the second half of the 18th century and the early examples were hand-made. The idea had become so popular by 1800 that a considerable industry had established itself. One of the best-known companies was H. Dobbs and Company of London, who started in 1803. Their cards tended to be highly elaborate and to use such devices as the 'flower-cage', so named because the card had a frame of thin material at its centre which could be raised by pulling a thread, revealing a message hidden underneath. Lace-like embossing was common on early 19th century cards, achieved by stamping the card on an engraved die and then filling the raised surfaces. Artists who designed Valentine cards included Kate Greenaway, Walter Crane and Robert Cruickshank.

The popularity of the Valentine card declined after the 1850s, while Christmas cards grew in popularity. The first Christmas card was designed and published in 1843 on the inspiration of Sir Henry Cole. The first printers of Christmas cards included Goodall's of Camden, Kronheim, Dean & Sons, Marcus Ward and Raphael Tuck. The German firm of S. Hildescheimer & Co. began printing cards in Manchester in 1876.

Much printed ephemera is related to the history of advertising, and so such a collection can express very graphically the development of the consumer society. Since its growth in the 19th century, the styles and psychology of advertising have undergone dramatic changes, many of which can be expressed perfectly by surviving printed material. To collect all the paraphernalia of advertising – packaging, labels, free offers, wrappers as well as the actual posters and advertisements – is to bring together an interesting and valuable record of the changes in society. Such items also reflect contemporary styles in typography and design quite forcefully, as they are prone to demonstrate the extremes of any particular period. Thus an enthusiasm for old cigarette packets, chocolate boxes, tea cartons and advertisements for Guinness, Pears Soap or Singer sewing machines is quite understandable, although to have to eat several packets of breakfast cereal each week in order to keep up with changes in packaging may be taking an interest in ephemera too far.

Perhaps the most popular of all ephemeral fields is the picture postcard. These have been collected as souvenirs, as nostalgia and as decoration since their development in the latter part of the 19th century.

The world's first postcard was issued by the Austrian Post Office on October 1, 1869 as the result of an idea submitted to them by Dr Emanuel Herrman, a professor of economics in Vienna. These first cards were plain, buff-coloured and bearing the Austrian emblem above which were the words 'Correspondenz – Karte'. That the postcard was to have an enormously popular future became clear when some three million cards were sold in Austria-Hungary in the first three months. The next country to issue postcards was the North German Confederation on July 1, 1870; Switzerland and Britain followed suit on October 1 of that year. In Britain some 75 million postcards were posted in the first year. Like the Austrian cards, British cards were plain, buff-coloured with the words 'Post Card' above the Royal Arms which were printed in lilac; in the right-hand top corner the Queen's head was imprinted and a frame surrounded the whole card. The back of the card was used for the message.

There is considerable debate as to the origins of the first pictorial postcard. One of the earliest reported was from France at the time of the Franco-Prussian War in 1870. Leon Besnardeau, a bookseller of Sille-le-Guillaume near Le Mas, produced special postcards illustrated with military and patriotic designs for the use of troops stationed at the nearby town of Conlie. Forty years after the event Besnardeau laid claim to be the originator of the postcard.

The Prussians issued Field Post Cards in 1870 some with humourous, risqué designs and verses. Possibly the first non-military, pictorial cards were made by A. Schwartz, a bookseller and printer from Oldenburg in the North German Confederation. The cards were printed with a small figure of a soldier and cannon; the only known example of this card is postmarked July 16, 1870. Since it was printed on a government-issued card many collectors consider it to be the world's first pictorial card. Not until 1872 did the German Post Office allow private companies to issue postcards, so this year is probably the date for the first German pictorial cards. In the same year a Zurich printer issued the first known set of views of Zurich on cards. Many of these early cards bore uncoloured pictures and views of well-known places, notably castles.

Britain's first pictorial cards were really advertisements printed on Post Office halfpenny cards and issued on October 1, 1870. The Swiss were among the first to issue coloured postcards around 1881. On early examples the picture covers most of the card, only a small space being left for a message. They show scenic views, towns and so on; particularly common was a view of the Rigi Kulm Hotel near Lake Lucerne. Among the first French pictorial cards were many celebrating the opening of the Eiffel Tower in 1889, while the first American cards were issued at the opening of the World's Columbian Exposition in Chicago on May 1, 1893.

By the end of 1899, when publishers had been allowed to issue larger postcards than previously, the age of the postcard had truly arrived. By 1902 designs were so varied and plentiful that collectors began their first albums.

Posters

Although poster collecting has achieved considerable popularity, the development of the poster itself is a comparatively modern phenomenon. Today, it is not uncommon for posters to be produced specifically to appeal to collectors, the design and decorative aspects often being more important than the message they have to carry. Similarly, many old posters have been reprinted to sell as modern wall decorations and have achieved a longevity and fame far beyond the wildest dreams of their creators.

Posters, placards and playbills date back to the 18th century and beyond, but they did not become commonplace until the second half of the 19th century. Early posters tend to be wholly typographical, relying on the size and variety of letter-forms used by the printer to make their impact. Illustrations are rare, largely because of the technical problems involved in their reproduction, and colours are limited. The best known is probably the theatrical playbill, in which the diverse qualities of the entertainments advertised were expressed by the mixed styles and sizes of the typography. However, these displays of the printer's virtuosity inevitably have a limited appeal, partly because of the rarity and partly because of their lack of visual detail.

The change came in the Victorian period. Firstly, technical developments such as chromolithography, high speed printing and photography gave the poster designer a new freedom. Chromolithography, or colour printing, was in regular use by about 1860, while the steam-powered printing press could produce up to 10,000 sheets an hour by the same date. Secondly, the rise of what is now called 'the consumer society' inspired a dramatic growth in advertising, affecting both its use and the subtlety of its presentation. More people were able to afford more and more things, and so they had to be increasingly persuaded that they actually needed them. Equally, the increasing availability of advertising sites on walls, hoardings and particularly in the new railway stations, encouraged competitiveness among manufacturers and suppliers of information. Thirdly, increased demand and the greater availability of money encouraged artists of greater skill and reputation to try their hands at poster designing; this was a change that immediately made posters more acceptable, and more memorable, to the educated middle classes.

The fourth, and in some ways the most important, factor was the revolution in artistic styles prompted by the reopening of the Japanese frontiers in the 1850s. Having been totally closed to the West for so long, Japan had acquired a magic and a fascination that knew no bounds within Europe. When the doors finally opened, they released Japanese artefacts into Europe that provoked an astonishing response affecting every field of artistic production. Spreading from France, the *Japonisme* movement swept across Europe, led by advanced designers such as the French engraver and artist F. Bracquemond and the English industrial designer and critic Dr Christopher Dresser. While all aspects of Japanese art and production made an impact, none was so immediate and dynamic as the discovery of Japanese colour prints. These magnificent designs, so simply drawn with their flat areas of bright colour, created a new style in European art. They affected particularly the French Impressionists and painters such as the Americans Whistler and Sargent, but their most direct influence was on poster design.

These elements combined to produce a wholly new sort of poster, in which colour and drama were vital elements. This developed first of all in France, in the work of Toulouse-Lautrec, Chéret, Grasset, Steinlen and de Faure, but spread rapidly to other countries. In England, Beardsley and Dudley Hardy followed the French lead, in America it was Will Bradley, while the Czech Mucha made his colourful and sinuous women familiar all over Europe.

Henri de Toulouse-Lautrec (1864–1901) was probably the first artist to apply his skills and imagination to the poster. Lautrec was introduced to lithography by Edouard Ancourt, a Parisian printer, and in 1890 he received a commission from Charles Zidler of Le Moulin Rouge to produce the series of posters he is now famous for. In fact Lautrec's total output for Zidler and others only numbers some 30 – the sum total of

Lautrec's poster work. He shunned the use of bright colours turning instead to muted yellows, greens and greys: he gave his characters such as Jane Avril and Aristide Bruant a reality not seen in earlier posters.

Théophile Alexandre Steinlein (1859–1923) drew on the work of both Lautrec and Chéret adding his own contribution as an excellent draughtsman. His best-known poster is probably the one for sterilised milk 'Lait pur de la Vingeanne sterilisé', and is typical of his relaxed style, quite different from Lautrec's harsher portrayal of aspects of Parisian life. Steinlein's animals, particularly his cats, are beautifully-drawn, appealing characters such as the fire-side cats in the Vingeanne poster and the aristocratic feline of Tournée du Chat Noir. Steinlein's posters were probably the first in a long line of animal posters.

Though born in Czechoslovakia, Alfons Maria Mucha (1860–1939), lived in Paris from 1888 and began his posterwork in 1894. By great fortune his first commission was for Sarah Bernhardt who wanted a poster of herself as Gismonda whom she was playing at the Théâtre de la Renaissance. Mucha's work is characterized by his use of pastel shades and tints and the air of unreality of his characters. Mucha has been said to have epitomized elements of the French Art Nouveau movement.

Aubrey Vincent Beardsley (1872–1898) established his early reputation by illustrating Malory's *Le Morte d'Arthur* and Oscar Wilde's *Salome*. His posters were extremely popular in his day and it is generally acknowledged that his poster designed for the Avenue Theatre in 1894 significantly influenced the subsequent development of the art in England. It has been said that Beardsley was not overly skilled in his use of colour, though this may have benefited his outstanding use of silhouettes and heavy shapes.

Much of Dudley Hardy's work (1865–1922) was with the theatre poster. He was influenced by both Chéret and Lautrec, but along with Beardsley and the Beggarstaffs, he set the standard for future English posterwork. He was probably the first to introduce the colour poster into Britain with his 'Yellow Girl'.

The work of Beardsley reached the United States in late 1893 and his popularity there soon knew no bounds. In 1894 a poster craze swept America as a result of his work. In the winter of 1894, Will Bradley's first posters appeared. His poster for The Masquerades by Henry Arthur Jones at the Empire Theatre in New York are the first signed theatrical posters by an American lithographer.

As *Japonisme* turned into Art Nouveau, the poster came of age. It had become a totally decorative artistic medium, brightly coloured, often garish, rich in pattern and sensuous drawing and universally applicable. The object being advertised, or the message to be broadcast, almost ceased to matter, the same decorative approach being applied freely to bicycles, cigarettes, theatres, cooking oil, sewing machines and politics. Posters had now achieved the status of works of art and so were able to outlive the ephemeral quality of actual advertising.

This pattern continued until the First World War. Because the war was fought at first by volunteers, the poster became an important means of encouraging recruitment and returned to its original role as the bearer of messages, slogans and information. However, the artistic aspects were not forgotten and all sides engaged in the conflict made extensive use of powerful propaganda posters, many of which were remarkably similar. After the war the gradual economic recovery inspired a return to conventional advertising, but this time the designers had to consider the marketing demands of the product. Despite this, many designers of the 1920s and 1930s are very remarkable, reflecting contemporary developments in art. Particularly memorable are the abstract designs of McKnight Kauffer and the modernist transport posters of the Frenchman Cassandre.

Since the 19th century impact of *Japonisme*, posters have always been closely allied to contemporary art movements. Leading avant-garde artists have often become poster designers, and so throughout this century posters have tended to mirror their period very precisely. While most examples can be dated by the product and their style of advertising, the relationship with art can be a more accurate guide. This is still true today, although more recently posters have fallen into groups determined by their subject matter. War, politics, protest, pop, as well as conventional advertising, all impose their own language and symbols, many of which are now international. These can limit decorative freedom in a way that 19th century designers would have found quite unacceptable. Despite this, the relationship between art and poster design continues to expand, especially in America, where contemporary artists have been quick to see the value of the poster in spreading their own message or style. A poster for national distribution is far more effective than a number of gallery shows.

It is probably this element, plus the obvious decorative and ephemeral qualities, that make poster collecting so appealing today. The continuing impact of the poster, regardless of its period, and its value as a living memorial to a past age has made it hard to collect. Originals by any of the great names will be as expensive as paintings, even though the quantity produced at the time may have been considerable, and so most collectors will have to content themselves with reproductions. However, it is a field where luck and perseverence can produce the most unexpected results. Many old posters have turned up unrecognized on market stalls, or framed into the backing for pictures. There is also such a wide choice of subject matter. The obvious themes, such as war or transport, will always be in demand, but it is not hard to find less popular areas for study.

Boxes

While the magnificent gold and silver boxes of the 18th century were never matched in the following century, there is much of interest for the collector of 19th century boxes, ranging from the novel, sumptuous, but now rare Fabergé boxes, to the more easily collectable tea caddies, cutlery boxes, lacquered boxes and painted ceramic pots.

A Russian, descended from French Huguenots, Peter Carl Fabergé

Nephrite box by Fabergé set with the Russian Imperial eagle.

(1846–1920) lived and worked in Russia for the last quarter of the century and much of his reputation is based on his use of enamelling in translucent colours on silver and gold. His boxes present a startling contrast to the theme expressed in the populist Arts and Crafts movement of William Morris who was working in England at this time, by being both exotic and expensive. In his boxes he successfully recaptured the mood of the 18th century and like the Dresden boxmakers of that century he was quick to exploit the deposits of semi-precious stones found in Russia – rhodonite, nephrite, gray jasper, quartz crystals, topaz and so on. The difference between Fabergé and the Dresden workers lay in the bold novelty of his designs and his technical skill. Collectors of Fabergé's boxes find that one of their attractions is the precise construction down to the last hinge. He was not afraid to use the stone with the minimum of mounting and decoration, as in his 'potato box' which was carved (roughly potato-shaped) from a piece of pink and brown veined and mottled jasper. The lid was formed by slicing some two-thirds the way along the upper half of the hollowed-out stone and simply hinging it in gold with a double-hinged fleur de-lys fastener.

Similar in concept were his nugget gold or roughcast gold boxes, work which the Russians call *samorodok*, meaning 'gold as it is born'. Also famous is his 'Gorilla head' box, carved out of hollowed purple porphyry with the lid at the back of the head a fluted golden shell with a ruby and diamond thumb-piece; for eyes the gorilla has yellow diamonds while the teeth are of gold inset with rose diamonds.

While Fabergé never produced two identical boxes, a particular 'uniform' style of box has come to be associated with him – flattish, often ovoid in section with the hinged lift-up lid flush with the surface. They were made in natural and multi-coloured gold with decorative chevrons, criss-cross fluting and similar geometric motifs deeply hand-tooled into the metal.

Tea Caddies and Lacquered Papier Mâché Boxes

18th and 19th century tea caddies are much prized by collectors today. The name caddy comes from a Malayan word 'kati' which is the name for a packet of tea weighing 1¾ lbs, about 780 grams. The ritual of tea-drinking in England became established in the 18th century and as it reached national proportions, tea caddies grew to match the ceremony. The first containers were bottle-shaped and made of porcelain, tin or silver, later changing to become squarer and held in wooden boxes. Ultimately the box itself became the container with one to three compartments to hold different kinds of tea. It was the double-compartment boxes that became known as caddies.

Most commonly, caddies were made in wood, usually deal, which was decorated. 19th century boxmakers experimented more widely than they had in the previous century with different kinds of decoration. Tortoiseshell, cut in thin sheets and glued over the deal, was used until about 1820. The surface of the shell was then polished or embossed. Ivory, mother-or-pearl and Sheffield silver were similarly used.

One type of early 19th century caddy that is popular with collectors is in the shape of various fruits and was sometimes made in the particular wood of the fruit. The lid was usually the top quarter of the box and was hinged. Caddies of quillwork and paper-mâché were also made.

Other boxes made from papier-mâché, dating from about 1820 to 1860, can be found today – snuff boxes, pen boxes, stationery boxes and so on. Most of these boxes were lacquered. The English papier mâché industry had its origins in 1772 when Henry Clay succeeded in making a new pulp that contained wood pulp as well as paper pulp. Clay established himself in Birmingham where his company was eventually succeeded in 1816 by Jennens and Bettridge. This firm is best known for its advances in mother-of-pearl inlay. The box, having had its shell pattern glued on, was then lacquered until it fully surrounded the shell. The box was then rubbed with pumice, polished and baked and the process repeated. The company closed in 1864.

Cutlery and Candle Boxes

Cutlery boxes were in use well into the 19th century and were long boxes that tapered slightly towards the bottom. They were made to be hung on the wall. Usually made in mahogany or oak, they had hinged lids and decorative inlay. Cutlery boxes can often be mistaken for candle boxes; the latter, however, often have two compartments, one of them for holding tinder. They were made in mahogany but pewter and brass examples can be found.

'Pot lid' Boxes

A type of pot popular with collectors are the 'pot lid' boxes in which potted meat, fishpaste and the like were marketed from the 1840s. Ceramic boxes, they were made mainly in Staffordshire by F. and R. Pratt of Fenton, the Cauldron Pottery Company in Shelton and Meyer and Company in Burslem. They are usually circular in shape, though some are rectangular and all have unhinged lids. The outstanding features of these boxes are the colourful pictures on the lid made by transfer printing and which required considerable skill. Favourite scenes are scenic or pastoral and occasionally portraits, notably Prince Albert and the Duke of Wellington.

Tunbridge Boxes

Boxes made in Tunbridge Wells in the 18th and 19th century became very popular partly because the town was a favourite spa. These wooden boxes are characterized by their mosaic-like patterns in coloured veneers which were glued to a rosewood or mahogany shell. The designs were made using slim strips of natural-coloured wood which were cut into tiny squares and it required great skill to find just the right natural woods to achieve an effective contrast. 19th century boxes are often identifiable by having a mosaic border. A large variety of boxes were made including cardcases, money boxes, stamp boxes and so on. Favourite motifs were birds, butterflies and flowers. Tunbridge wares, which became known as 'English mosaics', also included trays, tea caddies and small items of furniture.

Many other 19th century boxes too numerous to detail here are of interest to the collector, including dressing-table boxes in silver, glass or porcelain, needlework boxes, the most popular being imported Japanese lacquered ones and pictorial papier-mâché boxes which were produced in the Midlands from about 1800 and throughout Victorian times and jasperware boxes from Wedgwoods.

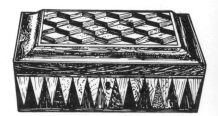

Cribbage box in Tunbridge ware.

Books and Bindings

To link together the development of printing with the spread of knowledge, and thus of civilization, is to state a broadly accepted historical truth. Although its actual development probably took place in China during the 6th century, the printing of books first took place in Europe between 1440 and 1460. The discovery is usually credited to a Mainz goldsmith, Johann Genzfleisch zum Gutenberg, although it would be inaccurate to say that Gutenberg invented printing. The realization that the creation of a stable society could be hastened by a rapid spread of knowledge had been well understood for several centuries.

Gutenberg brought together the results of many early attempts at mechanical reproduction, perhaps developed a means of casting large numbers of individual metal letters from one original matrix, discovered an ink that would adhere to these metal letters and then allow itself to be transferred under pressure on to paper, and adapted the familiar screw-driven wine-press into the first successful printing machine. Although Gutenberg himself made practically nothing from his efforts, he lit a fire that spread with dramatic speed. By the end of the 15th century, the mechanical reproduction of books by printing was under way in every country throughout Europe.

Prior to the development of printing, the spread of knowledge through the written word was in the hands of large numbers of scribes who painstakingly reproduced existing books and written documents by copying them by hand. This technique, of course, had existed in many earlier civilizations, such as classical Rome or ancient Egypt, but it reached a remarkably high level of sophistication and productivity during the early medieval period. Whole workshops of scribes, usually under monastic control, toiled to produce the religious, legal and governmental works that society demanded.

The need for large-scale production of literature had been understood well before Gutenberg's time, and so the reproduction of texts had become a recognized and lucrative trade by the 15th century. Booksellers and publishers, aided by armies of scribes, strove to produce the large number of volumes required to satisfy the ever-increasing demands of those wishing to read for education, for social development or simply for pleasure. Many of these early handwritten texts survive and so make possible the serious study of European history before the 15th century. Many were also finely made, the text meticulously written in a script specially developed for the purpose and interspersed with jewel-like illustrations that were included to clarify or illuminate the text. These manuscripts were then frequently bound with carved ivory or jewelled wooden panels to reflect the value of their contents and to safeguard them for the future.

Illuminated manuscripts are now usually only to be found in major public collections and so are accessible to study, not only for their contents, but also for their stylistic development. The changes in design, subject matter and method of illumination underline the many social upheavals of the early medieval period, making, for example, the close links between the manuscripts of Ireland and Scandinavia quite understandable. It is also important to realize that the early illuminated manuscripts established the form and style of the book as it is today. Printing merely continued the tradition, adding only speed and quantity to a well established pattern.

Although early illuminated manuscripts are outside the scope of this book, it would be wrong to assume that the production of such books and documents ceased with the coming of printing. To this day, the scribe and the illuminator are still called upon to produce the special book and the commemorative scroll. Such handmade documents frequently appear on the market once the reason for their original production has been forgotten and can often be bought quite cheaply. A royal visit, the opening of a factory, railway station or bridge, the launching of a ship, the laying of the foundation stone of a chapel, even the coming of age of the eldest son of an industrialist or landowner were the kinds of events commemorated by special illuminated scrolls, events of great importance at the time, but subsequently of little interest except to latter-day collectors.

The productions of Gutenberg and other early European printers followed closely the styles of handwritten manuscripts and so the letter forms they used were designed to resemble the formal characters used by the scribe. The full implication of the invention of printing from movable metal type was not realized until the last quarter of the 15th century and then the styles began to change dramatically. The Gothic, or blackletter, style of type was replaced by the more elegant Roman or antique form, a reflection of the humanism spreading across Europe from France and Italy. Venice and Paris became the centres of a new style of printing, epitomized by the work of Nicholas Jenson, and this style laid the foundations for modern printing. In Bologna, Francesco Griffo developed the first italic, or cursive type, and then in Paris Claude Garamond became the first to confine himself to the design and manufacture of typefaces to be used by other printers.

Aided by the demands of governments, churches, universities and private patrons, printing spread rapidly, so that by the 16th century it had already become the essential social force it is today. Because of their rarity, book collectors have traditionally specialized in the products of the 15th-century printers. The term 'incunabula' is used to refer to any book printed before 1500. Although arbitrary, this division is understandable; by 1500 printing had reached a stage of development that was then to remain unchanged for at least 300 years. The methods and the machinery did not greatly alter until the early 19th century, so much so that Gutenberg would certainly have been able to operate an 18th century press. The metal type and woodcut illustrations were produced in the same way and even the paper and the ink did not vary in any significant way. The general style and form of the book was finalized to such an extent that they do not vary greatly even today.

However, many changes did take place between 1500 and 1800, mostly in the actual design and appearance of the book. In the early 16th century, type designs proliferated, especially in Rome and Venice, where

Clarendon

SANS SERIF

Rockwell

Cloister

Four typefaces designed and first used in the 19th century.

printers such as Blado and Aldus developed an individuality of style lacking in the 15th century. In France, the highly personal pictorial manuscript style associated with the Books of Hours was adapted for books by printers such as Geofroy Tory.

The spread of the Renaissance through Europe encouraged the increased use of illustration and decorative detail. Arabesques, heraldic details and floral and geometric borders were used with increasing freedom, while new methods of reproducing illustrations, such as copper plate engraving and etching, were rapidly applied to books. By the 17th century, the design of books was closely allied to general changes in artistic styles, a relationship that has not altered since. This pattern of stylistic change continued into the 18th century, when typographers such as Fournier, Bodoni and Baskerville were able to increase still further the choice of typefaces available to printers.

In his *First Principles of Typography*, Stanley Morison wrote: 'The history of printing is in large measure the history of the title page.' Certainly no other part of the book reflects so precisely its period or style, or indeed expresses so clearly the nature of its contents. As a result, the book collector is likely to pay as much attention to this one page as to the rest of the book. It is also by the title page that the printer or designer of a book can be recognized, either because he has put his name on it, or because his style is distinctive. The development of the title page also reflects the gradual shift of emphasis from printer to publisher. Today, a book carries boldly the name of its publisher on the title page, and makes little mention of its printer. However, this is a relatively recent development, for it was only in the 19th century that the publisher emerged as the main producer of the book.

Originally, the printer published his own books and was responsible for all selling and distribution, either through book shops or by subscription. Then the printer worked in conjunction with a stationer or bookseller whose task was to sell the books, but the printer was still responsible for the origination, production and distribution of the books. As printers developed and diversified their activities, some set themselves up as publishers in order to control more precisely the production and selling of their books. However, in the 19th century, the whole system was turned round and the independent publisher appeared, his main function being to originate and sell books, this being done largely on a speculative basis. The publisher simply contracted the production of the book to the printer and therefore felt justified in replacing the printer's name on the title page with his own.

During the 19th century, printing was totally revolutionized by a number of technical developments and so the nature of the book was changed dramatically during the same period. First, the application of mechanical power to printing presses and other machinery enabled them to produce many more books. Secondly, new papers and inks were developed to match the speed and output of the new machines, and these in turn allowed a greater flexibility to the designers and manufacturers of books. Thirdly, large numbers of new typefaces were produced, many of which reflected the eclecticism and the successive fashions that followed and merged with each other throughout the 19th century.

Designers and printers made free use of the Tuscans, Egyptians, Sans Serifs and other new and exotic letter forms that were put before them. Fourthly, the method of printing by lithography, developed by A. Senefelder in 1798, was rapidly adapted into an adequate and accurate method of reproducing all kinds of illustrations in large quantities to suit both commercial and artistic demands. This facility was not available to printers and publishers until the 19th century, and so before then illustrated books had only been produced in limited quantities and then only by rather laborious methods. Once the principle of lithography was generally established, it was soon developed into a means of reproducing illustrations in colour. From the middle of the century, chromolithography was in general use, and so for the first time large quantities of books, illustrated throughout in full colour, could be quickly and cheaply produced.

There were also changes in marketing. The production of large numbers of books was dependent upon there being already in existence a market ready to absorb them, and so various changes in selling and distribution took place, most of which were aimed at reducing the cost of books. Publishers began to advertise their products more widely and developed new ways of selling. For example, books were produced in paper covers, or were sold in instalments in magazine style. At the same time, the gradual spread of education throughout the 19th century ensured that new markets were continually becoming available. Ultimately, the establishment of a general standard of education and literacy in one country after another throughout the world only became possible because the books were available to act as bricks upon which this concept of civilization could be firmly based.

In the 20th century, further changes have taken place in the methods of book production, but their impact has been rather less than those of the previous century. Book production has been advanced by technical developments such as computer-aided typesetting and the metal type itself has largely been replaced by film. Photographs in colour and black-and-white can now be reproduced in any book, almost regardless of its price. International co-editions have increased both the range and the quantity of published material. However, despite developments such as these, the book is still produced in the form ultimately finalized by the publishers and printers of the 19th century.

Of all collectors, the book collector is perhaps the oldest. The tradition was well established in classical Greece and Rome, and by the Middle Ages was generally accepted as a suitable activity for learned or wealthy gentlemen.

Many of the illuminated manuscripts produced during this period were immediately hoarded by collectors, both private and public. Indeed the fruits of these early collectors are still to be seen in university libraries throughout Europe. The development of printing merely encouraged the enthusiasm of early collectors, who seized the new books as they came from the presses.

Many scholars of this period, for example Erasmus, were known as much for their libraries as for their actual writing. Even in this early period, there is evidence of collectors specializing in the work of particular printers and paying less attention to the subject matter of the books they were collecting than to the typography. Once established, the habit rapidly spread and developed, aided by the efforts of the booksellers, who were as willing to keep old books in circulation as to sell the new. By the 18th century, the antiquarian and second-hand bookseller were essential parts of any civilized community, a pattern that has not really altered since then.

The development of an interest in old books was felt to be a necessary part of any young man's education and the acquisition of the interest was made as easy as possible. Auction houses were established which specialized in the sale and resale of old books, ensuring that as soon as one library was broken up others would be formed to take its place. The broad acceptability of book collecting made it stand apart from other forms of collecting, which by comparison were made to seem less neccessary and rather underhand. To collect books was to collect knowledge, even though the collector may have in fact paid little attention to the words within the covers.

As a result, the famous book collectors of the 18th and 19th centuries were far better known, both during and after their lifetimes, than collectors in other fields. To give one example, the collection of Sir Horace Walpole at Strawberry Hill was known throughout Europe. When it was dispersed at auction, its contents were judiciously scattered through the libraries of Europe, having been made more attractive by their connection with Walpole. Even today, a book known to have come from Walpole's library will command an interest greater than that aroused by its contents or typography alone. Indeed, the association of books with famous collectors of the past is one of their permanent attractions. To own a book with such associations is to own a part of that person, albeit temporarily.

Book collectors have a rich choice before them. They can concentrate on particular printers and so develop a knowledge of the changes in typographic styles. They can collect the works of particular authors in all their various editions. They can pursue a particular subject or theme, which is perhaps the widest choice of all, because there is no subject that has not been written about at one time or another. They can study a particular technique of illustration, or the work of a particular illustrator. They can collect books associated with famous people. They can collect authors' presentation copies, or first editions of 20th century novels. The choice is almost infinite and it is made even richer by its ability to fit any size of pocket. Browsing in second-hand bookshops is a universally attractive pastime and can be practised at any time and on any level of the market. Whether the collector is buying incunabula at auction, or old paperbacks in junk markets, the fascination is much the same.

One particular aspect of the book which is often overlooked by collectors is the binding. The cover of a book is often taken for granted, simply as a means of protecting the more delicate material inside, but in fact a study of bindings can be as rewarding as the books themselves. Manuscripts were frequently given splendid bindings, both to protect them and reflect the sacred significance of the contents. With the development of printing, this pattern was altered, for early printers rarely made

335

any attempt to bind their books themselves. Most books were bought on subscription by a limited number of purchasers, all of whom would expect the books to conform with the styles already established in their libraries or collections. The books were therefore supplied unbound by the printer and the purchaser would arrange for his own binder to complete the work. This pattern continued until the early 19th century, when changes in marketing and production methods completely altered the nature of the book.

Traditionally, leather has been the usual material for book binding, as it combines the necessary qualities of flexibility and permanence. Anyone with only a general interest in books will be aware that old books are likely to be bound in leather and decorated with embossed gold tooling, but they may not understand the complexities of style and technique that these bindings can conceal. In terms of style, binding has generally followed the fashions of contemporary typography and so the Renaissance arabesques of the 16th-century printers would also be echoed in the gold blocking on the binding. Similarly, the typographic elegance of the 18th century and the stylistic eclectism of the 19th century were reflected in the book bindings of those periods. Collectors should not forget, however, that books have frequently been re-bound, in which case the binding is likely to have followed its own period style rather than that of the original book.

The bindings of the 19th century are particularly interesting and are well worth collecting because they are both varied and available. The rise of the independent publisher meant that books were now required to have their own binding, for the public would no longer be willing or able to pay for individual custom-made binding. Printers therefore developed binderies and mechanized equipment to produce the new kind of book. Secondly, the far greater quantities of books being produced meant that leather had to be replaced by cheaper materials and so the technique still practised today of binding with stiff cloth-covered cardboard was developed. New materials did not, however, mean a reduction in standards or inventiveness, for during the 19th century book binding shows a greater use of imagination than at any earlier period. Imitation and substitute leathers were used with great freedom, many of which were embossed and blocked in sharp relief. The Gothic styles of the 1840s and 1850s were particularly suitable for this kind of treatment. Cloth bindings could be printed and decorated in a variety of ways, some of the most interesting and exciting being those used on children's books during the latter part of the century. Bindings could range from simple paper covers to elaborate confections inlaid with exotic materials such as ivory or tortoiseshell, while lacquer and papier-mâché could produce a finish beyond the wildest dreams of the early binders.

However, even in this period of expansion and novelty, the traditional methods of binding survived. There was a continuing demand for the work of the specialist book-binder who was able to produce an individually designed and made binding in the finest materials. Like the tools and the materials, the styles were also now quite old-fashioned and so it was rare for a Victorian binder to match the inventiveness of his newer and cheaper rivals.

The quality and the craftsmanship was as powerful as ever, but the designs had been gradually weakened by constant repetitition.

During the last quarter of the 19th century, there were some attempts at revitalizing the designs by returning to the early medieval sources, but the real change did not occur until the 1920s and 1930s, when there was a total renaissance of craft book binding in France. There, for the first time, avant-garde design was applied to book binding and whole new techniques of leather-working, matching and embossing were developed to interpret correctly the designs of artists such as Matisse.

From France the techniques and the dynamic modern styles spread to other countries, bringing about an international revival in book binding. This movement also brought together the design of the book and the design of the binding, which now combined to produce a unified whole. The influence of these avant-garde designers was not limited to craft book binding, but affected equally the cheaper mass-produced bindings. These and the paper book jackets, which did not come into common use until the 1920s, helped to revitalize typography and graphic design in Europe and America during the interwar period.

Domestic Metalwork

During the 19th century most of the wrought iron household artefacts of the 18th century were still made with little difference, except that there was a growing tendency to supply some parts in cast-iron. In fact, the 19th century became the foundry age *par excellence* and everything possible was made in this metal: useful objects like door knockers, boot scrapers, door porters and pavement covers for coal chutes, and useless objects like cast-iron razors; large objects like baths and kitchen ranges, and small objects like ears for roundabout horses; mechanical objects like penny-in-the-slot machines and coffee grinders, and toys like mechanical money-boxes.

One very attractive group included the Wardian case, a glass case, often with cast-iron framework and decoration, invented by Dr Nathaniel Bagshaw Ward (1791–1868) for growing plants, particularly ferns, in sealed conditions. There was an infinite variety of types, patterns and sizes. There were also hand-glass frames, a kind of cloche in cast-iron framing, and aquaria framed in cast-iron and supported on cast-iron stands.

Cast-iron furniture was not uncommon, especially for the garden, where favourite designs included concoctions of Gothic motifs, fern leaves, ivy and animal life. Similar to this were tables and chairs designed especially for public houses and gin palaces. But there was also house furniture, one of the most indefatigable designers of which was Mr Mallet of Dublin, Ireland, who assembled his furniture from units of easily-cast shapes; some of it was very attractive and included Gothic, honeysuckle and purely functional designs.

Great Britain was one of the most important centres for foundrywork and products of such firms as Steven Bros. and Co. of London, S. Adams and Co. of Oldbury, Birminghan, Jobson and Co. of Sheffield, Skidmore of Clerkenwell and High Holborn, London, Macfarlane and Co. of Glasgow, and the Coalbrookdale Co. of Shropshire were sent all over the world.

But first-class cast-ironwork was also produced elsewhere. Some very delectable things were made in the U.S.A., wood-burning stoves and kitchen ranges providing a very vivid evocation of the American spirit in design as, in another sphere, did the cast-iron Columbian printing press with a great eagle with outspread wings on its bar.

German cast-ironwork was notable for its fine finish. Chimney ornaments, not unlike door porters, some of them illustrating Biblical scenes such as Christ and the woman of Samaria, form one group. Cast-iron chessmen and chess tables were made by Zimmerman of Hanan, Berlin, and, in 1849, by Seebafs and Co. of Offenbach. Imagination was used in making the sets: some have Romans on one side, barbarians on the other, others depict characters from the story of Reynard the Fox.

These things might be thought to represent the ultimate refinement in cast-iron, but even finer was the cast-iron jewelry made from about 1820 by the Royal Prussian Iron Foundry, Berlin, and later given in exchange for valuable jewels handed in by Prussian ladies to help the war effort against France in 1870 so that to be seen wearing cast-iron jewelry was a sign of patriotism. The lacy quality of this jewelry has to be seen to be believed.

Cast-iron was made in France throughout the 19th century, but the best was made during the first Empire, when decorative panels, lanterns and shop signs of very pleasing quality were made. But later there was much mediocre work, and to see the best French ironwork of the second half of the century one must look to blacksmithery, although there was a second blooming of overripe and pompous cast work during the second Empire.

Most of the blacksmithery was architectural, though smaller objects of everyday use were made both in France and elsewhere, and some good bench work was still turned out. But during the 19th century, all over the western world these things were made more cheaply and often more efficiently, though not always so beautifully, in cast-iron.

Yet wrought iron design did have something of a revival with the coming of the Art Nouveau style at the end of the century, and many small artefacts such as candlesticks, fire irons, brackets and table lamps were forged in the curvaceous, drooping-tulip lines of the style.

Jardinières, window boxes and stands made of bent steel wire and painted white are an attractive subdivision of ironwork. They were popular throughout much of the 19th century and were made up to the beginning of the First World War (1914). Shapes and sizes are of considerable variation.

There was a blooming of bronze and brass work during the 19th century, especially in the France of Napoleon I, when it was, in common with other arts and crafts, dominated by the classical style. Among the great workers of this period was Pierre-Philippe Thomire (1751–1843), who had earlier been patronized by Marie-Antoinette. His works include

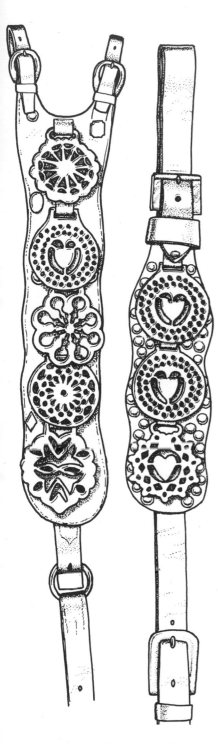

Some of the many designs of 19th-century horse brasses.

perfume burners in the form of a Greek tripod with winged griffins at the base and three female trumpeters at the top (Louvre, Paris). In collaboration with J.-B. Claude Odiot, Thomire made the cradle of the King of Rome (The Treasury, Hofburg, Vienna). This piece of furniture is richly constructed and decorated and has an eagle perched at its foot and above its canopy a winged Nike carrying a wreath. It is an impressive piece of craftsmanship, combining bronze casting and sculpture.

Despite the often turbulent changes of national administration, good work continued to be turned out in France throughout the 19th century. Some of the best products were smaller objects, among which we may include a pretty little bronze statuette of a bather by E. M. Falconet (1850–75) in the Wallace Collection, London. In France there were hundreds of manifestations of the craft of the bronzeworker: lighting fittings in the form of torches, chandeliers, candelabra, suspension fittings, stair rods and furniture decorations among them. As in the case of wrought iron, Art Nouveau later in the century held sway over the design of many of these things.

In Germany much bronzework was Gothic in design. Typical of this are the enormous candelabra and chandeliers in the singers' hall of Ludwig II's castle, Neuschwanstein in Bavaria. Assemblies of Gothic units, heavy and highly polished, they are masterpieces of their kind. Much similar work was made in England, in particular in Birmingham, a great deal of it stemming from the artistic theories of Augustus Welby Pugin, but more often it was of little artistic merit.

Horse brasses, used for the decoration of harness from the middle of the 18th century until the present day, make an interesting group of English brasswork. They embrace a whole range of metalworking techniques. The earliest brasses were made by simple benchwork, but after 1800 most of them were cast in alloys that varied considerably. There was calamine brass (copper together with zinc carbonate) in use from about 1850, pinchbeck brass (half copper, half zinc), Emerson's brass (copper and zinc but more golden in colour than the others) in use from before 1840 to about 1860 onwards. Early cast horse-brasses were often chased and brilliantly polished and burnished, and some of them were given an almost coppery hue by applications of heat and acid. After 1860, brasses were often made by stamping; these are lighter than the cast or hand-made specimens. Modern brasses, which are not really intended for use on a harness, but are merely curiosities, are cast and very roughly finished.

Hundreds of different types of decorative motifs and designs may be collected. One of the most pleasing – and incidentally an early pattern – is the sunflash, a rimmed and usually ribbed cone worn on the strap on the horse's face, so it flashes in the sun. Sometimes, in the later years of the 19th century, it was fitted with a glass or enamel boss. But there are others equally attractive in their way, including portraits of royalty, statesmen and heroes, stars and moons, birds, animals, devices and abstract patterns. Sometimes the horse's head-stall was surmounted by a decorative disc set in a ring, or with a polished bell, traditionally to frighten away the 'evil eye', but more practically to warn approaching traffic.

339

Closely related to horse brasses, is loriner's work: the metal mountings of horses' bridles, in which category, for convenience, spurs are sometimes included, although strictly speaking they are the specialized products of the spurrier. This group of artefacts was made throughout most of the periods previously discussed.

The parts that are in contact with the horse's mouth, the curb chain and curb hooks and the bit, snaffle or curb, are usually made of steel. But the branches, the parts that lie beside the animal's muzzle, are frequently of other metals or alloys, such as bronze or brass, and are beautifully decorated by casting, chasing or engraving or by all three together. Spurs, too, are made of steel or other metals and are often brilliantly decorated.

Guns

The flintlock, which made its appearance in the 17th century, was notable for its ease of manufacture, maintenance and certainty of operation, making it very suitable for military weapons and from early in the 18th century most European armies were equipped with flintlock muskets and pistols.

One of the best known and widely collected of these muskets was that of the British army, known as Brown Bess. This was produced in several styles which varied in detail although the basic shape and pattern remained the same. The earliest ones have a 116.8 cm (46 in) barrel with a bore of about 1.9 cm ($\frac{3}{4}$ in). The lockplates, since they were government weapons, normally carried the Royal cypher, the word Tower and, until 1764, the date and name of the manufacturer. The walnut stock had a brass butt plate and trigger guard. In a slot cut in the stock beneath the barrel was the ramrod. On the early models this was of wood but it was soon replaced by a metal one. The ramrod was held in position by small brass pipes set into the stock.

About 1768 the barrel was shortened to 106.7 cm (42 in) and in 1794 a shorter, and in many ways cruder, version of the Brown Bess, known as the India pattern, was taken into service, and this had a 99.1 cm (39 in) barrel. By about 1810, the New Land Model was introduced and this reverted to a 106.7 cm (42 in) barrel.

Military muskets are occasionally to be found with identifying regimental marks engraved on the barrel or on the butt plate and these are very desirable pieces. Many Brown Besses were produced by private suppliers for the volunteer movement which flourished during the period of the Napoleonic wars. These will often bear the name of a gunsmith and, quite often, a series of initials which identify the particular volunteer unit to which they were issued. The muskets and pistols of the European powers France, Prussia, Austria and Russia conform to much the same style as that of the Brown Bess.

The pistols of the same period are fitted with walnut stocks, a 30.5 cm (12 in) or 22.9 cm (9 in) barrel and a lock plate with the word Tower

Navy issue Colt with ivory grips, 1851.

and a crowned cypher and, like the musket, there may be on the barrel the initials of a regiment or ship to which they were issued.

The European military musket differed from the Brown Bess in the method of attaching the barrel to the stock. The British used a series of lugs under the barrel which were secured to the stock by pins which passed through holes in the lugs and stock. The French and other European nations favoured a simpler system using a ring or band which encircled the stock and barrel and at the muzzle end there was usually a more elaborate band. Most European weapons bear some marks, such as the name of the arsenal – Tula (Russia) or Suhl (Austria) or a proof mark or national emblem which will usually help identify the country of origin.

The flintlock pistol was produced in a tremendous range of patterns. There were tiny ones, known as muff pistols, intended for self-protection. They derived their name from the fact that they were small enough to be secreted inside a muff or in a pocket or a purse. Pocket pistols were slightly larger and these too were intended primarily as self defence weapons. They fired a small ball and instead of the cock and frizzen being mounted on the right hand side of the stock they were fitted with a device known as a box lock. The cock and frizzen were mounted centrally in the stock, just behind the breech. These pistols are frequently decorated with inlaid silver wire or by the use of special woods to enhance the appearance with the patterning and, less often, with some other form of inlay.

Very much sought-after by collectors are duelling pistols. They appeared first towards the end of the 18th century when they were basically just a form of officer's holster pistol, with a fairly long barrel.

At the end of the 18th century and certainly during the first part of the 19th century, specially made pistols intended solely for duelling, were produced. These were sold in pairs complete with accessories such as a flask to hold the powder, a mould in which to cast the lead bullets, sundry cleaning rods and leather bags to hold bullets. All these were fitted inside a case of oak or mahogany, together with a pair of flintlock pistols which were, as far as possible, identical. These duelling sets are very highly prized, particularly if by one of the better known British makers such as Manton, Mortimer, Twigg or Parker. France and Belgium excelled in the production of superb percussion duelling pistols. They were usually cased in trays with contoured compartments and often included extra accessories such as small mallets for tapping down the tight-fitting ball. The pistols were usually very ornate with chiselling and carving on barrels and stocks.

The barrels of most flintlock pistols were of steel but some were of brass, especially if the weapon was likely to be exposed to sea air or constant damp since brass does not rust.

One type of flintlock weapon which has always been popular with collectors is the blunderbuss. These weapons vary in detail but basically all have a bore which expands gradually from the breech towards the muzzle. The blunderbuss was loaded with 10 or 20 small pistol bullets with the idea that the widening bore would ensure that the shot spread over a wider area. In fact the widening of the muzzle only had a limited effect on the spread of shot but they were, nonetheless, very popular weapons. They were often fitted with a spring-operated bayonet fixed above or below the barrel. Either the trigger guard or a separate catch could be pressed so that the bayonet, which was folded back along the barrel, was driven by a spring to snap into the extended position in front of the barrel. These blunderbusses were carried by the guards on Royal Mail coaches, and those examples bearing post office markings or stage coach identification are extremely desirable. These inscriptions are normally to be found engraved round the muzzle.

Most of the pistols and muskets were, by modern standards, wildly inaccurate, but an improvement in accuracy could be obtained by rifling the barrel, that is cutting a number of quite shallow, spiral grooves on the inside face of the barrel. The idea was that the bullet, which was made of lead, would grip these ridges and as it moved down the length of the barrel the bullet would be forced to turn so that as it left the muzzle the ball was spinning. This spinning motion produced a gyroscopic effect which helped to cancel out the variations in shape, size and weight of the bullet, so resulting in far greater accuracy.

This basic ballistic fact had been known from the earliest days of gunpowder but the limiting factor was the difficulty of cutting the grooving or rifling on the inside surface of the barrel. It could be done and many of the wheellock guns were, in fact, rifled, but it was not until the middle of the 19th century that mass-produced rifled barrels became possible.

One of the best known of all rifles was the so-called Pennsylvanian or long rifle also known, erroneously, as the Kentucky rifle. It was an American weapon which had been developed from the European hunting rifle. The distinguishing feature of these very attractive and desirable rifles was the long barrel, around 94–101.6 cm (37–40 in) long, which fired quite a small diameter ball. The combination of a small bullet and a long, rifled barrel resulted in a standard of accuracy far in advance of the old, smooth-bored Brown Bess.

The Pennsylvanian rifle was frequently stocked with maple or other figured woods which gave it a very attractive appearance. Another distinguishing feature of these rifles was the graceful, down-drooping butt found on most of them, and the deep curve cut at the back of the butt where it fitted against the shoulder.

During the American War of Independence the colonists were largely armed with British style weapons although a number of muskets were supplied by the French. When, eventually, the new colonists were able to create their own arms industry they rather copied the French style.

The flintlock mechanism worked well, indeed its long life indicates this for it was in general use from about 1650 until the 1830s, but it was not without its faults. Probably the biggest inconvenience was the so-called hangfire which was the cumulative effect of a number of quite small delays. When the trigger was pressed a small period of time passed as the tumbler turned and the cock swung forward to strike the frizzen. The priming flashed and there was a further slight delay while the flame passed through the touchhole to ignite the main charge, which then fired. These small delays all added together to produce the hangfire which was particularly irritating to the hunter whose target was moving.

The flintlock mechanism was, like the matchlock, also somewhat at the mercy of the weather. If the priming powder got damp then the chances of a misfire were very high, or a strong wind might well blow most of the priming away. There were many attempts, some very ingenious, to overcome the hangfire problem and susceptibility to damage from weather. It was eventually a Scottish clergyman, the Reverend Alexander Forsyth, who pointed the way to a solution to these problems.

Forsyth used fulminates, very unstable chemicals, to ignite the main charge. His first practical system was the so-called scent bottle, a device which deposited a few grains of the fulminate just above a touchhole communicating with the main charge. A solid nosed hammer banged a small rod down on to the grains of fulminate causing it to explode and

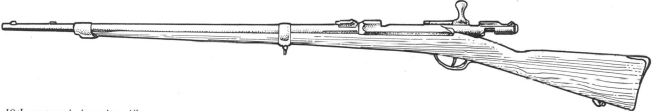

19th century bolt-action rifle.

produce a flash to fire the main charge. Forsyth patented his percussion system in 1807 but as yet it was not a really practical proposition. By the 1820s a simpler method of using the fulminate had been developed. A thin layer of fulminate was deposited on the inside of a thimble-like copper cap which was placed on top of a small pillar which had a tiny hole drilled through it to connect with the main charge. When the hammer swung forward it struck against the top of the cap forcing it down against the nipple, so causing the fulminate to explode.

The use of the percussion cap increased the efficiency of the firearms very considerably and the number of misfires was greatly reduced and priming was made so much simpler. With the matchlock, wheellock and flintlock priming had always been rather a slow business. After some powder had been poured down the barrel another pinch had to be deposited in the pan. Sometimes this was done using a special container known as a powder horn or powder flask which usually had some simple, automatic measuring device fitted at the nozzle.

From the mid-17th century onwards it became increasingly common to use a paper cartridge which was simply a tube of paper holding a charge of powder and a bullet. To load the weapon the end of the cartridge was bitten or torn, a pinch of powder was placed in the pan and the rest of the powder, followed by the ball and the paper case, was poured down the barrel and pushed home with the ramrod. With the percussion cap the system was simpler and the cartridge was merely torn open and the paper, powder and bullet poured down the barrel but instead of the priming powder a copper percussion cap was placed over the nipple and the weapon was then ready for firing.

One big problem for firearms makers and the military authorities brought about by the adoption of the percussion cap was that they were now left with quantities of obsolete flintlock weapons. From the 1830s onwards many of the military flintlocks were converted to the percussion system in a variety of styles. The most common way was to fit a nipple into the touchhole and replace the cock with a solid nosed hammer and remove the pan and frizzen. This type of conversion was quite effective and was carried out on all types of flintlocks.

Converted flintlock firearms are never as desirable as the original flintlock and some restorers will re-convert and restore the percussion weapon to its original flintlock state. Neither the flintlock converted to percussion nor the reconverted weapon is as desirable as one in its original condition.

Another great virtue of the percussion cap was that it made possible a simple, practical, multishot weapon. The great majority of matchlocks, wheellocks and flintlocks were single shot weapons. There had been many attempts to make them multishot and double and triple barrelled weapons were not uncommon. Not all of them were efficient and most suffered from some limitation. The big problem with all multishot flintlock and wheellock weapons was the complexity of the mechanism needed to discharge them. However, with the adoption of the percussion cap the problem was simplified.

The pepperbox revolver consisted of a large, metal cylinder drilled with five or six bores each connected to a nipple. Each bore was loaded separately with powder and ball and each was primed by placing a cap on the nipple. The whole barrel assembly was mounted in a frame with a hammer operated by a trigger and, either by mechanical means or by hand, the barrel assembly was rotated so that the hammer fell on a nipple and fired one shot, then the trigger was pulled again and the next unfired chamber was brought into position for firing. These pepperboxes, so called because of a similarity between the pepper pot in the kitchen and the end view of the block with its five or six holes, are desirable – especially if cased with all accessories.

As weapons pepperboxes were barrel-heavy, clumsy and, at best, rather inaccurate. Across the Atlantic an American, Samuel Colt, was developing a much more efficient percussion revolver. He saw the great possibilities of applying 'modern' manufacturing methods to the fire-arms industry. In 1848, after many ups and downs, he produced the Colt Dragoon pistol. This was a heavy weapon which weighed over 2 kg (4½ lbs) and fired six .44 bullets.

The charges were housed in a cylinder and as the hammer was cocked with the thumb the cylinder was turned to bring an unfired charge in line with a rifled barrel. This system made for accuracy and rapid shooting and soon Colt was leading the world in the design and supply of percussion revolvers. He produced many models, a particular favourite being the 1851 Navy Colt, which fired a 9 mm (.36 in) bullet, and took its name from the fact that the cylinder was decorated with the engraving of a naval battle. In 1861 he produced the Army Colt which fired an 11 mm (.44 in) bullet.

In 1851 Colt visited Britain to display his goods at the Great Exhibition in London. He promoted himself and his products with verve and skill and upset the majority of the British gunmakers who had nothing to offer in competition to his superb percussion revolvers. Stimulated by the impudence of this Yankee businessman British manufacturerers such

Pair of French export flintlock pistols made by Claude Bizouard of Marseilles in 1857 and presented to Emperor Franz Joseph I.

Left: *Pendant cross of diamonds and garnets made in c.1800.*

Right: *Emerald and diamond bracelet (top)* by Cartier; centre: *a pair of ruby and diamond earclips by Cartier and a ruby and diamond brooch by Van Cleef and Arpels;* bottom: *a ruby and diamond bracelet by Cartier.*

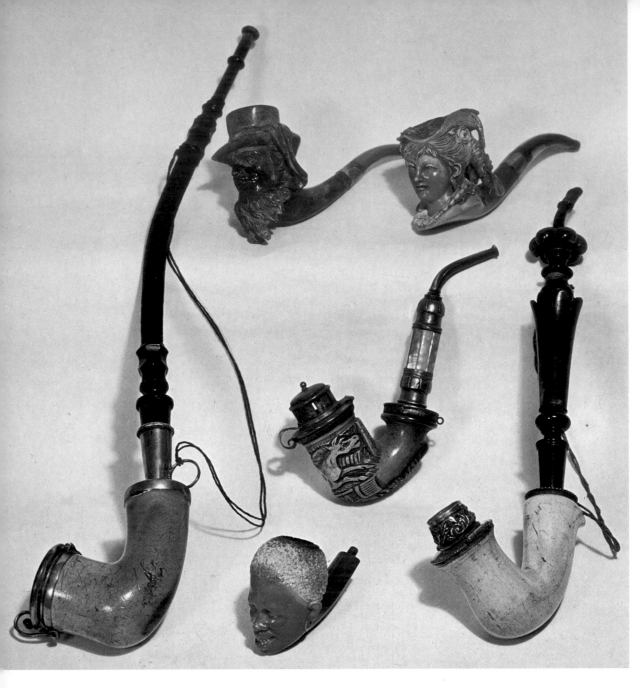

Above: *Group of variously carved and decorated 19th-century meerschaum pipes.*
Right: *Different styles of Chinese waterpipe popular in the 19th century.*

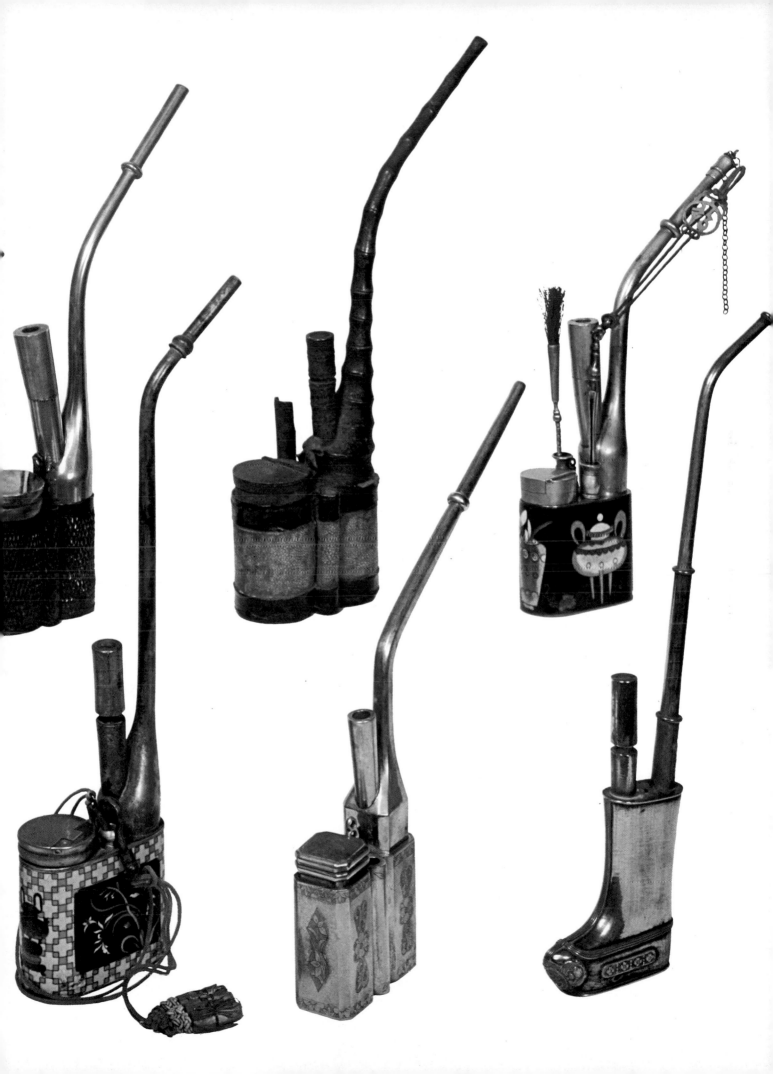

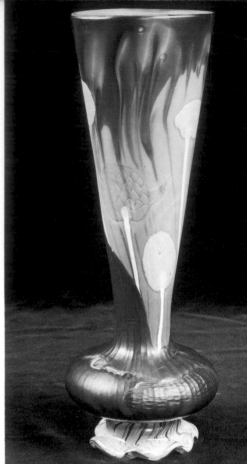

Top: *vase by Emile Galle in marqueterie de verre, c.1900.*
Above: *Enamel painted and acid etched glass c.1900.* Left: *Glass vase held in bronze mount. The outer layer of glass has been partly carved away to reveal the paler layer beneath.* Opposite above: *Design for a music room by M. H. Baillie Scott, 1902, showing the influence of William Morris's ideas.* Below: *Art Nouveau furniture made in Germany in the 1920s.*

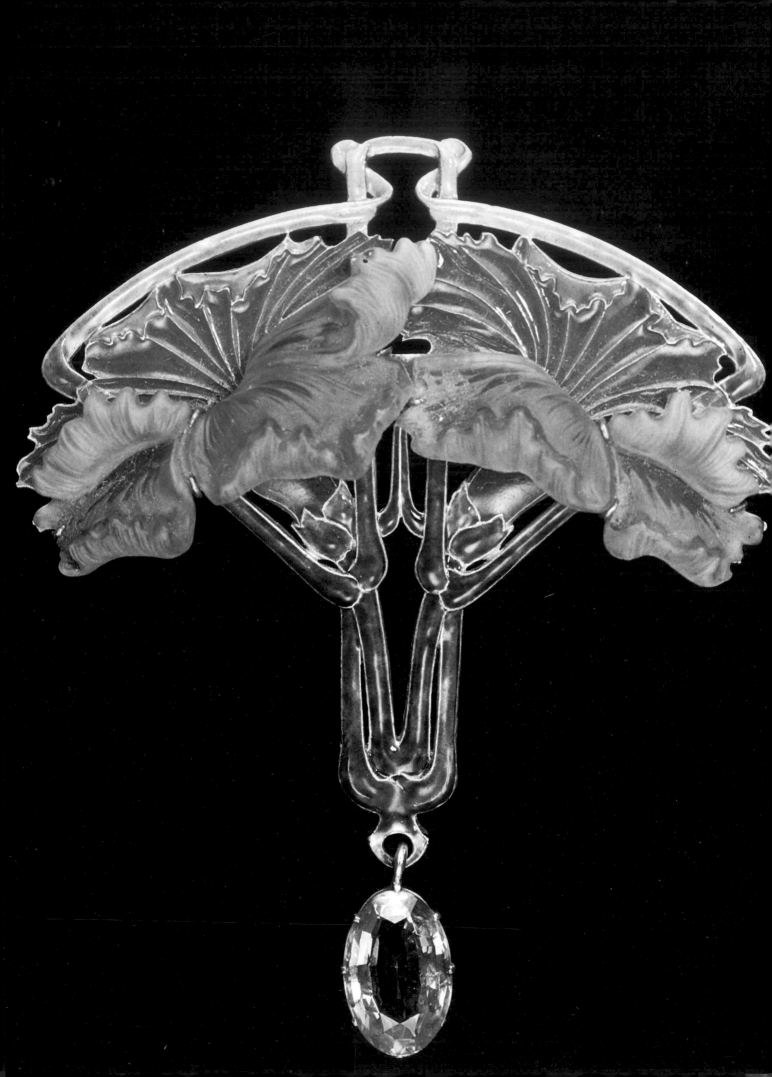

as Adams, Daws, Webley and Tranter, were soon producing their own models of percussion revolvers. At the time there was a great deal of controversy as to whether the Colt or British revolver was preferable. All Colt's weapons were single action and they had to be cocked manually, that is hammer pulled back by the thumb, before each shot could be fired. The British used another system whereby the hammer was cocked by pressure on the trigger and continuing pressure fired the charge.

Later, British manufacturers produced a double action version in which the hammer could be cocked either manually with the thumb or mechanically by means of the trigger. By the 1860s the number of percussion revolvers on the market was considerable.

Colts have long been prized by collectors, but British percussion revolvers have only recently begun to climb in price as collectors are turning to their study and collection, for they are fine examples of mid-19th century British craftsmanship.

Another big innovation around the mid-19th century was the general issue of rifled weapons to the armies of the world. The British Enfield rifle was one of the best and in the United States there were rifles and carbines such as the Spencer and the Sharps, and many others which were excellent weapons in their own right.

Another very important development was taking place at the same time and that was the adoption of breech loading systems. The majority of flintlock, wheellock, matchlock and percussion weapons were muzzle loading, the charge and bullet being poured down from the muzzle. The idea that loading from the breech end was simpler, easier and quicker, was not new – some of the earliest weapons, for example one owned by Henry VIII, were breech loading. The main problem was that in order to gain access to the breech there had to be some opening, and when the charge was fired gas escaped through this opening unless it was very effectively sealed. This gas escape was injurious to the firer as well as reducing the velocity of the bullet. During the 1850s and 1860s there were many systems devised to overcome this problem and there is a very rich field for collectors in these capping breech-loaders.

The other development which was in full flood at this time was the introduction of a metal cased cartridge. Paper cartridges were not a new idea, dating back to the 16th century, but what was being developed was a metal cartridge which contained the means of ignition as well as the propellant and bullet. One of the earliest was the pin-fire cartridge developed by Lefaucheux in 1835. This was a small copper case and in the base was a pinch of fulminate and touching this was a small, metal rod which projected through the wall of the case. The propellant was also inside the case and the mouth was sealed by the bullet. The pinfire cartridge was inserted into the breech and as the hammer fell it struck the pin which, in turn, hit against the fulminate exploding it and the flash fired the main charge. However, this system, efficient that it was, left much to be desired, being awkward and a little dangerous to handle because of the projecting pins.

In 1860 the firm of Smith and Wesson produced a copper case cartridge which could be loaded into the rear of a revolver cylinder or into the

Art Nouveau enamelled pendant of a pair of flowers.

breech of a rifle. The fulminate was deposited on the inside base of the case which was struck with the hammer to fire the cartridge. From then on muzzle loading was obsolete and cartridge weapons came into their own.

There was the usual problem of converting old weapons to the new system. Various stop-gap methods of converting old muzzle loading weapons to the new breech loading were adopted. In Britain the Snider system was approved; in the United States it was the Allin system. However, most countries sought a completely new weapon. A system designed by an American, Henry Peabody, was popular and was taken up by several countries, including France, Switzerland and Mexico.

A great flood of breech loading cartridge weapons were produced; one of the best known was the Colt revolver introduced in 1873 and known as the Single Action Army Colt. It was extremely efficient and has continued in production, virtually unchanged, ever since. Numerous breech loading rifles were also introduced and then, in 1890, came the latest development, the introduction of self-loading pistols.

With the revolver the hammer had to be cocked either with the thumb or by pressing the trigger before another shot could be fired. In 1893 Hugo Borchardt designed one of the first, really practical, self-loading pistols. The design was later developed by George Luger who produced, in 1898, the famous Luger or Parabellum pistol. This weapon was loaded by means of a separate magazine which slipped into the butt. An ingenious recoil mechanism operated and once the first shot had been fired it would throw out the empty case, insert a fresh cartridge ino the breech and make ready the action for firing. To discharge a shot all that was needed was a comparatively light pressure on the trigger, and the action could be repeated as long as there was any ammunition in the magazine.

Webley, Tranter, Mauser, Colt, Browning, Smith & Wesson were just a few of the manufacturers who produced metallic cartridge weapons, including many self-loading models.

The early 20th century was a period rich in mechanical devices, many of which came to nothing. But from a collector's point of view, these are still of considerable interest. However, collectors of these later weapons are at risk, for many of them are still quite capable of being fired and ammunition is still available; that means that in many parts of the world these are viewed as modern firearms and, in consequence, fall within the scope of firearms legislation and control. Anybody planning to begin such a collection would be well advised to check the legal position.

Prints

The possibilities of reproducing their work by mechanical means have always intrigued artists, and there is ample evidence of experimentation in many early civilizations. However, it was not until the Middle Ages that this possibility became a reality in the West.

The development of mechanical reproduction was closely related to the invention of printing from movable type, a technique pioneered in Germany by Johann Gutenberg during the late 1440s. The realization that an impression, or print, could be taken from carved letters in relief was quickly applied to illustrations carved in similar three-dimensional forms, and so engraving developed. Although an inaccurate term, engraving has come to be accepted as a generic title for all kinds of mechanical reproduction of illustrative material. In fact, there are three main types of engraving: the relief, or cameo, process; the intaglio process and the surface, or planographic process. Each type is quite distinct and so has developed its own methods and styles.

In its simplest form, the relief or cameo process can be expressed as a potato-cut or a lino-cut. A design can be carved on to a soft, flat material in such a way that it is left standing in relief, all the surplus surrounding material having been cut away. The carved design can then be covered with ink and its image transferred by pressure on to paper or some other equally flexible and absorbent surface. The process can then be repeated as many times as required to produce a number of virtually identical impressions, or prints, from the original carved design.

The material most suitable for this process is wood, especially the hard fruit woods such as pear, lime and box. The technique of woodcutting dates from the 14th century. With a strong, close-grained wood, the design left standing in relief could be quite fine and, at the same time, the carved block would be strong enough to produce hundreds, or even thousands, of impressions. The woodcut was developed extensively during the medieval period, and in the hands of artists such as Dürer attained a level of artistic quality that has rarely been equalled. It was widely used for illustrating the predominantly religious publications of the period and some secular designs were also produced. The best known example is probably the manual on chess printed by William Caxton during the early 1470s. As technique and style improved, so the tools used by the woodcutter became more sophisticated, which in turn allowed a greater artistic freedom to develop.

At the start of the history of mechanical reproduction there was already a kind of division of labour between the artist who was also capable of cutting his own designs on to wood and the professional engraver who simply used his technical skills to cut and print the designs of others. This division has remained a feature of printmaking ever since, regardless of technique or style. From the point of view of the collector, prints made by the artist himself have always been more desirable than those produced by the professional engraver.

From the woodcut there developed the wood engraving, which is effectively the reverse process, Here, the design is cut into the wood, leaving all the surplus material untouched. When printed, this produces a white design on a solid black ground, and so gives both artist and engraver a far finer control of line. Although developed at the same time as the woodcut, the wood engraving was not used extensively until the 18th century, when the combination of fine detail and a slow rate of wear of the block when in use made it suitable for book, magazine and newspaper illustrations. The most effective use of wood engraving can be seen either in the late 18th century natural history illustrations by Thomas

Bewick, or in the great variety of large scale illustrations in Victorian magazines and newspapers, whose immediacy, impact and speed of production could ultimately be bettered only by the photograph.

The second process, intaglio, is infinitely more flexible, although it also developed at about the same time as the woodcut. Here the design is cut into a metal plate with a series of small, sharp chisels, or burins. Until the development of the steel plate in the 19th century, the metal generally used was copper, as it was soft enough to be engraved by hand but firm enough to withstand the pressures of printing. When the engraving of the plate is complete, it is rolled all over with a stiff ink. The surface of the plate is then wiped clean, leaving ink only in the engraved lines. A damped piece of paper is then laid carefully on the plate and both are forced through a press, rather like a domestic mangle. The great pressure transfers the ink from the grooves in the plate on to the surface of the paper. This technique produces a far more precise result, with an infinitely greater range of tonal control. By the use of cross-hatching, a variable range of mid tones can be created, allowing the engraver to impart a surprising amount of 'colour' into his work and giving greater flexibility than the simple black and white of the woodcut. However, because of the pressure of the printing, engraved copper plates wear out quickly, so only a limited number of impressions can be taken. In many cases the deterioration of the plate is quite apparent, the lines becoming softer and more blurred as the run progresses. Collectors should always look closely at the sharpness of the printed line, as this can be a useful guide to the age of the plate when the print was actually produced.

The most common form is the line engraving, so called because the design is formed entirely of lines. However, many other engraving techniques were developed during the 17th and 18th centuries, mostly designed to improve the reproductive quality of the process. These included the stipple engraving, in which the design was created in dots rather than lines, a technique stylistically similar to that used for the reproduction of photographs in many newspapers today, and the mezzotint. In the latter, the whole surface of the copper plate is covered by a fine mesh of burred dots. The design is then created by alternatively smoothing or roughening areas of the plate to produce tonal contrasts of light and shade. This process was popular during the late 18th century because it was capable of reproducing many of the tonal qualities of paint. These techniques were often used in combination and so, by the end of the 18th century, engravings were in universal use for both artistic and reproductive purposes.

Other processes, such as etching and aquatint, involved the use of acid to etch or bite the design into the plate, instead of the tools and muscle power of the engraver. In this, the design is drawn with a needle on the surface of a plate coated with an acid-resistant wax. The plate is then immersed in an acid bath and the acid attacks only the areas exposed by the needle. Using his skill and control over a series of immersions in the acid, the etcher could produce a remarkably precise design with a far greater tonal range than the engraving and with a far softer quality. Etching was developed early in the 16th century, but its greatest period was in the 17th century in the hands of artists such as Rembrandt. There was also a significant etching revival during the late 19th and early 20th centuries, expressed particularly by the work of the American, J. M. Whistler. Variations of the etching process, such as aquatint and soft ground, were developed during the late 18th century as part of the move towards greater realism and tonal control, especially in landscape work. Most of these developments were designed to remove the hard outlines of etched or engraved work, bringing print-making nearer to painting.

The 18th century was the greatest period of the engraver, for the great explosion of technique at this time allowed him to work on so many levels. First there were the trade engravers, reproducing designs for catalogues, visiting and trade cards, magazines and books and for transfer printing on to ceramics and producing copies of popular paintings of the day. Highly professional and technically skilled, these engravers rarely produced original designs of their own. However, they frequently signed their work in the plate and so they are relatively easy to collect. Then there were the engravers of fashion plates, comic and satirical designs and miscellaneous sporting, social and topographical scenes. Some of these were artists of great originality, while others were content for their work to be largely reproductive. The output and range of this type of engraver was enormous and many examples are still available quite cheaply to present-day collectors. The third category were the artist engravers, who simply used the print-making processes as an extension of their work. This type of print has always been keenly collected, so the collector needs both money and judgment, plus a thorough understanding of the refinements of the techniques involved.

It is essential to remember that wood blocks or copper plates can often outlive the artist or engraver who originally produced them, and so can be reprinted many years later. There is no technical reason to prevent a block cut by Dürer being printed today. It takes considerable experience to judge the actual age of a print, experience that should include an understanding of ink and paper technology as well as the ability to judge the degree of wear on the plate. Many prints include the name of both engraver and artist cut into the plate, but these are of no use as a guide unless the names are actual signatures in pencil or ink. During the 19th century it became a common practice for artist engravers to sign their work and give some indication of the number of prints produced, a practice that is widely used today. These details obviously help the collector. Many artists also now insist that a plate be destroyed or defaced on the completion of the planned print run to make reprinting impossible. In the past these rules did not often apply and so the practice has developed among collectors of referring to prints by states. First state indicates a first proof printed by the artist or engraver, or at least one of the first edition to be produced, while second, third and successive states refer to subsequent or later editions of the print, often after alterations have been made by the engraver to the design. These alterations, combined with the sharpness of the line, are the best ways of distinguishing the states from each other. With popular or well-known artists, further editions of their work were frequently issued after their death, but with experience these later editions can usually be distinguished.

Another feature of the late 18th century was the search for a means of reproducing designs in colour. During this period there were many experiments in colour printing in France and elsewhere, most of which used the principle of printing several successive plates on top of each other. Each plate was inked with a separate colour, a technique that produced a fully coloured result when the plates were printed precisely in register. However, this process was both laborious and slow and, until the development of chromolithography in the mid-19th century prints were usually coloured by hand. This was done simply with flat washes of colour, all the tones and shadows already being present on the print. Many engravings were designed to be so coloured; others, intended to be left in the black, often acquired colour at a later date.

The third main process, the planographic, is not really engraving at all. In 1798, A. Senefelder first developed lithography, and thereby set in train all the various techniques that have revolutionized mechanical reproduction. The high speed colour printing that is generally taken for granted today could not exist without the early experiments in lithography and the development of trichromatics, that is to say, the realization that all colours can be formed from combinations of the three primaries, red, blue and yellow.

The lithographic process is based on the mutual antagonism of oil and water. The design is drawn with a greasy chalk on a smooth surface, originally stone, but generally a zinc plate today. The surface is then wetted and rolled with a greasy ink. The wet surface repels the ink, which adheres only to the areas drawn with the greasy chalk. A print is then taken and the process can be repeated, with almost no limit to the number of prints that can be made from one original. A lithograph also accurately reproduces very fine detail, and so could imitate closely the soft quality of drawing. It is therefore not surprising that its rapid development in the early 19th century was in part due to its popularity with artists such as Goya, Daumier and Turner.

It was not long before the colour lithograph was also developed, which clearly changed dramatically both fine and applied, or commercial, art. Once again, artists played a major part in this development, bringing about a general change in the status of the print maker. Although the commercial possibilities of chromolithography were startling, the artistic potential was even more exciting, for here was a development that gave the print-maker a position in the artistic hierarchy that was higher than any he had achieved since the invention of engraving in the Middle Ages.

This change has naturally affected also the collector of prints, as he now has a greater choice than ever before. He can specialize in art prints, either of the present or dating from the early years of this century. He can pursue particular artists, particular periods, unusual techniques, or simply specialize by subject, such as sport, topography, marine, architecture, or natural history. He can buy cheaply from the folders of the print dealers in antique markets, hoping for a rare find, or buy extravagant rarities at the top of the market, such as plates from Audubon's *Birds of America*. There is still a wealth of 18th century prints available at cheap prices. Equally, there are many interesting fields, most of them still scarcely considered by collectors, such as early 19th-century steel engravings.

20th
CENTURY

Introduction

Looking back on the history of the decorative arts from the vantage point of the 20th century, a cyclical pattern which has its roots in the arts of ancient Greece, Egypt and Rome, clearly characterizes the evolution of form and design. From the Romanesque and Gothic periods onwards the history of the decorative arts is very much the history of the reinterpretation and occasionally replication of those ancient art forms. By the 19th century this urge to historicism seems to have run its full course and the Victorian era was notable for its hotch-potch of styles which echoed the previous 500 years. In part this was perhaps due to the advent of industrialization and mass production which opened the decorative arts to almost everyone.

It was probably inevitable that a reaction against historicism, particularly the 19th century approach, would eventually find expression and in the last years of the 19th century and the first decade or so of the 20th century, Art Nouveau seemed to fill this need. The style had its origins in England with the paintings of William Blake, the curved, sinuous lines of his work providing ideal inspiration for those designers who were deliberately trying to break with the past. As a result Art Nouveau is characterized by its undulating asymmetrical lines which rely very often on natural forms such as flowers and buds, insects and vine tendrils.

The sources of Art Nouveau were many. Following the rediscovery of William Blake's art by the Pre-Raphaelites in the mid-19th century the challenge was taken up by Aubrey Beardsley who used sinuous lines in the same emotive way that Blake had done. The Arts and Crafts movement of William Morris also provided further stimulus to the new evolving style. Japanese styles which had reached England after about 1860 were also a formative influence. Curiously, although Art Nouveau originated in England it never fully flowered there – that dèvelopment was left to continental European designers. The work of Beardsley and Charles Rennie Mackintosh, for instance, was frequently condemned in England even though it was highly popular and influential in both Europe and America. Ultimately, Art Nouveau was condemned by the members of the Arts and Crafts movement; the textile designer William Crane described it as a 'strange decorative disease'.

Art Nouveau spread from England to the Continent during the 1890s. In France it was known as the 'Modern style', in Germany, *Jugendstil* and in Italy *Stile Florcale* or *Stile Liberty* (after the London store). The French school of Art Nouveau produced some of the most notable designers and craftsmen, particularly in the fields of furniture and glassware. The glassware of Emile Gallé is still much admired today as is the glass of the American Louis Tiffany. Gallé also produced furniture but the unique furniture of the period was made by such craftsmen as Louis Majorelle, Victor Prouvé and Eugène Vallin.

The Art Nouveau style lasted until about 1915 when it disappeared in the cataclysm of war. A revival of interest in the style arose in the 1950s

Top of the Chrysler Building, New York, designed by William van Alen, 1929.

and in recent years Art Nouveau has become extremely popular among collectors.

The final style of the first half of the 20th century that is of interest to collectors today was Art Deco which held sway during the 1930s. Art Deco is said to have begun with the Exposition Internationale des Arts Decoratifs et Industriels Modernes, held in Paris in 1925, which placed much emphasis on individuality. The origins of the style are to be found in Art Nouveau, the Bauhaus and Diaghilev's Ballets Russes. Art Deco is characterized by its rectilinear and symmetrical forms which were manifested in such motifs as sun-rays, rainbows and stylized foliage. Although France led the way in the new style the United States challenged that position and subsequently changed the style to a highly popular commercial one.

Furniture

The era that would dismiss the swirls of the Art Nouveau style for the streamlined rationality of machine-age design also witnessed the Art Deco style, which shared some qualities of each. At the turn of the century, European interest in Indo-Persian exotica was aroused by the displays at the Asian Pavilion of the International Exhibition in Paris in 1900, and was heightened by the publication of a French translation of the *Tales of the Arabian Nights*.

The Art Deco style was launched by the erotic, sensuous and spectacularly exotic productions of the Ballets Russes which, beginning with such dazzling displays as R. and S. Delaunay's *Cleopâtre* in 1909, drew its ornamental schemes at first from the lingering Art Nouveau style, and then increasingly from Russian, antique and Far Eastern sources.

Designed by such artists as Leon Bakst, A. Benois, and Alexander Kolovine, the rich and colourful decors and costumes of subsequent productions, including *Scheherazade* and the *L'Apres Midi d'un Faune*, enchanted and enraged the Parisian élite. Meeting success also in Rome, London and Monte Carlo, the Ballets Russes inspired a decorative style that relied for its effects on sumptuous, rich textiles and Ottoman affectations such as tapestries and opulent floor cushions.

In Paris, the firm of Poiret, and its branch the Atelier Martine, designed costumes and interiors that closely paralleled those of the Ballets Russes stage, pronouncing a stylistic dogma that balanced rich materials with simple forms.

Shaped by designers such as Josef Hoffman (1870–1956) and Koloman Moser (1868–1918) of the Viennese Secession Movement, and by other artists including Eileen Gray, Andre Groult, Edgar Brandt, J. E. Ruhlmann, A. A. Rateau, Ambrose Heal and E. W. Gimson, the Art Deco interior style combined highly decorative surface treatments with simple geometric forms, the latter foreshadowing the reductionism of the era that was to follow.

Cabinets, chairs, mirrors and tables designed by Heal, Gimson and

Hoffmann showed almost classical principles of restraint and geometricity in form. Stained woods, boxwood, ebony, mother-of-pearl, shagreen and lacquer covered these simple shapes, as did sparingly applied line ornament. Though cheerful, fresh, and often sparkling with colour, Art Deco ornament took on a similar restraint and geometric order. Furniture was inlaid with geometric shapes, small panels containing flowers, clustered discs, or layered arcs, or surfaced with plain lacquer or geometric compositions of such materials as lacquer and eggshell.

Elements such as disc-like flowers shown frontally, simplified unserrated leaves with thick, straight veins, and flat carvings of birds, figures and clouds, reflected the stylization of contemporary architectural sculpture, which was similarly executed in low relief.

The delight in surface texture and ornament that the Art Deco movement embraced was eschewed by the less productive, though seminally influential, de Stijl school of Holland in the first several decades of the century. Formulated in 1917 by the writer, painter and architect Theodore von Doesburg, the painter Piet Mondrian (1872–1944) and others, the movement sought to strip all superfluous decoration from essential forms, and to dissolve these forms into abstractions.

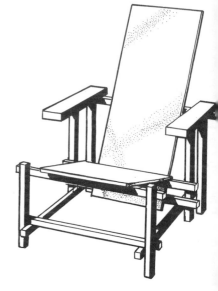

In the decorative arts, the most important product of this school was the chair designed by architect Gerrit Rietveld (1888–1964), commissioned with the request that it be based on the furniture of American architect Frank Lloyd Wright. Although singularly uncomfortable, and thus never made in large quantities, the chair reached European designers through the de Stijl magazine, in which it was published in 1919. The chair also appeared at an exhibition at the Bauhaus school of design in Germany in 1923, where some of the most progressive decorative artists of the era saw it.

The Bauhaus school was founded in 1919 by Walter Gropius, who designed the building that housed it in Dessau. The school attempted to approach modernity rationally and to embrace it fully, by welding high quality design with innovations in technology, materials and efficiency. The Bauhaus adhered to the precepts of the international style architect, Le Corbusier, who prescribed the clear presentation of pure geometric volumes and shapes. The school produced furniture, ceramics, and other items in a style that was simple, functional, streamlined and aesthetically pleasing, giving the appearance of industrial manufacture, for which each object was meant to be suited.

Tubular Steel Furniture

In addition to creating a wealth of fresh, clean new designs, the Bauhaus initiated the use of tubular steel in furniture, and also developed furniture that was easily stacked.

At the Bauhaus, Marcel Breuer created a series of chairs based on the Rietveld example. The first few of these followed the de Stijl model closely; the fifth, known as the 'Wassily' chair of 1925, was constructed of nickel-plated steel tubing, and transformed the rigid Rietveld precedent into a lightweight, airier structure, with arms and legs formed of continuous, pleasing lines of tubing, and arm, back and seat supports formed of flexible, supple leather or canvas.

This construction allowed, for the first time, an avoidance of the

Top: *Gerrit Rietveldt's Red-Blue chair, designed 1917–18.*
Below: *The 'Wassily' chair designed in 1925 by Marcel Breuer.*

visual clutter that chair legs had traditionally imposed on interior design. The chair also paved the way for the revolutionary 'cantilever' form chair, which was first developed in 1926 by the Dutch designer Mart Stam, in his attempts to create furniture that was light, mobile, and simply and perfectly scaled to the human body. Mies van der Rohe developed the similar 'MR' chair in the same year, and in 1928 Breuer perfected his own cantilever chair which, consisting of a rectangle of tubing bent sinusoidally, achieved maximum bounce, lightness and fluidity of form. Fitted with back and seat of canvas, leather caning, or vinyl upholstery, this chair has since been popularized internationally. Breuer also made use of the light, tensile qualities of steel tubing in his designs for glass-topped tables, which similarly expressed the simple beauty of structural form with their continuous linear supports.

Mies, whose pioneering work in glass-sheathed skyscrapers initiated an entire new phase of modern architecture, designed the German Government Pavilion at the International Exhibition at Barcelona in 1929, and the Tugenhadt House in Brno in 1930. Simple forms, flat planes, screen-like walls and rich materials characterized these interiors, for which he also designed two extremely significant 20th century chairs: the Barcelona chair and the super-streamlined Brno cantilever chair.

In the wake of these examples other designers have created furniture with steel frames – from Le Corbusier and others in the late 1920s, to the Danish Poul Kjaerholm, the Italian Claudio Salocchi and the Finnish Antti Nurmesniemi in very recent years. The firm of Thonet, which with its bent beechwood furniture of the 19th century had provided a prototype for bent steel construction, produced a great quantity of such furniture which was exported throughout Europe.

Beginning in the late 1930s, Danish furniture designers such as Borge Mogensen, Kaarl Klint, Mogens Koch and Hans Wegner began designing chairs which, relying on the natural beauty of curvaceously sculpted wood, were light and fluid, often with caned seats, sweeping crest rails and slightly undulating back uprights. Swedish, Finnish, Swiss and Italian designers similarly incorporated a light, linear approach to furniture design.

Alvar Aalto's first foray into furniture design was while he was building a convalescent home at Paimo between 1929 and 1933. One of his designs was a convertible sofa-bed with a thick wool upholstered seat and back, set on a chromium-plated tubular steel frame. However, surrounded by the vast forests of Finland, Aalto soon realized that, from an economic point of view if nothing else, wood should be the choice of medium for constructing Finnish furniture, and birchwood in particular was ideal for its colour, grain and final polished texture; laminated as plywood it was also as resilient as tubular steel.

Aalto, like Le Corbusier, was influenced in his first designs by the work of Michael Thonet. In 1931, he designed a chair with a sinusoidal seat-back comprised of a piece of bent plywood. The tables which he also designed in the 1930s are composed of upturned 'U's supporting a surface of wood or glass. Aalto was not concerned with ornamentation and ultimately his work was designed for mass production.

The American designer Charles Eames further developed the ideas advanced by Aalto. Eames was born in 1907 and trained as an architect at several institutions including Washington University and the Cranbrook Academy of Art, Michigan. He worked with Eero Saarinen in 1939 and the moulded plywood chair with a continuous curved surface they designed together was one of the prize-winning designs submitted for an exhibition called 'Organic Design in the Home', held at the Museum of Modern Art in New York in 1941. In 1946, based on the 1941 chair, he designed his shell chairs, first using steel for the seat but then turning to glass fibre-reinforced plastic. His first well-known model, made in 1948, was mounted on a light metal rod. Eames also designed collapsible tables and panel screens. In 1940 he worked with Saarinen on designs for standardized storage units.

The invention early in the century of latex foam meant that upholstery could be preformed into strong, shaped curves. Plastic furniture, with smooth continuous surfaces enclosing backs, seats and sides of chairs or curving gently from table into central leg into round base, was designed in a light, fluid style by Eero Saarinen in the 1950s.

These modern furniture pieces are not found in middle-class houses even today, although cheap mass production is more efficient than ever. Wall-to-wall carpeting, built-in cabinets and drawers and other innovations have had their effect on modern interior design. As in preceding centuries, past styles persist along with the most progressive, and most homes are likely to include antiques, attractive reproductions of old styles, and generally useful but stylistically homogenized pieces, in eclectic collections of styles. Rather than new stylistic forms, it is changes in standards of living that have probably most affected interior design today.

The unprecedented informality in domestic life, increasing 'furniturization' of such technological devices as televisions, radios, air conditioners and refrigerators have made their mark. And reduced dependence on servants for cleaning, the constant availability of electric lighting, improved insulation and heating systems, and such new materials as laminated boards, thermo-plastics, acrylics, vinyls and linoleum, have altered interior design far more drastically than any of the innovations that the rapid stylistic changes of a century ago could have wrought.

Glass

The work of René Lalique (1860–1945) helped to bring glassware into the modern age. A highly successful jeweller turned glassmaker, his first commercial success was the result of scent bottles produced for Monsieur Coty. His individual opalescent milky and frosted glass creations are moulded, and consequently mass produced. Embellishments by lacquer-type enamelling are particularly effective when they do occur, colour glass is more rare and in general Lalique relies for effect on form and texture. Lalique was one of the first artists to exploit the architectural possibilities of the glass material by creating doors, chandeliers and fountains. The firm today makes high quality crystal glass, and still produces pieces of earlier mould designs. After Lalique's death, the initial R was omitted from the signature.

The studio glass of Maurice Marinot (1882–1960) is the result of artistic concepts which produce striking effects. In 1911 Marinot, who was then a painter, visited the glass house of Eugène and Gabriel Villard and the sight of the glass in its molten state inspired him to begin designing some vases, bowls and bottles which were then made under his direction and decorated with enamels. By 1913 he was able to display a collection of glassware at the annual Salon d'Automne, which was widely admired. In the same year he began to teach himself to blow glass with the help of the Villards and was soon making as well as enamelling his own glass.

His motifs included stylized flowers, women's heads, nudes and dancers, showing again the innovative spirit that had characterized him as a painter. He also began to experiment with a reject glass called *malfin*, which was imperfectly refined. From 1922, Marinot's glass falls into two groups – smooth glass and engraved glass. The smooth wares were solid and chunky with the decorative effects all internal achieved by catching bubbles or films of metallic oxides between the layers of glass. The films of oxide produced coloured clouds and even coloured bubbles occasionally. With his engraved glass he took the smooth ware a step further, etching and/or wheel-cutting them to reveal the layers of decoration. The surfaces of these wares are usually polished but often the etched sections are left contrastingly rough.

England

From the early 1920s John Moncrieff in Perth produced a series of attractive glass. Moncrieff had founded his North British Glassworks in Perth in the 1880s and for the first few years made primarily medical and chemical glassware and bottles. In 1922 the company was joined by Salvador Ysart (1877–1955) from Barcelona, who created the so-called 'Monart' ware (Moncrieff Art Glass). A wide variety of Monart ware was made in a wide spectrum of colours, including bowls, decanters, plates, vases, boxes and paperweights. The glass is distinguished by its smooth, undecorated surface, the decoration lying instead in the thick walls of the glass in the form of bubbles, regular and random swirls of colour and marbling. The company eventually changed its name to John Moncrieff Ltd. and Ysart's son took over, after his father's death, as principal designer. The glass now produced by the company is called 'Monax'.

Many of the Stourbridge factories have survived, such as Webb Corbett, Steven Williams and Thomas Webb and Sons. Wedgwood have taken over the Lynn Glassworks production, now Wedgwood Glass, and Powells are now manufacturing as Whitefriars Glass. Many excellent artists design glass for the modern factories and the establishment of first-rate training centres for glassmaking and design such as the departments at the Stourbridge School of Art, the Edinburgh College of Art and the Royal College of Art in London has resulted in art glass of internationally high standard.

A revival of stippling techniques has extended the work of the engraver

'The Mausoleum' goblet engraved by Lawrence Whistler, 1960.

Laurence Whistler to a highly individual dimension, with tremendous influence on contemporary glass decoration. In a different vein, the glass engraving of New Zealander John Hutton produces a powerful impact of almost three-dimensional effect as seen in his figures on doors and panels at the Shakespeare Centre Stratford-on-Avon and at Coventry Cathedral. Organized exhibitions by the Guild of Glass Engravers and other associations encourage appreciation and interest in these fine achievements.

Holland and Italy

A new factory, the Royal Dutch Glassworks, was established at Leerdam in 1765. This was re-established in 1878 with the aim of improving the quality of Dutch glass and expanding the industry to curtail imports from Belgium. A small glassworks was founded in Maastricht in 1834 by Petrus Regout, a descendant from the Italian glassmaking family of Rigo. Leerdam, as a meaningful glass factory, did not come into its own until after 1915, when the director, P. M. Cochius, decided to engage two enterprising designers, Berlage and de Bazel. This was the beginning of a great new development at Leerdam, which had been bypassed by the Art Nouveau movement. A new designer, Andries Dirk Copier, who had studied glass techniques after his traineeship at the Utrecht school of graphic art, became the moving spirit of the factory. He joined Leerdam at 16 as a designer and in 1923, after the departure of one of the most gifted artist designers, Chris Lebeau, was made artistic director. Lebeau had initiated the Unica Studio at Leerdam and Copier extended the Unica glass ware and the Serica series to represent a range of studio glass which was desired by private collectors for its exciting and original treatment.

In the early 1920s, monumental, sculptured shapes with heavy cutting in clear coloured and colourless glass followed the designs of Berlage and de Bazel. Copier was interested in using both colour and blowing techniques to exploit the properties of the metal. Bubbles, inclusions, plain heavy and thin blown glass with perhaps one added colour effect, and glass forms inspired by early eastern or oriental glassmakers fascinate him. Today, a number of excellent young designers – including Lanooy, Valkema, Meydam and Brigitte Altenburger – have been engaged by Leerdam to produce glass at studio level.

Signatures vary greatly, sometimes they enclose the initials of the designer within a right-angle, sometimes they spell out in full the Unica and Serica studio products with Copier's name added, or the initials of the designer are added to form a geometric pattern.

During the 1920s, Ercole Barovier, a descendant of the Renaissance glassmaking family of Beroviero, made some original pieces in his desire for unusual colour glass effects. The company exists today as Barovier and Toso, very much catering for the tourist trade, but they have also developed a range of lightweight glass, well designed and of gentle colouring, which is original enough to stand apart from the popular Murano product. If signed, glass by Venini is marked with the full name and the additon of 'Murano'. Barovier and Toso use labels, but specially designed pieces or pieces that have been done for a commission carry the artist's signature.

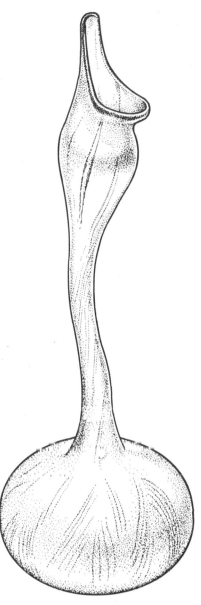

Tiffany gooseneck glass vase, c.1900.

America

In 1903 Frederick Carder of Stevens Williams (Stourbridge) and Thomas G. Hawkes founded the Steuben Glass Works. At first influenced by the work of Galle, Lalique and Tiffany, they succumbed to popular concepts of novelty glass with the creation of several attractive designs including:

Aurenne – a trade name for an iridescent glassware produced from 1904–30. It was made in blue and gold in a variety of shapes from table glasses to candlesticks and lampshades. Some examples are engraved.

Verre-de-Soie – this was similar to the European variety and was made by applying a layer of tin chloride solution to the glass to give a translucent effect. Steuben livened the European style by making the handles, stoppers and so on in coloured glass.

Moss Agate – made by rolling the hot glass on pulverized coloured glass then reheating to simulate moss agate.

Jade glass – an opaline glass made in blue, green, yellow, amethyst, rosaline and alabaster. The stems and feet of these wares were often a different colour from the bodies.

Rouge Flambe – a rare red glass.

Ivory   an opaque, pale-yellow glass which looks like polished alabaster and made by adding uranium slats to opal glass.

Glassmaking by the *cire perdue* technique was a particular hobby of Carder's. In 1918 the firm was taken over by the industrial Corning Glassworks and in 1933 was incorporated as Corning's artistic division under the direction of Arthur A. Houghton, with the cooperation of Jack Gates and Sydney Waugh. Steuben have developed a particularly brilliant and soft crystal which lends itself to the more individual glass sculptures, a unique facet of Steuben today which establishes the factory as the leading American crystal glasshouse. Signatures are present in full, and specially designed pieces may carry a date and the name of the artist.

Caucasian Carpets

During recent years antique Caucasian rugs have exerted a greater appeal to connoisseurs than was hitherto the case. Prayer rugs or *namazliks* are not so dominant as they are in the Turkish group, though quite a large number occur from time to time, particularly in Daghestans. In general, Caucasian rugs are very colourful, and therein lies their appeal. All Caucasians are made with a Turkish knot.

Kazak

The largest group is undoubtedly the Kazak, wherein there are a number of subdivisions which are generally ignored by most collectors, with the exception of Chelaberds, often called 'Eagle Kazaks', which are really from the Karabagh area and Bordjalous. Kazaks, in general, are woven from thick lustrous wool with a longer pile than most other rugs, and the texture is sturdy and usually fairly coarse, with knotting varying between 6.5 and 14 sq cm (42 to 90 sq in). Colours are strong, and include green, red, blue, yellow, white and brown, and the drawing of the designs is clear-cut and vigorous. Warp and weft are both of wool; the weft, usually dyed red or brown, crosses two, three or even four times between every two rows of knots.

Patterns are very varied, ranging from extreme simplicity with large areas of solid colour bearing disjointed motifs to several large medallions of different colours on a ground filled with small motifs. Borders are small in comparison with the remainder of the rug. The main stripe can vary from the most common 'crab' pattern, to the leaf-and-wineglass, or the reciprocal sloping latch hook, or consist of rows of stylized rosettes.

The so-called 'Eagle Kazaks' have similar wool, but the whole of the field is occupied by one, two or three sunburst patterns that give a wild and untamed effect. Borders are usually in the 'crab' pattern.

Shirvan

Equally as numerous as Kazaks are the antique Shirvans, but usually they are very different in styling, design and texture. Knotting varies from 8.75 to 22.25 to the sq cm (56 to 144 sq in) and the rows of knots have a slightly wavy appearance from the back, which is not ridged. Colours are mostly blue, red, ivory, with some yellowish tan and occasionally green, and the designs mostly tend to be a number of angular medallions occupying the centre of the field, with the remainder of the space filled with small unrelated motifs as in the manner of nomad rugs. There are many other designs to be found in this group however, both in field and border, but by far the commonest border design is the leaf-and-wineglass.

Soumak

Currently very popular, but rapidly becoming scarcer, are the flatweave Soumaks, a form of *kelim* with loose ends of weft threads hanging at the back, and the design on the surface effected in a flat chain stitch, while there are also separate weft threads additional to those employed in creating the design. The field usually contains three or four large diamond-shaped medallions stretching the full width of the field, with flattened octagons in their centres and in the triangular areas remaining at the sides of the medallions. The main colours employed are blue, red, brown, a little yellow and some ivory, and the warp and weft are both of wool.

Daghestan

Although less frequently encountered than the Shirvans, the Daghestan rugs are very popular with collectors. They have a short pile, which gives an incisive clarity to the designs, and they are some of the firmest textured rugs in the Caucasian group. Both prayer rugs and other types of rugs are encountered, the only difference in their treatment being the inclusion of a geometrical *mihrab*.

The fields and spandrels are covered with the same design, which is usually a diaper pattern in which the diamond shapes carry a very highly stylized small floral spray, the whole designed in blue, red, ivory, green and yellow on an ivory ground. The main border stripe is usually composed of a series of triangular shapes in contrasting colours.

Knotting varies from coarse, at 8.75 knots, to fine, with 28 knots to the sq cm (56 to 180 sq in). Unlike Shirvans, the rows of knots at the back look straight.

Khila (Baku)

At one time these rugs were more often called Baku, but today's opinion comes down on the side of Khila, although they come from the Baku area. They are different from all other Caucasian rugs in colouring and in design. The colour is duller and not so vivid, and consists of dark and light blue, shades of brown, yellow and tan and black. The main design – and the most usual – is a long narrow field carrying two or more rhomboidal medallions delineated by stepped outlines, with the corners of the field matching the medallions. If several medallions are present, they are set on larger rhombs in a contrasting colour, the intervening half rhombs matching the inner medallions.

The main ornamentation consists of larger *boteh* or cones which cover the field and are very heavily ornamented and of a strong rectangular form. Knotting is on the coarse side, varying from 6.5 to 15.25 to the sq cm (42 to 99 sq in) and the texture is fairly firm.

Derbend

Mostly on the coarse side, with knotting varying between a mere 4.5 and 16.75 to the sq cm (30 and 100 sq in). However, there are few to be found at the finer end of the scale, representing the earlier productions. There are two or three shoots of wool weft between every two rows of knots. Warp is usually wool, though frequently brown goat hair was used. Designs are varied, often with the field occupied by a number of medallions, sometimes filled with small stepped rhombs and similar devices. Usually, there are three border stripes, but more in the older and finer pieces. The main colours are red, blue, brown and ivory.

Chichi

These rugs are nearly always in small sizes, and the fields are covered with either horizontal or diagonal rows of small stepped polygons in differing colours. The most distinctive feature, however, is the main border stripe, which consists of alternate rosettes and diagonal bands which have been squared by the addition of stylized trifoliate forms. Colours are rich, and include light and dark blue, red and ivory, with a little yellow, green and brown. Texture is fairly firm, with knotting varying from 8.75 to 18.50 to the sq cm (56 to 120 sq in), the back being flat and not ribbed.

Talish

These rugs are always long and narrow and have an air of character; they are not very common. The most characteristic feature is the main border stripe which is invariably composed of a large rosette alternating with four tiny squared rosettes arranged in a square. Both the rosettes and squares appear in a variety of colours. The field, always long and narrow, is usually blue, often plain, though there might be one or two small rosettes capriciously placed in any position on the field. Very occasionally, the field is covered with eight-pointed stars arranged in a diaper pattern. Texture is rather loose, and knotting coarse, around 16.50 to the sq cm (100 sq in).

Kuba

From the Kuba district comes a great variety of designs and styles, and this also includes the border designs. Nevertheless, they are not difficult to place, having silky wool, fine ordered patterning with a rather Persian styling and a general air of sophistication.

Knotting varies from 6.5 to around 18.5 to the sq cm (42 to 120 sq in), with a fairly closed look on the back, with very little of the warps showing, yet the overall texture is rather loose. Patterns may closely follow the Shirvan medallion type or, on the other hand, they may consist of refulgent star shapes arranged in horizontal and diagonal rows, in differing colours, in glowing colours. Again, they might borrow formalized rosettes and other devices from other areas, but arrange them in an ordered fashion of their own.

Borders often are of the rosette and bracket type, and usually with three border stripes. But there are many other main stripes, a popular one being of alternate diamond-shaped rosettes and four serrated leaves arranged in a quadrangular form. Colours are rich, with medium and dark blue, red, ivory, sable brown, green and yellow.

Lesghi

Lesghi rugs are sometimes mistaken for Shirvans, but generally the large eight-pointed medallions occupying the field are flatter than those of Shirvan, and the corners at the diagonals where the straight lines intersect have arrowhead forms. Generally, there are more colours in Lesghi rugs, with red, blue, ivory and green predominating, and some tan and yellow. Texture is firm though the knots may be as few as 5.5 to the sq cm (36 sq in), but they may also range up to around 16.50 sq cm (100 sq in).

Gendje

These rugs, which often resemble Kazaks, are much more loosely woven, so less survived to become antiques. In the Gendje there may be as many as four to eight shoots of red weft between every two rows of knots and the warps are visible from the back, and may be of wool or goat-hair. There are no designs that are typical, and this also applies to the borders.

Karabagh

These rugs are woven in an area adjacent to the Persian border, and the Persian influence is very apparent in the flowing type of design, especially in the borders, which may consist of a wavy vine and flora arrangement. The reds of these rugs are very characteristic, having a marked pinkish tendency not seen in any other Caucasian pieces, while the indigo blues are almost black. Medium and light blues are also used, though somewhat sparingly, and ivory white and yellow. Occasionally there is green.

In the field the patterns tend towards the use of medallions, which can be either lightly or heavily ornamented. Knotting tends to be coarse, varying from 6.5 to 16.5 to the sq cm (42 to 100 sq in), while the texture is loose. The warp is wool and is not very apparent from the back of the rug, which has a ribbed appearance. The weft is also of wool, which is sometimes dyed red, and there are two shoots between every two rows of knots.

Fereghan

Within this group there are two main types – in one the field is covered with an all-over pattern, and in the other a pole medallion is set upon a shaped field of plain colour and the corners covered with a closely packed all-over design.

In the first type the most common design is the Herati, so called because it was very common in rugs from Herat. It consists of a central quadrant with a rosette in the centre, from the corners of which palmettes spring. From the sides of the quadrant stalks extend with curved serrated leaves. This pattern is repeated all over the field, so closely set that it almost obscures the ground colour of the carpet. When the Herati pattern is used there are usually small cut-off corners to the field.

Less frequently seen is a repetitive form of the Gul-i-Hinnai pattern – a design based upon the henna plant, with light coloured flowers.

The most common border design is the well-known 'turtle' style, which is really a palmette with an extension on either side at the top which gives the impression of a turtle with clippers. These are alternatively reversed and joined together by dainty tendrils and vines. Most frequently the borders have an almond green ground which has been attacked by the dye used so that the border is embossed against the green ground. Other borders used are generally based upon a vine and rosette combination.

Colours used are a deep indigo blue and red, with some light blue, green, yellow and ivory. Texture is firm, and knotting varies from coarse with 8.75 knots to the sq cm (56 sq in) to fairly fine with up to 36.25 (234), the knots being Persian. Warp and weft are made of cotton.

Ispahans

It is normal to refer to antique carpets from this area as Ispahans, and modern products as Isfahans. Both types demonstrate superb workmanship, the antique types going back to late 16th and 17th centuries when Isfahan was the newly created capital of Shah Abbas.

The most usual design is, appropriately, the Shah Abbas, which consists of intricate scrolls and arabesques terminating in palmettes. In the very old pieces cloudbands were often introduced. Borders were wide, with large palmettes and other floral and foliate motifs. In the 16th century the motifs were small and the design well balanced, but with time the designs became larger. Usual colours were a red field with dark blue border, though occasionally a blue field turns up with a dark green border. Touches of ivory and yellow were also used. Almost all the pieces from this period are large carpet sizes.

Warps and wefts are mostly cotton, though wool was also used; sometimes cotton and wool were twisted together. The Turkish knot is used, varying from 7.5 to 19.5 knots to the sq cm (48 to 126 sq in). The texture is firm and the back flat.

Kashan

The weavers of Kashan produced an astonishing number of excellent pieces of tight stout weave and superb designing, especially in the 16th and 17th centuries.

The later pieces are all well designed with the fields filled with flowing foliate designs in rich ruby reds, shades of blue, green, ivory, yellow and a characteristic light brown. The outer guard stripe of the border almost invariably consists of a reciprocal trefoil or more rarely a sawtooth pattern, while the secondary guards carry a flower and tendril pattern.

Texture is extremely firm and the Persian knots very fine, varying from 39.75 to 74.5 to the sq cm (256 to 480 sq in) the weave being so tight that the sides often curl under. Warps are usually cotton, and the fine cotton wefts are normally dyed blue giving the back of the rug a characteristic blue appearance.

20th Century

Sehna

Most rugs from Kurdistan are stout and heavy but Sehna produces some of the lightest, thinnest rugs in all Persia. The workmanship is superb. Unlike most weavers, those of Sehna only use one shoot of weft between every two rows of knots and this shows up on the back with a quincunx appearance, and also leads to a very characteristic feel of roughness when the hand is rubbed over the back of a Sehna rug.

Designs are mostly small all-over diaper patterns, using the *boteh* or cone design, small floral designs, and the Herati pattern. Some of the older pieces have a medallion on which a further small medallion is superimposed, both covered with small repeated motifs. Borders of only three stripes and occasionally just two are the rule, the main stripe mostly being of the 'turtle' type on a yellow ground. Knotting is fine, varying between 20.25 and 74.5 to the sq cm (130 and 480 sq in), and is almost invariably in the Turkish knot. Warps are generally cotton and the overcasting in wool, but sometimes the warps are of linen or silk and the overcasting at the sides silk, usually in a purple shade.

Tabriz

This is one of the greatest weaving areas of Persia and has produced many fine pieces. This area, like most of Western Persia, used the Turkish knot, and knotting varies from medium, at 18.5 to the sq cm (120 sq in), to very fine at 68.25 (740).

There are no really typical designs of this area, for the weavers copied anything, but the workmanship is good. Many of the patterns are of the medallion and corner type, and the drawing is good. In both wool and silk products the red has a typical brick tone which helps to distinguish this type, the other main colours being blue and ivory, though a great number of subsidiary colours are employed.

Heriz

Rugs from this area are noted for their stout construction, the Turkish knotting varying from a mere 4.5 to the sq cm (30 sq in) to as many as 18.5 (120). Designs are extremely geometric, hard and angular, with no suggestion of softening. All are carried out in light blue, red, yellow, reddish-brown, green and ivory, and usually a little black. Both warp and weft is white cotton, with two shoots between every two rows of knots, the weft showing at the back of the rug. Heriz rugs are rather more square than most Persian carpets.

Kirman

Unlike many of the modern products, antique Kirmans are attractive pieces, beautifully made and designed, with lovely soft colourings, including characteristic rose red and rose pink. Designs are very varied, covering such styles as floral designs, medallions and corner hunting carpets and figured rugs, all depicted with charm and delicacy.

The weavers of Kirman used more colours in their rugs than almost any other type, as many as 15 appearing in one rug. In addition to rose red and rose pink there may also be green, yellow, brown, ash grey, ivory and shades of blue. The Sehna knot is used, with anything from 18.5 to 62 to sq cm (120 to 400 sq in), giving a very fine texture. Warps are cotton, while the fine wefts are usually wool, often dyed blue. The main border stripe is always floral in character.

Shiraz

Rugs from this area were and are made from a soft flocky wool which is semi-translucent and imparts a brilliance to the colours that enriches the appearance of the whole rug. Unfortunately the wool was not very hard wearing, and antiques from this area are usually well worn. Most of the pieces on the market today are from the latter half of the 19th century.

Designs vary, owing mainly to tribal differences, for they are the product of nomads, and the motifs are the usual disjointed agglomeration typical of nomads. In the finer qualities the arrangement of the motifs is more regular and also more balanced. Typically there is an extra chequered border at either end of the rug. Sometimes the field design may consist of vertical or diagonal rows of *boteh* in differing colours. Sides of the rugs are invariably overcast with a two colour effect or in short lengths of different colours. Warps are of wool or of goat hair, and the weft is wool, usually dyed red. Texture is loose. Both Persian and Turkish knotting occurs, according to the sub-tribe producing the rug, and there are from 8.75 to 22.25 knots to the sq cm (56 to 144 sq in).

Joshaghan

The Joshaghan area has produced many fine pieces in the past, and the most common design covers the field with small diamond-shaped panels in a diaper pattern, each panel being enlivened with small floral motifs, the main colours being dark indigo blue and red with the addition of green, yellow, brown and ivory. There is usually a small diamond-shaped medallion in the centre bearing a similar design to the field, while the corners are cut off with narrow saw toothed lines. The main border stripe is usually floral, often arranged in a rather quadrangular form.

Knotting varies between 8.75 to 21.75 Turkish knots to the sq cm (56 to 140 sq in). The back is slightly ribbed, and the texture on the firm side. The warp is cotton, and the weft is wool usually of natural colour but sometimes dyed red or brown.

Bidjar

These rugs are noted for their stoutness, both in substance and in wearing qualities. They have stout wool warps and the weavers pull the knots so tightly when knotting that one warp thread encircled by the pile is pulled behind the other, doubling the thickness of the back. This gives a fabric feeling as firm as a board which should never be folded, only rolled. Wefts, too, are of wool, which is fairly coarse and usually dyed red.

Designs vary, often consisting of a central medallion and corners set on a plain field, or a field covered with a lattice bearing small floral forms. The field may be covered with sprays of roses, or may be a hotchpotch of flowers, and animal and human forms. Colours are a rosy red, light and dark blue, ivory, yellow, green and brown.

Meshed

These have a medallion set in a field of floral traceries. A characteristic is the peculiar red with a slight purple tinge that local dyers produce. There are two types of Meshed: those tied with the Persian knot called Farsibaff and the finer Turkbuff pieces tied with the Turkish knot.

Texture is fairly firm, and the weave is medium, the knotting varying from between 15 and 31 to the sq cm (96 and 200 sq in). Apart from the purplish red, there are also blues, green, yellow and ivory.

Care and Repair

Restoration of antiques and works of art is usually concerned with returning the object to its original state. This sometimes involves removing later additions which alter the original appearance, or replacing parts which have been damaged or lost. Restoration may go a step further and attempt to regain the original structural strength to prolong usage and life.

Conservation, in its purest sense, aims at keeping as much of the original as possible and preventing further deterioration. Restoration and conservation should be compatible, indeed restoration performed without regard to conservation can prove a disastrous waste of time and money. In many cases, preventative conservation makes it possible to avoid the need for restoration altogether.

When viewing an antique it is important to remember that it is a product of ageing and of history. Careless restoration can remove this quality. Repairs and even blatant additions must be considered historical evidence of usage and may, therefore, be an integral part of the object. Sometimes a repair can be of great interest in itself by exhibiting technical ingenuity or by showing the importance an antique may have held throughout its history. With ethnographic material, this concept of history is vital. The form in most recent use is just as valid as the original, and legitimate 'field repairs' tend to be left.

Often, however, one is faced with bad and disfiguring repairs of no historical significance, or damage or deterioration that make restoration inevitable.

It is important to bear in mind the effect of natural ageing and usage. Normal handling over time produces signs of wear, while environmental factors produce colour changes, cracks and splits. There may be evidence of insect and mould attack, and corroded metals. And of course, there is the almost inevitable accumulation of dirt and grime. All this produces what is known as age-related surface, or patina.

Patina lends authenticity to an antique, and it can have an attractive mellowing effect. It can just as easily be unsightly and obscure or alter the appearance completely. It is often a question of degree – too much or the wrong type.

Any restoration must take the patina into consideration. What has taken centuries to form can be removed by the restorer in seconds, and all antique quality erased. Re-patination can be achieved, but it is rarely completely successful and is often obvious. Cleaning should be a compromise. Enough patina should remain to keep the feeling of age, yet the original should be allowed to show without disfigurement.

In certain cases, patinas are very important in themselves. Some are a deliberate part of the manufacture and design. With antiquities, patinas may be so prized that great attempts are made to preserve and enhance them.

Underneath the old restorations, the alterations, and the patina, lies the often much disguised original. How can it be recognized? Experience and a knowledge of antiques are obviously important guides in knowing what to expect. Research and comparisons are also helpful.

Visual examination can yield a lot of information. Most restoration ages at a different rate from the original and this may be obvious through a variation in colour, tone, texture or depth. Joins in repairs or additions may be noticeable. Examination should include the backs, undersides and in the crevices of objects, where less careful faking and matching is likely. Signs of wear and patina should be consistent. Restoration materials may be different from the original and thus show up under ultra-violet light, on X-rays or through solubility tests.

Whenever possible, restoration should be reversible. It may be necessary to get back to the original in order to correct a misconception in restoration. Made-up areas and colours age at a different rate from the original and may become too obvious in time. The restorer may also wish to make changes while working and re-do certain steps. New materials or methods may prove unsatisfactory and need to be removed. So, it is a good principle to ensure that all restoration can be removed without harming the original. Sometimes though, strength and permanence cannot be achieved without resorting to irreversible methods.

Another important aspect of any restoration to be undertaken is that of sympathetic media and materials. All restoration must be compatible with the original – when it is not, restoration becomes destructive. Materials added must respond to the environment in the same way as the original, moving with a similar coefficient of expansion. Adhesives should also be selected with this in mind. For example, it would be unwise to stick a flexible object together with a rigid adhesive. Chemical compatibility is equally important since a support, lacquer, or anything in contact with the original may be or become unstable and cause damage. Materials which would attract problems such as insects or mould growth should also be avoided.

Restorations may be needed on purely aesthetic grounds to remove falsifying additions or bad restoration or to improve the appearance where damage has been extensive. Action may be necessary when weakness or damage threaten the safety and existence of a specimen.

The question of 'do-it-yourself' versus the professional restorer must be considered. There is much published information on every aspect of restoration which should indicate exactly what is involved and the degree of difficulty and skill to be expected. Even if it then appears to be a job for the professional, armed with some knowledge of the subject and what is involved, it is easier to negotiate with the restorer.

Obviously, value helps to justify the expense of professional attention, and good restoration can often enhance the value of an object. In some cases, the expense involved in purchasing the materials and equipment needed for a single restoration job at home may be greater than that charged by the professional restorer. However, if a professional restorer is used, it is essential that he is ethical and reliable.

The best approach to restoration is to avoid the need for it altogether. In many cases, damage and deterioration can be prevented by measures designed to eliminate the cases. This may involve dealing with environmental factors or those of use and handling. The approach might best be called 'preventive conservation'. It may appear perfectly obvious and simple, but its importance and understanding are fundamentally vital to any collector.

Relative Humidity

Perhaps the most important single factor in deterioration is humidity. It is the controlling factor for most deterioration processes, and it can be destructive in itself through fluctuations and extremes.

Relative humidity is a measure of the amount of moisture present in the air, expressed as a percentage of the amount of possible moisture in the air at a given temperature. A high relative humidity would mean a high moisture content while a low value would reflect a drier atmosphere. Most organic materials attempt to stay in equilibrium with the environment and respond to changes in relative humidity by releasing or absorbing moisture. Extremes and rapid fluctuations cause problems. There is a range of relative humidity and moisture content best suited to each material, and reasonably constant values within this safe limit can be achieved either by keeping the temperature constant and altering the moisture content of the atmosphere with humidifiers and dehumidifiers or by changing the temperature. Any change, however, should be achieved slowly to avoid stresses. Absolute values of relative humidity can be read with a hygrometer.

Light

Damage by light takes two forms. The most obvious is usually a colour change which can be a colour loss or fading or a change in hue and tone. The second form is fibre deterioration in which light has an acceleratory influence on normal chemical degradation, and fibre strength is lost at a rate related to the amount of light and length of exposure. Obviously, different dyes and types of fibres are affected in different ways.

There are basically two factors in light which cause this deterioration. The first is related to the brightness or intensity of light present. Absolute values are read in lux from a device called a lux meter. Particularly light-sensitive materials need low levels of illumination. The type of light is also critical, and it is the ultra-violet content which is destructive. Daylight and most fluorescent light is high in ultra-violet rays.

Light can be controlled by filters, shades and baffles, dimmers, and by careful selection of light-fittings and their placement. Certain bulbs and tubes are less harmful than others.

Insect and Mould Attack

Organic materials are potential food for both insects and moulds. Such environmental components as temperature and moisture are contributory and controlling factors. Unfortunately, those conditions ideal for the well-being of most organic materials and often found in the home are equally suitable for insects. Woollen textiles, furs and feathers can be attacked while in storage by the larvae of the clothes moth. Carpet-beetle and fur beetle can also be a problem.

The larvae of the furniture beetle, *Anobium punctatum*, commonly known as woodworm, is the main culprit where wood is concerned, though termites and powder-post beetles can also be destructive in certain parts of the world. Insecticides are available for their control, but professional advice should be sought as treatment can be dangerous and ineffective unless done correctly.

Moulds prefer a dark and moist environment with little air movement, but once established can tolerate normal domestic conditions. Fungicides are available and are especially useful where dampness persists. The usual treatment is to increase ventilation and dry out the atmosphere slowly to an acceptable level. After airing and drying, the mould can be brushed off.

Dust and Chemical Pollution

Air-borne pollution in the form of dust and the chemical pollutants of an industrial atmosphere are other destructive agents. Not only is dust unsightly, it can work its way into textile fibres where it can act as an abrasive to make the fibres brittle and weak. It can also be hygroscopic and, by attracting moisture, encourage metal corrosion.

Chemical pollutants may use dust particles as nuclei of activity. Most industrial and urban atmospheres are high in sulphides which can combine with moisture and form sulphuric acid. Sulphides also tarnish silver. Ozone may be present in some situations and accelerate chemical reactions of deterioration. Air-conditioning is the best solution to the problem, though obviously this is not always possible. Alternatives that can be used are dust sheets, plastic bags, acid-free tissue and tarnish-resistant tissues, all of which help to isolate articles from the atmosphere.

Water

The effects of atmospheric moisture are related to levels of relative humidity and this has already been described. Aside from the obvious destruction caused by flooding or soaking, one of the most frequent instances of water damage in the home is that caused by wet objects being set on wooden furniture, with the resulting formation of bloom or rings. These are caused by moisture getting under the polish. In some cases it dries out, but often only refinishing will remove it. Water, being a solvent, can dissolve gesso, size, dyes and some paints. Most adhesives and varnishes will also absorb water, and many will break down and lose their adhesion after prolonged soaking. Before using any water treatment in cleaning, it is essential to test first in some inconspicuous place.

Abrasion and Over-Cleaning

Most normal abrasion or wear can be minimized by sensible care and handling. Where necessary, surfaces can be protected. Cleaning agents which are too strong or abrasive and objects likely to cause scratches are easily avoided.

Over-zealous cleaning can remove patinas and finishes, so routine cleaning is best done using the mildest methods available which still manage the job. Cleaning as part of restoration should be approached with caution, testing first and perhaps cleaning in stages to reach the final appearance.

Storage and Handling

The more an antique is handled, the greater the risk of damage. Even while a piece is in storage, where handling is minimal, safety cannot be assumed. Poor storage conditions such as adverse relative humidity or light may also be a problem, and insect and mould damage may develop

377

undetected. Certain packing materials such as newspapers, standard cardboard and foam rubber can deteriorate and release harmful chemicals.

Adequate support and protection is important for pieces in store – they can prevent crushing and distortion which may be irreversible.

Heat

The relationship between temperature and relative humidity has been mentioned, and the low relative humidity caused by excessive heat can be especially damaging. However, heat itself can cause problems. Resins and waxes can melt or distort. Furniture finishes and paint layers can be blistered and ruined. Heat can accelerate both ageing and chemically induced deterioration.

Restoration and Conservation of Organic Material – Wood and Furniture

Wood is probably the most common of the organic materials in the home and a likely component of most collections. Its wide usage is based not only on beauty and versatility, but also on its strength and resilience. However, it is extremely prone to damage through abuse and environmental factors.

The moisture content of wood is self-adjusting to reach equilibrium with the enrivonment. Seasoned wood is deliberately brought to a moisture content compatible with its intended atmosphere. The ideal relative humidity generally accepted for wood is in the range 50–60 per cent at 20°C (68°F). Trouble occurs when adjustments are required which are too extreme or occur too quickly. Under very dry conditions, as may be caused by central heating, sufficient moisture may be lost to cause wood cells to collapse, then splits and cracks appear. Swelling is the opposite phenomenon, and is caused by high humidity. Rapid fluctuations increase the risk of stresses being formed which can result in splitting, lifting veneers and so on. Warping is caused by a number of factors including long-term support faults, but more especially, by uneven exposure to moisture. This can occur when one surface is polished, painted or covered while its opposite surface is free to swell or shrink to produce curling.

Insect damage is common and the pests vary with the district. The type of destruction usually consists of a network of tunnels eaten away under the surface with the result that structural strength can be lost. Flight holes can be unsightly.

The usual indication of infestation is the formation of fresh frass, resembling sawdust, falling from flight holes. Such obvious activity is most likely in late spring when the adult emerges from the wood. Fumigation can be extremely dangerous and is best done professionally, but there are several insecticides on the market which can be applied either by injection or by surface application. Care should be taken with these poisons. Many insecticides have strong solvent properties and can dissolve finishes and paint. Instructions should be followed carefully and tests made for solubility and colour change before treatment.

Finishes can be damaged in other ways. Abrasion through scratches or coarse cleaning agents is common. Some are affected by alcohol, and most by water. Heat can cause blistering. Excessive light can accelerate deterioration and discoloration.

Breaks can usually be repaired simply. Joins may break down and veneers lift due to glue embrittlement, insect and mould activity, or wood movement. It is generally advisable to remain consistent with adhesives throughout a piece so that all joins react in the same manner to stresses and future restoration efforts will be simplified. All traces of old glue should be removed before resticking, to produce a strong and clean join.

Adhesive should be applied to both surfaces to be joined and the pieces stuck together. Taking care not to bruise the wood, clamps, weight, or tourniquets can be applied to squeeze out excess adhesive and ensure a tight fit. Extruded adhesive should be carefully removed at this stage. Animal glue, soluble in warm water, is the adhesive generally found in antique pieces and used for repairs, but later restoration may have been done with synthetic adhesives. Where the repair is of a break rather than resticking a join, stronger synthetic adhesives may be advisable. Dowelling or new pieces of wood may be required.

Splits present an interesting problem. In some cases, small splits can be permanently closed by correcting the humidity or by pressing the split together and holding it with an adhesive. However there is a risk that the stress will seek an outlet elsewhere, and a new split form.

An alternative is to fill the split though fillers harder than wood should be avoided as they will not react to normal wood movement and can act like a solid wedge and so create more problems. Wood is the ideal filler, and it is possible to insert slivers of similar wood shaped to fit the split and held in place with an adhesive. This can be brought to the same surface plane, colour matched, and finished to be virtually invisible. Often splits are better watched and left alone.

Careful cleaning can return a newly acquired antique to its original appearance and yet leave enough patina. Any cleaning method should be carefully tested in an inconspicuous area. This is very important where solvents are to be used. Finishes and varnishes are of various compositions and a method of cleaning should be sought which will remove accumulated wax, dirt and grime without harming the original finish. In some cases, a good quality paste wax can be massaged into the surface and will remove the top wax layers and grime and replace it with fresh wax. Gentle abrasives such as metal polishes may be useful in other instances.

A good standard cleaner can be made from an emulsion of two parts turpentine, two parts white vinegar, two parts methylated spirit and one part linseed oil. The strength can be reduced by using less methylated spirit in the solution. This is not, however, intended for regular use on the same piece.

Where total refinishing is necessary, the old polish or varnish, and in some cases paint, must be removed. This can be done with various solvents ranging in strength from water through alcohols and the organic solvents, white spirit, toluene and xylene, to paint strippers. Alternatively, mechanical methods such as sandpaper or steel-wool could be used.

A new finish should be selected which is in character with the original appearance. French polish is the most common finish encountered in antiques, but it is difficult to apply without a great deal of practice. Varnishes can be simpler to apply though the result can be disappointing.

Reference

Pumice powder or jeweller's rouge applied with a soft brush helps reduce a new high gloss to a softer sheen. A good coat of wax will help to protect the final finish as well as improve its appearance.

Basketry and Vegetable Fibres

With the increase in interest and value in ethnography, basketry and articles made of natural fibre are finding a place in collections. The problems are much the same as those encountered in both wood and textiles. Most damage would seem to occur in storage, where crushing is likely. Desiccation features heavily as a problem and increases the risk of breakage.

Reshaping is usually accomplished by damping with distilled water applied by spray and, when flexible, gently manipulating into shape. Adequate ventilation must be available for drying to avoid the formation of mould.

Leather and Skin

Leather is made up of protein fibres, and its flexibility is dependent on the ability of these fibres to move in relation to each other. When allowed to become too dry or when lubricants have been soaked out or become rigid, this ability is lost, and the leather becomes brittle and stiff. The ideal relative humidity is 50–60 per cent.

Under damp conditions mould can form. Insects can also be a problem. Liquid insecticides are best avoided, but small-scale and safe fumigation is possible by enclosing the infected article in a plastic bag with para-dichlorobenzene crystals for a few weeks.

Some dyes are extremely light sensitive and require a low intensity of light, and the exclusion of ultraviolet rays. Leather dressings are available which can be massaged into the skin to replace lost lubricants. Too liberal an application can cause subsequent weeping and a sticky surface.

Paper

The repair and restoration of paper is a specialist's field. Tempting home remedies such as adhesive tapes, bleaches and glues can have disastrous results. It is far better to recognize and avoid, if possible, the problems involved.

The formation of brown spots or 'foxing' is common with paper behind glass. This is caused by the paper's close proximity to the glass, which encourages mould to develop. A mount would increase this space and reduce the problems. All mounts and supports should be of acid-free conservation board.

Paper can also be attacked by wood-eating insects and by silver-fish. Fumigation is preferable to liquid insecticides, and paradichlorobenzene crystals can be used as a fumigant by enclosing the article with the crystals for several weeks in a plastic bag.

Light can cause dyes and pigments to fade, and where water-colours are concerned very low levels of light in the range of 50 lux would be sensible.

Atmospheres high in sulphides are destructive. Also dry environments cause paper embrittlement, while mould can develop in the opposite extreme; a relative humidity of 50–60 per cent is about right.

Ivory and Bone

Ivory is very much affected by moisture and relative humidity fluctuations, and is prone to splitting and warping under dry conditions. If a split is forced together and stuck, there is a considerable danger that the split will occur elsewhere. Generally, it is better to fill splits with a plastic adhesive such as polyvinyl acetate with a marble flour filler. Such treatment may prevent the split from getting larger yet be plastic enough to give with any expansion or contraction. An ideal relative humidity for ivory and bone is about 50–65 per cent.

Textiles

Of all the organic materials commonly encountered in antiques, textiles are probably the most subject to environmental damage in the home. They are also especially beset by inherent problems which make them seem almost self-destructive. Some dyes can become acidic, and, in time, whole areas of the textile so coloured can disintegrate. Fabrics of mixed thread composition can suffer from different responses to the environment and rates of deterioration. In many cases, the unsupported weight of the textile can cause it to split and tear.

To these inherent fabric faults must be added the problems of dust and pollution which can be abrasive and cause the physical breakdown of individual fibres. Conditions of low relative humidity accelerate this deterioration by drying out the fibres and making them brittle, while the opposite extreme produces conditions ideal for mould growth. Again, a range of 50–60 per cent should be acceptable.

Insects can be a real threat to fabrics. Moths can ruin wool and fur unless prevented by frequent inspection and the use of naphthalene or paradichlorobenzene crystals.

Restoration is rarely straightforward or simple. Short-cuts are few. Even washing is complicated by fugitive dyes and differential swelling and shrinking of fibres. Textiles may be so fragile that they need to be attached to supports to be washed or handled and, indeed, to survive at all. Even in storage, it may be necessary to pad and support to prevent folds and creases breaking delicate fibres.

Restoration and Conservation of Inorganic Material

Archeological metals may be a part of a collection of antiques which can lead to problems. During periods of burial, chlorides from the soil form compounds with the metals which are stable in anaerobic conditions, but once excavated can enter into chemical cycles using oxygen and moisture to form acids that will destroy the metal. With iron, droplets of brown liquid form on the surface which indicate the problem, while with copper and its alloys, a pale green powdery substance, 'bronze disease', is formed. Because atmospheric moisture is required, archeological metals should be kept dry and never allowed in conditions of high humidity. Ideally, chlorides should be removed in the laboratory.

Iron

Cleaning is usually involved with the removal of layers of oxides called rust. There are instances where most of the metal has been replaced with products of corrosion and their total removal would destroy or disfigure too much. Examination with a magnet or by X-ray is a first step in determining the type of treatment.

Chemical rust removers, based on phosphoric acid, are fast and involve little labour. However, since they remove all rust, a pitted and etched surface is likely, and the protective layer of phosphates formed alters the colour of the metal.

Mechanical cleaning methods are generally to be preferred because of the control possible. Corrosion is physically abraded away down to the surface of the metal or, in instances of extensive corrosion, to the original surface. Pits and crevices can be left filled with corrosion to leave a smooth surface. The abrasive used depends on the extent of corrosion and on the desired finish and varies in degree of coarseness from metal polishes through wire-wool and finally to emery paper. It is often advisable to work through a series of emery papers from coarse to fine, using a light machine oil as a lubricant.

Future formation of rust can be inhibited by degreasing the metal with acetone and then lacquering with a good nitro-cellulose lacquer. Graphite powder can be mixed with the lacquer to offer additional protection and to intensify black patination. A microcystalline-based wax applied over or instead of the lacquer is also helpful and reduces the shine. Relative humidity should not exceed 60 per cent.

Copper and its Alloys

One of the most frequently encountered metals in antiques and in antiquities is copper. It may appear in its pure form or in alloys such as bronze and brasses. Even silver and gold often contain copper for hardness and strength. The behaviour of copper and its deterioration should be understood. Alloys, even those of low copper content, can show a dominant activity on the part of copper and suffer the effects of its corrosion.

'Bronze disease' is an active corrosion which forms a powdery, pale green corrosion in a relative humidity greater than about 50 per cent. This is best treated by a specialist. Copper acetate or verdigris can have a similar appearance but is more wax-like in texture. It is organic in origin, usually more unsightly than harmful and easily removed by the appropriate solvent or by light mechanical treatment. Copper carbonates may also be formed under burial conditions. These are usually highly prized as green patinas, but some degree of expert mechanical cleaning may be needed to form a good surface.

Surface oxides or tarnish can be removed to reveal a bright metal surface. Cleaning with a mild abrasive is generally best as it can be controlled to leave varying amounts of patina and yet polish the metal. Too coarse an abrasive can scratch and wear away the surface. Chemical cleaners can also be very helpful, especially when tackling very tarnished metals but these can overclean and plate copper on to the surface. A reversible clear lacquer, such as nitrocellulose lacquer, can be applied to prevent the need for repeated future cleaning in the case of objects not subjected to much handling.

Silver

For the most part a stable metal, silver in the home is subject to two forms of corrosion. Copper, alloyed with silver for hardness and used as a base metal in silver plate, can be attacked by organic acids and produce copper corrosion products which can disrupt or cover the surface. These can be removed by cleaning with mild abrasives in most cases, but swabbing with dilute ammonia or formic acid may be necessary. Avoid prolonged contact with vinegar, pickles, or salt and the like.

The second and by far more common form of corrosion is that caused by sulphides – tarnish or silver sulphide. Though relatively harmless in itself, the danger lies more in repeated cleaning. The more abrasive the cleaning agent and the more often cleaning is required, and the more rapidly the silver is worn away.

Air-borne sulphides, prevalent in urban and industrial atmospheric pollution, can be removed through air-conditioning. Some paints and textiles, rubber, linoleum and eggs can be avoidable sources. Silver in storage can often be effectively protected by using storage bags and shelf liners of fabric treated to prevent tarnish. Objects intended for display alone can be lacquered with a sulphur-free, reversible and non-yellowing lacquer manufactured specially for silver.

Chemical cleaners are available which remove tarnish on immersion. They are easy to use and ideal for cleaning areas impossible to reach. However, it must be realized that they remove all tarnish and thus patina, and contrast in engraved and raised surface decoration is reduced. Some objects cannot take immersion in a liquid. Chemical cleaners contain acid which can destroy coral and pearls and may etch the silver. After repeated usage, enough silver finds its way into the solution to begin plating back on to the surface, giving a frosted and quickly tarnished surface.

The alternative is mechanically cleaning with commercially prepared silver cleaners. These contain mild abrasives and usually have certain chemical additives. Paste cleaners and creams must be carefully and completely removed to avoid a build up of dried deposits in decorated areas. Impregnated waddings and cloths may be preferable from this point of view. The mildest effective method should be used.

Gold

Pure gold is virtually non-reactive and free from deterioration. Where alloyed with copper tarnishing and even copper corrosion can occur. For the most part, the problem is one of accumulated dirt, which can be removed by gentle swabbing with cotton or a soft cloth dampened with a soap solution.

Lead, Pewter and Tin

The amphoteric metals, lead, tin and zinc, are attacked by acids, but unlike iron, copper and silver, are also corroded by alkalis. Pewter, an alloy of lead and tin, is also amphoteric. Vinegar and acidic wines can corrode pewter food containers. Prolonged contact with poor quality paper and card, certain paints, and indeed anything likely to be acidic or alkaline, should be avoided. Some detergents therefore can create problems.

Cleaning is straightforward unless corrosion is extensive or active in which case professional advice should be sought. Mechanical cleaning with a mild abrasive cream or wadding or just polishing with a soft cloth should be sufficient. Chemical cleaners should be avoided. A light coat of microcrystalline wax often improves the final appearance.

Ceramics

Most damage to ceramics is through mishandling and should be avoidable. In some cases, inherent problems do exist. Through burial or usage, pottery can contain soluble salts which are affected by changes in relative humidity and crystallize on the surface pushing glazes and surface away. Intensive and prolonged washing under laboratory control is the usual treatment.

Generally though, ceramics are stable and not noticeably affected by normal environmental factors. However, repairs and some glazes are sensitive to light and heat. Except with unfired pottery, cleaning should simply be a matter of washing or gentle swabbing with mild soap and water. It is best to use lukewarm water because sudden temperature changes can cause glazes to craze and crack. Restored areas and adhesives can react badly to water and especially strong solvents, such as acetone or methylated spirit, which may sometimes be needed. Concretions and heavy deposits may require abrasive metal polishes or even acid for removal. Gilding and lustre glazes are less able to stand abrasion and strong cleaning.

The first step in ceramic restoration is to ensure that joins are clean and all old glue and adhesives removed. Sometimes it is necessary to take apart an old restoration. Most old adhesives come down on soaking in water. Methylated spirit or acetone may prove to be the solvent in other cases. Epoxy resins and other resistant adhesives may be broken down in commercial paint strippers.

Clean edges will help produce tight and less visible joins. Bleaching cracks and edges before sticking is also advisable. Clean dry pieces can be stuck with a suitable adhesive. Epoxy resins and other non-reversible adhesives, although strong, are difficult to work with and are best left to those with experience. A clear non-yellowing and reversible adhesive such as a nitrocellulose adhesive is best for most purposes. A sand tray is helpful for positioning pieces for drying. It is important to work out the logical sequence of sticking. Normally, a small amount of adhesive is applied to both edges to be stuck to ensure good coverage and then the pieces pressed together. Excess glue extruded from the join can be cleaned away with an appropriate solvent.

Missing pieces and gaps can be completed after sticking. The choice of gap-filler depends on the size, type and texture of the material to be replaced and the strength required. Gap-fillers may include plaster, wax, proprietory fillers and epoxy fillers. Reversibility is usually advisable. Fillers should be modelled or sanded down to the correct level and textured and coloured to match. Varnishes and resins are available to reproduce a glazed appearance.

Glass

Repairs to broken glass can be very unrewarding. Strength is difficult to achieve because the edges of broken glass are too smooth to allow an adhesive to key well. And the adhesive must have the same refractive index as the glass or the join will show. Also, it must be an exact colour match. The same problems exist in making up missing pieces.

Adhesives which set on drying shrink on loss of solvent and draw air into the join producing visible bubbles. Contact adhesives for glass repair are being used, but these seem to lose strength in time. The most successful adhesive to date would seem to be a two-part resin adhesive manufactured for glass restoration. However, the ideal adhesive for glass repair has yet to be produced.

Painted Surfaces

The first step in treating any painted surface must be examination to determine the cause of deterioration. This must be put right or all restoration will be a pointless exercise.

Often a layer of dirt or grease or a layer of discoloured varnish may be obscuring the paint beneath. Should it be necessary to remove these superficial layers, it must be done so that no solvent is used which adversely affects the paint layer, ground, or support, and abrasion must be avoided. The value of these layers as a form of patina must be considered.

The paint film itself should be examined for deterioration due to excess light, heat and damage through pollution, solvents and abrasion. Flaking may be caused by a loss of adhesion, and a suitable binding medium must be introduced between the appropriate layers. Heat and a vacuum may be required to make the flakes and blisters return to the correct level. The fault often lies in the support where deterioration can lead to a loss of structural strength. Excess movement in the support may also be contributory.

Before retouching can be carried out, areas of paint loss must be filled to a similar level and texture to the existing paint film. Wax with various fillers is commonly used. Pigments in water colours, tempera, acrylic or oil media may be used to replace lost areas of colour. Care should be taken to avoid over-painting original paint. Where varnishes are to be replaced, reversible varnishes should be used with a solvent which will not harm the paint film.

Glossary

Acanthus. A popular decorative motif used since the Renaissance, notably carved on furniture; also to be found on Corinthian and Composite capitals. The motif is derived from the leaf of *Acanthus spinosus* which is native to the shores of the Mediterranean.

Aigrette. An 18th-century piece of jewelry in the form of a spray of flowers and worn in the hair. Aigrettes were set with diamonds and other precious gems.

Andiron. A metal utensil used in hearths to support logs. Used in pairs, they were made principally of iron until the 17th century when more decorative examples made in silver, bronze and brass began to appear. The vertical section or standard is usually decorated with classic motifs, heraldic emblems or mythological figures.

An-hua decoration. Faint engraving or painting in white slip under the glaze of some Ming and 18th-century white porcelain. This form of decoration is often known as 'secret' decoration since it can only be seen if the piece is held against the light.

Aquatint. A form of 18th-century etching which imitates wash tints. Often used successfully for reproducing water colours.

Armadio. A tall, usually movable, Italian cupboard introduced during the Renaissance. A 16th-century version was made with two tiers. Sometimes decorated in low relief carving, it is similar to the French *armoire*.

Armillary sphere. A medieval astronomical instrument composed of a series of rings representing the equator, meridian, ecliptic and so on. A small globe in the centre of the device represents the earth. It was usually mounted on a turned or carved wooden stand.

Beehive clock. A mid-19th century form of small Connecticut shelf clock; named because of its resemblance to a beehive or flatiron, hence its alternative name of 'flatiron' clock.

Bell seat. A Queen Anne style chair, often in walnut, with a rounded or bell-shaped seat. Made in America in the early 18th century.

Bentside. The curved side of a harpsichord, piano or spinet.

Berlin wool work. A fashion in needlework during the Victorian era, characterized by its bright colours and use of tent or cross stitch.

Blackwork. The name given to a type of embroidery introduced during the reign of Henry VIII. This work was usually done in black silk thread on linen in backstitch.

Block book. A type of book produced before movable type was invented in which each page was printed from a single block which comprised both the illustration and text.

Block front. A feature of some American furniture made from about 1750–80 in which the front of the piece is made from thick boards – usually mahogany – cut so that the centres recede in a flattened curve while the ends curve outward in a flattened bulge. Pieces made in this way include chests, drawers, and slant-front desks.

Blown-moulded glass. A method of making glass in which the molten glass was blown in a mould in order to shape it. As well as being a useful method for impressing designs on a piece, blown moulding was a quick and cheap method of production.

Blue and white porcelain. Decoration with painting in cobalt blue under the glaze introduced during the Ming dynasty. The finest of this porcelain was produced during the reigns of Hsüan Tê and Ch'eng Hua. In the Ch'ing dynasty it was exported in large quantities to the West where it was extensively reproduced.

Blunderbuss. A pistol or short gun introduced into England from the Continent in the 16th century. It had a large bore and a flaring nozzle and was designed to fire a number of small metal balls at one time.

Bracket foot. Supporting foot on case furniture consisting of two pieces of wood joined at the corner. The side piece is usually cut out in a simple design.

Brittania metal. An alloy of tin, copper and antimony often with some bismuth or zinc, which closely resembled silver when polished. First used towards the end of the 18th century.

Broderie anglais. Embroidery of Eastern European origin introduced into England in the Middle Ages. The designs were composed of holes punched in the material oversewn around the edges in chain stitch, satin stitch and overcast stitch.

Cabochon. A method of cutting precious stones in a round or oval convex form; also any decorative motif made in this style. As a motif it was popular in England from 1740–60 when a kidney shape in the current Rococo style was also used.

Cabriole leg. A style of furniture leg on which the top curves outward as a knee, then curves inwards until just above the foot where it curves outward again. The style probably had its origins in China and was introduced into Europe in the late 17th century and into England in 1700.

Canton ware. This name is most frequently applied to enamelled porcelain made at the **Ching-tê Chên** kilns in China and exported through Canton to Europe in the 18th century. The decoration was often applied in Canton itself, notably the **famille rose**.

Cartel clock. An 18th-century French wall clock often decorated in flamboyant Rococo style. French examples are usually made of cast bronze and gilt or cast brass. English cartel clocks were made in wood.

Cartonnier. An open-sided box or small cupboard with compartments intended for storing papers. It usually stood at one end of a writing table.

Caryatid. A carved, draped female figure used as a decorative motif in place of a pilaster in furniture. First used in Italian Renaissance furniture design in the mid-16th century.

Caudle cup. A two-handled silver cup usually fitted with a cover and used for drinking caudle, a mixture of gruel and wine or ale and spices. The best-known shape is bulbous and pear-shaped. The handles often represented the heads of women.

Celadon ware. A Chinese stoneware with a beautiful translucent green glaze. The glaze itself is feldspathic and the slip contains iron. The colour, which was developed to imitate jade is applied to body which varies from grey to white and yellowish to reddish brown.

Chafing dish. A brazier made of silver or other metal and used to hold burning charcoal, introduced in America in the 17th century. The body was usually cylindrical with pierced ornament and it rested on three brackets with claw and wooden ball feet.

Chapter ring. The circular band on a clock dial on which the hour numerals appear.

Chatelaine. An elaborate silver or other metal ensemble with a clip and hook which was worn on a woman's belt and to which was attached her watch, keys, scissors and other small personal items.

Chelsea porcelain. Wares produced in the foremost English porcelain manufactory from about 1745 until 1784. The form of the wares was Rococo, while the designs were derivative. Japanese **imari** and **kakiemon** designs were particularly favoured in the early period and Sèvres in the later years.

Chiaroscuro. An Italian term meaning 'light and dark'. In painting it describes a technique for handling shadows. It also refers to a process of wood-engraving in which prints are made from several blocks to produce pictures in varying tones of one colour.

Chiffonier. A combination of chest and sideboard with drawers and cupboard below and a set of shelves above used for displaying china. The term was first used during the Chippendale period and the chiffonier became a popular piece of Regency furniture.

Ching-tê chên. A renowned ceramic centre in Kiangsi province, China. The kilns had been in existence for some time before they were rebuilt in 1369 to become the Imperial manufactory. The outstanding porcelains of the Ming and Ch'ing dynasties were developed there.

Cinqueda. A 15th-century Italian dagger with a straight, double-edged blade, wide at the hilt and tapering to a point; often elaborately decorated. Also known as an *anelace*.

Coalport porcelain. Porcelain manufactured in Coalport, Shropshire, by John Rose around 1796. The porcelain is distinguished by its feldspathic glaze which was highly translucent. Early wares were Rococo in form although from 1820–50 the wares were mainly imitative.

Cobiron. Plain **andirons** used in the kitchen. The vertical shafts are fitted with hooks or loops to hold the spits.

Compostiera. A container in the form of a salver carrying a pair of silver jars with glass linings and used for stewed fruit. The containers are often richly worked with a highly elaborate knob.

Creamware. Cream-coloured earthenware with a fine lead glaze principally made in Staffordshire and mainly by Wedgwood. It was developed as a substitute for porcelain by Wedgwood, but was later imitated by many potteries in the area.

Crewelwork. A type of embroidery in crewel stitch usually on linen dating from at least the 16th century. The best examples are considered to be Jacobean.

Glossary

C-scroll. A decorative motif in the form of a Roman capital 'C' that was a favourite form of Baroque ornament. During the Rococo period these motifs became more slender and graceful.

Cuirassier armour. Armour used by the heavy cavalry of the first half of the 17th century, which covered the body down to the knees. *Cuirass* is the term used for the breast and backplate together.

Cup-hilt. A type of rapier hilt introduced in the second quarter of the 17th century, which had a bowl- or cup-shaped guard.

Cut-card work. A type of decoration found on 17th-century silver in which designs are cut from thin sheet-silver and then applied to the main piece.

Cylinder escapement. Type of **escapement** used in watches until the end of the 18th century when they were replaced by lever escapements. It was first patented in 1695 by Thomas Tompion.

Deadbeat escapement. Escapement invented by George Graham around 1715. It was the most accurate escapement for astronomical clocks for some 200 years. It is still in use for some mantel and longcase clocks.

Derby porcelain. Porcelain made at Cockpit Hill, Derby, from the mid-18th century. From 1770 the manufactory, owned by William Duesbury, worked in association with the **Chelsea** manufactory. Particularly noted for beautifully painted figures.

Dropleaf. A wooden board, hinged to the front of some early keyboard chordophones that hung down when open; a hinged flap on a table which hangs down when not in use.

Dry-point. A type of engraving done with a fine-pointed instrument that leaves grooves whose edges are burred giving a soft, hazy line on the final print.

Écuelle. A French term for a porringer, a shallow, covered bowl with a dome-shaped cover surmounted by two handles that were horizontal to the rim. Introduced in the 17th century.

Épergne. The French name for an elaborate centrepiece. The large finely-wrought bowl, supported on a stand, had several arms incorporating small dishes. It was fashionable in England from the middle of the 18th century.

Escapement. In clocks and watches the mechanism which controls the movement of the spring or weight regulator.

Escutcheon. A decorative metal plate surrounding a keyhole; a small plate on a gun or clock bearing the maker's name; also an heraldic term applied to a shield with armorial bearings.

Etui. A small box or case used for carrying toilet articles and other personal items. Usually a small flat case in gold, silver or ivory, but some, used for carrying needles, toothpicks or pins, were in the form of a cylinder. They were often lavishly ornamented.

Faience. A type of earthenware covered with a tin glaze. The term is generally applied to Dutch imitations of Chinese wares made in the 17th century but was later applied to tin-glazed wares made in Germany, France and other countries.

Famille rose. A type of porcelain made in China after the early 18th century; it is characterized by the use of the different shades of pink. This type of porcelain supplanted **famille verte**.

Famille verte. Enamelled polychrome porcelains first made in China during the reign of K'ang Hsi (1662–1722). Although the distinguishing colour was a brilliant green, red, yellow and purple wares were also made. Supplanted by famille rose in the early 18th century.

Fireback. A cast-iron slab or plate used to protect the brickwork at the back of the fireplace, popular in the 16th century. It was decorated with heraldic emblems, fleur-de-lis and so on.

Fire-polishing. A method of working blown-moulded glass to remove tool marks. The designs and polish given to the edges of the glass make it almost indistinguishable from cut glass.

Flint glass. Brilliant, colourless glass, the silica for which comes from flint. The name was retained when sand was substituted for flint and is still used for English glass that uses potash and lead oxide as fluxing agents. First made in the 17th century.

Fluting. In cabinetwork, the term used to describe the long grooves or furrows cut in the surface of wood. Fluting was a favourite decoration on Adam furniture.

Form watch. A watch made in an unconventional shape, or form. Watches made to look like books, crucifixes, dogs, skulls and so on, were popular in the 17th century. In the late 18th century lyre, mandoline and fruit shapes were common.

Frit. In ceramics, the term applied to the glassy ingredients of soft paste porcelain; in glass, it is the raw molten glass.

Fusee. A conical, grooved pulley that equalizes the pull of the mainspring of a clock or watch.

It was first invented around 1460–70 and is still used in spring-driven clocks. It is also an early name for friction matches.

Gadroon. A continuous ornamental border, frequently carved along the edges of furniture. In appearance, usually a series of convex curves, it was first used in England during the 16th century. The same motif, either hammered or cast was used on silverware.

Girandole. A decorative candelabrum or branched candlestick, most frequently made of silver, that came into use in the second half of the 17th century. The term has come to mean all branched candlesticks, particularly fixed wall appliqués with branched supports for candles. Girandole mirrors were fitted with candleholders. In jewelry the term describes a gem hung with several pendants.

Guéridon. A candlestand introduced in France in the middle of the 17th century. Early stands were often made in the form of a young negro with a candleholder in his raised hand. Later examples conformed more to a small table-like design.

'Gothic' armour. A style of plate armour characterized by slender elegant lines with decorated borders and a ripple effect, developed in Germany in the 15th century.

Highboy. A tall chest of drawers usually in two sections: a **lowboy,** or commode, with a chest of drawers on top. It was introduced in America around 1700 and was popular for nearly 100 years. Early highboys were designed in the William and Mary style and later in Queen Anne and Chippendale style.

Hunting carpets. Persian carpet design with elaborate hunting scenes enacted among realistically worked flowers, leaves and arabesques.

Jacobite glass. English drinking glasses of the first half of the 18th century made to commemorate the Old and Young Pretenders. They were engraved with supporters of the exiled Stuarts.

Jadeite. One of the two types of jade, the other being **nephrite**. Jadeite is a silicate of aluminium and soda. Nephrite is a silicate of magnesium and lime.

Japanning. A method of imitating Japanese lacquer work by applying varnishes to the surface of wood and then baking it in an oven. Although commonly done in black, other colours are also used. Japanning was first introduced after the Restoration in 1660 and achieved its greatest popularity in England in the early 18th century.

Kakiemon. Japanese porcelain with coloured enamel decoration first made by Sakaida Kakiemon around 1650. The wares are decorated in underglaze blue and red, blue-green, violet, light blue and greyish yellow enamels.

Knop. A small rounded protuberance ornamenting the stem of a drinking vessel or candlestick.

Lambeth ware. The name given to **faience** or delftware made in a number of London potteries during the 17th century. Some late 19th century examples from the Doulton family were decorated in the tradition of Italian **maiolica**. Some of these wares were left undecorated, while others were painted in blue.

Latten. An impure type of brass which used unrefined zinc. It was used in medieval times for hanging lights, chandeliers and so on.

Line-engraving. An engraving method in which the line is cut out or incised, unlike woodcuts where the design is cut in relief and the areas to be left white are cut out.

Lithograph. A print made from a design done on either a polished or grained stone with ink or a greasy crayon respectively.

'Lobster-tail' helmet. A modern term for a form of cavalry helmet worn in the 17th century. It had a laminated tail, cheek pieces and a peak from which bars extended across the face. A type with three bars was used during the English Civil War.

Lowboy. An American term (as is **highboy**) and known in England as a dressing table or side table, a lowboy has a rectangular top over a valanced apron which was fitted with drawers. Queen Anne and Chippendale lowboys had **cabriole legs**.

Maiolica. Or majolica. A type of Italian tin-glazed earthenware characteristically decorated in blue, green, yellow, orange and manganese purple, and made in the 16th and 17th centuries; similar to **faience** and delftware. The use of the alternative 'majolica' is sometimes applied only to a pale brown stoneware made by Minton in the mid-19th century.

Mezzotint. A method of engraving on copper to produce a print with tonal variations, popular from the 17th to the 19th century. A special tool with fine teeth was used to cover the plate with raised particles of copper rather than single close lines.

Glossary

Millefiori. A Venetian method of glass-decorating which utilizes slender glass rods of every colour fused to form glass canes which were then cut across to reveal a pattern. The term means 'a thousand flowers'. First used in Venice in the mid-16th century, it was originally made by the Egyptians and Romans.

Miquelet-lock. A type of flint-lock used in Southern Italy and Spain from the early 17th century onwards.

Morion. A 16th-century open helmet worn by foot soldiers. It usually had a small brim which peaked upward at the front and back.

Napier's bones. An early pocket calculator invented by John Napier (1550–1617). The most usual form is a set of loose square-sectioned bones made of wood or ivory, with a series of numbers divided by diagonal lines on both sides. They lie on a small tray that fits into a box.

Nef. A medieval centrepiece, usually made of silver but occasionally gold, that was designed to hold knives and other table utensils. It was in the shape of a sailing ship.

Nephrite. One of the two types of jade (see **jadeite**).

Niello. Inlay work in which a black metal amalgam was used to fill incised designs on a highly polished surface, usually silver, but occasionally gold and bronze.

Nocturnal. An astronomical instrument used for finding out the time at night. It was composed of a large disc with a handle, and a smaller disc with a pointer attached to the centre of the larger disc. The small disc was set to the date and the pole star sighted through a hole in the centre of the instrument. By setting the handle to the Great or Little Bear the time could be determined.

Ogee or O.G. clock. A mid-19th century Connecticut shelf clock that uses decorative moulding in the shape of a reverse curve like the letter S. Large numbers of this clock were made until the first quarter of the 20th century.

Orrery. A hand or clockwork-driven instrument used for demonstrating the motion of the planets about the sun and, in more elaborate instruments, the moons of the planets. They were first made by George Graham and Thomas Tompion, c. 1709.

Pappenheimer. A type of rapier with a hilt having a perforated guard in the form of two shells. It was used during the first half of the 17th century.

Pierced work. A type of embroidery in which part of the cloth is cut away to form the design. Fine examples are called cutwork.

Pietra dura. A variety of inlaid mosaic work generally used for table tops. The technique, which originated in Renaissance Italy, used tesserae of semi-precious stones; the motifs were flowers, birds and butterflies. This type of work achieved its greatest perfection in the first half of the 17th century.

Pinchbeck. An alloy of zinc and copper invented by Christopher Pinchbeck (1670–1732) which looks like gold.

Polonaise carpet. Persian carpet first made during the reign of Shah Abbas (1588–1629) and woven in silk with gold and silver threads for the ground. The carpets show great freedom of design. The name comes from a collection of carpets exhibited in Paris in 1878 which were Polish-owned.

Porringer. A two-handled silver cup generally with a cover and used for serving hot wine drinks; also a single-handed, small silver bowl. The two-handled variety was first introduced in England around 1600 and the lower portion of the cup was usually elaborately worked. Porringers are related to **caudle cups**.

Prie-dieu. A wooden prayer-stand used in both medieval times and the 19th-century. It most commonly consisted of an upright portion supporting an arm rest or book rest and with a kneeler at the base.

Quadrant. Instrument used for calculating the elevation of a star. It consisted of a flat plate of wood or metal in the shape of a quarter of a circular disc with a 90° scale along the curved edge and a plumb-line and bob suspended from the apex of the right-angle. It was used in medieval Europe but was probably invented by the Arabs.

Rat-tail hinge. A cupboard hinge in which there is a downward extension in the shape of a rat's tail to brace the pintle.

Reliquary. A small box or chest used to hold sacred relics. They took many forms, most of them richly decorated, including tabernacles, monstrances and chests of ivory.

Reticello. A technique in which the rims or edges of glassware is made of threads of different coloured glass.

Ribbon work. Embroidery work that was particularly fashionable during the Georgian period. Pieces of ribbon about one-eighth of an inch thick were drawn through the fabric with a needle. It was used on articles such as dresses, work-boxes and fire screens.

Salt-glazed stoneware. Stoneware characterized by a hard clear glaze formed by throwing common salt into the kiln when the maximum temperature has been reached. The brown colour of this stoneware is made by applying a wash of iron oxide-rich clay to the pot before firing.

Sampler. Usually a small piece of embroidery used to show a sample of stitches or patterns or as a record of a person's achievement in the craft. Early samplers were worked by adults but later became a display of the skill of a child.

Sector. A mathematical instrument dating from the 17th century composed of two flat, equal rulers hinged together. The rulers bore various scales which were used for numerous mathematical problems in geometry, gunnery, surveying and so on.

Sévigné. A jeweled brooch in the form of a graduated bow popular in the 17th century and named after Mme de Sévigné, a famous letter writer.

Sgraffito. A term used in ceramics to describe a technique of scratching or inscribing with a pointed instrument through the slip to the body beneath to create a design of two contrasting colours. The method is of early origin, the most notable examples of which are probably the Gabri wares from 8th and 9th century Persia.

Slipware. Pottery decorated with coloured slips (clay diluted with water) applied to a contrasting coloured body. The technique is very old but the best examples of this work come from Egypt during the 13th and 14th centuries.

Snaphance. A variety of gun-lock first made in the 16th century. It has a pan with a flat steel pivoted above it; when the gun is fired a flint, held in the jaws of a spring-operated cock, strikes the steel spraying sparks into the priming.

Spandrels. The triangular area between the outer curve of an arch and the rectangle enclosing it. In cabinetwork it describes the arcaded façade of a Gothic chest; also the corners of a clock face and the decorative brass pieces that fit therein.

S-scroll. A decorative curve in the shape of Roman capital S. See **C-scroll**.

Stackfreed. A device used in early clocks and watches to check the rate at which the mainspring uncoils and to limit winding only to those number of turns that produce more or less equal tension in the spring.

Stirrup cup. A drinking vessel or cup in silver or china which was filled with a strong drink and offered to a traveller about to depart on a journey. Frequently in the form of a fox's or hound's head. First known in England in the late 17th century.

Stock lock. Plate lock let into a block of oak which was attached to the door by bolts or rivets. Some stock locks had the mechanism covered over by a decorated iron plate; from the 18th century the mechanism was covered by a solid iron plate.

Strapwork. Ornamentation consisting of a narrow band that has been folded, crossed or interlaced to form different designs and carved in low relief in furniture or chased on silver.

Stump leg. A term used in American cabinetwork to describe plain rear legs, slightly curved, on which there is no obviously separate foot. It was characteristic of the Philadelphia school of Chippendale furniture.

Stumpwork. A type of needlework quite common from the 15th to the 17th centuries; the design was in relief over cotton or wool.

Surveyor's cross. A sighting instrument consisting of a box or cylinder with slits at 90° and sometimes 45°. It was often combined with a compass.

Tassets. Laminated pieces of plate used as thigh armour, which first appeared in the second quarter of the 15th century.

Tazza. Derived from the Persian word *tas* meaning a goblet, and applied to a drinking vessel with a saucer-like cup mounted on a stem and foot or foot alone. They were made in silver, Limoges enamel and Venetian glass and other similar materials.

Tou ts'ai. Designs in underglaze blue set off by transparent enamel colours on some Chinese porcelain. The style was perfected in the reign of Ch'eng Hua (1465–87).

Turkey work. A type of English needlework which imitated Oriental carpets woven with a knotted pile. It was used for chair coverings, cushions and occasionally for rugs.

Vambrace. Plate armour for the arm from below the shoulder to the wrist.

Wirework. Silver and gold wares made from wire that had first been drawn through holes in steel sheets.

Collections to Visit

Australia
Art Gallery of South Australia
North Terrace, Adelaide,
South Australia
Museum of Applied Arts & Sciences
659–695 Harris Street,
Broadway, Sydney
National Gallery of Victoria
180 St Kilda Road, Melbourne
Victoria

Austria
Kunsthistorisches Museum
Maria Theresienplatz, Vienna

Belgium
Royal Museum of Art & History
Ave des Nreviens, Brussels 4

Canada
Art Gallery of Greater Victoria
1040 Moss Street, Victoria
British Columbia
Royal Ontario Museum
Queen's Park, Toronto 5
Winnipeg Art Gallery
Memorial Boulevard, Winnipeg
Manitoba

Czechoslovakia
Museum of Glass
Jablonc
Museum of Applied Art
Prague

Denmark
Kunstindustrimuseet
Copenhagen
National Museum
Copenhagen
Rosenberg Castle Museum
Ostervoldegade 4a, 1350 Copenhagen

Eire
National Museum of Ireland
Merrion Square, Dublin

Formosa
National Palace Museum
Taipei (Taiwan)

France
Conde Museum

Chateau de Chantilly, Chantilly
Oise
Louvre Museum
Palais de Louvre
Paris
Musée des Arts Décoratifs
Paris
Musée des Beaux Arts
Rouen
Musée Guimet
Paris
Museum of the School of Nancy
(Glass Museum), Nancy
National Ceramic Museum
Sèvres, Paris

German Democratic Republic
Bode Museum
Monbijoubrucke am Kupfergraben
Berlin (East)
Porzellan Galerie
Dresden

German Federal Republic
Art Museum
4 Dusseldorf-Nord, Ehrenhof 5
Dusseldorf
Bayerisches National Museum
Munich
Charlottenburg Palace Museums
Schloss Strasse 70
D-1 Berlin (West)
Dahlem Museum
Arnimallee 23/27, D-1 Berlin (West)
Herzog Anton Ulrich Museum
33 Braunschweig, Museumstrasse 1
Brunswick
Hessisches Landes Museum
Darmstadt
Museum fur Kunst und Gewerbe
Hamburg
Residenz Museum
Munich

Greece
Benaki Museum
1 Odos Koumbari, Athens

Hungary
Francis Hopp Museum of Eastern
Asiatic Arts
Nepkoztarsasag u. 103, Budapest 6
Hungarian National Museum

Muzeum krt 14016, Budapest 8

Italy
Bargello National Museum
via del proconsolo 4, Florence
Capodimonte National Museum
Parco di Capodimonte, Naples
Civic Museum of Ancient Art
Palazzo Madama, Piazzo Castello
Turin
Correr Museum
Piazza San Marco 52
Venice
National Ceramic Museum
Faenza
National Museum
viale delle Terme di Diocleziano
Rome
Pitti Gallery
Piazza Pitti, Florence
Poldi Pezzoli Museum
via Manzoni 12, Milan

Japan
National Museum
Ueno Park, Tokyo

Netherlands
Boymans-van Beuningen Museum
Mathenesserlaan 18–20, Rotterdam
Frans Hals Museum
Groot Heiligland 62, Haarlem
Rijksmuseum
Stadhouderskade 42, Amsterdam

New Zealand
Auckland City Art Gallery
Kitchener Street, Auckland
National Art Gallery
Buckle Street, Wellington

Norway
Kunstindustrimuseet
(Applied Arts Museum), Oslo

Poland
Wawelu Castle State Art Collection
Crakow

Portugal
Gulbenkian Foundation
Calouste Gulbenkian Park
Avenida Berne, Lisbon

South Africa
Art Gallery
Joubert Park, Johannesburg
Art Museum
Arcadia Park, Pretoria
South African National Gallery
Government Avenue, Cape Town

Sweden
Ostasiatiska Museet
Stockholm

Thailand
National Museum
Bangkok

Turkey
Topkapi Palace Museum
Istanbul

UK
American Museum in Britain
Claverton Manor, near Bath, Avon
Art Gallery & Museum
Kelvingrove, Glasgow
Ashmolean Museum
Beaumont Street, Oxford
Bethnal Green Museum
Museum of Childhood
London E8
Bristol Art Gallery
Queen's Road, Bristol BS8 1RL
British Museum
Great Russell Street, London WC1
Cecil Higgins Museum
Castle Close, Bedford
City Art Gallery
Moseley Street, Manchester
City Museum & Art Gallery
Congreve Street, Birmingham B33
City Museum & Art Gallery
Broad Street, Hanley
Stoke-on-Trent, Staffs
Clockmakers' Company Collection
Guildhall, London EC2
Dyson Perrins Museum of
Worcester Porcelain
Severn Street, Worcester
Fitzwilliam Museum
Trumpington Street, Cambridge
London Museum
London Wall EC2
Merseyside County Museums

William Brown Street, Liverpool 3
Museum & Art Gallery
Church Street, Brighton
East Sussex
Museum of Costume
Assembly Rooms, Bath, Avon
National Museum of Wales
Cardiff, South Glamorgan
Percival David Foundation of
Chinese Art
53 Gordon Square, London WC1
Pilkington Glass Museum
Prescot Road, St Helens, Lancs
Royal Scottish Museum
Chambers Street, Edinburgh EH1 1JF
Science Museum
South Kensington, London SW7
Temple Newsam House
Leeds
Victoria & Albert Museum
Brompton Road, London SW7
Wallace Collection
Manchester Square, London W1
Wedgwood Museum
Barlaston, Stoke-on-Trent
Staffordshire
William Morris Gallery
Water House, Forest Road
Walthamstow
London E17

USA
American Clock & Watch Museum
Bristol, Connecticut
Art Institute
Michigan Avenue, Chicago, Illinois
Art Museum
Cincinnati, Ohio
Avery Brundage Asian Art Collection
Golden Gate Park, San Francisco
California
Bayou Bend Collection of Americana
1 Westcott Street, Houston, Texas
Buten Museum of Wedgwood
Merion, Pennsylvania
Corning Glass Museum
Corning, New York
Fine Arts Museum
479 Huntington Ave, Boston, Mass
Fogg Art Museum
Harvard University, Cambridge, Mass
Freer Gallery of Art
(Smithsonian Institution)

Jefferson Drive SW, Washington DC
Frick Collection
1 East 70th Street, New York
Henry E Huntington Art Gallery
San Marino, California
Henry Ford Museum
Dearborn
H.F. Dupont Museum
Winterthur
Institute of Fine Arts
5200 Woodward, Detroit, Michigan
John Paul Getty Museum
Los Angeles, California
Los Angeles County Museum of Art
5905 Wiltshire Boulevard, Los Angeles
California
Metropolitan Museum
82nd Street, New York
M H de Young Memorial Museum
Palace of the Legion of Honour
Golden Gate Park, San Francisco
California
Museum of Art
11150 East Boulevard, Cleveland, Ohio
Museum of Art
26th Street, Philadelphia, Pennsylvania
Museum of Arts
Toledo, Ohio
National Gallery of Art
Constitution Avenue, Washington DC
Shaker Historical Society
Shaker Heights, Ohio
600 Main Street
Hartford, Connecticut
Walker Art Center
Minneapolis, Minnesota
William Rockhill Nelson
Collection
4525 Oak Street, Kansas City
Colonial Williamsburg
Yale University Art Collection
New Haven, Connecticut

USSR
Hermitage Museum
Leningrad D-65
Tretiakov Gallery
Lavrushinski per 10, Moscow

Yugoslavia
National Museum
Republike Sq, Belgrade

Index

Aalto, Alvar 363, 364
Abbe, Ernst 300
Abbotsford 262
Abbott, Anne W. 313
Aberdeen 191
Absolon, William 183
Acco 24
Adam, Robert 162, 164, 165, 166, 183, 218, 256
Adams 353
Adams, Dudley 214, 301
Adams, George 212, 213, 214
Adams, James 256
Adams, John 272
Adams, Robert 256
Adams and Co., S. 338
Adie, Alexander 301
Ailesbury, Earl of 230–1
Aki 129
Akins, William H. 285
Albert, Prince Consort 259, 330
Alberti, Leon Battista 60
Albrechtsburg 169–70
Album 261
Aldbourne 241
Aldobrandini family 86
Aldus 332–3
Aleppo 29
Alexander 111, 223
Alexandria 25, 26, 27
Allard 241
Allgeyer 311
Altare 31
Altenburger, Brigitte 366
Altona 271
Amelung, John Frederick 186
American Glass 277
American Pottery Company 268
American Waltham Watch Company, The 288
Amsterdam 71, 88, 89, 105, 107, 164, 175, 216
Ancourt, Edouard 326
Andreoli, Giorgio 66
Angelo, Michael 261
Angelo, Peter 261
Anne, Queen 147, 149–50, 210, 214, 231
Ansbach 175
Antioch 26
Antiquities of Athens 162
Antonibon, Pasquale 169
Antwerp 62, 68, 69, 78, 94, 107
Apis Altar 188
Apology for the Revival of Christian Architecture in England 263
Aquileia 30
Arabia factory 272
Argy-Rousseau, G. 276
Arione, F. 302
Arita 92, 93, 270
armour, 16th Century 81–2
Arsenius family 131
Art Deco style 361–2
Art Nouveau style 230, 258, 261, 263, 264, 265–6, 270, 275, 276, 278, 279, 283, 304, 327, 338, 339, 360–1, 366
Ascot Cup 280
Ashbee, Christopher 264, 283
Ashworth & Bros., G. L. 272
Asshoff, Bruno 271
Asshoff, Ingeborg 271
Astbury, John 180
Audubon 358
Augsburg 36, 71, 78, 91, 132–3, 134, 220
Auguste, R. J. 191
Augustus 60, 188
Augustus 11, 169, 170

Autun 207
Aytoun, William 191

Baccarat, Compagnie des Cristalliers de 110, 275
Bagatti Valsecchi House 340
Baglione, Giovanni 72
Bain, Alexander 286
Bakalowitz Söhne 275
Baker-Troll 241
Bakewell, Benjamin 276, 277
Bakst, Leon 361
Baku carpets *see* Khila carpets
Ballets Russes 361
Baltimore 165, 268
Banks, Joseph 210
Banks, William 267
Barberini family 86
Barbin, François 173
Barcelona 265, 363, 365
Barlow, Hannah 272
Baroni, Giovanni 169
Baroque style 62, 71, 79, 84–91, 111, 112, 119, 121, 123, 146, 147, 148, 150, 164, 168, 170, 171, 182, 187, 220, 229, 258
Barovier and Toso 366
Barrière, Jean-Joseph 219
Bartlam, John 182
Baskerville 333
Baschenis 232
Bassano 169
Bath 300
Battersea 217
Bauhaus school 361, 362
Bausch and Lomb Optical Company 301
Baxter, Thomas 266
Bayer, J. C. 176
Bayonne 143
Beatrice of Naples 22
Beaconsfield 87
Beardmore, Hilda 272
Beardsley, Aubrey Vincent 326, 327, 360
Beauweltz 107
Beck 311
Bedford, Stephen 208
Beggerstaff family 327
Beilby, Mary 183
Belfast 184
Bellange, L. F. 167
Bellange, P. A. 167, 262
Belluno 87
Belter, Henry 259, 265
Belvedere 91
Bembé, Anton 264
benchwork *see* metalwork
Bennett, E. & W. 268
Bennington 268
Benois, A. 361
Bentley, Thomas 181
Bérain, Jean 87, 91, 148, 149, 162
Bereman, Guillaume 163
Berge, Matthew 301
Berlage 366
Berlin 171, 177, 220, 232, 261, 270, 271, 274, 303–4, 338
Bernaes, Jean 207
Bernhardt, Sarah 327
Bernini, Gianlorenzo 84, 86
Beroviero family 31, 366
Berthevin, Pierre 176
Berthoud, Ferdinand 192, 201
Bertin, Rose 314
Besnard, Jean 271
Besnardeau, Leon 324–5
Bettally, C. 302
Bettigne family 175
Bevan, Charles 263
Beverly 313
Bewick, Thomas 355–6

Bexley Heath 263
Beyer, Jean 271
Bianchi 301
Bidjar carpets 373
Biedermeier style 258, 261, 274–5
Beilefiled, Charles 265
Biennais, M. G. 280
Bierzy, Joseph-Etienne 219
Big Ben 286
Billingsley, William 179, 266–7
Billington, Dora 272
Bilston 49, 217–18
Biman, Dominic 274
Bindesbølle, Thorwald 271
Bion 133
Bird, John 214, 300
Birds of America 358
Birmingham 190, 208, 210, 217, 272, 279, 281, 298, 330, 338, 339
Blado 332–3
Blake, William 360
Blakeway, Edward 180
Blenheim Palace 256, 311
Blois 116
Blond, Charles 133
Blond, Jacques 133
Blond, Jean 133
Bloor, Robert 179
Bluhmel 247
Bochum 271
Boehm, Theobald 247
Bohne, Ernst 168–9
Bolin, Lars 161
Bologna 242
Bongen, Andries 164
Bonhomme 187
Bonniksen 288
Bonnin, Gouse 182
Bontemps, George 275
Bonzanigo, Guiseppe Maria 162
Book of Architecture 150
Book of Jeweller's Work Designed by Thomas Flach in London, A 210
books, 19th Century 331–7
Boppard 260
Borchardt, Hugo 354
Boreman, Zachariah 179, 266
Borghese family 86
Borgis, Ortensio 122
Boston 113, 150, 165, 202, 213, 222, 248, 264, 270, 276, 277, 288
Bottger, Johann Friedrich 169
Botticelli 52
Botticelli, Sandro 15
Boucher, François 148, 173, 175, 217, 229
Bouilhet, Henri 281–2
Boulle, André Charles 87–8, 90, 147, 148, 164, 201
Boulton, Matthew 190–1
Bourbon, Louis Henri de 172
Bourg-la-Reine 173, 271
Bow 177–8, 182
Bowes, Sir Jerome 69
boxes
    18th Century 227–32
    19th Century 312, 328–30
    see also musical-boxes
Boyle, Charles 214
Boyle, John 268
Bracquemond, F. 326
Braden, Nor 273
Bradley, Milton 314
Bradley, Will 326, 327
Bradwell Wood 105
Brameld family 268
Brandt, Edgar 361
Breguet, Abraham Louis 203
Bremond 241
Brescia 244
Breton, Jean-François 218
Breuer, Marcel 362–3

Bridgens, Robert 262
Brighton 260
Briot, François 76
Brislington 95
Bristol 95, 178, 179, 183, 184, 285
Britain, William 311
British United Clock Company 286
Brno 363
Broadwood 246
Brocard, Joseph 29, 276
Brogden 297
Brossamer, Hans 63
Broseley 179
Browne, Robert 178
Browning 354
Bru 315
Bruges 93
Bruhl, Count 170, 228
Brunelleschi, Filippo 14, 52
Brunswick 37, 287
Brussels 107, 265
Brustolon, Andrea 87
Buchwald, Johann 1976
Budapest 248
Buen Retiro 168
Buffet 247
Buffon 175
Bugatti, Carlo 265
Bullard, Charles 284
Bunshojo 306
Buquoy, Count 274
Burges, William 261, 262–3
Burlington, Earl of 256
Burne-Jones, Edward 263, 304
Burnett, Thomas 184
Burnham, Lord 87
Burritt, Joseph C. 285
Burslem 96, 181, 330
Burwash 49
Burwell & Carter 285
Bustelli, Franz Anton 171
Bute, Lord 302
Buthaud, René 271
Butler, Frank 272
Butterfield, Michael 133, 212
Butterfield, William 261, 263
Butti 301
Byzantium 28

Cabinet-Maker and Upholsterer's Drawing Book 164
Cabinet-Maker and Upholsterer's Guide 164, 261, 264
Cabinet-Maker's London Book of Prices 164
Cafaggioli 22
Caffieri, Jacques 87, 148, 206–7
Cairoli, Giuseppe 261
Callot, Jacques 169
Cambrai 126
Cambridge 39
Campani, Giuseppe 212
Campbell, Colin Minton 268
Cantagalli 66
Canton 64
Caparra *see* Grosso, Nicolo
Capodimonte, Palace of 168
Carandolet, Archbishop 51
Carder, Frederick 366
Cardew, Michael 273
care of antiques 374–85
Carey, James 287
Carl 1, Duke 171
Carl Eugen, Duke 171
Carl Theodor, Elector 171
Carlin, Martin 164
carpets, Caucasian
    20th Century 367–73
Carpets, Chinese
    19th Century 316–19
carpets, Turkish
    17th Century 135–7
Carré, Jean 69

Cassandre 328
Cassel 36
Cassini 214
Casteldurante 22
Castellani brothers 297
Catherine II 174, 176, 181
Catherine the Great 147, 167, 191
Caughley 178, 179–80, 266, 267
Cauldron Pottery Company 330
Caxton, William 355
Cellini, Benvenuto 31, 71, 78, 106
ceramics
   pre 1500 16–22, 32
   16th Century 64–6
   17th Century 92–105, 123
   18th Century 168–82, 189, 224, 225, 229
   19th Century 266–75, 309, 320, 321, 330
   restoration of 383–4
Cersne, Eberhardt 246
Cetti, J. 302
Chamberlain, Richard 180
Chamberlain, Robert 266
Chambers, William 151, 166
Champion, Richard 179
Chance, William 183
Chantilly 172–3, 175, 180
Chaplet, Ernest 271
Chapotot 133
Chareau, Pierre 265
Charlemagne 32, 38
Charles I 123, 143
Charles II 89, 111, 114, 125
Charles VI 314
Charles VIII 16
Charles of Bourbon 168
Charleston 150, 165
Charlotte, Queen 181
Charlottenburg 91
Châteaudun 115, 123
Château de Malmaison 167
Chatsworth 95
Chaulnes, Duc de 213
Cheam 49
Chelaberds carpets 367, 368
Chelsea 175, 177, 178, 179, 189, 272
Chénavard, Aimé 262
Chêng Hua, Emperor 18
Chêng-tê 65
Chéret 326, 327
Chesnau, Aimé 281
Chia-ching 65, 225
Chicago 260, 264, 325
Chicaneux, Pierre 172
Chichester 49
Chichi carpets 369
Ch'ien Lung 224, 225, 250–1
Ch'ing Dynasty 224, 250
Ching-tê-chên 18, 65
Chippendale, Thomas 147, 151, 162, 166
Chiswick House 256
Choisy Le Roi 275
Chou Dynasty 17, 249
Christoffe, G. 281
Christofori, Bartolomeo 246
Chronicle of Galvano Fiammi 35
churches and cathedrals 10, 11, 12, 14, 28, 31, 33, 38, 39, 49–50, 51, 63, 71, 72, 84, 87, 124, 204, 207
Cie 276
Cima, Giuseppe 264
Cincinnati 269
Cirencester 50
Ciron, Ciquaire 172
Clay, Henry 330
Clements, William 115
Clerkenwell 338
Clichy 275
Clive, Kitty 177
clocks

pre 1500 34–6
16th Century 72–4
17th Century 114–15
18th Century 192–202, 221, 231
19th Century 283–6
see also watches
Clouet, François 53
Coalbrookdale Co. 338
Coalport 180, 266, 268
Cob, John 151
Cocclaeus, Johannes 74
Cochin, C. N. 163
Cochius, P. M. 366
Cockerell, C. R. 261
Coke, John 266
Colbert, Jean Baptiste 85, 87, 126
Colchester 27
Colditz 169
Cole, Sir Henry 259, 263, 324
Collard & Collard 264
Collcutt, T. E. 263
Colnett, John 109
Cologne 27, 72, 262
Colt, Samuel 344–53, 354
Columbus, Christopher 227
Coney, John 113
Constantine 1, Emperor 28
Constantinople 28
Cook, Captain 210
Cookworthy, William 179
Copeland, William 267
Copeland, William Taylor 267
Copenhagen 89, 161, 175–6, 272
Copier, Andries Dirk 366
Corbett, Webb 365
Cordova 72
Cork Glass Company 184
Corning Glass Works 367
Correr family 87
Cosmographia Pomponiae Melas 74
Coster, Salomon 114
Coteau 201
Cotterill, Edmund 280
Coty, Monsieur 364
Couper and Sons, James 279, 280
Courtrai 207
Conventry 366
Cox, James 201, 231
Cozzi, Geminiano 168, 169
Crane, Walter 304, 324
Crane, William 360
Cremona 244
Crescent, Charles 147, 148
Criseby 176
Crookes 302
Cros, H. and J. 276
Crowhurst 49
Cruickshank, Robert 324
Crutched Friars Hall 69
Crystal Palace 259
Culpeper, Edmund 211–12
Curtis, Samuel 288
cutlery
   pre 1500 32, 34
   16th Century 72
   17th Century 111, 113
Cuvillies, François 161

Daghestan carpets 367, 368
Dagly, Gerard 91
Dagnia 187
Dagnia-Williams 183
Dalpuyrat, Adrien 271
Damascus 29, 39
Dammouse, H. 276
Dancer 300
Danhauser, Josef 261
Danish Porcelain Factory, Royal 176
Darly, Matthew 151
Daroca Cope, the 55

d'Arre, Monsieur 122
Dauber, F. 175
Daum Frères 276
Daumier 358
Davidson and Co., George 279
Davis, Alexander 263
Davis, William 202
Daws 353
Dean & Sons 324
De Architectura 60
de Arfe, Antonio 72
de Arfe, Enrique 72
Debaufre, Jacob 203
Debaufre, Peter 203
de Bazel 366
de Bruy, Theodore 78
Debut, Jules 298
de Caylus, Comte 163
de Choiseul, Duc 229
Deck, Théodore 271
Decker, Paul 91
Decorchement, F. 276
de Cotte, Robert 148, 149
de'Dondi, Giovanni 36
de Duillier, Nicholas 203
Deerfield 315
de Feure, Georges 276, 326
de Fulvy, Orry 173
de Gama, Vasco 71
de Gault, Jacques-Joseph 219
Delaherche, Auguste 271
de la Hire, Philippe 131
de Lamerie, Paul 113
de la Mosson, Bonnier 212
Delaunay, R. and S. 361
Delaune, Etienne 78
Delftware 94–6
de Lisle, Anthony 69
del Vaga, Perino 63
de Marigny, Marquis 163
de Morgan, William 272
Denner 246
Dennison, Aaron L. 287–8
Dent, Edward John 286
De Paquier 169, 170
de Paquier 169, 170
de Pompadour, Madame 147, 163, 218, 229
de Pompadour, Marquis 213
Derbend carpets 369
Derby 173, 175, 179, 182, 266, 268, 286
Deruta 21, 66
Desiderio da Firenze 49
Designs of Chinese Buildings, Furniture, and Dresses 151
Despret, G. 276
Dessau 362
de Stijl school 362
De Thellusson 216
de Varennes, Robert 314
De Vez 276
de Villeroy, Duc 173
Devonshire, Duke of 95
de Vries, Hans Vredeman 16, 62, 63, 90, 261
de Vries, Paul 16, 62
Diaghilev 361
Diana, Bath of 188–9
di Bondone, Giotto 14
Dickens, Charles 269–70
Dieppe 133
Digges, Leonard 214
Dijon 63
Dillwyn, L. W. 266
Dinglinger, J. M. 188–9
Directoire style 257
Director 151
di Vieri, Ugolino 33
Dobbs and Company, H. 324
Doccia 168
Dolland, P. & J. 212, 301
dolls
   19th Century 314–15
Dolny Polubny 274

Dordrecht 108
Dortu, Jacob 177
Dosho, Kagai 307
Doulton Tableware Group, Royal 268
Doulton 272
Dowbiggon & Co. 264
Dresden 169, 179, 185, 188, 216, 220–1, 231–2, 329
Dresser, Christopher 263, 279–80, 282, 283, 326
Drummer, William 222
du Barry, Madame 163, 207
Dublin 37, 95, 297, 304, 337
Dubois, Gillies 172, 173
Dubois, Jacques 163
Dubois, Robert 172, 173
Duboule, Martin 117
Dubuisson, 201
du Cerceau, Jacques Androuet 63, 71, 78, 261
Duche, Andrew 182
Ducrollay, Jean 219
Duesbury, William 179
Du Paquier 170
Durand Glass Company 278
Dürer, Albrecht 62, 355, 357
Dutch Glassworks, Royal 366
Dwight, John 96–105
Dyers Cross 31
Dyrham Park 95

Eames, Charles 363–4
East, Edward 115
Eckenforde 176
Eco period 309
Edinburgh 134, 191, 301, 365
Edkins, Michael 183
Edlin, Martha 125
Edo period 305, 209
Edward III 35
Edwards, Benjamin 184
Egerman, Friedrich 274
Ehrenreich, J. L. E. 176
Elers, David 105
Elers, John 105
Elizabeth I 61, 63, 69, 80
Elizabeth Furnace 185
Elizabeth of Bohemia 248
Elizabeth of Russia 147, 229
Elkington's 281, 282
Ellison Glassworks 279
embroidery
   pre 1500 10, 54–5
   16th Century 79–81
   17th Century 124–7
   18th Century 251–4
   19th Century 303–4
Empire style 164, 167, 175, 257–8, 267, 274, 277, 280
Empoli 68
Enderlein, Kaspar 77
Ennion 26–7
Ensell, Edward 276
Erasmus 334
Ertel 300
Escorial, the 71
Eugène of Savoy, Prince 214

Faber 105
Fabergé, Peter Carl 222–3, 230, 299, 328–9
Faenza 21–2
Falconet, Etienne-Maurice 174, 229, 339
Falize, Lucien 298
fans
   18th Century 226–7
Farnese, Cardinal Alessandro 71–2
Fawkener, Sir Everard 177
Feilner, Simon 171
Fenoglio, Pietro 265

Index

Fenton 330
Ferdinand, King 21
Fereghan carpets 370–1
Feuchère 207
Fitzwilliam, Earl 268
Flach, Thomas 210
Flack 66
Flamboyant style 11
Flora Danica service 176
Flora of the Danish Kingdom 176
Florence 14, 21, 32–3, 39–40, 61, 66, 68, 168, 298
Floris, Cornelius 16, 62, 71
Flötner, Peter 62
Flowers, Fruits, Birds and Beasts 124
Fogelberg, Andrew 191
Fontaine, Pierre 167, 257
Fontainebleu 63
Fontana, Orazio 66
Fontenay, Eugène 298
Forster, Anne 49
Forsyth 343
Fortner, Franz Xavier 262
Foulet, Antoine 163
Fournier 333
Fournier, Louis 175
Fragonard, Jean Honoré 148
François I 16, 31, 61, 62–3, 71, 73, 78
Frankenthal 171
Frankfurt 105, 161
Franklin, Benjamin 322
Frauenhofer 300
Frederick 186
Frederick II 220, 229
Frederick the Great 161, 170, 171, 220, 232
Freiberg 105
Frisius, Gemma 131, 133
Fritsche, William 278
Frodsham 288
'Frog' service 181
Fromanteel family 114
Froment-Meurice 297, 298
Fromery, Alexander 220
Fromery, Pierre 220
Frontinus 27
Fulham 96–105, 272, 321
furniture
    pre 1500 10, 11, 12–16
    16th Century 40, 61–1, 62–4
    17th Century 32, 84–5, 85–91, 123
    18th Century 147, 148–67, 210, 251
    19th Century 257, 258–66
    20th Century 361–4
    restoration of 378–80
Fürstenberg 171
Furth 311
Furttenbach, Joseph 91

Gabriel 133
Gale, Daniel Jackson 285
Galileo 131
Gallatin, Albert 186
Gallé, Emile 265, 276, 360, 367
Gallien, F.-P. 207
Galliland, John 277
games
    19th Century 312–14
Gani mines 122
Garaku 309
Garamond, Claude 332
Garrards 280, 281
Garrett, Thomas 267
Garthorne, Francis 113
Garthorne, George 113
Gatchell, George 184
Gatchell, Jonathan 184
Gates, Jack 367
Gateshead 279
Gaudi, Antoni 265

Gauron, N. J. 175
Geissler 302
Gendje carpets 370
Geneva 116, 117, 221, 241
Genoa 28
Genroku 309
Gentili, Antonio 71–2
George III 212
George IV 231, 257, 260, 280
Germain, Thomas 188
Gerverot, L. V. 175
Gerz 1, S.M. 105
Ghiberti, Lorenzo 33
Ghiberti, Vittorio 33
Ghiordes 135
Ghirlandaio, Domenico 15
Gibb, James 150
Gibbons, Grinling 89–90
Gierlof, Christian 176
Giles, James 183
Gillot 149
Gimson, E. W. 361–2
Ginori, Carlo 168
Girod, Duconmum 241
Glasgow 95, 191, 279, 283, 338
glass
    pre 1500 22–31
    16th Century 60, 67–70
    17th Century 85, 106–10
    18th Century 182–7, 224, 225
    19th Century 275–80
    20th Century 364–7
    restoration of 384
Gloucester 37, 49, 95
Gobelins, the 87–8, 148
Goddard, Luther 287
Godfrey, Thomas 214
Godwin, William 263
Golconda mines 122
gold
    pre 1500 10, 11, 31–4, 52
    16th Century 60, 61, 70–2, 78–9
    17th Century 85, 110–13
    18th Century 147, 187–91, 209, 215–16, 218–19, 220, 221, 222–3, 228, 229, 230, 231–2
    19th Century 280–3
    restoration of 383
Gold Coffee Set 188
Gonzaga family 14
Goodall's of Camden 324
Gorham Manufacturing Company 282
Gosbertus 37
Gothic style 10–11, 12, 13, 14, 15, 16, 38, 39, 40, 49, 51, 55, 61, 62, 64, 71, 72, 81, 147, 151, 205, 256, 258, 260–1, 262–3, 282, 297, 304, 321, 336, 337, 339, 360
Goto School 129
Gottschalk 311
Gotzkowsky, J. C. 171
Gough and Co. 282
Gouldings 247
Gouthière, Pierre 163, 207
Govers, Daniel 216
Goya 358
Grafton 284
Graham, George 115, 192, 202, 214, 300
Granby, Marquis of 177
Grasset 326
Gravant, François 173
Gravelot, H. F. 150
Gray, Eileen 361
Greatbatch, William 181
Great Mogul diamond 122
Great Mogul's Birthday Party 188
Great Yarmouth 183
Greenaway, Kate 322, 324
Greene, John 107

Greener and Co. 279
Greenwich Observatory 115
Greenwood, Frans 108, 186
Greiner 241
Griffet, Rolyn 76
Grimthorpe, Lord 286
Grohé, Guillaume 264
Gropius, Walter 362
Grosso, Nicolo 39–40
Groult, André 361
Gruber, Jacques 265
Grueby Faience Company 270
Grunow Brothers 300
Guadagni Palace 40
Guarneri del Gesu, Giuseppe 244
Gubbio 66
Guerard 133
Guiliano, Carlo 297
Guimard, Hector 265
guns
    17th Century 137–41, 143–4
    18th Century 340–54
Gunter, Edmund 132
Gustavsberg 272
Gutenbrunn 185
Gutenberg, Johann Genzfleisch zum 331–2, 355
Gyokuzan 309

Haarlem 187
Hadeland 186
Hadley, John 214
Hafner 105
Halsey, James 213
Hamada, Shoji 273
Hamburg 105, 166, 303
Hampton Court 95
Hanau 105
Hancock, Joseph 190
Hancock, Robert 178
Handwerck 315
Han dynasty 17, 249–50
Hanley 272
Hannong, Paul 171
Hans of Antwerp 78
Hardy, Dudley 326, 327
Harff 72
Harland, Thomas 287
Harrach glassworks 275
Harrison, John 192, 214
Haubach 315
Haupt, George 166
Hawes, John H. 285
Hawkes, Thomas G. 367
Hayes, Atwell 184
Heal, Ambrose 361–2
Heckel 247
Hedebo 254
Hedwig Glasses 29
Heel 105
Heinrichsen, Ernst 311
Heintze, J. G. 170
Helmhack 105
Helsinki 272
Henlein, Peter 73, 74
Henley-on-Thames 108
Henri II 16, 61, 63, 261
Henri IV 87, 226
Henry VIII 63, 77, 78, 353
Henry the Lion 37
Henvey family 69
Hepplewhite, George 164, 165
Herculaneum 147, 161, 170, 256, 288, 297
Heriz carpets 372
Herold, C. F. 170
Herreboe 176
Herrman, Dr Emanuel 324
Hida school 306
Hildescheimer and Co., S. 324
Hill, John 184
Hilpert family 311
Hilton, J. & W. 264
Hilversum 175

Hirosige 323
Hittorf 302
Hizen 129
Hobbs-Brockunier and Company 278
Hoc family 69
Höchst 171, 175
Hodgetts, Joshua 278
Hoffman, Benjamin Gottlob 231
Hoffman, Josef 361, 362
Hoffmeister 274
Hoffnagel, Peter 176
Holbein, Hans 53, 71, 77–8, 254, 297
Holden, Henry 109
Hollins, Daintry 268
Homer, Edward 183
Hooke, Dr Robert 115, 116, 134
Hoppesteyn, Rochus 95
Horchhaimer, Nicholas 76–7
Horikawa School 129
Horoldt, Hohann Gregor 169–70
Horta, Victor 265
Horton, Henry B. 285
Hôtel de Soubise 256
Hotel van Eetveldte 265
Hotteterre, Jean 246, 247
Houghton, Arthur A. 367
Howard, Edward 287, 288
Howson, J. 272
Hsüan Tê, Emperor 18, 19, 250
Huaud family 116
Huguenots, the 69, 84, 110, 112–13, 126, 222, 223, 275, 328
Hull, John 113
Hung-chih 65
Hunger, C. K. 168, 170
Hung Li 224
Hunt and Roskell 281, 282
Hurd, Jacob 222
Hurdals Verk 186
Hutton, John 366
Huygens, Christian 114, 192

Iles, Frank 272
Ince, William 151
Ingersoll 288
Ingraham Company, E. 285
inro
    19th Century 307–10
Insectorum 124
Irminger 169
Isabeau de Barrière, Queen 314
Isabella, Queen 12, 314
Isfahan carpets *see* Ispahan
Isleworth 321
Isnik 20
Ispahan 130, 371
Issai, Ogusawara 306
Issan 309
Istanbul 18
Ithaca Calendar Glass Company 285
Ives, Joseph S. 284
Iyemitsu 130

Jackson and Son, G. 265
Jacob, Georges 163
Jacob-Desmalter, F. H. G. 167
Jacobs family 183
'Jacob Zech' 73, 74
jade, Chinese
    18th Century 248–51
James I 124, 248
Jamestown 185
Jaminitzer, Wenzel 71
Jansen, Jacob 95
Janssen, Stephen Theodore 217
Japanese Palace 170
Japy Frères 285, 287
Jardin, Nicolas Henri 166
Jarves, Deming 277

Jean de Paris 74
Jeanne of Burgundy, Queen 13
Jeannest, Pierre Emile 281
Jeanselme, J. P. F. 264
Jeckyll, Thomas 263
Jefferson, Thomas 165
Jelliff, John 263
Jena 300
Jennens and Bettridge 330
Jenson, Nicholas 332
Jerome, Chauncy 284
Jerome of Pesaro 246
Jersey City 268
jewelry
    pre 1500 26, 33, 34, 39, 50–4
    16th Century 60, 77–9
    17th Century 121–4
    18th Century 189, 209–11
    19th Century 288–99, 338
    see also objects of vertu *and*
    snuff bottles, Chinese
Jobson and Co. 338
John le Alemagne 31
Johnson, Thomas 151
Joi 309
Jones, Henry Arthur 327
Jones, Inigo 89
Jones, Thomas 301
Jones, W. & S. 213, 301
Josephine, Empress 288
Joshaghan carpets 373
Joubert, Gilles 163
Journal d'un Voyageur à Paris
    122
Journal of Design 259
Jumeau 315
Junghan family 285
Jurgensen 288

Kabuke 307
Kaendler, J. J. 170, 171, 189
Kähler, Herman A. 271
Kaiserpokal, the 71
Kajikawa 308
Kakiemon, Sakaida 92–3
Kolvine, Alexander 361
Kamble, Jean-Melchoir 207
Kamman 306
Kammer & Reinhardt 315
Kaneyuki, Matsuda 306
K'ang Hai 224, 251
Kano 129
Karabagh carpets 370
Kashan 20, 371–2
Kauffer, McKnight 328
Kazak carpets 367–8, 370
Kenelm Digby, Sir 109
Kent, William 150
Ker, James 191
Kestner 315
Ketterer, Franz Anton 202
Khila carpets 369
Khlebnikov 223
Kiel 176
Kimbel 262
Kinzing, Peter 167
Kirchner, Gottlieb 170
Kirman carpets 372
Kir-Shehir 137
Kjaerholm, Poul 363
Klieber family 132
Klint, Kaarl 363
Klostermühle 275
Knibb, Joseph 115
Knie, Balthazar 301
knives
    17th Century 141–2, 143, 144
Knole 90
Knütgen 66
Kny, Frederick 278
Koch, Mogens 363
Kocks, Adrianus 94–5
Köhler, Heinrich Gottliev 186

Kokusai 306
Kolovrat, Count 106
Koma family 308
Konieh 135, 136
Konoe, Emperor 309–10
Kopplesdorf 315
Koryō kingdom 19
König, Josef Pallme 275
Kothgasser, Anton 274
Kreussen 105
Kronheim 324
Kuba carpets 369–70
Kulah 135
Kungsholm Glasbruk 186
Kunihiro 129
Kutani 93
Kyoto 129, 305

La Granja de San Ildefonso,
    Royal Factory of 186
Lalique, René 364–5, 367
Lambeth 272
Lancaster 95
Langing, Jacob Gerritse 222
Langlois 133
Lanooy 366
Latrobe, Benjamin 261
Lauderdale, Duke of 230–1
Lausanne 37
Lavasseur, Etienne 164
Leach, Bernard 272–3
Lebeau, Chris 366
le Brun, Charles 87
Lechaudel, Fermier Antoine 207
Le Corbusier 260, 362, 363
Lecoultre 241
Leeds 181, 286
Leerdam 366
Lefaucheux 353
Légaré 123
Legras 276
Lehman, Caspar 106
Leighton, William 278
Leistler, Carl 260, 262, 264
Leland, Charles 283
Leleu, Jean François 163
Leningrad 181 *see also*
    St Petersburg
Le Nove 169
Leo III 28
Léon 72
Leonardo da Vinci 15, 73
le Pautre, Jean 87, 91, 148
Le Roux, Charles 222
Le Roy, Lulien 192, 201
Lesel, Michael 132
Lesghi carpets 370
Leveille, E. 276
Lewis, Benjamin B. 285
Libbey, Edward D. 278
Liberty and Co. 283
Liège 27, 37, 68, 107, 187, 189
Lille 126
Lillie, Joseph Christian 166
Limoges 174
Lincoln 49
Lindberg, Stig 272
Lindner, Edmund 315
Linnel, John 151, 162
Lisbon 184, 204
Little Gidding 125
Liu Sheng 250
Liverpool 95, 178, 179, 217
Lobmeyr, Louis 275
Lock, Matthias 151
Locke, Joseph 277, 278
Lombard style 11
London 18, 20, 37, 38, 50, 54, 55,
    69, 73, 89, 95, 96, 109, 113,
    114, 134, 149, 166, 179, 189,
    191, 201, 207, 212, 213, 214,
    216, 217, 222, 230, 244, 246,
    247, 248, 259, 263, 264, 266,
    267, 270, 272, 279, 282, 283,

297–8, 300, 302, 314, 315,
    322, 324, 338, 339, 344, 361,
    365
Long Bridge Glass House 184
Longleat 63
Longton Hall 178–9
Lonhuda Pottery 269–70
Lorne, Marquis of 323
Loudon, J. C. 262
Louis II 16
Louis IX 11
Louis XI 74
Louis XIII 61, 87
Louis XIV 32, 85, 86, 87–8, 112,
    119, 122, 125–6, 146, 148,
    188, 201, 216, 219, 228, 256,
    264
Louis XV 146, 147, 149, 174,
    188, 201, 213, 216, 229,
    256–7, 264, 265, 285
Louis XVI 162, 163–5, 166, 201,
    227, 256–7, 264, 265, 299
Louis, J. J. 171–2
Louis-Napoleon 264
Louvain 131
Louveciennes 163
Lowestoft 178
Lucas, John Robert 183
Lucca 68, 119
'Luck of Edenhall' 29
Lucotte 311
Ludlow 50
Ludwig II 339
Ludwigsburg 171–2
Luger, George 354
Lund and Miller 178
Lunéville 276
Lung-ch'ing 65
Lusuergh, Domenico 134
Lusuergh, Giacomo 134
Lutz, Nicholas 277
Lyncker, Anton 175
Lyndhurst and Ericstan 263
Lynn 182–3, 365
Lyons 76–7, 126, 242

Maastricht 366
McCarthy, Daniel 175
Macfarlane and Co. 338
McIntyre, Samuel 165
Mckearin, H. and G. S. 277
McKenzie, Colic 191
Mackintosh, Charles Rennie
    264, 283, 360
Mackmurdo, A. H. 264
Madrid 39, 55, 168
Maggiolini, Giuseppe 164
Magny, Alexis 212–13
Mainz 27, 264, 331
Majorelle, Louis 265, 360
Makri 137
Malaga 20
Maler, Laux 242–3
Maler, Sigismund 242
Mallard, Prudent 264
Mallet, Mr 337
Malmaison Palace 257
Malory 327
Manchester 300, 324
Manheim 185
Mannerism 61–2, 72, 79, 110,
    120, 121, 123
Mansell, Sir Robert 108
Manton 341
Manwaring, Robert 151
Marcot, Daniel 262
Maria Feodorovna 223
Maria Leszcyneki, Queen 216
Maria Theresa 147, 170, 174
Marie Antoinette 163, 314, 338
Marieberg 176
Marie-Joseph of Saxe 218
Marinot, Maurice 365
Markneukirchen 244

Marot, Daniel 87, 88, 91, 94,
    149
Marseille, Armand 315
Marsh, Charles 315
Martin, Benjamin 213, 214
Martin, Johann 132, 133
Martin family 226–7, 270, 272,
    321
Martine, Atelier 361
Marvel, Captain 322
Mary II 95
Mary Tudor 131
Mason, Miles 268
Masquerades, The 327
Mathematical-Mechanical
    Institute of Reichenbach,
    Utzschneider and
    Leibherr 300
Matisse 337
Ma-ts'ang 65
Matthias Corvinus, King 22
Mauser 354
Max Emanuel 161
Mayhew, John 151
Mayoden, Jean 271
Mazarin, Junes 87, 122
Maximilian I, Emperor 81–2
Medici family 14, 22, 146, 168
Meech 315
Meeks, Joseph 261, 262
Meiningen 315
Meissen 168, 169–70, 171, 173–4,
    175, 176, 177, 198, 218
Meissonnier, Juste Aurèle 149,
    188, 217, 231
Melas 135, 136
Melillio 297
Mennecy 173, 175, 176
Mercier, Charles 257
'Merckelsche' table-centre 71
Mertz 300
Mesangere 261
Meshed carpets 373
metalwork
    pre 1500 10, 13, 36–50
    16th Century 60, 75–7
    17th Century 85, 117–21
    18th Century 147, 189, 204–9,
    224
    19th Century 337–40
    restoration of 381
Metz, Bishop of 110, 275
Meydam 366
Meyer, Johann Fridrich 185
Meyer and Company 330
Michelangelo 62, 71–2, 84
Micrographia 134
Middleburgh 107
Miekle, W. 248
Mies van der Rohe 363
Mignot, Daniel 78
Milan 15, 33, 35, 36, 40, 79, 161,
    164, 264, 270
Mildner, Joseph 185
Milton shield 281
Ming Dynasty 17, 18, 20, 64–6,
    225, 250, 251, 316
Minton, Herbert 268
Minton, Thomas 267–8
Miotti 68
Mirecourt 244
Mittenwald 244
Modena 134
Moderna, Carlo 84
Mogensen, Borge 363
Mohn, Samuel 185
Mol, Johannes de 175
Moleyser, Willem 108
Moncrieff, John 365
Mondrian, Piet 362
Montanari, Madame 315
Monte Carlo 361
Monticello 165
Montreal 264
Moore, Bernard 272

Index

Moreau fils, Georges-Alexandre 207
Morel-Laudeuil, Léonard 281
Moriset 231
Morris, George 182
Morris, John 202
Morris, William 258, 260, 263, 264, 299, 304, 329, 360
Morris, Marshall, Faulkner and Company 263
Morte D'Arthur, Le 327
Mortimer 341
Mortlocks 267
Moscow 260
Moselini, Paolini 261
Moser 231
Moser, Koloman 361
Moser & Söhne, Ludwig 275
Moufet, Thomas 124
Mount Vernon 40
Mount Washington Glass Company 277–8
Moxon, Joseph 214
Mozart 246
Mucha, Alfons Maria 326, 327
Mudge, Thomas 286
Mudjar 135, 137
Mudge, Thomas 286
Müller 302
Müller, F. H. 176
Muller Frères 276
Munich 78, 161, 264, 271, 300
Muona, Toini 272
Murano 29, 30–1, 61, 68, 106, 366
Murillo 81
Murry, Keith 271
Musayuki, Hamano 309
museums and galleries
American Antiquarian Society 322
American Museum of Natural History 34
Archaeological Museum 39
Ashmolean Museum 261
Bibliothèque Nationale 322
British Museum 34, 38, 117, 125, 261, 315
Ca'Rezzonico 86, 87
Cluny Museum 38, 119
Corning Museum 69
Gulbenkian Collection 149
Hermitage Museum 181
Hofburg 339
Industrial Art Museum 106
Kunsthistorisches Museum 31, 71
Le Secq des Tournelles Museum 38, 119, 204
Louvre 87, 339
Mazarine Library 207
Metropolitan Museum of Art 72, 117
Museo Arqueológico 55
Musée des Arts Decoratifs 119, 120
Museo dell'Opera del Duomo 33
Museum of Fine Arts 222, 248
Museum of Modern Art 364
National Museum 37
National Palace Museum 17
New York Public Library 322
Northampton Museum 108, 109
Percival David Collection 18, 66
Philadelphia Museum 269
Public Library, Siena 38
Rijksmuseum 71
St Bride's Library 322
Schatzkammer der Residenz 78
Sicilian Ethnographical Museum 40

Victoria and Albert Museum 20, 29, 37, 38, 51, 55, 80, 106, 123, 125, 187, 208, 246, 282
Wallace Collection 123, 149, 207, 230, 339
Wrightsman Collection 229
musical-boxes
18th Century 241
musical instruments
18th Century 232–48, 311
Mutz, Herman 271
Mutz, Richard 271
Myōju, Umetada 129

Nabeshima 93
Nachet 300
Naestved 271
Nagasaki 93
Nagasone School 129
Nailsea 183
Nairne and Blunt 301
Namur 27
Nancy 221–2, 276
Nantes, Revocation of the Edict of 84, 88, 112, 126, 222
Nantgarw 266, 267
Napier, John 134
Naples 168, 241
Napoleon 167, 220, 222, 230, 257, 280, 288, 338
Napoleon III 281
Nara School 129
Nash, John 260
Nash, Joseph 262
Natural History 175
Nauka, Schimuke 309
Needlework, Royal Schools of Art 304
Neffe, Adolf Meyers 275
Negoro 307
Neo-classical style 111, 147, 161–5, 166–7, 170, 176, 179, 191, 211, 218, 219, 229, 244, 252, 256–7, 261, 262, 274, 280, 288, 297
Nero, Golden Home of 60
netsuke
19th Century 305–7, 308, 309
see also pipes *and* smoking equipment
Neuber, Johann Christian 221, 232
Neuchatel 203
Neuschwanstein 339
Neuwelt 274
Neuwied-am Rhein 166, 167
Nevers 110
Newark 298
New Bremen Glass manufactory 186
Newcastle 183, 187
New England Glass Company 276–7, 278
New Geneva Glassworks 186
New Hall 179, 268
New Haven 300
New Orleans 264
Newport 150, 165
New York 34, 69, 72, 117, 150, 213, 222, 229, 259, 260, 262, 263, 264, 265, 300, 322, 327, 364
Nicholas II 223
Nichols, Maria Longworth 269
Nicole Frères 241
Nicot, Jean 227
Nieuwer Amstel 175
Non-Such Flint Glass Manufactory 183
Norbert 300
Norman style 10
Northampton 108, 109
North British Glassworks 365

Northill 115
Northwood, John 278
Norwich 95, 182–3
Nøstetangen 186
Novy Bor 274
Nuremberg 36, 71, 73, 74, 76–7, 78, 91, 106, 120, 132, 176, 311
Nurmesniemi, Antti 363
Nymphenburg 171

Oberhauser 300
objects of vertu
18th Century 215–23
Obrisset, John 222
Odiot, J.-B. Claude 280, 339
Oeben, Jean François 163
Oeder, G. C. 176
Oeuvre de la diversité des Termes. dont on use en Architecture 63
Oem 66
Offenbach 338
Ohrmark, Erik 166
ojime
19th Century 307–10
Okawachi 93
Okisato, Kotetsu 129
Oldbury 338
Oldenburg 325
Old Moore's Almanac 322
O'Loughlin, Donal 37
O'Neill Wilson, Rose 311
Oppenord, A. J. 148
Orleans 110, 175
Ortman, Mathias 161
Orvieto 33
Osaka 129, 305
Osterley Park 162, 256
Oude Amstel 175
Oude Loosdrecht 175
Oughtred 133
Oushak 135, 136–7
Owens-Illinois Glass Company 278
Oxford 55, 261

Padua 14, 36, 242–3
Pagani 301
Paillard 241
Paimo 363
Palermo 51
Palladian style 256
Palladio, Andrea 89, 150, 165
Palladio Londonensis 150
Pamfili family 86
Pantin 276
Paris 11, 38, 51, 71, 73, 74, 85, 93, 119, 120, 147, 148, 166–7, 173, 174, 207, 212, 216, 219, 221, 222, 226, 228, 229, 256, 260, 264, 270, 271, 280, 281, 282, 297–8, 300, 302, 322, 327, 332, 339, 361
Parker 341
Parodi, Filipo 87
Parolin, Francesco 169
Passenger, Charles 272
Passenger, Fred 272
Pastorelli, F. 302
Paul III, Pope 84
Paxton, Joseph 259
Peabody, Henry 354
Peck, Lucy 315
Peking 224
Pelagi, Pelagio 261, 262
Pellipatio, Nicola 22
Penniman, John R. 284
Penrose, George 184
Penrose, William 184
Penshurst Place 13
Percier, Charles 167

Permoser 189
Perrot, Bernard 110
Perth 365
Peruzzi, Vincenzo 209
Peterinck, François Joseph 174–5
Peter the Great 229
Petitot, Jean 116, 123, 216, 220
Petrus, Baths of 52
Petworth House 90
Peytowe family 69
Pfohl, K. 274
Philadelphia 150, 182, 202, 214, 268, 269, 283, 284, 299, 300
Philip II 71, 131
Philippe, Duke of Orleans 146, 148, 216
Phillips 297
Phillipson 303
Phyfe, Duncan 257, 261
Piffetti, Pietro 161
Pike, Benjamin 213
Pinchbeck, Christopher 210
Pineau, Nicolas 148
Pinxton 266, 268
pipes
19th Century 320–1
Piranese, Giovanni Battista 161, 191
Pisa 68
Pisani family 87
Pistoia 246
Pitkin brothers 287
Pittsburgh Glass Manufactory 276
Plateresque style 61
Pleydell-Bouverie, Katherine 273
Pliny 25
Ploessel 300
Plücker 302
Plymouth 179
Poiret 361
Polidoro 63
Pollaiuolo, Antonio del 33, 52
Polyphon 241
Poor Richard's Almanack 322
Pommersfelden 91
Pompeii 147, 161, 162, 170, 256, 288, 297
Pompe, W. 207
porcelain *see* ceramics
Portland Vase 278, 282
Pössenbacher 264
posters
19th Century 325–8
Poterat, Louis 172
Potsdam 207
potteries, the 96–105
pottery *see* ceramics
Pounder, Thomas 49
Powell and Lealand 300
Powell, Harry J. 279, 365
Practical Cabinet-Maker, The 261
Prague 106
Pratt, F. and R. 330
Preissensin, Albrecht 77
Preissler, Ignaz 106
printed ephemera
19th Century 321–8
prints
19th Century 354–8
Prouvé, Victor 360
Providence 298
Prussian Iron, Royal 338
Pugin, Augustus Welby Northmore 262–3, 282, 339
Pyne, Benjamin 113

Quare, Daniel 115
Queen's Cup 280
Quellin, Artus 88

Rackham, Arthur 265

Ragard of Nancy 221–2
Raimondi, Marcantonio 66
Ramsden 300
Raphael 52, 66
Raqqa 20, 29
Rateau, A. A. 361
Ravenet 217
Ravenna 30
Ravenscroft, George 108, 109, 122
Rayonnant style 11, 13
Rayy 20
Reballio 301
Reed and Barton 282
Régence style 146, 149, 187
Regency style 167, 257–8, 280, 304
Regent, Prince *see* George IV
Regina 241
Regout, Petrus 366
Reimerschmid, Richard 265
Reinman, Paulus 132
Rembrandt 356
Renaissance, the 11–12, 13, 14–16, 33, 40, 49, 52, 60–3, 72, 76, 77, 78, 79, 80, 84, 89, 90, 150, 162, 211, 215, 216, 244, 257, 258, 261, 297, 333, 336
Renard, Jacques 207
repairing antiques 374–85
Repsold 300
restoring antiques 374–6
Revett, Nicholas 162
Richard Coeur-de-Lion 38
Richard-Ginori 168
Richard of Wallingford 36
Richardsons of Wordsley 278
Richelieu, Armand Jean de 87
Richter, Jean Louis 221
Ridgeways 268
Riedel, Josef 274
Riesener, Jean Henri 163
Rietveld, Gerrit 362
Rigo family 366
Ringler, Johann Josef 171
Ritsuo 309
Rochester 300
Rockingham 268
Rococo style 91, 106, 119, 146–61, 163, 166, 170, 171, 176, 177, 183, 186–7, 187–8, 191, 201, 204, 205, 207, 210, 212–13, 217, 219, 229, 231, 256–7, 258, 261, 264–5, 274, 277, 288, 298
Roemers Visscher, Anna 107
Roemers Visscher, Maria Tesselschade 107
Roentgen, Abraham 166
Roentgen, David 166–7
Roettiers, Jacques 191
Rogers, W. G. 262
Rogers, W. H. 262
Romanesque style 10, 12, 55, 360
Romani, Alessandro 38
Romano, Guilio 71
Romanticism 256–8
Rome 26, 60, 61, 70, 71, 84, 87, 134, 162, 212, 242–3, 297, 298, 332, 361
Rookwood Pottery 269
Rörstrand 272
Rosbury 202
Rose, John 180, 266
Rose, Richard 180
Rosenborg Castle 112
Ross 300
Rossetti 263
Rössler 105
Rouen 36, 38, 49, 119, 172, 204, 297
Rousseau, David 117
Rousseau, Eugène 276
Rousseau, Jean 117

Rousseau, Jean-Jacques 117
Roux, Alexander 263, 264
Roux, David Etienne 221
Rowe, Francis Richard 184
Roweau 74
Rowley, John 214
Roxbury 288
Royal Pavilion, the 260
Rudolph II, Emperor 79, 106
Rudolstadt 169
Ruhlmann, J. E. 361
Ruins of Palmyra 162
Ruins of the Palace of Diocletian at Spalatro 162
Rundell 282
Rundell and Bridge 280
Ruskin Pottery 272
Ryukei 306
Ryukoku 306

Saarinen, Eero 364
Sacro Catino cup 28
Sadler & Green 179
Sahagún 72
St Albans 36
St Claude 320
Saint-Cloud 172, 175
St Croix 241
St Denis 10
Sainte-Anne Glasshouse 275
St Ives 273
St Louis 275, 276, 277
St Patrick's bell 37
St Petersburg 167, 223, 229, 260
    see also Leningrad
St Quentin 126
Saint Yrieix 174
Salem 165
Salisbury 35, 36
Salmon, W. 150
Salocchi, Claudio 363
Salome 327
Salopian Porcelain Factory, Royal 179
Salto, Oxel 272
Salviati 67
Samarra 19
Sambin, Hugues 63
Saminiati Palace 119
Sampei, Ri 92
Samson of Paris 173
Sanderson, Robert 113
Sandwich Glass Company 277
Sang, Jacob 187
Sanssouci 161
Santiago di Compostella 72
Sargent 326
Sasikoff, Ovtchinnikoff 223
Sax, Adolphe 247–8
Saxon Porcelain Manufactory, Royal 169
Scapitta, Giacomo 186
Sceaux 175
Schaffgotsch Josephinenhutte, Count 275
Schaper, Johann 105, 106
Scharvogel, Julius 271
Schedula diversarum arta 30
Schilling 315
Schinkel, Karl Friedrich 261
Schissler family 132, 134
Schleswig 176
Schmidt, H. W. 105, 106
Schneider 276
Schofield, John 191
Schübler, J. J. 91
Schurman, Anna Maria 107
Schurterre family 69
Schwanhardt, George 106
Schwanhardt, Henry 106
Schwartz, A. 325
Schwinger, Hermann 106
scientific instruments
    17th Century 130–4

18th Century 211–15
19th Century 300–3
Scott, Mackay Hugh Baillie 264
Scott, Sir Walter 262
Seebafs and Co. 338
Sehna carpets 372
Senecal 133
Senefelder, A. 334, 358
Senex, John 214
Serre, George 271
Seto 270
Sevenoaks 90
Sèvres 162, 163–4, 169, 170, 171, 173–4, 175, 177, 179, 218, 226, 271
Seymour, John 165
Seymour, Thomas 165
S.F.B.J., the 315
Sforza family 14
Shang Dynasty 249
Shanghai 225
Shaw, Norman 262–3
Shearer, Thomas 164, 165
Sheffield 338
Shelton 180, 330
Sheraton, Thomas 164, 165, 257
S'Hertogenbosch 107
Shiraz 29, 373
Shirley, Frederick S. 277
Shirvan carpets 368, 370
Shogetsu 306
Short 300
Shrewsbury 267, 287
Shun-chih 224
Shuzan 306
Sidoli, Alessandro 264
Sidon 24, 25, 26
Siegburg 66
Sienna 21, 33, 38
Silla kingdom 19
Sille-le-Guillaume 324–5
silver
    pre 1500 10, 11, 31–4
    16th Century 60, 61, 63, 70–2
    17th Century 91, 110–13
    18th Century 187–91, 209, 218, 222, 223, 231
    19th Century 280–3
    restoration of 382–3
Simon & Halbig 315
Simpson 124
Sisson, Mr 214
Sivas 135
Six Dynasties 17
Sixtus V, Pope 84
Skidmore 338
Smee, William 264
Smethwick 272
Smith, George 261, 264
Smith and Wesson 353–4
smoking equipment
    19th Century 320–1
snuff bottles, Chinese
    18th Century 224–5
    see also boxes
Socchi, Giovanni 163
Solis, Vergil 78
Somerset, Duke of 64
Spathe 246
Spenser 300
Spode, Josiah 179, 267, 268
Spode, William 267
Sprimont, Nicholas 177, 178, 189
Staffordshire pottery 20, 178–9, 180–1
Stalhane, Harry 272
Stam, Mark 363
Stein, Johann Andreas 246
Steinder, Edmund Ulrich 315
Steinder, Jules Nicolas 315
Steinlein, Théophile Alexandre 326, 327
Stephens, William 182
Steuben Glass Works 367

Steubenville 269
Steven Bros. and Co. 338
Stevens Williams 278–9, 367
Stiegel, Henry William 185
Stockholm 176, 186
Stöer, Lorenz 62
Stokel 247
Stoke-on-Trent 96, 267, 272
Stolzel, Samuel 169, 170
Store Kongensgade 176
Storr, Paul 280
Storr and Flaxman 282
Stourbridge 69, 184, 277, 278, 279, 365
Stradivari 244
Stras 209–10
Strasbourg 171, 176
Stratford-on-Avon 366
Street, G. E. 263
Strozzi Palace 39
Stuart, James 'Athenian' 162
Stumpf 276
Sue et Mare 265
Suger, Abbot 10, 11
Sukehiro 129
Sukenaga 306
Sukenao 129
Sung Dynasty 17, 19, 271
Swansea 266
Swan Service 170
Swinton 268
swords
    17th Century 127–30, 142–3
Symonds 66
Symphonica 241
Sympsone, James 191
Syon Cope, the 55

Tabriz carpets 372
Taddel, Heinrich 232
Taiwan 17
Talbert, Bruce 263
Tales of the Arabian Nights 361
Talish carpets 369
Tamerlane 29, 136
T'ang dynasty 17, 19
Tangudani 92
Tannich, J. S. F. 176
Tassie, James 211
Taunton (Mass.) Britannia Manufacturing Company 282
Taylor, William Howson 272
Taylor, William Watts 269
Teams glassworks 279
Temminck, Leonhardus 175
Temperantia Dish, the 76, 77
Ten Books on Architecture 60
Teniers 218, 229
Terry, Eli 284
Terry, Silas 284
The Hague 175
Theodosius II 28
Thomas Clock Company, Seth 285
Thomire, Pierre-Philippe 338–9
Thonet, Michael 260, 261, 264, 363
Thorpe, W. A.
Thorvaldsen 176
Tiffany, C. F. 282
Tiffany, Charles 298
Tiffany, Louis Comfort 265, 278, 360, 367
Tinworth, George 272
Tittery family 69
Titus, Baths of 60
Tokugawa, Ieyasu 305
Tokuku, Suzuki 307, 309
Toledo 28, 72, 278
Tomiharu 306
Tompion, Thomas 115, 116, 192, 203, 214

Index

Tontegen, W. T. 302
Topkapi Sarayi Palace 18
Töplwer 215
Toricelli 301
Torres, Antonio 243–4
Tory, Geofroy 333
Toshinaga, Nara 129
Toshiteru, Nara 129
Toulouse-Laurec, Henri de 326–7
Tournai 174–5
Toutin, Jean 115, 123
Touvier, 276
Tou Wan 250
Townsend family 165
toys
  19th Century 310–12
Tranter 353, 354
Treatise of Japanning, Varnishing and Guilding 89
Trenton 268
Treves 27
Trier 37
Trou, Henri 172
Troughton, J. & E. 300, 301
True Principles of Pointed or Christian Architecture, The 263
Tschirnhaus, Count von 169
Tsin state 17
Tsuta School 129
Tuck, Raphael 324
Tucker, William Ellis 268–9
Tuileries, the 167
Tunbridge Wells 330
Turin 162
Turner 358
Turner, Thomas 178, 179–80, 266, 267
Turner, W. & J. 267
Tuscan style 11
Tussaud, Madame 315
Tuttel, Thomas 133
Twickenham 256
Tyxach family 69

Ulm 36
Unica Studio 366
United States Pottery 268
Unteutsch, Friederich 91
Utamaro 323
Utrecht 105, 111, 366

Vacheron 288
Vachette, Adrian Maximilian 216, 220
Valenciennes 126
Vallin, Eugène 260
van Beeck, Bontjes 271
Van Blarenberghe family 219, 229
Vanbrugh, John 256
Van der Hoeve, Cornelius 95
van de Velde, Henry 265
Van Dyck 123
van Eenhorn, Samuel 94
van Heemskerk, Willem Jacob 207
van Mekeren, Jan 88
van Rijswijk, Dirk 88
van Vianen family 111
Vasa Diatreta 27
Vatican, the 52, 55
Veneto, Bartolommeo 53
Veneziano, Agostino 63
Venicc 28, 29–31, 61, 67 9, 86, 87, 107, 168, 242 3, 212, 332
Venier, Pietro 87
Verrochio 52
Versailles 86, 88, 91, 120, 125, 148, 163, 173, 187, 207
Verzelini, Jacopo 69
Vetter, Johann Wilhelm 262

Vezzi, Francesco 168
Vicenze 150
Victoria, Queen 231, 315
Victorian style 258
Vienna 32, 71, 169, 170–1, 260, 264, 270, 274, 275, 300, 324, 339
Vile, William 151
Villard, Eugène 365
Villard, Gabriel 365
Villa Rotunda 165
Villiers, Charles 108, 122
Vincennes 171, 172, 173–4, 175
Vinter, Villas 186
Viollet 276
Vitrearius, Laurence 31
Vitrearius, William 31
Vitruvius 60
Vivant-Denon, Baron 167
von Doesburg, Theodore 362
von Sorgenthal, Konrad 170
von Spaun, Max 275
Voyage dans la Basse et Haute Egypte 167
Voysey, C. F. A. 264

Wakelin, John 280
Walker, Samuel 267
Wall, Dr 178, 180
Walpole, Horace 256, 335
Walter, Almeric 276
Walton, George 279, 280
Wan-li 65, 105
Ward, Dr Nathaniel Bagshaw 337
Ward, Marcus 324
Washington, George 40
watches
  16th Century 74–5, 78
  17th Century 115–17, 122–3
  18th Century 202–4, 221
  19th Century 287–8
  see also clocks

Waterford Glass House 184
Watteau 173, 217, 229, 231
Waugh, Sydney 367
weapons
  pre 1500 49, 56–8
  17th Century 127–30, 137–44
  see also guns
Wear Glassworks 279
Webb, Captain 323
Webb, Philip 263–4
Webb, Thomas 277, 279, 365
Webb and Bruce 259
Webley 353, 354
Wedgwood, Josiah 180–1, 191, 211, 266, 271, 272, 321, 330, 365
Wegner, Hans 363
Wei state 17
Weisweiler, Adam 163, 164
Welch, Spring & Company 285
Weller, Samuel 269
Wellington, Duke of 330
Wells, Robert 241
Werner, Caspar 73
Westminster, Palace of 263
Wheeling Glass Factory 278
Whieldon, Thomas 180, 181, 267
Whistler, J. M. 326, 357
Whistler, Laurence 366
Whitefriars Glass 279, 365
Wiese, Jules 297
Wilde, Oscar 327
Wilkes, E. E. 272
Wilkinson & Co., Henry 282
Willard family 202
Willems, Joseph 175, 177
William II 183
William and Mary 85, 89, 90, 119, 183
William of Wykeham, Bishop 55
Williams, Steven 365
Williard, Simon 284
Willibrand, Johann 132, 133
Wills, W.D. & H.O. 323

Wilms, Albert 281
Wilpe, Bishop Yso 49
Winckelmann, Johann Joachim 161
Wistar, Caspar 185
Witwe, Lötz 175
Wolfe, General 177
Wolff, David 108, 186–7
Wolverhampton 217
Woodall family 279
Wood family 181
Wood, George 248
Wood, Robert 162
Woodward, Henry 177
Worcester 175, 178, 179–80, 182, 184, 266
Wordsley 278
Wornum, Robert 244
Wright, Frank Lloyd 264, 362
Wright, Thomas 214
Wurttembergische Metallwaren fabrik 275
Würzburg 161
Wyatt, James 162

Yasuchika 309
Yedo 129
Yi Dynasty 19, 273
Yoshimune 18
Ysart, Salvador 365
Yüan Dynasty 17, 18
Yung Chêng 225, 251
Yung Lo 18

Zanesville 269
Zech, Joseph 114
Zeiss 300
Zentmayer 300
Zidler, Charles 326–7
Zimmerman of Hanan 338
Zurich 325
Zweisel 275

Acknowledgements

The publishers would like to thank the following organizations and individuals for their kind permission to reproduce the photographs in this book:

American Museum in Britain, Bath (Cooper-Bridgeman Library) 292–293; Bavaria-Verlag 42–43, 351 below; Bethnal Green Museum (Cooper-Bridgeman Library) 295 above, 296; N. Bloom and Son 233, 346; Brighton Pavilion 289; British Horological Institute (R. B. Fleming) 237 above; The Trustees of the British Museum 44, 45, 48; Brooklyn Museum 156 above; Cecil Higgins Museum, Bedford 200; Charleston, South Carolina Museum, exhibited in the Heyward Washington House (Helga Studio photo, courtesy magazine 'Antiques') 153; Christie, Manson and Woods Ltd. 160, 240, (Cooper-Bridgeman Library) 235, 236, 347; Cooper-Bridgeman Library 46, 195, (Private Collection) 199 inset, 290–291; De Havilland Antiques Ltd., London (Angelo Hornak) 239; Editions Graphiques (Cooper-Bridgeman Library) 295 below; Henry Ford Museum (Cooper-Bridgeman Library) 157; Henry Francis du Pont Winterthur Museum (Cooper-Bridgeman Library) 98 above, 156–157; Courtesy of Roger Fresco Corbu 348, 348–349; Gros Collection (Cooper-Bridgeman Library) 290; Hamlyn Publishing Group 351 above; Angelo Hornak 100, 294–295; Instituto Vendite Guidiziarie, Florence 98 below; John Jesse Collection (A. C. Cooper) 350 below right; Metropolitan Museum of Art: Bequest of A. T. Clearwater 158–159; Edwin Meyer, Vienna 345; Museum Vandekar (Antique Porcelain Company) 194 below; National Trust (Clandon Park) 97; Osterly Park (Cooper-Bridgeman Library) 154–155; Percival David Foundation of Chinese Art, University of London 47 below; S. J. Phillip Ltd. 234; Peter Philp, Cardiff 156 below; P. P. Pryce Collection (Cooper-Bridgeman Library) 291; Joseph Sataloff 352; Scala 41, 104; Simon Spero Collection (Cooper-Bridgeman Library) 194–195; Sotheby Parke Bernet and Company 350 left, (Alain Lesieutre Collection) 350 above right; Oliver Sutton Antiques (A. C. Cooper) 294 above and below; Victoria and Albert Museum, London 238, (A. C. Cooper) 101, 155, (Cooper-Bridgeman Library) 47 above, 99, 102, 102–103, 198–199; Waddesdon Manor (Angelo Hornak) 155 above; Winifred Williams (Antiques) 196, 197; Worcester Royal Porcelain Company 193.